Stuart Reges | Marty Stepp

University of Washington

Building
Java™
Programs

A Back to Basics
Approach

PEARSON
Addison
Wesley

Boston San Francisco New York
London Toronto Sydney Tokyo Singapore Madrid
Mexico City Munich Paris Cape Town Hong Kong Montreal

Publisher	Greg Tobin
Executive Editor	Michael Hirsch
Acquisitions Editor	Matt Goldstein
Editorial Assistant	Maurene Goo
Manager, Product Development	Patty Mahtani
Associate Managing Editor	Jeffrey Holcomb
Cover Design	Joyce Cosentino Wells
Digital Assets Manager	Marianne Groth
Media Producer	Bethany Tidd
Senior Marketing Manager	Michelle Brown
Marketing Assistant	Sarah Milmore
Senior Prepress Supervisor	Caroline Fell
Senior Manufacturing Buyer	Carol Melville
Media Manufacturing Buyer	Ginny Michaud
Text Design	Susan Carsten Raymond
Production Coordination	Argosy Publishing
Composition and Illustrations	Argosy Publishing

Cover Image: © Roz Woodward/age fotostock

Many of the designations used by manufacturers and sellers to distinguish their products are claimed as trademarks. Where those designations appear in this book, and Addison-Wesley was aware of a trademark claim, the designations have been printed in initial caps or all caps.

The interior of this book was composed in QuarkXPress 4.1 using ETM version 1.

Library of Congress Cataloging-in-Publication Data

Reges, Stuart.
  Building Java programs / Stuart Reges, Marty Stepp.
    p. cm.
  ISBN 0-321-38283-8 (pbk.)
  1. Java (Computer program language) I. Stepp, Martin. II. Title.
  QA76.73.J38R447 2007
  005.13'3--dc22
                                                    2006038885

ISBN-13: 978-0-321-38283-2
ISBN-10: 0-321-38283-8

1 2 3 4 5 6 7 8 9 10—CRW—10 09 08 07 06

Preface

Building Java Programs is a textbook designed for use in a first course in computer science. We have written the book for a broad student audience, not just computer science majors. The material was class-tested with thousands of undergraduates at the University of Washington (most of whom were not CS majors) over the course of two and a half years.

The first course in computer science has a long history at many schools of being a "killer" course with high failure rates. But as Douglas Adams says in *The Hitchhiker's Guide to the Galaxy,* "Don't panic." Students can master this material if they can learn it gradually.

Many instructors have experimented with new ways to teach introductory computer science. The most visible experiment has been the approach of teaching "objects early." Our sense is that these experiments have largely failed. While the top students in the course seem to learn the material well, there is a broad group of students in the middle who struggle with the object concept.

Building Java Programs uses a "back to basics" approach that stresses procedural programming early. We know from years of experience that a broad range of scientists, engineers, and others can learn how to program in a procedural manner. Once we have built a solid foundation of procedural techniques we turn to object-oriented programming. So by the end of the course, students will have learned both styles of programming.

Here are some of the key features of the approach taken in *Building Java Programs:*

- *Use* **objects early.** Java provides a wealth of useful objects that allow students to write interesting programs using traditional procedural programming techniques. Using these objects early and often eases the transition to defining them later.

- *Define* **objects later.** Students can become overwhelmed if they have to learn how to define objects while they are also trying to master basic programming skills. We teach the basics first and then teach students how to define objects later.

- **Focus on problem solving.** Many textbooks focus on language details when introducing new constructs. We focus instead on problem solving. What new problems can be solved with each construct? What pitfalls are novices likely to encounter along the way? What are the most common ways to use a new construct?

- **Emphasis on algorithmic thinking.** Our procedural approach allows us to emphasize algorithmic problem solving: breaking a large problem into smaller problems, using pseudocode to refine an algorithm, and grappling with the challenge of expressing a problem algorithmically.

- **Layered approach.** Programming in Java involves many concepts that are difficult to learn all at once. Teaching Java to a novice is like trying to build a house of cards. Each new card has to be placed carefully. If the process is rushed and you try to place too many cards at once, the entire structure collapses. We teach new concepts gradually, layer by layer, allowing students to expand their understanding at a manageable pace.

- **Full use of Java 5 features.** Our book was written from the beginning with Java 5 in mind. We make full use of the `Scanner` class, generics, the for-each loop, and boxing/unboxing. Java 6 was an incremental change to Java that will have no effect on our approach. Our book is fully compatible with Java 6.

- **Case studies.** We end each chapter with a significant case study that shows students how to develop a complex program in stages and how to test it as it is being developed. This allows us to demonstrate each new programming concept in a rich context that can't be achieved with short code examples.

- **Optional graphics supplement.** We have produced a custom `DrawingPanel` class that facilitates students' access to Java's extensive graphics capabilities. Many students enjoy the chance to produce complex graphical images, but this section of the book is entirely optional.

Layers and Dependencies

Many introductory CS books are language-oriented, but the early chapters of our book are layered. For example, Java has many control structures to master (including `for` loops, `while` loops, and `if/else` statements), and many books include all of these control structures in a single chapter. While that might make sense to someone who already knows how to program, it can be overwhelming for a novice who is learning how to program. We find it much more effective to spread out these control structures into different chapters so that students learn one at a time rather than trying to learn them all at once.

The following table shows how the layered approach works in the first six chapters:

Chapter	Control flow	Data	Programming techniques	Input/Output
1	methods	`String` literals	procedural decomposition	`println`
2	definite loops (`for`)	variables expressions `int`, `double`	local variables class constants pseudocode	`print`
3	return values	using objects	parameters	console input graphics (optional)
4	conditional execution (`if`/`else`)	`char`	pre/postconditions throwing exceptions	`printf`
5	indefinite loops (`while`)	`boolean`	assertions robust programs	
6		`Scanner`	token-based processing line-based processing	file input/output

Chapters 1–6 are designed to be worked through in order, with greater flexibility beginning in Chapter 7.

Chapter 6 is dedicated to file processing, a topic that has disappeared from many Java CS1 courses. Most likely, this is because prior to Java 5 it was not easy to manipulate files from a Java program. With the addition of the `Scanner` class in Java 5, we feel that files are now a reasonable topic to include. Including files opens up a world of interesting programming examples and data-intensive projects. Even so, we know that some instructors will not want to spend a lot of time on this subject, so we have made it possible for them to cover just the first part of our file-processing chapter.

The following is a dependency chart for the book:

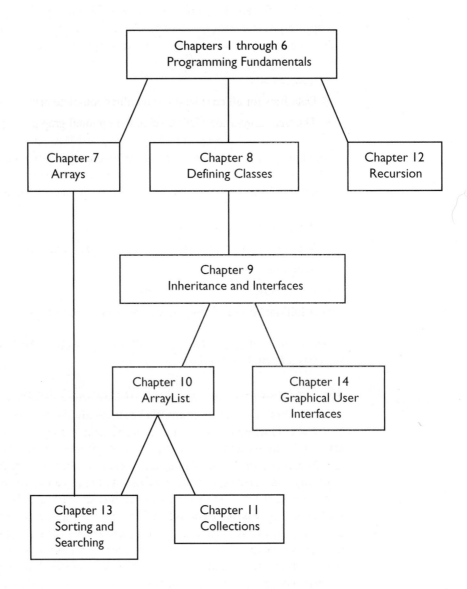

Support Material

We provide a wealth of supporting material for both instructors and students. Answers for all self-check exercises appear in Appendix A. In addition, students can access the following resources at www.aw-bc.com/cssupport

- Source code
- Data files for all case studies and other complete program examples
- The DrawingPanel class used in the optional graphics supplement to Chapter 3

   In addition, the student CD that accompanies the book contains the source code as well as numerous Java development environments (see the CD for a complete listing).
   Qualified instructors can also access the following resources:

- PowerPoint® slides
- Solutions to programming exercises and programming projects
- Sample exams
- Lab handouts
- Additional programming exercises with solution keys

To access the instructor resources, contact your Addison-Wesley sales representative or send an email to computing@aw.com.

My Code Mate–Your Own T.A. Just a Click Away

Addison-Wesley's *MyCodeMate* is a book-specific Web resource that provides tutorial help and evaluation of student programs. Example programs throughout the book and selected Exercises and Programming Projects from every chapter have been integrated into *MyCodeMate*. Using this tool, a student is able to write and compile programs from any computer with Internet access, and receive guidance and feedback on how to proceed and on how to address compiler error messages. Instructors can track each student's progress on Exercises and Programming Projects from the text or can develop projects of their own. **A complimentary subscription to *MyCodeMate* is offered when the access code is ordered in a package with a new copy of this text.** Subscriptions can also be purchased online. For more information visit www.mycodemate.com, or contact your campus Addison-Wesley representative.

Acknowledgments

First, we would like to thank the many students and teaching assistants who have used and commented on early drafts of this text. We could not have written this book without their input. Special thanks go to Hélène Martin, who pored over early versions of these chapters to find errors and to identify rough patches that needed work.

Second, we would like to thank our colleagues in the Computer Science & Engineering Department at the University of Washington. The faculty collectively decided to take a chance by hiring us and giving us the freedom to develop our course. We would particularly like to thank Hank Levy (current chair), David Notkin (former chair), and Richard Anderson (Associate Chair for Education) for their unwavering support. We would also like to thank Steve Gribble and Carl Ebeling for class-testing the book and providing us with valuable feedback.

Third, we would like to thank the talented pool of reviewers who have guided us in the process of turning a set of class notes into a full-fledged textbook:

Delroy A. Brinkerhoff, Weber State University
Ed Brunjes, Miramar Community College
Tom Cortina, Carnegie Mellon University
H.E. Dunsmore, Purdue University
Mary Anne Egan, Siena College
Ahmad Ghafarian, North Georgia College & State University
Raj Gill, Anne Arundel Community College
Michael Hostetler, Park University
David Hovemeyer, York College of Pennsylvania
Chenglie Hu, Carroll College
Philip Isenhour, Virginia Polytechnic Institute
Andree Jacobson, University of New Mexico
David C. Kamper Sr., Northeastern Illinois University
Simon G.M. Koo, University of San Diego
Evan Korth, New York University
Joan Krone, Denison University
Eric Matson, Wright State University
Kathryn S. McKinley, University of Texas, Austin
Jerry Mead, Bucknell University
George Medelinskas, Northern Essex Community College
John Neitzke, Truman State University
Richard E. Pattis, Carnegie Mellon University
Frederick Pratter, Eastern Oregon University
Roger Priebe, University of Texas, Austin

Dehu Qi, Lamar University
Amala V S Rajan, Middlesex University
Mike Scott, University of Texas, Austin
Tom Stokke, University of North Dakota
Leigh Ann Sudol, Fox Lane High School
Ronald F. Taylor, Wright State University
Scott Thede, DePauw University
Megan Thomas, California State University, Stanislaus
Jeannie Turner, Sayre School
Tammy VanDeGrift, University of Portland
Thomas John VanDrunen, Wheaton College
Neal R. Wagner, University of Texas, San Antonio
Jiangping Wang, Webster University
Yang Wang, Missouri State University
Stephen Weiss, University of North Carolina at Chapel Hill
Laurie Werner, Miami University
Dianna Xu, Bryn Mawr College
Carol Zander, University of Washington, Bothell

We would like to thank our copy editor, Rachel Head, as well as the staff at Argosy Publishing, including Nancy Kotary and Kathleen Kenny.

Finally, we would like to thank the great staff at Addison-Wesley who have kept us on track for the past two years: Michelle Brown, who "gets it" and is helping us figure out how to explain it to others; Jeff Holcomb, who promised and delivered a simple yet elegant design; Maurene Goo, who took care of the little details; Patty Mahtani, who quietly holds everything together; and especially our editor Matt Goldstein, who has believed in the concept of our book from day one. We couldn't have finished this job without all of their support.

Feature Walkthrough

1940s, when the first computers were built, the idea of storing complex data in integer form was fairly unusual.

Not only are computers digital, storing all information as integers, they are also *binary,* which means they store integers as *binary numbers.*

> **Binary Number**
> A number composed of just 0s and 1s, also known as a base-2 number.

Humans generally work with *decimal* or base-10 numbers, which match our physiology (10 fingers and 10 toes). However, in the case of computers, we wanted systems that would be easy to create and very reliable. It turned out to be simpler

Defined Terms   Throughout the text, key terms are pulled out and defined for quick reference.

"Did You Know" Boxes   These sections offer interesting anecdotal background to topics or terms used throughout the book.

Did You Know?

Hello, World!

The "hello world" tradition was started by Brian Kernighan and Dennis Ritchie, who invented a programming language known as C in the 1970s. The first complete program in their 1978 book describing the C language was a "hello world" program. Kernighan and Ritchie and their book *The C Programming Language* have both been affectionately referred to as "K & R" ever since.

Many major programming languages have borrowed the basic C syntax as a way to leverage the popularity of C and to encourage programmers to switch. The languages C++ and Java both borrow a great deal of their core syntax from C.

Kernighan and Ritchie also had a distinctive style for where to place curly braces and how to indent their programs that has become known as "K & R style." This is the style that Sun recommends and that we use in this book.

Common Programming Error

File Name Does Not Match Class Name

As mentioned earlier, Java requires that a program's class name and file name match. For example, a program that begins with `public class Hello` must be stored in a file called `Hello.java`.

If you use the wrong file name (say, saving it as `WrongFileName.java`), you'll get an error message like this:

```
WrongFileName.java:1: class Hello is public, should be
    declared in a file named Hello.java
public class Hello {
       ^
1 error
```

"Common Programming Error" Boxes   These sections warn of common errors that can bedevil beginning programmers.

Here's how to modify the header for the `main` method to include a `throws` clause indicating that it can throw a `FileNotFoundException`:

```java
public static void main(String[] args)
        throws FileNotFoundException {
    Scanner input = new Scanner(new File("hamlet.txt"));
    ...
}
```

With the `throws` clause, the line becomes so long that we have to break it into two lines to allow it to fit in the margins of the textbook. On your own computer, you will

Try typing the following simple program in your IDE:

```java
1  public class Hello {
2      public static void main(String[] args) {
3          System.out.println("Hello, world!");
4      }
5  }
```

Code Listings   There are abundant code listings throughout the text. Key lines in a listing are highlighted. Reserved words are printed in colored font. In syntax templates, placeholders meant to be replaced by the programmer are surrounded by <brackets> and highlighted in gray.

Simple methods are like verbs: They command the computer to perform some action. Inside the curly braces for a class, you can define several different methods. At a minimum, a complete program requires a special method that is known as the main method. It has the following syntax:

```java
public static void main(String[] args) {
    <statement>;
    <statement>;
    ...
    <statement>;
}
```

Just as the first line of a class is known as a class header, the first line of a method is known as a *method header*. The header for main is rather complicated. Most people

You can initialize the variable `input` to `null` as a way to say, "This variable doesn't yet point to an actual object." The primary advantage of initializing the variable to `null` is that you can test whether it's `null` in the `while` loop.

The pseudocode should now look like this:

```
Scanner input = null;
while (input == null) {
    prompt for name.
    try to open file, generating error message if illegal.
}
```

Start the variable with the value `null`, so it enters the `while` loop the first time through. If the code in the `try` block fails to properly open the file, the variable will still be `null` and you'll execute the loop a second time, prompting for another file

Pseudocode listings   Pseudocode listings are colored, and use a different "code" font than the Java listings.

This code does a great job of deleting the long sequences of spaces from the String, but it goes too far: It eliminates all of the spaces. To get one space between each pair of words, you'll have to include some spaces:

```
Scanner data = new Scanner(text);
while (data.hasNext()) {
    output.print(data.next() + " ");
}
```

This ends up looking pretty good, but it prints an extra space at the end of the line. To get rid of that space so that you truly have spaces appearing only between pairs of words, you'll have to change this slightly. This is a classic fencepost problem; you

"Thumbs-down" Incorrect Code Icon
On occasion, *Building Java Programs* uses flawed or incorrect code to illustrate common coding pitfalls that often trip up inexperienced programmers. The thumbs-down symbol indicates that the associated code listing is flawed or incorrect in some way.

Chapter Summary

Computers execute sets of instructions called programs. Computers store information internally as sequences of 0s and 1s (binary numbers).

Programming and computer science deal with algorithms, which are step-by-step descriptions for solving problems.

Java is a modern object-oriented programming language developed by Sun Microsystems that has a large set of libraries you can use to build complex programs.

A programs is translated from text into computer instructions by another program called a compiler. Java's compiler turns Java programs into a special format called Java byte-codes, which are executed using a special program called the Java runtime environment.

Java programmers typically complete their work using an editor called an Integrated Development Environment (IDE). The commands may vary from environment to environment, but the same three-step process is always involved:

1. Type in a program as a Java class.
2. Compile the program file.
3. Run the compiled version of the program.

Chapter Summaries
Located at the end of each chapter, summaries provide a concise overview of the fundamental concepts presented in the chapter.

Self-Check Problems

Section 6.1: File-Reading Basics

1. What is a file? How can we read data from a file in Java?

2. What is wrong with the following line of code?

   ```
   Scanner input = new Scanner("test.dat");
   ```

3. Write code to construct a Scanner object to read the file input.txt, which exists in the same folder as your program.

Section 6.2: Details of Token-Based Processing

4. What is wrong with the following line of code?

   ```
   Scanner input = new Scanner(new File("C:\temp\new files\test.dat"));
   ```
   (Hint: Try printing the above String.)

Self-Check Problems
These end-of-chapter problems offer readers an opportunity to assess their mastery of key topics in each section. Solutions to all self-check problems are available to all readers in Appendix A of the book.

Exercises These intermediate problems require computation, the analysis or writing of code fragments, and a deeper understanding about the chapter content. Solutions to all exercises are available to instructors.

Programming Projects Along with the problems and exercises, Programming Projects challenge readers to design and implement Java programs. They vary in level of difficulty, but generally take more time to complete than exercises. Example solutions to many programming projects are available to instructors.

MyCodeMate Working online, students can view, compile, run, and edit select programming problems as well as all code listings from the textbook. Look for this MyCodeMate icon to see which Programming Projects are available with a subscription to MyCodeMate.

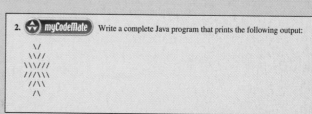

Contents

Chapter 6 File Processing   331

Chapter 7 Arrays   375

Chapter 1

Introduction to Java Programming

Introduction

This chapter begins with a review of some basic terminology about computers and computer programming. Many of these concepts will come up in later chapters, so it will be useful to review them before we start delving into the details of how to program in Java.

We will begin our exploration of Java by looking at simple programs that produce output. This will allow us to explore many elements that are common to all Java programs, while working with programs that are fairly simple in structure.

After we have reviewed the basic elements of Java programs, we will explore the technique of procedural decomposition by learning how to break up a Java program into several methods. Using this technique, we can break up complex tasks into smaller subtasks that are easier to manage and we can avoid redundancy in our program solutions.

1.1 Basic Computing Concepts

Computers are pervasive in our daily lives, and, thanks to the Internet, they give us access to nearly limitless information. Some of this information is essential news, like the headlines at cnn.com. Some of it is more frivolous: If you're concerned about whether the guy you met last night cheats on his girlfriends, perhaps you've visited dontdatehimgirl.com. Computers let us share photos with our families and map directions to the nearest pizza place for dinner.

Lots of real-world problems are being solved by computers, some of which don't much resemble the one on your desk or lap. The human genome is sequenced and searched for DNA patterns using powerful computers. There are computers in recently manufactured cars, monitoring each vehicle's status and motion. Digital music players such as Apple's iPod are actually computers underneath their small casings. Even the Roomba vacuum-cleaning robot houses a computer with complex instructions about how to dodge furniture while cleaning your floors.

But what makes a computer a computer? Is a calculator a computer? Is a human being with a paper and pencil a computer? The next several sections attempt to address this question while leading you toward putting computers into your command through programming.

Why Programming?

At most universities, the first course in computer science is predominantly a programming course. Many computer scientists are bothered by this because it leaves people with the impression that computer science = programming. While it is true that many trained computer scientists spend time programming, there is a lot more to the discipline. So why do we study programming first?

A Stanford computer scientist named Don Knuth answers this question by saying that the common thread for most computer scientists is that we all in some way work with *algorithms*.

> **Algorithm**
> A step-by-step description of how to accomplish a task.

Knuth is an expert in algorithms, so he is naturally biased toward thinking of them as the center of computer science. Still, he claims that what is most important is not the algorithms themselves, but rather the thought process that computer scientists employ. Knuth has said:

> It has often been said that a person does not really understand something until after teaching it to someone else. Actually a person does not *really* understand something until after teaching it to a *computer*, i.e., expressing it as an algorithm.[1]

---

[1] Knuth, Don. *Selected Papers on Computer Science.* Stanford. CA: Centre for the Study of Language and Information, 1996.

Knuth is describing a thought process that is common to most of computer science, which he refers to as *algorithmic thinking.* So, we study programming not because it is the most important aspect of computer science, but because it is the best way to explain the approach computer scientists take to solving problems.

Algorithms are expressed as computer programs, and that is what this book is all about. But before we look at how to program, it will be useful to review some basic concepts about computers.

Hardware and Software

A *computer* is a machine that manipulates data and executes lists of instructions known as *programs.*

> **Program**
>
> A list of instructions to be carried out by a computer.

One key feature that differentiates a computer from a simpler machine like a calculator is its versatility. The same computer can perform many different tasks (playing games, computing income taxes, connecting to other computers around the world), depending on what program it is running at a given moment. A computer can run not only the programs that exist on it currently, but also new programs that haven't even been written yet.

The physical components that make up a computer are collectively called *hardware.* One of the most important pieces of hardware is the central processing unit, or *CPU.* The CPU is the "brain" of the computer: It is what executes the instructions. Also important is the computer's *memory* (often called random access memory, or *RAM,* because the computer can access any part of that memory at any time). The computer uses its memory to store programs that are being executed, along with their data. RAM is limited in size and does not retain its contents when the computer is turned off. Therefore, computers generally also use a *hard disk* as a larger permanent storage area.

Computer programs are collectively called *software.* The primary piece of software running on a computer is its operating system. An *operating system* provides an environment in which many programs may be run at the same time, as well as providing a bridge between those programs and the hardware and user. The programs that run inside the operating system are often called *applications.*

When the user selects a program to be run by the operating system (e.g., by double-clicking the program's icon on the desktop), several things happen: The instructions for that program are loaded into the computer's memory from the hard disk, the operating system allocates memory for that program to use, and the instructions of the program are fed from memory to the CPU and executed sequentially.

The Digital Realm

In the last section, we saw that a computer is a general-purpose device that can be programmed. You will often hear people refer to modern computers as *digital* computers because of the way that they operate.

> **Digital**
>
> Based on numbers that increase in discrete increments, such as the integers 0, 1, 2, 3, etc.

Because computers are digital, everything that is stored on a computer is stored as a sequence of integers. This includes every program and every piece of data. An MP3 file, for example, is simply a long sequence of integers that stores audio information. Today we're used to digital music, digital pictures, and digital movies, but in the 1940s, when the first computers were built, the idea of storing complex data in integer form was fairly unusual.

Not only are computers digital, storing all information as integers, they are also *binary*, which means they store integers as *binary numbers*.

> **Binary Number**
>
> A number composed of just 0s and 1s, also known as a base-2 number.

Humans generally work with *decimal* or base-10 numbers, which match our physiology (10 fingers and 10 toes). However, in the case of computers, we wanted systems that would be easy to create and very reliable. It turned out to be simpler to build these systems on top of binary phenomena (e.g., a circuit being open or closed) rather than having 10 different states to distinguish (e.g., 10 different voltage levels).

From a mathematical point of view, you can store things just as easily using binary numbers as you can using base-10 numbers. But since it is easier to construct a physical device that uses binary numbers, that's what computers use.

This does mean, however, that people who aren't used to computers find their conventions unfamiliar. As a result, it is worth spending a little time reviewing how binary numbers work. In binary, as in base-10, you start with 0 and count up, but you run out of digits much faster. So, counting in binary, you say:

```
0
1
```

And already you've run out of digits. This is like reaching 9 when you count in base-10. After you run out of digits, you carry over to the next digit. So, the next two binary numbers are:

10
11

And again, you've run out of digits. This is like reaching 99 in base-10. Again, you carry over to the next digit to form the three-digit number 100. In binary, whenever you see a series of ones, as in 111111, you know you're just one away from the digits all flipping to 0s with a 1 added in front, in the same way that in base-10, when you see a number like 999999, you know that you are one away from all those digits turning to 0s with a 1 added in front.

The following table shows how to count up to the base-10 number 8 using binary.

decimal	binary
0	0
1	1
2	10
3	11
4	100
5	101
6	110
7	111
8	1000

There are several useful observations to make about binary numbers. Notice in the table that the binary numbers 1, 10, 100, and 1000 are all perfect powers of 2 (2^0, 2^1, 2^2, 2^3). In the same way that in base-10 we talk about a ones digit, tens digit, hundreds digit, and so on, we can think in binary of a ones digit, twos digit, fours digit, eights digit, sixteens digit, and so on.

Computer scientists quickly found themselves needing to refer to the sizes of different binary quantities, so they invented the term *bit* to refer to a single binary digit and the term *byte* to refer to 8 bits. To talk about large amounts of memory, they invented the terms kilobytes (KB), megabytes (MB), gigabytes (GB), and so on. Many people think that these correspond to the metric system, where "kilo" means 1000, but that is only approximately true. We use the fact that 2^{10} is appromixately equal to 1000 (it actually equals 1024). So, a kilobyte is 2^{10} bytes (1024 bytes), a megabyte is 2^{20} bytes (1,048,576 bytes), a gigabyte is 2^{30} bytes (1,073,741,824 bytes), and so on.

The Process of Programming

The word *code* describes program fragments ("these four lines of code") or the act of programming ("Let's code this into Java."). Once a program has been written, you can *execute* it.

> **Program Execution**
>
> The act of carrying out the instructions contained in a program.

The process of execution is often called *running.* This term can also be used as a verb ("When my program runs it does something strange") or as a noun ("The last run of my program produced these results").

A computer program is stored internally as a series of binary numbers known as the *machine language* of the computer. In the early days, programmers entered numbers like these directly into the computer. Obviously, this is a tedious and confusing way to program a computer, and we have invented all sorts of mechanisms to simplify this process.

Modern programmers write in what are known as "high-level" programming languages, such as Java. Such programs cannot be run directly on a computer: They first have to be translated into a different form by a special program known as a *compiler.*

> **Compiler**
>
> A program that translates a computer program written in one language into an equivalent program in another language (often, but not always, translating into machine language).

A compiler that translates directly into machine language creates a program that can be executed directly on the computer, known as an *executable.* We refer to such compilers as *native compilers* because they compile code to the lowest possible level (the native machine language of the computer).

This approach works well when you know exactly what computer you want your program to execute on. But what if you want to execute a program on many different computers? Using this approach, you'd need a compiler that generates different machine language output for each of them. The designers of Java decided to use a different approach. They cared a lot about their programs being able to run on many different computers, because they wanted to create a language that worked well for the Web. People who write *applets* (Java programs that live inside web pages) want those programs to run on as many computers as possible.

Instead of compiling into machine language, Java programs are compiled into what are known as *Java bytecodes.* One set of bytecodes can execute on many different machines. These bytecodes represent an intermediate level: They aren't quite as high-level as Java or as low-level as machine language. In fact, they are the machine language of a theoretical computer known as the Java Virtual Machine, or *JVM.*

> **Java Virtual Machine (JVM)**
>
> A theoretical computer whose machine language is the set of Java bytecodes.

A JVM isn't an actual machine, but it's similar to one. By compiling down to this level, there isn't as much work left to turn the Java bytecodes into actual machine instructions.

In the Java programming language, nothing can exist outside of a *class*.

> **Class**
>
> A unit of code that is the basic building block of Java programs.

The notion of a class is much richer than this, as you'll see when we get to Chapter 8, but for now all you need to know is that each of your Java programs will be stored in a class.

To actually execute a Java class file, you need another program that will execute the Java bytecodes. Such programs are known generically as *Java runtimes,* and the standard environment distributed by Sun is known as the Java Runtime Environment, or *JRE.*

> **Java Runtime**
>
> A program that executes compiled Java class files.

Most people have Java runtimes on their computers, even if they don't know about them. For example, Apple's Mac OS X includes a Java runtime, and many Windows applications install a Java runtime.

Why Java?

When Sun Microsystems released Java in 1995, they published a document called a "white paper" describing their new programming language. Perhaps the key sentence from that paper is the following:

> Java: A simple, object-oriented, network-savvy, interpreted, robust, secure, architecture neutral, portable, high-performance, multithreaded, dynamic language.[2]

This sentence covers many of the reasons why Java is a good introductory programming language. For starters, Java is reasonably simple for beginners to learn, and it embraces object-oriented programming, a style of writing programs that has been shown to be very successful for creating large and complex software.

Java also includes a large amount of prewritten software that programmers can utilize to enhance their programs. Such off-the-shelf software components are often called *libraries*. For example, if you wish to write a program that connects to a site on the internet, Java contains a library to simplify the connection for you. Java contains libraries to draw graphical user interfaces (GUIs), retrieve data from databases, and perform complex mathematical computations, among many other things. These libraries collectively are called the *Java class libraries.*

---

[2]http://java.sun.com/docs/overviews/java/java-overview-1.html

> **Java Class Libraries**
>
> Java's collection of preexisting code that provides solutions to common programming problems.

The richness of Java's class libraries has been an extremely important factor in the rise of Java as a popular language. As of version 1.5, the class libraries include over 3200 entries.

Another reason to use Java is that it has a vibrant programmer community. A large amount of online documentation and tutorials are available to help programmers learn new skills. Many of these documents are written by Sun themselves, including an extensive reference to Java's class libraries called the *API Specification* ("API" stands for Application Programming Interface).

Java is extremely platform-independent; unlike programs written in many other languages, the same Java program can be executed on many different operating systems, such as Windows, Linux, and Mac OSX.

Java is used extensively for both research and business applications, which means that a large number of programming jobs exist in the marketplace today for skilled Java programmers. A sample Google search for the phrase "Java jobs" returns 124,000,000 hits.

The Java Programming Environment

You must become familiar with your computer setup before you start programming. Each computer provides a different environment for program development, but there are some common elements that deserve comment. No matter what environment you use, you will follow the same basic three steps:

1. Type in a program as a Java class.
2. Compile the program file.
3. Run the compiled version of the program.

The basic unit of storage on most computers is a *file*. Every file has a name. A file name ends with an *extension*, which is the part of a file's name that follows the period. A file's extension indicates the type of data contained in the file. For example, files with the extension `.doc` are Microsoft Word documents, and files with the extension `.mp3` are MP3 audio files.

The Java program files that you create must use the extension `.java`. When you compile a Java program, the resulting Java bytecodes are stored in a file with the same name and the extension `.class`.

Most Java programmers use what are known as Integrated Development Environments, or IDEs, which provide an all-in-one environment for creating, editing, compiling, and executing program files. Some of the more popular choices for introductory computer science classes are Eclipse, DrJava, BlueJ, and TextPad. Your instructor will tell you what environment you should use.

Try typing the following simple program in your IDE:

```
1  public class Hello {
2      public static void main(String[] args) {
3          System.out.println("Hello, world!");
4      }
5  }
```

Don't worry about the details of this program right now. We will explore those in the next section.

Once you have created your program file, move to step 2 and compile it. The command to compile will be different in each development environment, but the process is the same (typical commands are "compile" or "build"). If any errors are reported, go back to the editor, fix them, and try to compile the program again. (We'll discuss errors in more detail later in this chapter.)

Once you have successfully compiled your program, you are ready to move to step 3, running the program. Again, the command to do this will differ from one environment to the next, but the process is similar (the typical command is "run").

The diagram in Figure 1.1 summarizes the steps you would follow in creating a program called Hello.java.

In some IDEs (most notably Eclipse), the first two steps are combined. In these environments the process of compiling is more incremental; you are warned about errors as you type in code. It is generally not necessary to formally ask such an environment to compile your program because it is compiling as you type.

When your program is executed, it will typically interact with the user in some way. The Hello.java program involves an onscreen window known as the *console*.

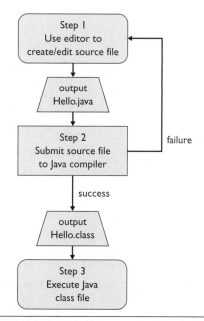

Figure 1.1   Creation and execution of a Java program

> **Console Window**
>
> A special text-only window in which Java programs interact with the user.

The console window is a classic interaction mechanism wherein the computer displays text on the screen and sometimes waits for the user to type responses. This is known as *console* or *terminal interaction*. The text the computer prints to the console window is known as the *output* of the program. Anything typed by the user is known as the console *input*.

To keep things simple, most of the sample programs in this book involve console interaction. Keeping the interaction simple will allow you to focus your attention and effort on other aspects of programming. For those who are interested, Chapter 14 describes how to write programs that use more modern graphical user interfaces.

1.2 And Now—Java

It's time to look at a complete Java program. It is a tradition in computer science that when you describe a new programming language, you should start with a program that produces a single line of output with the words, "Hello, world!" The "hello world" tradition has been broken by many authors of Java books because the program turns out not to be as short and simple when written in Java as in other languages, but we'll use it here anyway.

Here is our "hello world" program:

```
1  public class Hello {
2      public static void main(String[] args) {
3          System.out.println("Hello, world!");
4      }
5  }
```

This defines a class called `Hello`. (The line numbers are not part of the program but are included as an aid.) Sun has established the convention that class names always begin with a capital letter, which makes it easy to recognize them. Java requires that the class name and the file name match, so this program must be stored in a file called `Hello.java`. You don't have to understand all the details of this program just yet, but you do need to understand the basic structure.

Remember that the basic unit of code in Java is the class. Every program must be contained within a Java class. The basic form of a Java class is as follows:

```
public class <name> {
    <method>
    <method>
    ...
    <method>
}
```

This type of description is known as a *syntax template* because it describes the basic form of a Java construct. Java has rules that determine its legal *syntax* or grammar. Each time we introduce a new element of Java, we'll begin by looking at its syntax template. By convention, we use the less-than (<) and greater-than (>) characters in a syntax template to indicate items that need to be filled in (in this case, the name of the class and the methods). When we write ". . . " in a list of elements, we're indicating that any number of those elements may be included.

The first line of the class is known as the *class header.* The word `public` in the header indicates that this class is available to anyone to use. Notice that the program code in a class is enclosed in curly brace characters (`{ }`). These characters are used in Java to group together related bits of code.

Grouping Characters

The curly brace characters { and }, used in Java to group together related lines of code.

In this case, the curly braces are indicating that everything defined within them is part of this public class.

So what exactly can appear inside the curly braces? What can be contained in a class? All sorts of things, but for now, we'll limit ourselves to *methods.* Methods are the next-smallest unit of code in Java. A method represents a single action or calculation to be performed.

Method

A program unit that represents a particular action or computation.

Simple methods are like verbs: They command the computer to perform some action. Inside the curly braces for a class, you can define several different methods. At a minimum, a complete program requires a special method that is known as the `main` method. It has the following syntax:

```
public static void main(String[] args) {
    <statement>;
    <statement>;
    ...
    <statement>;
}
```

Just as the first line of a class is known as a class header, the first line of a method is known as a *method header.* The header for `main` is rather complicated. Most people memorize this as a kind of magical incantation. You want to open the door to Ali Baba's cave? You say, "Open sesame." You want to create an executable Java program? You say, `public static void main(String[] args)`. A group of Java teachers make fun of this with a website called publicstaticvoidmain.com.

Just memorizing magical incantations is never satisfying, especially for computer scientists who like to know everything that is going on in their programs. But this is a place where Java shows its ugly side, and you'll just have to live with it. New programmers, like new drivers, must learn to use something complex without fully understanding how it works. Fortunately, by the time you finish this book, you'll understand every part of the incantation.

Notice that the `main` method has a set of curly braces of its own. They are again used for grouping, indicating that everything that appears between them is part of the `main` method. The lines in between the curly braces specify the series of actions to perform in executing the program. We refer to these as the *statements* of the program. Just as you put together an essay by stringing together complete sentences, you put together a method by stringing together statements.

> **Statement**
>
> An executable snippet of code that represents a complete command.

The sample "hello world" program has just a single statement that is known as a `println` statement:

```
System.out.println("Hello, world!");
```

Notice that this statement ends with a semicolon. The semicolon has a special status in Java; it is used to terminate statements in the same way that periods terminate sentences in English.

> **Statement Terminator**
>
> The semicolon character ; used in Java to terminate statements.

In the basic "hello world" program there is just a single command to produce a line of output, but consider the following variation (called `Hello2`), which has four lines of code to be executed in the `main` method:

```
1  public class Hello2 {
2      public static void main(String[] args) {
3          System.out.println("Hello, world!");
4          System.out.println();
5          System.out.println("This program produces four");
6          System.out.println("lines of output.");
7      }
8  }
```

Notice that there are four semicolons in the `main` method, one at the end of each of the four `println` statements. The statements are executed in the order in which they appear, from first to last, so the `Hello2` program produces the following output:

```
Hello, world!

This program produces four
lines of output.
```

Let's summarize the different levels we just looked at:

- A Java program is stored in a class.
- Inside the class you can include methods. At a minimum, a complete program requires that you have a special method called `main`.
- Inside a method like `main`, you include a series of statements that each represent a single command for the computer to execute.

It may seem odd to put the opening curly brace at the end of a line rather than on a line by itself. Some people would use this style of indentation for the program instead:

```
1  public class Hello3
2  {
3      public static void main(String[] args)
4      {
5          System.out.println("Hello, world!");
6      }
7  }
```

Different people will make different choices about the placement of curly braces. The style we use follows Sun's official Java coding conventions, but the other style has its advocates too. Often people will passionately argue that one way is much better than the other, but it's really a matter of personal taste because each choice has some advantages and some disadvantages. Your instructor may require a particular style; if not, you should choose a style that you are comfortable with and then use it consistently.

Now that you've seen an overview of the structure, let's examine some of the details of Java programs.

String Literals (Strings)

When writing Java programs (such as the preceding "hello world" program), you'll often want to include some literal text to send to the console window as output. Programmers have traditionally referred to text such as this as a *string* because it is composed of a sequence of characters that we string together. The Java language specification uses the term *string literals*.

In Java you specify a string literal by surrounding the literal text in quotation marks, as in:

```
"This is a bunch of text surrounded by quotation marks."
```

You must use double quotation marks, not single quotation marks. The following is not a valid string literal:

```
'Bad stuff here.'
```

Did You Know?

Hello, World!

The "hello world" tradition was started by Brian Kernighan and Dennis Ritchie, who invented a programming language known as C in the 1970s. The first complete program in their 1978 book describing the C language was a "hello world" program. Kernighan and Ritchie and their book *The C Programming Language* have both been affectionately referred to as "K & R" ever since.

Many major programming languages have borrowed the basic C syntax as a way to leverage the popularity of C and to encourage programmers to switch. The languages C++ and Java both borrow a great deal of their core syntax from C.

Kernighan and Ritchie also had a distinctive style for where to place curly braces and how to indent their programs that has become known as "K & R style." This is the style that Sun recommends and that we use in this book.

The following is a valid string literal:

```
"This is a quote even with 'these' quotes inside."
```

String literals must not span more than one line of a program. The following is not a valid string literal:

```
"This is really
bad stuff
right here."
```

System.out.println

As you have seen, the `main` method of a Java program contains a series of statements for the computer to carry out. They are executed sequentially, starting with the first statement, then the second, then the third, and so on until the final statement has been executed. One of the simplest and most common statements is `System.out.println`, which is used to produce a line of output. This is another "magical incantation" that you should commit to memory. As of this writing, Google lists over 6,000,000 web pages that mention `System.out.println`. The key thing to remember about this statement is that it's used to produce a line of output that is sent to the console window.

The simplest form of the `println` statement has nothing inside its parentheses and produces a blank line of output:

```
System.out.println();
```

You need to include the parentheses even if you don't have anything to put inside them. Notice the semicolon at the end of the line. All statements in Java must be terminated with a semicolon.

More often, however, you use println to output a line of text:

```
System.out.println("This line uses the println method.");
```

The above statement commands the computer to produce the following line of output:

```
This line uses the println method.
```

Each `println` statement produces a different line of output. For example, if you execute the following three statements:

```
System.out.println("This is the first line of output.");
System.out.println();
System.out.println("This is the third, below a blank line.");
```

the following three lines of output are produced (the second is blank):

```
This is the first line of output.

This is the third, below a blank line.
```

Escape Sequences

Any system that involves quoting text will lead you to certain difficult situations. For example, string literals are contained inside of quotation marks, so how can you include a quotation mark inside a string literal? String literals also aren't allowed to break across lines, so how can you include a line break inside a string literal?

The solution is to embed what are known as *escape sequences* in the string literals. Escape sequences are two-character sequences that are used to represent special characters. They all begin with the backslash character (\). The following table lists some of the more common escape sequences.

Common Escape Sequences

Sequence	Represents
\t	tab character
\n	new line character
\"	quotation mark
\\	backslash character

Keep in mind that each of these two-character sequences actually stands for just a single character. For example, if you were to execute the following statement:

```
System.out.println("What \"characters\" does this \\ print?");
```

you would get the following output:

```
What "characters" does this \ print?
```

The string literal in the println has three escape sequences that are each two characters long, but they each produce a single character of output.

While string literals themselves cannot span multiple lines (that is, you cannot use a carriage return within a string literal to force a line break), you can use the \n escape sequence to embed newline characters in a string. This leads to the odd situation where a single println statement can produce more than one line of output.

For example, if you execute this statement:

```
System.out.println("This\nproduces 3 lines\nof output.");
```

you will get the following output:

```
This
produces 3 lines
of output.
```

The println itself produces one line of output, but the string literal contains two newline characters that cause it to be broken up into a total of three lines of output. To produce the same output without newline characters, you would have to issue three separate println statements.

This is another programming habit that tends to vary according to taste. Some people (including the authors) find it hard to read string literals that contain \n escape sequences, but other people prefer to write fewer lines of code. Once again, you should make up your own mind about when to use the newline escape sequence.

Identifiers and Keywords

The words used to name parts of a Java program are called *identifiers.* An identifier specifies the name of a class, method, or other entity in your program.

> **Identifier**
> A name given to an entity in a program, such as a class or method.

Identifiers must start with a letter, which can be followed by any number of letters or digits. The following are all legal identifiers:

```
first         hiThere      numStudents    TwoBy4
```

The Java language specification defines the set of letters to include the underscore and dollar-sign characters (_ and $), which means that the following are legal identifiers as well:

```
two_plus_tw    _count       $2donuts       MAX_COUNT
```

The following are illegal identifiers:

```
two+two       hi there     hi-There       2by4
```

Java has conventions for capitalization that are followed fairly consistently by programmers. All class names should begin with a capital letter, as with the Hello,

Hello2, and Hello3 classes introduced earlier. The names of methods should begin with lowercase letters, as in the main method. When putting several words together to form a class or method name, capitalize the first letter of each word after the first. In the next chapter we'll discuss constants, which have yet another capitalization scheme, with all letters in uppercase and words separated by underscores. These different schemes might seem like tedious constraints, but using consistent capitalization in your code allows viewers to quickly identify the various code elements.

For example, suppose that you were going to put together the words "all my children" into an identifier. The result would be:

- AllMyChildren for a class name (each word starts with a capital)
- allMyChildren for a method name (starts with a lowercase letter, subsequent words capitalized)
- ALL_MY_CHILDREN for a constant name (all uppercase, with words separated by underscores; described in Chapter 2)

Java is case sensitive, so the identifiers class, Class, CLASS, and cLASs are all considered different. Keep this in mind as you read error messages from the compiler. People are good at understanding what you write, even if you misspell words or make little mistakes like changing the capitalization of a word. However, mistakes like these cause the Java compiler to become hopelessly confused.

Don't hesitate to use long identifiers. The more descriptive your names are, the easier it will be for people (including yourself) to read your programs. Descriptive identifiers are worth the time they take to type. Java's String class, for example, has a method called compareToIgnoreCase.

Be aware, however, that Java has a set of predefined identifiers called *keywords* that are reserved for particular uses. As you read this book, you will learn many of these keywords and what they are used for. You can only use keywords for their intended purposes. You must be careful to avoid using these words for definitions that you make. For example, if you name a method short or try, this will cause a problem, because short and try are reserved keywords. Here is the complete list of reserved keywords.

List of Java Keywords

abstract	continue	for	new	switch
assert	default	goto	package	synchronized
boolean	do	if	private	this
break	double	implements	protected	throw
byte	else	import	public	throws
case	enum	instanceof	return	transient
catch	extends	int	short	try
char	final	interface	static	void
class	finally	long	strictfp	volatile
const	float	native	super	while

A Complex Example: DrawFigures1

The `println` statement can be used to draw text figures as output. Consider this more complicated program example. Notice that it uses two empty `println` statements to produce blank lines.

```
 1  public class DrawFigures1 {
 2      public static void main(String[] args) {
 3          System.out.println("   /\\");
 4          System.out.println("  /  \\");
 5          System.out.println(" /    \\");
 6          System.out.println(" \\    /");
 7          System.out.println("  \\  /");
 8          System.out.println("   \\/");
 9          System.out.println();
10          System.out.println(" \\      /");
11          System.out.println("  \\    /");
12          System.out.println("   \\  /");
13          System.out.println("    \\/");
14          System.out.println("    /\\");
15          System.out.println("   /  \\");
16          System.out.println("  /    \\");
17          System.out.println();
18          System.out.println("    /\\");
19          System.out.println("   /  \\");
20          System.out.println("  /    \\");
21          System.out.println("+------+");
22          System.out.println("|      |");
23          System.out.println("|      |");
24          System.out.println("+------+");
25          System.out.println("|United|");
26          System.out.println("|States|");
27          System.out.println("+------+");
28          System.out.println("|      |");
29          System.out.println("|      |");
30          System.out.println("+------+");
31          System.out.println("   /\\");
32          System.out.println("  /  \\");
33          System.out.println(" /    \\");
34      }
35  }
```

The following is the output it generates. Notice that the program includes double backslash characters (\ \), but the output has single backslash characters. This is an example of an escape sequence, as described previously.

Comments and Readability

Java is a free-format language. This means you can put in as many or as few spaces and blank lines as you like, as long as you put at least one space or other punctuation mark between words. However, you should bear in mind that the layout of a program can enhance (or detract from) its readability. The following program is legal, but hard to read:

```
1   public class Ugly{public static void main(String[] args)
2   {System.out.println("How short I am!");}}
```

Here are some simple rules to follow that will make your programs more readable:

- Put class and method headers on lines by themselves.
- Put no more than one statement on each line.
- Indent your program properly. When an opening brace appears, increase the indentation of the following lines. When a closing brace appears, reduce the indentation. Indent statements inside curly braces by a consistent number of spaces (a common choice is four spaces per level of indentation).
- Use blank lines to separate parts of the program (e.g., methods).

Using these rules to rewrite the Ugly program yields the following:

```
1   public class Ugly {
2       public static void main(String[] args) {
3           System.out.println("How short I am!");
4       }
5   }
```

Well-written Java programs can be quite readable, but often you will want to include some explanations that are not part of the program itself. You can annotate programs by putting notes called *comments* in them.

> **Comment**
> Text included by programmers to explain their code. The compiler ignores comments.

There are two comment forms in Java. In the first form, you open the comment with a slash followed by an asterisk and you close it with an asterisk followed by a slash:

```
/* like this */
```

You must not put spaces between the slashes and the asterisks:

```
/ * this is bad * /
```

You can put almost any text you like, including multiple lines, inside the comment:

```
/* Thaddeus Martin
   Assignment #1
   Instructor:  Professor Walingford
   Grader:      Bianca Montgomery      */
```

The only thing you aren't allowed to put inside a comment is the comment end character(s). The following is not legal:

```
/* This comment has an asterisk/slash /*/ in it,
   which prematurely closes the comment.  This is bad. */
```

Java also provides a second comment form for shorter, single-line comments. You can use two slashes in a row to indicate that the rest of the current line (everything to the right of the two slashes) is a comment. For example, you can put a comment after a statement:

```
System.out.println("You win!");   // Good job!
```

Or you can create a comment on its own line:

```
// give an introduction to the user
System.out.println("Welcome to the game of blackjack.");
System.out.println();
System.out.println("Let me explain the rules.");
```

You can even create blocks of single-line comments:

```
// Thaddeus Martin
// Assignment #1
// Instructor:  Professor Walingford
// Grader:      Bianca Montgomery
```

Some people prefer to use the other comment form for comments that span multiple lines but it is safer to use the second form because you don't have to remember to close the comment. It also makes the comment stand out more. This is another case where, if you are not told to use a particular comment style by an instructor or colleague, you should decide for yourself which style you prefer and use it consistently.

Don't confuse comments with the text of `println` statements. The text of your comments will not be displayed as output when the program executes. The comments are there only to help readers examine and understand the program.

It is a good idea to include comments at the beginning of each class file to indicate what the class does. You might also want to include information about who you are, what course you are taking, your instructor and/or grader's name, the current date, and so on. You should also comment each method to indicate what it does.

Commenting becomes more useful in larger and more complicated programs, as well as programs that will be viewed or modified by more than one programmer. Clear comments are extremely helpful to explain to another person, or to yourself at a later time, what your program is doing and why it is doing it.

In addition to the two comment forms discussed above, Java supports a particular style of comments known as *Javadoc comments*. Their format is more complex, but they have the advantage that you can use a program to extract the comments to make HTML files suitable for reading with a web browser. Javadoc comments are useful in more advanced programming and are discussed in more detail in Appendix C.

1.3 Program Errors

In 1949, Maurice Wilkes, an early pioneer of computing, expressed a sentiment that still rings true today:

> As soon as we started programming, we found out to our surprise that it wasn't as easy to get programs right as we had thought. Debugging had to be discovered. I can remember the exact instant when I realized that a large part of my life from then on was going to be spent in finding mistakes in my own programs.

You will also have to face this reality as you learn to program. You're going to make mistakes, just like every other programmer in history, and you're going to need strategies for eliminating those mistakes. Fortunately, the computer itself can help you with some of the work.

There are three kinds of errors that you'll encounter as you write programs:

- *Syntax errors* occur when you misuse Java. They are the programming equivalent of bad grammar and are caught by the Java compiler.
- *Logic errors* occur when you write code that doesn't perform the task it is intended to perform.
- *Runtime errors* are logic errors that are so severe that Java stops your program from executing.

Syntax Errors

Human beings tend to be fairly forgiving about minor mistakes in speech. For example, we might find it odd, but we generally understand Master Yoda when he says, "Unfortunate that you rushed to face him . . . that incomplete was your training. Not ready for the burden were you."

The Java compiler will be far less forgiving. The compiler reports syntax errors as it attempts to translate your program from Java into bytecodes if your program breaks any of Java's grammar rules. For example, if you misplace a single semicolon in your program, you can send the compiler into a tailspin of confusion. The compiler may report several error messages, depending on what it thinks is wrong with your program.

A program that generates compilation errors cannot be executed. If you submit your program to the compiler and errors are reported, you must fix the errors and resubmit the program to the compiler. You will not be able to proceed until your program is free of compilation errors.

Some development environments, such as Eclipse, help you along the way by underlining syntax errors for as you write your program. This makes it easy to spot exactly where errors occur.

An error can be introduced before you even start writing your program, if you choose the wrong name for its file.

Common Programming Error

File Name Does Not Match Class Name

As mentioned earlier, Java requires that a program's class name and file name match. For example, a program that begins with `public class Hello` must be stored in a file called `Hello.java`.

If you use the wrong file name (say, saving it as `WrongFileName.java`), you'll get an error message like this:

```
WrongFileName.java:1: class Hello is public, should be
    declared in a file named Hello.java
public class Hello {
       ^
1 error
```

The file name is just the first hurdle. A number of other errors may exist in your Java program. One of the most common syntax errors is to misspell a word. Aside from spelling, you may have punctuation errors, such as missing semicolons. Semicolons are not the only items that you can forget when writing a program. It's also easy to forget an entire word, such as a required keyword.

The error messages the compiler gives may or may not be helpful. If you don't understand the content of the error message, look for the caret marker (∧) below the line, which points at the position in the line where the compiler became confused. This can help you pinpoint the place where a required keyword might be missing.

Common Programming Error

Misspelled Words

Java (like most programming languages) is very picky about spelling. You need to spell each word correctly, including proper capitalization. Suppose, for example, that you were to replace the `println` statement in the "hello world" program with the following:

```
System.out.pruntln("Hello, world!");
```

When you try to compile this program, it will generate an error message similar to the following:

```
Hello.java:3: cannot find symbol
symbol  : method pruntln(java.lang.String)
location: class java.io.PrintStream
        System.out.pruntln("Hello, world!");
                    ^
1 error
```

The first line of this output indicates that the error occurs in the file `Hello.java` on line 3 and that the error is that the compiler cannot find a symbol. The second line indicates that the symbol it can't find is a method called `pruntln`. That's because there is no such method; the method is called `println`. The error message can take slightly different forms depending on what you have misspelled. For example, if you forget to capitalize the word `System`:

```
system.out.println("Hello, world!");
```

you will get the following error message:

```
Hello.java:3: package system does not exist
        system.out.println("Hello, world!");
                ^
1 error
```

Again, the first line indicates that the error occurs in line 3 of the file `Hello.java`. The error message is slightly different here, though, indicating that it can't find a package called `system`. The second and third lines of this error message include the original line of code with an arrow (caret) pointing to where the compiler got confused. The compiler errors are not always very clear, but if you pay attention to where the arrow is pointing, you'll have a pretty good sense of where the error occurs.

If you still can't figure out the error, try looking at the error's line number and comparing the contents of that line with similar lines in other programs. You can also ask someone else, such as an instructor or lab assistant, to examine your program.

Yet another common syntax error is to forget to close a string literal.

Common Programming Error

Forgetting a Semicolon

All Java statements must end with semicolons, but it's easy to forget to put a semicolon at the end of a statement, as is done in the following program:

```
1  public class MissingSemicolon {
2      public static void main(String[] args) {
3          System.out.println("A rose by any other name")
4          System.out.println("would smell as sweet");
5      }
6  }
```

In this case, the compiler produces output similar to the following:

```
MissingSemicolon.java:4: ';' expected
        System.out.println("would smell as sweet");
        ^
1 error
```

The odd thing about the compiler's output is that it has listed line 4 as the cause of the problem, not line 3, where the semicolon was actually forgotten. This is because the compiler is looking forward for a semicolon and isn't upset until it finds something that isn't a semicolon, which it does when it reaches line 4. Unfortunately, as this case demonstrates, compiler error messages don't always direct you to the correct line to be fixed.

A good rule of thumb to follow is that the first error reported by the compiler is the most important one to pay attention to. The rest might be the result of that first error. Many programmers don't even bother to look at errors beyond the first, as fixing that error and recompiling may cause the other errors to disappear.

Logic Errors (Bugs)

Logic errors are also called *bugs*. Computer programmers use words like "bug-ridden" and "buggy" to describe poorly written programs, and the process of finding and eliminating bugs from programs is called *debugging*.

The word "bug" is an old engineering term that predates computers; early computing bugs sometimes occured in hardware as well as software. Admiral Grace Hopper, an early pioneer of computing, is largely credited with popularizing the use of the term in the context of computer programming. She often told the the true story of a group of programmers at Harvard University in the mid-1940s who couldn't figure out what was wrong with their programs, until they opened up the computer and found an actual moth trapped inside.

The form that a bug takes may vary. Sometimes your program will simply behave improperly. For example, it might produce the wrong output. Other times it will ask the computer to perform some task that is clearly a mistake, in which case your program will have a runtime error that stops it from executing. In this chapter, since

---

Common Programming Error

Forgetting a Required Keyword

Another common syntax error is to forget a required keyword when typing your program, such as `static` or `class`. Double-check your programs against the examples in the textbook to make sure you haven't omitted an important keyword.

The compiler will give different error messages depending on which keyword is missing, but the messages can be hard to understand. For example, you might write a program called `Bug4` and forget the keyword `class` when writing its class header. In this case, the compiler will provide the following error message:

```
Bug4.java:1: 'class' or 'interface' expected
public Bug4 {
       ^
1 error
```

However, if you forget the keyword `void` when declaring the `main` method, the compiler generates a different error message:

```
Bug5.java:2: invalid method declaration; return type required
    public static main(String[] args) {
                  ^
1 error
```

---

your knowledge of Java is limited, generally the only type of logic error you will see is a mistake in program output from an incorrect `println` statement or method call.

We'll look at an example of a runtime error in the next section.

1.4 Procedural Decomposition

Brian Kernighan, one of the creators of the C programming language, has said, "Controlling complexity is the essence of computer programming." People have only a modest capacity for detail. We can't solve complex problems all at once. Instead, we structure our problem solving by dividing the problem into manageable pieces and conquering each piece individually. We often use the term *decomposition* to describe this principle as applied to programming.

> **Decomposition**
>
> A separation into discernible parts, each of which is simpler than the whole.

With procedural programming languages like Kernighan's C, decomposition involves dividing a complex task into a set of subtasks. This is a very verb- or action-oriented approach, involving dividing up the overall action into a series of smaller actions. This technique is called *procedural decomposition.*

Common Programming Error

Not Closing a String Literal or Comment

Every string literal has to have an opening quote and a closing quote, but it's easy to forget the closing quotation mark. For example, you might say:

```
System.out.println("Hello, world!);
```

This produces two different error messages, even though there is only one underlying syntax error:

```
Hello.java:3: unclosed string literal
        System.out.println("Hello, world!);
                           ^
Hello.java:4: ')' expected
    }
    ^
2 errors
```

In this case, the first error message is quite clear, including an arrow pointing at the beginning of the string literal that wasn't closed. The second error message was caused by the first. Because the string literal was not closed, the compiler didn't notice the right parenthesis and semicolon that appear at the end of the line.

A similar problem occurs when you forget to close a multiline comment by writing */, as in the first line of the following program:

```
/* This is a bad program.

public class Bad {
    public static void main(String[] args){
        System.out.println("Hi there.");
    }
} /* end of program */
```

The preceding file is not a program; it is one long comment. Because the comment on the first line is not closed, the entire program is swallowed up.

Luckily, many Java editor programs color the parts of a program to help you identify them visually. Usually, if you forget to close a string literal or comment, the rest of your program will turn the wrong color, which can help you spot the mistake.

Java was designed for a different kind of decomposition that is more noun- or object-oriented. Instead of thinking of the problem as a series of actions to be performed, we think of it as a collection of objects that have to interact.

As a computer scientist, you should be familiar with both types of problem solving. This book begins with procedural decomposition and devotes many chapters to mastering various aspects of the procedural approach. Only after you have thoroughly practiced procedural programming will we turn our attention back to object decomposition and object-oriented programming.

As an example of procedural decomposition, consider the problem of baking a cake. You can divide this problem into the following subproblems:

- Make the batter.
- Bake the cake.
- Make the frosting.
- Frost the cake.

Each of these four tasks has details associated with it. To make the batter, for example, you:

- Mix the dry ingredients.
- Cream the butter and sugar.
- Beat in the eggs.
- Stir in the dry ingredients.

Thus, you divide the overall task into subtasks, which you further divide into even smaller subtasks. Eventually, you reach descriptions that are so simple they require no further explanation (i.e., primitives).

A partial diagram of this decomposition is shown in Figure 1.2. "Make Cake" is the highest-level operation. It is defined in terms of four lower-level operations called "Make Batter," "Bake," "Make Frosting," and "Frost Cake." The "Make Batter" operation is defined in terms of even lower-level operations, and the same could be done for the other three operations. We use diagrams like this throughout the book. They are called structure diagrams, and are intended to show how a problem is broken down into subproblems. In this diagram, you can also tell in what order operations are performed by reading from left to right. That will not be true of most structure diagrams. To determine the actual order in which subprograms are performed, you will usually have to refer to the program itself.

Two styles of approaching problems are called *bottom-up* and *top-down*. To make a cake, you might start at the top and reason, "I can make a cake by first making batter, then baking it, then making frosting, and finally putting the frosting on the cake. I

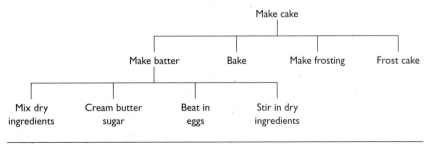

Figure 1.2 Decomposition of "Make cake" task

could make the batter by first...." This is a top-down solution; it starts at the highest level and proceeds downward.

A bottom-up solution involves reasoning like, "What can I do now? I could put together dry ingredients. If I then creamed the butter and sugar, and then beat in eggs, and then mixed in dry ingredients, I'd have some batter. If I then baked that batter, I'd have an unfrosted cake. If I then...." This is a bottom-up solution because it starts with low-level operations and puts them together to form higher-level operations.

One final problem-solving term has to do with the process of programming. Professional programmers develop programs in stages. Instead of trying to produce a complete working program all at once, they choose some piece of the problem to implement first. Then another piece is added, and another, and another. The overall program is built up slowly, piece by piece. This process is known as *iterative enhancement* or *stepwise refinement*.

> ### Iterative Enhancement
>
> The process of producing a program in stages, adding new functionality at each stage. A key feature of each iterative step is that you can test it to make sure that piece works before moving on.

Now, let's look at a construct that will allow you to iteratively enhance your Java programs to improve their structure and reduce their redundancy: static methods.

Static Methods

Java is designed for objects, and programming in Java usually involves decomposing a problem into various objects, each with methods that perform particular tasks. You will see how this works in later chapters, but for now, we are going to explore procedural decomposition. This will allow us to postpone examining some of Java's details while we discuss programming in general.

Consider the following program, which draws two text boxes on the console:

```
 1  public class DrawBoxes {
 2      public static void main(String[] args) {
 3          System.out.println("+------+");
 4          System.out.println("|      |");
 5          System.out.println("|      |");
 6          System.out.println("+------+");
 7          System.out.println();
 8          System.out.println("+------+");
 9          System.out.println("|      |");
10          System.out.println("|      |");
11          System.out.println("+------+");
12      }
13  }
```

The program works correctly, but the four lines used to draw the box appear twice. This redundancy is undesirable for several reasons. For example, you might wish to change the appearance of the boxes, in which case you'll have to make all of the edits twice. Also, you might wish to draw additional boxes, which would require you to type additional copies of (or copy and paste) the redundant lines.

A preferable solution would be to create a Java command that specifies how to draw the box, and then execute that command twice. Java doesn't have a "draw a box" command, but you can create one. Such a named command is called a *static method*.

> ### Static Method
> A block of Java statements that is given a name.

Static methods are units of procedural decomposition. We typically break a class into several static methods, each of which solves some piece of the overall problem. For example, here is a static method to draw a box:

```java
public static void drawBox() {
    System.out.println("+------+");
    System.out.println("|      |");
    System.out.println("|      |");
    System.out.println("+------+");
}
```

You have already seen a static method called main in earlier programs. Recall that the main method has the following form:

```java
public static void main(String[] args) {
    <statement>;
    <statement>;
    ...
    <statement>;
}
```

The static methods you'll write have a similar structure:

```java
public static void <name>() {
    <statement>;
    <statement>;
    ...
    <statement>;
}
```

The first line is known as the *method header*. You don't yet need to fully understand what each part of this header means in Java; for now, just remember that you'll need to write public static void, followed by the name you wish to give the method, followed by a set of parentheses. Briefly, here is what the words in the header mean:

- The keyword public indicates that this method is available to be used by all parts of your program. All methods you write will be public.

- The keyword static indicates that this is a static (procedural-style, not object-oriented) method. For now, all methods you write will be static, until you learn about defining objects in Chapter 8.
- The keyword void indicates that this method executes statements but does not produce any value. (Other methods you'll see later compute and *return* values.)
- <name> (e.g., drawBox) is the name of the method.
- The empty parentheses specify a list (in this case, an empty list) of values that are sent to your method as input; such values are called *parameters* and will not be used by your methods until Chapter 3.

Including the keyword static for each method you define may seem cumbersome. Other Java textbooks often do not discuss static methods as early as we do here; instead, other techniques are shown for decomposing problems. But even though static methods require a bit of work to create, they are powerful and useful tools for improving basic Java programs.

After the header in our sample, you see a series of println statements that make 0up the body of this static method. As in the main method, the statements of this method are executed in order from first to last when the method executes.

By defining the method drawBox, you have given a simple name to this sequence of println statements. It's like saying to the Java compiler, "Whenever I tell you to 'drawBox,' I really mean that you should execute the println statements in the drawBox method." But the command won't actually be executed unless our main method explicitly says that it wants to do so. The act of executing a static method is called a *method call*.

> **Method Call**
>
> A command to execute another method, which causes all of the statements inside that method to be executed.

To execute the drawBox command, include this line in your program's main method:

```
drawBox();
```

Since we want to execute the drawBox command twice (to draw two boxes), the main method should contain two calls to the drawBox method. The following program uses the drawBox method to produce the same output as the original DrawBoxes program:

```
1  public class DrawBoxes2 {
2      public static void main(String[] args) {
3          drawBox();
4          System.out.println();
5          drawBox();
6      }
7
8      public static void drawBox() {
9          System.out.println("+------+");
10         System.out.println("|      |");
11         System.out.println("|      |");
12         System.out.println("+------+");
13     }
14 }
```

A better version of the preceding program adds an additional method for each redundant section of output. The redundant sections are the top and bottom halves of the diamond shape, and the box used in the rocket. Here is the improved program:

```
1   public class DrawFigures3 {
2       public static void main(String[] args) {
3           drawDiamond();
4           drawX();
5           drawRocket();
6       }
7
8       public static void drawDiamond() {
9           drawCone();
10          drawV();
11          System.out.println();
12      }
13
14      public static void drawX() {
15          drawV();
16          drawCone();
17          System.out.println();
18      }
19
20      public static void drawRocket() {
21          drawCone();
22          drawBox();
23          System.out.println("|United|");
24          System.out.println("|States|");
25          drawBox();
26          drawCone();
27          System.out.println();
28      }
29
30      public static void drawBox() {
31          System.out.println("+------+");
32          System.out.println("|      |");
33          System.out.println("|      |");
34          System.out.println("+------+");
35      }
36
37      public static void drawCone() {
38          System.out.println("   /\\");
39          System.out.println("  /  \\");
40          System.out.println(" /    \\");
41      }
42
43      public static void drawV() {
44          System.out.println(" \\    /");
45          System.out.println("  \\  /");
46          System.out.println("   \\/");
47      }
48  }
```

This program, now called DrawFigures3, has seven static methods defined within it. The first static method is the usual main method, which calls three methods. These three methods in turn call three other methods, which appear next.

Analysis of Flow of Execution

The structure diagram in Figure 1.3 shows which static methods `main` calls and which static methods each of them calls. As you can see, this program has three levels of structure and two levels of decomposition. The overall task is split into three subtasks, each of which has two subtasks.

A program with methods has a more complex flow of control than one without them, but the rules are still fairly simple. Remember that when a method is called, the computer executes the statements in the body of that method. Then, control proceeds to the next statement after the method call. Also remember that the computer always starts with the `main` method, executing its statements from first to last.

So, in executing the `DrawFigures3` program, the computer first executes its `main` method. That, in turn, first executes the body of the method `drawDiamond`. `drawDiamond` executes the methods `drawCone` and `drawV` (in that order). When `drawDiamond` finishes executing, control shifts to the next statement in the body of the `main` method, the call on the `drawX` method.

A complete breakdown of the flow of control from static method to static method in `DrawFigures3` follows:

```
1st   main
2nd       drawDiamond
3rd           drawCone
4th           drawV
5th       drawX
6th           drawV
7th           drawCone
8th       drawRocket
9th           drawCone
10th          drawBox
11th          drawBox
12th          drawCone
```

Recall that the order in which you define methods does not have to parallel the order in which they are executed. The order of execution is determined by the body of the main method and by the bodies of methods called from `main`. A static method declaration is like a dictionary entry—it defines a word, but it does not specify how the word will be used. The body of this program's `main` method says to first execute `drawDiamond`, then `drawX`, then drawRocket. This is the order of execution, regardless of the order in which the methods are defined.

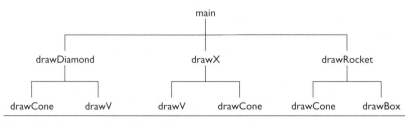

Figure 1.3 Decomposition of DrawFigures3

```
16
17       public static void main(String[] args) {
18           first();
19           third();
20           second();
21           third();
22       }
23   }
```

17. What would have been the output of the preceding program if the `third` method had contained the following statements?

```
public static void third() {
    first();
    second();
    System.out.println("Inside third method");
}
```

18. What would have been the output of the `Strange` program if the `main` method had contained the following statements? (Use the original version of `third`, not the modified version from the most recent exercise.)

```
public static void main(String[] args) {
    second();
    first();
    second();
    third();
}
```

19. What is the output of the following program? You may wish to draw a structure diagram first.

```
1    public class Confusing {
2        public static void method2() {
3            method1();
4            System.out.println("I am method 2.");
5        }
6
7        public static void method3() {
8            method2();
9            System.out.println("I am method 3.");
10           method1();
11       }
12
13       public static void method1() {
14           System.out.println("I am method 1.");
15       }
16
17       public static void main(String[] args) {
18           method1();
19           method3();
20           method2();
21           method3();
22       }
23   }
```

20. What would have been the output of the preceding program if the `method3` method had contained the following statements?

```java
public static void method3() {
    method1();
    method2();
    System.out.println("I am method 3.");
}
```

21. What would have been the output of the `Confusing` program if the `main` method had contained the following statements? (Use the original version of `method3`, not the modified version from the most recent exercise.)

```java
public static void main(String[] args) {
    method2();
    method1();
    method3();
    method2();
}
```

22. The following program contains at least 10 syntax errors. What are they?

```java
1    public class LotsOf Errors {
2        public static main(String args) {
3            System.println("Hello, world!");
4            message()
5        }
6
7        public static void message {
8            System.out println("This program surely cannot";
9            System.out.println("have any "errors" in it");
10       }
```

23. Consider the following program, saved into a file named `Example.java`:

```java
1    public class Example {
2        public static void displayRule() {
3            System.out.println("The first rule ");
4            System.out.println("of Java Club is,");
5            System.out.println();
6            System.out.println("you do not talk about Java Club.");
7        }
8
9        public static void main(String[] args) {
10           System.out.println("The rules of Java Club.");
11           displayRule();
12           displayRule();
13       }
14   }
```

What would happen if each of the following changes was made to the `Example` program? For example: no effect, syntax error, or different program output. Treat each change independently of the others.

- Change line 1 to: `public class Demonstration`
- Change line 9 to: `public static void MAIN(String[] args) {`
- Insert a new line after line 11 that reads: `System.out.println();`

```
I don't know why she swallowed that fly,
Perhaps she'll die.
There was an old lady who swallowed a dog,
What a hog to swallow a dog.
She swallowed the dog to catch the cat,
She swallowed the cat to catch the bird,
She swallowed the bird to catch the spider,
She swallowed the spider to catch the fly,
I don't know why she swallowed that fly,
Perhaps she'll die.

There was an old lady who swallowed a horse,
She died of course.
```

4. Write a program that produces as output the words of "The Twelve Days of Christmas." (Static methods simplify this task.) Here are the first two verses and the last verse of the song:

```
On the first day of Christmas,
my true love sent to me
a partridge in a pear tree.

On the second day of Christmas,
my true love sent to me
two turtle doves, and
a partridge in a pear tree.

...

On the twelfth day of Christmas,
my true love sent to me
Twelve drummers drumming,
eleven pipers piping,
ten lords a-leaping,
nine ladies dancing,
eight maids a-milking,
seven swans a-swimming,
six geese a-laying,
five golden rings,
four calling birds,
three French hens,
two turtle doves, and
a partridge in a pear tree.
```

Chapter 2

Primitive Data and Definite Loops

Introduction

Now that you know something about the basic structure of Java programs, you are ready to learn how to solve more complex problems. For the time being we will still concentrate on programs that produce output, but we will begin to explore some of the aspects of programming that require problem-solving skills.

The first half of this chapter fills in two important areas. First, it examines expressions: how to express simple computations in Java, particularly those involving numeric data. Second, it discusses program elements called variables that can change in value as the program executes.

The second half of the chapter introduces your first control structure: the for loop. You use this structure to repeat actions in a program. This is useful whenever you find a pattern in a task such as the creation of a complex figure, because you can use a for loop to repeat an action that creates a particular pattern. The challenge is finding each pattern and figuring out what repeated actions will reproduce it. In exploring this process, we will examine a variation of println known as print that allows you to break up a complex line of output into several pieces.

The for loop is a flexible control structure that can be used for many tasks, but in this chapter we use it for *definite loops,* where you know exactly how many times you want to perform a particular task. In Chapter 5 we will discuss how to write *indefinite loops,* where you don't know in advance how many times to perform a task.

2.1 Basic Data Concepts

Programs manipulate information, and information comes in many forms. Java is a *strongly typed* language, which means that it requires you to be explicit about what kind of information you intend to manipulate. Everything that you manipulate in a Java program will be of a certain *type,* and you will constantly find yourself telling Java what types of data you intend to use.

> **Data Type**
> A name for a category of data values that are all related, as in type `int` in Java that represents integer values.

A decision was made early in the design of Java to support two different kinds of data: primitive data and objects. The designers admit that this decision was made purely on the basis of performance, to make Java programs run faster. Unfortunately, it means that you have to learn two sets of rules about how data works, but this is one of those times when you simply have to pay the price if you want to use an industrial-strength programming language. To make things a little easier, we will study the primitive data types first, in this chapter; in the next chapter, we will turn our attention to objects.

Primitive Types

There are eight primitive data types in Java, four of which are considered fundamental. The other four types are variations that exist for programs that have special requirements. The four fundamental types that we will explore are listed in Table 2.1.

The type names (`int`, `double`, `char`, and `boolean`) are Java keywords that you will use in your programs to let the compiler know that you intend to use that type of data.

It may seem odd to have one type for integers and another type for real numbers. Isn't every integer a real number? The answer is yes, but these are fundamentally different types of numbers. The difference is so great that we make this distinction even in English. We don't ask, "How much sisters do you have?" or "How many do you weigh?" We realize that sisters come in discrete integer quantities (0 sisters, 1 sister, 2 sisters, 3 sisters, and so on), and we use the word "many" for integer quantities ("How

TABLE 2.1   Commonly Used Primitive Types in Java

Type	Description	Examples
int	integers (whole numbers)	42, −3, 18, 20493, 0
double	real numbers	7.35, 14.9, −19.83423
char	single characters	'a', 'X', '!'
boolean	logical values	true, false

many sisters do you have?"). Similarly, we realize that weight can vary by tiny amounts (175 pounds versus 175.5 pounds versus 175.25 pounds, and so on), and we use the word "much" for these real-valued quantities ("How much do you weigh?").

In programming this distinction is even more important, because integers and reals are represented in a different way in the computer's memory: Integers are stored exactly, while reals are stored as approximations with a limited number of digits of accuracy. You will see that storing values as approximations can lead to round-off errors when you use real values.

The name `double` for real values isn't very clear. It's an accident of history in much the same way that we still talk about "dialing" a number on our telephones even though modern telephones don't have dials. The C programming language introduced a type called `float` (short for "floating-point number") for storing real numbers. But `float`s had limited accuracy, so another type was introduced, called `double` (short for "double precision"; i.e., double the precision of a simple float). As memory became cheaper, people began using `double` as the default for floating-point values. In hindsight, it might have been better to use the word `float` for what is now called `double` and a word like "half" for the values with less accuracy, but it's tough to change habits that are so ingrained. So, programming languages will continue to use the word `double` for floating-point numbers, and people will still talk about "dialing" people on the phone even if they've never touched a telephone dial.

Expressions

When writing programs, you will often need to include values and calculations. The technical term for these is *expressions*.

> **Expression**
> A simple value or a set of operations that produces a value.

The simplest expression is a specific value, like `42` or `28.9`. We call these "literal values," or *literals*. More complex expressions involve combining simple values. Suppose, for example, that you want to know how many bottles of water you have. If you have two six-packs, four four-packs, and two individual bottles, you can compute the total number of bottles with the following expression:

```
(2 * 6) + (4 * 4) + 2
```

Notice that we use an asterisk to represent multiplication and that we use parentheses to group parts of the expression. The computer determines the value of an expression by *evaluating* it.

> **Evaluation**
> The process of obtaining the value of an expression.

The value obtained when an expression is evaluated is called the *result*.

Complex expressions are formed using *operators*.

> **Operator**
>
> A special symbol (like + or *) used to indicate an operation to be performed on one or more values.

The values used in the expression are called *operands*. For example, consider the following simple expressions:

```
3 + 29
4 * 5
```

The operators here are the + and *, and the operands are simple numbers.

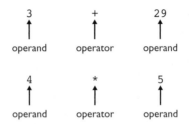

When you form complex expressions, these simpler expressions can in turn become operands for other operators. For example, consider the following expression:

```
(3 + 29) - (4 * 5)
```

which has two levels of operators:

The addition operator has simple operands of 3 and 29 and the multiplication

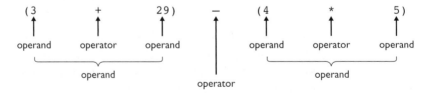

operator has simple operands of 4 and 5, but the subtraction operator has operands that are each parenthesized expressions with operators of their own. Thus, complex expressions can be built from smaller expressions. At the lowest level you have simple numbers. These are used as operands to make more complex expressions, which in turn can be used as operands in even more complex expressions.

There are many things you can do with expressions. One of the simplest things you can do is to print the value of an expression using a `println` statement. For example, if you say:

```
System.out.println(42);
System.out.println(2 + 2);
```

you will get the following two lines of output:

```
42
4
```

Notice that for the second `println`, the computer evaluates the expression (adding 2 and 2) and prints the result (in this case, 4).

You will see many different operators as you progress through this book, all of which can be used to form expressions. Expressions can be arbitrarily complex, with as many operators as you like. For that reason, when we tell you, "An expression can be used here," we will often point out that we mean "arbitrary expressions" to emphasize that you can use complex expressions as well as simple values.

Literals

The simplest expressions refer to values directly using what are known as *literals*. An integer literal (considered to be of type `int`) is a sequence of digits with or without a leading sign:

```
3    482    −29434    0    92348    +9812
```

A floating-point literal (considered to be of type `double`) will include a decimal point, as in:

```
298.4    0.284    207.    .2843    −17.452    −.98
```

Notice that `207.` is considered a `double` even though it coincides with an integer, because of the decimal point. Literals of type `double` can also be expressed in scientific notation (a number followed by `e` followed by an integer), as in:

```
2.3e4    1e-5    3.84e92    2.458e12
```

The first of these numbers represents 2.3 times 10 to the 4th power, which equals 23,000. Even though this value happens to coincide with an integer, it is considered to be of type `double` because it is expressed in scientific notation. The second number represents 1 times 10 to the –5th power, which is equal to 0.00001. The third value represents 3.84 times 10 to the 92nd power. The fourth represents 2.458 times 10 to the 12th power.

Character literals (of type `char`) are enclosed in single quotation marks and can include just one character:

```
'a'    'm'    'X'    '!'    '3'    '\\'
```

All of these are of type `char`. Notice that the last example uses an escape sequence to represent the backslash character. You can even refer to the single quotation character using an escape sequence:

```
'\''
```

Finally, the primitive type `boolean` stores logical information. Logic deals with just two possibilities: true and false. These two Java keywords are the two literal values of type `boolean`:

```
true    false
```

Arithmetic Operators

The basic arithmetic operators are shown in Table 2.2. The addition and subtraction operators will, of course, look familiar to you, as should the asterisk as a multiplication operator and the forward slash as a division operator. However, as you'll see, Java has two different division operations. The remainder or mod operation may be unfamiliar.

Division presents a problem when the operands are integers. When you divide 119 by 5, for example, you do not get an integer result. Therefore, the results of integer division are expressed as two different integers, a quotient and a remainder:

$$\frac{119}{5} = 23 \text{ (quotient) with 4 (remainder)}$$

In terms of the arithmetic operators:

```
119 / 5 evaluates to 23
119 % 5 evaluates to 4
```

Long-division calculations are performed like this:

```
      31
34)1079
   102
    59
    34
    25
```

Here, dividing 1079 by 34 yields 31 with a remainder of 25. Using arithmetic operators, the problem would be described like this:

TABLE 2.2   Arithmetic Operators in Java

Operator	Meaning	Example	Result
+	addition	2 + 2	4
−	subtraction	53 − 18	35
*	multiplication	3 * 8	24
/	division	4.8 / 2.0	2.4
%	remainder or mod	19 % 5	4

Sometimes you want Java to go the other way, converting a double into an int. You can ask Java for this conversion with a *cast*. Think of it as "casting a value in a different light." You request a cast by putting the name of the type you want to cast to in parentheses in front of the value you want to cast. For example, if you say:

```
(int) 4.75
```

you will get the int value 4. When you cast a double value to an int, it simply truncates anything after the decimal point. If you want to cast the result of an expression, you have to be careful to use parentheses. For example, suppose that you have some books that are 0.15 feet wide and you want to know how many of them will fit in a bookshelf that is 2.5 feet wide. You could do a straight division of 2.5 / 0.15, but that evaluates to a double result that is between 16 and 17. Americans use the phrase "16 and change" as a way to express the idea that a value is larger than 16 but not as big as 17. In this case, we don't care about the "change"; we only want to compute the 16 part. You might form the following expression:

```
(int) 2.5 / 0.15
```

Unfortunately, this expression evaluates to the wrong answer because the cast is applied to whatever comes right after it (here, the value 2.5). This casts 2.5 into the integer 2, divides by 0.15, and evaluates to 13 and change, which isn't an integer and isn't the right answer. Instead, you want to form this expression:

```
(int) (2.5 / 0.15)
```

This expression first performs the division to get 16 and change, and then casts that value to an int by truncating it. It thus evaluates to the int value 16, which is the answer you're looking for.

In later chapters we'll see other expressions involving mixed types. For example, in Chapter 4 we will see that every value of type char has a corresponding integer value, which allows for strange expressions like the following:

```
2 * 'a'              // produces 194
(char) ('f' + 2)     // produces 'h'
```

2.2 Variables

Primitive data can be stored in the computer's memory in a *variable*.

> **Variable**
> A memory location with a name and a type that stores a value.

Think of the computer's memory as being like a giant spreadsheet that has many cells where data can be stored. When you create a variable in Java, you are asking it to set aside one of those cells for this new variable. Initially the cell will be empty, but you will have the option to store a value in the cell. And as with a spreadsheet, you will have the option to change the value in that cell later.

Java is a little more picky than a spreadsheet, though, in that it requires you to tell it exactly what kind of data you are going to store in the cell. For example, if you want to store an integer, you need to tell Java that you intend to use type int. If you want to store a real value, you need to tell Java that you intend to use a double. You also have to decide on a name to use when you want to refer to this memory location. The normal rules of Java identifiers apply (the name must start with a letter, which can be followed by any combination of letters and digits). The standard convention in Java is to start variable names with a lowercase letter, as in number or digits, and to capitalize any subsequent words, as in numberOfDigits.

To explore the basic use of variables, let's examine a program that computes an individual's *body mass index,* or BMI. Health professionals use this number to advise people about whether or not they are overweight. Given an individual's height and weight, we can compute a BMI. A simple BMI program, then, would naturally have three variables for these three pieces of information. There are several details that we need to discuss about variables, but it can be helpful to look at a complete program first to see the overall picture. The following program computes and prints the BMI for an individual who is 5 feet 10 inches tall and weighs 195 pounds:

```
1   public class BMICalculator {
2       public static void main(String[] args) {
3           // declare variables
4           double height;
5           double weight;
6           double bmi;
7
8           // compute BMI
9           height = 70;
10          weight = 195;
11          bmi = weight / (height * height) * 703;
12
13          // print results
14          System.out.println("Current BMI:");
15          System.out.println(bmi);
16      }
17  }
```

Notice that the program includes blank lines to seperate the sections and comments to indicate what the different parts of the program do. It produces the following output:

```
Current BMI:
27.976530612244897
```

Let's now examine the details of this program to understand how variables work. Before variables can be used in a Java program, they must be declared. The line of code that declares the variable is known as a variable *declaration.*

> **Declaration**
>
> A request to set aside a new variable with a given name and type.

Each variable is declared just once. If you declare a variable more than once, you will get an error message from the Java compiler. Simple variable declarations are of the following form:

```
<type> <name>;
```

as in the three declarations at the beginning of our sample program:

```
double height;
double weight;
double bmi;
```

Notice that a variable declaration, like a statement, ends with a semicolon. These declarations can appear anywhere a statement can occur. The declaration indicates the type and the name of the variable. Remember that the name of each primitive type is a keyword in Java (`int`, `double`, `char`, `boolean`). We've used the keyword `double` to define the type of these three variables.

Once a variable is declared, Java sets aside a memory location to store its value. However, with the simple form of variable declaration used in our program, Java does not store initial values in these memory locations. We refer to these as *uninitialized* variables, and they are similar to blank cells in a spreadsheet:

height <code>?</code>   weight <code>?</code>   bmi <code>?</code>

So how do we get values into those cells? The easiest way to do so is using an *assignment statement.* The general syntax of the assignment statement is:

```
<variable> = <expression>;
```

as in:

```
height = 70;
```

This statement stores the value `70` in the memory location for the variable `height`, indicating that this person is 70 inches tall (5 feet 10 inches). We often use the phrase "gets" or "is assigned" when reading a statement like this, as in "`height` gets `70`" or "`height` is assigned `70`."

When the statement executes, the computer first evaluates the expression on the right side; then, it stores the result in the memory location for the given variable. In this case the expression is just a simple literal value, so after executing this statement, the memory looks like this:

height <code>70.0</code>   weight <code>?</code>   bmi <code>?</code>

Notice that the value is stored as 70.0 because the variable is of type `double`. The variable `height` has now been initialized, but the variables `weight` and `bmi` are still uninitialized. The second assignment statement gives a value to `weight`:

```
weight = 195;
```

After executing this statement, the memory looks like this:

     height `70.0`   weight `195.0`   bmi `?`

The third assignment statement includes a formula (an expression to be evaluated):

```
bmi = weight / (height * height) * 703;
```

To calculate the value of this expression, the computer divides the weight by the square of the height and then multiplies the result of that operation by the literal value 703. The result is stored in the variable `bmi`. So, after executing the third assignment statement, the memory looks like this:

     height `70.0`   weight `195.0`   bmi `27.976530612244897`

The last two lines of the program report the BMI result using `println` statements:

```
System.out.println("Current BMI:");
System.out.println(bmi);
```

Notice that we can include a variable in a `println` statement the same way that we include literal values and other expressions to be printed.

As its name implies, a variable can take on different values at different times. For example, consider the following variation of the BMI program, which computes a new BMI assuming the person lost 15 pounds (going from 195 pounds to 180 pounds).

```
1  public class BMICalculator2 {
2      public static void main(String[] args) {
3          // declare variables
4          double height;
5          double weight;
6          double bmi;
7
8          // compute BMI
9          height = 70;
10         weight = 195;
11         bmi = weight / (height * height) * 703;
12
13         // print results
14         System.out.println("Previous BMI:");
15         System.out.println(bmi);
16
17         // recompute BMI
18         weight = 180;
19         bmi = weight / (height * height) * 703;
20
```

```
21              // report new results
22              System.out.println("Current BMI:");
23              System.out.println(bmi);
24      }
25  }
```

The program begins the same way, setting the three variables to the following values and reporting this initial value for BMI:

height `70.0`   weight `195.0`   bmi `27.976530612244897`

But the new program then includes the following assignment statement:

```
weight = 180;
```

This changes the value of the `weight` variable:

height `70.0`   weight `180.0`   bmi `27.976530612244897`

You might think that this would also change the value of the `bmi` variable. After all, earlier in the program we said that the following should be true:

```
bmi = weight / (height * height) * 703;
```

But even though Java uses the equals sign for assignment, don't confuse this with a statement of equality. The assignment statement does not represent an algebraic relationship. In algebra, you might say:

$$x = y + 2$$

In mathematics you state definitively that x is equal to y plus two, a fact that is true now and forever. If x changes, y will change accordingly, and vice versa. Java's assignment statement is very different.

The assignment statement is a command to perform an action at a particular point in time. It does not represent a lasting relationship between variables. That's why we usually say "gets" or "is assigned" rather than saying "equals" when we read assignment statements.

Getting back to the program, resetting the variable called `weight` does not reset the variable called `bmi`. To recompute `bmi` based on the new value for weight, we must include the second assignment statement:

```
weight = 180;
bmi = weight / (height * height) * 703;
```

Otherwise, the variable `bmi` would store the same value as before. That would be a rather depressing outcome to report to someone who's just lost 15 pounds. By including both of these statements, we reset both the `weight` and `bmi` variables so that memory looks like this:

height `70.0`   weight `180.0`   bmi `25.82448979591837`

The output of the new version of the program is:

```
Previous BMI:
27.976530612244897
Current BMI:
25.82448979591837
```

One very common assignment statement that points out the difference between algebraic relationships and program statements is:

```
x = x + 1;
```

Remember not to think of this as "x equals x + 1." There are no numbers that satisfy that equation. We use a word like "gets" to read this as, "x gets the value of x plus one." This may seem a rather odd statement, but you should be able to decipher it given the rules outlined earlier. Suppose that the current value of x is 19. To execute the statement, you first evaluate the expression to obtain the result 20. The computer stores this value in the variable named on the left, x. Thus, this statement adds one to the value of the variable. We refer to this as *incrementing* the value of x. It is a fundamental programming operation because it is the programming equivalent of counting (1, 2, 3, 4, and so on). The following statement is a variation that counts down, which we call *decrementing* a variable:

```
x = x - 1;
```

We will discuss incrementing and decrementing in more detail later in this chapter.

Assignment/Declaration Variations

Java is a complex language that provides a lot of flexibility to programmers. In the last section we saw the simplest form of variable declaration and assignment, but there are many variations on this theme. It wouldn't be a bad idea to stick with the simplest form while you are learning, but you'll come across other forms as you read other people's programs, so you'll want to understand what they mean.

The first variation is that Java allows you to provide an initial value for a variable at the time that you declare it. The syntax is as follows:

```
<type> <name> = <expression>;
```

as in:

```
double height = 70;
double weight = 195;
```

This variation combines declaration and assignment in one line of code. These two have the same effect as providing two declarations followed by two assignment statements:

```
double height;
double weight;
height = 70;
weight = 195;
```

Another variation is to declare several variables all of the same type. The syntax is as follows:

```
<type> <name>, <name>, <name>, . . . , <name>;
```

as in:

```
double height, weight;
```

This example declares two different variables, both of type `double`. Notice that the type appears just once, at the beginning of the declaration.

The final variation is a mixture of the previous two. You can declare multiple variables all of the same type, and you can initialize them at the same time. For example, you could say:

```
double height = 70, weight = 195;
```

This statement declares the two `double` variables `height` and `weight` and gives them initial values (70 and 195, respectively). Java even allows you to mix initializing and not initializing, as in:

```
double height = 70, weight = 195, bmi;
```

This declares three `double` variables called `height`, `weight`, and `bmi` and provides initial values to two of them (`height` and `weight`). The variable `bmi` is uninitialized.

Common Programming Error

Accidentally Declaring a Variable Twice

One of the things to keep in mind as you learn is that you can declare any given variable just once. You can assign it as many times as you like once you've declared it, but the declaration should appear just once. Think of variable declaration as being like checking into a hotel and assignment as being like going in and out of your room. You have to check in first to get your room key, but then you can come and go as often as you like. If you tried to check in a second time, the hotel would be likely to ask you if you really want to pay for a second room.

If Java sees you declaring a variable more than once, it generates a compiler error. For example, say your program contains the following lines:

```
int x = 13;
System.out.println(x);
int x = 2;             // this line does not compile
System.out.println(x);
```

The first line is okay. It declares an integer variable called `x` and initializes it to 13. The second line is also okay, because it simply prints the value of `x`. But the third line will generate an error message indicating that "x is already defined." If you want to change the value of `x` you need to use a simple assignment statement instead of a variable declaration:

```
int x = 13;
System.out.println(x);
x = 2;
System.out.println(x);
```

We have been referring to the "assignment statement," but in fact assignment is an operator, not a statement. When you assign a value to a variable, the overall expression evaluates to the value just assigned. That means that you can form expressions that have assignment operators embedded within them. Unlike most other operators, the assignment operator evaluates from right to left, which allows programmers to write statements like the following:

```
int x, y, z;
x = y = z = 2 * 5 + 4;
```

Because the assignment operator evaluates from right to left, this statement is equivalent to:

```
x = (y = (z = 2 * 5 + 4));
```

The expression 2 * 5 + 4 evaluates to 14. This value is assigned to z. The assignment is itself an expression that evaluates to 14, which is then assigned to y. The assignment to y evaluates to 14 as well, which is then assigned to x. The result is that all three variables are assigned the value 14.

While you can do assignments like these, it's not always wise to do so. The previous chained assignment statement is not that difficult to read, but try to figure out what the following statement does:

```
x = 3 * (y = 2 + 2) / (z = 2);
```

It's easier to see what is going on when you write this code as three separate statements:

```
y = 2 + 2;
z = 2;
x = 3 * y / z;
```

String Concatenation

You saw in Chapter 1 that you can output string literals using System.out.println. You can also output numeric expressions using System.out.println:

```
System.out.println(12 + 3 - 1);
```

This statement causes the computer first to evaluate the expression, which yields the value 14, and then to write that value to the console window. You'll often want to output more than one value on a line, but unfortunately, you can pass only one value to println. To get around this limitation, Java provides a simple mechanism called *concatenation* for putting together several pieces into one long string literal.

> **String Concatenation**
>
> Combining several strings into a single string, or combining a string with other data into a new, longer string.

The addition (+) operator concatenates the pieces together. Doing so forms an expression that can be evaluated. Even if the expression includes both numbers and text, it can be evaluated just like the numeric expressions we have been exploring. Consider, for example, the following:

```
"I have " + 3 + " things to concatenate"
```

You have to pay close attention to the quotation marks in an expression like this to keep track of which parts are "inside" a string literal and which are outside. This expression begins with the text `"I have "` (including a space at the end), followed by a plus sign and the integer literal 3. Java converts the integer into a textual form (`"3"`) and concatenates the two pieces together to form `"I have 3"`. Following the 3 is another plus and another string literal, `" things to concatenate"` (which starts with a space). This piece is glued onto the end of the previous string to form the string `"I have 3 things to concatenate"`.

Because this expression produces a single concatenated string, we can include it in a `println` statement:

```
System.out.println("I have " + 3 + " things to concatenate");
```

This statement produces a single line of output:

```
I have 3 things to concatenate
```

String concatenation is often used to report the value of a variable. Consider, for example, the following program that computes the number of hours, minutes, and seconds in a standard year:

```
 1  public class Time {
 2      public static void main(String[] args) {
 3          int hours = 365 * 24;
 4          int minutes = hours * 60;
 5          int seconds = minutes * 60;
 6          System.out.println("Hours in a year = " + hours);
 7          System.out.println("Minutes in a year = " + minutes);
 8          System.out.println("Seconds in a year = " + seconds);
 9      }
10  }
```

Notice that the three `println` commands at the end each have a string literal concatenated with a variable. The program produces the following output:

```
Hours in a year = 8760
Minutes in a year = 525600
Seconds in a year = 31536000
```

You can use concatenation to form arbitrarily complex expressions. For example, if you had variables x, y, and z and you wanted to write out their values in coordinate format with parentheses and commas, you could say:

```
System.out.println("(" + x + ", " + y + ", " + z + ")");
```

If x, y, and z had the values 8, 19, and 23, respectively, this statement would output the string "(8, 19, 23)".

The + used for concatenation has the same level of precedence as the normal arithmetic + operator, which can lead to some confusion. Consider, for example, the following expression:

```
2 + 3 + " hello " + 7 + 2 * 3
```

This expression has four addition operators and one multiplication operator. Because of precedence, we evaluate the multiplication first:

```
2   +   3   +   " hello "   +   7   +   2   *   3

2   +   3   +   " hello "   +   7   +       6
```

This grouping might seem odd, but that's what the precedence rule says to do: We don't evaluate any additive operators until we've first evaluated all of the multiplicative operators. Once we've taken care of the multiplication, we're left with the four addition operators. These will be evaluated from left to right.

We first find ourselves asked to add together two integer values. Even though the overall expression involves a string, because this little subexpression has just two integers we perform integer addition:

```
2   +   3   +   " hello "   +   7   +   6

    5       +   " hello "   +   7   +   6
```

The next addition involves adding the integer 5 to the string literal "hello". If either of the two operands is a string, we perform concatenation. So, in this case, we convert the integer into a text equivalent ("5") and glue the pieces together to form a new string value:

```
5   +   " hello "   +   7   +   6

     "5 hello "     +   7   +   6
```

You might think that Java would add together the 7 and 6 the same way it added the 2 and 3 to make 5. But it doesn't work that way. The rules of precedence are simple, and Java follows them with simple-minded consistency. Precedence tells us that addition operators are evaluated from left to right, so first we add the string "5 hello" to

7. That is another combination of a string and an integer, so Java converts the integer to its textual equivalent (`"7"`) and concatenates the two parts together to form a new string:

```
"5 hello "  +  7  +  6
```

```
     "5 hello 7"    +  6
```

Now there is just a single remaining addition to perform, which again involves a string/integer combination. We convert the integer to its textual equivalent (`"6"`) and concatenate the two parts together to form a new string:

```
     "5 hello 7"  +  6
```

```
        "5 hello 76"
```

Clearly, such expressions can be confusing, but you wouldn't want the Java compiler to have to try to guess what you mean. Our job as programmers is easier if we know that the compiler is going to follow simple rules consistently. You can make the expression clearer, and specify how it is evaluated, by adding parentheses. For example, if we really did want Java to add together the 7 and 6 instead of concatenating them separately, we could have written the original expression in a much clearer way as:

```
(2 + 3) + " hello " + (7 + 2 * 3)
```

Because of the parentheses, Java will evaluate the two numeric parts of this expression first and then concatenate the results with the string in the middle. This expression evaluates to `"5 hello 13"`.

Increment/Decrement Operators

In addition to the standard assignment operator, Java has several special operators that are useful for a particular family of operations that are common in programming. As mentioned earlier, you will often find yourself increasing the value of a variable by a particular amount, which we call incrementing. You will also often find yourself decreasing the value of a variable by a particular amount, which we call decrementing. To accomplish this, you write statements like the following:

```
x = x + 1;
y = y - 1;
z = z + 2;
```

Likewise, you'll frequently find yourself wanting to double or triple the value of a variable or to reduce its value by a factor of 2, in which case you might write code like the following:

```
x = x * 2;
y = y * 3;
z = z / 2;
```

Java has a shorthand for these situations. You glue together the operator character (+, −, *, etc.) with the equals sign to get a special assignment operator (+=, −=, *=, etc.). This variation allows you to rewrite assignment statements like the previous ones as follows:

```
x += 1;
y -= 1;
z += 2;

x *= 2;
y *= 3;
z /= 2;
```

This convention is yet another detail to learn about Java, but the code can be clearer to read. Think of a statement like x += 2 as saying, "add 2 to x." That's more concise than saying x = x + 2.

Java has an even more concise way of expressing the particular case where you want to increment by 1 or decrement by 1. In this case, you can use the increment and decrement operators (++ and −−). For example, you can say:

```
x++;
y--;
```

There are actually two different forms of each of these operators, because you can also put the operator in front of the variable:

```
++x;
--y;
```

The two versions of ++ are known as the preincrement (++x) and postincrement (x++) operators. The two versions of -- are similarly known as the predecrement (--x) and postdecrement (x--) operators. The pre versus post distinction doesn't matter when you include them as statements by themselves, as in these two examples. The difference comes up only when you embed these inside of more complex expressions, which we don't recommend.

Now that we've seen a number of new operators, it is worth revisiting the issue of precedence. Updated precedence Table 2.5 includes the assignment operators and the increment and decrement operators. Notice that the increment and decrement operators are grouped with the unary operators and have the highest precedence.

TABLE 2.5 **Java Operator Precedence**

Description	Operators
unary operators	++, −−, +, −
multiplicative operators	*, /, %
additive operators	+, −
assignment operators	=, +=, −=, *=, /=, %=

Did you Know?

++ and --

The ++ and -- operators were first introduced in the C programming language. Java has them because the designers of the language decided to use the syntax of C as the basis for Java syntax. Many languages have made the same choice, including C++ and C#. There is almost a sense of pride among C programmers that these operators allow you to write extremely concise code, but many other people feel that they can make code unnecessarily complex. In this book we always use these operators as separate statements so that it is obvious what is going on, but in the interest of completeness we will look at the other option here.

The pre and post variations both have the same overall effect—the two increment operators increment a variable and the two decrement operators decrement a variable—but they differ in terms of what they evaluate to. When you increment or decrement, there are really two values involved: the original value that the variable had before the increment or decrement operation, and the final value that the variable has after the increment or decrement operation. The post versions evaluate to the original (older) value and the pre versions evaluate to the final (later) value.

Consider, for example, the following code fragment:

```
int x = 10;
int y = 20;
int z = ++x * y--;
```

What value is z assigned? The answer is 220. The third assignment increments x to 11 and decrements y to 19, but in computing the value of z, it uses the new value of x (++x) times the old value of y (y--), which is 11 times 20, or 220.

There is a simple mnemonic to remember this: When you see x++, read it as "give me x, then increment," and when you see ++x, read it as "increment, then give me x." Another memory device that might help is to remember that C++ is a bad name for a programming language. The expression "C++" would be interpreted as "evaluate to the old value of C and then increment C." In other words, even though you're trying to come up with something new and different, you're really stuck with the old awful language. The language you want is ++C, which would be a new and improved language rather than the old one. Some people have suggested that perhaps Java is ++C.

Variables and Mixing Types

You already know that when you declare a variable, you must tell Java what type of value it will be storing. For example, you might declare a variable of type `int` for integer values or of type `double` for real values. The situation is fairly clear when you have just integers or just reals, but what happens when you start mixing the types? For example, the following code is clearly okay:

```
int x;
double y;
x = 2 + 3;
y = 3.4 * 2.9;
```

Here, we have an integer variable that we assign an integer value and a double variable that we assign a double value. But what if we try to do it the other way around?

```
int x;
double y;
x = 3.4 * 2.9; // illegal
y = 2 + 3;     // okay
```

As the comments indicate, you can't assign an integer variable a `double` value, but you can assign a `double` variable an integer value. Let's consider the second case first. The expression `2 + 3` evaluates to the integer `5`. This value isn't a `double`, but every integer is a real value, so it is easy enough for Java to convert the integer into a `double`. The technical term is that Java *promotes* the integer into a `double`.

The first case is more problematic. The expression `3.4 * 2.9` evaluates to the `double` value `9.86`. This value can't be stored in an integer because it isn't an integer. If you want to perform this kind of operation, you'll have to tell Java to convert this value into an integer. As described earlier, you can cast a `double` to an `int`, which will truncate anything after the decimal point:

```
x = (int) (3.4 * 2.9);  // now legal
```

This statement first evaluates `3.4 * 2.9` to get `9.86` and then truncates that value to get the integer `9`.

Common Programming Error

Forgetting to Cast

We often write programs that involve a mixture of integers and doubles, so it is easy to make mistakes when it comes to combinations of the two. For example, suppose that you want to compute the percentage of correctly answered questions on a student's test, given the total number of questions on the test and the number of questions the student got right. You might declare the following variables:

```
int totalQuestions;
int numRight;
double percent;
```

Java allows great flexibility in deciding what to include in the initialization part and the update, so we can use the for loop to solve all sorts of programming tasks. For now, though, we will restrict ourselves to a particular kind of loop that declares and initializes a single variable that is used to control the loop. This variable is often referred to as the *control variable* of the loop. In the test we compare the control variable against some final desired value, and in the update we change the value of the control variable, most often incrementing it by 1. Such loops are very common in programming. By convention, we often use names like i, j, and k for the control variables.

Each execution of the controlled statement of a loop is called an *iteration* of the loop (as in, "The loop finished executing after four iterations"). Iteration also refers to looping in general (as in, "I solved the problem using iteration").

Consider another for loop:

```
for (int i = -100; i <= 100; i++) {
    System.out.println(i + " squared = " + (i * i));
}
```

This loop executes a total of 201 times, producing the squares of all the integers between −100 and +100 inclusive. The values used in the initialization and the test, then, can be any integers. They can, in fact, be arbitrary integer expressions:

```
for (int i = (2 + 2); i <= (17 * 3); i++) {
    System.out.println(i + " squared = " + (i * i));
}
```

This loop will generate the squares of all the integers between 4 and 51 inclusive. The parentheses around the expressions are not necessary but improve readability. Consider the following loop:

```
for (int i = 1; i <= 30; i++) {
    System.out.println("+--------+");
}
```

This loop generates 30 lines of output, all exactly the same. It is slightly different from the previous one because the statement controlled by the for loop makes no reference to the control variable. Thus:

```
for (int i = -30; i <= -1; i++) {
    System.out.println("+--------+");
}
```

generates exactly the same output. The behavior of such a loop is determined solely by the number of iterations it performs. The number of iterations is given by:

```
<ending value> - <starting value> + 1
```

It is much simpler to see that the first of these loops iterates 30 times, so it is better to use. In general, if you want a loop to iterate exactly *n* times, you will use one of two standard loops. The first standard form looks like the ones you have already seen:

```
for (int <variable> = 1; <variable> <= n; i++) {
    <statement>;
    <statement>;
    . . .
    <statement>;
}
```

It's pretty clear that this loop executes *n* times because it starts at 1 and continues as long as it is less than or equal to *n*. Often, however, it is more convenient to start our counting at 0 instead of 1. That requires a change in the loop test to allow you to stop when *n* is one less:

```
for (int <variable> = 0; <variable> < n; i++) {
    <statement>;
    <statement>;
    . . .
    <statement>;
}
```

Notice that in this form when you initialize the variable to 0, you test whether it is strictly less than *n*. Either form will execute exactly *n* times, although there are some situations where the zero-based loop works better.

Let's look at some borderline cases. Consider this loop:

```
for (int i = 1; i <= 1; i++) {
    System.out.println("+--------+");
}
```

According to our rule it should iterate once, and it does. It initializes the variable i to 1 and tests to see if this is less than or equal to 1, which it is. So it executes the println, increments i, and tests again. The second time it tests, it finds that i is no longer less than or equal to 1, so it stops executing. Now consider this loop:

```
for (int i = 1; i <= 0; i++) {
    System.out.println("+--------+"); // never executes
}
```

This loop performs no iterations at all. It will not cause an execution error; it just won't execute the body. It initializes the variable to 1 and tests to see if this is less than or equal to 0. It isn't, so rather than executing the statements in the body, it stops there.

When you construct a `for` loop, you can include more than one statement inside the curly braces. Consider, for example, the following code:

```
for (int i = 1; i <= 20; i++) {
    System.out.println("Hi!");
```

```
        System.out.println("Ho!");
}
```

This will produce 20 pairs of lines, the first of which has the word "Hi!" on it and the second of which has the word "Ho!"

When a for loop controls a single statement, you don't have to include the curly braces. The curly braces are required only for situations like the previous one, where you have more than one statement that you want the loop to control. However, the Sun coding convention includes the curly braces even for a single statement, and we follow this convention in this book. There are two advantages to this convention:

- Including the curly braces prevents future errors. Even if you need only one statement in the body of your loop now, your code is likely to change over time. Having the curly braces there ensures that, if you add an extra statement to the body later, you won't accidentally forget to include them. In general, including curly braces in advance is cheaper than locating obscure bugs later.

- Always including the curly braces reduces the level of detail you have to consider as you learn new control structures. It takes time to master the details of any new control structure, and it will be easier to master those details if you don't have to also be thinking about when to include and when not to include the braces.

print versus println

So far you have been producing entire lines of output using println commands. Now that you know how to write for loops, you will want to be able to produce complex lines of output piece by piece. For example, if you want to produce a line of output that has 80 stars on it, it would be easier to use a loop that prints one star at a time and have it execute 80 times rather than using a single println. Before you can do that, though, you have to learn about a variation of the println command.

Java has a variation of the println command called print that allows you to produce output on the current line without going to a new line of output. The println command really does two different things: It sends output to the current line, and then it moves to the beginning of a new line. The print command does only the first of these. Thus, a series of print commands will generate output all on the same line. Only a println command will cause the current line to be completed and a new line to be started. For example, consider these six statements:

```
System.out.print("To be ");
System.out.print("or not to be.");
System.out.print("That is ");
System.out.println("the question.");
System.out.print("This is");
System.out.println(" for the whole family!");
```

Common Programming Error

Forgetting Curly Braces

You should use indentation to indicate the body of a `for` loop, but indentation alone is not enough. Java ignores indentation when deciding how different statements are grouped. Suppose, for example, that you were to write the following code:

```
for (int i = 1; i <= 20; i++)
    System.out.println("Hi!");
    System.out.println("Ho!");
```

The indentation indicates to the reader that both of the `println` statements are in the body of the `for` loop, but there aren't any curly braces to indicate that to Java. As a result, this code is interpreted as follows:

```
for (int i = 1; i <= 20; i++) {
    System.out.println("Hi!");
}
System.out.println("Ho!");
```

Only the first `println` is considered to be in the body of the `for` loop. The second `println` is considered to be outside the loop. So, this code would produce 20 lines of output that all say "Hi!" followed by one line of output that says "Ho!" To include both `println`s in the body, you need curly braces around them:

```
for (int i = 1; i <= 20; i++) {
    System.out.println("Hi!");
    System.out.println("Ho!");
}
```

These statements produce two lines of output. Remember that every `println` statement produces exactly one line of output; because there are two `println` statements here, there are two lines of output. After the first statement executes, the current line looks like this:

```
To be
     ^
```

The arrow below the output line indicates the position where output will be sent next. We can simplify our discussion if we refer to the arrow as the *output cursor*. Notice that the output cursor is at the end of this line and that it appears after a space. That is so because the command was a `print` (don't go to a new line) and the string literal in the `print` ended with a space. Java will not insert a space for you unless you specifically request it. After the next `print`, the line looks like this:

```
To be or not to be.
                   ^
```

There's no space at the end now because the string literal in the second `print` command ends in a period, not a space. After the next `print`, the line looks like this:

```
To be or not to be.That is
                          ^
```

There is no space between the period and the word "That" because there was no space in the `print` commands, but there is a space at the end of the string literal in the third statement. After the next statement executes, the output looks like this:

```
To be or not to be.That is the question.
^
```

Because this fourth statement is a `println` command, it finishes the output line and positions the cursor at the beginning of the second line. The next statement is another `print` that produces this:

```
To be or not to be.That is the question.
This is
       ^
```

The final `println` completes the second line and positions the output cursor at the beginning of a new line:

```
To be or not to be.That is the question.
This is for the whole family!
^
```

These six statements are equivalent to these two single statements:

```
System.out.println("To be or not to be.That is the question.");
System.out.println("This is for the whole family!");
```

Using the `print` and the `println` commands together to produce lines like these may seem a bit silly, but you will see that there are more interesting applications of `print` in combination with `for` loops.

Remember that it is possible to have an empty `println` command:

```
System.out.println();
```

Because there is nothing inside of the parentheses to be written to the output line, this positions the output cursor at the beginning of the next line. If there are `print` commands before this empty `println`, it finishes out the line made by those `print` commands. If there are no previous `print` commands, it produces a blank line. An empty `print` command is meaningless and illegal.

Nested for Loops

The `for` loop controls a statement, and the `for` loop is itself a statement, which means that one `for` loop can control another `for` loop. For example, you can write code like the following:

```
for (int i = 1; i <= 10; i++) {
    for (int j = 1; j <= 5; j++) {
        System.out.println("Hi there.");
    }
}
```

This code is probably easier to read from the inside out. The `println` statement produces a single line of output. The inner `j` loop executes this statement five times, producing five lines of output. The outer `i` loop executes the inner loop 10 times, which produces 10 sets of 5 lines, or 50 lines of output. The preceding code, then, is equivalent to:

```
for (int i = 1; i <= 50; i++) {
    System.out.println("Hi there.");
}
```

This example shows that a `for` loop can be controlled by another `for` loop. Such a loop is called a *nested loop*. This example wasn't very interesting, though, because the nested loop can be eliminated. Let's look at a more interesting nested loop that does something useful:

```
for (int i = 1; i <= 6; i++) {
    for (int j = 1; j <= 10; j++) {
        System.out.print("*");
    }
    System.out.println();
}
```

When you write code that involves nested loops, you have to be careful to indent the code correctly to make the structure clear. At the outermost level, the preceding code is a simple `for` loop that executes six times:

```
for (int i = 1; i <= 6; i++) {
    ...
}
```

We use indentation for the statements inside this `for` loop to make it clear that they are the body of this loop. Inside, we find two statements: another `for` loop and a `println`. Let's look at the inner `for` loop:

```
for (int j = 1; j <= 10; j++) {
    System.out.print("*");
}
```

This loop is controlled by the outer `for` loop, which is why it is indented, but it itself controls a statement (the `print` statement), so we end up with another level of indentation. The indentation thus indicates that the `print` statement is controlled by the inner `for` loop, which in turn is controlled by the outer `for` loop. So what does this inner loop do? It prints 10 stars on the current line of output. They all appear on the same line because we are using a `print` instead of a `println`. Notice that after this loop we perform a `println`:

```
System.out.println();
```

The net effect of the `for` loop followed by the `println` is that we get a line of output with 10 stars on it. But remember that these statements are contained in an outer loop that executes six times, so we end up getting six lines of output, each with 10 stars:

```
**********
**********
**********
**********
**********
**********
```

Let's examine one more variation. In the code above, the inner `for` loop always does exactly the same thing: It prints exactly 10 stars on a line of output. But what happens if we change the test for the inner `for` loop to make use of the outer `for` loop's control variable (`i`)?

```
for (int i = 1; i <= 6; i++) {
    for (int j = 1; j <= i; j++) {
        System.out.print("*");
    }
    System.out.println();
}
```

In the old version the inner loop always executes 10 times, producing 10 stars on each line of output. With the new test (`j <= i`), the inner loop will execute i times with each iteration. But i is changing: It takes on the values 1, 2, 3, 4, 5, and 6. On the first iteration of the outer loop, when i is 1, the test `j <= i` is effectively testing `j <= 1`, and a line with one star on it is produced. On the second iteration of the outer loop, when i is 2, the test is effectively testing `j <= 2`, and a line with two stars on it is produced. On the third iteration of the outer loop, when i is 3, the test is effectively testing `j <= 3`, and a line with three stars on it is produced. This continues through the sixth iteration.

In other words, this code produces a triangle as output:

```
*
**
***
****
*****
******
```

2.4 Managing Complexity

You've learned about several new programming constructs in this chapter, and it's time to put the pieces together to solve some complex tasks. As we pointed out in Chapter 1, Brian Kernighan, one of the creators of the C programming language, has said that "Controlling complexity is the essence of computer programming." In this section we will examine several techniques that computer scientists use to solve complex problems without being overwhelmed by complexity.

Scope

As programs get longer, there is an increasing possibility of different parts of the program interfering with each other. Java helps us to manage this potential problem by enforcing rules of *scope.*

> **Scope (of a Declaration)**
> The part of a program in which a particular declaration is valid.

As you've seen, when it comes to declaring static methods, you can put them in any order whatsoever. The scope of a static method is the entire class in which it appears. Variables work differently. The simple rule is that the scope of a variable declaration extends from the point where it is declared to the right curly brace that encloses it. In other words, find the pair of curly braces that directly enclose the variable declaration. The scope of the variable is from the point where it is declared to the closing curly brace.

This scope rule has several implications. Consider first what it means for different methods. Each method has its own set of curly braces to indicate the statements to be executed when the method is called. Any variables declared inside of a method's curly braces won't be available outside the method. We refer to such variables as *local variables,* and we refer to the process of limiting their scope as *localizing* variables.

> **Local Variable**
> A variable declared inside a method that is accessible only in that method.

> **Localizing Variables**
> Declaring variables in the innermost (most local) scope possible.

In general, you will want to declare variables in the most local scope possible. You might wonder why we would want to localize variables to just one method. Why not just declare everything in one outer scope? That certainly seems simpler, but there are some important drawbacks. Localizing variables leads to some duplication (and possibly confusion) but provides more security. As an analogy, consider the use of refrigerators in dormitories. Every dorm room can have its own refrigerator, but if you are outside of a room, you don't know whether it has a refrigerator in it. The contents of the room are hidden from you.

Java programs use variables to store values just as students use refrigerators to store beer, ice cream, and other valuables. The last time we were in a dorm we noticed that most of the individual rooms had refrigerators in them. This seems terribly redundant, but the reason is obvious. If you want to guarantee the security of something, you put it where nobody else can get it. You will use local variables in your programs in much the same way. If each individual method has its own local variables to use, you don't have to consider possible interference from other parts of the program.

Let's look at a simple example involving two methods:

```
1   // This program does not compile.
2   public class ScopeExample {
3       public static void main(String[] args) {
4           int x = 3;
5           int y = 7;
6           computeSum();
7       }
8
9       public static void computeSum() {
10          int sum = x + y; // illegal, x/y are not in scope
11          System.out.println("sum = " + sum);
12      }
13  }
```

In this example, the main method declares local variables x and y and gives them initial values. Then it calls the method computeSum. Inside of this method, we try to make use of the values of x and y to compute a sum. However, because the variables x and y are local to the main method and are not visible inside of the computeSum method, this doesn't work. (In the next chapter, we will see a technique for allowing one method to pass a value to another.)

The program produces error messages like the following:

```
ScopeExample.java:10: cannot find symbol
symbol  : variable x
location: class ScopeExample
        int sum = x + y;  // illegal, x/y are not in scope
                  ^
ScopeExample.java:10: cannot find symbol
symbol  : variable y
location: class ScopeExample
        int sum = x + y;  // illegal, x/y are not in scope
                      ^
```

It's important to understand scope when discussing the local variables of one method versus another method, but it also has implications for what happens inside a single method. You have seen that curly braces are used to group together a series of statements. But you can have curly braces inside of curly braces, and this leads to some scope issues. For example, consider the following code:

```
for (int i = 1; i <= 5; i++) {
    int squared = i * i;
    System.out.println(i + " squared = " + squared);
}
```

This is a variation of the code we looked at earlier in the chapter to print out the squares of the first five integers. In this version, a variable called squared is used to keep track of the square of the `for` loop control variable. This code works fine, but consider this variation:

```java
for (int i = 1; i <= 5; i++) {
    int squared = i * i;
    System.out.println(i + " squared = " + squared);
}
System.out.println("Last square = " + squared); // illegal
```

This code generates a compiler error. The variable `squared` is declared inside the `for` loop. In other words, the curly braces that contain it are the curly braces for the loop. It can't be used outside of this scope, so when you attempt to refer to it outside of the loop, you'll get a compiler error.

If for some reason you need to write code like this that accesses the variable after the loop, you have to declare the variable in the outer scope before the loop:

```java
int squared = 0;   // declaration is now in outer scope
for (int i = 1; i <= 5; i++) {
    squared = i * i;   // change this to an assignment statement
    System.out.println(i + " squared = " + squared);
}
System.out.println("Last square = " + squared); // now legal
```

There are a few special cases for scope, and the `for` loop is one of them. When a variable is declared in the initialization part of a `for` loop, its scope is just the `for` loop itself (the three parts in the `for` loop header and the statements controlled by the `for` loop). That means you can use the same variable name in multiple `for` loops:

```java
for (int i = 1; i <= 10; i++) {
    System.out.println(i + " squared = " + (i * i));
}
for (int i = 1; i <= 10; i++) {
    System.out.println(i + " cubed = " + (i * i * i));
}
```

The variable `i` is declared twice in the preceding code, but because the scope of each variable is just the `for` loop in which it is declared, this isn't a problem. (It's like having two dorm rooms, each with its own refrigerator.) Of course, you can't do this with nested `for` loops. The following code, for example, will not compile:

```java
for (int i = 1; i <= 5; i++) {
    for (int i = 1; i <= 10; i++) { //illegal
        System.out.println("hi there.");
    }
}
```

When Java encounters the inner `for` loop, it will complain that the variable `i` has already been declared within this scope. You can't declare the same variable twice within the same scope. You have to come up with two different names to distinguish between them, just as when there are two Carls in the same family they tend to be called "Carl Junior" and "Carl Senior" to avoid any potential confusion.

As we saw earlier, a control variable that is used in a `for` loop doesn't have to be declared in the initialization part of the loop. You can separate the declaration of the `for` loop control variable from the initialization of the variable, as in the following:

```
int i;
for (i = 1; i <= 5; i++) {
    System.out.println(i + " squared = " + (i * i));
}
```

Doing so extends the variable's scope to the end of the enclosing set of curly braces. One advantage of this approach is that it enables you to refer to the final value of the control variable after the loop. Normally you wouldn't be able to do this, because its scope would be limited to the loop itself. However, declaring the control variable outside the loop is a dangerous practice, and it provides a good example of the problems you can encounter when you don't localize variables. Consider the following code, for example:

```
int i;
for (i = 1; i <= 5; i++) {
    for (i = 1; i <= 10; i++) {
        System.out.println("hi there.");
    }
}
```

As noted earlier, you shouldn't use the same control variable when you have nested loops. But unlike the previous example, because here the variable declaration is outside the outer `for` loop, this code actually compiles. So, instead of getting a helpful error message from the Java compiler, you get a program with a bug in it. You'd think from reading these loops that the code will produce 50 lines of output, but it actually produces just 10 lines of output. The inner loop increments the variable `i` until it becomes 11, and that causes the outer loop to terminate after just one iteration. It can be even worse. If you reverse the order of these loops:

```
int i;
for (i = 1; i <= 10; i++) {
    for (i = 1; i <= 5; i++) {
        System.out.println("hi there.");
    }
}
```

you get something known as an *infinite loop.*

> **Infinite Loop**
>
> A loop that never terminates.

This loop is infinite because no matter what the outer loop does to the variable `i`, the inner loop always sets it back to 1 and iterates until it becomes 6. The outer loop then increments the variable to 7 and finds that 7 is less than or equal to 10, so it always goes back to the inner loop, which once again sets the variable back to 1 and iterates up to 6. This process goes on indefinitely. These are the kinds of interference problems you can get when you fail to localize variables.

Common Programming Error

Referring to the Wrong Loop Variable

The following code attempts to print a triangle of stars. However, it has a subtle bug that causes it to print stars infinitely:

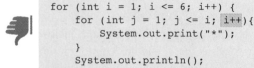

```java
for (int i = 1; i <= 6; i++) {
    for (int j = 1; j <= i; i++){
        System.out.print("*");
    }
    System.out.println();
}
```

The problem is on the second line, in the inner `for` loop header's update statement. The programmer meant to write `j++` but instead accidentally wrote `i++`. A trace of the code is shown in Table 2.7.

TABLE 2.7

Step	Code	Description
initialization	`int i = 1;`	variable i is created and initialized to 1
initialization	`int j = 1;`	variable j is created and initialized to 1
test	`j <= i`	true because 1 <= 1, so we enter the inner loop
body	`{...}`	execute the `print` with j equal to 1
update	`i++`	increment i, which becomes 2
test	`j <= i`	true because 1 <= 2, so we enter the inner loop
body	`{...}`	execute the `print` with j equal to 1
update	`i++`	increment i, which becomes 3
...	...	...

The variable `j` should be increasing, but `i` is instead. The effect of this mistake is that the variable `j` is never incremented in the inner loop, and therefore the test of `j <= i` never fails, so the inner loop doesn't terminate.

Here's another broken piece of code. This one tries to print a 6 × 4 box of stars, but it also prints infinitely:

```java
for (int i = 1; i <= 6; i++) {
    for (int j = 1; i <= 4; j++) {
        System.out.print("*");
    }
    System.out.println();
}
```

The problem is on the second line, this time in the inner `for` loop header's test. The programmer meant to write `j <= 4` but instead accidentally wrote `i <= 4`. Since the value of `i` is never incremented in the inner loop, the test of `i <= 4` never fails, so the inner loop again doesn't terminate.

Pseudocode

As you write more complex algorithms, you will find that you can't just write the entire algorithm immediately. Instead, you will increasingly make use of the technique of writing *pseudocode*.

> **Pseudocode**
>
> English-like descriptions of algorithms. Programming with pseudocode involves successively refining an informal description until it is easily translated into Java.

For example, you can describe the problem of drawing a box as:

```
draw a box with 50 lines and 30 columns of asterisks.
```

While this describes the figure, it is not specific about how to draw (that is, what algorithm to use). Do you draw the figure line by line or column by column? In Java, figures like these must be generated line by line, because once a `println` has been performed on a line of output, that line cannot be changed. There is no command for going back to a previous line in the output. Therefore, you must output the first line in its entirety first, then the second line in its entirety, and so on. As a result, your decompositions for figures such as these will be line-oriented at the top level. Thus, a closer approximation is:

```
for (each of 50 lines) {
    draw a line of 30 asterisks.
}
```

Even this can be made more specific by introducing the idea of repeatedly writing a single character on the output line and then moving to a new line of output:

```
for (each of 50 lines) {
    for (each of 30 columns) {
        write one asterisk on the output line.
    }
    go to a new output line.
}
```

Using pseudocode, you can gradually convert an English description into something easily translated into a Java program. The simple examples we've looked at so far are hardly worth the application of pseudocode, so we will now examine the problem of generating a more complex figure:

```
* * * * * * * *
 * * * * * * *
  * * * * *
   * * *
    *
```

This figure must also be generated line by line:

```
for (each of 5 lines) {
    draw one line of the triangle.
}
```

Unfortunately, each line is different. Therefore, you must come up with a general rule that fits all the lines. The first line of this figure has a series of asterisks on it with no leading spaces. The subsequent lines each have a series of spaces followed by a series of asterisks. Using your imagination a bit, you can say that the first line has 0 spaces on it followed by a series of asterisks. This allows you to write a general rule for making this figure:

```
for (each of 5 lines) {
    write some spaces (possibly 0) on the output line.
    write some asterisks on the output line.
    go to a new output line.
}
```

In order to proceed, you must determine a rule for the number of spaces and a rule for the number of asterisks. Assuming that the lines are numbered 1 through 5, looking at the figure, you can fill in Table 2.8.

You want to find a relationship between line number and the other two columns. This is simple algebra, because these columns are related in a linear way. The second column is easy to get from the line number. It equals (`line` − 1). The third column is a little tougher. Because it goes down by 2 every time and the first column goes up by 1 every time, you need a multiplier of −2. Then you need an appropriate constant. The number 11 seems to do the trick, so that the third column equals (`11` − 2 * `line`). You can improve your pseudocode, then, as follows:

```
for (line going 1 to 5) {
    write (line − 1) spaces on the output line.
    write (11 − 2 * line) asterisks on the output line.
    go to a new output line.
}
```

TABLE 2.8

Line	Spaces	Asterisks
1	0	9
2	1	7
3	2	5
4	3	3
5	4	1

This is simple to turn into a program:

```
1  public class DrawV {
2      public static void main(String[] args) {
3          for (int line = 1; line <= 5; line++) {
4              for (int i = 1; i <= (line - 1); i++) {
5                  System.out.print(" ");
6              }
7              for (int i = 1; i <= (11 - 2 * line); i++) {
8                  System.out.print("*");
9              }
10             System.out.println();
11         }
12     }
13 }
```

A Decrementing for Loop

Sometimes we manage complexity by taking advantage of work that we have already done. For example, how would you produce this figure?

```
    *
   ***
  *****
 *******
*********
```

You could follow the same process you did above and find new expressions that produce the appropriate number of spaces and asterisks. However, there is an easier way. This figure is the same as the previous one, except the lines appear in reverse order. You can achieve this result by running the for loop backwards: Instead of starting at 1 and going up to 5 with a ++ update, you can start at 5 and go down to 1 using a -- update.

For example, the following loop:

```
for (int i = 10; i >= 1; i--) {
    System.out.println(i + " squared = " + (i * i));
}
```

will produce the squares of the first 10 integers, but in reverse order. The simple way to produce the upward-pointing triangle, then, is:

```
1  public class DrawCone {
2      public static void main(String[] args) {
3          for (int line = 5; line >= 1; line--) {
4              for (int i = 1; i <= (line - 1); i++) {
5                  System.out.print(" ");
6              }
7              for (int i = 1; i <= (11 - 2 * line); i++) {
8                  System.out.print("*");
9              }
10             System.out.println();
```

```
11              }
12         }
13   }
```

Class Constants

The `DrawCone` program in the last section draws a cone with five lines. How would you modify it to produce a cone with three lines? Your first thought might be to simply change the 5 in the code to a 3. However, that would cause the program to produce the following output:

```
  *****
 *******
*********
```

which is obviously wrong. If you work through the geometry of the figure, you will discover that the problem is with the use of the number 11 in the expression used to calculate the number of asterisks to print. The number 11 comes from this formula:

```
2 * (number of lines) + 1
```

Thus, for five lines the appropriate value is 11, but for three lines the appropriate value is 7. Programmers call numbers like these *magic numbers*. They are magic in the sense that they seem to make the program work, but their definition is not always obvious. Glancing at the `DrawCone` program, one is apt to ask, "Why 5? Why 11? Why 3? Why 7? Why me?"

To make programs more readable and more adaptable, you should try to avoid magic numbers whenever possible. You do so by storing the magic numbers. You can use variables to store these values, but that is misleading, given that you are trying to represent values that don't change. Fortunately, Java offers an alternative: You can declare values that are similar to variables but are guaranteed to have constant values. Not surprisingly, they are called *constants*. We most often define *class constants,* which can be accessed throughout the entire class.

| **Constant, Class Constant** |
| A named value that cannot be changed. A class constant can be accessed anywhere in the class (i.e., its scope is the entire class). |

You can choose a descriptive name for a constant that explains what it represents. You can then use that name instead of referring to the specific value to make your programs more readable and adaptable. For example, in the `DrawCone` program, you might want to introduce a constant called `LINES` that represents the number of lines (recall from Chapter 1 that we use all uppercase letters for constant names). You can use that constant in place of the magic number 5 and as part of an expression to calculate a value. This approach allows you to replace the magic number 11 with the formula from which it is derived (`2 * LINES + 1`).

Constants are declared with the keyword `final` that indicates the fact that their values cannot be changed once assigned. For example:

```
final int LINES = 5;
```

You can declare a constant anywhere you can declare a variable, but because they are often used by several different methods, we generally declare constants outside of methods. This causes another run-in with our old pal, the `static` keyword. If you want your static methods to be able to access your constants, the constants themselves must be static. Likewise, just as we declare our methods to be public, we usually declare our constants to be public. The following is the general syntax for constant definitions:

```
public static final <type> <name> = <expression>;
```

For example, here are definitions for two constants:

```
public static final int HEIGHT = 10;
public static final int WIDTH = 20;
```

These definitions create constants called `HEIGHT` and `WIDTH` that will always have the values `10` and `20`. These are known as class constants, because we declare them in the outermost scope of the class, along with the methods of the class. That way, they are visible in each method of the class.

We've already mentioned that we can avoid using a magic number in the `DrawCone` program by introducing a constant for the number of lines. Here's what the constant definition looks like:

```
public static final int LINES = 5;
```

We can now replace the `5` in the outer loop with this constant and replace the `11` in the second inner loop with the expression `2 * LINES + 1`. The result is the following program:

```
1  public class DrawCone2 {
2      public static final int LINES = 5;
3
4      public static void main(String[] args) {
5          for (int line = LINES; line >= 1; line--) {
6              for (int i = 1; i <= (line - 1); i++) {
7                  System.out.print(" ");
8              }
9              int stars = 2 * LINES + 1 - 2 * line;
10             for (int i = 1; i <= stars; i++) {
11                 System.out.print("*");
12             }
13             System.out.println();
14         }
15     }
16 }
```

Notice that in this program the expression for the number of stars has become sufficiently complex that we've introduced a local variable called `stars` to store the value. The advantage of this program is that it is more readable and more adaptable. A simple change to the constant `LINES` will make it produce a figure with a different number of lines.

2.5 Case Study: A Complex Figure

Now we'll consider an example that is even more complex. To solve it, we will go through three basic steps:

1. Decompose the task into subtasks, each of which will become a static method.

2. For each subtask, make a table for the figure and compute formulas for each column of the table in terms of the line number.

3. Convert the tables into actual `for` loop code for each method.

The output we want to produce is the following:

```
+------+
|\    /|
| \  / |
|  \/  |
|  /\  |
| /  \ |
|/    \|
+------+
```

Problem Decomposition and Pseudocode

To generate this figure, you have to first break it down into subfigures. In doing so, you should look for lines that are similar in one way or another. The first and last lines are exactly the same. The three lines after the first line all fit one pattern, and the three lines after that fit another:

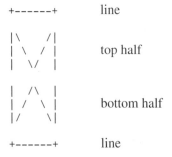

```
+------+          line

|\    /|
| \  / |          top half
|  \/  |

|  /\  |
| /  \ |          bottom half
|/    \|

+------+          line
```

Thus, you can break down the overall problem as:

```
draw a solid line.
draw the top half of the hourglass.
```

```
draw the bottom half of the hourglass.
draw a solid line.
```

You should solve each subproblem independently. Eventually you'll want to incorporate a class constant to make the program more flexible, but let's first solve the problem without worrying about magic numbers.

The solid line task can be further specified as:

```
write a plus on the output line.
write 6 dashes on the output line.
write a plus on the output line.
go to a new output line.
```

This translates easily into a static method:

```java
public static void drawLine() {
    System.out.print("+");
    for (int i = 1; i <= 6; i++) {
        System.out.print("-");
    }
    System.out.println("+");
}
```

The top half of the hourglass is more complex. Here is a typical line:

```
| \ / |
```

There are four printing characters, separated by spaces:

| \   / |
bar   spaces backslash spaces slash spaces bar

Thus, a first approximation in pseudocode might look like this:

```
for (each of 3 lines) {
    write a bar on the output line.
    write some spaces on the output line.
    write a backslash on the output line.
    write some spaces on the output line.
    write a slash on the output line.
    write some spaces on the output line.
    write a bar on the output line.
    go to a new line of output.
}
```

Again, you can make a table to figure out the required expressions. Writing the individual characters will be easy enough to translate into Java, but you need to be more specific about the spaces. Each line in this group contains three sets of spaces. Table 2.9 shows how many to use.

The first and third sets of spaces fit the rule ($line - 1$), and the second number of spaces is ($6 - 2 * line$). Therefore, the pseudocode should read:

```
for (line going 1 to 3) {
    write a bar on the output line.
    write (line - 1) spaces on the output line.
```

TABLE 2.9

Line	Spaces	Spaces	Spaces
1	0	4	0
2	1	2	1
3	2	0	2

```
        write a backslash on the output line.
        write (6 − 2 * line) spaces on the output line.
        write a slash on the output line.
        write (line − 1) spaces on the output line.
        write a bar on the output line.
        go to a new line of output.
}
```

Initial Structured Version

The pseudocode for the top half of the hourglass is easily translated into a static method called drawTop. A similar solution exists for the bottom half of the hourglass. Put together, the program looks like this:

```
 1  public class DrawFigure {
 2      public static void main(String[] args) {
 3          drawLine();
 4          drawTop();
 5          drawBottom();
 6          drawLine();
 7      }
 8
 9      // produces a solid line
10      public static void drawLine() {
11          System.out.print("+");
12          for (int i = 1; i <= 6; i++) {
13              System.out.print("−");
14          }
15          System.out.println("+");
16      }
17
18      // produces the top half of the hourglass figure
19      public static void drawTop() {
20          for (int line = 1; line <= 3; line++) {
21              System.out.print("|");
22              for (int i = 1; i <= (line − 1); i++) {
23                  System.out.print(" ");
24              }
25              System.out.print("\\");
26              for (int i = 1; i <= (6 − 2 * line); i++) {
27                  System.out.print(" ");
28              }
29              System.out.print("/");
30              for (int i = 1; i <= (line − 1); i++) {
```

```
31                        System.out.print(" ");
32                    }
33                    System.out.println("|");
34                }
35          }
36
37          // produces the bottom half of the hourglass figure
38          public static void drawBottom() {
39              for (int line = 1; line <= 3; line++) {
40                  System.out.print("|");
41                  for (int i = 1; i <= (3 - line); i++) {
42                      System.out.print(" ");
43                  }
44                  System.out.print("/");
45                  for (int i = 1; i <= 2 * (line - 1); i++) {
46                      System.out.print(" ");
47                  }
48                  System.out.print("\\");
49                  for (int i = 1; i <= (3 - line); i++) {
50                      System.out.print(" ");
51                  }
52                  System.out.println("|");
53              }
54          }
55  }
```

Adding a Class Constant

The `DrawFigure` program works in that it produces the desired output, but it is not very flexible. What if we wanted to produce a similar figure of a different size? The original problem involved an hourglass figure that had three lines in the top half and three lines in the bottom half. What if we wanted the following output, with four lines in the top half and four lines in the bottom half?

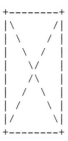

Obviously the program would be more useful if we could make it flexible enough to produce either output. We do so by eliminating the magic numbers with the introduction of a class constant. You might think that we need to introduce two constants—one for the height and one for width—but because of the regularity of this figure, the height is determined by the width and vice versa. Consequently, we only need to introduce a single class constant. Let's use the height of the hourglass halves:

```
public static final int SUB_HEIGHT = 4;
```

We've called the constant SUB_HEIGHT rather than HEIGHT because it refers to the height of each of the two halves, rather than the figure as a whole. Notice how we use the underscore character to separate the different words in the name of the constant.

So, how do we modify the original program to incorporate this constant? We look through it for any magic numbers and insert the constant or an expression involving it where appropriate. For example, the drawLine method draws six dashes for the sub-height of 3. If you look at the new figure, you will see that it draws eight dashes for the subheight of 4. You can use the same kind of reasoning that we used with our tables. If the number of dashes goes up by 2 when the subheight goes up by 1, we need a multiplier of 2. So, the expression to compute the number of dashes will involve (2 * SUB_HEIGHT). We might also need a constant, although not in this case because the expression gives us exactly what we are looking for (six dashes for a sub-height of 3, eight dashes for a subheight of 4).

So, the drawLine method would be rewritten as follows:

```
public static void drawLine() {
    System.out.print("+");
    for (int i = 1; i <= (2 * SUB_HEIGHT); i++) {
        System.out.print("-");
    }
    System.out.println("+");
}
```

There are quite a few magic numbers in the drawTop and drawBottom methods. In particular, the numbers 1, 2, 3, and 6 appear several times. In some cases, it is fairly obvious what to do. For example, each method has an outer for loop that uses the magic number 3. Why 3? Because each subfigure has a height of 3. Obviously, that 3 should be replaced with SUB_HEIGHT. The number 6 is not quite so obvious, but you can make an educated guess that if the magic number is 6 when the subheight is 3, perhaps it's equal to twice the subheight. In fact, that turns out to be the right answer.

If guessing doesn't work, you can always fall back on the table technique. Work out a new table for the figure of subheight 4 and figure out what expressions to use for it. If you do so, you'll find that the magic number 6 in the old expressions is replaced by the magic number 8. If the magic number needs to go up by 2 when the subheight goes up by 1, clearly we need a multiplier of 2.

The magic numbers 1 and 2 turn out not to be related to the subheight. Again, this is something you can make an educated guess about and verify by executing the program, or you can work out a new set of formulas to see whether these numbers change with a new subheight.

Here is the new version of the program with a class constant for the subheight. It uses a SUB_HEIGHT value of 4, but we could change this to 3 to produce the smaller version or to some other value to produce yet another version of the figure.

```
1  public class DrawFigure2 {
2      public static final int SUB_HEIGHT = 4;
3
4      public static void main(String[] args) {
```

```
 5              drawLine();
 6              drawTop();
 7              drawBottom();
 8              drawLine();
 9          }
10
11      // produces a solid line
12      public static void drawLine() {
13          System.out.print("+");
14          for (int i = 1; i <= (2 * SUB_HEIGHT); i++) {
15              System.out.print("-");
16          }
17          System.out.println("+");
18      }
19
20      // produces the top half of the hourglass figure
21      public static void drawTop() {
22          for (int line = 1; line <= SUB_HEIGHT; line++) {
23              System.out.print("|");
24              for (int i = 1; i <= (line - 1); i++) {
25                  System.out.print(" ");
26              }
27              System.out.print("\\");
28              int spaces = 2 * SUB_HEIGHT - 2 * line;
29              for (int i = 1; i <= spaces; i++) {
30                  System.out.print(" ");
31              }
32              System.out.print("/");
33              for (int i = 1; i <= (line - 1); i++) {
34                  System.out.print(" ");
35              }
36              System.out.println("|");
37          }
38      }
39
40      // produces the bottom half of the hourglass figure
41      public static void drawBottom() {
42          for (int line = 1; line <= SUB_HEIGHT; line++) {
43              System.out.print("|");
44              for (int i = 1; i <= (SUB_HEIGHT - line); i++) {
45                  System.out.print(" ");
46              }
47              System.out.print("/");
48              for (int i = 1; i <= 2 * (line - 1); i++) {
49                  System.out.print(" ");
50              }
51              System.out.print("\\");
52              for (int i = 1; i <= (SUB_HEIGHT - line); i++) {
53                  System.out.print(" ");
54              }
55              System.out.println("|");
56          }
57      }
58  }
```

Notice that the SUB_HEIGHT constant is declared with class-wide scope, rather than locally in the individual methods. While localizing variables is a good idea, the same is not true for constants. We localize variables to avoid potential interference, but that argument doesn't hold for constants, since they are guaranteed not to change. Another argument for using local variables is that it makes static methods more independent. That argument has some merit when applied to constants, but not enough. It is true that class constants introduce dependencies between methods, but often that is what you want. For example, the three methods in `DrawFigure2` should not be independent of each other when it comes to the size of the figure. Each subfigure has to use the same size constant. Imagine the potential disaster if each method had its own `SUB_HEIGHT`, each with a different value—none of the pieces would fit together.

Further Variations

The solution we have arrived at may seem cumbersome, but it is easier to adapt to a new task. For example, suppose that you want to generate the following output:

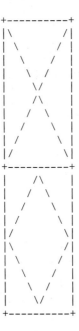

This output uses a subheight of 5 and includes both a diamond pattern and an X pattern. You can produce this output by changing the `SUB_HEIGHT` constant to 5:

```
public static final int SUB_HEIGHT = 5;
```

and rewriting the `main` method as follows to produce both the original x pattern and the new diamond pattern, which you get simply by reversing the order of the calls on the two halves:

```
public static void main(String[] args) {
    drawLine();
    drawTop();
    drawBottom();
```

8. 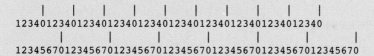 Write `for` loops to produce the following output:

```
    1
   22
  333
 4444
55555
```

9. Write `for` loops to produce the following output, with each line 40 characters wide:

```
----------------------------------------
_-^-__-^-__-^-__-^-__-^-__-^-__-^-__-^-__-^-
1122334455667788990011223344556677889900
----------------------------------------
```

10. It's common to print a rotating, increasing list of single-digit numbers at the start of a program's output as a visual guide to number the columns of the output to follow. With this in mind, write nested `for` loops to produce the following output, with each line 60 characters wide:

```
         |         |         |         |         |         |
123456789012345678901234567890123456789012345678901234567890
```

11. Modify your code from the previous exercise so that it could easily be modified to display a different range of numbers (instead of 1234567890) and a different number of repetitions of those numbers (instead of 60 total characters), with the vertical bars still matching up correctly. Use class constants instead of "magic numbers." Example outputs that could be generated by changing your constants would be:

```
     |    |    |    |    |    |    |    |    |    |
12340123401234012340123401234012340123401234012340
       |       |       |       |       |       |       |
12345670123456701234567012345670123456701234567012345670
```

12. Write nested `for` loops that produce the following output.

```
000111222333444555666777888999
000111222333444555666777888999
000111222333444555666777888999
```

13. Modify the code so that it now produces the following output:

```
999998888877777666665555544444333332222211111100000
999998888877777666665555544444333332222211111100000
999998888877777666665555544444333332222211111100000
999998888877777666665555544444333332222211111100000
999998888877777666665555544444333332222211111100000
```

14. Modify the code so that it now produces the following output:

```
9999999999888888888777777766666665555554444333221
9999999999888888888777777766666665555554444333221
9999999999888888888777777766666665555554444333221
9999999999888888888777777766666665555554444333221
```

15. Write a method called `printDesign` that produces the following output. Use `for` loops to capture the structure of the figure.

```
-----1-----
----333----
---55555---
--7777777--
-999999999-
```

16. Write a pseudocode algorithm that will produce the following figure as output:

```
+===+===+
|   |   |
|   |   |
|   |   |
+===+===+
|   |   |
|   |   |
|   |   |
+===+===+
```

17. Use your pseudocode from the previous exercise to write a Java program that produces the preceding figure as output. Use `for` loops to print the repeated parts of the figure. Once you get it to work, add a class constant so that the size of the figure can be changed simply by changing the constant's value.

Programming Projects

1. Write a program that produces the following output:

```
****** ////////////  ******
*****  ///////////\\   *****
****   //////////\\\    ****
***    /////\\\\\\       ***
**     ////\\\\\\\\        **
*      //\\\\\\\\\\         *
       \\\\\\\\\\\\
```

2.   Write a program that produces the following output:

```
+-------+
|  ^^   |
| ^  ^  |
|^    ^|
|  ^^   |
| ^  ^  |
|^    ^|
+-------+
|v     v|
| v  v  |
|  vv   |
|v     v|
| v  v  |
|  vv   |
+-------+
```

3. Write a program that produces the following output:

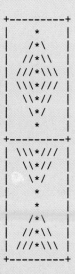

4. Write a program that produces the following output. Use a class constant to make it possible to change the number of stairs in the figure.

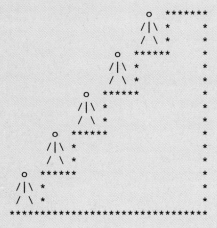

5. Write a program that produces the following rocket ship figure as its output. Use a class constant to make it possible to change the size of the rocket (the following output uses a size of 3).

```
      /**\
     //**\\
    ///**\\\
   ////**\\\\
  /////**\\\\\
 +=*=*=*=*=*=*+
 |../\..../\..|
 |./\/\../\/\.|
 |/\/\/\/\/\/\|
 |\/\/\/\/\/\/|
 |.\/\/..\/\/.|
 |..\/....\/..|
 +=*=*=*=*=*=*+
 |/\/\/\/\/\/\|
 |.\/\/..\/\/.|
 |..\/....\/..|
 |../\..../\..|
 |./\/\../\/\.|
 |/\/\/\/\/\/\|
 +=*=*=*=*=*=*+
      /**\
     //**\\
    ///**\\\
   ////**\\\\
  /////**\\\\\
```

Chapter 3

Introduction to Parameters and Objects

Introduction

Chapter 2 introduced techniques for managing complexity, including the use of class constants, which make programs more flexible. This chapter explores a more powerful technique for obtaining such flexibility. Here, you will learn how to use parameters to create methods that solve not just single tasks, but whole families of tasks. Creating such methods requires an insight into problems called generalization, which involves looking beyond a specific task to find the more general category of task it exemplifies. The ability to generalize is one of the most important qualities of a good software engineer, and the generalization technique you will study in this chapter is one of the most powerful techniques programmers use. After exploring parameters, we'll discuss some other issues associated with methods, such as the ability of a method to return a value.

This chapter then introduces the idea of objects and how to use them in Java programs. We aren't going to explore the details of defining objects for a while, but we want to begin using objects early. One of the most attractive features of Java is that it comes with a rich library of predefined objects that can be used to solve many common programming tasks.

The chapter concludes with an exploration of a very important kind of object known as a `Scanner`. Using a `Scanner` object, you can write programs that obtain values from the user. This will allow you to write interactive programs that prompt for input as well as producing output.

3.1 Parameters

Humans are very good at learning new tasks. In doing so, we often group a family of related tasks into one generalized solution. For example, someone might ask you to take 10 steps forward or 20 steps forward. These are different tasks, but they both involve taking a certain number of steps forward. We think of this action as a single task of taking steps forward, but we understand that the number of steps will vary from one task to another. In programming terms, we refer to the number of steps as a *parameter* that allows us to generalize the task.

> **Parameter (Parameterize)**
>
> Any of a set of characteristics that distinguish different members of a family of tasks. To parameterize a task is to identify a set of its parameters.

For a programming example, let's return to the `DrawFigure2` program of Chapter 2. It performs its task adequately, but there are several aspects that can be improved. For example, there are six different places where a `for` loop writes out spaces. This approach is redundant and can be consolidated into a single method that performs all space-writing tasks.

Each space-writing task requires a different number of spaces, so you need some way to tell the method how many spaces to write. The methods you've written so far have a simple calling mechanism where you say:

```
writeSpaces();
```

You might consider setting a variable to a particular value before the method is called, as in:

```
int number = 10;
writeSpaces();
```

Then the method could look at the value of the variable `number` to see how many spaces to write. Unfortunately, this approach won't work. Recall from Chapter 2 that scope rules determine where variables can be accessed. Following those rules, the variable `number` would be a local variable in `main` that could not be seen inside `writeSpaces`.

Instead, you want to be able to somehow include this value in the call, so that if you want to write 10 spaces you say:

```
writeSpaces(10);
```

and if you want to write 20 spaces you say:

```
writeSpaces(20);
```

You can do this using parameters. In Java, you can specify one or more parameters to a method. The idea is that instead of writing a method that performs just one version of a task, you write a more flexible version that solves a family of related tasks that all differ by one or more parameters. In the case of the `writeSpaces` method, the parameter is the number of spaces to write.

The following is the definition of `writeSpaces` with a parameter for the number of spaces to write:

```java
public static void writeSpaces(int number) {
    for (int i = 1; i <= number; i++) {
        System.out.print(" ");
    }
}
```

The parameter appears in the method header, after the name and inside the parentheses that you have, to this point, been leaving empty. The `writeSpaces` method uses a parameter called `number` of type `int`. As indicated earlier, you can no longer call the parameterized method by using just its name:

```java
writeSpaces();
```

You must now say something like:

```java
writeSpaces(10);
```

When a call like this is made, the value `10` is used to initialize the `number` parameter. You can think of this as information flowing into the method from the call:

```java
writeSpaces(10);
```

```java
public static void writeSpaces(int number) {
    ...
}
```

The parameter `number` is a local variable, but it gets its initial value from the call. Calling this method with the value `10` is equivalent to including the following declaration at the beginning of the `writeSpaces` method:

```java
int number = 10;
```

Of course, this mechanism is more flexible than a specific variable declaration, because you can instead say:

```java
writeSpaces(20);
```

and it will be as if you had said:

```java
int number = 20;
```

at the beginning of the method. You can even use an integer expression for the call:

```java
writeSpaces(3 * 4 - 5);
```

In this case, Java evaluates the expression to get the value 7 and then calls writeSpaces, initializing number to 7.

Computer scientists use the word "parameter" liberally to mean both what appears in the method header (the *formal parameter*) and what appears in the method call (the *actual parameter*).

> **Formal Parameter**
>
> A variable that appears inside parentheses in the header of a method that is used to generalize the method's behavior.

> **Actual Parameter**
>
> A specific value or expression that appears inside parentheses in a method call.

The term "formal parameter" is not very descriptive of its purpose. A better name would be "generalized parameter." In the writeSpaces method, number is the generalized parameter that appears in the method declaration. It is a placeholder for some unspecified value. The values appearing in the method calls are the actual parameters, because each call indicates a specific task to perform. In other words, each call provides an actual value to fill the placeholder.

The word "argument" is often used as a synonym for "parameter," as in, "These are the arguments I'm passing to this method." Some people prefer to reserve the word "argument" for actual parameters and the word "parameter" for formal parameters.

Let's look at an example of how you might use this writeSpaces method. Remember that the DrawFigure2 program had the following method, called drawTop:

```java
// produces the top half of the hourglass figure
public static void drawTop() {
    for (int line = 1; line <= SUB_HEIGHT; line++) {
        System.out.print("|");
        for (int i = 1; i <= (line - 1); i++) {
            System.out.print(" ");
        }
        System.out.print("\\");
        int spaces = 2 * SUB_HEIGHT - 2 * line;
        for (int i = 1; i <= spaces; i++) {
            System.out.print(" ");
        }
        System.out.print("/");
        for (int i = 1; i <= (line - 1); i++) {
            System.out.print(" ");
        }
        System.out.println("|");
    }
}
```

Using the `writeSpaces` method, you can rewrite this as follows:

```java
public static void drawTop() {
    for (int line = 1; line <= SUB_HEIGHT; line++) {
        System.out.print("|");
        writeSpaces(line - 1);
        System.out.print("\\");
        writeSpaces(2 * SUB_HEIGHT - 2 * line);
        System.out.print("/");
        writeSpaces(line - 1);
        System.out.println("|");
    }
}
```

Notice that `writeSpaces` is called three different times, specifying how many spaces are requred in each case. You could modify the `drawBottom` method from the `DrawFigure2` program similarly to simplify it.

The Mechanics of Parameters

When Java executes a call on a method, it initializes the method's parameters. For each parameter, it first evaluates the expression passed as the actual parameter and then uses the result to initialize the local variable whose name is given by the formal parameter. Let's use an example to clarify this process:

```java
 1  public class ParameterExample {
 2      public static void main(String[] args) {
 3          int spaces1 = 3;
 4          int spaces2 = 5;
 5
 6          System.out.print("*");
 7          writeSpaces(spaces1);
 8          System.out.println("*");
 9
10          System.out.print("!");
11          writeSpaces(spaces2);
12          System.out.println("!");
13
14          System.out.print("'");
15          writeSpaces(8);
16          System.out.println("'");
17
18          System.out.print("<");
19          writeSpaces(spaces1 * spaces2 - 5);
20          System.out.println(">");
21      }
22
23      // writes "number" spaces on the current output line
24      public static void writeSpaces(int number) {
25          for (int i = 1; i <= number; i++) {
26              System.out.print(" ");
27          }
28      }
29  }
```

In the first two lines of the `main` method, the computer finds instructions to allocate and initialize two variables:

spaces1 [3]   spaces2 [5]

The next three lines of code produce an output line with three spaces bounded by asterisks on either side:

```
System.out.print("*");
writeSpaces(spaces1);
System.out.println("*");
```

You can see where the asterisks come from, but look at the method call that produces the spaces. When Java executes the call on `writeSpaces`, it must set up its parameter. To set up the parameter, Java first evaluates the expression being passed as the actual parameter. The expression is simply the variable `spaces1`, which has the value 3. Therefore, the expression evaluates to 3. Java uses this result to initialize a local variable called `number`.

The following diagram indicates how the computer's memory would look as the `writeSpaces` method is entered the first time. Because there are two methods involved (`main` and `writeSpaces`), the diagram indicates which variables are local to `main` (`spaces1` and `spaces2`) and which are local to `writeSpaces` (the parameter `number`):

The net effect of this process is that the `writeSpaces` method has a local copy of the value stored in the variable `spaces1` from the `main` method. The `println` that comes after the call on `writeSpaces` puts an asterisk at the end of the line and then completes the line of output.

Let's now trace the next three lines of code:

```
System.out.print("!");
writeSpaces(spaces2);
System.out.println("!");
```

This first prints an exclamation mark on the second line of output, then calls `writeSpaces` again, this time with the variable `spaces2` as its actual parameter. The computer evaluates this expression, obtaining the result 5. This value is used to initialize `number`. Thus, this time it creates a copy of the value stored in the variable `spaces2` from the `main` method:

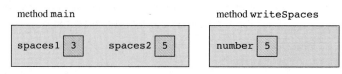

Because `number` has a different value this time (5 instead of 3), the method produces a different number of spaces. After the method executes, the `println` finishes the line of output with a second exclamation mark.

Here are the next three lines of code:

```
System.out.print("'");
writeSpaces(8);
System.out.println("'");
```

This code writes a single quotation mark at the beginning of the third line of output and then calls `writeSpaces` again. This time it uses the integer literal 8 as the expression, which means it initializes the parameter `number` as a copy of the number 8:

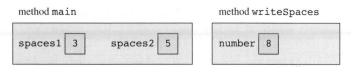

Again, the method will behave differently because of the different value of `number`. It prints eight spaces on the line and finishes executing. Then the `println` completes the line of output by printing another single quotation mark at the end of the line.

Finally, the last three lines of code in the `main` method are:

```
System.out.print("<");
writeSpaces(spaces1 * spaces2 - 5);
System.out.println(">");
```

This code prints a less-than character at the beginning of the fourth line of output and then makes a final call on the `writeSpaces` method. This time the actual parameter is an expression, not just a variable or literal value. Thus, before the call is made, the computer evaluates the expression to determine its value:

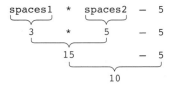

The computer uses this result to initialize `number`:

`number` is now a copy of the value described by this complex expression. Therefore, the total output of this program is:

```
*     *
!     !
'           '
<           >
```

Common Programming Error

Confusing Actual and Formal Parameters

Many students get used to seeing declarations of formal parameters and mistakenly believe that their syntax is identical to that for passing actual parameters. It's a common mistake to write the type of a variable as it's being passed to a parameter:

```
writeSpaces(int spaces1);    // this doesn't work
```

This confusion is due to the fact that parameters' types are written in the declaration of the method, like this:

```
public static void writeSpaces(int number)
```

Types must be written when variables or parameters are declared, but when variables are used, such as when calling a method and passing them as actual parameters, their types are not written. Actual parameters are not declarations, so therefore types should not be written before them:

```
writeSpaces(spaces1);    // much better!
```

Limitations of Parameters

We've seen that a parameter can be used to provide input to a method. But while you can use a parameter to send a value into a method, you can't use a parameter to get a value out of a method.

When a parameter is set up, a local variable is created and is initialized to the value being passed as the actual parameter. The net effect is that the local variable is a copy of the value coming from the outside. Since it is a local variable, it can't influence any variables outside the method. Consider the following sample program:

```
 1  public class ParameterExample2 {
 2      public static void main(String[] args) {
 3          int x = 17;
 4          doubleNumber(x);
 5          System.out.println("x = " + x);
 6          System.out.println();
 7
 8          int number = 42;
 9          doubleNumber(number);
10          System.out.println("number = " + number);
11      }
12
13      public static void doubleNumber(int number) {
14          System.out.println("Initial value = " + number);
15          number *= 2;
16          System.out.println("Final value = " + number);
17      }
18  }
```

This program begins by declaring and initializing an integer variable called x with the value 17:

It then calls the method doubleNumber, passing x as a parameter. The value of x is used to initialize the parameter number as a local variable of the method called doubleNumber:

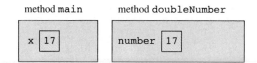

The program then executes the statements inside of doubleNumber. doubleNumber begins by printing the initial value of number (17). Then it doubles number:

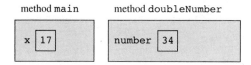

Notice that this has no effect on the variable x. The parameter called number is a copy of x, so even though they started out the same, changing the value of number does not impact x. doubleNumber then reports the new value of number (34).

At this point, doubleNumber finishes executing and we return to main:

The next statment in the main method reports the value of x, which is 17. Then it declares and initializes a variable called number with the value 42:

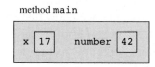

The following statement calls doubleNumber again, this time passing it the value of number. This is an odd situation because the parameter has the same name as the variable in main, but Java doesn't care. It always creates a new local variable for the doubleNumber method:

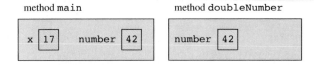

So, at this point there are two different variables called number, one in each method. Now it's time to execute the statements of doubleNumber again. It first reports the value of number (42), then doubles it:

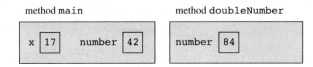

Again, notice that doubling number inside of doubleNumber has no effect on the original variable number in main. These are separate variables. The method then reports the new value of number (84) and returns to main:

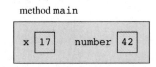

The program then reports the value of number and terminates. So, the overall output of the program is as follows:

```
Initial value = 17
Final value = 34
x = 17

Initial value = 42
Final value = 84
number = 42
```

The local manipulations of the parameter do not change these variables outside the method. The fact that variables are copied is an important aspect of parameters. On the positive side, we know that the variables are protected from change because the parameters are copies of the originals. On the negative side, it means that although parameters will allow us to send values into a method, they will not allow us to get values back out of a method.

Multiple Parameters

So far, our discussion of parameter syntax has been informal. It's about time that we wrote down more precisely the syntax we use to declare static methods with parameters. Here it is:

```
public static void <name>(<type> <name>, ..., <type> <name>) {
    <statement or variable declaration>;
```

```
    <statement or variable declaration>;
    ...
    <statement or variable declaration>;
}
```

This template indicates that we can declare as many parameters as we want inside the parentheses that appear after the name of a method in its header. We use commas to separate different parameters.

As an example of a method with multiple parameters, let's consider a variation of `writeSpaces`. It is convenient that we can tell it a different number of spaces to write, but it always writes spaces. What if we want 18 asterisks or 23 periods or 17 question marks? We can generalize the task even further by having the method take two parameters: both a character and a number of times to write that character:

```
public static void writeChars(char ch, int number) {
    for (int i = 1; i <= number; i++) {
        System.out.print(ch);
    }
}
```

The character to be printed is a parameter of type `char`, which we will discuss in more detail in the next chapter. Recall that character literals are enclosed in single quotation marks.

The syntax template for calling a method that accepts parameters is the following:

```
<method name>(<expression>, <expression>, ..., <expression>);
```

By calling the `writeChars` method you can write code like the following:

```
writeChars('=', 20);
System.out.println();
for (int i = 1; i <= 10; i++) {
    writeChars('>', i);
    writeChars(' ', 20 - 2 * i);
    writeChars('<', i);
    System.out.println();
}
writeChars('=', 20);
System.out.println();
```

which produces the following output:

```
====================
>                  <
>>                <<
>>>              <<<
>>>>            <<<<
>>>>>          <<<<<
>>>>>>        <<<<<<
>>>>>>>      <<<<<<<
>>>>>>>>    <<<<<<<<
>>>>>>>>>  <<<<<<<<<
>>>>>>>>>><<<<<<<<<<
====================
```

You can include as many parameters as you want when you define a method. Each method call must provide exactly that number of parameters, in the same order. For example, consider the first call on `writeChars` in the preceding code fragment, and the header for `writeChars`. Java lines up the parameters in sequential order (with the first actual parameter going into the first formal parameter and the second actual parameter going into the second formal parameter):

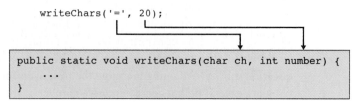

When you're writing methods that accept many parameters, the method header can become very long. It is common to wrap long lines (ones that exceed roughly 80 characters in length) by inserting a line break after an operator or parameter and indenting the following line by twice the normal indentation width. For example:

```
// method's header is too long, so we'll wrap it
public static void printTriangle(int xCoord1, int yCoord1,
        int xCoord2, int yCoord2, int xCoord3, int yCoord3) {
    ...
}
```

Parameters versus Constants

In Chapter 2, you saw that class constants are a useful mechanism to increase the flexibility of your programs. By using such constants, you can make it easy to modify a program to behave differently. Parameters provide much of the same flexibility, and more. Consider the `writeSpaces` method. Suppose you wrote it using a class constant:

```
public static final int NUMBER_OF_SPACES = 10;
```

This approach would give you the flexibility to produce a different number of spaces, but it has one major limitation: The constant can change only from execution to execution; it cannot change within a single execution. In other words, you can execute the program once with one value, edit the program, recompile, and then execute it again with a different value, but you can't use different values in a single execution of the program using a class constant.

Parameters are more flexible. Because you specify the value to be used each time you call the method, you can use several different values in a single program execution. As you have seen, you can call the method many different times within a single program execution and have it behave differently every time. However, using parameters involves more work for the programmer than using class constants. It makes your method headers and method calls more tedious, not to mention making the execution (and, thus, the debugging) more complex.

Therefore, you will probably find occasion to use each technique. The basic rule is to use a class constant when you only want to change the value from execution to execution. If you want to use different values within a single execution, use a parameter.

Overloading of Methods

You'll often want to create slight variations of the same method, passing different parameters. For example, you could have a `drawBox` method that allows you to specify a particular height and width, but you might also want to have a version that draws a box of default size. In other words, sometimes you want to specify these values:

```
drawBox(8, 10);
```

and other times you want to just tell it to draw a box with the standard height and width:

```
drawBox();
```

Some programming languages require you to come up with different names for these versions, such as `drawBox` and `drawDefaultBox`. As you can imagine, coming up with new names for each variation becomes tedious. Fortunately, Java allows you to have more than one method with the same name, as long as they have different parameters. This is called *overloading*. The primary requirement for overloading is that the different methods that you define must have different *method signatures*.

> **Method Signature**
> The name of a method, along with its number and type of parameters.

> **Method Overloading**
> The ability to define two or more different methods with the same name but different method signatures.

The two example `drawBox` versions would clearly have different method signatures, because one has two parameters and the other has zero parameters. It would be obvious from any call on the method which version to use: If you see two parameters, you execute the version with two parameters; if you see zero parameters, you execute the version with zero parameters.

It gets more complicated when overloading involves the same number of parameters, but this turns out to be one of the most useful applications of overloading. For example, the `println` method is actually a series of overloaded methods. We can call `println` passing it a `String`, an `int`, a `double`, and so on. This flexibility is implemented as a series of different methods, all of which take one parameter: One version takes a `String`, another version takes an `int`, another version takes a `double`, and so on. Obviously, you do slightly different things to print one of these kinds of data versus another, which is why it's useful to have these different versions of the method.

3.2 Methods That Return Values

The last few methods we've looked at have been action-oriented methods that perform some specific task. You can think of them as being like commands that you could give someone, as in "Draw a box" or "Draw a triangle." Parameters allow these commands to be more flexibile, as in "Draw a box that is 10 by 20."

You will also want to be able to write methods that compute values. These methods are more like questions, as in "What is the square root of 2.5?" or "What do you get when you carry 2.3 to the 4th power?" Consider, for example, a method called `sqrt` that would compute the square root of a number.

It might seem that the way to write such a method would be to have it accept a parameter of type `double` and `println` its square root to the console. But you may want to use the square root as part of a larger expression or computation, such as solving a quadratic equation or computing the distance between points on an x/y plane.

A better solution would be a square root command where the number of interest is passed as a parameter, and its square root comes back to the program as a result. You could then use the result as part of an expression, store it into a variable, or print it on the console. Such a command is a new type of method that is said to *return* a value.

> **Return**
>
> To send a value out as the result of a method that can be used in an expression in your program. Void methods do not return any value.

If you had such a method, you could ask for the square root of 2.5 by writing code like this:

```
// assuming you had a method named sqrt
double answer = sqrt(2.5);
```

The `sqrt` method has a parameter (the number to find the square root of), but it also returns a value (the square root). The actual parameter `2.5` goes "into" the method, and the square root comes out. In the preceding code, the returned result is stored in a variable called `answer`.

You can tell whether or not a method returns a value by looking at its header. All the methods you've written so far have begun with `public static void`, as in:

```
public static void drawTriangle(int height)
```

The word `void` is known as the *return type* of the method.

The `void` return type is a little odd because, as the word implies, it means that the method returns nothing. Instead of `void`, you can use any legal type. So, you can write methods that return an `int`, a `double`, or any other type. In the case of the `sqrt` method, you want it to return a `double`, so you would write its header as follows:

```
public static double sqrt(double n)
```

As in the previous case, the word that comes after `public static` is the return type of the method:

`public static double sqrt(double n)`

return type

Fortunately, you don't actually need to write a method for computing the square root of a number, because Java has one that is built in. The method is included in a class known as `Math` that includes many useful computing methods. So, before we discuss the details of writing methods that return values, let's explore the `Math` class and what it has to offer.

The `Math` Class

In Chapter 1 we mentioned that a great deal of predefined code, collectively known as the Java class libraries, has been written for Java. One of the most useful classes is `Math`. It includes predefined mathematical constants and a large number of common mathematical functions. The `Math` class should be available on any machine on which Java is properly installed.

As noted in the previous section, the `Math` class has a method called `sqrt` that computes the square root of a number. The method has the following header:

```
public static double sqrt(double n)
```

This header says that the method is called "sqrt," that it takes a parameter of type `double`, and that it returns a value of type `double`.

Unfortunately, you can't just call this method directly by referring to it as `sqrt` because it is in another class. Whenever you want to refer to something declared in another class, you use *dot notation:*

```
<class name>.<element>
```

So, you would refer to this method as `Math.sqrt`. Here's a sample program that uses this method:

```
1  public class WriteRoots {
2      public static void main(String[] args) {
3          for (int i = 1; i <= 20; i++) {
4              double root = Math.sqrt(i);
5              System.out.println("sqrt(" + i + ") = " + root);
6          }
7      }
8  }
```

It produces the following output:

```
sqrt(1) = 1.0
sqrt(2) = 1.4142135623730951
```

```
sqrt(3) = 1.7320508075688772
sqrt(4) = 2.0
sqrt(5) = 2.23606797749979
sqrt(6) = 2.449489742783178
sqrt(7) = 2.6457513110645907
sqrt(8) = 2.8284271247461903
sqrt(9) = 3.0
sqrt(10) = 3.1622776601683795
sqrt(11) = 3.3166247903554
sqrt(12) = 3.4641016151377544
sqrt(13) = 3.605551275463989
sqrt(14) = 3.7416573867739413
sqrt(15) = 3.872983346207417
sqrt(16) = 4.0
sqrt(17) = 4.123105625617661
sqrt(18) = 4.242640687119285
sqrt(19) = 4.358898943540674
sqrt(20) = 4.47213595499958
```

Notice that we're passed a value of type `int` to `Math.sqrt`, but the header says that it expects a value of type `double`. Remember that if Java is expecting a `double` and gets an `int`, it converts the `int` into a corresponding `double`.

The `Math` class also defines two frequently used constants, *e* and *pi* (see Table 3.1). Following the Java convention, we use all uppercase letters for their names and refer to them as `Math.E` and `Math.PI`.

Table 3.2 lists some of the most useful static methods from the `Math` class. You can see a complete list of methods defined in the `Math` class by checking out the API documentation for your version of Java. The API describes how to make use of the standard libraries that are available to Java programmers. It can be a bit over-whelming, because the Java libraries are vast. Wander around a bit if you are so inclined, but don't be dismayed that there are so many libraries to choose from in Java.

If you do look into the `Math` API, you'll notice that the `Math` class has several overloaded methods. For example, there is a version of the absolute value method (`Math.abs`) for integers and another for doubles. The rules that govern which method is called are complex, so we won't cover them here. The basic idea, though, is that Java tries to find the method that is the best fit. For the most part, you don't have to think much about this issue; you can just let Java choose for you, and it will generally make the right choice.

TABLE 3.1   Math Constants

Constant	Description
E	base used in natural logarithms (2.71828. . .)
PI	ratio of circumference of a circle to its diameter (3.14159. . .)

TABLE 3.2 Useful Static Methods in the `Math` Class

Method	Description	Example
abs	absolute value	`Math.abs(-308)` returns 308
ceil	ceiling (rounds upward)	`Math.ceil(2.13)` returns 3.0
cos	cosine (radians)	`Math.cos(Math.PI)` returns –1.0
exp	exponent base *e*	`Math.exp(1)` returns 2.7182818284590455
floor	floor (rounds downward)	`Math.floor(2.93)` returns 2.0
log	logarithm base *e*	`Math.log(Math.E)` returns 1.0
log10	logarithm base 10	`Math.log10(1000)` returns 3.0
max	maximum of two values	`Math.max(45, 207)` returns 207
min	minimum of two values	`Math.min(3.8, 2.75)` returns 2.75
pow	power (general exponentiation)	`Math.pow(3, 4)` returns 81.0
random	random value	`Math.random()` returns a random double value k such that $0.0 \leq k < 1.0$
sin	sine (radians)	`Math.sin(0)` returns 0.0
sqrt	square root	`Math.sqrt(2)` returns 1.4142135623730951
toDegrees	converts radian angles to degrees	`Math.toDegrees(Math.PI)` returns 180.0
toRadians	converts degree angles to radians	`Math.toRadians(270.0)` returns 4.71238898038469

Defining Methods That Return Values

You can write your own methods that return values by using a special statement known as a `return` statement. For example, here is a method that takes a distance specified as a number of feet that returns the corresponding number of miles:

```
public static double miles(double feet) {
    return feet / 5280.0;
}
```

The `miles` method could be used by the `main` method in code such as the following:

```
System.out.println("15000 feet is " + miles(15000) + " miles.");
```

Notice once again that in the header for the method the familiar word `void` (indicating no return value) has been replaced with the word `double`. Remember that when you declare a method that returns a value, you have to tell Java what kind of value it will return. Thus, we can update our syntax template for static methods once more to clarify that the header includes a return type (`void` for none):

```
public static <type> <name>(<type> <name>, ... , <type> <name>) {
    <statement or variable declaration>;
    <statement or variable declaration>;
    ...
    <statement or variable declaration>;
}
```

The syntax of the `return` statement is:

```
return <expression>;
```

When Java encounters a `return` statement, it evaluates the given expression and immediately terminates the method, returning the value it obtained from the expression. Because of this, it's not legal to have any other statements after a `return` statement; the `return` must be the last statement in your method. It is also an error for a Java method with a non-`void` return type to terminate without a `return`.

There are exceptions to the previous rules, as you'll see later. For example, it is possible for a method to have more than one `return` statement; this will come up in the next chapter, when we discuss conditional execution using `if` and `if`/`else` statements.

Let's look at another example method that returns a value. The Pythagorean Theorem of right triangles (as stated by the scarecrow in *The Wizard of Oz*) says that the length of the hypotenuse of a right triangle is equal to the square root of the sums of the squares of the two remaining sides. If you know the lengths of two sides *a* and

Common Programming Error

Ignoring the Returned Value

When you call a method that returns a value, the expectation is that you'll do something with the value that's returned. You can print it, store it into a variable, or use it as part of a larger expression. It is legal (but unwise) to simply call the method and ignore the value being returned from it:

```
miles(15000);   // doesn't do anything
```

However, the preceding call doesn't print the number of miles or have any noticeable effect. If you want the value printed, you must include a `println` statement:

```
double vacation = miles(15000);    // better
System.out.println("I drove " + vacation + " miles.");
```

A shorter form of the fixed code would be the following:

```
System.out.println("I drove " + miles(15000) + " miles.");
```

b of a right triangle and want to find the length of the third side c, you compute it as follows:

$$c = \sqrt{a^2 + b^2}$$

Say you want to print out the lengths of the hypotenuses of two right triangles: one with side lengths of 5 and 12, and the other with side lengths of 3 and 4. You could write code such as the following:

```
double c1 = Math.sqrt(Math.pow(5, 2) + Math.pow(12, 2));
System.out.println("hypotenuse 1 = " + c1);
double c2 = Math.sqrt(Math.pow(3, 2) + Math.pow(4, 2));
System.out.println("hypotenuse 2 = " + c2);
```

The preceding code is correct, but it's a bit hard to read, and you'd have to duplicate the same complex math a third time if you wanted to include a third triangle. A better solution would be to create a method that computes and returns the hypotenuse length when given the lengths of the two other sides as parameters. Such a method would look like this:

```
public static double hypotenuse(double a, double b) {
    double c = Math.sqrt(Math.pow(a, 2) + Math.pow(b, 2));
    return c;
}
```

This method can be used to craft a more concise and readable `main` method, as shown here.

```
 1   public class Triangles {
 2       public static void main(String[] args) {
 3           System.out.println("hypotenuse 1 = " +
 4                               hypotenuse(5, 12));
 5           System.out.println("hypotenuse 2 = " +
 6                               hypotenuse(3, 4));
 7       }
 8
 9       public static double hypotenuse(double a, double b) {
10           double c = Math.sqrt(Math.pow(a, 2) + Math.pow(b, 2));
11           return c;
12       }
13   }
```

A few variations of this program are possible. For one, it isn't necessary to store the `hypotenuse` method's return value into the variable c. If you prefer, you can simply compute and return the value in one line. In this case, the body of the hypotenuse method would become the following:

```
return Math.sqrt(Math.pow(a, 2) + Math.pow(b, 2));
```

Also, some programmers avoid using `Math.pow` for low powers such as 2 and just manually do the multiplication. Using that approach, the body of the hypotenuse method would look like this:

```
return Math.sqrt(a * a + b * b);
```

Common Programming Error

Statement After Return

It's illegal to place other statements immediately after a `return` statement, because those statements can never be reached or executed. New programmers often accidentally do this when trying to print the value of a variable after returning. Say you've written the `hypotenuse` method but have accidentally written the parameters to `Math.pow` in the wrong order, so the method is not producing the right answer. You would try to debug this by printing the value of c that is being returned. Here's the faulty code:

```
// trying to find the bug in this buggy version of hypotenuse
public static double hypotenuse(double a, double b) {
    double c = Math.sqrt(Math.pow(2, a) + Math.pow(2, b));
    return c;
    System.out.println(c);  //   this doesn't work
}
```

The compiler complains about the `println` statement being unreachable, since it follows a `return` statement. The compiler error output looks something like this:

```
Triangles.java:10: unreachable statement
        System.out.println(c);
        ^
Triangles.java:11: missing return statement
    }
    ^
2 errors
```

The fix is to move the `println` statement earlier in the method, before the `return` statement:

```
public static double hypotenuse(double a, double b) {
    double c = Math.sqrt(Math.pow(2, a) + Math.pow(2, b));
    System.out.println(c);    // better
    return c;
}
```

3.3 Using Objects

We've spent a considerable amount of time discussing the primitive types in Java and how they work, so it's about time that we started talking about objects and how they work.

The idea for objects came from the observation that as we start working with a new kind of data (integers, reals, characters, text, etc.), we find ourselves writing a lot of methods that operate on that data. Rather than completely separating them, it seemed to make sense to include some of the basic operations with the data itself.

This packaging of data and operations into one entity is the central idea behind objects. An *object* stores some data and has methods that act on its data.

> **Object**
>
> A programming entity that contains state (data) and behavior (methods).

As we said in Chapter 1, classes are the basic building blocks of Java programs. But classes also serve another purpose: to describe new types of objects.

> **Class**
>
> A category or type of object.

When used this way, a class is like a blueprint of what the object looks like. Once you've given Java the blueprint, you can ask it to create actual objects that match that blueprint. We sometimes refer to the individual objects as *instances* of the class. We tend to use the words "instance" and "object" interchangeably.

This concept is difficult to understand in the abstract. To help you come to grips with what it means and how it works, we'll look at several different classes. In keeping with our idea of focusing on fundamental concepts first, in this chapter we'll study how to use existing objects that are already part of Java, but we aren't going to study how to define our own new types of objects just yet. We'll get to that in Chapter 8, after we've had time to practice using objects.

Using objects differs from using primitive types, so we'll have to introduce some new syntax and concepts. It would be nice if Java had a consistent model for using all types of data, but it doesn't. Consequently, if you want to understand how your programs operate, you'll have to learn two sets of rules: one for primitives and one for objects.

String Objects

Strings are one of the most useful and most commonly used types of objects in Java, so they make a good starting point. They aren't the best example of objects, though, because there are a lot of special rules that apply only to strings. In the next section, we'll look at a more typical kind of object.

Strings have the special property that there are literals that represent String objects (string literals). We've been using them in println statements since Chapter 1. What we haven't discussed is that these literal values represent objects of type String (instances of the String class). For example, in the same way that you can say:

```
int x = 8;
```

you can say:

```
String s = "hello there";
```

You can declare variables of type `String` and use the assignment statement to give values to these variables. You can also write code that involves `String` expressions:

```
String s1 = "hello";
String s2 = "there";
String combined = s1 + " " + s2;
```

This code defines two `String`s that each represent a single word and a third `String` that represents the concatenation of the two words with a space in between. You'll notice that the type `String` is capitalized (as are the names of all object types in Java), unlike the primitive types, such as `double` and `int`.

These examples haven't shown anything special about `String` objects, but we're getting there. Remember that the idea behind objects was to include basic operations with the data itself, the way we make cars that have controls built in. The data stored in a `String` is a sequence of characters. There are all sorts of operations you might want to perform on this sequence of characters. For example, you might want to know how many characters there are in the `String`. `String` objects have a `length` method that returns this information.

If the `length` method were static, you would call it by saying something like:

```
length(s)      // this isn't legal
```

But when performing operations on objects, you use a different syntax. Objects store data and methods, so the method to report a `String`'s length actually exists inside that `String` object itself. To call an object's method, you write the name of the variable first, followed by a dot, and then the name of the method:

```
s.length()
```

Think of it as talking to the `String` object. When you ask for `s.length()`, you're saying, "Hey, `s`. I'm talking to you. What's your length?" Of course, different `String` objects have different lengths, so you will get different answers when you communicate with different `String` objects.

The general syntax for calling a method of an object is the following:

```
<variable>.<method name>(<expression>, <expression>, . . . , <expression>)
```

For example, suppose that you have initialized two string variables as follows:

```
String s1 = "hello";
String s2 = "how are you?";
```

You can use a `println` to examine the length of each string:

```
System.out.println("Length of s1 = " + s1.length());
System.out.println("Length of s2 = " + s2.length());
```

which produces the following output:

```
Length of s1 = 5
Length of s2 = 12
```

What else might you want to do with a `String` object? With the `length` method you can figure out how many characters there are in a `String`, but what about getting the individual characters themselves? There are several ways to do this, but one of the most common is to use a method called `charAt` that returns the character at a specific location in the string.

This leads us to the problem of how to specify locations in a sequence. Obviously there is a first character, a second character, and so on, so it makes sense to use an integer to refer to a specific location. We call this the *index*.

> **Index**
>
> An integer used to specify a location in a sequence of values. Java generally uses zero-based indexing (with 0 as the first index value, followed by 1, 2, 3, and so on).

Each character of a `String` object is assigned an index value, starting with 0. For example, for the variable `s1` that refers to the string `"hello"`, the indexes are:

0	1	2	3	4
h	e	l	l	o

It may seem intuitive to consider the letter "h" to be at position 1, but there are advantages to starting with an index of 0. It's a convention that was adopted by the designers of the C language and has been followed by the designers of C++ and Java, so it's a convention you'll have to learn to live with.

For the longer string `s2`, the positions are:

0	1	2	3	4	5	6	7	8	9	10	11
h	o	w		a	r	e		y	o	u	?

Notice that the spaces in the string have positions as well (here, positions 3 and 7). Also notice that the indexes for a given string always range from 0 to one less than the length of the string.

Using the `charAt` method, you can request specific characters of a string. The return type is `char`. For example, if you ask for `s1.charAt(1)` you'll get `'e'` (the 'e' in "hello"). If you ask for `s2.charAt(5)`, you'll get `'r'` (the 'r' in "how are you?"). For any `String`, if you ask for `charAt(0)`, you'll get the first character of the string.

When working with `String` objects, you'll often find it useful to write a `for` loop to handle the different characters of the `String`. Because `Strings` are indexed starting at 0, this task is easier to write with `for` loops that start with 0 rather than 1. Consider, for example, the following code that prints out the individual characters of `s1`:

```java
String s1 = "hello";
for (int i = 0; i < s1.length(); i++) {
    System.out.println(i + ": " + s1.charAt(i));
}
```

This code produces the following output:

```
0: h
1: e
2: l
3: l
4: o
```

Remember that when we start loops at 0, we usually test with less than (<) rather than less than or equal to (<=). The string s1 has five characters in it, so the call on s1.length() will return 5. But because the first index is 0, the last index will be one less than 5 (4). This convention takes a while to get used to, but zero-based indexing is used throughout Java, so you'll eventually get the hang of it.

Another useful string method is the substring method. It takes two integer arguments representing a starting and ending index. When you call the substring method, you provide two of these indexes: the index of the first character you want and the index just past the last index that you want.

Recall that the string s2 has the following positions:

0	1	2	3	4	5	6	7	8	9	10	11
h	o	w		a	r	e		y	o	u	?

If you want to pull out the individual word "how" from this string, you'd ask for:

```
s2.substring(0, 3)
```

Remember that the second value that you pass to the substring method is supposed to be one beyond the end of the substring you are forming. So, even though there is a space at position 3 in the original string, it will not be part of what you get from the call on substring. Instead, you'll get all the characters just before position 3.

Following this rule means that sometimes you will give a position to a substring at which there is no character. For instance, the last character in the string that s2 refers to is at index 11 (the question mark). If you want to get the substring "you?" including the question mark, you'd ask for:

```
s2.substring(8, 12)
```

There is no character at position 12 in s2, but this call asks for characters starting at position 8 that come before position 12, so this actually makes sense.

You have to be careful about what indexes you use, though. With the substring method you can ask for the position just beyond the end of the string, but you can't ask for anything beyond that. For example, if you ask for:

```
s2.substring(8, 13)    // out of bounds!
```

your program will generate an execution error. Similarly, if you ask for the `charAt` at a nonexistent position, your program will generate an execution error. These errors are known as *exceptions*.

Exceptions are runtime errors as mentioned in Chapter 1.

> **Exception**
>
> A runtime error that prevents a program from continuing its normal execution.

We say that an exception is *thrown* when an error is encountered. When an exception is thrown, Java looks to see if you have written code to handle it. If not, program execution is halted and you will see what is known as a *stack trace* or *back trace*. The stack trace shows you the series of methods that have been called, in reverse order. In the case of bad `String` indexes, the exception prints a message such as the following to the console:

```
Exception in thread "main"
    java.lang.StringIndexOutOfBoundsException:
    String index out of range: 13
    at java.lang.String.substring(Unknown Source)
    at ExampleProgram.main(ExampleProgram.java:3)
```

You can use `Strings` as parameters to methods. For example, the following program uses `String` parameters to eliminate some of the redundancy in a popular children's song:

```
1   public class BusSong {
2       public static void main(String[] args) {
3           verse("wheels", "go", "round and round");
4           verse("wipers", "go", "swish, swish, swish");
5           verse("horn", "goes", "beep, beep, beep");
6       }
7
8       public static void verse(String item, String verb,
9                                String sound) {
10          System.out.println("The " + item + " on the bus " +
11                             verb + " " + sound + ",");
12          System.out.println(sound + ",");
13          System.out.println(sound + ".");
14          System.out.println("The " + item + " on the bus " +
15                             verb + " " + sound + ",");
16          System.out.println("All through the town.");
17          System.out.println();
18      }
19  }
```

It produces the following output:

```
The wheels on the bus go round and round,
round and round,
round and round.
The wheels on the bus go round and round,
All through the town.
```

```
The wipers on the bus go swish, swish, swish,
swish, swish, swish,
swish, swish, swish.
The wipers on the bus go swish, swish, swish,
All through the town.

The horn on the bus goes beep, beep, beep,
beep, beep, beep,
beep, beep, beep.
The horn on the bus goes beep, beep, beep,
All through the town.
```

Table 3.3 lists some of the most useful methods that you can call on `String` objects. Strings in Java are *immutable,* which means that once they are constructed, their values can never be changed.

> **Immutable Object**
>
> An object whose value cannot be changed.

It may seem odd that strings are immutable and yet have methods like `toUpperCase` and `toLowerCase`. But if you read the descriptions in the table carefully, you'll see that these methods don't actually change a given `String` object; instead they return a new string. Consider the following code:

TABLE 3.3   Useful Methods of `String` Objects

Method	Description	Example (assuming s is "hello")
charAt(index)	character at a specific index	s.charAt(1) returns 'e'
endsWith(text)	whether or not the string ends with some text	s.endsWith("llo") returns true
indexOf(text)	index of a particular character or String (–1 if not present)	s.indexOf("o") returns 4
length()	number of characters in the string	s.length() returns 5
startsWith(text)	whether or not the string starts with some text	s.startsWith("hi") returns false
substring(start, stop)	characters from start index to just before stop index	s.substring(1, 3) returns "el"
toLowerCase()	a new string with all lowercase letters	s.toLowerCase() returns "hello"
toUpperCase()	a new string with all uppercase letters	s.toUpperCase() returns "HELLO"

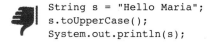

```
String s = "Hello Maria";
s.toUpperCase();
System.out.println(s);
```

You might think that this will turn the string s into its uppercase equivalent, but it doesn't. The second line of code constructs a new string that has the uppercase equivalent of the value of s, but we don't do anything with this new value. The key is to either store this new string in a different variable or reassign the variable s to point to the new string:

```
String s = "Hello Maria";
s = s.toUpperCase();
System.out.println(s);
```

This version of the code produces the following output:

```
HELLO MARIA
```

The toUpperCase and toLowerCase methods are particularly helpful when you want to perform string comparisons in which you ignore the case of the letters involved.

Point Objects

Strings are extremely useful objects, but the rules for creating and using them don't completely match those of other types of objects. We'll now examine a more typical type of object: Point. A Point object stores the (x, y) coordinates of a point in 2-D space. These coordinates are expressed as integers, although there are also variations for storing points expressed using floating-point numbers.

Strings are special cases that have literal values that can be referred to directly. Most objects have to be explicitly constructed by calling a special method known as a *constructor.*

> **Constructor (Construct)**
>
> A method that creates and initializes an object. Objects in Java programs must be constructed before they can be used.

Remember that a class is like a blueprint for a family of objects. Calling a constructor is like sending an order to the factory asking it to follow the blueprint to get you an actual object that you can manipulate. When you send in your order to the factory, you sometimes specify certain parameters (e.g., what color you want the object to be).

In Java, constructors are called using the special keyword new, followed by the object's type and any necessary parameters. For example, to construct a specific Point object, you have to pass the values you want for x and y:

```
Point p = new Point(3, 8);
```

This code performs a call on a constructor of the `Point` class. Constructors always have the same name as the class. In this case, we pass the constructor two integer values as parameters to specify the x- and y-coordinates of the point.

After executing the line of code above, you have the following situation:

Once you have constructed a `Point` object, what can you do with it? One of the most common things you do with an object is print it to the console. A `Point` object, like many Java objects, can be printed with the `println` statement.

```
System.out.println(p);
```

The `println` statement produces the following output:

```
java.awt.Point[x=3,y=8]
```

The output produced begins with the full name of the class, `java.awt.Point` (the "java.awt" part of this name will be explained in a moment). After the name of the class, the x and y coordinates are listed inside square brackets. This format is a little ugly, but it lets you see the x and y values inside a given `Point`.

`Point` objects also have a method called `translate` that can be used to shift the coordinates by a specific delta-x and delta-y, which are passed as parameters. When you translate a `Point`, you shift its location by the specified amount. For example, you might say:

```
p.translate(-1, -2);   // subtract 1 from x, subtract 2 from y
```

Given that the `Point` started out with coordinates (3, 8), this translation would leave the `Point` with coordinates (2, 6). Thus, after this line of code is executed, you'd end up with the following situation:

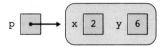

One of the other things you can do with a `Point` object is to refer to its x and y values using the dot notation:

```
int sum = p.x + p.y;
System.out.println("Sum of coordinates = " + sum);
```

You can even change these internal values directly, as in:

```
p.x = 12;
p.y = 15;
```

TABLE 3.4 Useful Methods of `Point` Objects

Method	Description
`translate(dx, dy)`	translates the coordinates by the given amounts
`setLocation(x, y)`	sets the coordinates to the given values
`distance(p2)`	returns the distance from this point to p2

Table 3.4 includes some useful methods of the `Point` class.

Here is a complete program that constructs a `Point` object and translates its coordinates, using `println` statements to examine the coordinates before and after the call:

```
1   import java.awt.*;
2
3   public class PointExample1 {
4       public static void main(String[] args) {
5           Point p = new Point(3, 8);
6           System.out.println("initially p = " + p);
7           p.translate(-1, -2);
8           System.out.println("after translating p = " + p);
9       }
10  }
```

This code produces the following output:

```
initially p = java.awt.Point[x=3,y=8]
after translating p = java.awt.Point[x=2,y=6]
```

There is something new at the beginning of this class file called an *import declaration*. Remember that Java has a large number of classes included in what are collectively known as the Java class libraries. To help manage these classes, Java provides an organizational unit known as a *package*. Related classes are combined together into a single package. For example, the `Point` class is stored in a package known as `java.awt`, which is an abbreviation for the "Java Abstract Window Toolkit." Java programs don't normally have access to a package unless they include an import declaration.

> **Package**
>
> A collection of related Java classes.

> **Import Declaration**
>
> A request to access a specific Java package.

We haven't needed an `import` declaration yet because Java automatically imports every class stored in a package called `java.lang`. The `java.lang` package includes basic classes that most Java programs are likely to use (e.g., `System`, `String`, `Math`). Because Java does not automatically import `java.awt`, you have to do it yourself.

Java allows you to use an asterisk to import all classes from a package:

```
import java.awt.*;
```

But some people prefer to specifically mention each class they import. The import declaration allows you to import just a single class from a package, as in:

```
import java.awt.Point;
```

The problem is that once you start importing one class from a package, you're likely to want to import others as well. We will use the asterisk version of `import` in this book to keep things simple.

Reference Semantics

Objects are stored in the computer's memory in a different way than primitive data. For example, when we declare an integer variable:

```
int x = 8;
```

the variable stores the actual data. So, we've drawn pictures like the following:

The situation is different for objects. With objects, the variable doesn't store the actual data. Instead, the data is stored in an object and the variable stores a reference to where the object is stored. So, we have two different elements in memory: the variable and the object. Thus, when we construct a `Point` object:

```
Point p = new Point(3, 8);
```

we end up with the following:

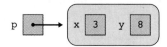

As the diagram indicates, two different values are stored in memory: the `Point` object itself, which appears on the right side of the diagram, and a variable called `p`, which stores a reference to the `Point` object (represented in this picture as an arrow). We say that `p` *refers* to the object.

It may take some time to get used to the two different approaches to storing data, but these approaches are so common that computer scientists have technical terms to describe them. The system for the primitive types like `int` is known as *value semantics,* and those types are often referred to as *value types.* The system for `Point`s and other objects is known as *reference semantics,* and those types are often referred to as *reference types.*

Value Semantics (Value Types)

A system in which values are stored directly and copying involves the creation of independent copies of values. Types that use value semantics are called value types.

Reference Semantics (Reference Types)

A system in which references to values are stored and copying involves copying references. Types that use reference semantics are called reference types.

It will take us a while to explore all of the implications of this difference. The key thing to remember is that when you are working with objects, you are always working with references to data rather than the data itself.

At this point you are probably wondering why Java has two different systems. Java was designed for object-oriented programming, so the first question to consider is why Sun decided that objects should have reference semantics. There are two primary reasons:

- **Efficiency.** Objects can be complex, which means that they can take up a lot of space in memory. We don't want to have to make copies of such objects because we would quickly run out of memory. For example, a `String` object that stores a large number of characters might take up a lot of space in memory. But even if the `String` object is very large, a reference to it can be fairly small, in the same way that even a mansion has a simple street address. As another analogy, think of how we use cell phones to communicate with people. The phones can be very tiny and easy to transport because cell phone numbers don't take up much space. Imagine how different it would be if, instead of carrying around a set of cell phone numbers, you tried to carry around the actual people!

- **Sharing.** It is often the case that having a copy of something is not good enough. Suppose that your instructor tells all of the students in the class to put their tests into a certain box. Imagine how pointless and confusing it would be if each student made a copy of the box. The obvious intent is that all of the students use the same box. With reference semantics, you can have many references to a single object, which allows different parts of your program to share a certain object.

So without reference semantics, Java programs would be more difficult to write. Then why did Sun also decide to include primitive types that have value semantics? The reasons are primarily historical. Sun wanted to leverage the popularity of C and C++, which had similar types, and to guarantee that Java programs would run quickly, which was easier to accomplish with the more traditional primitive types. If Sun had a chance to redesign Java today, they might well get rid of the primitive types and go with a consistent object model with just reference semantics.

Multiple Objects

In the last section you saw how to manipulate a single object. Consider the following lines of code that construct two different objects:

```
Point p1 = new Point(3, 8);
Point p2 = new Point();
```

Each object must be constructed separately by a call on `new`. Remember that we call these *instances* of the class. The first call passes the x- and y-coordinates of the `Point`. The second call uses a different constructor with a different method signature (zero parameters instead of two parameters). This constructor sets the x- and y-coordinates to `0`. The zero-argument constructor is often referred to as the *default constructor*. After executing these statements, the memory would look as follows:

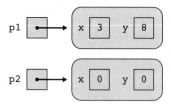

To underscore the fact that variables and objects are stored separately, consider what will happen if you now execute the following code:

```
Point p3 = p2;
```

This declares a third `Point` variable but doesn't include a third call on `new`. This means that you still have just two `Point` objects, even though you now have three `Point` variables:

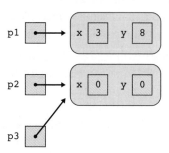

The variables `p2` and `p3` both refer to the same `Point` object. This situation doesn't arise when you use value types like `int`; it happens only with objects.

Let's look at a complete program to explore how this works:

```
1   import java.awt.*;
2
```

Remember that a parameter becomes a copy of whatever is passed in the call. With the value types, such as `int`, any changes you make to the parameter have no effect on any variable passed to the method. The situation is more complicated for objects because of their reference semantics. Suppose you define a `Point` variable and you pass it to this method:

```
Point test = new Point(6, 15);
manipulate(test);
```

Does the method end up translating the coordinates of the object? The answer is yes, even though you're using a parameter that creates a copy. Think of what is happening in the computer's memory. When you declare the `test` variable, you end up with this situation:

When you call the `manipulate` method, Java makes a copy of the variable `test` and stores this in the parameter `p`. But the variable `test` isn't itself an object: It simply stores a reference to an object. So, when you make a copy of it, you end up with this situation in memory:

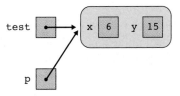

You now have two variables that refer to the same `Point` object. It doesn't matter that `p` is a copy, because it refers to the same object as the original. So, any calls on `translate` using `p` will change the object referred to by `test`.

There is one other case worth considering. Say you'd written the `manipulate` method this way instead:

```
public static void manipulate(Point p) {
    p.translate(2, 3);
    p = new Point(17, 45);
}
```

Let's look at this in detail. When the method is called, the variable `p` is set up as a copy of the variable `test`, which leads to two variables referring to the same `Point` object:

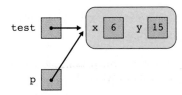

The coordinates for p are translated by 2 in the x direction and 3 in the y direction, as in the old version of the method:

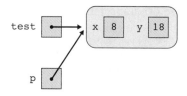

The variable p is then reset to a new `Point` object with a different set of coordinates. Does this affect the `test` variable? The answer is no. Because p is a local copy, changing its value has no effect on `test`:

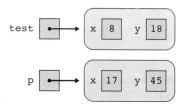

The bottom line is that when you pass an object as a parameter, you can change the object itself but you can't change the variable that points to the object.

Phone numbers provide a useful analogy. Suppose that you have a piece of paper on which you have written down a person's phone number. That gives you the ability to call that person. You can make a copy of that piece of paper and give it to a friend, which is similar to what happens when you pass an object as a parameter to a method. Because you have your own piece of paper with the phone number on it, you can still call the person. But your friend has the phone number too, so the friend can also make the call.

3.4 Interactive Programs

As you've seen, you can easily produce output in the console window by calling `System.out.println` and `System.out.print`. You can also write programs that pause and wait for the user to type a response. Such programs are known as *interactive* programs, and the responses typed by the user are known as *console input*.

> **Console Input**
>
> Responses typed by the user when an interactive program pauses for input.

When you refer to `System.out`, you are accessing an object in the `System` class known as the standard output stream, or "standard out" for short. There is a corresponding object for standard input known as `System.in`, but Java wasn't designed for console input, and `System.in` has never been particularly easy to use for this purpose. Fortunately for us, there is an easier way to read console input: `Scanner` objects.

Scanner Objects

As of version 1.5, Java has a class called `Scanner` that simplifies reading from the console and from files. It is part of the `java.util` package, so you will have to remember to include the following import declaration in your programs that use `Scanner`:

```
import java.util.*;   // for Scanner
```

To use a `Scanner` object, you must first construct it. You can construct a `Scanner` by passing it a reference to an input stream. To read from the console window, pass it `System.in`:

```
Scanner console = new Scanner(System.in);
```

Once you've constructed it, you can ask the `Scanner` to return a value of a particular type. A number of methods, all beginning with the word "next," are available to obtain the various types of values. Table 3.5 lists them.

Typically, you will use variables to keep track of the values returned by these methods. For example, you might say:

```
int n = console.nextInt();
```

The call on the `console` object's `nextInt` method pauses for user input. Whenever the computer pauses for input, it will pause for an entire line of input. In other words, whenever the computer pauses for input, it will wait until the user hits the Enter key before continuing execution.

You can use the `Scanner` class to read input line by line using the `nextLine` method, although we won't be using `nextLine` very much for now. The other "next" methods are all *token*-based (that is, they read single elements of input rather than entire lines).

> **Token**
> A single element of input (e.g., one word, one number).

TABLE 3.5   Scanner Methods

Method	Description
`next()`	reads and returns the next token as a `String`
`nextDouble()`	reads and returns a `double` value
`nextInt()`	reads and returns an `int` value
`nextLine()`	reads and returns the next line of input as a `String`

By default, the `Scanner` uses *whitespace* to separate tokens.

> **Whitespace**
> Spaces, tab characters, and newline characters.

A `Scanner` object looks at what the user types and uses the whitespace on the input line to break it up into individual tokens. For example, the following line of input:

```
hello      there. how are      "you?"  all-one-token
```

would be split into six tokens:

```
hello
there.
how
are
"you?"
all-one-token
```

Notice that the `Scanner` includes punctuation characters such as periods, question marks, and quotation marks in the tokens it generates. It also includes dashes, so, because there is no whitespace in the middle to break it up into different tokens, we get just one token for "all-one-token." You can control how a `Scanner` turns things into tokens (a process called *tokenizing* the input), but we won't be doing anything that fancy.

It is possible to read more than one value from a `Scanner`, as in:

```
double x = console.nextDouble();
double y = console.nextDouble();
```

Because there are two different calls on the `console` object's `nextDouble` method, this code will cause the computer to pause until the user has entered two numeric values. The values can be entered on the same line or on separate lines. In general, the computer continues to pause for user input until it has obtained whatever values you have asked the `Scanner` to obtain.

If a user types something that isn't an integer when you call `nextInt`, such as `xyzzy`, the `Scanner` object generates an exception. Recall from the section on `String` objects that exceptions are runtime errors that halt program execution. In this case, you'll see runtime error output such as the following:

```
Exception in thread "main" java.util.InputMismatchException
       at java.util.Scanner.throwFor(Unknown Source)
       at java.util.Scanner.next(Unknown Source)
       at java.util.Scanner.nextInt(Unknown Source)
       at Example.main(Example.java:13)
```

You will see in a later chapter how to test for user errors. In the meantime, we will assume that the user provides appropriate input.

Sample Interactive Program

Using the `Scanner` class, we can write a complete interactive program that performs a useful computation for the user. If you ever find yourself buying a house, you'll want to know what your monthly loan payment is going to be. The following is a complete program that asks for information about a loan and prints the monthly payment:

```
1    // This program prompts for information about a loan and
2    // computes the monthly loan payment.
3
4    import java.util.*;    // for Scanner
5
6    public class Mortgage {
7        public static void main(String[] args) {
8            Scanner console = new Scanner(System.in);
9
10           // obtain values
11           System.out.println("This program computes monthly " +
12                               "loan payments.");
13           System.out.print("loan amount     : ");
14           double loan = console.nextDouble();
15           System.out.print("number of years : ");
16           int years = console.nextInt();
17           System.out.print("interest rate   : ");
18           double rate = console.nextDouble();
19           System.out.println();
20
21           // compute result and report
22           int n = 12 * years;
23           double c = rate / 12.0 / 100.0;
24           double payment = loan * c * Math.pow(1 + c, n) /
25                            (Math.pow(1 + c, n) - 1);
26           System.out.println("payment = $" + (int) payment);
27       }
28   }
```

The following is a sample execution of the program (user input is in bold):

```
This program computes monthly loan payments.
loan amount     : 275000
number of years : 30
interest rate   : 6.75

payment = $1783
```

The first thing we do in the program is construct a `Scanner` object, which we will use for console input. Next, we explain what the program is going to do, printing a description to the console. This is essential for interactive programs. You don't want a program to pause for user input until you've explained to the user what is going to happen.

Below the `println`, you'll notice several pairs of statements like these:

```
System.out.print("loan amount     : ");
double loan = console.nextDouble();
```

The first statement is called a *prompt,* a request for information from the user. We use a `print` statement instead of a `println` so that the user will type the values on the same line as the prompt (i.e., to the right of the prompt). The second statement calls the `nextDouble` method of the `console` object to read a value of type `double` from the user. This value is stored in a variable called `loan`. This pattern of prompt/read statements is common in interactive programs.

After prompting for values, the program computes several values. The formula for computing monthly mortgage payments involves the loan amount, the total number of months involved (a value we call n) and the monthly interest rate (a value we call c). The payment formula is given by the following equation:

$$payment = loan \, \frac{c(1 + c)^n}{(1 + c)^n - 1}$$

You will notice in the program that we use the `Math.pow` method for exponentiation to translate this formula into a Java expression.

The final line of the program prints out the monthly payment. You might imagine that we would simply say:

```
System.out.println("payment = $" + payment);
```

However, because the payment is stored in a variable of type `double`, this would print all of the digits of the number. For example, for the log listed above, it would print the following:

```
payment = $1783.6447655625927
```

That is a rather strange-looking output for someone used to dollars and cents. For the purposes of this simple program, it's easy to cast the `double` to an `int` and report just the dollar amount of the payment:

```
System.out.println("payment = $" + (int) payment);
```

Most people trying to figure out their mortgage payments aren't that interested in the pennies, so the program is still useful. In the next section, we will see how to round a `double` to two decimal places.

3.5 Case Study: Projectile Trajectory

It's time to pull together the threads of this chapter with a more complex example that will involve parameters, methods that return values, mathematical computations, and the use of a `Scanner` object for console input.

Physics students are often asked to calculate the trajectory that a projectile will follow, given its initial velocity and its initial angle relative to the horizontal. For example, the projectile might be a football that someone has kicked. We want to compute the path it follows given Earth's gravity. To keep the computation reasonable, we will ignore air resistance.

There are several questions that we might want to answer for such a problem:

- When does the projectile reach its highest point?
- How high does it reach?
- How long does it take to come back to the ground?
- How far does it land from where it was launched?

There are several ways to answer these questions. One simple approach is to provide a table that displays the trajectory step by step, indicating the x position, y position, and elapsed time.

To make such a table, we need to obtain three values from the user: the initial velocity, the angle relative to the horizontal, and the number of steps to include in the table we will produce. We could ask for the velocity in either meters/second or feet/second, but given that this is a physics problem, we'll stick to the metric system and ask for meters/second.

We also have to think about how to specify the angle. Unfortunately, most of the Java methods that operate on angles require angles in radians rather than degrees. We could request the angle in radians, but that would be highly inconvenient for the user, who would be required to make the conversion. Instead, we can allow the user to enter the angle in degrees and then convert it to radians using the built-in method `Math.toRadians`.

So, the interactive part of the program will look like this:

```java
Scanner console = new Scanner(System.in);
System.out.print("velocity (meters/second)? ");
double velocity = console.nextDouble();
System.out.print("angle (degrees)? ");
double angle = Math.toRadians(console.nextDouble());
System.out.print("number of steps to display? ");
int steps = console.nextInt();
```

Notice that for the velocity and angle we call the `nextDouble` method of the `console` object, because we want to let the user specify any number (including one with a decimal point), but for the number of steps we call `nextInt`, because the number of lines in our table needs to be an integer.

Look more closely at this line of code:

```java
double angle = Math.toRadians(console.nextDouble());
```

Some beginners would write this as two separate steps:

```java
double angleInDegrees = console.nextDouble();
double angle = Math.toRadians(angleInDegrees);
```

Both approaches work and are reasonable, but keep in mind that you don't need to divide this operation into two separate steps. You can write it in the more compact form as a single line of code.

Once we have obtained these values from the user, we are ready to begin the computations for the trajectory table. First, we need to compute the x component of the velocity versus the y component of the velocity. From physics, we know that these can be computed as follows:

```
double xVelocity = velocity * Math.cos(angle);
double yVelocity = velocity * Math.sin(angle);
```

Because we are ignoring the possibility of air resistance, the x-velocity will not change. The y-velocity, however, is subject to the pull of gravity. Physics tells us that on the surface of the Earth, gravity is approximately 9.81 meters/second^2. This is an appropriate value to define as a class constant:

```
public static final double ACCELERATION = -9.81;
```

Notice that we define gravity as a negative number, because it decreases the y-velocity of an object (pulling it down as opposed to pushing it away).

Our goal is to display x, y, and elapsed time as the object goes up and comes back down again. The y-velocity decreases steadily until it becomes 0. From physics, we know that there is a symmetry in this problem. The projectile will go upward until its y-velocity reaches 0, and then it will follow a similar path back down that takes an equal amount of time. Thus, the total time involved in seconds can be computed as follows:

```
double totalTime = -2.0 * yVelocity / ACCELERATION;
```

Now, how do we compute the values of x, y, and elapsed time to include in our table? Two of these are relatively simple. We want steady time increments for each entry in the table, so we can compute the time increment by dividing total time by the number of steps we want to include in our table:

```
double timeIncrement = totalTime / steps;
```

As noted earlier, the x-velocity does not change, so for each of these time increments, we move the same distance in the x-direction:

```
double xIncrement = xVelocity * timeIncrement;
```

The tricky value to compute here is the y-position. Because of gravity, the y-velocity changes over time. But from physics, we have the following general formula for computing the displacement of an object given the velocity *v*, time *t*, and acceleration *a*:

$$\text{displacement} = vt + \frac{1}{2}at^2$$

```
17                System.out.print("number of steps to display? ");
18                int steps = console.nextInt();
19                System.out.println();
20
21                printTable(velocity, angle, steps);
22          }
23
24          // prints a table showing the trajectory of an object given
25          // its initial velocity and angle and including the given
26          // number of steps in the table
27          public static void printTable(double velocity,
28                                        double angle, int steps) {
29                double xVelocity = velocity * Math.cos(angle);
30                double yVelocity = velocity * Math.sin(angle);
31                double totalTime = -2.0 * yVelocity / ACCELERATION;
32                double timeIncrement = totalTime / steps;
33                double xIncrement = xVelocity * timeIncrement;
34
35                double x = 0.0;
36                double y = 0.0;
37                double t = 0.0;
38                System.out.println("step\tx\ty\ttime");
39                System.out.println("0\t0.0\t0.0\t0.0");
40                for (int i = 1; i <= steps; i++) {
41                    t += timeIncrement;
42                    x += xIncrement;
43                    y = displacement(yVelocity, t, ACCELERATION);
44                    System.out.println(i + "\t" + round2(x) + "\t" +
45                                       round2(y) + "\t" + round2(t));
46                }
47          }
48
49          // gives a brief introduction to the user
50          public static void giveIntro() {
51                System.out.println("This program computes the");
52                System.out.println("trajectory of a projectile given");
53                System.out.println("its initial velocity and its");
54                System.out.println("angle relative to the");
55                System.out.println("horizontal.");
56                System.out.println();
57          }
58
59          // returns the vertical displacement for a body given
60          // initial velocity v, elapsed time t, and acceleration a
61          public static double displacement(double v, double t,
62                                            double a) {
63                return v * t + 0.5 * a * t * t;
64          }
65
66          // rounds n to 2 digits after the decimal point
67          public static double round2(double n) {
68                return (int) (n * 100.0 + 0.5) / 100.0;
69          }
70    }
```

This version executes the same way as the earlier version.

Chapter Summary

Methods may be written to accept parameters, which are values given from the calling code into the methods. Parameters allow data values to flow into a method, which can change the way the method executes. A method declared with a set of parameters can perform an entire family of similar tasks instead of exactly one task.

———

When primitive values such as those of type `int` or `double` are passed as parameters, their values are copied into the method. Primitive parameters send values into a method, but not out of it; the method can use the data values but cannot affect the value of any variables outside of it.

———

Two methods can have the same name if they declare different parameters. This is called overloading.

———

Methods can be written to return values to the calling code. This allows a method to perform a complex computation and then provide its result back to the calling code. The type of the return value must be declared in the method's header and is called the method's return type.

———

Java has a class called `Math` that contains several useful static methods that you can use in your programs, such as powers, square roots, and logarithms.

———

An object is an entity that combines data and operations. Some objects in Java include `Strings`, which are sequences of text characters, and `Points`, which hold Cartesian (x, y) coordinates.

———

Objects contain methods that implement their behavior. To call a method on an object, write its name, followed by a dot, followed by the method name.

———

A `String` object holds a sequence of characters. The characters have indexes, starting with 0 for the first character.

———

A `Point` object holds two `int` values, `x` and `y`, representing a two-dimensional point. A `Point` can be constructed, translated (moved to a new location), and converted into a `String` to be printed on the console.

———

An exception is an error that occurs when a program has performed an illegal action and is unable to continue executing normally.

———

Java objects use reference semantics, where variables store references to objects rather than the actual objects themselves. This means that two variables can refer to the same object. If an object is modified through one of its references, the modification will also be seen in the other.

———

Objects that are passed as parameters to methods behave differently from primitive parameters because the methods refer to the same objects that were passed in, not to copies of the objects. If a method modifies an object's data, the modification will also be seen when the method returns.

———

3. Write a program that shows the total number of presents received on each day according to the song "The Twelve Days of Christmas," as indicated in Table 3.6.

TABLE 3.6

Day	Presents received	Total presents
1	1	1
2	2	3
3	3	6
4	4	10
5	5	15
...	...	...

4. Write a program that prompts for the lengths of the sides of a triangle and reports the three angles.

5. Write a program that computes the spherical distance between two points on the surface of the Earth, given their latitudes and longitudes. This is a useful operation because it tells you how far apart two cities are if you multiply it by the radius of the Earth, which is roughly 6372.795 km.

Let φ_1, λ_1, and φ_2, λ_2 be the latitude and longitude of two points, respectively. $\Delta \lambda$, the longitudinal difference, and $\Delta\sigma$, the angular difference/distance in radians, can be determined from the spherical law of cosines as:

$$\Delta\sigma = \arccos(\sin \varphi_1 \sin \varphi_2 + \cos \varphi_1 \cos \varphi_2 \cos \Delta\lambda)$$

For example, consider the latitude and longitude of two major cities:

- Nashville, TN, USA: N 36°7.2′, W 86°40.2
- Los Angeles, CA, USA: N 33°56.4′, W 118°24.0′

You must convert these coordinates to radians before you can use them effectively in the formula. After conversion, the coordinates become:

- Nashville: $\varphi_1 = 36.12° = 0.6304$ rad, $\lambda_1 = -86.67° = -1.5127$ rad
- Los Angeles: $\varphi_2 = 33.94° = 0.5924$ rad, $\lambda_2 = -118.40° = -2.0665$ rad

Using these values in the angular distance equation, you get:

r $\Delta\sigma$ = 6372.795 × 0.45306 = 2887.259 km

Thus, the distance between these cities is about 2887 km, or 1794 miles. (Note: To solve this problem, you will need to use the `Math.acos` method, which returns an arccosine angle in radians.)

Graphics (Optional)

Introduction

One of the most compelling reasons to learn about using objects is that they allow us to draw graphics in Java. Graphics are used for games, rendering complex images, computer animation, and modern graphical user interfaces (GUIs). In this optional supplement we will examine a few of the basic classes from Java's graphical framework and use them to draw patterned two-dimensional figures of shapes and text onto the screen.

3G.1 Introduction to Graphics

Java's original graphical tools were collectively known as the Abstract Window Toolkit, or AWT. The classes associated with the AWT (including the `Point` class discussed in Chapter 3) reside in the package `java.awt`. In order to create graphical programs like those you'll see in this section, you'll need to include the following `import` declaration at the top of your programs:

```java
import java.awt.*;    // for graphics
```

To keep things simple, we'll use a custom class called `DrawingPanel` that was written by the authors of this textbook to simplify some of the more esoteric details of Java graphics. It is less than a page long, so we aren't hiding much. You won't need to import `DrawingPanel`, but you will need to place the file `DrawingPanel.java` in the same folder as your program.

The drawing panel keeps track of the overall image, but the actual drawing will be done with an object of type `Graphics`. The `Graphics` class is also part of the `java.awt` library.

DrawingPanel

You can create a graphical window on your screen by constructing a `DrawingPanel` object. You must specify the width and height of the drawing area:

```java
DrawingPanel <name> = new DrawingPanel(<width>, <height>);
```

`DrawingPanel` objects have two public methods, listed in Table 3.7.

The typical usage of the `DrawingPanel` will be to construct a panel of a particular height and width, set its background color (if you don't want the default white background), and then draw something on it using its `Graphics` object. The `DrawingPanel` appears on the screen at the time that you construct it.

All coordinates are specified as integers. Each (x, y) position corresponds to a different pixel on the computer screen. The word *pixel* is shorthand for "picture element" and represents a single dot on the computer screen.

The coordinate system assigns the upper-left corner of a panel the position (0, 0). As you move to the right of this position, the x value increases. As you move down

TABLE 3.7   Useful Methods of `DrawingPanel` Objects

Method	Description
`getGraphics()`	returns a reference to the `Graphics` object that can be used to draw onto the panel
`setBackground (color)`	sets the background color of the panel to the given color (the default is white)

from this position, the y value increases. For example, suppose that you construct a `DrawingPanel` with a width of 200 pixels and a height of 100 pixels. The upper-left corner will have the coordinates (0, 0), and the lower-right corner will have the coordinates (199, 99).

```
(0, 0) ┌──────────┐
       │          │
       │          │
       └──────────┘
              (199, 99)
```

This is likely to be confusing at first, because you're probably used to coordinate systems where y values decrease as you move down. However, you'll soon get the hang of it.

Drawing Lines and Shapes

So, how do you actually draw something? To draw shapes and lines, you don't talk directly to the `DrawingPanel`, but rather to a related object of type `Graphics`. Think of the `DrawingPanel` as a canvas and the `Graphics` object as the paintbrush. The `DrawingPanel` class has a method called `getGraphics` that returns a reference to its `Graphics` object.

One of the simplest drawing commands is `drawLine`, which takes four integer arguments. For example:

```
g.drawLine(<x1>, <y1>, <x2>, <y2>);
```

This draws a line from the point (x1, y1) to the point (x2, y2).

Here is a sample program that puts these pieces together:

```
1   // Draws a line onto a DrawingPanel.
2
3   import java.awt.*;    // for graphics
4
5   public class DrawLine1 {
6       public static void main(String[] args) {
7           // create the drawing panel
8           DrawingPanel panel = new DrawingPanel(200, 100);
9
10          // draw a line on the panel using
11          // the Graphics paintbrush
12          Graphics g = panel.getGraphics();
13          g.drawLine(25, 75, 175, 25);
14      }
15  }
```

When you run this program, the window shown in Figure 3.1 appears. Though it isn't text on the console, as in previous chapters, we'll still refer to this as the "output" of the program.

(Java can be run on a variety of operating systems. The screenshots of graphical output in this chapter will differ slightly in appearance to reflect the fact that they were taken in different environments.)

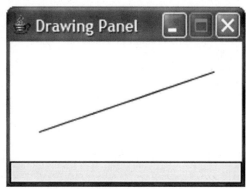

Figure 3.1 : Output of DrawLine1

The first statement in `main` constructs a `DrawingPanel` with a width of 200 and a height of 100. Once constructed, the window will pop up on the screen. The second statement draws a line from (25, 75) to (175, 25). The first point is in the lower-left part of the window (25 over from the left, 75 down from the top). The second point is in the upper-right corner (175 over from the left, 25 down from the top).

Notice these particular lines of code:

```
Graphics g = panel.getGraphics();
g.drawLine(25, 75, 175, 25);
```

You might wonder why you can't just say:

```
panel.drawLine(25, 75, 175, 25);   // this is illegal
```

The problem is that there are two different objects involved in this program: the `DrawingPanel` itself (the canvas) and the `Graphics` object associated with the panel (the paintbrush). The panel doesn't know how to draw a line; only the `Graphics` object knows how to do this. You have to be careful to make sure that you are talking to the right object when you give a command.

This can be confusing, but it is a common occurrence in Java programs. In fact, in a typical Java program, there are hundreds (if not thousands) of objects interacting with each other. These interactions aren't so unlike interactions between people. If you want to schedule a meeting, a busy corporate executive might tell you, "Talk to my secretary about that." Or if you're asking difficult legal questions, a person might tell you, "Talk to my lawyer about that." In this case, the `DrawingPanel` doesn't know how to draw, so if it could talk it would say, "Talk to my `Graphics` object about that."

It would also have been legal to use the `Graphics` object without storing it in a variable, like this:

```
panel.getGraphics().drawLine(25, 75, 175, 25);   // also legal
```

But you'll often want to send several commands to the `Graphics` object, so it's more convenient to give it a name and store it in a variable.

Let's look at a more complicated example:

```
1   // Draws three lines to make a triangle.
2
3   import java.awt.*;
4
5   public class DrawLine2 {
6       public static void main(String[] args) {
7           DrawingPanel panel = new DrawingPanel(200, 100);
8
9           // draw a triangle on the panel
10          Graphics g = panel.getGraphics();
11          g.drawLine(25, 75, 100, 25);
12          g.drawLine(100, 25, 175, 75);
13          g.drawLine(25, 75, 175, 75);
14      }
15  }
```

This program draws three different lines to form a triangle, as shown in Figure 3.2. The lines are drawn between three different points. In the lower-left corner we have the point (25, 75). In the middle at the top we have the point (100, 25). And in the lower-right corner we have the point (175, 75). The various calls on drawLine simply draw the lines that connect these three points.

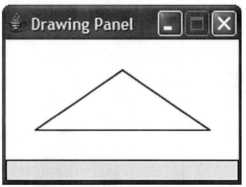

Figure 3.2: Output of DrawLine2

The Graphics object also has methods for drawing particular shapes. For example, you can draw rectangles with the drawRect method:

```
g.drawRect(<x>, <y>, <width>, <height>);
```

This draws a rectangle with upper-left coordinates (x, y) and the given height and width.

Another figure you'll often want to draw is a circle, or, more generally, an oval. But how do you specify where it appears and how big it is? What you actually specify is what is known as the "bounding rectangle" of the circle or oval. Java will draw the largest oval possible that fits inside that rectangle. So, this:

```
g.drawOval(<x>, <y>, <width>, <height>);
```

draws the largest oval that fits within the rectangle with upper-left coordinates (x, y) and the given height and width.

Notice that the first two values passed to drawRect and drawOval are coordinates, while the next two values are a width and a height. For example, here is a short program that draws two rectangles and two ovals:

```
 1  // Draws several shapes.
 2
 3  import java.awt.*;
 4
 5  public class DrawShapes1 {
 6      public static void main(String[] args) {
 7          DrawingPanel panel = new DrawingPanel(200, 100);
 8
 9          Graphics g = panel.getGraphics();
10          g.drawRect(25, 50, 20, 20);
11          g.drawRect(150, 10, 40, 20);
12          g.drawOval(50, 25, 20, 20);
13          g.drawOval(150, 50, 40, 20);
14      }
15  }
```

Figure 3.3 shows the output of the program.

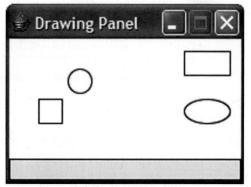

Figure 3.3: Output of DrawShapes1

The first rectangle has its upper-left corner at the coordinates (25, 50). Its width and height are each 20, so this is a square. The coordinates of its lower-right corner would be (45, 70), or 20 more than the (x, y) coordinates of the upper-left corner. The program also draws a rectangle with its upper-left corner at (150, 10) that has a width of 40 and a height of 20 (wider than it is tall). The bounding rectangle of the first oval has upper-left coordinates (50, 25) and a width and height of 20. In other words, it's a circle. The bounding rectangle of the second oval has upper-left coordinates (150, 50), a width of 40, and a height of 20 (it's an oval that is wider than it is tall).

Sometimes you don't just want to draw the outline of a shape; you want to paint the entire area with a particular color. There are variations of the drawRect and drawOval methods known as fillRect and fillOval that do exactly that, drawing a rectangle or oval and filling it in with the current color of paint (the default is black). Let's change two of the calls in the previous program to be "fill" operations instead of "draw" operations:

```
1   // Draws and fills several shapes.
2
3   import java.awt.*;
4
5   public class DrawShapes2 {
6       public static void main(String[] args) {
7           DrawingPanel panel = new DrawingPanel(200, 100);
8
9           Graphics g = panel.getGraphics();
10          g.fillRect(25, 50, 20, 20);
11          g.drawRect(150, 10, 40, 20);
12          g.drawOval(50, 25, 20, 20);
13          g.fillOval(150, 50, 40, 20);
14      }
15  }
```

Now we get the output shown in Figure 3.4 instead.

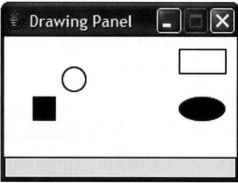

Figure 3.4: Output of DrawShapes2

Colors

All of the shapes and lines drawn by the preceding programs were black, and all of the panels had a white background. These are the default colors, but you can change the background color of the panel, and you can change the color being used by the Graphics object as many times as you like. To change these colors, you use the standard Color class, which is part of the java.awt package.

There are a number of predefined colors that you can refer to directly. They are defined as class constants (just like the constants we used in Chapter 2). The names of these constants are all in uppercase and are self-explanatory. To refer to one of these colors, you have to precede it with the class name and a dot, as in Color.GREEN or Color.BLUE. The predefined Color constants are listed in Table 3.8.

As mentioned earlier the DrawingPanel object has a method that can be used to change the background color that covers the entire panel:

```
<panel>.setBackground(<color>);
```

Likewise, the Graphics object has a method that can be used to change the current drawing filling color for shapes and lines:

```
g.setColor(<color>);
```

TABLE 3.8 `Color` Constants

Color.BLACK	Color.GREEN	Color.RED
Color.BLUE	Color.LIGHT_GRAY	Color.WHITE
Color.CYAN	Color.MAGENTA	Color.YELLOW
Color.DARK_GRAY	Color.ORANGE	
Color.GRAY	Color.PINK	

Calling `setColor` is like dipping your paintbrush in a different color of paint. From that point on, all drawing and filling will be done in the specified color. For example, here is another version of the previous program that uses a cyan (light blue) background color and fills in the oval and square with white instead of black:

```
 1   // Draws and fills shapes in different colors.
 2
 3   import java.awt.*;
 4
 5   public class DrawColoredShapes {
 6       public static void main(String[] args) {
 7           DrawingPanel panel = new DrawingPanel(200, 100);
 8           panel.setBackground(Color.CYAN);
 9
10           Graphics g = panel.getGraphics();
11           g.drawRect(150, 10, 40, 20);
12           g.drawOval(50, 25, 20, 20);
13           g.setColor(Color.WHITE);
14           g.fillOval(150, 50, 40, 20);
15           g.fillRect(25, 50, 20, 20);
16       }
17   }
```

It produces the output shown in Figure 3.5.

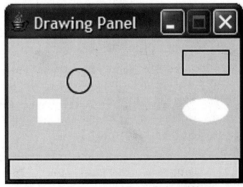

Figure 3.5:Output of DrawColoredShapes

Notice that you tell the panel to set the background color, while you tell the `Graphics` object to set the foreground color. The reasoning is that the background color is a property of the entire window, while the foreground color affects only the particular shapes that you then draw.

Notice also that the order of the calls has been rearranged. The two drawing commands appear first, then the call on `setColor` that changes the color to white, then the two filling commands. This ensures that the drawing is done in black and the filling is done in white. The order of operations is very important in these drawing programs, so you'll have to keep track of what your current color is each time you give a new command to draw or fill something.

In each of the preceding examples we used simple constants for the drawing and filling commands, but it is possible to use expressions. For example, suppose that we stick with our `DrawingPanel` size of 200 pixels wide and 100 pixels tall and we want to produce a diagonal series of four rectangles that extend from the upper-left corner to the lower-right corner, each with a white oval inside. In other words, we want to produce the output shown in Figure 3.6.

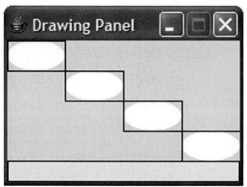

Figure 3.6: Desired Output of DrawLoop1

The overall width of 200 and overall height of 100 are divided evenly into four rectangles, which means that they must all be 50 pixels wide and 25 pixels high. So, width and height values for the four rectangles are the same, but the positions of their upper-left corners are different. The first rectangle's upper-left corner is at (0, 0), the second is at (50, 25), the third is at (100, 50), and the fourth is at (150, 75). We need to write code to generate these different coordinates.

This is a great place to use a `for` loop. Using the techniques introduced in Chapter 2, we can make a table and develop a formula for the coordinates. In this case it is easier to have the loop start with 0 rather than 1, which will often be the case with drawing programs. Here is a program that is a good first stab at generating the desired output:

```
1   // Draws boxed ovals using a for loop (flawed version).
2
3   import java.awt.*;
4
```

```
 5  public class DrawLoop1 {
 6      public static void main(String[] args) {
 7          DrawingPanel panel = new DrawingPanel(200, 100);
 8          panel.setBackground(Color.CYAN);
 9
10          Graphics g = panel.getGraphics();
11          for (int i = 0; i < 4; i++) {
12              g.drawRect(i * 50, i * 25, 50, 25);
13              g.setColor(Color.WHITE);
14              g.fillOval(i * 50, i * 25, 50, 25);
15          }
16      }
17  }
```

It produces the output shown in Figure 3.7.

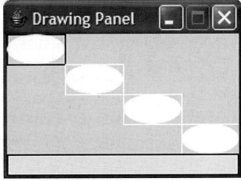

Figure 3.7: Output of DrawLoop1

The coordinates and sizes are right, but not the colors. Instead of getting four black rectangles with white ovals inside, we're getting one black rectangle and three white rectangles. That's because we only have one call on setColor inside the loop. Initially the color will be set to black, which is why the first rectangle comes out black. But once we make a call on setColor changing the color to white, every subsequent drawing and filling command is done in white, including the second, third, and fourth rectangles.

So, we need to include calls to set the color to black to draw the rectangles and to set the color to white to draw the filled ovals. While we're at it, it's a good idea to switch the order of these tasks. The rectangles and ovals overlap slightly, and we would rather have the rectangle drawn over the oval than the other way around. The following program produces the correct output:

```
 1  // Draws boxed ovals using a for loop.
 2
 3  import java.awt.*;
 4
 5  public class DrawLoop2 {
 6      public static void main(String[] args) {
 7          DrawingPanel panel = new DrawingPanel(200, 100);
 8          panel.setBackground(Color.CYAN);
 9
```

```
10              Graphics g = panel.getGraphics();
11              for (int i = 0; i < 4; i++) {
12                  g.setColor(Color.WHITE);
13                  g.fillOval(i * 50, i * 25, 50, 25);
14                  g.setColor(Color.BLACK);
15                  g.drawRect(i * 50, i * 25, 50, 25);
16              }
17          }
18      }
```

It's also possible to create custom `Color` objects of your own, rather than using the constant colors provided in the `Color` class. Computer monitors use red, green, and blue (RGB) as their primary colors, so when you construct a `Color` object you pass your own parameter values for the redness, greenness, and blueness of the color:

```
new Color(<red>, <green>, <blue>)
```

The red/green/blue components should be integer values between 0 and 255. The higher the value, the more of that color is mixed in. All 0 values produce black, and all 255 values produce white. Values of (0, 255, 0) produce a pure green, while values of (128, 0, 128) make a dark purple color (because red and blue are mixed). Search for "RGB table" in your favorite search engine to find tables of many common colors.

The following program demonstrates the use of custom colors. It uses a class constant for the number of rectangles to draw and produces a blend of colors from black to white:

```
1   // Draws a smooth color gradient from black to white.
2
3   import java.awt.*;
4
5   public class DrawColorGradient {
6       public static final int RECTS = 32;
7
8       public static void main(String[] args) {
9           DrawingPanel panel = new DrawingPanel(256, 256);
10          panel.setBackground(new Color(255, 128, 0)); // orange
11
12          Graphics g = panel.getGraphics();
13
14          // from black to white, top left to bottom right
15          for (int i = 0; i < RECTS; i++) {
16              int shift = i * 256 / RECTS;
17              g.setColor(new Color(shift, shift, shift));
18              g.fillRect(shift, shift, 20, 20);
19          }
20      }
21  }
```

It produces the output shown in Figure 3.8.

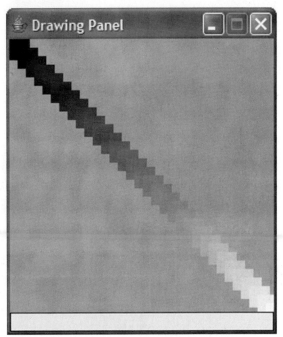

Figure 3.8: Output of DrawColorGradient

Text and Fonts

There is another drawing command worth mentioning, which can be used to include text in your drawings. The `drawString` method of the `Graphics` object:

```
g.drawString(<message>, <x>, <y>);
```

draws the given `String` with its lower-left corner at coordinates (x, y).

This is a slightly different convention than we used for `drawRect`. With `drawRect`, we specified the coordinates of the upper-left corner. Here we specify the coordinates of the lower-left corner. By default, text is drawn approximately 10 pixels high. Here is a sample program that uses a loop to draw a particular `String` 10 different times, each time indenting it 5 pixels to the right and moving it down 10 pixels from the top:

```
1   // Draws a message several times.
2
3   import java.awt.*;
4
5   public class DrawStringMessage1 {
6       public static void main(String[] args) {
7           DrawingPanel panel = new DrawingPanel(200, 100);
8           panel.setBackground(Color.YELLOW);
9
```

```
10              Graphics g = panel.getGraphics();
11              for (int i = 0; i < 10; i++) {
12                  g.drawString("There is no place like home",
13                                  i * 5, 10 + i * 10);
14              }
15          }
16  }
```

It produces the output shown in Figure 3.9.

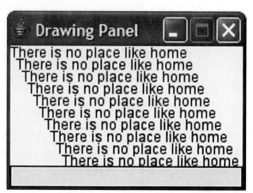

Figure 3.9: Output of DrawStringMessage

If you'd like to change the style or size in which the onscreen text is drawn, you can use the setFont method of the Graphics object:

g.setFont(<font>)

This changes the text size and style in which strings are drawn.

The parameter to setFont is a Font object. A Font object is constructed by passing three parameters: the font's name as a String, its style (such as bold or italic), and its size as an integer. For example:

new Font(<name>, <style>, <size>)

Common font styles such as bold are implemented as constants in the Font class. The available constants and some popular font names are listed in Tables 3.9 and 3.10.

TABLE 3.9   Useful Constants of the Font Class

Constant	Displays
Font.BOLD	**Bold text**
Font.ITALIC	*Italic text*
Font.BOLD + Font.ITALIC	***Bold/Italic text***
Font.PLAIN	Plain text

TABLE 3.10   Common Font Names

Name	Description
`"Monospaced"`	a typewriter font, such as `Courier New`
`"SansSerif"`	a font without curves (serifs) at letter edges, such as Arial
`"Serif"`	a font with curved edges, such as Times New Roman

As with colors, setting the font affects only strings drawn after the font is set. The following program sets several fonts and uses them to draw strings:

```
1   // Draws several messages using different fonts.
2
3   import java.awt.*;
4
5   public class DrawFonts {
6       public static void main(String[] args) {
7           DrawingPanel panel = new DrawingPanel(200, 100);
8           panel.setBackground(Color.PINK);
9
10          Graphics g = panel.getGraphics();
11          g.setFont(new Font("Monospaced",
12                  Font.BOLD + Font.ITALIC, 36));
13          g.drawString("Too big", 20, 40);
14
15          g.setFont(new Font("SansSerif", Font.PLAIN, 10));
16          g.drawString("Too small", 30, 60);
17
18          g.setFont(new Font("Serif", Font.ITALIC, 18));
19          g.drawString("Just right", 40, 80);
20      }
21  }
```

It produces the output shown in Figure 3.10.

Figure 3.10: Output of DrawFonts

3G.2 Procedural Decomposition with Graphics

If you write complex drawing programs, you will want to break them down into several static methods to structure the code and to remove redundancy. In doing so, you'll have to pass a reference to the `Graphics` object to each static method that you introduce. For a quick example, the `DrawStringMessage1` program from the previous section could be split into a `main` method and a `drawText` method, as follows:

```
1   // Draws a message several times using a static method.
2
3   import java.awt.*;
4
5   public class DrawStringMessage2 {
6       public static void main(String[] args) {
7           DrawingPanel panel = new DrawingPanel(200, 100);
8           panel.setBackground(Color.YELLOW);
9
10          Graphics g = panel.getGraphics();
11          drawText(g);
12      }
13
14      public static void drawText(Graphics g) {
15          for (int i = 0; i < 10; i++) {
16              g.drawString("There is no place like home",
17                           i * 5, 10 + i * 10);
18          }
19      }
20  }
```

It produces the same output as the original program (Figure 3.9).

The program wouldn't compile without passing `Graphics g` to the `drawText` method, because `g` is needed to call drawing methods such as `drawString` and `fillRect`.

A Larger Example: `DrawDiamonds`

Now let's consider a slightly more complicated task: drawing the largest diamond figure that will fit into a box of a particular size. The largest diamond that can fit into a box of size 50×50 looks a bit like the following diagram:

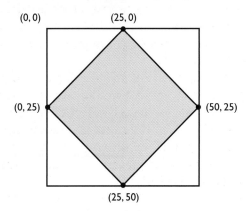

The overall drawing panel has a size of 350×250. Each pyramid is 100 pixels high and 100 pixels wide. The pyramids consist of centered flights of colored stairs that widen toward the bottom, with black outlines around each stair. Table 3.12 lists the attributes of each pyramid.

TABLE 3.12

Fill color	Top-left corner	Number of stairs	Height of each stair
white	(0, 0)	10 stairs	10 pixels
red	(80, 140)	5 stairs	20 pixels
blue	(220, 50)	20 stairs	5 pixels

Unstructured Partial Solution

When trying to solve a larger and more complex problem like this, it's important to tackle it piece by piece and make iterativ-e enhancements toward a final solution. Let's begin by trying to draw the top-left white pyramid correctly.

Each stair is centered horizontally within the pyramid. The top stair is 10 pixels wide. Therefore, it is surrounded by $\frac{90}{2}$ or 45 pixels of empty space on either side. That means that the 10×10 rectangle's top-left corner is at (45, 0). The second stair is 20 pixels wide, meaning that it's surrounded by $\frac{80}{2}$ or 40 pixels on each side:

The following program draws the white pyramid at its correct position:

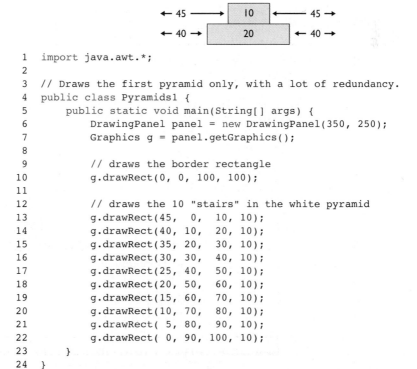

```
1   import java.awt.*;
2
3   // Draws the first pyramid only, with a lot of redundancy.
4   public class Pyramids1 {
5       public static void main(String[] args) {
6           DrawingPanel panel = new DrawingPanel(350, 250);
7           Graphics g = panel.getGraphics();
8
9           // draws the border rectangle
10          g.drawRect(0, 0, 100, 100);
11
12          // draws the 10 "stairs" in the white pyramid
13          g.drawRect(45,  0,  10, 10);
14          g.drawRect(40, 10,  20, 10);
15          g.drawRect(35, 20,  30, 10);
16          g.drawRect(30, 30,  40, 10);
17          g.drawRect(25, 40,  50, 10);
18          g.drawRect(20, 50,  60, 10);
19          g.drawRect(15, 60,  70, 10);
20          g.drawRect(10, 70,  80, 10);
21          g.drawRect( 5, 80,  90, 10);
22          g.drawRect( 0, 90, 100, 10);
23      }
24  }
```

Looking at the code, it's clear that there's a lot of redundancy in the 10 lines to draw the stairs. Examining the patterns of numbers in each column reveals that the x value decreases by 5 each time, the y value increases by 10 each time, the width increases by 10 each time, and the height stays the same.

Another way of describing a stair's x value is to say that it is half of the overall 100 minus the stair's width. With that in mind, the following `for` loop draws the 10 stairs without the previous redundancy:

```
for (int i = 0; i < 10; i++) {
    int stairWidth = 10 * (i + 1);
    int stairHeight = 10;
    int stairX = (100 - stairWidth) / 2;
    int stairY = 10 * i;
    g.drawRect(stairX, stairY, stairWidth, stairHeight);
}
```

Generalizing the Drawing of Pyramids

Next let's add code to draw the bottom (red) pyramid. Its (x, y) position is (80, 140) and it has only five stairs. That means each stair is twice as tall and wide as those in the white pyramid:

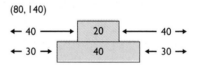

Based on this, the top stair's upper-left corner is at (120, 140) and its size is 20×20, the second stair's upper-left corner is at (110, 160) and its size is 40×20, and so on.

For the moment, let's focus on getting the coordinates of the stairs right, and not on the red fill color. Here is a redundant bit of code to draw the red pyramid's stairs, without the coloring:

```
// draws the border rectangle
g.drawRect(80, 140, 100, 100);
// draws the 5 "stairs" of the red pyramid
g.drawRect(120, 140,  20, 20);
g.drawRect(110, 160,  40, 20);
g.drawRect(100, 180,  60, 20);
g.drawRect( 90, 200,  80, 20);
g.drawRect( 80, 220, 100, 20);
```

Noticing that we again have redundancy between the five lines to draw the stairs, let's look for a pattern between them. We'll use a loop to eliminate the redundancy like we did for the last pyramid, but with appropriate modifications. Each stair's height is now 20 pixels, and each stair's width is now 20 times the number for that stair. The x- and y-coordinates are a bit trickier. The x-coordinate formula is similar to the (100 – stairWidth) / 2 from before, but this time it must be shifted right by 80 to account for the position of it's bounding box's top-left corner. The y-coordinate must similarly be shifted downward by 140 pixels. Here's the correct loop:

```
// draws the 5 "stairs" of the red pyramid
for (int i = 0; i < 5; i++) {
    int stairWidth = 20 * (i + 1);
    int stairHeight = 20;
    int stairX = 80 + (100 - stairWidth) / 2;
    int stairY = 140 + 20 * i;
    g.drawRect(stairX, stairY,
               stairWidth, stairHeight);
}
```

Can you spot the pattern between these two loops? The x- and y-coordinates differ only in the addition of the offset from (0, 0) in the second loop. The stairs' widths and heights differ only in that one pyramid's stairs are 20 pixels tall and the other's are 10 (the result of dividing the overall size of 100 by the number of stairs).

Using the preceding information, let's turn the code for drawing a pyramid into a method that we can call three times to avoid redundancy. As parameters, we'll pass the (x, y) coordinates of the top-left corner of the pyramid's bounding box, and the number of stairs in the pyramid. We'll also need to pass Graphics g as a parameter so that we can draw onto the DrawingPanel. The main modification we'll make to the for loop is to compute the stair height first, then use this to compute the stair width, and finally use the width and height to help compute the (x, y) coordinates of the stair. Here's the code:

```
public static void drawPyramid(Graphics g, int x,
                                  int y, int stairs) {
    // draws the border rectangle
    g.drawRect(x, y, 100, 100);

    // draws the stairs of the pyramid
    for (int i = 0; i < stairs; i++) {
        int stairHeight = 100 / stairs;
        int stairWidth = stairHeight * (i + 1);
        int stairX = x + (100 - stairWidth) / 2;
        int stairY = y + stairHeight * i;
        g.drawRect(stairX, stairY,
                   stairWidth, stairHeight);
    }
}
```

The preceding code is now generalized to draw a pyramid at any location with any number of stairs. But one final ingredient is missing: the ability to give a different color to each pyramid.

Complete Structured Solution

The preceding code is correct except that it doesn't allow us to draw the pyramids in the proper colors. Let's add an additional parameter, a Color, to our method and use it to fill the pyramid stairs as needed. We'll pass Color.WHITE as this parameter's value for the first white pyramid; it'll fill the stairs with white, even though this isn't necessary.

The way to draw a filled shape with an outline of a different color is to first fill the shape, then use the outline color to draw the same shape. For example, to get red rectangles with black outlines, first we'll use fillRect with red, then we'll use drawRect with black with the same parameters.

Here's the new version of the drawPyramid method that uses the fill color as a parameter:

```java
public static void drawPyramid(Graphics g, Color c,
        int x, int y, int stairs) {
    g.drawRect(x, y, 100, 100);

    for (int i = 0; i < stairs; i++) {
        int stairHeight = 100 / stairs;
        int stairWidth = stairHeight * (i + 1);
        int stairX = x + (100 - stairWidth) / 2;
        int stairY = y + stairHeight * i;

        g.setColor(c);
        g.fillRect(stairX, stairY,
                   stairWidth, stairHeight);
        g.setColor(Color.BLACK);
        g.drawRect(stairX, stairY,
                   stairWidth, stairHeight);
    }
}
```

Using this method, we can now draw all three pyramids easily by calling drawPyramid three times with the appropriate parameters:

```java
drawPyramid(g, Color.WHITE, 0, 0, 10);
drawPyramid(g, Color.RED, 80, 140, 5);
drawPyramid(g, Color.BLUE, 220, 50, 20);
```

One last improvement we can make to our Pyramids program is to turn the overall pyramid size of 100 into a constant, so there aren't so many 100s lying around in the code. Here is the complete program:

```java
1   // This program draws three colored pyramid figures.
2
3   import java.awt.*;
4
5   public class Pyramids {
6       public static final int SIZE = 100;
7
8       public static void main(String[] args) {
9           DrawingPanel panel = new DrawingPanel(350, 250);
10          Graphics g = panel.getGraphics();
11
12          drawPyramid(g, Color.WHITE, 0, 0, 10);
13          drawPyramid(g, Color.RED, 80, 140, 5);
14          drawPyramid(g, Color.BLUE, 220, 50, 20);
15      }
16
17      // draws one pyramid figure with the given
18      // number of stairs at the given (x, y) position
19      // with the given color
20      public static void drawPyramid(Graphics g, Color c,
21              int x, int y, int stairs) {
22
23          // draws the border rectangle
24          g.drawRect(x, y, SIZE, SIZE);
```

```
25
26              // draws the stairs of the pyramid
27              for (int i = 0; i < stairs; i++) {
28                  int stairHeight = SIZE / stairs;
29                  int stairWidth = stairHeight * (i + 1);
30                  int stairX = x + (SIZE − stairWidth) / 2;
31                  int stairY = y + stairHeight * i;
32
33                  // fills the rectangles with the fill colors
34                  g.setColor(c);
35                  g.fillRect(stairX, stairY,
36                          stairWidth, stairHeight);
37
38                  // draws the black rectangle outlines
39                  g.setColor(Color.BLACK);
40                  g.drawRect(stairX, stairY,
41                          stairWidth, stairHeight);
42              }
43          }
44      }
```

Chapter Summary

DrawingPanel is a custom class provided by the authors to easily show a graphical window on the screen. A DrawingPanel contains a Graphics object, which can be used to draw lines, text, and shapes on the screen using different colors.

———

A Graphics object has many useful methods for drawing shapes and lines, such as drawLine, fillRect, and setColor. Shapes can be "drawn" (drawing only the outline) or "filled" (coloring the entire shape).

———

The Graphics object can write text on the screen with its drawString method. Different font styles and sizes can be specified with the setFont method.

———

Graphical programs that are decomposed into methods must pass appropriate parameters to those methods (for example, the Graphics object, as well as any (x, y) coordinates, sizes, or other values that guide the figures to be drawn).

———

Self-Check Exercises

Section 3G.1: Introduction to Graphics

1. There are two mistakes in the following code, which attempts to draw a line from coordinates (50, 86) to (20, 35). What are they?

```
DrawingPanel panel = new DrawingPanel(200, 200);
panel.drawLine(50, 20, 86, 35);
```

2. The following code attempts to draw a filled black outer rectangle with a white filled inner circle inside it:

```
DrawingPanel panel = new DrawingPanel(200, 100);
```

```
Graphics g = panel.getGraphics();
g.setColor(Color.WHITE);
g.fillOval(10, 10, 50, 50);
g.setColor(Color.BLACK);
g.fillRect(10, 10, 50, 50);
```

However, it has the incorrect appearance shown in Figure 3.14. What must be changed for it to look as intended?

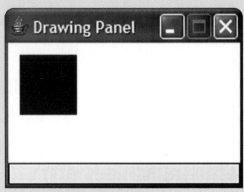

Figure 3.14

3. The following code attempts to draw a black rectangle from (10, 20) to (50, 40) with a line across its diagonal:

```
DrawingPanel panel = new DrawingPanel(200, 100);
Graphics g = panel.getGraphics();
g.drawRect(10, 20, 50, 40);
g.drawLine(10, 20, 50, 40);
```

However, it looks like Figure 3.15. What must be changed for it to look as intended?

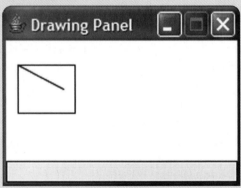

Figure 3.15

4. What sort of figure will be drawn by the following program? Can you draw a picture that will approximately match its appearance without running it first?

```
1   import java.awt.*;
2
3   public class Draw7 {
4       public static void main(String[] args) {
5           DrawingPanel panel = new DrawingPanel(200, 200);
6           Graphics g = panel.getGraphics();
```

```
 7              for (int i = 0; i < 20; i++) {
 8                  g.drawOval(i * 10, i * 10, 200 - (i * 10),
 9                          200 - (i * 10));
10              }
11          }
12      }
```

Exercises

1. Write a program that uses the DrawingPanel to draw Figure 3.16.

Figure 3.16

The window is 220 pixels wide and 150 pixels tall. The background is yellow. There are two blue ovals of size 40 × 40 pixels. They are 80 pixels apart, and the left oval is located at position (50, 25). There is a red square whose top two corners exactly intersect the centers of the two ovals. Lastly, there is a black horizontal line through the center of the square.

2. Modify your program from the previous exercise so that the figure is drawn by a method called drawFigure. The method should accept two arguments: the Graphics g of the DrawingPanel on which to draw, and a Point specifying the location of the top-left corner of the figure. Use the following heading for your method:

```
public static void drawFigure(Graphics g, Point location)
```

Set your DrawingPanel's size to 450 × 150 pixels, and use your drawFigure method to place two figures on it, as shown in Figure 3.17. One figure should be at position (50, 25) and the other should be at position (250, 45).

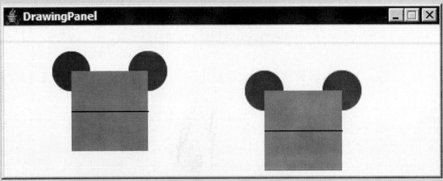

Figure 3.17

3. 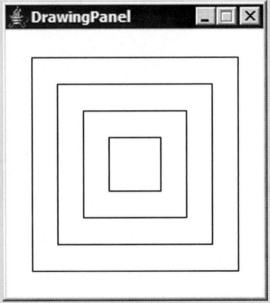 Write a program with a static method called showDesign that uses the DrawingPanel to draw Figure 3.18.

Figure 3.18

The window is 200 pixels wide and 200 pixels tall. The background is white and the foreground is black. There are 20 pixels between each of the four rectangles, and the rectangles are concentric (their centers are at the same point). Use a loop to draw the repeated rectangles.

4. Modify your showDesign method from the previous exercise so that it accepts parameters for the window width and height and displays the rectangles at the appropriate sizes. For example, if your showDesign method was called with values of 300 and 100, the window would look like Figure 3.19.

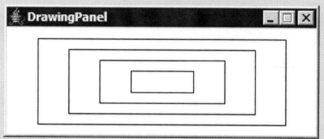

Figure 3.19

5. 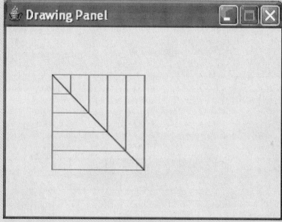 Write a program that uses the DrawingPanel to draw the shape shown in Figure 3.20.

Figure 3.20

The drawing panel is 300 pixels wide by 200 pixels high. Its background is cyan. The horizontal and vertical lines are drawn in red and the diagonal line is drawn in black. The upper-left corner of the diagonal line is at (50, 50). Successive horizontal and vertical lines are spaced 20 pixels apart.

6. Modify your code from the previous exercise to produce the pattern shown in Figure 3.21.

The drawing panel is now 400×300 pixels in size. The first figure is at the same position, (50, 50). The other figures are at positions (250, 10) and (180, 115), respectively. Use one or more parameterized static methods to reduce the redundancy of your solution.

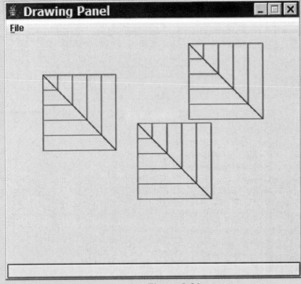

Figure 3.21

7. Write a program that uses the `DrawingPanel` to draw the spiral shown in Figure 3.22.

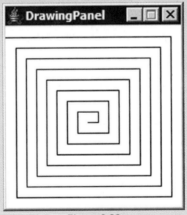

Figure 3.22

The window is 170 pixels wide and 170 pixels tall. The background is white and the foreground is black. The spiral line begins at point (0, 10) and spirals inward. There are 10 pixels between each arm of the spiral. Eight spirals are made in total. The initial spiral touches points (0, 10), (160, 10), (160, 160), (10, 160), and (10, 20).

For an additional challenge, parameterize your program with parameters such as the window size and the number of spiral loops desired.

Programming Projects

1. Write a program that draws the patterns shown in Figure 3.23 onto a `DrawingPanel`.

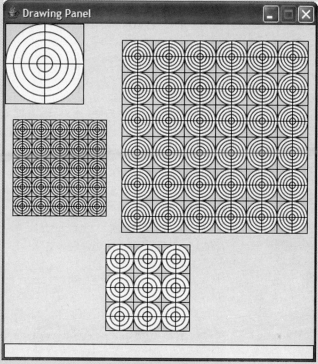

Figure 3.23

The drawing panel's size is 400×400 and its background color is cyan. It contains four figures of concentric yellow circles with black outlines, all surrounded by a green rectangle with a black outline. The four figures on your drawing panel should have the properties shown in Table 3.13.

TABLE 3.13

Description	(x, y) position	Size of subfigures	Number of circles	Number of rows/cols
top left	(0, 0)	100×100	5	1×1
bottom left	(10, 120)	24×24	4	5×5
top right	(150, 20)	40×40	5	6×6
bottom right	(130, 275)	36×36	3	3×3

Break down your program into methods for drawing one subfigure as well as larger grids of subfigures, such as the 5×5 grid at (10, 120).

2. Write a program that draws the image shown in Figure 3.24 onto a `DrawingPanel` of size 200×200. Each stamp is 50×50 pixels in size.

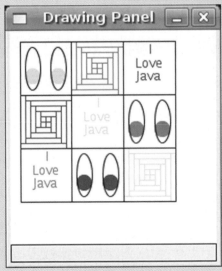

Figure 3.24

3. 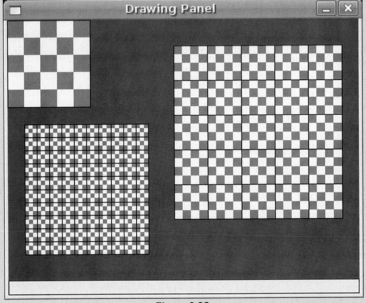 Write a program that draws checkerboards like these shown in Figure 3.25 onto a `DrawingPanel` of size 420×300.

Figure 3.25

4. Write a modified version of the `Projectile` case study program from Chapter 3 that draws a graph of the projectile's flight onto a `DrawingPanel` of size 420×220. For example, the panel shown in Figure 3.26 draws a projectile with an initial velocity of 30 meters per second, an angle of 50 degrees, and 10 steps.

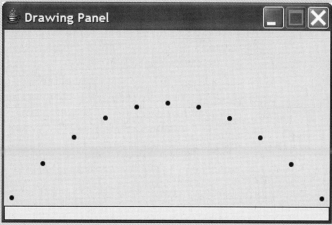

Figure 3.26

Chapter 4

Conditional Execution

Introduction

In the last few chapters, you've seen how to solve complex programming problems using `for` loops to repeat certain tasks many times. You've also seen how to introduce some flexibility into your programs through the use of class constants and how to read values input by the user with a `Scanner` object. Now we are going to explore a much more powerful technique for writing code that can adapt to different situations.

In this chapter, we'll look at *conditional execution* in the form of a control structure known as the `if/else` statement. With `if/else` statements, you can instruct the computer to execute different lines of code depending upon whether certain conditions are true. The `if/else` statement, like the `for` loop, is so powerful that you will wonder how you managed to write programs without it.

This chapter will also expand your understanding of common programming situations. It begins with an exploration of loop techniques we haven't yet examined and includes a discussion of text-processing issues. Adding conditional execution to your repertoire will also require us to revisit methods, parameters, and return values so that you can better understand some of the fine points.

4.1 Loop Techniques

The more you program, the more you will find that certain patterns emerge. Before we delve into conditional execution, we are going to look at two common loop patterns that come up often in programming: cumulative sum and fencepost loops.

Cumulative Sum

You'll often want to find the sum of a series of numbers. You might imagine declaring a different variable for each value you want to include, but that would not be practical: If you have to add a hundred numbers together, you won't want to have to declare a hundred different variables. Fortunately, there is a simpler way.

The trick is to keep a running tally and process one number at a time. If you had a variable called sum, for example, you would add in the next number by saying:

```
sum = sum + next;
```

or using the shorthand assignment operator:

```
sum += next;
```

This statement says to take the existing value of sum, add the value of a variable called next, and store this as the new value of sum. This operation is performed for each number to be summed. There is a slight problem when executing this statement for the first number, though, because the first time around sum does not have a value. To get around this, you initialize sum to a value that will not affect the answer: 0.

Here is a pseudocode description of the cumulative sum algorithm:

```
sum = 0.
for (all numbers to sum) {
    obtain "next".
    sum += next.
}
```

To implement this algorithm, you must decide how many times to go through the loop and how to obtain a next value. Here is an interactive program that prompts the user for how many numbers to sum together and for the numbers themselves:

```
1  // Finds the sum of a sequence of numbers.
2
3  import java.util.*;
4
5  public class ExamineNumbers1 {
6      public static void main(String[] args) {
7          System.out.println("This program adds a sequence of");
8          System.out.println("numbers.");
9          System.out.println();
10
11         Scanner console = new Scanner(System.in);
12
13         System.out.print("How many numbers do you have? ");
14         int totalNumber = console.nextInt();
15
```

```
16              double sum = 0.0;
17              for (int i = 1; i <= totalNumber; i++) {
18                  System.out.print("    #" + i + "? ");
19                  double next = console.nextDouble();
20                  sum += next;
21              }
22              System.out.println();
23
24              System.out.println("sum = " + sum);
25          }
26  }
```

The program's execution will look something like this (as usual, user input is boldface):

```
This program adds a sequence of
numbers.

How many numbers do you have? 6
    #1? 3.2
    #2? 4.7
    #3? 5.1
    #4? 9.0
    #5? 2.4
    #6? 3.1

sum = 27.5
```

Let's trace the execution in detail. Before we enter the for loop, we initialize the variable sum to 0.0:

sum | 0.0 |

On the first execution of the for loop, we read in a value of 3.2 from the user and add this value to sum:

sum | 3.2 | next | 3.2 |

The second time through the loop, we read in a value of 4.7 and add this to the value of sum:

sum | 7.9 | next | 4.7 |

Notice that the sum now includes both of the numbers entered by the user because we have added the new value, 4.7, to the old value, 3.2. The third time through the loop, we add in the value 5.1:

sum | 13.0 | next | 5.1 |

Notice that the variable sum now contains the sum of the first three numbers (3.2 + 4.7 + 5.1). Now we read in 9.0 and add it to the sum:

sum [22.0]   next [9.0]

Then we add in the fifth value, 2.4:

sum [24.4]   next [2.4]

And finally, the sixth value, 3.1:

sum [27.5]   next [3.1]

We then exit the for loop and print the value of sum.

There is an interesting scope issue in this particular program. Notice that the variable sum is declared outside the loop, while the variable next is declared inside the loop. We have no choice but to declare sum outside the loop because it needs to be initialized and it is used after the loop. But the variable next is used only inside the loop, so it can be declared in that inner scope. It is best to declare variables in the innermost scope possible.

The cumulative sum algorithm and variations on it will be useful in many of the programming tasks you solve. How would you do a cumulative product, for example? Here is the pseudocode:

```
product = 1.
for (all numbers to multiply) {
    obtain "next".
    product *= next.
}
```

Fencepost Loops

Another common programming problem involves a particular kind of loop known as a *fencepost loop*. Consider the following problem: You want to put up a fence that is 100 yards long and you want to have a post every 10 yards. How many posts do you need? If you do a quick division in your head, you might say that you need 10 posts, but actually you need 11 posts. That's because fences begin and end with posts. In other words, a fence looks like Figure 4.1.

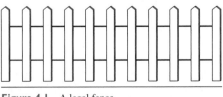

Figure 4.1   A legal fence

Because you want posts on both the far left and the far right, you can't use the following simple loop because it doesn't plant the final post:

```
for (the length of the fence) {
    plant a post.
    attach some wire.
}
```

If you use the preceding loop, you'll get a fence that looks like Figure 4.2.

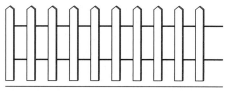

Figure 4.2 A flawed fence

Switching the order of the two operations doesn't help, because then you miss the first post. The problem with this loop is that it produces the same number of posts as sections of wire, but we know we need an extra post. That's why this problem is also sometimes referred to as the "loop and a half" problem—we want to execute one half of this loop (planting a post) one extra time.

One solution is to plant one of the posts either before or after the loop. The usual solution is to do it before:

```
plant a post.
for (the length of the fence) {
    attach some wire.
    plant a post.
}
```

Notice that the order of the two operations in the body of the loop is now reversed because the initial post is planted before the loop is entered.

As a simple example, consider the problem of writing out the integers between 1 and 10, separated by commas. In other words, we want to get this output:

```
1, 2, 3, 4, 5, 6, 7, 8, 9, 10
```

This is a classic fencepost problem because we want to write out 10 numbers but only 9 commas. In our fencepost terminology, writing a number is the "post" part of the task and writing a comma is the "wire" part. So, implementing the pseudocode above, we print the first number before the loop:

```
System.out.print(1);
for (int i = 2; i <= 10; i++) {
    System.out.print(", " + i);
}
System.out.println();
```

4.2 `if/else` Statements

You will often find yourself writing code that you want to execute some of the time but not all of the time. For example, if you are writing a game-playing program, when a new high score is reached you might want to print a message and store that score. You can accomplish this by putting the required two lines of code inside an `if` statement:

```java
if (currentScore > maxScore) {
    System.out.println("A new high score!");
    maxScore = currentScore;
}
```

The idea is that you will sometimes want to execute the two lines of code inside the `if` statement, but not always. The test in parentheses determines whether or not the statements inside the `if` are executed. In other words, the test describes the conditions under which we want to execute the code.

The general form of the `if` statement is as follows:

```java
if (<test>) {
    <statement>;
    <statement>;
    . . .
    <statement>;
}
```

The `if` statement, like the `for` loop, is a control structure. Notice that we once again see a Java keyword (`if`) followed by parentheses and a set of curly braces enclosing a series of controlled statements.

The diagram in Figure 4.3 indicates the flow of control for the simple `if` statement. The computer performs the test, and if it evaluates to true, the computer executes the controlled statements. If the test evaluates to false, the computer skips the controlled statements.

You'll use the simple `if` statement when you have code that you sometimes want to execute and sometimes want to skip. Java also has a variation known as the `if/else` statement that allows you to choose between two alternatives. Suppose, for example, that you want to set a variable called `answer` to the square root of a number:

```java
answer = Math.sqrt(number);
```

There's a potential problem in that you don't want to ask for the square root if the number is negative. You could use a simple `if` statement to avoid the problem:

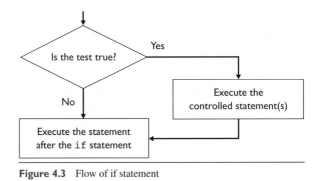

Figure 4.3   Flow of if statement

```
if (number >= 0) {
    answer = Math.sqrt(number);
}
```

This will avoid asking for the square root of a negative number, but what value will it assign to `answer` if `number` is negative? This is a case where you'll probably want to give a value to `answer` either way. Suppose you want `answer` to be -1 when `number` is negative. You can express this pair of alternatives with an `if/else` statement:

```
if (number >= 0) {
    answer = Math.sqrt(number);
} else {
    answer = -1;
}
```

The idea behind the `if/else` statement is that two alternatives are provided, and one or the other is executed. So, in the code above, you know that `answer` will be assigned a value regardless of whether `number` is positive or negative.

The general form of the `if/else` statement is as follows:

```
if (<test>) {
    <statement>;
    <statement>;
    . . .
    <statement>;
} else {
    <statement>;
    . . .
    <statement>;
    <statement>;
}
```

This control structure is unusual in that it has two sets of controlled statements and two different keywords (`if` and `else`). Figure 4.4 indicates the flow of control. The computer performs the test and, depending upon whether it evaluates to true or false, executes one or the other group of statements.

As with the `for` loop, if you have a single statement to execute, you don't need to include the curly braces. However, the Sun convention is to include the curly braces even if you don't need them, and we follow that convention in this book.

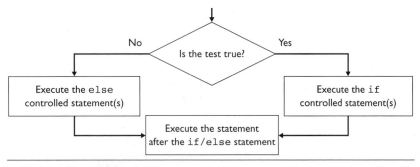

Figure 4.4 Flow of if/else statement

Relational Operators

An if/else statement is controlled by a test. Simple tests compare two expressions to see if they are related in some way. Such tests are themselves expressions of the following form that return either true or false:

```
<expression> <relational operator> <expression>
```

To evaluate such a test of this form, you first evaluate the two expressions and then see if the given relation holds between the value on the left and the value on the right. If the relation does hold, the test evaluates to true. If not, the test evaluates to false.

The relational operators are listed in Table 4.1. Notice that the equality operator consists of two equals signs (==). This is to distinguish it from the assignment operator (=).

Because we use the relational operators as a new way of forming expressions, we must reconsider precedence. Table 4.2 is an updated version of Table 2.5. It includes these new operators. You will see that technically the equality comparisons are considered at a slightly different level of precedence than the other relational operators, but both sets of operators have a lower precedence than the arithmetic operators.

Let's look at an example. The following expression is made up of the constants 3, 2, and 9 and contains addition, multiplication, and equality operations:

```
3 + 2 * 2 == 9
```

TABLE 4.1   Relational Operators

Operator	Meaning	Example	Value
==	equal to	2 + 2 == 4	true
!=	not equal to	3.2 != 4.1	true
<	less than	4 < 3	false
>	greater than	4 > 3	true
<=	less than or equal to	2 <= 0	false
>=	greater than or equal to	2.4 >= 1.6	true

TABLE 4.2   Java Operator Precedence

Description	Operators
unary operators	++, --, +, -
multiplicative operators	*, /, %
additive operators	+, -
relational operators	<, >, <=, >=
equality operators	==, !=
assignment operators	=, +=, -=, *=, /=, %=

Which of the operations is performed first? Because the relational operators have a lower level of precedence than the arithmetic operators, the answer is that the multiplication is performed first, then the additions, then the equality test. In other words, Java will perform all of the "math" first before it tests for one of these relationships. This precedence scheme frees you from the need to parenthesize the left and right sides of a test using a relational operator. Using Java's precedence rules, the sample expression is evaluated as follows:

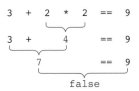

You can put arbitrary expressions on either side of the relational operator as long as they are of a compatible type. Here is a test with complex expressions on either side:

```
(2 - 3 * 8) / (435 % (7 * 2)) <= 3.8 - 4.5 / (2.2 * 3.8)
```

One limitation of the relational operators is that they should only be used with primitive data. Later in this chapter we will talk about how to compare objects for equality, and in a later chapter we'll discuss how to perform less-than and greater-than comparisons on objects.

Cumulative Sum with `if`

Let's now explore how you can use `if/else` statements to create some interesting variations on the cumulative sum algorithm. Suppose you want to read a sequence of numbers and compute the average. This seems like a straightforward variation of the cumulative sum code. You can compute the average as the sum divided by the number of numbers, as in:

```
double average = sum / totalNumber;
System.out.println("average = " + average);
```

But there is one minor problem with this code. Suppose that when you ask how many numbers to process, the user enters 0. The cumulative sum loop will not be entered, and your code will try to compute the value of 0 divided by 0. Java will then print that the average is NaN, a cryptic message short for "Not a Number." It would be better to print out some other kind of message that would indicate that there weren't any numbers to average. You can use an `if/else` statement for this purpose:

```
if (totalNumber <= 0) {
    System.out.println("No numbers to average");
} else {
    double average = sum / totalNumber;
    System.out.println("average = " + average);
}
```

Another use of `if` statements would be to count how many negative numbers the user enters. You will often find yourself wanting to count how many times something occurs in a program. This goal is easy to accomplish with an `if` statement and an integer variable called a *counter.* You start by initializing the counter to 0:

```
int negatives = 0;
```

You can use any name you want for the variable. Here we used `negatives` because that is what you're counting. The other essential step is to increment the counter inside the loop if it passes the test you're interested in:

```
if (next < 0) {
    negatives++;
}
```

Putting this all together and modifying the comments and introduction, you end up with the following variation of the cumulative sum program:

```
 1 // Finds the average of a sequence of numbers as well as
 2 // reporting how many of the user-specified numbers were negative.
 3
 4 import java.util.*;
 5
 6 public class ExamineNumbers2 {
 7     public static void main(String[] args) {
 8         System.out.println("This program examines a sequence");
 9         System.out.println("of numbers to find the average");
10         System.out.println("and count how many are negative.");
11         System.out.println();
12
13         Scanner console = new Scanner(System.in);
14
15         System.out.print("How many numbers do you have? ");
16         int totalNumber = console.nextInt();
17
18         int negatives = 0;
19         double sum = 0.0;
20         for (int i = 1; i <= totalNumber; i++) {
21             System.out.print("    #" + i + "? ");
22             double next = console.nextDouble();
23             sum += next;
24             if (next < 0) {
25                 negatives++;
26             }
27         }
28         System.out.println();
29
30         if (totalNumber <= 0) {
31             System.out.println("No numbers to average");
32         } else {
33             double average = sum / totalNumber;
34             System.out.println("average = " + average);
35         }
36         System.out.println("# of negatives = " + negatives);
```

```
37     }
38 }
```

The program's execution will look something like this:

```
This program examines a sequence
of numbers to find the average
and count how many are negative.

How many numbers do you have? 8
    #1? 2.5
    #2? 9.2
    #3? -19.4
    #4? 208.2
    #5? 42.3
    #6? 92.7
    #7? -17.4
    #8? 8

average = 40.7625
# of negatives = 2
```

Fencepost with `if`

Many of the fencepost loops that you write will require conditional execution. In fact, the fencepost problem itself can be solved with an `if` statement. Remember that the classic solution to the fencepost is to handle the first post before the loop begins:

```
plant a post.
for (the length of the fence) {
    attach some wire.
    plant a post.
}
```

This solution solves the problem, but it can be confusing because inside the loop you do things in reverse order. With an `if` statement, you can keep the original order of the steps:

```
for (the length of the fence) {
    plant a post.
    if (this isn't the last post) {
        attach some wire.
    }
}
```

This variation isn't used as often as the classic solution because it involves both a loop test and a test inside the loop. Often these tests are nearly identical, so it is inefficient to test the same thing twice each time through the loop. But there will be situations where you might use this approach. For example, in the classic approach, the lines of code that correspond to planting a post are repeated. If there is a lot of code involved, you might decide that the `if` inside the loop is a better approach, even if it leads to some extra testing.

As an example, consider writing a method called `multiprint` that will print a string a particular number of times. Suppose that you want the output on a line by itself, inside square brackets and separated by commas. Here are two example calls:

```
multiprint("please", 4);
multiprint("beetlejuice", 3);
```

You would expect these calls to produce the following output:

```
[please, please, please, please]
[beetlejuice, beetlejuice, beetlejuice]
```

Your first attempt might be a simple loop that prints square brackets outside the loop and prints the string and a comma inside the loop:

```
public static void multiprint(String s, int times) {
    System.out.print("[");
    for (int i = 1; i <= times; i++) {
        System.out.print(s + ", ");
    }
    System.out.println("]");
}
```

Unfortunately, this code produces an extraneous comma after the last value:

```
[please, please, please, please, ]
[beetlejuice, beetlejuice, beetlejuice, ]
```

Because the commas are separators, you want to print one more string than comma (e.g., two commas to separate the three occurrences of "beetlejuice"). You can use the classic solution to the fencepost problem to get this behavior by printing one string outside the loop and reversing the order of the printing inside the loop:

```
public static void multiprint(String s, int times) {
    System.out.print("[" + s);
    for (int i = 2; i <= times; i++) {
        System.out.print(", " + s);
    }
    System.out.println("]");
}
```

Notice that because you're printing one of the strings before the loop begins, you have to modify the loop so that it won't print as many strings as it did before. Adjusting the loop variable `i` to start at 2 accounts for the first value that is printed before the loop.

Unfortunately, this solution does not quite work properly. Think of what happens when you ask the method to print a string zero times, as in:

```
multiprint("please don't", 0);
```

This call produces the following incorrect output:

```
[please don't]
```

It should be possible to request zero occurrences of a string, so the method shouldn't do this. The problem is that the classic solution to the fencepost problem involves printing one value before the loop begins. To get it to behave correctly for the zero case, you can include an if/else statement:

```java
public static void multiprint(String s, int times) {
    if (times == 0) {
        System.out.println("[]");
    } else {
        System.out.print("[" + s);
        for (int i = 2; i <= times; i++) {
            System.out.print(", " + s);
        }
        System.out.println("]");
    }
}
```

Alternatively, you can use the approach of including an if statement inside the loop (the double-test approach):

```java
public static void multiprint(String s, int times) {
    System.out.print("[");
    for (int i = 1; i <= times; i++) {
        System.out.print(s);
        if (i < times) {
            System.out.print(", ");
        }
    }
    System.out.println("]");
}
```

Although this code performs a similar test twice on each iteration, it is simpler than using the classic fencepost solution and its special case. Neither solution is better than the other, as there is a tradeoff involved. If you think the code will be executed often with the loop iterating many times, you might be more inclined to use the efficient solution. Otherwise, you might choose the simpler code.

Nested if/else Statements

Many beginners write code that looks like this:

```java
if (<test1>) {
    <statement1>;
}
if (<test2>) {
    <statement2>;
}
if (<test3>) {
    <statement3>;
}
```

This sequential structure is appropriate if you want to execute any combination of the three statements. For example, you might write this code in a program for a questionnaire with three optional parts, any combination of which might be applicable for a given person.

The diagram in Figure 4.5 shows the flow of the sequential `if` code. Notice that it's possible to execute none of the controlled statements (if all tests are false), just one of them (if only one test happens to be true), or many of them (if multiple tests are true).

Often, however, you only want to execute one of a series of statements. In such cases, it is better to nest the `if` statements:

```
if (<test1>) {
    <statement1>;
} else {
    if (<test2>) {
        <statement2>;
    } else {
```

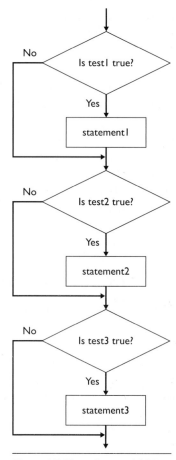

Figure 4.5 Flow of sequential `if`s

```
                if (<test3>) {
                    <statement3>;
                }
            }
        }
    }
```

With this construct, you can be sure that one statement at most is executed: the statement corresponding to the first test to evaluate to `true`. If no tests evaluate to `true`, no statement is executed. If executing at most one statement is your objective, this construct is more appropriate than the sequential `if` statements. It reduces the likelihood of errors and simplifies the testing process.

As you can see, nesting `if` statements like this leads to a lot of indentation. The indentation also isn't all that helpful, because we really think of this as choosing one of a number of alternatives. K&R style has a solution for this as well. If an `else` is followed by an `if`, we put them on the same line:

```
if (<test1>) {
    <statement1>;
} else if (<test2>) {
    <statement2>;
} else if (<test3>) {
    <statement3>;
}
```

This way, the various statements that we are choosing from all appear at the same level of indentation. Sun recommends that nested `if/else` statements be indented in this way.

The diagram in Figure 4.6 shows the flow of the nested `if/else` code. Notice that it is possible to execute one of the controlled statements (the first one whose test is true), or none (if no tests are true).

There is a variation of this structure in which the final statement is controlled by an `else` instead of a test:

```
if (<test1>) {
    <statement1>;
} else if (<test2>) {
    <statement2>;
} else {
    <statement3>;
}
```

In this construct, the final branch will always be taken when all the tests fail, and thus the construct will always execute exactly one of the three statements. The diagram in Figure 4.7 shows the flow of this modified nested `if/else` code.

To explore these variations, consider the task of writing out whether a number is positive, negative, or zero. You could structure this as three simple `if` statements, as follows:

```java
if (number > 0) {
    System.out.println("Number is positive.");
}
if (number == 0) {
    System.out.println("Number is zero.");
}
if (number < 0) {
    System.out.println("Number is negative.");
}
```

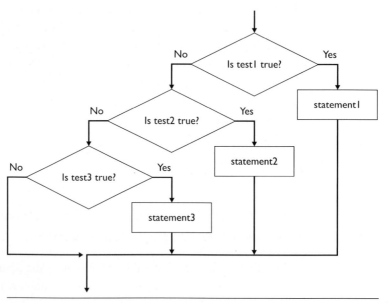

Figure 4.6 Flow of nested `if`s ending in test

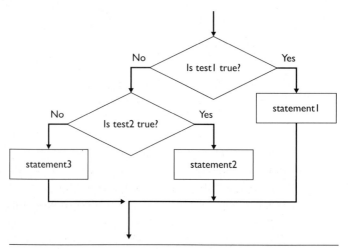

Figure 4.7 Flow of nested `if`s ending in `else`

To determine how many of the `println`s are potentially executed, you have to stop and think about the tests being performed. But you shouldn't have to put that much effort into understanding this code. The code is clearer if you nest the `if` statements:

```java
if (number > 0) {
    System.out.println("Number is positive.");
} else if (number == 0) {
    System.out.println("Number is zero.");
} else if (number < 0) {
    System.out.println("Number is negative.");
}
```

This solution, however, is not the best. You know that you want to execute one and only one `println` statement, but this nested structure does not preclude the possibility of no statement being executed (which would happen if all three tests failed). Of course, with these particular tests that will never happen: If a number is neither positive nor zero, it must be negative. Thus, the final test here is unnecessary and misleading. You must think about the tests to determine whether or not it is possible for all three branches to be skipped.

In this case, the best solution is the nested `if/else` approach with a final branch that is always taken if the first two tests fail:

```java
if (number > 0) {
    System.out.println("Number is positive.");
} else if (number == 0) {
    System.out.println("Number is zero.");
} else {
    System.out.println("Number is negative.");
}
```

You can glance at this construct and see immediately that exactly one `println` will be executed. You don't have to look at the tests being performed in order to realize this; it is a property of this kind of nested `if/else` structure. If you want, you can include a comment to make it clear what is going on:

```java
if (number > 0) {
    System.out.println("Number is positive.");
} else if (number == 0) {
    System.out.println("Number is zero.");
} else { // number must be negative
    System.out.println("Number is negative.");
}
```

One final benefit of this approach is efficiency. With three simple `if` statements, all three tests are always performed. With the nested `if/else` approach, tests are carried out only until a match is found. For example, in the preceding code we only need to perform one test for positive numbers and at most two tests overall.

When you find yourself writing code to pick among alternatives like these, you have to analyze the particular problem to figure out how many of the branches you potentially want to execute. If any combination can be taken, use sequential `if` statements. If you

TABLE 4.3 `if/else` Options

Situation	Construct	Basic form

you want to execute any combination of controlled statements	sequential `ifs`	`if (<test1>) {`
		    `<statement1>;`
		`}`
		`if (<test2>) {`
		    `<statement2>;`
		`}`
		`if (<test3>) {`
		    `<statement3>;`
		`}`

you want to execute zero or one of the controlled statements	nested `ifs` ending in test	`if (<test1>) {`
		    `<statement1>;`
		`} else if (<test2>) {`
		    `<statement2>;`
		`} else if (<test3>) {`
		    `<statement3>;`
		`}`

you want to execute exactly one of the controlled statements	nested `ifs` ending in `else`	`if (<test1>) {`
		    `<statement1>;`
		`} else if (<test2>) {`
		    `<statement2>;`
		`} else {`
		    `<statement3>;`
		`}`

want one or none of the branches to be taken, use nested `if/else` statements with a test for each statement. If you want exactly one branch to be taken, use nested `if/else` statements with a final branch controlled by an `else` rather than by a test. Table 4.3 summarizes these choices.

4.3 Subtleties of Conditional Execution

The last section presented the basic idea behind `if` statements and `if/else` constructs. You'll find as we get deeper into programming that many of the new constructs we study aren't overly complex, but they take time to master. This is true of any craft. For example, it would probably take only a day to learn each of the major tools used by a carpenter, but learning when to use which tool, how to use them together, and how to use them well would require much more than a day of training.

In this section we will explore some of the issues that arise when you start using conditional execution.

Choosing the Wrong `if/else` Construct

Suppose that your instructor has told you that grades will be determined as follows:

> A for scores ≥ 90
> B for scores ≥ 80
> C for scores ≥ 70
> D for scores ≥ 60
> F for scores < 60

You can translate this into code as follows:

```
String grade;
if (score >= 90) {
    grade = "A";
}
if (score >= 80) {
    grade = "B";
}
if (score >= 70) {
    grade = "C";
}
if (score >= 60) {
    grade = "D";
}
if (score < 60) {
    grade = "F";
}
```

However, if you then try to use the variable `grade` after this code, you'll get this error from the compiler:

```
variable grade might not have been initialized
```

This should be a clue that there is a problem. The Java compiler is saying that it believes there are paths through this code that will leave the variable `grade` uninitialized. In fact, the variable will always be initialized, but the compiler is not able to figure this out. We can fix this by giving an initial value to `grade`:

```
String grade = "no grade";
```

This change allows the code to compile. But if you compile and run it, you will find that it gives out only two grades: D and F. Anyone who has a score of at least 60 ends up with a D and anyone with a grade below 60 ends up with an F. And even though the compiler complained that there was a path that would allow `grade` not to be initialized, no one ever gets a grade of "no grade."

The problem here is that you want to execute exactly one of the assignment statements, but with sequential `if` statements, several of them can be executed. For example, if someone has a score of 95, `grade` is set to `"A"`, then reset to `"B"`, then reset to `"C"`, and finally reset to `"D"`. You can fix this problem by using a nested `if/else` construct:

```
String grade;
if (score >= 90) {
    grade = "A";
} else if (score >= 80) {
    grade = "B";
} else if (score >= 70) {
    grade = "C";
} else if (score >= 60) {
    grade = "D";
} else { // score < 60
    grade = "F";
}
```

You don't need to set `grade` to `"no grade"` now because the compiler can see that no matter what path is followed, the variable `grade` will be assigned a value (exactly one of the branches will be executed).

Object Equality

You saw earlier in the chapter that you can use the `==` and `!=` operators to test for equality and nonequality of primitive data, respectively. Unfortunately, these operators do not work as you might expect when testing for equality and nonequality of objects like `Strings` and `Points`. You will have to learn a new way to test objects for equality.

Suppose you were to execute the following lines of code:

```
Point p1 = new Point(3, 4);
Point p2 = new Point(3, 4);
Point p3 = p2;
```

This would lead to the creation of three variables and two objects:

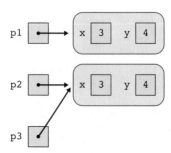

There are two `Point` objects, both of which have coordinates (3, 4). You would normally think of these points as being equal, but if you were to test whether `p1 == p2`, the answer would be `false`. In performing this test, Java looks at whether the variables `p1` and `p2` store exactly the same value. These variables store references to `Point` objects, but they aren't `Point` objects themselves. So, this test is asking whether `p1` and `p2` refer to the same object. Since they refer to different objects, the `==` test evaluates to `false`.

If you were instead to ask whether `p2 == p3`, the answer would be `true`. That's because `p2` and `p3` store the same value. In other words, they both refer to the same object.

Java provides a second way of testing for equality that is intended for testing object equality. Every Java object has a method called `equals` that takes another object as an argument. So, you ask an object whether it equals another object. For example, given the variables `p1` and `p2`, you could test them for equality as follows:

```java
if (p1.equals(p2)) {
    System.out.println("points are equal");
}
```

In this case you are not comparing the variables themselves; you are calling a method of the `Point` object referred to by `p1`. For `Point` objects, the `equals` method compares the x- and y-coordinates stored in each point to see if they are the same. In effect, you are saying, "Hey, `p1`, do you store the same x- and y-coordinates as `p2`?" In this case, the test evaluates to `true`.

Occasionally, you will want to use the `equals` method to test for equality of `String`s. For example, you might write code like the following to read a token from the console and to call one of two different methods depending upon whether the user responded with "yes" or "no." If the user types neither word, this code prints an error message:

```java
System.out.print("yes or no? ");
String s = console.next();
if (s.equals("yes")) {
    processYes();
} else if (s.equals("no")) {
    processNo();
} else {
    System.out.println("You didn't type yes or no");
}
```

As with other object comparisons, this code will not work as intended with `==` tests.

Java also has a special variation of the `equals` method for the `String` class that ignores case differences (uppercase versus lowercase letters). The method is called `equalsIgnoreCase`. For example, you could rewrite the preceding code as follows to recognize responses like "Yes," "YES," "No," "NO," yES", and so on:

```java
System.out.print("yes or no? ");
String s = console.next();
if (s.equalsIgnoreCase("yes")) {
    processYes();
```

```
    } else if (s.equalsIgnoreCase("no")) {
        processNo();
    } else {
        System.out.println("You didn't type yes or no");
    }
```

Roundoff Errors

Earlier in the chapter we looked at a program called `ExamineNumbers2` that reads a series of numbers, computes their average, and counts how many negative numbers are in the sequence. Here is a sample execution that produces an unusual final result:

```
This program examines a sequence of numbers to
find the average as well as counting how many
are negative.

How many numbers do you want me to examine? 4
    #1? 2.1
    #2? -3.8
    #3? 5.4
    #4? 7.4

average = 2.7750000000000004
# of negatives = 1
```

If you use a calculator, you will find that the four numbers add up to 11.1. If you divide this number by 4, you get 2.775. Yet Java reports the result as `2.7750000000000004`. Where do all of those zeros come from, and why does the number end in 4? The answer is that floating-point numbers can lead to *roundoff errors*.

> **Roundoff Error**
>
> A numerical error that occurs because floating-point numbers are stored as approximations rather than as exact values.

Roundoff errors are generally small and can occur in either direction (slightly high or slightly low). In the previous case, we got a roundoff error that was slightly high.

Floating-point numbers are stored in a format similar to scientific notation, with a set of digits and an exponent. Think of how you would store the value one-third in scientific notation using base-10. We describe this number as 3.33333 (repeating) times 10 to the –1 power. We can't store an infinite number of digits on a computer, though, so we'll have to stop repeating the 3s at some point. Suppose we can store 10 digits. This value will be stored as 3.333333333 times 10 to the –1. If we multiply that by 3, we don't get back 1. Instead, we get 9.999999999 times 10 to the −1 (which is equal to 0.9999999999).

You might wonder why the numbers used in the previous example caused a problem when they didn't have any repeating digits. You have to remember that the computer stores numbers in base-2. Numbers like 2.1 and 5.4 might look like simple numbers in base-10, but they have repeating digits when stored in base-2.

Roundoff errors can lead to rather surprising outcomes. For example, consider the following short program:

```
1 public class Roundoff {
2     public static void main(String[] args) {
3         double n = 1.0;
4         for (int i = 1; i <= 10; i++) {
5             n += 0.1;
6             System.out.println(n);
7         }
8     }
9 }
```

This is a classic cumulative sum where we add 0.1 to the number n each time through the loop. We start with n equal to 1.0 and the loop iterates 10 times, so this should print the numbers 1.1, 1.2, 1.3, and so on through 2.0. Instead, it produces the following output:

```
1.1
1.2000000000000002
1.3000000000000003
1.4000000000000004
1.5000000000000004
1.6000000000000005
1.7000000000000006
1.8000000000000007
1.9000000000000008
2.000000000000001
```

The problem occurs because 0.1 cannot be stored exactly in base-2 (it produces a repeating set of digits, just as one-third does in base-10). Each time through the loop the error is compounded, which is why the roundoff error gets worse each time.

As another example, consider the task of adding up a penny, a nickel, a dime, and a quarter. If we use variables of type int, we will get an exact answer no matter what order we add the numbers in:

```
int cents1 = 1 + 5 + 10 + 25;
int cents2 = 25 + 10 + 5 + 1;
System.out.println(cents1);
System.out.println(cents2);
```

The output of this code is as follows:

```
41
41
```

Regardless of the order, these numbers always add up to 41 cents. But suppose that instead of thinking of these values as whole cents, we think of them as fractions of a dollar that we store as doubles:

```
double dollars1 = 0.01 + 0.05 + 0.10 + 0.25;
double dollars2 = 0.25 + 0.10 + 0.05 + 0.01;
System.out.println(dollars1);
System.out.println(dollars2);
```

This code has surprising output:

```
0.41000000000000003
0.41
```

Even though we are adding up exactly the same numbers, the fact that we add them in a different order makes a difference. The reason is roundoff errors.

There are several lessons to draw from this:

- Be aware that when you store floating-point values (e.g., doubles), you are storing approximations and not exact values. If you need to store an exact value, store it using type int.
- Don't be surprised when you see numbers that are slightly off from the expected values.
- Don't expect to be able to compare variables of type double for equality.

To follow up on the third point, consider what would happen with the preceding code if we were to perform the following test:

```
if (dollars1 == dollars2) {
    . . .
}
```

The test would evaluate to false because the values are very close, but not close enough for Java to consider them equal. We rarely use a test for exact equality when we work with doubles. Instead, we can test to see if numbers are close to each other using a test like this:

```
if (Math.abs(dollars1 - dollars2) < 0.001) {
    . . .
}
```

We use the absolute value (abs) method from the Math class to find the magnitude of the difference and then test whether it is less than some small epsilon (in this case, 0.001).

Later in this chapter we'll introduce a variation on print/println called printf that will make it easier to print numbers like these without all of the extra digits.

Factoring if/else Statements

Suppose you are writing a program that plays a betting game with a user and you want to give different warnings about how much cash the user has left. The following nested if/else construct distinguishes three different cases: money less than $500, which is considered low; money between $500 and $1000, which is considered okay; and money over $1000, which is considered good. Notice that the user is given different advice in each branch:

```
if (money < 500) {
    System.out.println("You have, $" + money + " left.");
    System.out.print("Cash is dangerously low. Bet carefully.");
```

```
      System.out.print("How much do you want to bet? ");
      bet = console.nextInt();
} else if (money < 1000) {
      System.out.println("You have, $" + money + " left.");
      System.out.print("Cash is somewhat low. Bet moderately.");
      System.out.print("How much do you want to bet? ");
      bet = console.nextInt();
} else {
      System.out.println("You have, $" + money + " left.");
      System.out.print("Cash is in good shape. Bet liberally.");
      System.out.print("How much do you want to bet? ");
      bet = console.nextInt();
}
```

This construct is repetitious and can be reduced using a technique called *factoring*. Using this simple technique, you factor out common pieces of code from the different branches of the `if`/`else` construct. Here, there are three different branches, depending upon the value of the variable `money`. Start by writing down the series of actions being performed in each branch and comparing them, as shown in Figure 4.8.

You can factor at both the top and the bottom of a construct like this. If you notice that the top statement in each branch is the same, you factor it out of the branching part and put it before the branch. Similarly, if the bottom statement in each branch is the same, you factor it out of the branching part and put it after the loop. You can factor the top statement in each of these branches and the bottom two statements, as shown in Figure 4.9.

Thus, the preceding code can be reduced to the following, which is more succinct:

```
System.out.println("You have, $" + money + " left.");
if (money < 500) {
    System.out.print("Cash is dangerously low. Bet carefully.");
} else if (money < 1000) {
    System.out.print("Cash is somewhat low. Bet moderately.");
} else {
    System.out.print("Cash is in good shape. Bet liberally.");
}
System.out.print("How much do you want to bet? ");
bet = console.nextInt();
```

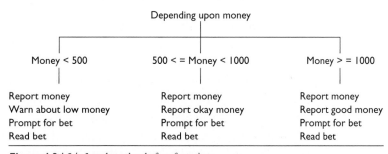

Figure 4.8 `if`/`else` branches before factoring

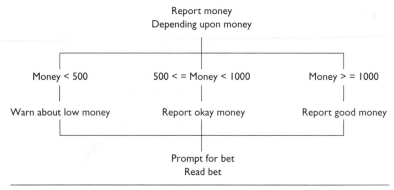

Figure 4.9 `if/else` branches after factoring

Min/Max Loops

You've already seen how to compute the average of a sequence of numbers. Another common programming task is to keep track of the maximum and/or minimum values in a sequence. For example, with an average temperature of around 50 degrees below 0 Fahrenheit, the surface of the Moon is clearly inhospitable. But the much greater challenge of living on the Moon is that the range of temperatures is from around 240 degrees below 0 to around 250 degrees above 0.

To compute the maximum of a sequence of values, you can keep track of the largest value you've seen so far and use an `if` statement to update the maximum if you come across a new value that is larger than the current maximum. This approach can be described in pseudocode as follows:

```
initialize max.
for (all numbers to examine) {
    obtain "next".
    if (next > max) {
        max = next;
    }
}
```

Initializing the maximum isn't quite as simple as it sounds. For example, novices often initialize max to 0. But what if the sequence of numbers you are examining is composed entirely of negative numbers? For example, you might be asked to find the maximum of this sequence:

$$-84, -7, -14, -39, -410, -17, -41, -9$$

The correct answer is that –7 is the maximum value in this sequence, but if you've initialized max to 0, 0 will be incorrectly reported as the maximum.

There are two classic solutions to this problem. First, if you know the range of the numbers you are examining, you have an appropriate choice for max. In that case, you can set max to the lowest value in the range. That seems counterintuitive because normally we think of the maximum as being large, but the idea is to set max to the smallest possible value it could ever be so that anything larger will cause max to be reset to that value. For example, if you knew that the preceding sequence of numbers were temperatures in degrees Fahrenheit, you would know that they could never be smaller than absolute zero (around –460 degrees Fahrenheit), so you could initialize max to that value.

The second possibility is to initialize max to the first value in the sequence. That won't always be convenient because it means obtaining one of the numbers outside the loop.

Combining these two possibilities, the pseudocode becomes:

```
initialize max either to lowest possible value or to first value.
for (all numbers to examine) {
    obtain "next".
    if (next > max) {
        max = next;
    }
}
```

The pseudocode for computing the minimum is a slight variation of this:

```
initialize min either to highest possible value or to first value.
for (all numbers to examine) {
    obtain "next".
    if (next < min) {
        min = next;
    }
}
```

To help you understand this better, let's put the pseudocode into action with a real problem. In mathematics, there is an open problem that involves what are known as *hailstone sequences*. They have that name because they have the property that they often rise and fall in unpredictable patterns, which is somewhat analogous to the process that forms hailstones.

A hailstone sequence is a sequence of numbers in which each value x is followed by either:

$(3x + 1)$, if x is odd

$\left(\dfrac{x}{2}\right)$, if x is even

For example, if you start with 7 and construct a sequence of length 10, you get:

7, 22, 11, 34, 17, 52, 26, 13, 40, 20

In this sequence, the maximum and minimum values are 52 and 7, respectively. If you extend this to a sequence of length 20, you get:

7, 22, 11, 34, 17, 52, 26, 13, 40, 20, 10, 5, 16, 8, 4, 2, 1, 4, 2, 1

In this case, the maximum and minimum values are 52 and 1, respectively.

You will notice that once you get to any of the numbers 1, 2, or 4, the sequence repeats itself. It is conjectured that all integers eventually reach 1, like hailstones that fall to the ground. This is an unsolved problem in mathematics. Nobody has been able to disprove it, but nobody has proven it either.

Let's write a method that takes a starting value and a sequence length and prints the maximum and minimum values obtained in a hailstone sequence formed with that starting value and of that length. Our method will look like this:

```
public static void printHailstoneMaxMin(int value, int length) {
    . . .
}
```

We can use the starting value to initialize `max` and `min`:

```
int min = value;
int max = value;
```

We then need a loop that will generate the other values. We are passed a parameter telling us how many times to go through the loop, but we don't want to execute `length` times: Remember that the starting value is part of the sequence, so if we want to use a sequence of the given length, we have to make sure that the number of iterations is one less than `length`. Combining this idea with the `max/min` pseudocode, we know the loop will look like this:

```
for (int i = 1; i <= length - 1; i++) {
    compute next number.
    if (value > max) {
        max = value;
    }
    if (value < min) {
        min = value;
    }
}
print max and min.
```

To fill out the pseudocode for "compute next number", we need to translate the hailstone formula into code. The formula is different depending upon whether the current value is odd or even. We can use an `if/else` statement to solve this task. For the test, we can use a "mod 2" test to see what remainder we get when we divide by 2. Even numbers have a remainder of 0 and odd numbers have a remainder of 1. So, the test should look like this:

```
if (value % 2 == 0) {
    do even computation.
} else {
    do odd computation.
}
```

Translating the hailstone mathematical formulas into Java expressions, we get:

```
if (value % 2 == 0) {
    value = value / 2;
} else {
    value = 3 * value + 1;
}
```

The only part of our pseudocode that we haven't filled in yet is the printing part after the loop. That is fairly easy to complete, which gives us the following complete method:

```java
public static void printHailstoneMaxMin(int value, int length) {
    int min = value;
    int max = value;
    for (int i = 1; i <= length - 1; i++) {
        if (value % 2 == 0) {
            value = value / 2;
        } else {
            value = 3 * value + 1;
        }
        if (value > max) {
            max = value;
        }
        if (value < min) {
            min = value;
        }
    }
    System.out.println("max = " + max);
    System.out.println("min = " + min);
}
```

4.4 Text Processing

Programmers commonly face problems that require them to create, edit, examine, and format text. Collectively, we call these *text-processing* tasks.

> **Text Processing**
>
> Editing and formatting strings of text.

In this section, we'll look in more detail at the char primitive type and introduce a new command called System.out.printf. Both of these are very useful for text-processing tasks.

The char Type

The primitive type char represents a single character of text. It's legal to have variables, parameters, and return values of type char if you so desire. Literal values of type char are expressed by placing the character within single quotes, as in:

```java
char ch = 'A';
```

It is also legal to create a char value that represents an escape sequence, such as:

```java
char newline = '\n';
```

In the previous chapter we discussed String objects, which can consist of zero to many characters. The distinction between char and String is a subtle one that confuses many new Java programmers. Why have two types for such similar data? As you might have guessed, the char type exists primarily for historical reasons; it dates back to older languages such as C that influenced the design of Java.

So why would a person ever use the `char` type when `String` is available? It's often necessary to use `char`, because some methods in Java's API use this as a parameter or return type. But there are also a few cases where using `char` can be more useful or simpler than using `String`.

Values of type `char` can be used in simple arithmetic expressions and in loops to cover ranges of letters. The `char` values can also be compared using relational operators such as `<` or `==`. `Strings` don't have either of these abilities. For example, the following code prints every letter of the alphabet:

```
// prints abcdefghijklmnopqrstuvwxyz
for (char letter = 'a'; letter <= 'z'; letter++) {
    System.out.print(letter);
}
```

The main bridge between the types `String` and `char` is the `String` object's `charAt` method, which accepts an integer index as a parameter and returns the character found at that index in the `String`. We often break apart `Strings` based on characters, or loop over `Strings` to examine or change each character. For example, the following loop creates a `String` that contains all of the nonspace characters from another `String`:

```
String phrase = "the rain in Spain";
String noSpaces = "";
for (int i = 0; i < phrase.length(); i++) {
    char ch = phrase.charAt(i);
    if (ch != ' ') {
        noSpaces += ch;
    }
}
// noSpaces stores "theraininSpain" here
```

This example uses an interesting technique in that it builds a `String` using a loop, starting with an empty `String` and concatenating individual characters onto it. This is sometimes called a *cumulative concatenation* and is a variation of the cumulative sum technique shown earlier in this chapter. At the end of the preceding code, the variable noSpaces stores the `String` "theraininSpain". The code also illustrates that `char` values can be concatenated onto a `String` just like other primitive values.

There are several useful methods that can be called to check information about a character or convert one character into another. Remember that `char` is a primitive type, which means that you can't use the dot syntax used with `strings`. Instead, the methods are static methods in the `Character` class that accept `char` parameters and return appropriate values. Some of the most useful `Character` methods are listed in Table 4.4.

For example, the following program counts the number of letters in a `strings`, ignoring all nonletter characters:

```
1  // Counts letter characters in a String.
2  import java.util.*;    // for Scanner
3
4  public class CountLetters {
5      public static void main(String[] args) {
6          Scanner console = new Scanner(System.in);
```

```
 7            System.out.print("Type a word: ");
 8            String s = console.next();
 9
10            int count = 0;
11            for (int i = 0; i < s.length(); i++) {
12                char ch = s.charAt(i);
13                if (Character.isLetter(ch)) {
14                    count++;
15                }
16            }
17            System.out.println("Letters: " + count);
18        }
19 }
```

The following is a sample execution of the program:

```
Type a word: test123TEST
Letters: 8
```

Every character also has a corresponding integer value. Java is willing to automatically convert a value of type char into an int whenever it is expecting an int. For example, consider the following rather strange expression:

```
2 * 'a'
```

Java sees a value of type char where it was expecting an int, but it's happy to convert this for you. It turns out that the integer value for 'a' is 97, so the expression's result is 194.

TABLE 4.4   Useful Methods of the Character Class

Method	Description	Example
getNumericValue(ch)	converts a character that looks like a number into that number	Character.getNumericValue('6') returns 6
isDigit(ch)	whether or not the character is one of the digits '0' through '9'	Character.isDigit('X') returns false
isLetter(ch)	whether or not the character is in the range 'a' to 'z' or 'A' to 'Z'	Character.isLetter('f') returns true
isLowerCase(ch)	whether or not the character is a lowercase letter	Character.isLowerCase('Q') returns false
isUpperCase(ch)	whether or not the character is an uppercase letter	Character.isUpperCase('Q') returns true
toLowerCase(ch)	the lowercase version of the given letter	Character.toLowerCase('Q') returns 'q'
toUpperCase(ch)	the uppercase version of the given letter	Character.toUpperCase('x') returns 'X'

Java will not, however, automatically convert in the other direction. That is because the type char is in a sense a subset of the type int. Every char value has a corresponding int, but not every int has a corresponding char. Thus, while Java can always turn a char into an int, it may not always be able to turn an int into a char. So, in this case, Java insists on a cast. This allows you to form expressions like the following:

```
(char) ('a' + 3)
```

Inside the parentheses are a char value and an int value, so Java converts the char to an int (97) and then performs the addition operation, yielding the value 100. This integer is then converted to a char value because of the cast, which yields the character 'd' (the character that appears three later in the sequence than the character 'a').

System.out.printf (Optional)

So far we've used System.out.println and System.out.print for console output. There's a third method, System.out.printf, which is a bit more complicated than the others but gives us some useful new abilities. The "f" in printf stands for "formatted," implying that System.out.printf gives you more control over the format in which your output is printed.

Imagine that you'd like to print a multiplication table from 1x1 up to 10x10. The following code prints the correct numbers, but it doesn't look very nice:

```
for (int i = 1; i <= 10; i++) {
    for (int j = 1; j <= 10; j++) {
        System.out.print(i * j + " ");
    }
    System.out.println();
}
```

The output is the following. Notice that the numbers don't line up vertically:

```
1 2 3 4 5 6 7 8 9 10
2 4 6 8 10 12 14 16 18 20
3 6 9 12 15 18 21 24 27 30
4 8 12 16 20 24 28 32 36 40
5 10 15 20 25 30 35 40 45 50
6 12 18 24 30 36 42 48 54 60
7 14 21 28 35 42 49 56 63 70
8 16 24 32 40 48 56 64 72 80
9 18 27 36 45 54 63 72 81 90
10 20 30 40 50 60 70 80 90 100
```

Separating the numbers by tabs is better, but the numbers are automatically left-aligned, as in this shortened table:

```
1       2       3       4       5
2       4       6       8       10
3       6       9       12      15
4       8       12      16      20
5       10      15      20      25
```

Did You Know?

ASCII and Unicode

We store data on a computer as binary numbers (sequences of 0s and 1s). To store textual data, we need an encoding scheme that will tell us what sequence of 0s and 1s to use for any given character. Think of it as being like a giant secret decoder ring that says things like, "If you want to store a lowercase 'a,' use the sequence 01100001."

In the early 1960s IBM developed an encoding scheme called *EBCDIC* that worked well with their punched cards, which had been in use for decades before computers were even invented. But it soon became clear that EBCDIC wasn't a convenient encoding scheme for computer programmers. For example, there were gaps in the sequence, such that characters like 'i' and 'j' appeared far apart even though we think of them as coming one after the other.

In 1967 the American Standards Association published a scheme known as *ASCII* (pronounced "AS-kee") that has been in common use ever since. The acronym is short for "American Standard Code for Information Interchange." In its original form, ASCII defined 128 characters that could be stored with 7 bits of data.

The biggest problem with ASCII is that it is an *American* code. There are many characters in common use in other countries that were not included in ASCII. For example, the British pound (£) and the Spanish variant of the letter n (ñ) are not included in the standard 128 ASCII characters. Various attempts have been made to extend ASCII, doubling it to 256 characters so that it can include many of these special characters. However, it turns out that 256 characters is simply not enough to capture the incredible diversity of human communication.

Around the time that Java was created, a consortium of software professionals introduced a new standard for encoding characters known as *Unicode*. They decided that the 7 bits of standard ASCII and the 8 bits of extended ASCII were simply not big enough and chose not to set a limit on how many bits they might use for encoding characters. At the time of this writing, the consortium has identified over 90,000 characters, which require a little over 16 bits to store. Unicode includes the characters used in most modern languages and even some ancient languages. It does not yet include Egyptian or Mayan hieroglyphs, and the consortium has rejected a proposal to include Klingon characters.

The designers of Java used Unicode as the standard for the type char, which means that Java programs are capable of manipulating a full range of characters. Fortunately, the Unicode Consortium decided to incorporate the ASCII encodings, so ASCII can be seen as a subset of Unicode. If you are curious about the actual ordering of characters in ASCII, type "ASCII table" into your favorite search engine and you will find millions of hits to explore.

What if you want them right-aligned? It would be a pain to try to right-align the numbers manually, because you'd have to use if/else statements to check whether a given number was in a certain range and, if necessary, pad it with a given number of spaces. A much easier way to print values aligned in fixed-width fields is to use the System.out.printf command. The printf method accepts a specially written String called a *format string* specifying the general appearance of the output, followed by any parameters to be printed:

```
System.out.printf(<format String>, <parameters>);
```

A format String is like a normal String except that it can contain placeholders called *format specifiers* that allow you to specify a location for insertion of a variable's value, along with the format you'd like to give that value. Format specifiers begin with a % sign and end with a letter specifying the kind of value, such as d for decimal integers (int) or f for floating-point real numbers (double). For example:

```
int x = 38, y = -152;
System.out.printf("%d %d\n", x, y);
System.out.printf("location: (%d, %d)\n", x, y);
```

The preceding printf statements produce the following output:

```
38 -152
location: (38, -152)
```

The %d is not actually printed but is instead replaced with the corresponding parameter written after the format String. The number of format specifiers in the format String must match the number of parameters that follow it. The first specifier will be replaced by the first parameter, the second specifier by the second parameter, and so on. System.out.printf is a bizarre method in this way, because it can accept a varying number of parameters.

The printf command is like System.out.print in that it doesn't move to a new line unless you explicitly tell it to do so. Notice that in the previous code we had to say "location: (%d, %d)\n" to complete the line of output.

Format specifiers can contain information between the % and the letter for the type, to specify the width, precision, and alignment of the value. For example, %8d specifies an integer right-aligned in an 8-space-wide area, and %12.4f specifies a double value right-aligned in a 12-space-wide area rounded to four digits past the decimal point. Table 4.5 lists some common format specifiers you may wish to use in your programs.

As a comprehensive example, suppose that the following variables have been declared:

```
int x = 38, y = -152;
int grade = 86;
double angle = 87.4163;
String veggie = "carrot";
```

```
    }
    return product;
}
```

You can then test the method for various values with a loop:

```
for (int i = 0; i <= 10; i++) {
    System.out.println(i + "! = " + factorial(i));
}
```

which produces the following output:

```
0! = 1
1! = 1
2! = 2
3! = 6
4! = 24
5! = 120
6! = 720
7! = 5040
8! = 40320
9! = 362880
10! = 3628800
```

It seems odd that the `factorial` method should return 1 when you ask for 0!, but that is actually part of the mathematical definition of the factorial function. It returns 1 because the local variable `product` in the `factorial` method is initialized to 1, and the loop is never entered when the parameter n has the value 0. So, this is actually desirable behavior for 0!.

But what if you're asked to compute the factorial of a negative number? The method returns the same value, 1. The mathematical definition of factorial says that the function is undefined for negative values of n, so it actually shouldn't even compute an answer when n is negative. This is a precondition of the method that can be described in the documentation:

```
// pre : n >= 0
// post: returns n factorial (n!)
```

Adding comments about this restriction is helpful, but what if someone calls the `factorial` method with a negative value anyway? The best solution is to throw an exception. The general syntax of the `throw` statement is as follows:

```
throw <exception>;
```

In Java, exceptions are objects. Before you can throw an exception, you have to construct an exception object using `new`. You'll normally construct the object as you are throwing it, because the exception object includes information about what was going on when the error occurred. Java has a class called `IllegalArgumentException` that is meant to cover a case like this where someone has passed an inappropriate value as an argument. So, you can construct the exception object and include it in a `throw` statement as follows:

```
throw new IllegalArgumentException();
```

Of course, you'll only want to do this in the case where the precondition fails, so you need to include this inside of an `if` statement:

```
if (n < 0) {
    throw new IllegalArgumentException();
}
```

You can also include some text when you construct the exception that will be displayed when the exception is thrown:

```
if (n < 0) {
    throw new IllegalArgumentException("negative n");
}
```

Incorporating the `pre/post` comments and the exception code into the method definition, you get the following:

```
// pre : n >= 0
// post: returns n factorial (n!)
public static int factorial(int n) {
    if (n < 0) {
        throw new IllegalArgumentException("negative n");
    }
    int product = 1;
    for (int i = 2; i <= n; i++) {
        product *= i;
    }
    return product;
}
```

You don't need an `else` after the `if` that throws the exception, because when an exception is thrown, it halts the execution of the method. So, if someone calls the `factorial` method with a negative value of `n`, Java will never execute the code that comes after the `throw` statement.

You can test this with the following `main` method:

```
public static void main(String[] args) {
    System.out.println(factorial(-1));
}
```

When you execute this program, it stops executing with the following message:

```
Exception in thread "main" java.lang.IllegalArgumentException:
    negative n
      at Factorial2.factorial(Factorial2.java:8)
      at Factorial2.main(Factorial2.java:3)
```

The message indicates that the program `Factorial2` stopped running because an `IllegalArgumentException` was thrown. The system then shows you a backward trace of how it got there. The illegal argument appeared in line 8 of the `factorial` method of the `Factorial2` class. It got there because of a call in line 3 of the `main` of the `Factorial2` class. This kind of information is very helpful in figuring out where the bugs are in your programs.

Throwing exceptions is an example of *defensive programming.* We don't intend to have bugs in the programs we write, but we're only human, so we want to build in mechanisms that will give us feedback when we make mistakes. Testing the values passed to methods and throwing an `IllegalArgumentException` when a value is not appropriate is a great way to provide that feedback.

Revisiting Return Values

In Chapter 3 we looked at some examples of simple calculating methods that return a value, as in this method for converting feet to miles:

```
public static double miles(double feet) {
    return feet / 5280.0;
}
```

Now that you know how to write `if/else` statements, we can look at some more interesting examples involving return values. For example, earlier in this chapter you saw that the `Math` class has a method called `max` that returns the larger of two values. There are actually two different versions of the method, one that finds the max of two integers and one that finds the max of two doubles. Recall that this is called *overloading.*

Let's write our own version of the `max` method that returns the larger of two integers. Its header will look like this:

```
public static int max(int x, int y) {
    ...
}
```

We want to return either x or y, depending upon which is larger. This is a perfect place to use an `if/else` construct:

```
public static int max(int x, int y) {
    if (x > y) {
        return x;
    } else {
        return y;
    }
}
```

This code begins by testing whether x is greater than y. If it is, it executes the first branch by returning x. If not, it executes the `else` branch by returning y. There are three different cases to consider, though: x might be larger, y might be larger, or they might be equal. The preceding code executes the `else` branch when the values are equal, but it doesn't actually matter which `return` statement is executed when x and y are equal.

Remember that when Java executes a `return` statement, the method stops executing. It's like a command to Java to "get out of this method right now." That means that this method could also be written as follows:

```
public static int max(int x, int y) {
    if (x > y) {
        return x;
    }
    return y;
}
```

This version is equivalent in behavior because the statement `return x` inside the `if` statement will cause Java to exit the method immediately and not to execute the `return y` statement that comes after the `if`. If, on the other hand, we don't enter the `if`, we proceed directly to the statement that follows it (`return y`).

Whether you choose to use the first form or the second in your own programs depends somewhat on personal taste. The `if`/`else` construct makes it more clear that the method is choosing between two alternatives, but some people prefer the second alternative because it is shorter. Unfortunately, we can't rely on Sun to break the tie, because the Java source code solves this problem using something known as the "ternary operator" (a minor detail of Java that you can read about by doing a Web search for "Java ternary operator").

As another example, consider the `indexOf` method of the `String` class. If we define a variable `s` that stores a `String`:

```
String s = "four score and seven years ago";
```

we can write expressions like the following to determine where a particular character appears in the `String`:

```
int r = s.indexOf('r');
int v = s.indexOf('v');
```

This code sets `r` to 3 because that is the index of the first occurrence of the letter `'r'` in the `String`. It sets `v` to 17 because that is the index of the first occurrence of the letter `'v'` in the `String`.

The `indexOf` method is part of the `String` class, but let's see how we could write a different method that performs the same task. Obviously, our method would be called differently. We would have to pass it both the `String` and the letter, as in:

```
int r = indexOf('r', s);
int v = indexOf('v', s);
```

So, the header for our method would look like this:

```
public static int indexOf(char ch, String s) {
    . . .
}
```

Remember that when a method returns a value, we must include the return type after the words `public` `static`. In this case, we have indicated that the method returns an `int` because the index will be an integer. This problem can be solved rather nicely with a `for` loop that goes through each possible index from first to last. We can describe this in pseudocode as follows:

```
for (int i = 0; i < s.length(); i++) {
    if char is at position i, we've found it.
}
```

To flesh this out, we have to think about how to test whether the character at position i is the one we are looking for. Remember that `String` objects have a method called `charAt` that allows us to pull out an individual character from the `String`, so we can refine our pseudocode as follows:

```
for (int i = 0; i < s.length(); i++) {
    if (s.charAt(i) == ch) {
        we've found it.
    }
}
```

To complete this, we have to refine what to do when "we've found it." If we find the character, we have our answer: the current value of the variable i. And if that is the answer we want to return, we can put a `return` statement there:

```
for (int i = 0; i < s.length(); i++) {
    if (s.charAt(i) == ch) {
        return i;
    }
}
```

To understand this code, you have to understand how the `return` statement works. For example, if the `String s` is the one from our example ("four score. . . ") and we are searching for the character `'r'`, we know that when i is equal to 3 we will find that `s.charAt(3)` is equal to `'r'`. That causes our code to execute the `return` statement, effectively saying:

```
return 3;
```

When a `return` statement is executed, the method is immediately exited, which means we break out of the loop and return 3 as our answer. Even though the loop would normally increment i to 4 and keep going, our code doesn't do that because we hit the `return` statement.

There is only one thing missing from our code. If we try to compile it as-is, we get this error message from the Java compiler:

```
missing return statement
```

This error message occurs because we haven't told Java what to do if we never find the character we are searching for. In that case, we will execute the `for` loop in its entirety and reach the end of the method without having returned a value. This is not acceptable. If we say that the method returns an `int`, we have to guarantee that every path through the method will return an `int`.

If we don't find the character, we want to return some kind of special value to indicate that the character was not found. We can't use the value 0, because 0 is a legal index for a `string` (the index of the first character). So, the convention in Java is to return −1 if the character is not found. This is easy to add after the `for` loop:

```java
public static int indexOf(char ch, String s) {
    for (int i = 0; i < s.length(); i++) {
        if (s.charAt(i) == ch) {
            return i;
        }
    }
    return -1;
}
```

Common Programming Error

String Index out of Bounds

It's very easy to forget that the last index of a `string` of length n is actually $n - 1$. Forgetting this fact can cause you to write incorrect text-processing loops like this one:

```java
// This version of the code has a mistake!
// The test should be i < s.length()
public static int indexOf(char ch, String s) {
    for (int i = 0; i <= s.length(); i++) {
        if (s.charAt(i) == ch) {
            return i;
        }
    }
    return -1;
}
```

The program will throw an exception if the loop runs past the end of the `String`. On the last pass through the loop, the value of the variable `i` will be equal to `s.length()`, meaning that when it executes the `if` statement test, the exception will occur. The error message will resemble the following:

```
Exception in thread "main"
    java.lang.StringIndexOutOfBoundsException:
    String index out of range: 11
        at java.lang.String.charAt(Unknown Source)
        at OutOfBoundsExample.indexOf(OutOfBoundsExample.java:9)
        at OutOfBoundsExample.main(OutOfBoundsExample.java:4)
```

An interesting thing about the bug in this example is that it only occurs if the `string` does not contain the character `ch`. If `ch` is contained in the `string`, the `if` test will be `true` for one of the legal indexes in `s`, so the code will return that index. Only if all characters from `s` have been examined without finding `ch` will the loop attempt its last fatal pass.

It may seem strange that we don't have a test for the final `return` statement that returns -1, but remember that the `for` loop tries every possible index of the `String` searching for the character. If the character appears anywhere in the `String`, the `return` statement inside the loop will be executed and we'll never get to the `return` statement after the loop. The only way to get to the `return` statement after the loop is to find that the character appears nowhere in the given `String`.

4.6 Case Study: Body Mass Index

In recent years, computing an individual body mass index has become a popular task. The Centers for Disease Control (CDC) has put together a website about body mass index at http://www.cdc.gov/nccdphp/dnpa/bmi/. As that site explains:

> Body Mass Index (BMI) is a number calculated from a person's weight and height. BMI provides a reliable indicator of body fatness for most people and is used to screen for weight categories that may lead to health problems.

It has also become popular to compare the statistics for two or more individuals to have a "fitness challenge," or to compare two sets of numbers for the same person to get a sense of how that person's BMI will vary if a person loses weight. In this section we will write a program that prompts the user for the height and weight of two individuals and reports the overall results for the two people. Here is a sample execution for the program we want to write:

```
This program reads data for two
people and computes their body
mass index and weight status.

Enter next person's information:
height (in inches)? 73.5
weight (in pounds)? 230

Enter next person's information:
height (in inches)? 71
weight (in pounds)? 220.5

Person #1 body mass index = 29.930121708547368
overweight
Person #2 body mass index = 30.75014878000397
obese
```

In Chapter 1 we introduced the idea of *iterative enhancement*, in which you develop a complex program in stages. Every professional programmer uses this technique, so it is important to learn to apply it yourself in the programs you write.

In this case, we eventually want to have a program that explains what it does to the user and computes BMI results for two different people. We also want the program to be well structured. But we don't have to do everything at once. In fact, if we try to do so, we are likely to be overwhelmed by the details. In writing this program, we will go through three different stages:

1. First, we'll write a program that computes results for just one person, without an introduction. We won't worry about program structure yet.

2. Next, we'll write a complete program that computes results for two people, including an introduction. Again, we won't worry about program structure at this point.

3. Finally, we will put together a well-structured and complete program.

One-Person Unstructured Solution

Even the first version of the program will prompt for user input, so we will need to construct a `Scanner` object to read from the console:

```
Scanner console = new Scanner(System.in);
```

To compute the BMI for an individual, we will need to know the height and weight of that person. This is a fairly straightforward "prompt and read" task. The only real decision here is what type of variable to use for storing the height and weight. People often talk about height and weight in whole numbers, but the question to ask is whether or not it makes sense for people to use fractions. Do people sometimes describe their heights using half-inches? The answer is yes. Do people ever describe their weights using half-pounds? Again the answer is yes. So it makes sense to store the values as doubles, to allow people to enter either integer values or fractions:

```
System.out.println("Enter next person's information:");
System.out.print("height (in inches)? ");
double height1 = console.nextDouble();
System.out.print("weight (in pounds)? ");
double weight1 = console.nextDouble();
```

Once we have the height and weight, we can compute the BMI. The CDC website says that the BMI formula for adults is as follows:

$$\frac{\text{weight (lb)}}{[\text{height (in)}]^2} \times 703$$

This is fairly easy to translate into a Java expression:

```
double bmi1 = weight1 / (height1 * height1) * 703;
```

If you look closely at the sample execution, you will see that we want to print blank lines to separate different parts of the user interaction. The introduction ends with a blank line, then there is a blank line after the "prompt and read" portion of the interaction. So, adding an empty `println` and putting all of these pieces together, our `main` method looks like this so far:

```
public static void main(String[] args) {
    Scanner console = new Scanner(System.in);
    System.out.println("Enter next person's information:");
    System.out.print("height (in inches)? ");
    double height1 = console.nextDouble();
```

```
            System.out.print("weight (in pounds)? ");
            double weight1 = console.nextDouble();
            double bmi1 = weight1 / (height1 * height1) * 703;
            System.out.println();
            . . .
}
```

This program prompts for values and computes the BMI. Now we need to include code to report the results. We could use a `println` for the BMI:

```
System.out.println("Person #1 body mass index = " + bmi1);
```

This would work, but it produces output like the following:

```
Person #1 body mass index = 29.930121708547368
```

The long sequence of digits after the decimal point is distracting and implies a level of precision that we simply don't have. It would be more appropriate and more appealing to the user to list just a few digits after the decimal point. So, this would also have been a good place to use a `printf`:

```
System.out.printf("Person #1 body mass index = %4.2f\n", bmi1);
```

Because the `printf` command is optional, it is not included in the program.

In the sample of execution we also see a report of the person's weight status. The CDC website includes the information shown in Table 4.6. There are four entries in this table, so we need four different `println` statements for the four possibilities. We will want to use `if` or `if/else` statements to control the four `println` statements. In this case, we know that we want to print exactly one of the four possibilities. Therefore, it makes most sense to use a nested `if/else` construct that ends with an `else`.

But what tests do we use for the nested `if/else`? If you look closely at the previous table, you will see that there are some gaps. For example, what if your BMI is 24.95? That isn't between 18.5 and 24.9 and it isn't between 25.0 and 29.9. It seems clear that the CDC intended their table to be interpreted slightly differently. They probably mean 18.5–24.999999 (repeating), but that would look rather odd in a table. In fact, if you understand nested `if/else` statements, this is a case where a nested `if/else` construct expresses the possibilities more clearly than a table like the CDC's:

TABLE 4.6   Weight Status by BMI

BMI	Weight status
below 18.5	underweight
18.5–24.9	normal
25.0–29.9	overweight
30.0 and above	obese

```
if (bmi1 < 18.5) {
    System.out.println("underweight");
} else if (bmi1 < 25) {
    System.out.println("normal");
} else if (bmi1 < 30) {
    System.out.println("overweight");
} else { // bmi1 >= 30
    System.out.println("obese");
}
```

So, putting all this together, we get a complete version of the first program:

```
 1 import java.util.*;
 2
 3 public class BMI1 {
 4     public static void main(String[] args) {
 5         Scanner console = new Scanner(System.in);
 6
 7         System.out.println("Enter next person's information:");
 8         System.out.print("height (in inches)? ");
 9         double height1 = console.nextDouble();
10         System.out.print("weight (in pounds)? ");
11         double weight1 = console.nextDouble();
12         double bmi1 = weight1 / (height1 * height1) * 703;
13         System.out.println();
14
15         System.out.println("Person #1 body mass index = " +
16                             bmi1);
17         if (bmi1 < 18.5) {
18             System.out.println("underweight");
19         } else if (bmi1 < 25) {
20             System.out.println("normal");
21         } else if (bmi1 < 30) {
22             System.out.println("overweight");
23         } else { // bmi1 >= 30
24             System.out.println("obese");
25         }
26     }
27 }
```

Here is a sample execution of the program:

```
Enter next person's information:
height (in inches)? 73.5
weight (in pounds)? 230

Person #1 body mass index = 29.930121708547368
overweight
```

Two-Person Unstructured Solution

Now that we have a program that computes one person's BMI and weight status, let's expand it to handle two different people. Experienced programmers would probably begin by adding structure to the program before trying to make it handle two sets of data, but for novice programmers it is often helpful to consider the unstructured solution first.

To make this program handle two people, we can copy and paste a lot of the code and make slight modifications. For example, instead of using variables called `height1`, `weight1`, and `bmi1`, for the second person we change the code to use variables `height2`, `weight2`, and `bmi2`.

We also have to be careful to do each step in the right order. Looking at the sample execution, you'll see that the program prompts for data for both individuals first and then reports results for both. Thus, we can't copy the entire program and simply paste a second copy; we have to rearrange the order so that all of the prompting happens first and all of the reporting happens later.

We've also decided that, in moving to this second stage, we will add code for the introduction. This code should appear at the beginning of the program and should include an empty `println` to produce a blank line to separate the introduction from the rest of the user interaction.

Combining these elements into a complete program, we get the following:

```
 1 // This program finds the body mass index (BMI) for two
 2 // individuals.
 3
 4 import java.util.*;
 5
 6 public class BMI2 {
 7     public static void main(String[] args) {
 8         System.out.println("This program reads data for two");
 9         System.out.println("people and computes their body");
10         System.out.println("mass index and weight status.");
11         System.out.println();
12
13         Scanner console = new Scanner(System.in);
14
15         System.out.println("Enter next person's information:");
16         System.out.print("height (in inches)? ");
17         double height1 = console.nextDouble();
18         System.out.print("weight (in pounds)? ");
19         double weight1 = console.nextDouble();
20         double bmi1 = weight1 / (height1 * height1) * 703;
21         System.out.println();
22
23         System.out.println("Enter next person's information:");
24         System.out.print("height (in inches)? ");
25         double height2 = console.nextDouble();
26         System.out.print("weight (in pounds)? ");
27         double weight2 = console.nextDouble();
28         double bmi2 = weight2 / (height2 * height2) * 703;
29         System.out.println();
30
31         System.out.println("Person #1 body mass index = " +
32                            bmi1);
33         if (bmi1 < 18.5) {
34             System.out.println("underweight");
35         } else if (bmi1 < 25) {
36             System.out.println("normal");
37         } else if (bmi1 < 30) {
38             System.out.println("overweight");
```

```
39              } else { // bmi1 >= 30
40                  System.out.println("obese");
41              }
42
43              System.out.println("Person #2 body mass index = " +
44                                  bmi2);
45              if (bmi2 < 18.5) {
46                  System.out.println("underweight");
47              } else if (bmi2 < 25) {
48                  System.out.println("normal");
49              } else if (bmi2 < 30) {
50                  System.out.println("overweight");
51              } else { // bmi2 >= 30
52                  System.out.println("obese");
53              }
54      }
55 }
```

This program compiles and works. When we execute it, we get exactly the interaction we wanted. However, the program lacks structure. All of the code appears in main, and there is significant redundancy. That shouldn't be a surprise, because we created this version by copying and pasting. Whenever you find yourself using copy and paste, you should wonder whether there isn't a better way to solve the problem. Most often there is.

Two-Person Structured Solution

Let's explore how static methods can improve the structure of the program. Looking at the code, you will notice a great deal of redundancy. For example, we have two code segments that look like this:

```
System.out.println("Enter next person's information:");
System.out.print("height (in inches)? ");
double height1 = console.nextDouble();
System.out.print("weight (in pounds)? ");
System.out.println();
```

The only difference between these two code segments is that the first uses variables height1, weight1, bmi1, and the second uses variables height2, weight2, and bmi2. We eliminate redundancy by moving code like this into a method that we can call twice. So, as a first approximation, we can turn this into a more generic form as a method:

```
public static void getBMI(Scanner console) {
    System.out.println("Enter next person's information:");
    System.out.print("height (in inches)? ");
    double height = console.nextDouble();
    System.out.print("weight (in pounds)? ");
    double weight = console.nextDouble();
    double bmi = weight / (height * height) * 703;
    System.out.println();
}
```

We have to pass in the `Scanner` from `main`, otherwise we have made all of the variables local to this method. From `main` we can call this method twice:

```
getBMI(console);
getBMI(console);
```

Unfortunately, introducing this change breaks the rest of the code. If we try to compile and run the program, we find that we get error messages in `main` whenever we refer to the variables `bmi1` and `bmi2`.

The problem is that the method computes a `bmi` value that we need later in the program. We can fix this by having the method return the `bmi` value that it computes:

```
public static double getBMI(Scanner console) {
    System.out.println("Enter next person's information:");
    System.out.print("height (in inches)? ");
    double height = console.nextDouble();
    System.out.print("weight (in pounds)? ");
    double weight = console.nextDouble();
    double bmi = weight / (height * height) * 703;
    System.out.println();
    return bmi;
}
```

Notice that the method header now lists the return type as `double`. We also have to change `main`. We can't just call the method twice the way we would call a `void` method. Because each call returns a BMI result that needs to be remembered, for each call we have to store the result coming back from the method in a variable:

```
double bmi1 = getBMI(console);
double bmi2 = getBMI(console);
```

Study this change carefully, because this technique can be one of the most challenging for novices to master. In writing the method, we have to make sure that it returns the BMI result. In writing the call, we have to make sure that we store the result in a variable so that we can access it later.

With this modification, the program would again compile and run properly. But there is another obvious redundancy in the `main` method, in that the same nested `if/else` construct appears twice. The only difference is that in one case we use the variable `bmi1`, and in the other case we use the variable `bmi2`. This is easily generalized with a parameter:

```
public static void reportStatus(double bmi) {
    if (bmi < 18.5) {
        System.out.println("underweight");
    } else if (bmi < 25) {
        System.out.println("normal");
    } else if (bmi < 30) {
        System.out.println("overweight");
    } else { // bmi >= 30
```

```
            System.out.println("obese");
        }
    }
```

With this method, we can replace the code in `main` with two calls:

```
System.out.println("Person #1 body mass index = " + bmi1);
reportStatus(bmi1);
System.out.println("Person #2 body mass index = " + bmi2);
reportStatus(bmi2);
```

That takes care of the redundancy in the program, but we can still use static methods to improve the program to indicate structure. It is best to keep the `main` method short if possible, to reflect the overall structure of the program. The problem breaks down into three major phases: introduction, compute BMI, report results. We already have a method for computing the BMI, but we haven't yet introduced methods for the introduction and reporting of results. These are fairly simple to add.

There is one other method that makes sense to add to the program. We are using a formula from the CDC website for calculating the BMI of an individual given the person's height and weight. Whenever you find yourself programming a formula, it is a good idea to introduce a method for that formula so that it is easy to spot and so that it has a name.

Applying all these ideas, we end up with the following version of the program:

```
 1 // This program finds the body mass index (BMI) for two
 2 // individuals. This variation includes several methods
 3 // other than main.
 4
 5 import java.util.*;
 6
 7 public class BMI3 {
 8     public static void main(String[] args) {
 9         giveIntro();
10         Scanner console = new Scanner(System.in);
11         double bmi1 = getBMI(console);
12         double bmi2 = getBMI(console);
13         reportResults(bmi1, bmi2);
14     }
15
16     // introduces the program to the user
17     public static void giveIntro() {
18         System.out.println("This program reads data for two");
19         System.out.println("people and computes their body");
20         System.out.println("mass index and weight status.");
21         System.out.println();
22     }
23
24     // prompts for one person's statistics, returning the BMI
25     public static double getBMI(Scanner console) {
26         System.out.println("Enter next person's information:");
27         System.out.print("height (in inches)? ");
```

```
28          double height = console.nextDouble();
29          System.out.print("weight (in pounds)? ");
30          double weight = console.nextDouble();
31          double bmi = BMIFor(height, weight);
32          System.out.println();
33          return bmi;
34      }
35
36      // this method contains the body mass index formula for
37      // converting the given height (in inches) and weight
38      // (in pounds) into a BMI
39      public static double BMIFor(double height, double weight) {
40          return weight / (height * height) * 703;
41      }
42
43      // reports the overall bmi values and weight status
44      public static void reportResults(double bmi1,
45                                       double bmi2) {
46          System.out.println("Person #1 body mass index = " +
47                             bmi1);
48          reportStatus(bmi1);
49          System.out.println("Person #2 body mass index = " +
50                             bmi2);
51          reportStatus(bmi2);
52      }
53
54      // reports the weight status for the given BMI value
55      public static void reportStatus(double bmi) {
56          if (bmi < 18.5) {
57              System.out.println("underweight");
58          } else if (bmi < 25) {
59              System.out.println("normal");
60          } else if (bmi < 30) {
61              System.out.println("overweight");
62          } else { // bmi >= 30
63              System.out.println("obese");
64          }
65      }
66 }
```

This solution has the same behavior as the unstructured solution, but it has a much nicer structure. The unstructured program is in a sense simpler, but the structured solution is easier to maintain if we want to expand the program or make other modifications. These structural benefits aren't so important in short programs, but they become essential as programs become longer and more complex.

Chapter Summary

A cumulative sum loop declares a sum variable and incrementally adds to that variable's value inside the loop.

A fencepost loop executes a "loop-and-a-half" by executing part of a loop's body once before the loop begins.

An `if` statement lets you write code that will execute only if a certain condition is met. An `if/else` statement lets you execute one piece of code if a condition is met, and another if not. Conditions are Boolean expressions and can be written using relational operators such as <, >=, and !=.

———

`if/else` statements can be nested to test a series of conditions and execute the appropriate block of code based on which condition is true.

———

The == operator that tests primitive data for equality doesn't behave the way we would expect with objects, so we test objects for equality by calling their `equals` method instead.

———

Since the `double` type does not store all values exactly, small roundoff errors can occur when performing calculations on real numbers. Avoid these by providing a small amount of tolerance in your code for values near those you expect.

———

Common code that appears in every branch of an `if/else` statement should be factored out so that it is not replicated multiple times in the code.

———

The `char` type represents individual characters of text. Each letter of a `String` is stored internally as a `char` value, and you can access these characters by index using the `String`'s `charAt` method.

———

The `System.out.printf` method prints formatted text. You can specify complex format `String`s to control the width, alignment, and precision by which values are printed.

———

You can "throw" (generate) exceptions in your own code. This can be useful in cases where your code reaches an unrecoverable error condition, such as an invalid argument value being passed to a method.

———

Self-Check Problems

Section 4.1: Loop Techniques

1. What is wrong with the following code, which attempts to add all numbers from 1 to a given maximum? Describe how to fix the code so that it will behave properly.

```java
public static int sumTo(int n) {
    for (int i = 1; i <= n; i++) {
        int sum = 0;
        sum += i;
    }
    return sum;
}
```

2. What is wrong with the following code, which attempts to print all numbers from 1 to a given maximum, separated by commas? Describe how to fix the code so that it will behave properly.

```java
for (int i = 1; i <= n; i++) {
    System.out.print(i + ", ");
}
System.out.println();
```

3. Write code to produce a cumulative product by multiplying together many numbers read from the console.

Section 4.2: if/else Statements

4. Translate each of the following English statements into logical tests that could be used in an if/else statement. Write the appropriate if statement with your logical test. Assume that three int variables, x, y, and z, have been declared.

- z is odd.
- z is not greater than y's square root.
- y is positive.
- One of x and y is even, and the other is odd.
- y is a multiple of z.
- z is not zero.
- y is greater in magnitude than z.
- x and z are of opposite signs.
- y is a non-negative one-digit number.
- z is non-negative.
- x is even.
- x is closer in value to y than z is.

5. Given the following variable declarations:

```
int x = 4;
int y = -3;
int z = 4;
```

what are the results of the following relational expressions?

- x == 4
- x == y
- x == z
- y == z
- x + y > 0
- x - z != 0
- y * y <= z
- y / y == 1
- x * (y + 2) > y - (y + z) * 2

6. Consider the following Java method, which is written incorrectly:

```
// This method should return how many of its three
// arguments are odd numbers.
public static void printNumOdd(int n1, int n2, int n3) {
    int count = 0;

    if (n1 % 2 == 1) {
        count++;
    } else if (n2 % 2 == 1) {
        count++;
    } else if (n3 % 2 == 1) {
        count++;
    }
```

```
        System.out.println(count + " of the 3 numbers are odd.");
    }
```

Under what cases will the method print the correct answer, and when will it print an incorrect answer? What should be changed to fix the code? Can you think of a way to write the code correctly without any if/else statements?

7. Write Java code to read an integer from the user, then print even if that number is an even number or odd otherwise. You may assume that the user types a valid integer.

8. The following code contains a logic error:

```
Scanner console = new Scanner(System.in);
System.out.print("Type a number: ");
int number = console.nextInt();

if (number % 2 == 0) {
    if (number % 3 == 0) {
        System.out.println("Divisible by 6.");
    } else {
        System.out.println("Odd.");
    }
}
```

Examine the preceding code and describe a case where the code would print something that is untrue about the number that was entered. Explain why. Then correct the code so that the logic error is fixed.

9. What is wrong with the following code, which attempts to return the number of factors of a given integer n? Describe how to fix the code so that it will behave properly.

```
public static int countFactors(int n) {
    for (int i = 1; i <= n; i++) {
        if (n % i == 0) { // factor
            return i;
        }
    }
}
```

Section 4.3: Subtleties of Conditional Execution

10. The following code is poorly structured:

```
int sum = 1000;
Scanner console = new Scanner(System.in);
System.out.print("Is your money multiplied 1 or 2 times? ");
int times = console.nextInt();

if (times == 1) {
    System.out.print("And how much are you contributing? ");
    int donation = console.nextInt();
    sum = sum + donation;
    count1++;
    total = total + donation;
}
if (times == 2) {
    System.out.print("And how much are you contributing? ");
    int donation = console.nextInt();
```

```
    sum = sum + 2 * donation;
    count2++;
    total = total + donation;
}
```

Rewrite it so that it has a better structure and avoids redundancy. To simplify things, you may assume that the user always types 1 or 2. (How would the code need to be modified if the user might type any number?)

11. The following code is poorly structured:

```
Scanner console = new Scanner(System.in);
System.out.print("How much will John be spending? ");
double amount = console.nextDouble();
System.out.println();

int numBills1 = (int) (amount / 20.0);
if (numBills1 * 20.0 < amount) {
    numBills1++;
}

System.out.print("How much will Jane be spending? ");
amount = console.nextDouble();
System.out.println();

int numBills2 = (int) (amount / 20.0);
if (numBills2 * 20.0 < amount) {
    numBills2++;
}

System.out.println("John needs " + numBills1 + " bills");
System.out.println("Jane needs " + numBills2 + " bills");
```

Rewrite it so that it has a better structure and avoids redundancy. You may wish to introduce a method to help capture redundant code.

12. Describe a problem with the following code:

```
Scanner console = new Scanner(System.in);
System.out.print("What is your favorite color?");
String name = console.next();
if (name == "blue") {
    System.out.println("Mine, too!");
}
```

13. What is the output of the following code?

```
Point p1 = new Point(3, -2);
Point p2 = new Point(3, -2);

if (p1 == p2) {
    System.out.println("equal");
} else {
    System.out.println("non-equal");
}
```

14. What is the output of the following code?

```
Point p1 = new Point(3, -2);
Point p2 = new Point(4, 0);

if (p1.equals(p2)) {
    System.out.println("first");
}

p2.translate(-1, -2);
if (p1.equals(p2)) {
    System.out.println("second");
}

p2 = p1;
p2.translate(2, 5);
if (p1.equals(p2)) {
    System.out.println("third");
}

p2 = new Point(5, -3);
p1.translate(1, 1);
if (p1.equals(p2)) {
    System.out.println("fourth");
}
```

15. Write a piece of code that reads a shorthand text description of a color and prints the longer equivalent. Acceptable color names are B for Blue, G for Green, and R for Red. If the user types something other than B, G, or R, print an error message. Make your program case-insensitive so that the user can type an uppercase or lowercase letter. Here are some example executions:

```
What color do you want? B
You have chosen Blue.

What color do you want? g
You have chosen Green.

What color do you want? Bork
Unknown color: Bork
```

16. Write a piece of code that reads a shorthand text description of a playing card and prints the longhand equivalent. The shorthand description of the card is the card's rank (2 through 10, J, Q, K, or A) followed by its suit (C, D, H, or S). You should expand the shorthand into the form "<Rank> of <Suit>". You may assume that the user types valid input. Here are two example executions:

```
Enter a card: 9 S
Nine of Spades

Enter a card: K C
King of Clubs
```

17. The following expression in Java should equal 6.8, but it does not. Why does this occur?

```
0.2 + 1.2 + 2.2 + 3.2
```

Program Logic and Indefinite Loops

Introduction

The chapter begins by examining a new construct called a `while` loop that allows you to loop an indefinite number of times. The `while` loop will allow you to solve a new class of programming problem where you don't know in advance how many times you want a loop to execute. For example, game-playing programs often involve `while` loops because it isn't known beforehand how the user will play the game. Because we will be exploring game programs, we will also explore how to generate random numbers inside a Java program.

The chapter then discusses the final primitive type, `boolean`. The `boolean` type is used to store logical (true/false) information. Once you understand the details of the `boolean` type, you will be able to write complex loops involving multiple tests.

Next, we'll briefly examine the important topic of handling user errors. The chapter then concludes with a discussion of loop variations and assertions. Using assertions, you can reason about the formal properties of programs (what is true at different points in program execution).

5.1 The `while` Loop

The `for` loops we have been writing since Chapter 2 are fairly simple loops that execute a predictable number of times. Recall that we call them *definite* loops because we know before the loops begin executing exactly how many times they will execute. Now we want to turn our attention to *indefinite* loops, which execute an unknown number of times. Indefinite loops come up often in interactive programs and file processing. For example, you don't know in advance how many times a user might want to play a game, and you won't know before you look at a file exactly how much data it stores.

The `while` loop is the first indefinite loop we will study. It has the following syntax:

```
while (<test>) {
    <statement>;
    <statement>;
    . . .
    <statement>;
}
```

The diagram in Figure 5.1 indicates the flow of control for the `while` loop. It performs its test and, if the test evaluates to true, executes the controlled statements. It repeatedly tests again and executes again if the test evaluates to true. Only when the test evaluates to false does the loop terminate.

As Figure 5.1 indicates, the `while` loop performs its test at the top of the loop, before the body of the loop is executed. A `while` loop will not execute its controlled statements if its test evaluates to false the first time it is evaluated.

Here is an example of a `while` loop:

```
int number = 1;
while (number <= 200) {
    number *= 2;
}
```

Recall that the `*=` operator multiplies a variable by a certain amount (in this case, 2). Thus, this loop initializes an integer variable called `number` to 1 and then doubles it

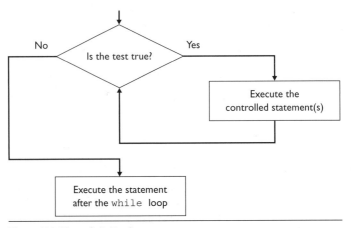

Figure 5.1 Flow of `while` loop

while it is less than or equal to 200. On the surface, using an `if` statement would look similar:

```
int number = 1;
if (number <= 200) {
    number *= 2;
}
```

The difference between the two is that the `while` loop executes multiple times, looping until the test evaluates to false. The `if` statement executes the doubling statement only once, leaving `number` equal to 2. The `while` loop executes the doubling statement until the test evaluates to false, executing the assignment statement eight times, setting `number` to the value `256` (the first power of 2 that is greater than 200).

Here is a `while` loop containing two statements:

```
int number = 1;
while (number <= max) {
    System.out.println("Hi there");
    number++;
}
```

This `while` loop is almost the same as the following `for` loop:

```
for (int number = 1; number <= max; number++) {
    System.out.println("Hi there");
}
```

The only difference between these two loops is the scope of the variable `number`. In the `while` loop, `number` is declared in the scope outside the loop. In the `for` loop, `number` is declared inside the loop.

A Loop to Find the Smallest Divisor

Suppose you want to find the smallest divisor of a number other than 1. Table 5.1 gives examples of what you are looking for.

Here is a pseudocode description of how you might do this:

```
start divisor at 2.
while (the current value of divisor does not work) {
    increase divisor.
}
```

TABLE 5.1 Examples of Factors

Number	Factors	Smallest divisor
10	2 * 5	2
15	3 * 5	3
25	5 * 5	5
31	31	31
77	7 * 11	7

You don't start `divisor` at 1 because you are looking for the first divisor greater than 1. To refine this pseudocode, you must be more explicit about what makes a divisor work. A divisor of a number has no remainder when the number is divided by it. You can rewrite this as:

```
start divisor at 2.
while (the remainder of number/divisor is not 0) {
    increase divisor.
}
```

Here is a use for the mod operator, which gives the remainder for integer division. The following `while` loop performs this task:

```
int divisor = 2;
while (number % divisor != 0) {
    divisor++;
}
```

One problem you will undoubtedly encounter in writing your `while` loops is the infamous infinite loop. Consider the following code:

```
int number = 1;
while (number > 0) {
    number++;
}
```

Because `number` begins as a positive value and the loop makes it larger, this loop will continue indefinitely. You must be careful in formulating your `while` loops to avoid situations where a piece of code will never finish executing. Every time you write a `while` loop, you should consider when and how it will finish executing.

Sentinel Loops

Suppose you want to read a series of numbers from the user and compute their sum. You could ask the user in advance how many numbers to read, as we did in the last chapter, but that isn't always convenient. What if the user has a long list of numbers to enter? One way around this is to pick some special input value that will signal the end of input. We call this a *sentinel value*.

> **Sentinel**
> A special value that signals the end of input.

For example, you could tell the user to enter the value −1 to stop entering numbers. But how do you structure your code to make use of this sentinel? In general, you'll want to do the following:

```
sum = 0.
while (we haven't seen the sentinel) {
    prompt & read.
    add it to the sum.
}
```

Common Programming Error

Infinite Loop

It is relatively easy to write a while loop that never terminates, causing its body to repeat infinitely. One reason it's so easy to make this mistake is that a while loop doesn't have an update step in its header like a for loop does. A correct update step is crucial because it is needed to eventually cause the loop's test to fail.

Consider the following code, which tries to prompt the user for a number and repeatedly print that number divided in half until 0 is reached. This first attempt doesn't compile:

```
Scanner console = new Scanner(System.in);
System.out.print("Type a number: ");

// this code does not compile
while (number > 0) {
    int number = console.nextInt();
    System.out.println(number / 2);
}
```

The problem with the preceding code is that the variable number needs to be in scope during the loop's test, so it cannot be declared inside the loop. An incorrect attempt to fix this compiler error would be to cut and paste the line initializing number outside the loop:

```
// this code has an infinite loop
int number = console.nextInt(); // moved out of loop

while (number > 0) {
    System.out.println(number / 2);
}
```

This version has an infinite loop; if the loop is entered, it will never be exited. This problem arises because there is no update inside the while loop's body to change the value of number. If number is greater than 0, the loop will keep printing its value and checking the loop test, which will be true every time.

The following version of the code solves the infinite loop problem. The loop contains an update step on each pass that divides the integer in half and stores its new value. If the integer hasn't reached 0, the loop repeats:

```
// this code behaves correctly
int number = console.nextInt(); // moved out of loop

while (number > 0) {
    number = number / 2; // update step: divide in half
    System.out.println(number);
}
```

The key idea is that every while loop's body should contain code to update the terms being tested in the loop test. If the while loop test examines a variable's value, the loop body should potentially reassign a meaningful new value to that variable.

But you don't want to add the sentinel value into your sum. This is a classic fence-post or "loop-and-a-half" problem: You want to prompt for and read the sentinel, but you don't want to add it to the sum.

The usual fencepost solution of doing the first prompt and read before the loop and reversing the order of the two steps in the body of the loop works here:

```
sum = 0.
prompt & read.
while (we haven't seen the sentinel) {
    add it to the sum.
    prompt & read.
}
```

You can then refine this pseudocode by introducing a variable for the number read from the user:

```
sum = 0.
prompt & read a value into n.
while (n is not the sentinel) {
    add n to the sum.
    prompt & read a value into n.
}
```

This translates fairly easily into Java code:

```
Scanner console = new Scanner(System.in);

int sum = 0;
System.out.print("next integer (-1 to quit)? ");
int number = console.nextInt();
while (number != -1) {
    sum += number;
    System.out.print("next integer (-1 to quit)? ");
    number = console.nextInt();
}
System.out.println("sum = " + sum);
```

When this code is executed, the interaction looks like this:

```
next integer (-1 to quit)? 34
next integer (-1 to quit)? 19
next integer (-1 to quit)? 8
next integer (-1 to quit)? 0
next integer (-1 to quit)? 17
next integer (-1 to quit)? 204
next integer (-1 to quit)? -1
sum = 282
```

Random Numbers

We often want our programs to exhibit apparently random behavior. This often comes up in game-playing programs, where we want the programs to make up a number for the user to guess, shuffle a deck of cards, pick a word from a list for the user to guess, and so on. Programs are, by their very nature, predictable and nonrandom. But we can produce values that seem to be random. Such values are called *pseudorandom* because they are produced algorithmically.

> **Pseudorandom Numbers**
>
> Numbers that, although they are derived from predictable and well-defined algorithms, mimic the properties of numbers chosen at random.

Java provides several mechanisms for obtaining pseudorandom numbers. One option is to call the `random` method from the `Math` class to obtain a random value of type `double` that has the property that:

$$0.0 <= \text{Math.random()} < 1.0$$

This method provides a quick and easy way to get a random number, and you can use multiplication to change the range of the numbers produced. Java also provides a class called `Random` that can be easier to use. It is included in the `java.util` package, so you have to include an import declaration at the beginning of your program to use it.

`Random` objects have several useful methods related to generating pseudorandom numbers, listed in Table 5.2. Each time you call one of these methods, a new random number of the requested type will be generated and returned.

TABLE 5.2 Useful Methods of Random Objects

Method	Description
`nextInt()`	random integer between -2^{31} and $(2^{31} - 1)$
`nextInt(max)`	random integer between 0 and `(max - 1)`
`nextDouble()`	random real number between `0.0` (inclusive) and `1.0` (exclusive)
`nextBoolean()`	random logical value of `true` or `false`

To create random numbers, you first construct a `Random` object:

```
Random r = new Random();
```

You can then call its `nextInt` method, passing it a maximum integer. The number returned will be between 0 (inclusive) and the maximum (exclusive). For example, if you call `nextInt(100)`, you will get a number between 0 and 99. You can add 1 to the number to have a range between 1 and 100.

Let's look at a simple program that picks numbers between 1 and 10 until a particular number comes up. We'll use the `Random` class to construct an object for generating our pseudorandom numbers:

Our loop should look something like this (where `number` is the value the user has asked us to generate):

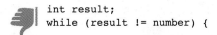
```
int result;
while (result != number) {
```

```
        result = r.nextInt(10) + 1; // random number from 1-10
        System.out.println("next number = " + result);
}
```

Notice that we have to declare the variable `result` outside the `while` loop, because `result` appears in the `while` loop test. The preceding code has the right approach, but Java won't accept it. The code generates an error message that the variable `result` might not be initialized. This is an example of a loop that needs *priming*.

| **Priming a Loop**
| Initializing variables before a loop to "prime the pump" and guarantee
| that the loop is entered.

We want to set the variable `result` to something that will cause the loop to be entered, but the value isn't important as long as it gets us into the loop. We do want to be careful not to set it to a value the user wants us to generate, though. We are dealing with values between 1 and 10 in this program, so we could set `result` to a value such as −1 that is clearly outside this range of numbers. We sometimes refer to this as a "dummy" value because we don't actually process it. Later in this chapter we will see a variation of the `while` loop that doesn't require this kind of priming.

The following is the complete program solution:

```
 1 import java.util.*;
 2
 3 public class Pick {
 4     public static void main(String[] args) {
 5         System.out.println("This program picks numbers from");
 6         System.out.println("1 to 10 until a particular");
 7         System.out.println("number comes up.");
 8         System.out.println();
 9
10         Scanner console = new Scanner(System.in);
11         Random r = new Random();
12
13         System.out.print("Pick a number between 1 and 10--> ");
14         int number = console.nextInt();
15
16         int result = -1;
17         int count = 0;
18         while (result != number) {
19             result = r.nextInt(10) + 1;
20             System.out.println("next number = " + result);
21             count++;
22         }
23         System.out.println("Your number came up after " +
24                             count + " times");
25     }
26 }
```

Depending upon the sequence of numbers returned by the `Random` object, it might end up picking the given number quickly, as in this sample execution:

```
This program picks numbers from
1 to 10 until a particular
number comes up.

Pick a number between 1 and 10--> 2
next number = 7
next number = 8
next number = 2
Your number came up after 3 times
```

or it might take a while to pick the number, as in this sample execution:

```
This program picks numbers from
1 to 10 until a particular
number comes up.

Pick a number between 1 and 10--> 10
next number = 9
next number = 7
next number = 7
next number = 5
next number = 8
next number = 8
next number = 1
next number = 5
next number = 1
next number = 9
next number = 7
next number = 10
Your number came up after 12 times
```

5.2 The boolean Type

George Boole was such a good logician that Java has a data type named after him. The Java type `boolean` is used to describe logical true/false relationships. Recall that `boolean` is one of the primitive types, like `int`, `double`, and `char`.

Without realizing it, you have already used `boolean`s. All of the control structures we have looked at—`if/else` statements, `for` loops, and `while` loops—are controlled by expressions that specify tests. For example, the following expression:

```
number % 2 == 0
```

is a test for divisibility by 2. It is also a Boolean expression. Boolean expressions are meant to capture the concepts of truth and falsity, so it is not surprising that the domain of type `boolean` has only two values: `true` and `false`. The words `true` and `false` are reserved words in Java. They are the literal values of type `boolean`. All Boolean expressions, when evaluated, will return one or the other of these literals.

To understand this better, remember what these terms mean for the type `int`. The literals of type `int` include 0, 1, 2, and so on. Because these are literals of type `int`, you can do things like the following with them:

```
int number1 = 1;
int number2 = 0;
```

Common Programming Error

Misusing the Random Object

A `Random` object creates a new random integer every time the `nextInt` method is called on it. When trying to produce a constrained random value, such as one that is odd, some students mistakenly write code such as the following:

```
// this code contains a bug
Random r = new Random();

if (r.nextInt() % 2 == 0) {
    System.out.println("Even number: " + r.nextInt());
} else {
    System.out.println("Odd number: " + r.nextInt());
}
```

The preceding code fails in many cases because the `Random` object produces one random integer for use in the `if/else` test, then another for use in whichever `println` statement is chosen to execute. For example, the `if` test might retrieve a random value of 47 from the `Random` object; it would see that 47 % 2 does not equal 0, so the code would proceed to the `else` statement. The `println` statement would then execute another call on `nextInt`, which would return a completely different number (say, 128). The output of the code would then be the following bizarre statement:

```
Odd number: 128
```

The solution to this problem is to store the randomly created integer into a variable and call `nextInt` again only if another random integer is truly needed. The following code accomplishes this task:

```
// this code behaves correctly
Random r = new Random();
int n = r.nextInt(); // save random number into a variable
if (n % 2 == 0) {
    System.out.println("Even number: " + n);
} else {
    System.out.println("Odd number: " + n);
}
```

Consider what you can do with variables of type `boolean`. Suppose you define two `boolean` variables, `test1` and `test2`. These variables can take on only two possible values: `true` and `false`. You can say:

```
boolean test1 = true;
boolean test2 = false;
```

You can also write a statement that copies the value of one `boolean` variable to another, as with variables of any other type:

```
test1 = test2;
```

Furthermore, you know that the assignment statement can use expressions:

```
number1 = 2 + 2;
```

and that the simple tests you have been using are Boolean expressions. That means you can say things like the following:

```
test1 = (2 + 2 == 4);
test2 = (3 * 100 < 250);
```

These assignment statements say, "Set this `boolean` variable according to the truth value returned by the following test." The first statement sets the variable `test1` to `true`, because the test evaluates to `true`. The second sets the variable `test2` to `false`, because the second test evaluates to `false`. The parentheses are not needed, but they make the statements more readable.

Many beginners don't understand these assignment statements and write code like the following:

```
if (x < y) {
    less = true;
} else {
    less = false;
}
```

This is a redundant `if/else` statement. First, it evaluates the truth value of the test `(x < y)`. If the test evaluates to true, it executes the `if` part and assigns `less` the value `true`. If the test evaluates to false, is executes the `else` part and assigns `less` the value `false`. Since you are assigning `less` the truth value of the `if/else` test, you should do it directly:

```
less = (x < y);
```

Obviously, then, assignment is one of the operations you can perform on variables of type `boolean`.

Logical Operators

In Java, you can form complicated Boolean expressions using what are known as the *logical operators* (Table 5.3).

The NOT operator (`!`) reverses the truth value of its operand. If an expression evaluates to true, its negation evaluates to false, and vice versa. You can express this

TABLE 5.3 Logical Operators

Operator	Meaning	Example	Value
&&	AND (conjunction)	(2 == 2) && (3 < 4)	true
||	OR (disjunction)	(1 < 2) || (2 == 3)	true
!	NOT (negation)	!(2 == 2)	false

using a truth table. The following truth table has two columns, one for a variable and one for its negation. For each value of the variable, the table shows the corresponding value of the negation.

Truth Table for NOT (!)

p	!p
true	false
false	true

In addition to the negation operator, there are two logical connectives you will use, AND (&&) and OR (||). You use these connectives to tie together two Boolean expressions, creating a new Boolean expression. The following truth table shows that the AND operator evaluates to `true` only when both of its individual operands are `true`.

Truth Table for AND (&&)

p	q	p && q
true	true	true
true	false	false
false	true	false
false	false	false

The following truth table shows that the OR operator evaluates to `true` except when both operands are `false`.

Truth Table for OR (||)

p	q	p || q
true	true	true
true	false	true
false	true	true
false	false	false

The Java OR operator has a slightly different meaning from the English word "or." In English you say, "I'll study tonight or I'll go to a movie." One or the other will be true, but not both. The OR operator is more like the English expression "and/or": If one or both operands are `true`, the overall proposition is `true`.

You generally use logical operators when what you have to say does not reduce to one test. For example, suppose you want to do something if a number is between 1 and 10. You might say:

```java
if (number >= 1) {
    if (number <= 10) {
```

```
        doSomething();
    }
}
```

But you can say this more easily using logical AND:

```
if (number >= 1 && number <= 10) {
    doSomething();
}
```

People use the words "and" and "or" all the time, but Java only allows you to use them in the strict logical sense. Be careful not to write code like the following:

```
// this does not compile
if (x == 1 || 2 || 3) {
    doSomething();
}
```

In English we would read this as "x equals 1 or 2 or 3," which makes sense to us, but not to Java. You might also be tempted to say:

```
// this does not compile
if (1 <= x <= 10) {
    doSomethingElse();
}
```

In mathematics, this expression would make sense and would test whether x is between 1 and 10 inclusive. However, the expression doesn't make sense in Java.

You can only use the logical AND and OR operators to combine a series of Boolean expressions. Otherwise, the computer will not understand what you mean. To express the "1 or 2 or 3" idea, combine three different Boolean expressions with logical ORs:

```
if (x == 1 || x == 2 || x == 3) {
    doSomething();
}
```

To express the "between 1 and 10 inclusive" idea, combine two Boolean expressions with a logical AND:

```
if (1 <= x && x <= 10) {
    doSomethingElse();
}
```

Now that we've introduced the AND, OR, and NOT logical operators, it's time to revisit our precedence table. The NOT operator appears at the top, with the highest level of precedence. The other two logical operators have fairly low precedence, lower than the arithmetic and relational operators but higher than the assignment operators. The AND operator has a slightly higher level of precedence than the OR operator. Table 5.4 includes these new operators.

According to these rules of precedence, when evaluating an expression like the following:

TABLE 5.4   Java Operator Precedence

Description	Operators
unary operators	`!, ++, --, +, -`
multiplicative operators	`*, /, %`
additive operators	`+, -`
relational operators	`<, >, <=, >=`
equality operators	`==, !=`
logical AND	`&&`
logical OR	`||`
assignment operators	`=, +=, -=, *=, /=, %=, &&=, ||=`

```
if (test1 || !test2 && test3) {
    doSomething();
}
```

the computer will evaluate the NOT first, the AND second, and then the OR.

Short-Circuited Evaluation

In this section we will explore the use of the logical operators to solve a complex programming task, and we'll introduce an important property of these operators. We will write a method called `firstWord` that takes a `String` as a parameter and returns the first word in the string. To keep things simple, we will adopt the convention that a `String` is broken up into individual words by spaces. If the `String` has no words at all, the method should return an empty string. Here are a few example calls:

Method Call	Value Returned
`firstWord("four score and seven years")`	`"four"`
`firstWord("all-one-word-here")`	`"all-one-word-here"`
`firstWord("   lots   of   space   here")`	`"lots"`
`firstWord(" ")`	`""`

Remember that we can call the `substring` method to pull out part of a string. We pass two parameters to the `substring` method: the starting index of the substring and the index one beyond the end of the substring. If the string is stored in a variable called s, our task basically reduces to the following steps:

```
set start to the first index of the word
set stop to the index just beyond the word
return s.substring(start, stop)
```

As a first approximation, let's assume that the starting index is 0. That won't work for strings that begin with spaces, but it will allow us to focus on the second step in the pseudocode. Consider a string that begins with `"four score"`. If we examine the individual characters of the string and their indexes, we find the following pattern:

[0]	[1]	[2]	[3]	[4]	[5]	[6]	[7]	[8]	[9]	...
'f'	'o'	'u'	'r'	' '	's'	'c'	'o'	'r'	'e'	...

We set `start` to `0`, and we want to set the variable `stop` to the index just beyond the end of the first word. In this example, the word we want is `"four"`, and it extends from indexes 0 through 3. So, if we want the variable `stop` to be one beyond the end of the desired substring, we want to set it to index 4, the location of the first space in the string.

So how do we find the first space in the string? We use a `while` loop. We simply start at the front of the string and loop until we get to a space:

```
set stop to 0.
while (the character at index stop is not a space) {
    stop++;
}
```

This is easily converted into Java code. Combining it with our assumption that `start` will be `0`, we get:

```java
public static String firstWord(String s) {
    int start = 0;
    int stop = 1;
    while (s.charAt(stop) != ' ') {
        stop++;
    }
    return s.substring(start, stop);
}
```

This version of the method works for many cases, including our sample string, but it doesn't work for all strings. It has two major limitations. We began by assuming that the string did not begin with spaces, so we know we have to fix that limitation. The second problem is that this version of `firstWord` doesn't work on one-word strings. For example, if we execute it with a string like `"four"`, it generates a `StringIndexOutOfBoundsException` indicating that 4 is not a legal index.

The exception occurs because our code assumes that we will eventually find a space, but there is no space in the string `"four"`: `stop` is incremented until it becomes equal to 4, and an exception is thrown because there is no character at index 4. This is sometimes referred to as "running off the end of the string."

To address this problem, we need to incorporate a test that involves the length of the string. Many novices attempt this using some combination of `while` and `if`, as in:

```java
int stop = 0;
while (stop < s.length()) {
    if (s.charAt(stop) != ' ') {
        stop++;
    }
}
```

This code works for one-word strings like `"four"` because as soon as `stop` becomes equal to the length of the string, we break out of the loop. However, it doesn't work for the original multiword cases like `"four score"`. We end up in an infinite loop because once `stop` becomes equal to 4, we stop incrementing it, but we get trapped inside the loop because the test says to continue as long as `stop` is less than the length of the string.

The point to recognize is that this is a case where there are two different conditions that we need to use in controlling the loop. We want to continue incrementing `stop` only if we know that we haven't seen a space *and* that we haven't reached the end of the string. We can express that idea using the logical AND operator:

```
int stop = 0;
while (s.charAt(stop) != ' ' && stop < s.length()) {
    stop++;
}
```

Unfortunately, even this test does not work. It expresses the two conditions properly, because we want to make sure that we haven't reached a space and we want to make sure that we haven't reached the end of the string. But think about what happens just as we reach the end of a string. Suppose that `s` is `"four"` and `stop` is equal to 3. We see that the character at index 3 is not a space and we see that `stop` is less than the length of the string, so we increment one more time and `stop` becomes 4. As we come around the loop, we test whether `s.charAt(4)` is a space. This test throws an exception. We also test whether `stop` is less than 4, which it isn't, but that test comes too late to avoid the exception.

Java offers a solution for this situation. The logical operators `&&` and `||` use *short-circuited evaluation.*

Short-Circuited Evaluation

The property of the logical operators `&&` and `||` that prevents the second operand from being evaluated if the overall result is obvious from the value of the first operand.

In our case, we are performing two different tests and asking for the logical AND of the two tests. If either test fails the overall result is `false`, so if the first test fails, the second test doesn't have to be performed. Because of short-circuited evaluation, we don't perform the second test at all because the overall result is obvious from the first test. In other words, the performance and evaluation of the second test are prevented (short-circuited) by the fact that the first test fails.

This means we need to reverse the order of our two tests:

```
int stop = 0;
while (stop < s.length() && s.charAt(stop) != ' ') {
    stop++;
}
```

If we run through the same scenario again with `stop` equal to 3, we pass both of these tests and increment `stop` to 4. Then, as we come around the loop again, we first test to see if `stop` is less than `s.length()`. It is not, which means the test evaluates to `false`. As a result, Java knows that the overall expression will evaluate to false and never evaluates the second test. This prevents the exception from occurring, because we never test whether s.charAt(4) is a space.

This solution gives us a second version of the method:

```
public static String firstWord(String s) {
    int start = 0;
    int stop = 0;
    while (stop < s.length() && s.charAt(stop) != ' ') {
        stop++;
    }
    return s.substring(start, stop);
}
```

But remember that we assumed that the first word starts at position 0. That won't necessarily be the case. For example, if we pass a string that begins with several spaces, this method will return an empty string. We need to modify the code so that it skips any leading spaces. Accomplishing that goal requires another loop. As a first approximation, we can say:

```
int start = 0;
while (s.charAt(start) == ' ') {
    start++;
}
```

This code works for most strings, but it fails in two important cases. The loop test assumes we will find a nonspace character. What if the string is composed entirely of spaces? In that case, we'll simply run off the end of the string, generating a StringIndexOutOfBoundsException. And what if the string is empty to begin with? We'll get an error immediately when we ask about s.charAt(0), because there is no character at index 0.

We could decide that these cases constitute errors. After all, how can you return the first word if there is no word? So, we could document a precondition that the string contains at least one nonspace character, and throw an exception if we find it doesn't. Another approach is to return an empty string in these cases.

To deal with the possibility of the string being empty, we need to modify our loop to incorporate a test on the length of the string. If we add it at the end of our while loop test, we get:

```
int start = 0;
while (s.charAt(start) == ' ' && start < s.length()) {
    start++;
}
```

But this code has the same flaw we saw before. It is supposed to prevent problems when start becomes equal to the length of the string, but when this occurs, a StringIndexOutOfBoundsException will be thrown before the test on the length of the string is reached. So these tests also have to be reversed to take advantage of short-circuited evaluation:

```
int start = 0;
while (start < s.length() && s.charAt(start) == ' ') {
    start++;
}
```

To combine this with our previous code, we have to change the initialization of `stop`. We no longer want to search from the front of the string. Instead, we need to initialize `stop` to be equal to `start`. Putting these pieces together, we get the following version of the method:

```
public static String firstWord(String s) {
    int start = 0;
    while (start < s.length() && s.charAt(start) == ' ') {
        start++;
    }
    int stop = start;
    while (stop < s.length() && s.charAt(stop) != ' ') {
        stop++;
    }
    return s.substring(start, stop);
}
```

This version works in all cases, skipping any leading spaces and returning an empty string if there is no word to return.

boolean Variables and Flags

All `if`/`else` statements are controlled by Boolean tests. The tests can be `boolean` variables or Boolean expressions. Consider, for example, the following code:

```
if (number > 0) {
    System.out.println("positive");
} else {
    System.out.println("not positive");
}
```

It could be rewritten as follows:

```
boolean positive = (number > 0);
if (positive) {
    System.out.println("positive");
} else {
    System.out.println("not positive");
}
```

Using `boolean` variables adds to the readability of your programs because it allows you to give names to tests. Consider the kind of code you would generate for a dating program. You might have some integer variables that describe certain attributes of a person: `looks`, to store a rough estimate of physical beauty (on a scale of 1–10); `IQ`, to store intelligence quotient; `income`, to store gross annual income; and `snothers`, to track intimate friends ("snother" is short for "significant other"). Given these variables to specify a person's attributes, you can develop various tests of suitability. `boolean` variables are useful here to give names to those tests, adding greatly to the readability of the code:

```
boolean cute = (looks >= 9);
boolean smart = (IQ > 125);
boolean rich = (income > 100000);
boolean available = (snothers == 0);
boolean awesome = cute && smart && rich && available;
```

You might find occasion to use a special kind of `boolean` variable called *a flag*. Typically we use flags within loops to record error conditions or to signal completion. Different flags test different conditions. As an analogy, consider a referee at a game who watches for a particular illegal action and throws a flag if it happens. You sometimes hear an announcer saying, "There is a flag down on the play."

Let's introduce a flag into the cumulative sum code we saw in the previous chapter:

```
double sum = 0.0;
for (int i = 1; i <= totalNumber; i++) {
    System.out.print("    #" + i + "? ");
    double next = console.nextDouble();
    sum += next;
}
System.out.println("sum = " + sum);
```

Suppose we want to know whether the sum ever goes negative at any point. Notice that this isn't the same as whether the sum ends up being negative. Like a bank account balance, the sum might switch back and forth between positive and negative. As you make a series of deposits and withdrawals, the bank will want to keep track of whether you overdraw your account along the way. Using a `boolean` flag, we can modify the preceding loop to keep track of whether the sum ever goes negative and report the result after the loop:

```
double sum = 0.0;
boolean negative = false;
for (int i = 1; i <= totalNumber; i++) {
    System.out.print("    #" + i + "? ");
    double next = console.nextDouble();
    sum += next;
    if (sum < 0.0) {
        negative = true;
    }
}
System.out.println("sum = " + sum);
if (negative) {
    System.out.println("Sum went negative");
} else {
    System.out.println("Sum never went negative");
}
```

Boolean Zen

In 1974, Robert Pirsig started a cultural trend with his book *Zen and the Art of Motorcycle Maintenance: An Inquiry into Values.* A slew of later books copied the title, so we got *Zen and the Art of X,* where *X* was Poker, Knitting, Writing, Foosball, Guitar, Public School Teaching, Making a Living, Falling in Love, Quilting,

Stand-up Comedy, the SAT, Flower Arrangement, Fly Tying, Systems Analysis, Fatherhood, Screenwriting, Diabetes Maintenance, Intimacy, Helping, Street Fighting, Murder, and on and on. There was even a book called *Zen and the Art of Anything.*

We now join this cultural trend by discussing Zen and the art of type `boolean`. It seems to take a while for many novices to get used to Boolean expressions. Novices often write overly complex expressions involving `boolean` values because they don't grasp the simplicity that is possible when you "get" how the `boolean` type works.

For example, suppose you wanted to write a method that determines whether or not a number is even. You might call the method `isEven`. It would take a value of type `int` and would return `true` if the `int` is even and `false` if it is not. So, the method would look like this:

```
public static boolean isEven(int n) {
    . . .
}
```

How would you write the body of this method? You can use the mod operator to see if the remainder when you divide n by 2 is 0. If (`n % 2`) is 0, you know the number is even. If it isn't, you know the number is not even (i.e., is odd). The method has a `boolean` return type, so you want to return the value `true` when (`n % 2`) is 0 and the value `false` when it is not. You can write the method as follows:

```
public static boolean isEven(int n) {
    if (n % 2 == 0) {
        return true;
    } else {
        return false;
    }
}
```

This works, but it is more verbose than it needs to be. The preceding code evaluates the expression (`n % 2 == 0`). That expression is of type `boolean`, which means that it evaluates to either `true` or `false`. The `if/else` statement says to return `true` if the expression evaluates to `true` and to return `false` if it evaluates to `false`. But why use this construct? If the method is going to return `true` when the expression evaluates to `true` and return `false` when it evaluates to `false`, you can just return the value of the expression directly:

```
public static boolean isEven(int n) {
    return (n % 2 == 0);
}
```

Even this version can be simplified, because the parentheses are not necessary (although they make it clearer exactly what is being returned). This code tests whether n `% 2` equals 0 and returns the result (`true` when it does equal 0, `false` when it does not).

Consider an analogy to integer expressions. To someone who understands Boolean Zen, the `if/else` version of this method looks as odd as the following code:

```
if (x == 1) {
    return 1;
} else if (x == 2) {
    return 2;
} else if (x == 3) {
    return 3;
} else if (x == 4) {
    return 4;
} else if (x == 5) {
    return 5;
}
```

If you always want to return the value of x, why not just say:

```
return x;
```

A similar confusion can occur when students use boolean variables. In the last section we looked at a variation of the cumulative sum algorithm that used a boolean variable called negative to keep track of whether or not the sum ever goes negative. We then used an if/else statement to print a message reporting the result:

```
if (negative) {
    System.out.println("Sum went negative");
} else {
    System.out.println("Sum never went negative");
}
```

Some novices would write this code as follows:

```
if (negative == true) {
    System.out.println("Sum went negative");
} else {
    System.out.println("Sum never went negative");
}
```

The comparison is unnecessary because the if/else statement expects an expression of type boolean to appear inside the parentheses. A boolean variable is already of the appropriate type, so we don't need to test whether it equals true; it either *is* true or it isn't (in which case it is false). To someone who understands Boolean Zen, the preceding test seems as redundant as saying:

```
if ((negative == true) == true) {
    . . .
}
```

Novices also often write tests like the following:

```
if (negative == false) {
    . . .
}
```

This makes more sense because the test is doing something useful, in that it switches the meaning of the boolean variable (evaluating to true if the variable is false and evaluating to `false` if the variable is `true`). But the negation operator is designed to do this kind of switching of `boolean` values, so this test is better written as:

```
if (!negative) {
    . . .
}
```

You should get used to reading the exclamation mark as "not", so this test would be read as "if not negative." To those who understand Boolean Zen, that is a more concise way to express this than to think about testing whether `negative` is equal to `false`.

5.3 User Errors

In the last chapter you learned that it is good programming practice to think about the preconditions of a method and to mention them in the comments for the method. You also learned that in some cases your code can throw exceptions if preconditions are violated.

When writing interactive programs, the simplest approach is to assume that the user will provide good input. You can then document your preconditions and throw exceptions when the user input isn't what was expected. In general, though, it's better to write programs that don't make assumptions about user input. You've seen, for example, that the `Scanner` object can throw an exception if the user enters the wrong kind of data. It's preferable to write programs that can deal with user errors. Such programs are referred to as being *robust*.

> **Robust**
>
> A program is said to be robust if it is able to execute even when presented with illegal data.

In this section we will explore how to write robust interactive programs. Before you can write robust code, though, you have to understand some special functionality of the `Scanner` class.

Scanner Lookahead

The `Scanner` class has methods that allow you to perform a test before you read a value. In other words, it allows you to look before you leap. For each of the "next" methods of the `Scanner` class, there is a corresponding "has" method that tells you whether or not you can perform the given operation.

For example, you will often want to read an `int` using a `Scanner` object. But what if the user types something other than an `int`? `Scanner` has a method called `hasNextInt` that tells you whether or not reading an `int` is currently possible. To determine this, the `Scanner` object looks at the next token and sees if it can be interpreted as an integer.

We tend to think of certain sequences of characters as representing particular types of data, but when we read tokens, they can be interpreted in different ways. The following program will allow us to explore this concept:

```
 1 import java.util.*;
 2
 3 public class ExamineInput1 {
 4     public static void main(String[] args) {
 5         System.out.println("This program examines the ways");
 6         System.out.println("a token can be read.");
 7         System.out.println();
 8
 9         Scanner console = new Scanner(System.in);
10
11         System.out.print("token? ");
12         System.out.println("  hasNextInt = " +
13                                 console.hasNextInt());
14         System.out.println("  hasNextDouble = " +
15                                 console.hasNextDouble());
16         System.out.println("  hasNext = " + console.hasNext());
17     }
18 }
```

Let's look at a few sample executions. Here is what happens when we enter the token 348:

```
This program examines the ways
a token can be read.

token? 348
  hasNextInt = true
  hasNextDouble = true
  hasNext = true
```

As you'd expect, the call on hasNextInt returns true, which means that we could interpret this token as an integer. The Scanner would also allow us to interpret this token as a double, so hasNextDouble also returns true. But notice that hasNext() returns true as well. That means that we could call the next method to read in this token as a String.

Here's another execution, this time for the token 348.2:

```
This program examines the ways
a token can be read.

token? 348.2
  hasNextInt = false
  hasNextDouble = true
  hasNext = true
```

This token cannot be interpreted as an int, but it can be interpreted as a double or a String. Finally, consider this execution for the token hello:

```
This program examines the ways
a token can be read.

token? hello
  hasNextInt = false
  hasNextDouble = false
  hasNext = true
```

The token `hello` can't be interpreted as an `int` or `double`; it can only be interpreted as a `String`.

Handling User Errors

Consider the following code fragment:

```
Scanner console = new Scanner(System.in);
System.out.print("How old are you? ");
int age = console.nextInt();
```

What if the user types something that is not an integer? If that happens, the `Scanner` will throw an exception on the call to `nextInt`. We saw in the previous section that we can test whether or not the next token can be interpreted as an integer with the `hasNextInt` method. So, we can test before reading an `int` whether the user has typed an appropriate value.

What if the user types something other than an integer? In this case, we want to discard the input, print out some kind of error message, and prompt for a second input. We want this code to execute in a loop so that we keep discarding input and generating error messages as necessary until the user gives us legal input.

Here is a first attempt at a solution in pseudocode:

```
while (user hasn't given us an integer) {
    prompt.
    discard input.
    generate an error message.
}
read the integer.
```

This reflects what we want to do, in general. We want to keep prompting, discarding, and generating error messages as long as the input is illegal, and when a legal value is entered, we want to read the integer. Of course, in that final case we don't want to discard the input or generate an error message. In other words, the last time through the loop we want to do just the first of these three steps (prompting, but not discarding and not generating an error message). This is another classic fencepost problem, and we can solve it in the usual way by putting the initial prompt before the loop and changing the order of the operations within the loop:

```
prompt.
while (user hasn't given us an integer) {
    discard input.
    generate an error message.
    prompt.
}
read the integer.
```

This pseudocode is fairly easy to turn into actual Java code:

```
Scanner console = new Scanner(System.in);
System.out.print("How old are you? ");
while (!console.hasNextInt()) {
    console.next(); // to discard the input
```

```
        System.out.println("Not an integer; try again.");
        System.out.print("How old are you? ");
    }
    int age = console.nextInt();
```

In fact, this is such a common operation that it is worth turning into a static method:

```
// prompts until a valid number is entered
public static int getInt(Scanner console, String prompt) {
    System.out.print(prompt);
    while (!console.hasNextInt()) {
        console.next();
        System.out.println("Not an integer; try again.");
        System.out.print(prompt);
    }
    return console.nextInt();
}
```

Using this method, we can rewrite our original code as follows:

```
Scanner console = new Scanner(System.in);
int age = getInt(console, "How old are you? ");
```

When you execute this code, the interaction looks like this:

```
How old are you? what?
Not an integer; try again.
How old are you? 18.4
Not an integer; try again.
How old are you? ten
Not an integer; try again.
How old are you? darn!
Not an integer; try again.
How old are you? help
Not an integer; try again.
How old are you? 19
```

5.4 Indefinite Loop Variations

The while loop is the standard indefinite loop, but Java provides several alternatives. Some programmers stick to the while loop and don't bother to learn the alternatives. But the alternatives are part of the language and many programmers do use them, so it is a good idea to explore how they work.

The do/while Loop

As we have seen, the while loop tests at the "top" of the loop, before it executes its controlled statement. Java has an alternative known as the do/while loop that tests at the "bottom" of the loop. The do/while loop has the following syntax:

```
do {
    <statement>;
    . . .
    <statement>;
} while (<test>);
```

For example:

```
int number = 1;
do {
    number *= 2;
} while (number <= 200);
```

This loop produces the same result as the corresponding `while` loop, doubling the variable `number` until its value reaches `256`, which is the first power of 2 greater than 200. But unlike the `while` loop, the `do/while` loop always executes its controlled statements at least once. The diagram in Figure 5.2 shows the flow of control in a `do/while` loop.

As an example, suppose that you want to simulate the rolling of two dice until you get doubles (the same number on both dice). This is easier to write as a `do/while` loop than as a `while` loop, because you know that you have to roll the dice at least once before you can get doubles.

To simulate the rolling of the dice, you need a `Random` object.

```
Random r = new Random();
```

The basic structure of the loop should be to simulate the rolling of the two dice each time through the loop until the values returned are the same. A first attempt might look like this:

```
// right idea, but doesn't compile
do {
    int roll1 = r.nextInt(6) + 1;
    int roll2 = r.nextInt(6) + 1;
} while (roll1 != roll2);
```

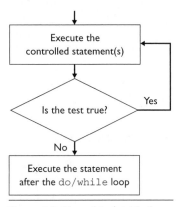

Figure 5.2 Flow of do/while loop

This code doesn't compile. Two compiler errors are reported:

```
Doubles.java:9: cannot find symbol
symbol : variable roll1
location: class Doubles
        } while (roll1 != roll2);
                 ^
Doubles.java:9: cannot find symbol
symbol : variable roll2
location: class Doubles
        } while (roll1 != roll2);
                         ^
2 errors
```

The compiler is complaining that it doesn't know about the variables `roll1` and `roll2` that it sees in the do/while test. That seems odd because they are declared right above the test. The issue is scope. Remember that to determine the scope of a variable declaration, you look for the set of curly braces that contains the declaration. The variables `roll1` and `roll2` are declared inside the curly braces for the do/while loop, but the test for the do/while loop is outside of those curly braces, which means it is outside of the scope of the variables.

To fix this problem, declare the variables in the outer scope so that they can be used in the do/while test. Assign the variables inside the loop (rolling the dice each time through the loop), but declare the variables outside the loop:

```
int roll1, roll2; // declare the variables in the outer scope
do {
    // assign the variables in the inner scope
    roll1 = r.nextInt(6) + 1;
    roll2 = r.nextInt(6) + 1;
} while (roll1 != roll2);
```

This code correctly simulates the rolling of two dice until doubles come up. You can improve the code by adding a counter and by printing the values each time through the loop. Here is a complete program that includes all of these elements:

```
 1 // This program simulates the rolling of two dice until
 2 // doubles (two dice that are the same) come up.
 3
 4 import java.util.*;
 5
 6 public class Doubles {
 7     public static void main(String[] args) {
 8         Random r = new Random();
 9         int count = 0;
10         int roll1, roll2;
11         do {
12             roll1 = r.nextInt(6) + 1;
13             roll2 = r.nextInt(6) + 1;
14             System.out.println("next roll = " + roll1 +
15                                ", " + roll2);
16             count++;
17         } while (roll1 != roll2);
18         System.out.println("Doubles after " + count +
19                            " rolls");
20     }
21 }
```

Here is a sample execution:

```
next roll = 3, 5
next roll = 5, 4
next roll = 1, 2
next roll = 6, 2
next roll = 3, 1
next roll = 2, 4
next roll = 3, 3
Doubles after 7 rolls
```

There are many programming problems where using do/while loops is appropriate. These loops are often useful in interactive programs where you know you want to do something at least once. For example, you might have a loop that allows a user to play a game multiple times, but you can be fairly sure that the user will want to play at least once. Likewise, if you are playing a guessing game with the user, you will always have to obtain at least one guess.

We saw a situation like this earlier with the program that picked pseudorandom numbers between 1 and 10 until a certain number was picked. Because at least one number must be picked, a do/while loop is appropriate. The while loop version required priming, which involved initializing a variable before the loop. With the do/while version, we don't need to initialize because we know the loop will execute at least once:

```java
 1 import java.util.*;
 2
 3 public class Pick2 {
 4     public static void main(String[] args) {
 5         System.out.println("This program picks numbers from");
 6         System.out.println("1 to 10 until a particular");
 7         System.out.println("number comes up.");
 8         System.out.println();
 9
10         Scanner console = new Scanner(System.in);
11         Random r = new Random();
12
13         System.out.print("Pick a number between 1 and 10--> ");
14         int number = console.nextInt();
15
16         int result;
17         int count = 0;
18         do {
19             result = r.nextInt(10) + 1;
20             System.out.println("next number = " + result);
21             count++;
22         } while (result != number);
23         System.out.println("Your number came up after " +
24                             count + " times");
25     }
26 }
```

Notice that, as always, we use curly braces to turn multiple statements into a block. You might be tempted to move the declaration for the variable `result` inside the do/while loop, but that won't work because it appears in the loop test, which is outside the curly braces. Also notice the semicolon that appears at the end of the `do/while` loop. The semicolon is a required part of the syntax for the loop.

break and "Forever" Loops (Optional)

The `while` loop has its test at the top of the loop and the `do/while` loop has its test at the bottom of the loop. That should lead you to wonder whether it might be desirable to have the test in the middle of the loop. There is a way to accomplish this in Java, although it requires some odd-looking code.

Java has a special statement called `break` that will exit a loop. You can use it to break out of any of the loops we have discussed (`while`, `do/while`, `for`). Loops with `break` statements can be difficult to understand, so using `break` is generally discouraged. But there is an interesting application of `break` to form a loop where the test occurs in the middle. The problem is that we still need to choose one of the standard loop constructs (`while`, `do/while`, `for`). One common choice is to form what appears to be an infinite loop with a `while` loop:

```
while (true) {
    <statement>;
    . . .
    <statement>;
}
```

Because the `boolean` literal `true` always evaluates to `true`, this `while` loop appears to execute indefinitely. But you can include a test in the middle of the loop with a `break` statement. This technique is useful for solving fencepost problems.

Recall that earlier in this chapter the following code was used to solve a fencepost problem:

```
Scanner console = new Scanner(System.in);

int sum = 0;
System.out.print("next integer (-1 to quit)? ");
int number = console.nextInt();
while (number != -1) {
    sum += number;
    System.out.print("next integer (-1 to quit)? ");
    number = console.nextInt();
}
System.out.println("sum = " + sum);
```

The code to prompt and read appears twice, once before the loop executes and once at the bottom of the loop. Using a `while` loop with a `break`, we can eliminate this redundancy:

```
Scanner console = new Scanner(System.in);

int sum = 0;
while (true) {
    System.out.print("next integer (-1 to quit)? ");
    int number = console.nextInt();
    if (number == -1) {
        break;
```

```
    }
    sum += number;
}
System.out.println("sum = " + sum);
```

Keep in mind that the `while` loop test is not the real test for this loop. The real test appears in the middle, when we see if `number` is equal to −1, in which case we break. Having the test in the middle makes for a simpler solution to the "loop and a half" problem: We exit the loop on the final iteration, after doing the "half" that we want.

Another way to solve this problem is to use a `for` loop that has none of the usual initialization, test, and update code. The `for` loop still needs the parentheses and semicolons, but the rest can be empty. This leads to the following rather odd-looking code:

```
Scanner console = new Scanner(System.in);

int sum = 0;
for (;;) {
    System.out.print("next integer (−1 to quit)? ");
    int number = console.nextInt();
    if (number == −1) {
        break;
    }
    sum += number;
}
System.out.println("sum = " + sum);
```

The `for (;;)` has the same effect as the `while (true)` loop. In other words, it would normally be an infinite loop, but it's okay in this case because the true loop test appears in the middle of the loop, with a `break`.

People tend to either love or hate this version of the `for` loop, usually for the same reason. The people who hate it say, "This looks too strange." The people who love it say, "I'm glad it looks strange because it makes it clear that the real loop test is somewhere else." Some people read the `for (;;)` as "forever" and refer to these as "forever loops."

5.5 Assertions and Program Logic

Logicians concern themselves with declarative statements called *assertions*.

> **Assertion**
> A declarative sentence that is either true or false.

The following are all assertions:

- 2 + 2 equals 4.
- The sun is larger than the Earth.
- x > 45.
- It was raining.
- The rain in Spain falls mainly on the plain.

Did You Know?

Controversy over break

The use of break and "forever" loops is controversial in the computer science community. A computer scientist named Edsger Dijkstra started an intense debate in 1968 when he wrote a letter to a magazine read by computer science professionals that was titled, "Goto Considered Harmful." He argued against a certain style of programming that was common at the time that relied heavily on "go to" commands that caused the computer to jump from one point of program execution to another. This style of programming was called "spaghetti code" by its critics because the various goto commands often led to a highly unpredictable flow of control.

Dijkstra's letter included an important defense of *structured programming*, which has since become the dominant style of programming. Java, C, and C++ are all derived from the structured programming approach. However, the break statement is a kind of "goto" that allows you to prematurely end the execution of a loop. As such, it is considered by some to be part of the "bad" programming of the past.

Many people have argued against being too puritanical about structured programming. Computer scientist Donald Knuth, for example, has argued that for situations like fencepost loops, using break statements simplifies the code and is therefore preferable.

A computer scientist named Elliot Soloway added fuel to the fire in 1983 when he published a study showing that novices can more easily learn to solve fencepost problems with forever loops and break than by using while loops. His study suggests that most programmers think more easily in terms of exit conditions than in terms of continuation conditions and that forever loops with break are more intuitive to novice programmers.

There are passionate advocates on both sides of this issue and the debate has lasted for several decades, so the controversy is likely to go on indefinitely. Individual programmers will have to make up their own minds about whether they like this construct or not.

The following are not assertions (the first is a question and the second is a command):

- How much do you weigh?
- Take me home.

Some assertions are true or false depending upon context:

- x > 45. (This depends on x.)
- It was raining. (This depends on when and where.)

You can pin down whether they are true or false by providing a context:

- when x = 13, x > 45.
- On July 4, 1776, in Philadelphia, it was raining.

To write programs correctly and efficiently, you must learn to make assertions about your programs and to understand the contexts in which those assertions will be true. For example, if you are trying to obtain a non-negative number from the user, you want the assertion "Number is non-negative" to be true. If you use a simple prompt and read, like this:

```
System.out.print("Please give me a nonnegative number--> ");
double number = console.nextDouble();
// is number non-negative here?
```

the user can ignore your request and input a negative number anyway. In fact, users often input values that you don't expect, most often because they are confused. Given the uncertainty of user input, this particular assertion may sometimes be true and sometimes false. But something later in the program may depend upon the assertion being true. For example, if you are going to take the square root of that number, you must be sure the number is non-negative. Otherwise, you might end up with a bad result.

Using a loop, you can guarantee that the number you get is non-negative:

```
System.out.print("Please give me a non-negative number--> ");
double number = console.nextDouble();
while (number < 0.0) {
    System.out.print("That is negative. Try again--> ");
    number = console.nextDouble();
}
// is number non-negative here?
```

You know that `number` will be non-negative after the loop; otherwise, you would not exit the `while` loop. As long as a user gives negative values, your program stays in the `while` loop and continues to prompt for input.

This doesn't mean that `number` *should* be non-negative after the loop. It means `number` *will* be non-negative after the loop. By working through the logic of the program, you can see that this is a certainty. It is an assertion of which you are sure. You could even prove it if need be. Such an assertion is called a *provable assertion*.

Provable Assertion

An assertion that can be proven to be true at a particular point in program execution.

Provable assertions help to identify unnecessary bits of code. Consider these statements:

```
int x = 0;
if (x == 0) {
    System.out.println("This is what I expect.");
} else {
    System.out.println("how can that be?");
}
```

The `if/else` construct is not necessary. You know what the assignment statement does, so you know that it sets x to 0. Testing whether x is 0 is like saying, "Before I proceed, I'm going to check that 2 + 2 equals 4." Because the `if` part of this `if/else` statement is always executed, you can prove that these lines of code always do the same thing as the preceeding lines:

```
int x = 0;
System.out.println("This is what I expect.");
```

This code is simpler and, therefore, better. Programs are complex enough without adding unnecessary code.

Reasoning About Assertions

The focus on assertions comes out of a field of computer science known as *program verification.*

> **Program Verification**
>
> A field of computer science that involves reasoning about the formal properties of programs to prove the correctness of a program.

For example, consider the properties of the simple `if` statement:

```
if (<test>) {
    // test is always true here
    . . .
}
```

You enter the body of the `if` statement only if the test is true, which is why you know that it must be true at that particular point in program execution. You can draw a similar conclusion about what is true in an `if/else` statement:

```
if (<test>) {
    // test is always true here
    . . .
} else {
    // test is never true here
    . . .
}
```

and about what is true inside the body of a `while` loop:

```
while (<test>) {
    // test is always true here
    . . .
}
```

But in the case of the `while` loop, you can draw an even stronger conclusion. You know that as long as the test evaluates to true, you'll keep going back into the loop. Thus, you can conclude that after the loop is done executing, the test can no longer be true:

```
while (<test>) {
    // test is always true here
    . . .
}
// test is never true here
```

The test can't be true after the loop because if it had been true, the body of the loop would have been executed again.

These observations about the properties of `if` statements, `if`/`else` statements, and `while` loops provide a good start for proving certain assertions about programs. But often, proving assertions requires a deeper analysis of what the code actually does. For example, suppose you have a variable x of type `int` and you execute the following `if` statement:

```
if (x < 0) {
    // x < 0 is always true here
    x = -x;
}
// but what about x < 0 here?
```

You wouldn't normally be able to conclude anything about x being less than 0 after the `if` statement, but you can if you think about the different cases. If x was greater than or equal to 0 before the `if` statement, it will still be greater than or equal to 0 after the `if` statement. And if x was less than 0 before the `if` statement, it will be equal to −x after. When x is less than 0, −x is greater than 0. Thus, in either case, you know that after the `if` statement executes, x will be greater than or equal to 0.

Programmers naturally apply this kind of reasoning when writing programs. Program-verification researchers are trying to figure out how to do this kind of reasoning in a formal, verifiable way.

A Detailed Assertions Example

To explore assertions further, let's take a detailed look at a code fragment and a set of assertions we might make about the fragment. Consider the following method:

```
public static void printCommonPrefix(int x, int y) {
    int z = 0;
    // Point A
    while (x != y) {
        // Point B
        z++;
        // Point C
        if (x > y) {
            // Point D
            x = x / 10;
        } else {
```

```
            // Point E
            y = y / 10;
        }
        // Point F
    }
    // Point G
    System.out.println("common prefix = " + x);
    System.out.println("digits discarded = " + z);
}
```

This method finds the longest sequence of leading digits that two numbers have in common. For example, the numbers 32845 and 328929343 each begin with the prefix 328. This method will compute that prefix and will also report the total number of digits that are discarded by the computation.

We will identify various assertions as being either always true, never true, or sometimes true/sometimes false at various points in program execution. The comments in the method indicate the points of interest. The assertions we will consider are:

```
x > y
x == y
z == 0
```

Normally computer scientists write assertions with mathematical notation, as in $z = 0$, but we will use a Java expression to distinguish this assertion of equality from assigning a value to the variable.

We can record our answers in a table with the words "always," "never," or "sometimes." So, we want to fill in a table like the following:

	$x > y$	$x == y$	$z == 0$
Point A			
Point B			
. . .	. . .	. . .	. . .

Let's start at point A. This appears near the beginning of the method's execution:

```
public static void printCommonPrefix(int x, int y) {
    int z = 0;
    // Point A
```

The variables x and y are parameters and get their values from the call to the method. Many calls are possible, so we don't really know anything about the values of x and y. Thus, the assertion x > y could be true but doesn't have to be. The assertion is sometimes true, sometimes false at point A. Likewise, the assertion x == y could be true depending upon what values are passed to the method, but it doesn't have to be true. However, we initialize the local variable z to 0 just before point A, so the assertion z == 0 will always be true at that point in execution. So, we can fill in the first line of the table as follows:

	x > y	x == y	z == 0
Point A	sometimes	sometimes	always

Point B appears just inside the `while` loop:

```
while (x != y) {
    // Point B
    z++;
    . . .
}
```

We get to point B only by entering the loop, which means that the loop test has to have evaluated to `true`. This means that at point B it will always be true that x is not equal to y, so the assertion x == y will never be true at that point. But we don't know which of the two is larger. Therefore, the assertion x > y is sometimes true and sometimes false.

You might think that the assertion z == 0 would always be true at point B because we were at point A just before being at point B, but that is not the right answer. Remember that point B is inside of a `while` loop. On the first iteration of the loop, we will have been at point A just before reaching point B, but not on later iterations of the loop. And if you look at the line of code just after point B, you will see that it increments z. There are no other modifications to the variable z inside the loop. Therefore, each time the body of the loop executes, z will increase by 1. So, it will be 0 at point A the first time through the loop, but it will be 1 on the second iteration, 2 on the third iteration, and so forth. Therefore, the right answer for the assertion z == 0 at point B is that it is sometimes true, sometimes false. So, the second line of the table should look like this:

	x > y	x == y	z == 0
Point B	sometimes	never	sometimes

Point C is right after the increment of the variable z. There are no changes to the values of x and y between point B and point C, so the same answers apply at point C for the assertions x > y and x == y. The assertion z == 0 will never be true after the increment, though z starts at 0 before the loop begins and there are no other manipulations of the variable inside the loop, so once it is incremented, it will never be 0 again. Therefore, we can fill in the table for point C as follows:

	x > y	x == y	z == 0
Point C	sometimes	never	never

Points D and E are part of the `if/else` statement inside the `while` loop, so we can do them as a pair. The `if/else` statement appears right after point C:

```
// Point C
if (x > y) {
    // Point D
    x = x / 10;
} else {
    // Point E
    y = y / 10;
}
```

No variables are changed between point C and points D and E. What happens is that Java performs a test and branches in one of two directions. The `if/else` test determines whether x is greater than y. If the test is true, we go to point D. If not, we go to point E. So, for the assertion x > y, we know it is always true at point D and never true at point E. The assertion x == y is a little more difficult to work out. We know it can never be true at point D, but could it be true at point E? Based solely on the `if/else` test, the answer would be yes. But remember that at point C the assertion could never be true. The values of x and y have not changed between point C and point E, so it still can never be true.

As for the assertion z == 0, the variable z hasn't changed between point C and points D and E, and z is not included in the test. So whatever we knew about z before still holds. Therefore, the right answers to fill in for points D and E are as follows:

	x > y	x == y	z == 0
Point D	always	never	never
Point E	never	never	never

Point F appears after the `if/else` statement. To determine the relationship between x and y at point F, we have to look at how the variables have changed. The `if/else` statement either divides x by 10 (if it is the larger value) or divides y by 10 (if it is the larger value). So, we have to ask whether it is possible for the assertion x > y to be true at point F. The answer is yes. For example, x might have been 218 and y might have been 6 before the `if/else` statement. In that case, x would now be 21, which is still larger than y. But does it have to be larger than y? Not necessarily. The values might have been reversed, in which case y will be larger than x. So, that assertion is sometimes true and sometimes false at point F.

What about the assertion x == y? We know it doesn't have to be true because we have looked at cases where x is greater than y or y is greater than x. Can it be true? Are there any values of x and y that would lead to this outcome? Consider if x had been 218 and y had been 21. Then we would have divided x by 10 and it would now be 21, which would equal y. So, this assertion also is sometimes true and sometimes false.

There was no change to z between points D and E and point F, so we simply carry our answer down from the previous columns. So we would fill in the table as follows for point F:

	x > y	x == y	z == 0
Point F	sometimes	sometimes	never

Point G appears after the `while` loop:

```
while (x != y) {
    . . .
}
// Point G
```

We can escape the `while` loop only if x becomes equal to y. So, at point G we know that the assertion x == y is always true. That means that the assertion x > y can never be true. The assertion z == 0 is a little tricky. At point F it was never true, so you might imagine that at point G it can never be true. But we weren't necessarily at point F just before we reached point G. We might never have entered the `while` loop at all, in which case we would have been at point A just before point G. At point A the variable z was equal to 0. Therefore, the right answer for this assertion is that it is sometimes true, sometimes false at point G. The final row of our table thus looks like this:

	x > y	x == y	z == 0
Point G	never	always	sometimes

Putting it all together, we would fill in the table as follows:

	x > y	x == y	z == 0
Point A	sometimes	sometimes	always
Point B	sometimes	never	sometimes
Point C	sometimes	never	never
Point D	always	never	never
Point E	never	never	never
Point F	sometimes	sometimes	never
Point G	never	always	sometimes

The Java assert Statement

The concept of assertions has become so popular among software practitioners that many programming languages provide support for testing assertions. Java added support for testing assertions starting with version 1.4 of the language. The syntax for the `assert` statement is:

```
assert <boolean test>;
```

as in:

```
assert (x < 0);
```

Parentheses have been included here to make the Boolean expression clear, but they are not required.

Programmers often build assertions into their programs to have the computer check to whether all of their assumptions are correct. In general, we expect these assertions to succeed. When an assertion fails, that signals a problem. It means that the programmer has a logic error that is preventing the assumptions from holding true. If the Boolean test in the `assert` statement evaluates to false, we say that the assertion fails. When an assertion fails, an exception is thrown that stops the program from executing.

Testing of assertions can be expensive, so Java lets you control whether this feature is enabled or disabled. You can enable assertion checking while you are developing and testing a program to make sure it works properly, and you can disable it when you're fairly confident that the program works and you want to speed it up. By default, assertion checking is disabled.

5.6 Case Study: NumberGuess

Combining indefinite loops, the ability to check for user errors, and random number generation, it's possible to create guessing games where the computer thinks of random numbers and the user tries to guess them. Let's consider an example game with the following rules. The computer thinks of a random two-digit number but keeps it secret from the player. We'll count numbers that begin with 0, so the acceptable range of numbers here is 00 through 99 inclusive. The player will try to guess the computer's number. If the player guesses correctly, the program will report the number of guesses needed.

To make the game more interesting, the computer will give the player hints for every incorrect guess. Specifically, the computer will tell the player how many digits from the guess are contained in the correct answer. The order of the digits doesn't affect how many are matching. For example, if the correct number is 57 and the player guesses 73, the computer will report one matching digit, because the correct answer contains a 7. If the player next guesses 75, the computer will report two matching digits. At this point the player knows that the computer's number must be 57, because 57 is the only two-digit number whose digits match 75's.

Since the players will be doing a lot of console input, it's likely that they might type incorrect numbers or non-numeric tokens by mistake. We'd like our guessing-game program to be robust against user input errors.

Initial Version Without Hinting

In previous chapters, we've talked about the idea of iterative enhancement. Since this is a challenging program, we'll tackle it in stages. One of the hardest parts of the program is giving correct hints to the player when a guess is wrong. For now, we'll simply write a game that tells players whether they are correct or incorrect on each guess and, once the game is done, reports the number of guesses needed. The program won't be robust against user input errors yet; that can be added later. To further simplify the game, rather than having the computer choose a random number, we'll fix the number at a known value so that the code can be tested more easily.

Since it's not known exactly how many tries a player will need to guess the number, it seems that the main loop for this game will have to be a `while` loop. It might be tempting to write the code to match the following pseudocode:

```
// flawed number guess pseudocode
think of a number.
while (user has not guessed the number) {
    prompt and read a guess.
    report whether the guess was correct or incorrect.
}
```

But the problem with this pseudocode is that you can't start the `while` loop if you don't have any `guess` value from the player yet. The following code doesn't compile, because the variable `guess` isn't initialized when the loop begins:

```
// this code doesn't compile
int numGuesses = 0;
int number = 42; // computer always picks same number
int guess;

while (guess != number) {
    System.out.print("Your guess? ");
    guess = console.nextInt();
    numGuesses++;
    System.out.println("Incorrect.");
}

System.out.println("You got it right in " + numGuesses +
                   " tries.");
```

We could try to solve the problem with the preceding code by priming the value of the `guess` variable, setting it to a value other than the correct number. However, a fencepost "loop-and-a-half" solution will work even better. It turns out that the game's main guess loop is a fencepost loop, because after each incorrect guess we must print an "Incorrect" message (and later a hint). For *n* guesses, there are *n* − 1 hints. Recall the following general pseudocode for fencepost loops:

```
plant a post.
for (the length of the fence) {
    attach some wire.
    plant a post.
}
```

This particular problem is an indefinite fencepost using a `while` loop. Let's look at some more specific pseudocode. The "posts" are the prompts for guesses, and the "wires" are the "Incorrect" messages:

```
// specific number guess pseudocode
think of a number.
ask for the player's initial guess.

while (the guess is not the correct number) {
    inform the player that the guess was incorrect,
    and ask for another guess.
}

report the number of guesses needed.
```

This pseudocode leads us to write the following Java program. Note that the computer always picks the value 42 for now:

```
 1  import java.util.*;
 2
 3  public class NumberGuess1 {
 4      public static void main(String[] args) {
 5          Scanner console = new Scanner(System.in);
 6          int number = 42; // always picks the same number
 7
 8          System.out.print("Your guess? ");
 9          int guess = console.nextInt();
10          int numGuesses = 1;
11
12          while (guess != number) {
13              System.out.println("Incorrect.");
14              System.out.print("Your guess? ");
15              guess = console.nextInt();
16              numGuesses++;
17          }
18
19          System.out.println("You got it right in " +
20                              numGuesses + " tries.");
21      }
22  }
```

A `do/while` loop or a `while` loop with priming would also do the trick at this stage, but in the next step of the program, we'll add new features that work better with the loop solution shown here.

We can test our initial program to verify the code we've written so far. A sample dialogue looks like this:

```
Your guess? 65
Incorrect.
Your guess? 12
Incorrect.
Your guess? 34
Incorrect.
Your guess? 42
You got it right in 4 tries.
```

Randomized Version with Hinting

Now that we've tested the code to make sure our main game loops, let's first make the game random by choosing a random value between 00 and 99 inclusive. To do so, we'll create a `Random` object and call its `nextInt` method, specifying the maximum value. Remember that the value passed to `nextInt` should be one more than the desired maximum, so we'll pass `100`:

```
// pick a random number between 00 and 99 inclusive
Random rand = new Random();
int number = rand.nextInt(100);
```

The next important feature our final game should have is the hint given to the player when an incorrect guess is made. The tricky part is figuring out how many digits of the player's guess match the correct number. Since this code is nontrivial to write, let's make a helping method named `matches` that does the work for us. To figure out how many digits match, the `matches` method needs the guess and correct number as parameters, and it will return the number of matching digits. Therefore, its header should look like this:

```
public static int matches(int number, int guess) {
    . . .
}
```

Our algorithm must count the number of matching digits. Either digit from the guess can match either digit from the correct number. Since the digits are somewhat independent—that is, whether the ones digit of the guess matches is independent of whether the tens digit matches—we should use sequential `if` statements rather than an `if`/`else` statement to represent these conditions.

The digit-matching algorithm does have a special case. If the player guesses a number such as 33 that contains two of the same digit, and if that digit is contained in the correct answer (say, 37), it would be misleading to report that two digits match. A better behavior would be to report one matching digit. Because of this case, our algorithm must check whether the guess contains two of the same digit and consider the second digit of the guess a match only if it is different from the first.

Here is the pseudocode for the algorithm:

```
matches = 0.
if (the first digit of the guess matches
        either digit of the correct number) {
    we have found one match.
}

if (the second digit of the guess is different from the first digit,
        AND it matches either digit of the correct number) {
    we have found another match.
}
```

We need to be able to split the correct number and the guess into their two digits so we can compare them. Using the division and remainder operators, we can express the digits of any two-digit number n as n / 10 for the tens digit and n % 10 for the ones digit.

Let's write the statement that tries to match the ones digit of the guess against the correct answer. Since the guess's ones digit can match either of the correct number's digits, we'll use an OR test with the || operator:

```java
int matches = 0;

// check the first digit for a match
if (guess / 10 == number / 10 || guess / 10 == number % 10) {
    matches++;
}
```

Writing the statement that tries to match the tens digit of the guess against the correct answer is slightly trickier, because of the special case described previously. We'll account for this by counting the second digit as a match only if it is unique *and* matches a digit from the correct number:

```java
// check the second digit for a match
if (guess / 10 != guess % 10 &&
        (guess % 10 == number / 10 || guess % 10 == number % 10)) {
    matches++;
}
```

The following version of the program uses the hinting code we've just written. It also adds the randomly chosen number and a brief introduction to the program:

```java
 1  // Two-digit number-guessing game with hinting.
 2  import java.util.*;
 3
 4  public class NumberGuess2 {
 5      public static void main(String[] args) {
 6          System.out.println("Try to guess my two-digit");
 7          System.out.println("number, and I'll tell you how");
 8          System.out.println("many digits from your guess");
 9          System.out.println("appear in my number.");
10          System.out.println();
11
12          Scanner console = new Scanner(System.in);
13
14          // pick a random number from 0 to 99 inclusive
15          Random rand = new Random();
16          int number = rand.nextInt(100);
17
18          // get first guess
19          System.out.print("Your guess? ");
20          int guess = console.nextInt();
21          int numGuesses = 1;
22
23          // give hints until correct guess is reached
24          while (guess != number) {
25              int numMatches = matches(number, guess);
26              System.out.println("Incorrect (hint: " +
27                                  numMatches + " digits match)");
28              System.out.print("Your guess? ");
```

```
29                    guess = console.nextInt();
30                    numGuesses++;
31            }
32
33            System.out.println("You got it right in " +
34                          numGuesses + " tries.");
35      }
36
37      // reports a hint about how many digits from the given
38      // guess match digits from the given correct number
39      public static int matches(int number, int guess) {
40            int numMatches = 0;
41
42            if (guess / 10 == number / 10 ||
43                  guess / 10 == number % 10) {
44                  numMatches++;
45            }
46
47            if (guess / 10 != guess % 10 &&
48                  (guess % 10 == number / 10 ||
49                  guess % 10 == number % 10)) {
50                  numMatches++;
51            }
52
53            return numMatches;
54      }
55 }
```

The following is a sample log of execution:

```
Try to guess my two-digit
number, and I'll tell you how
many digits from your guess
appear in my number.

Your guess? 13
Incorrect (hint: 0 digits match)
Your guess? 26
Incorrect (hint: 0 digits match)
Your guess? 78
Incorrect (hint: 1 digits match)
Your guess? 79
Incorrect (hint: 1 digits match)
Your guess? 70
Incorrect (hint: 2 digits match)
Your guess? 07
You got it right in 6 tries.
```

Final Robust Version

The last major change we'll make to our program is to make it robust against invalid user input. There are two types of bad input we may see:

1. Non-numeric tokens.

2. Numbers outside the range of 0–99.

Let's deal with these cases one at a time. Recall the `getInt` method discussed earlier in this chapter. It repeatedly prompts the user for input until an integer is typed:

```java
// prompts until a valid number is entered
public static int getInt(Scanner console, String prompt) {
    System.out.print(prompt);
    while (!console.hasNextInt()) {
        console.next();
        System.out.println("Not an integer; try again.");
        System.out.print(prompt);
    }
    return console.nextInt();
}
```

We can make use of `getInt` to get an integer between 0 and 99. We'll repeatedly call `getInt` until the integer returned is within the acceptable range:

```java
// prompts until a number in proper range is entered
// post: guess is between 0 and 99
public static int getGuess(Scanner console) {
    int guess = getInt(console, "Your guess? ");
    while (guess < 0 || guess >= 100) {
        System.out.println("Out of range; try again.");
        guess = getInt(console, "Your guess? ");
    }

    return guess;
}
```

Now, whenever we want to read user input in the main program, we'll call `getGuess`. It's useful to separate the input prompting in this way, to make sure that we don't accidentally count invalid inputs as guesses.

The final version of our code is the following:

```java
 1 // Robust two-digit number-guessing game with hinting.
 2 import java.util.*;
 3
 4 public class NumberGuess3 {
 5     public static void main(String[] args) {
 6         giveIntro();
 7         Scanner console = new Scanner(System.in);
 8
 9         // pick a random number from 0 to 99 inclusive
10         Random rand = new Random();
11         int number = rand.nextInt(100);
12
13         // get first guess
14         int guess = getGuess(console);
15         int numGuesses = 1;
16
17         // give hints until correct guess is reached
18         while (guess != number) {
19             int numMatches = matches(number, guess);
20             System.out.println("Incorrect (hint: " +
21                                 numMatches + " digits match)");
22             guess = getGuess(console);
```

```
23                numGuesses++;
24            }
25
26            System.out.println("You got it right in " +
27                                numGuesses + " tries.");
28        }
29
30        public static void giveIntro() {
31            System.out.println("Try to guess my two-digit");
32            System.out.println("number, and I'll tell you how");
33            System.out.println("many digits from your guess");
34            System.out.println("appear in my number.");
35            System.out.println();
36        }
37
38        // returns # of matching digits between the two numbers
39        // pre: number and guess are unique two-digit numbers
40        public static int matches(int number, int guess) {
41            int numMatches = 0;
42
43            if (guess / 10 == number / 10 ||
44                guess / 10 == number % 10) {
45                numMatches++;
46            }
47
48            if (guess / 10 != guess % 10 &&
49                (guess % 10 == number / 10 ||
50                 guess % 10 == number % 10)) {
51                numMatches++;
52            }
53
54            return numMatches;
55        }
56
57        // prompts until a number in proper range is entered
58        // post: guess is between 0 and 99
59        public static int getGuess(Scanner console) {
60            int guess = getInt(console, "Your guess? ");
61            while (guess < 0 || guess >= 100) {
62                System.out.println("Out of range; try again.");
63                guess = getInt(console, "Your guess? ");
64            }
65
66            return guess;
67        }
68
69        // prompts until a valid number is entered
70        public static int getInt(Scanner console, String prompt) {
71            System.out.print(prompt);
72            while (!console.hasNextInt()) {
73                console.next();
74                System.out.println("Not an integer; try again.");
75                System.out.print(prompt);
76            }
77            return console.nextInt();
78        }
79 }
```

Section 5.2: The boolean Type

11. Given the following variable declarations:

```
int x = 27;
int y = -1;
int z = 32;
boolean b = false;
```

what is the value of each of the following Boolean expressions?

- `!b`
- `b || true`
- `(x > y) && (y > z)`
- `(x == y) || (x <= z)`
- `!(x % 2 == 0)`
- `(x % 2 != 0) && b`
- `b && !b`
- `b || !b`
- `(x < y) == b`
- `!(x / 2 == 13) || b || (z * 3 == 96)`
- `(z < x) == false`
- `!((x > 0) && (y < 0))`

12. Write a method called `isVowel` that accepts a character as input and returns `true` if that character is a vowel (a, e, i, o, or u). For extra challenge, make your method case-insensitive.

13. The following code attempts to examine a number and return whether that number is prime (i.e., has no factors other than 1 and itself). A `boolean` flag named `prime` is used. However, the Boolean logic is not implemented correctly, so the method does not always return the correct answer. In what cases does the method report an incorrect answer? How can the code be changed so that it will always return a correct result?

```java
public static boolean isPrime(int n) {
    boolean prime = true;
    for (int i = 2; i < n; i++) {
        if (n % i == 0) {
            prime = false;
        } else {
            prime = true;
        }
    }

    return prime;
}
```

14. The following code attempts to examine a `String` and return whether it contains a given letter. A `boolean` flag named `found` is used. However, the Boolean logic is not implemented correctly, so the method does not always return the correct answer. In what cases does the method report an incorrect answer? How can the code be changed so that it will always return a correct result?

```java
public static boolean contains(String str, char ch) {
    boolean found = false;
    for (int i = 0; i < str.length(); i++) {
        if (str.charAt(i) == ch) {
            found = true;
        } else {
```

```
                found = false;
            }
        }

        return found;
    }
```

15. Using "Boolean Zen," write an improved version of the following method, which returns whether the given `String` starts and ends with the same character:

```
public static boolean startEndSame(String str) {
    if (str.charAt(0) == str.charAt(str.length() - 1)) {
        return true;
    } else {
        return false
    }
}
```

16. Using "Boolean Zen," write an improved version of the following method, which returns whether the given number of cents would require any pennies when making change:

```
public static boolean hasPennies(int cents) {
    boolean nickelsOnly = (cents % 5 == 0);
    if (nickelsOnly == true) {
        return false;
    } else {
        return true;
    }
}
```

17. Consider the following method:

```
public static int mystery(int x, int y) {
    while (x != 0 && y != 0) {
        if (x < y) {
            y -= x;
        } else {
            x -= y;
        }
    }
    return x + y;
}
```

For each of the following calls, indicate what value is returned:

```
mystery(3, 3)
mystery(5, 3)
mystery(2, 6)
mystery(12, 18)
mystery(30, 75)
```

Section 5.3: User Errors

18. The following code is not robust against invalid user input. Describe how to change the code so that it will not proceed until the user has entered a valid age and GPA. (Assume that any `int` is a legal age and that any `double` is a legal GPA.)

```
Scanner console = new Scanner(System.in);
System.out.print("Type your age: ");
int age = console.nextInt();

System.out.print("Type your GPA: ");
double gpa = console.nextDouble();
```

For added challenge, modify the code so that it rejects invalid ages (for example, numbers less than 0) and GPAs (say, numbers less than 0.0 or greater than 4.0).

19. Consider the following code:

```
Scanner console = new Scanner(System.in);
System.out.print("Type something for me! ");

if (console.hasNextInt()) {
    int number = console.nextInt();
    System.out.println("Your IQ is " + number);
} else if (console.hasNext()) {
    String token = console.next();
    System.out.println("Your name is " + token);
}
```

What is the output when the user types the following values?

- Jane

- 56

- 56.2

20. Write a piece of code that prompts the user for a number and then prints a different message depending on whether the number was an integer or a real number. Here are two example dialogues:

```
Type a number: 42.5
You typed the real number 42.5

Type a number: 3
You typed the integer 3
```

21. Write code that prompts for three integers and then averages them and prints the average. Make your code robust against invalid input. (You may want to use the getInt method discussed in this chapter.)

Section 5.4: Indefinite Loop Variations

22. For each of the following do/while loops, how many times will the loop execute its body? Remember that "zero," "infinity," and "unknown" are legal answers. Also, what is the output of the code in each case?

```
int x = 1;
  do {
      System.out.print(x + " ");
      x += 10;
  } while (x < 100);
```
```
• int max = 10;
  do {
      System.out.println("count down: " + max);
      max--;
  } while (max < 10);
```

- ```java
  int x = 250;
  do {
      System.out.println(x);
  } while (x % 3 != 0);
  ```
- ```java
  int x = 100;
  do {
      System.out.println(x);
      x = x / 2;
  } while (x % 2 == 0);
  ```
- ```java
  int x = 2;
  do {
      System.out.print(x + " ");
      x *= x;
  } while (x < 200);
  ```
- ```java
  String word = "a";
  do {
      word = "b" + word + "b";
  } while (word.length() < 10);
  System.out.println(word);
  ```
- ```java
  int x = 100;
  do {
      System.out.println(x / 10);
      x = x / 2;
  } while (x > 0);
  ```
- ```java
  String str = "/\\";
  do {
      str += str;
  } while (str.length() < 10);
  System.out.println(str);
  ```

23. Write a do/while loop that repeatedly prints a message until the user tells the program to stop. The do/while is appropriate because the message should always be printed at least one time, even if the user types n after the first message appears.

```
She sells seashells by the seashore.
Do you want to hear it again? y
She sells seashells by the seashore.
Do you want to hear it again? y
She sells seashells by the seashore.
Do you want to hear it again? n
```

24. Write a do/while loop that repeatedly prints random numbers between 0 and 1000 until a number above 900 is printed. At least one line of output should always be printed, even if the first random number is above 900. Here is a sample execution:

```
Random number: 235
Random number: 15
Random number: 810
Random number: 147
Random number: 915
```

25. Question 5 asked you to write a sentinel loop that read numbers from the console until the user typed −1 and then printed the maximum and minimum numbers entered. Rewrite this code to use a "forever" loop with a break statement. Here is a sample execution:

10. Write a method named `randomWalk` that takes an integer `n` as a parameter and performs `n` steps of a random one-dimensional walk, reporting the maximum position reached during the walk. The random walk should begin at position 0. On each step, you should either increase or decrease the position by 1 (each with equal probability). The output should look like this when the method is passed a parameter value of 7:

```
walking 7 steps
position = 1
position = 0
position = -1
position = 0
position = 1
position = 2
position = 1
max position = 2
```

11. Write a method named `season` that takes as parameters two integers representing a month and day and returns a `String` indicating the season for that month and day. Assume that the month is specified as an integer between 1 and 12 (1 for January, 2 for February, and so on) and that the day of the month is a number between 1 and 31.

    If the date falls between 12/16 and 3/15, you should return `"winter"`. If the date falls between 3/16 and 6/15, you should return `"spring"`. If the date falls between 6/16 and 9/15, you should return `"summer"`. And if the date falls between 9/16 and 12/15, you should return `"fall"`.

12. Write a method named `consecutive` that accepts three integers as parameters and returns `true` if they are three consecutive numbers; that is, if the numbers can be arranged into an order such that, assuming some integer `k`, the parameters' values are `k`, `k+1`, and `k+2`. Your method should return `false` if the integers are not consecutive. Note that order is not significant; your method should return the same result for the same three integers passed in any order.

    For example, the calls `consecutive(1, 2, 3)`, `consecutive(3, 2, 4)`, and `consecutive(-10, -8, -9)` would return `true`. The calls `consecutive(3, 5, 7)`, `consecutive(1, 2, 2)`, and `consecutive(7, 7, 9)` would return `false`.

13. Write a method named `numUnique` that takes three integers as parameters and returns the number of unique integers among the three. For example, the call `numUnique(18, 3, 4)` should return 3 because the parameters have three different values. By contrast, the call `numUnique(6, 7, 6)` should return 2 because there are only two unique numbers among the three parameters: 6 and 7.

Programming Projects

1. (**myCodeMate**) Write an interactive program that reads lines of input from the user and converts each line into "Pig Latin." Pig Latin is English with the initial consonant sound moved to the end of each word, followed by "ay." Words that begin with vowels simply have an "ay" appended. For example, the phrase:

   `The deepest shade of mushroom blue`

   would have the following appearance in Pig Latin:

   `e-Thay eepest-day ade-shay of-ay ushroom-may ue-blay`

   Terminate the program when the user types a blank line.

2. Write a reverse Hangman game where the user thinks of a word and the computer tries to guess the letters in that word. The user tells the computer how many letters the word contains.

3. Write a program that plays a guessing game with the user. The program should generate a random number between 1 and some maximum (such as 100), then prompt the user repeatedly to guess the number. When the user guesses incorrectly, the game should give the user a hint about whether the correct answer is higher or lower than the guess. Once the user guesses correctly, the program should print a message showing the number of guesses required.

   Consider extending this program by making it play multiple games until the user chooses to stop and then printing statistics about the player's total and average number of guesses.

4. Write a program that plays a reverse guessing game with the user. The user thinks of a number between 1 and 10, and the computer repeatedly tries to guess it by guessing random numbers. It's fine for the computer to guess the same random number more than once. At the end of the game, the program reports how many guesses were needed. Here is a sample execution:

```
This program has you, the user, choose a number
between 1 and 10, then I, the computer, will try
my best to guess it.

Is it 8? (y/n) n
Is it 7? (y/n) n
Is it 5? (y/n) n
Is it 1? (y/n) n
Is it 8? (y/n) n
Is it 1? (y/n) n
Is it 9? (y/n) y


I got your number of 9 correct in 7 guesses.
```

   For added challenge, consider having the user hint to the computer whether the correct number is higher or lower than the computer's guess. The computer should adjust its range of random guesses based on the hint.

5. Write a game that plays many rounds of Rock Paper Scissors. The user and computer will each choose between three items: rock (defeats scissors, but loses to paper), paper (defeats rock, but loses to scissors), and scissors (defeats paper, but loses to rock). If the player and computer choose the same item, the game is a tie.

   An extension of this program would be to write different algorithmic strategies for choosing the best item. Should the computer pick randomly? Should it always pick a particular item or a repeating pattern of items? Should it count the number of times the opponent chooses various items and base its strategy on this history?

Chapter 6

File Processing

Introduction

In Chapter 4 we discussed how to construct a Scanner object to read input from the console. Now we will look at how to construct Scanner objects to read input from files. The idea is fairly straightforward, but Java does not make it easy to read from input files. This is unfortunate because many interesting problems can be formulated as file-processing tasks. Many introductory computer science classes have abandoned file processing altogether or the topic has moved into the second course because it is considered too advanced for novices.

There is nothing intrinsically complex about file processing, but Java was not designed for it and Sun has not been particularly eager to provide a simple solution. Sun did, however, introduce the Scanner class as a way to simplify some of the details associated with reading files. The result is that file reading is still awkward in Java, but at least the level of detail is manageable.

Before we start writing file-processing programs, we have to explore some issues related to Java exceptions. Remember that exceptions are errors that halt the execution of a program. In the case of file processing, trying to open a file that doesn't exist or trying to read beyond the end of a file would generate an exception.

6.1 File-Reading Basics

In this section we'll look at the most basic issues related to file processing. What are files and why do we care about them? What are the most basic techniques for reading files in a Java program? Once you've mastered these basics, we'll move on to a more detailed discussion of the different techniques you can use for processing files.

Data, Data Everywhere

We seem to have a fascination with data. When the field of Statistics emerged in the nineteenth century, there was an explosion of interest in gathering and interpreting large amounts of data. Mark Twain reported that the British statesman Benjamin Disraeli complained to him, "There are three kinds of lies: lies, damn lies, and statistics."

The advent of the internet has only added fuel to the fire. Today, every person with an internet connection has access to a vast array of databases containing information about every facet of our existence. Here are just a few examples:

- Go to http://www.landmark-project.com and click on the link for "Raw Data," and you will find data files about earthquakes, air pollution, baseball, labor, crime, financial markets, US history, geography, weather, national parks, a "world values survey," and more.

- At http://www.gutenberg.org you'll find thousands of online books, including the complete works of Shakespeare and works by Sir Arthur Conan Doyle, Jane Austen, H.G. Wells, James Joyce, Albert Einstein, Mark Twain, Lewis Carroll, T.S. Eliot, Edgar Allan Poe, and many others.

- A wealth of genomic data is available on the Web from sites like http://www.gdb.org and http://www.ncbi.nih.gov. Biologists have decided that the vast quantities of data about the human genome and the genomes of other organisms should be publicly available to everyone to study.

- Many popular web sites, such as the Internet Movie Database, make their data available for download as simple data files (see http://www.imdb.com/interface).

- The US government produces reams of statistical data. The web site http://www.fedstats.gov provides a lengthy list of available downloads, including maps and statistics on employment, climate, manufacturing, demographics, health, crime, and so on.

Files and File Objects

When you store data on your own computer, you store it in a *file*.

> **File**
> A collection of information stored on a computer.

Every file has a name. For example, if you were to download the text of *Hamlet* from the Gutenberg site, you might store it on your computer in a file called

Did You Know?

Origin of Data Processing

The field of data processing predates computers by over half a century. It is often said that necessity is the mother of invention, and the emergence of data processing is a good example of this principle. The crisis that spawned the industry came from a requirement in Article 1, Section 2 of the US Constitution, which indicates that population will be used to decide how many representatives each state will get in the House of Representatives. To make such a calculation you need to know the population numbers, so the Constitution says, "The actual Enumeration shall be made within three Years after the first Meeting of the Congress of the United States, and within every subsequent Term of ten Years, in such Manner as they shall by Law direct."

The first census was completed relatively quickly in 1790. Since then, every 10 years the US government has had to perform another complete census of the population. This process became more and more difficult as the population of the country grew larger. By 1880 the government found that with old-fashioned hand-counting techniques, it barely completed the census within the 10 years allotted to it. So, the government announced a competition for inventors to propose machines that could be used to speed up the process.

Herman Hollerith won the competition with a system involving punched cards. Clerks punched over 62 million cards, which were then counted by 100 counting machines. This allowed the tabulation to be completed in less than half the time taken to hand-count the 1880 results, even though the population had increased by 25 percent.

Hollerith struggled for years to turn his invention into a commercial success. His biggest problem initially was that he had just one customer: the US government. Eventually he found other customers, and the company that he founded merged with competitors and grew into the company we now know as International Business Machines Corporation, or IBM.

We think of IBM as a computer company, but it sold a wide variety of data-processing equipment involving Hollerith cards long before computers became popular. Later, when it entered the computer field, IBM used Hollerith cards for storing programs and data. These cards were still being used when one of this book's authors took his freshman computer programming class in 1978.

`hamlet.txt`. A file name often ends with a special suffix that indicates the kind of data it contains or the format in which it has been stored. This suffix is known as a *file extension*. Table 6.1 lists some common file extensions.

TABLE 6.1   Common File Extensions

Extension	Description
.txt	text file
.dat	data file
.out	output file
.java	Java source code file
.class	compiled Java bytecode file
.doc	Microsoft Word file
.xls	Microsoft Excel file
.pdf	Adobe Portable Document File
.mp3	audio file
.jpg	image file
.exe	executable file

To access a file from inside a Java program, you need to construct an internal object that will represent the file. The Java class libraries include a class called `File` that performs this duty.

You construct a `File` object by passing in the name of a file, as in:

```
File f = new File("hamlet.txt");
```

Once you've constructed the object, you can call a number of methods to manipulate the file. For example, the following program calls a method that determines whether a file exists, whether it can be read, what its length is (i.e., how many characters are in the file), and what its absolute path is (i.e., where it is stored on the computer):

```
 1 // Report some basic information about a file.
 2
 3 import java.io.*; // for File
 4
 5 public class FileInfo {
 6     public static void main(String[] args) {
 7         File f = new File("hamlet.txt");
 8         System.out.println("exists returns " + f.exists());
 9         System.out.println("canRead returns " + f.canRead());
10         System.out.println("length returns " + f.length());
11         System.out.println("getAbsolutePath returns "
12                         + f.getAbsolutePath());
13     }
14 }
```

Notice that it includes an import from the package `java.io`, because the `File` class is part of that package. The term "io" (or I/O) is jargon used by computer

TABLE 6.2 Useful Methods of `File` Objects

Method	Description
`delete()`	deletes the given file
`exists()`	whether or not this file exists on the system
`getAbsolutePath()`	the full path where this file is located
`getName()`	the name of this file as a `String`, without any path attached
`isDirectory()`	whether this file represents a directory/folder on the system
`isFile()`	whether this file represents a file (non-folder) on the system
`length()`	the number of characters in this file
`mkdirs()`	creates the directory represented by this file, if it does not exist
`renameTo(file)`	changes this file's name to be the given file's name

science professionals to mean "input/output." Assuming you have stored the file
`hamlet.txt` in the same directory as the program, you'll get output like the following when you run the program:

```
exists returns true
canRead returns true
length returns 191734
getAbsolutePath returns C:\data\hamlet.txt
```

Table 6.2 lists some useful methods for `File` objects.

Reading a File with a Scanner

The `Scanner` class that we have been using since Chapter 3 is flexible in that
`Scanner` objects can be attached to many different kinds of input (see Figure 6.1).
You can think of a `Scanner` object as being like a faucet that you can attach to a pipe

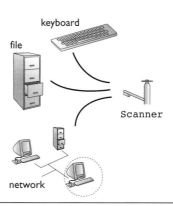

Figure 6.1 Scanners can be connected to many input sources.

that has water flowing through it. The water can come from various sources. For example, in a house you'd attach a faucet to a pipe carrying water from the city or from a well, but you'll also see faucets in places like mobile homes and airplanes, where the source of water is different.

Thus far, we have been constructing `Scanner` objects by passing `System.in` to the `Scanner` constructor:

```
Scanner console = new Scanner(System.in);
```

This instructs the computer to construct a `Scanner` that reads from the console (i.e., pausing for input from the user). Instead of passing `System.in` to the constructor, you can pass a `File` object:

```
File f = new File("hamlet.txt");
Scanner input = new Scanner(f);
```

In this case the variable `f` is not necessary, so we can shorten this to:

```
Scanner input = new Scanner(new File("hamlet.txt"));
```

This line of code, or something like it, will appear in all of your file-processing programs. When we were reading from the console window, we called our `Scanner` variable `console`. This variable is called `input`, to make it clear that it will read from an input file. Of course, you can name the variable anything you want, as long as you are consistent in how you refer to it.

Unfortunately, when you try to compile a program that constructs a `Scanner` in this manner, you'll run into a snag. Say you write a `main` method that begins by opening a `Scanner` as follows:

```
// flawed method--does not compile
public static void main(String[] args) {
    Scanner input = new Scanner(new File("hamlet.txt"));
    . . .
}
```

This program does not compile. It produces a message like the following:

```
CountWords.java:8:
unreported exception java.io.FileNotFoundException;
must be caught or declared to be thrown
        Scanner input = new Scanner(new File( hamlet.txt ));
                    ^
1 error
```

The issue involves exceptions, which were first introduced in Chapter 3. Remember that exceptions are errors that prevent a program from continuing normal execution. In this case the compiler is worried that it might not be able to find a file called `hamlet.txt`. What is it supposed to do if that happens? It won't have a file to read from, so it won't have any way to continue executing the rest of the code.

If the program is unable to locate the specified input file, it will generate an error by throwing what is known as a `FileNotFoundException`. This particular exception is known as a *checked exception.*

> **Checked Exception**
>
> An exception that *must* be caught or specifically declared in the header of the method that might generate it.

Because `FileNotFoundException` is a checked exception, you can't just ignore it. Java provides a construct known as the `try/catch` statement for handling such errors. Later in this chapter you will see how to use this construct, but for now you can use a less sophisticated but simpler approach. Java allows you to avoid handling this error as long as you clearly indicate the fact that you aren't handling it. All you have to do is include a `throws` clause in the header for the `main` method to clearly state the fact that your `main` method might generate this exception.

> **`throws` Clause**
>
> A declaration that a method will not attempt to handle a particular type of exception.

Here's how to modify the header for the `main` method to include a `throws` clause indicating that it can throw a `FileNotFoundException`:

```java
public static void main(String[] args)
        throws FileNotFoundException {
    Scanner input = new Scanner(new File("hamlet.txt"));
    . . .
}
```

With the `throws` clause, the line becomes so long that we have to break it into two lines to allow it to fit in the margins of the textbook. On your own computer, you will probably include all of it on a single line.

With this modification, the program compiles. Once you've constructed the `Scanner` so that it reads from the file, you can manipulate it like any other `Scanner`. Of course, while you should always prompt before reading from the console to give the user an indication of what kind of data you want, when reading from a file you don't need to prompt because the data is already there, stored in the file. For example, you could write a program like the following to count the number of words in *Hamlet*:

```java
1 // Counts the number of words in Hamlet.
2
3 import java.io.*;
4 import java.util.*;
5
6 public class CountWords {
7     public static void main(String[] args)
8             throws FileNotFoundException {
```

```
 9              Scanner input = new Scanner(new File("hamlet.txt"));
10              int count = 0;
11              while (input.hasNext()) {
12                  String word = input.next();
13                  count++;
14              }
15              System.out.println("total words = " + count);
16          }
17 }
```

Note that you have to include an import from `java.util` for the `Scanner` class and an import from `java.io` for the `File` class. The program generates the following output:

```
total words = 31956
```

Common Programming Error

Reading Beyond the End of a File

As you learn how to process input files, you are likely to accidentally attempt to read data when there is no data left to read. For example, the `CountWords` program we just looked at uses a `while` loop to keep reading words from the file as long as there are still words left to read. What if after the `while` loop you included an extra statement to read a word:

```
while (input.hasNext()) {
    String word = input.next();
    count++;
}
String extra = input.next(); // illegal, no more input
```

This new line of code causes the computer to try to read a word when there is no word to read. Java throws an exception when this occurs:

```
Exception in thread "main" java.util.NoSuchElementException
        at java.util.Scanner.throwFor(Scanner.java:817)
        at java.util.Scanner.next(Scanner.java:1317)
        at CountWords.main(CountWords.java:15)
```

As usual, the most important information appears at the end of this list of line numbers. The exception is indicating that the error occurred in line 15 of `CountWords`. The other line numbers come from the `Scanner` class and aren't helpful.

If you find yourself getting a `NoSuchElementException`, it is probably because you have somehow attempted to read beyond the end of the input. The `Scanner` is saying, "You've asked me for some data, but I don't have any such value to give you."

Common Programming Error

Forgetting "new File"

Suppose that instead of constructing a `Scanner` in this way:

```
Scanner input = new Scanner(new File("hamlet.txt"));
```

you accidentally forget to include the `File` object and instead write this line of code:

```
Scanner input = new Scanner("hamlet.txt"); // not right
```

This line of code may seem correct because it mentions the name of the file, but it won't work because it doesn't include the `File` object.

Normally, when you make a mistake like this Java warns you that you have done something illegal. In this case, however, you'll get no warning from Java. This is because, as you'll see later in this chapter, it is possible to construct a `Scanner` from a `String`, in which case Java reads from the `String` itself.

If you were to make this mistake in the `CountWords` program, you would get the following output:

```
total words = 1
```

The program would report just one word because the `String "hamlet.txt"` looks like a single word to the `Scanner`. So, whenever you construct a `Scanner` that is supposed to read from an input file, make sure that you include the call on `new File` to construct an appropriate `File` object.

6.2 Details of Token-Based Processing

Now that we've introduced some of the basic issues involved in reading an input file, let's explore reading from a file in more detail. One way to process a file is token by token.

> **Token-Based Processing**
>
> Processing input token by token (i.e., one word at a time or one number at a time).

Remember from Chapter 3 that the primary token-reading methods for the `Scanner` class are:

- `nextInt` for reading an `int` value
- `nextDouble` for reading a `double` value
- `next` for reading the next token as a `String`

For example, you might want to create a file called `numbers.dat` with the following content:

```
308.2 14.9 7.4
2.8


3.9 4.7 -15.4
2.8
```

You can create such a file with an editor like Notepad on a Windows machine or TextEdit on a Macintosh. Then you might write a program that processes this input file and produces some kind of report. For example, the following program reads the first five numbers from the file and reports their sum:

```
 1 // Program that reads five numbers and reports their sum.
 2
 3 import java.io.*;
 4 import java.util.*;
 5
 6 public class ShowSum1 {
 7     public static void main(String[] args)
 8             throws FileNotFoundException {
 9         Scanner input = new Scanner(new File("numbers.dat"));
10
11         double sum = 0.0;
12         for (int i = 1; i <= 5; i++) {
13             double next = input.nextDouble();
14             System.out.println("number " + i + " = " + next);
15             sum += next;
16         }
17         System.out.println("Sum = " + sum);
18     }
19 }
```

This is a variation of the cumulative sum code from Chapter 4. Remember that you need a `throws` clause in the header for `main` because of the potential `FileNotFoundException`. The program produces the following output:

```
number 1 = 308.2
number 2 = 14.9
number 3 = 7.4
number 4 = 2.8
number 5 = 3.9
Sum = 337.19999999999993
```

Notice that the numbers are not reported as adding up to 337.2. This is another example of a roundoff error (also described in Chapter 4).

The preceding program reads exactly five numbers from the file. More typically, you'll read as long as there are more numbers to read using a `while` loop. Remember that the `Scanner` class includes a series of `hasNext` methods that parallel the various `next` methods. In this case, `nextDouble` is being used to read a value of type `double`, so you can use `hasNextDouble` to test whether there is such a value to read:

```
1 // Reads an input file of numbers and prints the numbers and
2 // their sum.
3
4 import java.io.*;
```

```
 5 import java.util.*;
 6
 7 public class ShowSum2 {
 8     public static void main(String[] args)
 9             throws FileNotFoundException {
10         Scanner input = new Scanner(new File("numbers.dat"));
11
12         double sum = 0.0;
13         int count = 0;
14         while (input.hasNextDouble()) {
15             double next = input.nextDouble();
16             count++;
17             System.out.println("number " + count + " = "
18                                     + next);
19             sum += next;
20         }
21         System.out.println("Sum = " + sum);
22     }
23 }
```

This program would work on an input file with any number of numbers, `numbers.dat` happens to contain eight. This version of the program produces the following output:

```
number 1 = 308.2
number 2 = 14.9
number 3 = 7.4
number 4 = 2.8
number 5 = 3.9
number 6 = 4.7
number 7 = -15.4
number 8 = 2.8
Sum = 329.29999999999995
```

Structure of Files and Consuming Input

We think of text as being two-dimensional, like a sheet of paper, but from the computer's point of view, each file is just a one-dimensional sequence of characters. For example, consider the file `numbers.dat` used in the last section:

```
308.2 14.9 7.4
2.8


3.9 4.7 -15.4
2.8
```

We think of this as a six-line file with text going across and down and two blank lines in the middle. However, the computer views the file differently. When you typed the text in this file, you hit the Enter key to go to a new line. This inserts special "new line" characters in the file. You know that the escape sequence \n can be used to produce a newline character for output, so you can annotate the file with \n characters to indicate the end of each line:

```
308.2 14.9 7.4\n
2.8\n
\n
\n
```

Common Programming Error

Reading the Wrong Kind of Token

It's easy to write code that accidentally reads the wrong kind of data. For example, the ShowSum1 program always reads exactly five doubles from the input file numbers.dat. But suppose that the input file has some extraneous text in it, as in:

```
308.2 14.9 7.4
hello
2.8


3.9 4.7 −15.4
2.8
```

The first line of the file contains three numbers that the program will read properly. But when it attempts to read a fourth number, it will find that the next token in the file is the text "hello". This token cannot be interpreted as a double, so the program generates an exception:

```
number 1 = 308.2
number 2 = 14.9
number 3 = 7.4
Exception in thread "main" java.util.InputMismatchException
        at java.util.Scanner.throwFor(Scanner.java:819)
        at java.util.Scanner.next(Scanner.java:1431)
        at java.util.Scanner.nextDouble(Scanner.java:2335)
        at ShowSum1.main(ShowSum1.java:13)
```

Once again, the useful line number appears at the bottom of this list. The last line indicates that the exception occurred in line 13 of the ShowSum1 class. The other line numbers are from the Scanner class and aren't helpful.

You saw earlier that when you attempt to read beyond the end of a file, the Scanner throws a NoSuchElementException. Here, it throws an InputMismatchException. By paying attention to the kind of exception the Scanner throws, you can get better feedback about what the problem is.

```
3.9 4.7 −15.4\n
2.8\n
```

Once you've marked the end of each line, you no longer need to use a two-dimensional representation. You can collapse this text to a one-dimensional sequence of characters:

```
308.2 14.9 7.4\n2.8\n\n\n3.9 4.7 −15.4\n2.8\n
```

From this one-dimensional sequence, you can reconstruct the various lines of the file. This is how the computer views the file: as a one-dimensional sequence of characters including special characters that represent "new line". On some systems, including Windows machines, there are two different "new line" characters, but we'll

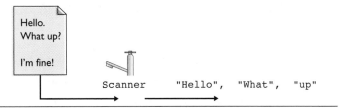

Figure 6.2 Scanners treat files as one-dimensional strings of characters and convert their contents into a series of whitespace-separated tokens.

use just \n here—objects like Scanner handle these differences for you, so you can generally ignore them. (For those who are interested, the brief explanation is that Windows machines end each line with a \r followed by a \n.)

When processing a file, the Scanner object keeps track of the current position in the file. You can think of this as a *cursor* or pointer into the file.

Input Cursor

A pointer to the current position in an input file.

When a Scanner object is first constructed, the cursor points to the beginning of the file. But as you perform various next operations, the cursor moves forward. The ShowSum2 program from the last section processes the file through a series of calls on nextDouble. Let's take a moment to examine in detail how that works. Again, when the Scanner is first constructed, the input cursor will be positioned at the beginning of the file (indicated with an up-arrow pointing at the first character):

```
308.2 14.9 7.4\n2.8\n\n\n3.9 4.7 -15.4\n2.8\n
↑
input
cursor
```

After the first call on nextDouble the cursor will be positioned in the middle of the first line, after the token "308.2":

We refer to this process as *consuming input*.

```
308.2 14.9 7.4\n2.8\n\n\n3.9 4.7 -15.4\n2.8\n
     ↑
     input
     cursor
```

Consuming Input

Moving the input cursor forward past some input.

The first call on nextDouble consumes the text "308.2" from the input file and leaves the input cursor positioned at the first character after this token. Notice that this leaves the input cursor positioned at a space. When the second call is made on nextDouble, the Scanner first skips past this space to get to the next token, then consumes the text "14.9" and leaves the cursor positioned at the space that follows it:

```
308.2 14.9 7.4\n2.8\n\n\n3.9 4.7 -15.4\n2.8\n
         ↑
         input
         cursor
```

The third call on `nextDouble` skips that space and consumes the text "7.4":

```
308.2 14.9 7.4\n2.8\n\n\n3.9 4.7 -15.4\n2.8\n
             ↑
             input
             cursor
```

At this point, the input cursor is positioned at the newline character at the end of the first line of input. The fourth call on `nextDouble` skips past this newline character and consumes the text "2.8":

```
308.2 14.9 7.4\n2.8\n\n\n3.9 4.7 -15.4\n2.8\n
                  ↑
                  input
                  cursor
```

Notice that in skipping past the first newline character, the input cursor has moved into data stored on the second line of input. At this point, the input cursor is positioned at the end of the second line of input, because it has consumed the "2.8" token. When a fifth call is made on `nextDouble`, the `Scanner` finds two newline characters in a row. This isn't a problem for the `Scanner`, because it simply skips past any leading whitespace characters (spaces, tabs, newline characters) until it finds an actual token. So, it skips both of these newline characters and consumes the text "3.9":

```
308.2 14.9 7.4\n2.8\n\n\n3.9 4.7 -15.4\n2.8\n
                          ↑
                          input
                          cursor
```

At this point the input cursor is positioned in the middle of the fifth line of input (the third and fourth lines were blank). The program continues reading in this manner, consuming the remaining three numbers in the input file. After it reads the final token, "2.8", the input cursor is positioned at the newline character at the end of the file:

```
308.2 14.9 7.4\n2.8\n\n\n3.9 4.7 -15.4\n2.8\n
                                          ↑
                                          input
                                          cursor
```

If you attempted to call `nextDouble` again, it would throw a `NoSuchElementException` because there are no more tokens left to process. But remember that the `ShowSum2` program has a `while` loop that calls `hasNextDouble` before calling `nextDouble`. When you call methods like `hasNextDouble`, the `Scanner` looks ahead in the file to see whether there is a next token and whether it can be interpreted as being of the specified type (in this case, a `double`). So, the `ShowSum2` program will continue executing until it reaches the end of the file or until it encounters a token that cannot be interpreted as a `double`.

When the input cursor reaches the newline at the end of the file, the `Scanner` notices that there are no more `double` values to read and returns `false` when `hasNextDouble` is called. That stops the `while` loop from executing and causes the program to exit.

`Scanner` objects are designed for file processing in a forward manner. They provide a great deal of flexibility for looking ahead in an input file, but no support for reading the input backwards. There are no "previous" methods, and there's no mechanism for resetting a `Scanner` back to the beginning of the input.

Scanner Parameters

Novices are sometimes surprised that the input cursor for a `Scanner` does not reset to the beginning of the file when it is passed as a parameter to a method. For example, consider the following variation of the `ShowSum1` program. It has a method that takes a `Scanner` as input and an integer specifying how many numbers to process:

```
 1 // Demonstrates a Scanner as a parameter to a method that
 2 // can consume an arbitrary number of tokens.
 3
 4 import java.io.*;
 5 import java.util.*;
 6
 7 public class ShowSum3 {
 8     public static void main(String[] args)
 9             throws FileNotFoundException {
10         Scanner input = new Scanner(new File("numbers.dat"));
11         processTokens(input, 2);
12         processTokens(input, 3);
13         processTokens(input, 2);
14     }
15
16     public static void processTokens(Scanner input, int n) {
17         double sum = 0.0;
18         for (int i = 1; i <= n; i++) {
19             double next = input.nextDouble();
20             System.out.println("number " + i + " = " + next);
21             sum += next;
22         }
23         System.out.println("Sum = " + sum);
24         System.out.println();
25     }
26 }
```

The `main` method creates a `Scanner` object that is tied to the `numbers.dat` file. It then calls the `processTokens` method several times, indicating the number of tokens to process. The first call instructs the method to process two tokens. It operates on the first two tokens of the file, generating the following output:

```
number 1 = 308.2
number 2 = 14.9
Sum = 323.09999999999997
```

The second call on the method indicates that three tokens are to be processed. Some people expect the method to process the first three tokens of the file, but that's not what happens. Remember that the `Scanner` keeps track of where the input cursor is positioned. After the first call on the method, the input cursor is positioned beyond the first two tokens. So, the second call on the method processes the next three tokens from the file, producing this output:

```
number 1 = 7.4
number 2 = 2.8
number 3 = 3.9
Sum = 14.1
```

The final call on the method asks the `Scanner` to process the next two tokens from the file, so it ends up processing the sixth and seventh numbers from the file:

```
number 1 = 4.7
number 2 = -15.4
Sum = -10.7
```

The program then terminates, never having processed the eighth number in the file.

The key point to remember is that a `Scanner` keeps track of the position of the input cursor, so you can process an input file piece by piece in a very flexible manner. Even when the `Scanner` is passed as a parameter to a method, it remembers how much of the input file has been processed so far.

Paths and Directories

Any given file will be stored in a particular *folder* or *directory*. Directories are organized in a hierarchy, starting from a root directory at the top. For example, most Windows machines have a disk drive known as `c:`. At the top level of this drive is the *root* directory, which we can describe as `c:\`. This root directory will contain various top-level directories. Each top-level directory can have subdirectories, each subdirectory can have subdirectories, and so on. Every file is stored in one of these directories. The description of how to get from the top-level directory to the particular directory that stores a file is known as the *path* of the file.

> **File Path**
>
> A description of a file's location on a computer, starting with a drive and including the path from the root directory to the directory where the file is stored.

We read the path information from left to right. For example, if the path to a file is `C:\school\data\hamlet.txt`, we know that the file is on the `c:` drive in a folder called `school` and in a subfolder called `data`.

In the previous section the file name `numbers.dat` was used. When Java finds you using a simple name like that (also called a relative file path), it looks in the *current directory* to find the file.

> **Current Directory (a.k.a. Working Directory)**
>
> The directory that Java uses as the default when a simple file name is used.

The default directory varies depending upon what Java environment you are using. In most environments, the current directory is the directory in which your program appears. This is the behavior we'll assume for the examples in this textbook.

You can also use a fully *qualified* file name (sometimes called an absolute file path). However, this approach works well only when you know exactly where your file is going to be stored on your system. For example, if you are on a Windows machine and you have stored the file in the `c:\data` directory, you could use a file name like this:

```
Scanner input = new Scanner(new File("C:/data/numbers.dat"));
```

Notice that the path is written with forward slash characters rather than backslash characters. On Windows you would normally use a backslash, but Java allows you to use a forward slash instead. If you wanted to use a backslash, you would have to use a \\ escape sequence. Most programmers use the simpler approach of using forward slash characters because Java does the appropriate translation on Windows machines.

Sometimes rather than writing a file's path name in the code yourself, you'll ask the user for a file name. For example, here is a variation of `ShowSum2` that prompts the user for the file name:

```java
 1 // Variation of ShowSum2 that prompts for a file name.
 2
 3 import java.io.*;
 4 import java.util.*;
 5
 6 public class ShowSum4 {
 7     public static void main(String[] args)
 8             throws FileNotFoundException {
 9         System.out.println("This program will add a series");
10         System.out.println("of numbers from a file.");
11         System.out.println();
12
13         Scanner console = new Scanner(System.in);
14         System.out.print("What is the file name? ");
15         String name = console.nextLine();
16         Scanner input = new Scanner(new File(name));
17         System.out.println();
18
19         double sum = 0.0;
20         int count = 0;
21         while (input.hasNextDouble()) {
22             double next = input.nextDouble();
23             count++;
24             System.out.println("number " + count + " = "
25                                 + next);
26             sum += next;
27         }
28         System.out.println("Sum = " + sum);
29     }
30 }
```

Notice that the program has two different `Scanner` objects: one for reading from the console and one for reading from the file. We read the file name using a call on `nextLine` to read an entire line of input from the user. This allows the user to type in file names that have spaces in them. Notice that we still need the `throws FileNotFoundException` in the header for `main` because even though we are prompting the user for a file name, there won't necessarily be a file of that name.

If we have this program read from the file `numbers.dat` used earlier, it will execute like this:

```
This program will add a series
of numbers from a file.

What is the file name? numbers.dat

number 1 = 308.2
number 2 = 14.9
number 3 = 7.4
number 4 = 2.8
number 5 = 3.9
number 6 = 4.7
number 7 = -15.4
number 8 = 2.8
Sum = 329.29999999999995
```

The user also has the option of specifying a full file path, as in:

```
This program will add a series
of numbers from a file.

What is the file name? C:\data\numbers.dat

number 1 = 308.2
number 2 = 14.9
number 3 = 7.4
number 4 = 2.8
number 5 = 3.9
number 6 = 4.7
number 7 = -15.4
number 8 = 2.8
Sum = 329.29999999999995
```

Notice that the user doesn't have to type two backslashes to get a single backslash. The `Scanner` object that reads the user's input is able to read it without escape sequences.

A More Complex Input File

Suppose you have an input file that contains information about how many hours each employee of a company has worked. For example, it might look like the following:

```
Erica 7.5 8.5 10.25 8 8.5
Erin 10.5 11.5 12 11 10.75
```

```
Simone 8 8 8
Ryan 6.5 8 9.25 8
Kendall 2.5 3
```

The idea is that you have a list of hours worked by each employee and you want to find out the total hours worked by each individual. You can construct a `Scanner` object linked to this file to solve this task. As you start writing more complex file-processing programs, you will want to divide the program into methods to break up the code into logical subtasks. In this case, you can open the file in `main` and write a separate method to process the file.

Most file processing will involve `while` loops, because you won't know in advance how much data the file contains. Different tests will be required depending upon the particular file being processed, but they will almost all be calls on the various `hasNext` methods of the `Scanner` class. You basically want to say, "While you have more data for me to process, let's keep reading."

In this case you have a series of input lines that each begin with a name. For this program you can assume that names are simple, with no spaces in the middle. That means you can read them with a call on the `next` method. As a result, the `while` loop test involves seeing if there is another name in the input file:

```
while (input.hasNext()) {
    process next person.
}
```

So, how do you process each person? You have to read that person's name and then read that person's list of hours. If you look at the sample input file, you will see that the list of hours is not always the same length. For example, some employees might have worked on five different days while others worked only two or three days. This is a common occurrence in input files, and you can deal with it using a nested loop. The outer loop will handle one person at a time and the inner loop will handle one number at a time. The task is a fairly straightforward cumulative sum:

```
double sum = 0.0;
while (input.hasNextDouble()) {
    sum += input.nextDouble();
}
```

Putting all this together, you end up with the following complete program:

```
 1 // This program reads an input file of hours worked by various
 2 // employees and reports the total hours worked by each.
 3
 4 import java.io.*;
 5 import java.util.*;
 6
 7 public class HoursWorked {
 8     public static void main(String[] args)
 9             throws FileNotFoundException {
10         Scanner input = new Scanner(new File("hours.dat"));
11         process(input);
12     }
13
```

```
14      public static void process(Scanner input) {
15          while (input.hasNext()) {
16              String name = input.next();
17              double sum = 0.0;
18              while (input.hasNextDouble()) {
19                  sum += input.nextDouble();
20              }
21              System.out.println("Total hours worked by " + name
22                              + " = " + sum);
23          }
24      }
25 }
```

Notice that you need the `throws FileNotFoundException` in the header for `main`. You don't need to include this in the `process` method because the code to open the file appears in method `main`.

If you put the input into a file called `hours.dat` and execute the program, you get the following result:

```
Total hours worked by Erica = 42.75
Total hours worked by Erin = 55.75
Total hours worked by Simone = 24.0
Total hours worked by Ryan = 31.75
Total hours worked by Kendall = 5.5
```

6.3 Line-Based Processing

So far we have been looking at programs that process input token by token. However, you'll often find yourself working with input files that are line-based, where each line of input represents a different case to be handled separately from the rest. This leads to a second style of file processing, called *line-based processing*.

> **Line-Based Processing**
>
> Processing input line by line (i.e., reading in entire lines of input at a time).

Most file processing involves a combination of line- and token-based styles, and the `Scanner` class is flexible enough to allow you to write programs that include both styles of processing. For line-based processing, you'll use the `nextLine` and `hasNextLine` methods of the `Scanner` object. For example, here is a program that echos an input file in uppercase:

```
1 // Reads a file and echos it in uppercase.
2
3 import java.io.*;
4 import java.util.*;
5
6 public class EchoUppercase {
7     public static void main(String[] args)
8             throws FileNotFoundException {
```

```
 9          Scanner input = new Scanner(new File("poem.txt"));
10          while (input.hasNextLine()) {
11              String text = input.nextLine();
12              System.out.println(text.toUpperCase());
13          }
14      }
15 }
```

This loop reads the input line by line until it runs out of lines to process, printing each line in uppercase. It reads from a file called `poem.txt`. Given this input file:

```
My candle burns at both ends
It will not last the night;
But ah, my foes, and oh, my friends -
It gives a lovely light.

    --Edna St. Vincent Millay
```

it produces the following output:

```
MY CANDLE BURNS AT BOTH ENDS
IT WILL NOT LAST THE NIGHT;
BUT AH, MY FOES, AND OH, MY FRIENDS -
IT GIVES A LOVELY LIGHT.

    --EDNA ST. VINCENT MILLAY
```

Notice that you could not have accomplished the same task with token-based processing. Here, the line breaks are significant because they are part of the poem. Also, when you read a file token by token, you lose the spacing within the line because the `Scanner` skips any leading whitespace when it reads a token. The final line of this input file is indented to make it clear that it is the name of the author and not part of the poem. That spacing would be lost if the file was read as a series of tokens.

String Scanners and Line/Token Combinations

In the last section we looked at a program called `HoursWorked` that processed the following data file:

```
Erica 7.5 8.5 10.25 8 8.5
Erin 10.5 11.5 12 11 10.75
Simone 8 8 8
Ryan 6.5 8 9.25 8
Kendall 2.5 3
```

The data is line-oriented, with each employee's information on a different line of input, but this aspect of the data wasn't incorporated into the program. The program processed the file in a token-based manner, but that won't always work. For example, consider a slight variation in the data where each line of input begins with an employee ID and a name rather than just a name:

```
101 Erica 7.5 8.5 10.25 8 8.5
783 Erin 10.5 11.5 12 11 10.75
```

```
114 Simone 8 8 8
238 Ryan 6.5 8 9.25 8
156 Kendall 2.5 3
```

This seems like a fairly simple change that shouldn't require major changes to the code. Recall that the program has a method to process the file:

```
public static void process(Scanner input) {
    while (input.hasNext()) {
        String name = input.next();
        double sum = 0.0;
        while (input.hasNextDouble()) {
            sum += input.nextDouble();
        }
        System.out.println("Total hours worked by " + name +
                           " = " + sum);
    }
}
```

Suppose you add a line of code to read the employee ID and modify the `println` to report it:

```
public static void process(Scanner input) {
    while (input.hasNext()) {
        int id = input.nextInt();
        String name = input.next();
        double sum = 0.0;
        while (input.hasNextDouble()) {
            sum += input.nextDouble();
        }
        System.out.println("Total hours worked by " + name +
                           " (id#" + id + ") = " + sum);
    }
}
```

When you run this version of the program on the new input file, you'll get one line of output and then an exception will be thrown:

```
Total hours worked by Erica (id#101) = 825.75
Exception in thread "main" java.util.InputMismatchException
        at java.util.Scanner.throwFor(Scanner.java:819)
        at java.util.Scanner.next(Scanner.java:1431)
        at java.util.Scanner.nextInt(Scanner.java:2040)
        . . .
```

The program correctly reads Erica's employee ID and reports it in the `println` statement, but then it dies. Also, notice that the program reports Erica's total hours worked as 825.75, when the number should be 42.75. Where did it go wrong?

If you compute the difference between the reported sum of 825.75 hours and the correct sum of 42.75 hours, you'll find it is equal to 783. That number appears in the data file: It's the employee ID of the second employee, Erin. In adding up the hours for Erica, the program has accidentally read Erin's employee ID and added it to the sum. That's also why the exception occurs—on the second iteration of the loop, the program tries to read an employee ID for Erin when the next token in the file is not an integer.

The solution is to somehow get the program to stop reading when it gets to the end of an input line. Unfortunately, there is no easy way to do this with a token-based approach. The loop asks whether the `Scanner` has a next `double` value to read, and the employee ID will look like a `double` that can be read. You might try to form a complex test that looks for a `double` that is not also an integer, but even that won't work because some of the hours are integers.

To make this work, you need to write a more sophisticated program that pays attention to the line breaks. The program must read an entire line of input at a time and process that line by itself. Recall that the `main` method for the program looks like this:

```
public static void main(String[] args)
        throws FileNotFoundException {
    Scanner input = new Scanner(new File("hours2.dat"));
    process(input);
}
```

If you incorporate a line-based loop, you'll end up with something like this:

```
public static void main(String[] args)
        throws FileNotFoundException {
    Scanner input = new Scanner(new File("hours2.dat"));
    while (input.hasNextLine()) {
        String text = input.nextLine();
        processLine(text);
    }
}
```

Reading the file line by line guarantees that you don't accidentally combine data for two employees. The downside to this approach is that you have to write a method called `processLine` that takes a `String` as a parameter, and you have to pull apart that `String`. It contains the employee ID, followed by the employee name, followed by the numbers indicating how many hours were worked on different days. In other words, the input line is composed of several pieces (tokens) that you want to process piece by piece. It's much easier to process this data in a token-based manner than to have it in a `String`.

Fortunately, there is a convenient way to do this. You can construct a `Scanner` object from an individual `String`. Remember that just as you can attach a faucet to different sources of water (a faucet in a house attached to city or well water versus a faucet on an airplane attached to a tank of water), you can attach a `Scanner` to different sources of input. You've seen how to attach it to the console (`System.in`) and to a file (passing a `File` object). You can also attach it to an individual `String`. For example, this code:

```
Scanner input = new Scanner("18.4 17.9 8.3 2.9");
```

constructs a `Scanner` that gets its input from the `String` used to construct it. This `Scanner` has an input cursor just like a `Scanner` linked to a file. Initially the input cursor is positioned at the first character in the `String`, and it moves forward as you read tokens from the `Scanner`.

Here is a short program that demonstrates this:

```
1  // Simple example of a Scanner reading from a String.
2
3  import java.util.*;
4
5  public class StringScannerExample {
6      public static void main(String[] args) {
7          Scanner input = new Scanner("18.4 17.9 8.3 2.9");
8          while (input.hasNextDouble()) {
9              double next = input.nextDouble();
10             System.out.println(next);
11         }
12     }
13 }
```

It produces the following output:

```
18.4
17.9
8.3
2.9
```

Notice that it produces four lines of output because there are four numbers in the String used to construct the Scanner.

When you have a file that requires this combination of line-based and token-based processing, you can use a slightly different approach by constructing a different String-based Scanner for each line of the input file. With this approach, you end up with a lot of Scanner objects. You have a Scanner object that is keeping track of the input file, and you use that Scanner to read entire lines of input. But each time you read a line of text from the file, you construct a mini-Scanner for just that line of input. You can then use token-based processing for these mini-Scanner objects, because each contains just a single line of data.

This combination of line-based and token-based processing is powerful. You will find that you can use this approach (and slight variations) to process a large variety of input files.

In the HoursWorked program, each input line contains information for a single employee. Processing the input line involves making a Scanner for the line and then reading its various parts in a token-based manner (ID, name, hours). You can put this all together into a new version of the program:

```
1  // Variation of HoursWorked that includes employee IDs.
2
3  import java.io.*;
4  import java.util.*;
5
6  public class HoursWorked2 {
7      public static void main(String[] args)
8              throws FileNotFoundException {
9          Scanner input = new Scanner(new File("hours2.dat"));
10         while (input.hasNextLine()) {
11             String text = input.nextLine();
12             processLine(text);
13         }
14     }
15
```

```
16        // processes the given String (ID, name, and hours worked)
17        public static void processLine(String text) {
18            Scanner data = new Scanner(text);
19            int id = data.nextInt();
20            String name = data.next();
21            double sum = 0.0;
22            while (data.hasNextDouble()) {
23                sum += data.nextDouble();
24            }
25            System.out.println("Total hours worked by " + name +
26                               " (id#" + id + ") = " + sum);
27        }
28 }
```

Notice that the main method includes the line-based processing of reading entire lines of input from the file. Each such line is passed to the processLine method. Each time you call processLine, you make a mini-Scanner for just that line of input and use token-based processing (calling the methods nextInt, next, and nextDouble).

This new version of the program produces the following output:

```
Total hours worked by Erica (id#101) = 42.75
Total hours worked by Erin (id#783) = 55.75
Total hours worked by Simone (id#114) = 24.0
Total hours worked by Ryan (id#238) = 31.75
Total hours worked by Kendall (id#156) = 5.5
```

While this version of the program is a little more complex than the original, it is much more flexible because it pays attention to line breaks.

6.4 Advanced File Processing

In this section we'll explore two advanced topics related to file processing: producing output files and handling errors using try/catch statements.

Output Files with PrintStream

All of the programs we've looked at so far have sent their output to the console window by calling System.out.print or System.out.println. But just as you can read input from a file instead of reading from the console, you can write output to a file instead of writing it to the console. There are many ways to accomplish this. The simplest approach is to take advantage of what you already know. You've already learned all about how print and println statements work, and you can leverage that knowledge to easily create output files.

If you look at Sun's Java documentation, you will find that System.out is a variable that stores a reference to an object of type PrintStream. The print and println statements you've been writing are calls on methods that are part of the PrintStream class. The variable System.out stores a reference to a special

`PrintStream` object that is tied to the console window. However, you can construct other `PrintStream` objects that send their output to other places. Suppose, for example, that you want to send output to a file called `results.txt`. You can construct a `PrintStream` object as follows:

```
PrintStream output = new PrintStream(new File("results.txt"));
```

This looks a lot like the line of code used to construct a `Scanner` tied to an input file. In this case, the computer is creating an output file. If there is no such file, the program creates it. If there is such a file, it overwrites the current version. Initially, the file will be empty. It will end up containing whatever output you tell it to produce through calls on `print` and `println`.

The preceding line of code can generate an exception if Java is unable to create the file you've described. There are many reasons this might happen: You might not have permission to write to the directory, or the file might be locked because another program is using it. Like the line of code that creates a file-based `Scanner`, this line of code potentially throws a `FileNotFoundException`. That means that Java requires you to include the `throws` clause in whatever method contains this line of code. The simplest approach is to put this line in `main`. In fact, it is common practice to have the `main` method begin with the lines of code that deal with the input and output files.

Once you have constructed a `PrintStream` object, how do you use it? You should already have a good idea of what to do. We have been making calls on `System.out.print` and `System.out.println` since Chapter 1. As it turns out, `System.out` is the name of a variable that stores a reference to a `PrintStream` object, so you've already had quite a bit of practice talking to the `PrintStream` known as `System.out`. The plan is to have a variable called `output` that will store a reference to your `PrintStream` object. If you think of everything you know about `System.out` you'll have a good idea of what to do, but for this program, you will call `output.print` instead of `System.out.print` and `output.println` instead of `System.out.println`.

As a simple example, remember that in Chapter 1 we looked at the following variation of the simple "hello world" program that produces several lines of output:

```
1 public class Hello2 {
2     public static void main(String[] args) {
3         System.out.println("Hello, world!");
4         System.out.println();
5         System.out.println("This program produces four");
6         System.out.println("lines of output.");
7     }
8 }
```

Here is a variation that sends its output to a file called `hello.txt`:

```
1 // Variation of Hello2 that prints to a file.
2
3 import java.io.*;
```

```
 4
 5
 6 public class Hello4 {
 7     public static void main(String[] args)
 8             throws FileNotFoundException {
 9         PrintStream output =
10             new PrintStream( new File("hello.txt"));
11         output.println("Hello world.");
12         output.println();
13         output.println("This program produces four");
14         output.println("lines of output.");
15     }
16 }
```

When you run this new version of the program, a curious thing happens. The program doesn't seem to do anything; no output appears on the console at all. In this case, the output was directed to a file instead. After the program finishes executing, you can open up the file called `hello.txt` and you'll find that it contains the following:

```
Hello world.

This program produces four
lines of output.
```

The main point is that everything you've learned to do with `System.out`, you can also do with `PrintStream` objects that are tied to files.

You can also write methods that take `PrintStream` objects as parameters. For example, consider the task of fixing the spacing for a series of words. Say you have a line of text that has erratic spacing, as in:

```
a       new   nation,      conceived  in      liberty
```

Suppose you want to print this text with exactly one space between each pair of words:

```
a new nation, conceived in liberty
```

How do you do that? Assume that you are writing a method that is passed a `String` to echo and a `PrintStream` object to send the output to:

```
public static void echoFixed(String text, PrintStream output) {
    ...
}
```

You can construct a `Scanner` from the `String` and then use the `next` method to read one word at a time. Recall that the `Scanner` class ignores whitespace, so you'll get just the individual words without all of the spaces between them. As you read words, you'll need to echo them to the `PrintStream` object. Here's a first attempt:

```
Scanner data = new Scanner(text);
while (data.hasNext()) {
    output.print(data.next());
}
```

This code does a great job of deleting the long sequences of spaces from the `String`, but it goes too far: It eliminates all of the spaces. To get one space between each pair of words, you'll have to include some spaces:

```
Scanner data = new Scanner(text);
while (data.hasNext()) {
    output.print(data.next() + " ");
}
```

This ends up looking pretty good, but it prints an extra space at the end of the line. To get rid of that space so that you truly have spaces appearing only between pairs of words, you'll have to change this slightly. This is a classic fencepost problem; you want to print one more word than you have spaces. You can use the typical solution of processing the first word before the loop begins and swapping the order of the other two operations inside the loop (printing a space and then the word):

```
Scanner data = new Scanner(text);
output.print(data.next());
while (data.hasNext()) {
    output.print(" " + data.next());
}
```

This now works well for almost all cases, but by including the fencepost solution of echoing the first word before the loop begins, you've introduced an assumption that there is a first word. If the `String` has no words at all, this call on next will throw an exception. So, you need a test for the case where the `String` doesn't contain any words. If you also want this to produce a complete line of output, you'll also have to include a call on `println` to complete the line of output after printing the individual words. Putting all of this together, you get the following:

```
public static void echoFixed(String text, PrintStream output) {
    Scanner data = new Scanner(text);
    if (data.hasNext()) {
        output.print(data.next());
        while (data.hasNext()) {
            output.print(" " + data.next());
        }
    }
    output.println();
}
```

Notice that you're now calling `output.print` and `output.println` instead of calling `System.out.print` and `System.out.println`. An interesting thing about this method is that it can be used to send output to an output file, but it can also be used to send output to `System.out`. The method header indicates that it works on any `PrintStream`, so you can call it to send output to a `PrintStream` object tied to a file, or to send output to `System.out`.

The following is a complete program that uses this method to fix the spacing in an entire input file of text. To underscore the flexibility of the method, the program sends its output to both a file (`words2.txt`) and the console:

```
 1  // This program removes excess spaces in an input file.
 2
 3  import java.io.*;
 4  import java.util.*;
 5
 6  public class FixSpacing {
 7      public static void main(String[] args)
 8              throws FileNotFoundException {
 9          Scanner input = new Scanner( new File("words.txt"));
10          PrintStream output =
11              new PrintStream( new File("words2.txt"));
12          while (input.hasNextLine()) {
13              String text = input.nextLine();
14              echoFixed(text, output);
15              echoFixed(text, System.out);
16          }
17      }
18
19      public static void echoFixed(String text,
20                                   PrintStream output) {
21          Scanner data = new Scanner(text);
22          if (data.hasNext()) {
23              output.print(data.next());
24              while (data.hasNext()) {
25                  output.print(" " + data.next());
26              }
27          }
28          output.println();
29      }
30  }
```

Given the following input file:

```
    four          score      and
seven     years ago     our
    fathers brought    forth on this      continent
a        new  nation,      conceived  in      liberty
   and  dedicated    to    the  proposition      that
   all    men     are      created    equal
```

it produces the following output file called words2.txt:

```
four score and
seven years ago our
fathers brought forth on this continent
a new nation, conceived in liberty
and dedicated to the proposition that
all men are created equal
```

The output also appears in the console window.

try/catch Statements

Including the clause throws FileNotFoundException in the header for main allows your programs to compile, but it's not a very satisfying solution to the underlying problem. To actually handle the potential error, you'll want to use something called a `try/catch` statement. We won't explore all of the details of `try/catch` here, but we will examine how to write some basic `try/catch` statements that you can use for file processing.

The general syntax of the `try/catch` statement is:

```
try {
    <statement>;
    <statement>;
    . . .
    <statement>;
} catch (<type> <name>) {
    <statement>;
    <statement>;
    . . .
    <statement>;
}
```

Notice that it is divided into two blocks using the keywords `try` and `catch`. The first block contains the code you want to execute. The second block contains error-recovery code that should be executed if an exception is thrown. So, think of this as saying, "Try to execute these statements, but if something goes wrong, I'm going to give you some other code in the `catch` part that you should execute if an error occurs."

Notice that after the `catch` keyword is a set of parentheses in which you include a type and name. The type should be the type of exception you are trying to catch. The name can be any legal identifier. For example, in the case of our `Scanner` code, you know that a `FileNotFoundException` might be thrown. What do you do if such an exception occurs? That's a tough question, but for now, just write an error message:

```
try {
    Scanner input = new Scanner(new File("numbers.dat"));
} catch (FileNotFoundException e) {
    System.out.println("File not found");
}
```

This code says to try constructing the `Scanner` from the file `numbers.dat` but, if the file is not found, to print an error message instead. This is the basic idea you'll want to follow, but there are several issues to address to make this code work for you. First of all, there is a scope issue. The variable `input` isn't going to be much use if it's trapped inside the `try` block, so you must declare the `Scanner` variable outside the `try/catch` statement:

```
Scanner input;
try {
    input = new Scanner(new File("numbers.dat"));
} catch (FileNotFoundException e) {
    System.out.println("File not found");
}
```

A bigger problem is that simply printing an error message isn't a good way to recover. How is the program supposed to proceed with execution if it can't read from the file? It probably can't. So what would be a more appropriate way to recover from the error? That depends on the particular program you are writing, so the answer is likely to vary.

Let's explore how you might handle this when you are prompting the user for a file name in the console window. In that case, you can keep prompting until the user gives you0 a legal file name. Let's begin by modifying the preceding code to prompt and read a file name:

```
Scanner input;
System.out.print("What is the name of the input file? ");
String name = console.nextLine();
try {
    input = new Scanner(new File(name));
} catch (FileNotFoundException e) {
    System.out.println("File not found");
}
```

This code catches the potential exception and prints an error message, but you'll want to add a loop that executes when the user does not provide a legal file name. It should look something like this:

```
Scanner input;
while (user hasn't given a legal name) {
    prompt for name.
    try to open file, generating error message if illegal.
}
```

We have a classic problem of how to prime this loop so that it enters the first time through. You're trying to construct a `Scanner` from a file. When you succeed, you'll be giving a value to the variable `input`. Can you initialize `input` to something that would indicate that you aren't yet done? The answer is yes. There is a special keyword in Java called `null` that is used to represent "no object".

> **null**
>
> A Java keyword signifying no object.

You can initialize the variable `input` to `null` as a way to say, "This variable doesn't yet point to an actual object." The primary advantage of initializing the variable to `null` is that you can test whether it's `null` in the `while` loop.

The pseudocode should now look like this:

```
Scanner input = null;
while (input == null) {
    prompt for name.
    try to open file, generating error message if illegal.
}
```

Start the variable with the value `null`, so it enters the `while` loop the first time through. If the code in the `try` block fails to properly open the file, the variable will still be `null` and you'll execute the loop a second time, prompting for another file name and trying to open that file. If the code in the `try` block fails again, you'll generate yet another error message and go through the loop a third time.

Now, combine this pseudocode with the earlier `try/catch` code, modifying the error message to make it clear that the user is being given another chance to enter a legal file name:

```
Scanner input = null;
while (input == null) {
    System.out.print("What is the name of the input file? ");
    String name = console.nextLine();
    try {
        input = new Scanner(new File(name));
    } catch (FileNotFoundException e) {
        System.out.println("File not found. "
                                + "Please try again.");
    }
}
```

This loop executes repeatedly until the call on new `Scanner` inside the `try` block succeeds and gives the variable `input` a non-null value. This code could be included in your `main` method, although you'd have to construct a `Scanner` for console input to be able to prompt the user for a file name.

Here is a variation of the `HoursWorked2` program that prompts for a file name:

```
 1 // Variation of HoursWorked2 that prompts for a file name.
 2
 3 import java.io.*;
 4 import java.util.*;
 5
 6 public class HoursWorked3 {
 7     public static void main(String[] args) {
 8         Scanner console = new Scanner(System.in);
 9         Scanner input = null;
10         while (input == null) {
11             System.out.print("input file name? ");
12             String name = console.nextLine();
13             try {
14                 input = new Scanner(new File(name));
15             } catch (FileNotFoundException e) {
16                 System.out.println("File not found. "
17                                         + "Please try again.");
18             }
19         }
20         while (input.hasNextLine()) {
21             String text = input.nextLine();
22             processLine(text);
23         }
24     }
25
26     // processes the given String (ID, name, and hours worked)
27     public static void processLine(String text) {
28         Scanner data = new Scanner(text);
29         int id = data.nextInt();
```

```
30            String name = data.next();
31            double sum = 0.0;
32            while (data.hasNextDouble()) {
33                sum += data.nextDouble();
34            }
35            System.out.println("Total hours worked by " + name +
36                               " (id#" + id + ") = " + sum);
37        }
38 }
```

Notice that you no longer need the `throws FileNotFoundException` in the header for `main` because you handle the potential exception. Here is a log of execution showing what happens when the user types in some illegal file names, followed by a legal file name:

```
input file name? ours2.dat
File not found. Please try again.
input file name? hours2.txt
File not found. Please try again.
input file name? data.txt
File not found. Please try again.
input file name? file.dat
File not found. Please try again.
input file name? hours2.dat
Total hours worked by Erica (id#101) = 42.75
Total hours worked by Erin (id#783) = 55.75
Total hours worked by Simone (id#114) = 24.0
Total hours worked by Ryan (id#238) = 31.75
Total hours worked by Kendall (id#156) = 5.5
```

This code for opening a file is complicated enough that you might want to put it in its own static method. The following final variation includes a method called `getInput` that prompts the user for a legal file name that can be used to construct a `Scanner`:

```
1 // Variation of HoursWorked3 with file opening in a method.
2
3 import java.io.*;
4 import java.util.*;
5
6 public class HoursWorked4 {
7     public static void main(String[] args) {
8         Scanner console = new Scanner(System.in);
9         Scanner input = getInput(console);
10        while (input.hasNextLine()) {
11            String text = input.nextLine();
12            processLine(text);
13        }
14    }
15
16    // prompt the user for a legal file name, create and return
17    // a Scanner tied to the file
18    public static Scanner getInput(Scanner console) {
19        Scanner result = null;
20        while (result == null) {
```

```
21                 System.out.print("input file name? ");
22                 String name = console.nextLine();
23                 try {
24                     result = new Scanner(new File(name));
25                 } catch (FileNotFoundException e) {
26                     System.out.println("File not found. "
27                                        + "Please try again.");
28                 }
29             }
30         return result;
31     }
32
33     // processes the given String (ID, name, and hours worked)
34     public static void processLine(String text) {
35         Scanner data = new Scanner(text);
36         int id = data.nextInt();
37         String name = data.next();
38         double sum = 0.0;
39         while (data.hasNextDouble()) {
40             sum += data.nextDouble();
41         }
42         System.out.println("Total hours worked by " + name +
43                            " (id#" + id + ") = " + sum);
44     }
45 }
```

The code for opening a file is fairly standard and could be used without modification in many programs. We refer to this as *boilerplate code*.

> **Boilerplate Code**
>
> Code that tends to be the same from one program to another.

The getInput method is a good example of the kind of boilerplate code that you might use in many different file-processing programs.

6.5 Case Study: Weighted GPA

The HoursWorked program requires that names in the input file have no spaces in them. However, this isn't a very practical restriction. It would be more convenient to be able to type anything for a name, including spaces. One way to enable that is to put the name on a separate line from the rest of the data. For example, suppose that we want to compute weighted GPAs for a series of students. Say, for example, that a student has a 3-unit 3.0, a 4-unit 2.9, a 3-unit 3.2, and a 2-unit 2.5. We can compute an overall GPA that is weighted by the individual units for each course.

The input file will have its data on pairs of lines. In each pair, the name will appear on the first line and the grade data will appear on the second line. For example, the input file might look like this:

```
Erica Kane
3 2.8 4 3.9 3 3.1
Greenlee Smythe
3 3.9 3 4.0 4 3.9
Ryan Laveree
2 4.0 3 3.6 4 3.8 1 2.8
Adam Chandler
3 3.0 4 2.9 3 3.2 2 2.5
Adam Chandler, Jr
4 1.5 5 1.9
```

This data is line-based, but some of the lines have individual tokens that we'll need to process, so we'll want to use a slight variation of the template given in the last section. Recall that in general the way to get a combination of line-based and token-based processing is to write code like this:

```
while (input.hasNextLine()) {
    String text = input.nextLine();
    Scanner data = new Scanner(text);
    process data.
}
```

We won't need to process the names token by token, but we'll need to process the grades as individual tokens. To accomplish this, we can use the following slight variation that reads two lines of data each time through the loop and constructs a `Scanner` object for the second line of input (which contains the grade information):

```
while (input.hasNextLine()) {
    String name = input.nextLine();
    String grades = input.nextLine();
    Scanner data = new Scanner(grades);
    process this student's data.
}
```

To complete this program, we have to figure out how to process the grade data in the `Scanner` called `data`. This is a good place to introduce a static method. The preceding code above involves processing the overall file, but the task of processing one list of grades should be split off into its own method. Let's call it `processGrades`. It can't do its work without the `Scanner` object that reads in the grades, so we'll pass that as a parameter. What exactly needs to be done in this method? The plan was to compute a weighted GPA for each student, so it needs to read the individual grades and turn them into a single GPA score.

Calculating weighted GPAs involve computing values known as "quality points" for each grade. The quality points are defined as the units times the grade. The weighted GPA is calculated by dividing the total quality points by the total units, so we just need to add up the total quality points, add up the total units, and then do the division. This involves a pair of cumulative sum tasks that we can express in pseudocode as follows:

```
set total units to 0.
set total quality points to 0.
while (more grades to process) {
    read next units and next grade.
    add next units to total units.
    add (next units) * (next grade) to total quality points.
}
set gpa to (total quality points) / (total units).
```

This is fairly simple to translate into Java code by incorporating the `data` `Scanner` object:

```
double totalQualityPoints = 0.0;
double totalUnits = 0;
while (data.hasNextInt()) {
    int units = data.nextInt();
    double grade = data.nextDouble();
    totalUnits += units;
    totalQualityPoints += units * grade;
}
double gpa = totalQualityPoints / totalUnits;
```

Because the `data` `Scanner` object was constructed from a single line of input, we can process just one person's grades with this loop.

There is still a potential problem. What if there are no grades? Some students might have dropped all of their classes. There are several ways to handle that situation, but let's assume that it is appropriate to use a GPA of 0.0 when there are no grades.

Making that correction and putting this into a method, we end up with the following code:

```
public static double processGrades(Scanner data) {
    double totalQualityPoints = 0.0;
    double totalUnits = 0;
    while (data.hasNextInt()) {
        int units = data.nextInt();
        double grade = data.nextDouble();
        totalUnits += units;
        totalQualityPoints += units * grade;
    }
    if (totalUnits == 0) {
        return 0.0;
    } else {
        return totalQualityPoints / totalUnits;
    }
}
```

Recall that our high-level code looked like this:

```
while (input.hasNextLine()) {
    String name = input.nextLine();
    String grades = input.nextLine();
    Scanner data = new Scanner(grades);
    process this student's data.
}
```

We can now start to fill in the details of what it means to "process this student's data." We will call the method we just wrote to process the student's grades, turn it into a weighted GPA, and then print the results:

```
double gpa = processGrades(data);
System.out.println("GPA for " + name + " = " + gpa);
```

This would complete the program, but let's add one more calculation to compute the maximum and minimum GPAs. We can accomplish this fairly easily with some simple `if` statements after the `println`:

```
if (gpa > max) {
    max = gpa;
}
if (gpa < min) {
    min = gpa;
}
```

We simply compare the current `gpa` against what we currently consider the `max` and `min`, resetting those values if the new `gpa` represents a new `max` or a new `min`. But how do we initialize these variables? There are two possible approaches. One approach involves initializing `max` and `min` to the first value in the sequence. We could do that, but it would make our loop much more complicated than it is currently. The second approach involves setting `max` to the lowest possible value and setting `min` to the highest possible value. This approach isn't always possible because we don't always know how high or low our values might go, but in the case of GPAs, we know that they will always be between 0.0 and 4.0. Thus, we can initialize the variables as follows:

```
double max = 0.0;
double min = 4.0;
```

It may seem odd to set `max` to 0.0 and `min` to 4.0, but that's because we are intending to have them reset inside the loop. If the first student has a GPA of 3.2, for example, this will constitute a new `max` (higher than 0.0) and a new `min` (lower than 4.0). Of course, it's possible that all students will end up with a 4.0, but in that case our choice of 4.0 for `min` is appropriate. Likewise, all students could end up with a 0.0, in which case our choice of a `max` of 0.0 is appropriate.

Putting all this together, we get the following complete program:

```
 1  // This program reads an input file with GPA data for a series
 2  // of students and reports a weighted GPA for each student as
 3  // well as the max and min GPAs.
 4
 5  import java.io.*;
 6  import java.util.*;
 7
 8  public class Gpa {
 9      public static void main(String[] args)
10              throws FileNotFoundException {
11          Scanner input = new Scanner(new File("gpa.dat"));
12          process(input);
13      }
```

```
14
15        public static void process(Scanner input) {
16            double max = 0.0;
17            double min = 4.0;
18            while (input.hasNextLine()) {
19                String name = input.nextLine();
20                String grades = input.nextLine();
21                Scanner data = new Scanner(grades);
22                double gpa = processGrades(data);
23                System.out.println("GPA for " + name + " = "
24                                    + gpa);
25                if (gpa > max) {
26                    max = gpa;
27                }
28                if (gpa < min) {
29                    min = gpa;
30                }
31            }
32            System.out.println();
33            System.out.println("max GPA = " + max);
34            System.out.println("min GPA = " + min);
35        }
36
37        public static double processGrades(Scanner data) {
38            double totalQualityPoints = 0.0;
39            double totalUnits = 0;
40            while (data.hasNextInt()) {
41                int units = data.nextInt();
42                double grade = data.nextDouble();
43                totalUnits += units;
44                totalQualityPoints += units * grade;
45            }
46            if (totalUnits == 0) {
47                return 0.0;
48            } else {
49                return totalQualityPoints / totalUnits;
50            }
51        }
52 }
```

Once again the main method has throws FileNotFoundException in its header.
This program executes as follows, assuming the data presented earlier is placed in a file
called gpa.dat:

```
GPA for Erica Kane = 3.3299999999999996
GPA for Greenlee Smythe = 3.9299999999999997
GPA for Ryan Laveree = 3.6799999999999997
GPA for Adam Chandler = 2.9333333333333336
GPA for Adam Chandler, Jr = 1.7222222222222223

max GPA = 3.9299999999999997
min GPA = 1.7222222222222223
```

The program could be modified to send its output to a file such as gpa.out. This
is left as an exercise.

Chapter Summary

Files are represented in Java as `File` objects. The `File` class is found in the `java.io` package.

A `Scanner` object can read input from a file rather than from the keyboard. This is achieved by passing `new File(`*filename*`)` to the `Scanner`'s constructor, rather than passing `System.in`.

A checked exception is a program error condition that must be caught or declared for the program to compile. For example, when constructing a `Scanner` that reads a file, you must write the phrase `throws FileNotFoundException` in the `main` method's header.

The `Scanner` treats as input file as a one-dimensional stream of data that is read in order from start to end. The input cursor consumes (moves past) input tokens as they are read and returns them to your program.

A `Scanner` that reads a file makes use of the various `hasNext` methods to discover when the file's input has been exhausted.

`Scanner`s can be passed as parameters to methods to read part or all of a file, since they are objects and therefore use reference semantics.

A file name can be specified as a relative path, as in `data/text/numbers.dat`, which would be assumed to exist in the `data/text/` subfolder of the current directory. Altenatively, a full file path can be specified, as in `C:/Documents and Settings/user/My Documents/data/text/numbers.dat`.

Many files have their input structured by lines, and it makes sense to process those files line by line. In such cases, it is common to use nested loops: an outer loop that iterates over each line of the file and an inner loop that processes the tokens in each line.

Output to a file can be achieved with a `PrintStream` object, which is constructed with a `File` and has the same methods as `System.out`, such as `println` and `print`.

Java has a `try/catch` statement that can be used to check for errors and handle them while the program is executing. A `try/catch` statement can be used when opening a file, to handle the possibility that the file does not exist.

Self-Check Problems

Section 6.1: File-Reading Basics

1. What is a file? How can we read data from a file in Java?

2. What is wrong with the following line of code?

```
Scanner input = new Scanner("test.dat");
```

3. Write code to construct a `Scanner` object to read the file `input.txt`, which exists in the same folder as your program.

Section 6.2: Details of Token-Based Processing

4. What is wrong with the following line of code?

```
Scanner input = new Scanner(new File("C:\temp\new files\test.dat"));
```

(Hint: Try printing the above String.)

5. If your Java program is located on a Windows machine in the folder `C:\Documents and Settings\amanda\My Documents\programs`, answer the following:

   - What are two legal ways you can refer to the file `C:\Documents and Settings\amanda\My Documents\programs\numbers.dat`?
   - What about the file `C:\Documents and Settings\amanda\My Documents\programs\data\home-work6\input.dat`?
   - How many legal ways can you refer to the file `C:\Documents and Settings\amanda\My Documents\homework\data.txt`? What is it/are they?

6. If your Java program is located on a Linux machine in the folder `/home/amanda/Documents/hw6`, answer the following:

   - What are two legal ways you can refer to the `file /home/amanda/Documents/hw6/names.txt`?
   - What about the file `/home/amanda/Documents/hw6/data/numbers.txt`?
   - How many legal ways can you refer to the file `/home/amanda/download/saved.html`? What is it/are they?

Section 6.3: Line-Based Processing

7. For the next several questions, consider a file called `readme.txt` that has the following contents:

```
6.7        This file has
       several input lines.

  10 20        30   40

test
```

   What would be the output from the following code when run on the `readme.txt` file?

```java
Scanner input = new Scanner(new File("readme.txt"));
int count = 0;
while (input.hasNextLine()) {
    System.out.println("input: " + input.nextLine());
    count++;
}
System.out.println(count + " total");
```

8. What would be the output from the code in the previous exercise if the calls to `hasNextLine` and `nextLine` were replaced by calls to `hasNext` and `next`, respectively?

9. What would be the output from the code in the previous exercise if the calls to `hasNextLine` and `nextLine` were replaced by calls to `hasNextInt` and `nextInt`, respectively? How about `hasNextDouble` and `nextDouble`?

10. Write a program that prints itself to the console as output. That is, if the program is stored in `Example.java`, it will open the file `Example.java` and print its contents to the console.

11. Write code that prompts the user for a file name and prints the contents of that file to the console as output. Assume that the file exists. You may wish to place this code into a method called `printEntireFile`.

Section 6.4: Advanced File Processing

12. What object is used to write output to a file? What methods does this object have available for you to use?

13. Write code to print the following four lines of text into a file named `message.txt`:

```
Testing,
1, 2, 3.

This is my output file.
```

14. Write code that repeatedly prompts the user for a file name until the user types the name of a file that exists on the system. You may wish to place this code into a method named `getFileName`, which will return that file name as a `String`.

15. Problem 11 had you write a piece of code to prompt the user for a file name and print that file's contents to the console. Modify your code so that it will repeatedly prompt the user for the file name until the user types the name of a file that exists on the system.

Exercises

1. Write a method called `doubleSpace` that accepts two `Strings` representing file names as its parameters, writing into the second file a double-spaced version of the text in the first file. You can achieve this by inserting a blank line between each line of output.

   To make it more challenging, try to make your code so that it will work even if the two `Strings` are the same (in other words, so it will write the double-spaced output back into the same file).

2. Write a method called `wordWrap` that accepts a `Scanner` representing an input file as its parameter and outputs each line of the file to the console, word-wrapping all lines that are longer than 60 characters. For example, if a line contains 112 characters, the method should replace it with two lines: one containing the first 60 characters and another containing the final 52 characters. A line containing 217 characters should be wrapped into four lines: three of length 60 and a final line of length 37.

3. Modify the preceding word-wrap method so that it outputs the newly wrapped text back into the original file. (Be careful—don't output into a file while you are reading it!) Also, modify it to use a class constant for the maximum line length rather than hard-coding 60.

4. Modify the preceding word-wrap method so that it only wraps whole words, never chopping a word in half. Assume that a word is any whitespace-separated token and that all words are under 60 characters in length.

5. Write a program that prompts the user for a file name, then reads that file (assuming that its contents consist entirely of integers) and prints the maximum, minimum, sum, count (number of integers in the file), and average of the numbers. For example, if the file `numberinput.dat` has the following contents:

   ```
   4 -2 18
   15 31

   27
   ```

   your program should produce the following output:

   ```
   input file name? numberinput.dat
   Maximum = 31
   Minimum = -2
   Sum = 93
   Count = 6
   Average = 15.5
   ```

6. Modify the previous program so that it works even on an input file that contains non-integer tokens. Your code should skip over any tokens that are not valid integers. For example, if the file `numberinput2.dat` has the following contents:

```
4 billy bob -2 18 2.54
15 31 NotANumber
```

```
true 'c' 27
```

your program should produce the same output as in the previous exercise.

7. (⊕ **myCodeMate**) Write a method called `collapseSpaces` that accepts a `Scanner` representing an input file as its parameter, then reads that file and outputs it with all its tokens separated by single spaces, collapsing any sequences of multiple spaces into single spaces. That is, if a line of the file contains the following text:

```
    many     spaces     on     this     line!
```

the same line of the file should be output as follows:

```
many spaces on this line!
```

8. Write a method called `readEntireFile` that accepts a `Scanner` representing an input file as its parameter, then reads that file and returns its entire text contents as a `String`.

9. Write a method called `stripHtmlTags` that accepts a `Scanner` representing an input file containing an HTML web page as its parameter, then reads that file and prints the file's text with all HTML tags removed. A tag is any text between < and > characters. For example, if the file contains the following text:

```
<html>
<head>
<title>My web page</title>
</head>
<body>
<p>There are many pictures of my cat here,
as well as my <b>very cool</b> blog page,
which contains <font color="red">awesome
stuff about my trip to Vegas.<p>

Here's my cat now:<img src="cat.jpg">
</body>
</html>
```

your program should output the following text:

```
My web page

There are many pictures of my cat here,
as well as my very cool blog page,
which contains awesome
stuff about my trip to Vegas.

Here's my cat now:
```

You may assume that the file is a well-formed HTML document and that no tag contains a < or > character inside itself.

10. (⊕ **myCodeMate**) Write a method called `stripComments` that accepts a `Scanner` representing an input file contaning a Java program as its parameter, then reads that file, and prints the file's text with all comments removed. A comment is any text on a line from // to the end of the line, and any text between /* and */ characters. For example, if the file contains the following text:

```
import java.util.*;

/* My program
```

```
by Suzy Student */
 public class Program {
     public static void main(String[] args) {

         System.out.println("Hello, world!"); // a println

     }

     public static /* Hello there */ void foo() {
         System.out.println("Goodbye!"); // comment here
     } /* */
 }
```

your program should output the following text:

```
import java.util.*;

public class Program {
    public static void main(String[] args) {

        System.out.println("Hello, world!");
    }

    public static  void foo() {
        System.out.println("Goodbye!");
    }
}
```

11. Write a program that takes as input lines of text like:

```
This is some
text here.
```

and produces as output the same text inside a box, as in:

```
+--------------+
| This is some |
| text here.   |
+--------------+
```

Your program will have to assume some maximum line length (e.g., 12 in this case).

Programming Projects

1. Students are often told that their term papers should contain a certain number of words. Counting words in a long paper is a tedious task, but the computer can help. Write a program that counts the number of words, lines, and total characters (not including whitespace) in a paper, assuming that consecutive words are separated either by spaces or end-of-line characters.

2. **myCodeMate** Write a program that compares two files and prints information about the differences between them. For example, if a file data1.txt exists with the following contents:

```
This file has a great deal of
text in it which needs to

be processed.
```

and another file data2.txt exists with the following contents:

```
This file has a grate deal of
text in it which needs to

bee procesed.
```

a dialogue with the user running your program might look like this:

```
Enter a first file name: data1.txt
Enter a second file name: data2.txt

Differences found:
Line 1:
< This file has a great deal of
> This file has a grate deal of

Line 4:
< be processed.
> bee procesed.
```

3. Write a program that prompts the user for a file name, assuming that the file contains a Java program. Your program should read the file and print its contents properly indented. When you see a left brace character ({) in the file, increase your indentation level by four spaces. When you see a right brace character (}), decrease your indentation level by four spaces. You may assume that the file has only one opening or closing brace per line, that every block statement (such as if or for) uses braces rather than omitting them, and that every relevant occurrence of a { or } character in the file occurs at the end of a line. Consider using a class constant for the number of spaces to indent (4), so that it can easily be changed later.

4. Write a program that reads a file of popularities of baby first names over time and displays the data about a particular baby's name. Each line of the file stores a first name followed by integers representing the name's popularity in each decade: 1900, 1910, 1920, and so on. The rankings range from 1 (most popular) to 1000 (least popular), or 0 for a name that was less popular than the 1000th name. The following is a sample of the file format:

```
Sally 0 0 0 0 0 0 0 0 0 0 886
Sam 58 69 99 131 168 236 278 380 467 408 466
Samantha 0 0 0 0 0 0 272 107 26 5 7
Samir 0 0 0 0 0 0 0 0 920 0 798
```

Your program should prompt the user for a name and search the file for that name. If the name is found, it should display data about the name on the screen.

```
This program allows you to search through the
data from the Social Security Administration
to see how popular a particular name has been
since 1900.

Name? Sam

Statistics on name "Sam"
    1900: 58
    1910: 69
    1920: 99
    1930: 131
    . . .
```

This program is more fun and challenging if you also draw the name's popularity on a **DrawingPanel** as a line graph. Plot the decades on the x-axis and the popularity on the y-axis.

Chapter 7

Arrays

Introduction

The sequential nature of files severely limits the number of interesting things you can easily do with them. The algorithms we have examined so far have all been sequential algorithms: algorithms that can be performed by examining each data item once, in sequence. There is an entirely different class of algorithms that can be performed when you can access the data items multiple times and in an arbitrary order.

This chapter examines a new object called an array that provides this more flexible kind of access. The concept of arrays is not complex, but it can take a while for a novice to learn all of the different ways that an array can be used. The chapter begins with a general discussion of arrays and then moves into a discussion of common array manipulations as well as advanced array techniques.

7.1 Array Basics

An *array* is a flexible structure for storing a sequence of values all of the same type.

> **Array**
> A structure that holds multiple values of the same type.

The values stored in an array are called *elements*. The individual elements are accessed using an integer *index*.

> **Index**
> An integer indicating the position of a value in a data structure.

As an analogy, consider post office boxes. The boxes are indexed with numbers, so you can refer to an individual box by using a description like "PO Box 884." You already have experience using an index to indicate positions within a `String`, when calling methods like `charAt` or `substring`. As was the case with `String` indexes, array indexes start with 0. This is a convention known as *zero-based indexing*.

> **Zero-Based Indexing**
> A numbering scheme used throughout Java in which a sequence of values is indexed starting with 0 (element 0, element 1, element 2, and so on).

It might seem more natural to have indexes that start with 1 instead of 0, but Sun decided that Java would use the same indexing scheme that is used in C and C++.

Constructing and Traversing an Array

Suppose you want to store some different temperature readings. You could keep them in a series of variables:

```
double temperature1;
double temperature2;
double temperature3;
```

This isn't a bad solution if you have just 3 temperatures, but suppose you need to store 3000 temperatures. Then you would want something more flexible. You can instead store the temperatures in an array.

When using an array, you first need to declare a variable for it, so you have to know what type to use. The type will depend on the type of elements you want to have in your array. To indicate that you want an array, follow the type name with a set of square brackets. For temperatures, you want a sequence of values of type `double`, so you use the type `double[ ]`. Thus, you can declare a variable for storing your array as follows:

```
double[] temperature;
```

Arrays are objects, which means they must be constructed. Simply declaring a variable isn't enough to bring the object into existence. In this case you want an array of three `double` values, which you can construct as follows:

```
double[] temperature = new double[3];
```

This is a slightly different syntax than you've used previously when asking for a new object. It is a special syntax for arrays only. Notice that on the left-hand side you don't put anything inside the square brackets, because you're describing a type. The variable `temperature` can refer to any array of `double` values, no matter how many elements it has. On the right-hand side, however, you have to mention a specific number of elements because you are asking Java to construct an actual array object and it needs to know how many elements to include.

The general syntax for declaring and constructing an array is as follows:

```
<element type>[] <name> = new <element type>[<size>];
```

You can use any type as the element type, although the left and right sides of this statement have to match. For example, any of the following would be legal ways to construct an array:

```
int[] numbers = new int[10];     // an array of 10 ints
char[] letters = new char[20];    // an array of 20 chars
boolean[] flags = new boolean[5];  // an array of 5 booleans
String[] names = new String[100];  // an array of 100 Strings
Point[] points = new Point[50];   // an array of 50 Points
```

There are some special rules that apply when you construct an array of objects such as an array of `Strings` or an array of `Points`, but we'll discuss those later in the chapter.

In executing the line of code to construct the array of temperatures, Java will construct an array of three `double` values, with the variable `temperature` referring to the array:

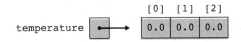

As you can see, the variable `temperature` is not itself the array. Instead, it stores a reference to the array. The array indexes are indicated in square brackets. To refer to an individual element of the array, you combine the name of the variable that refers to the array (`temperature`) with a specific index (`[0]`, `[1]`, or `[2]`). So, there is an element known as `temperature[0]`, an element known as `temperature[1]`, and an element known as `temperature[2]`.

In the `temperature` array diagram, the array elements are each indicated as having the value `0.0`. This is a guaranteed outcome when an array is constructed. Each element is initialized to a default value, a process known as *auto-initialization*.

Auto-Initialization

The initialization of variables to a default value, as in the initialization of array elements when an array is constructed.

TABLE 7.1   Zero-Equivalent Auto-Initialization Values

Type	Value
int	0
double	0.0
char	'\0'
boolean	false
objects	null

When Java performs auto-initialization, it always initializes to the zero-equivalent for the type. Table 7.1 indicates the zero-equivalent values for various types. Notice that the zero-equivalent for type `double` is `0.0`, which is why the array elements were initialized to that value. Using the indexes, you can store the specific temperature values you want to work with:

```
temperature[0] = 74.3;
temperature[1] = 68.4;
temperature[2] = 70.3;
```

This code modifies the array to have the following values:

Obviously an array isn't particularly helpful when you have just three values to store, but you can request a much larger array. For example, you could request an array of 100 temperatures by saying:

```
double[] temperature = new double[100];
```

This is almost the same line of code you executed before. The variable is still declared to be of type `double[]`, but in constructing the array you request 100 elements instead of 3, which constructs a much larger array:

Notice that the highest index is 99 rather than 100 because of zero-based indexing.

You are not restricted to simple literal values inside the brackets. You can use any integer expression. This allows you to combine arrays with loops, which greatly simplifies the code you write. For example, suppose you want to read a series of temperatures from a `Scanner`. You could read each value individually, as in:

```
temperature[0] = input.nextDouble();
temperature[1] = input.nextDouble();
temperature[2] = input.nextDouble();
...
temperature[99] = input.nextDouble();
```

But since the only thing that changes from one statement to the next is the index, you can capture this pattern in a `for` loop with a control variable that takes on the values 0 to 99:

```
for (int i = 0; i < 100; i++) {
    temperature[i] = input.nextDouble();
}
```

This is a very concise way to initialize all the elements of the array. The preceding code works when the array has a length of 100, but you can imagine the array having a different length. Java provides a useful mechanism for making this code more general. Each array keeps track of its own length. You're using the variable `temperature` to refer to your array, which means you can ask for `temperature.length` to find out the length of the array. By using `temperature.length` in the `for` loop test instead of the specific value 100, you make your code more general:

```
for (int i = 0; i < temperature.length; i++) {
    temperature[i] = input.nextDouble();
}
```

Notice that the array convention is different from the `String` convention. If you have a `String` variable s, you ask for the length of the `String` by referring to `s.length()`. For an array variable, you don't include the parentheses after the word "length." This is another one of those unfortunate inconsistencies that Java programmers just have to memorize.

The previous code provides a pattern that you will see often with array-processing code: a `for` loop that starts at 0 and that continues while the loop variable is less than the length of the array, doing something with element [i] in the body of the loop. This goes through each array element sequentially, which we refer to as *traversing* the array.

> **Array Traversal**
>
> Processing each array element sequentially from the first to the last.

This pattern is so useful that it is worth including it in a more general form:

```
for (int i = 0; i < <array>.length; i++) {
    <do something with array [i]>;
}
```

We will see this traversal pattern repeatedly as we explore common array algorithms.

Accessing an Array

As discussed in the last section, we refer to array elements by combining the name of the variable that refers to the array with an integer index inside square brackets:

```
<array variable>[<integer expression>]
```

Notice in this syntax description that the index can be an arbitrary integer expression. To explore this, let's see how we would access particular values in an array of integers. Suppose that we construct an array of length 5 and fill it up with the first five odd integers:

```java
int[] list = new int[5];
for (int i = 0; i < list.length; i++) {
    list[i] = 2 * i + 1;
}
```

The first line of code declares a variable `list` of type `int[]` and has it refer to an array of length 5. The array elements are auto-initialized to `0`:

	[0]	[1]	[2]	[3]	[4]
list →	0	0	0	0	0

Then the code uses the standard traversing loop to fill in the array with successive odd numbers:

	[0]	[1]	[2]	[3]	[4]
list →	1	3	5	7	9

Suppose we want to report the first, middle, and last values in the list. Looking at the preceding diagram, we can see that they occur at indexes 0, 2, and 4, which means we could write the following code:

```java
// works only for an array of length 5
System.out.println("first = " + list[0]);
System.out.println("middle = " + list[2]);
System.out.println("last = " + list[4]);
```

This works when the array is of length 5, but suppose that we change the length of the array. If the array has a length of 10, for example, this code will report the wrong values. We need to modify it to incorporate `list.length`, just as when writing the standard traversing loop.

The first element of the array will always be at index 0, so the first line of code doesn't need to change. You might at first think that we could fix the third line of code by replacing the 4 with `list.length`:

```java
// doesn't work
System.out.println("last = " + list[list.length]);
```

However, this code doesn't work. The culprit is zero-based indexing. In our example, the last value is stored at index 4 when `list.length` is 5. More generally, the last value will be at index `list.length` − 1. We can use this expression directly in our `println` statement:

```
// this one works
System.out.println("last = " + list[list.length - 1]);
```

Notice that what appears inside the square brackets is an integer expression (the result of subtracting 1 from `list.length`).

A simple approach to finding the middle value is to divide the length in half:

```
// is this right?
System.out.println("middle = " + list[list.length / 2]);
```

When `list.length` is 5, this expression evaluates to 2, which prints the correct value. But what about when `list.length` is 10? In that case the expression evaluates to 5, and we would print `list[5]`. But when the list has even length, there are actually two values in the middle, so it is not clear which one should be returned. For a list of length 10, the two values would be at `list[4]` and `list[5]`. In general, the preceding expression would always return the second of the two values in the middle for a list of even length.

If we wanted to instead get the first of the two values in the middle, we could subtract one from the length before dividing by two. Here is a complete set of `println` statements that follows this approach:

```
System.out.println("first = " + list[0]);
System.out.println("middle = " + list[(list.length - 1) / 2]);
System.out.println("last = " + list[list.length - 1]);
```

As you learn how to use arrays, you will find yourself wondering what exactly you can do with an array element that you are accessing. For example, with the array of integers called `list`, what exactly can you do with `list[i]`? The answer is that you can do anything with `list[i]` that you would normally do with any variable of type `int`. For example, if you have a variable called `x` of type `int`, you know that you can say any of the following:

```
x = 3;
x++;
x *= 2;
x--;
```

That means that you can say the same things for `list[i]` if `list` is an array of integers:

```
list[i] = 3;
list[i]++;
list[i] *= 2;
list[i]--;
```

From Java's point of view, because `list` is declared to be of type `int[ ]`, an array element like `list[i]` is of type `int` and can be manipulated as such. For example, to increment every value in the array, you could use the standard traversing loop as follows:

```
for (int i = 0; i < list.length; i++) {
    list[i]++;
}
```

This code would increment each value in the array, turning the array of odd numbers into an array of even numbers.

It is possible to refer to an illegal index of an array, in which case Java throws an exception. For example, for an array of length 5, the legal indexes are from 0 to 4. Any number less than 0 or greater than 4 is outside the bounds of the array:

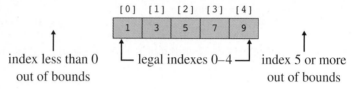

With this sample array, if you attempt to refer to `list[-1]` or `list[5]`, you are attempting to access an array element that does not exist. If your code makes such an illegal reference, Java will halt your program with an `ArrayIndexOutOfBoundsException`.

A Complete Array Program

Let's look at a program where an array allows you to solve a problem you couldn't solve before. If you tune in to any local news broadcast at night, you'll hear them report the high temperature for that day. It is usually reported as an integer, as in, "It got up to 78 today."

Suppose you want to examine a series of high temperatures, compute the average temperature, and count how many days were above average in temperature. You've been using `Scanner`s to solve problems like this, and you can almost solve the problem that way. If you just wanted to know the average, you could use a `Scanner` and write a cumulative sum loop to find it:

```
 1 // Reads a series of high temperatures and reports the average.
 2
 3 import java.util.*;
 4
 5 public class Temperature1 {
 6     public static void main(String[] args) {
 7         Scanner console = new Scanner(System.in);
 8         System.out.print("How many days' temperatures? ");
 9         int numDays = console.nextInt();
10         int sum = 0;
11         for (int i = 1; i <= numDays; i++) {
12             System.out.print("Day " + i + "'s high temp: ");
13             int next = console.nextInt();
14             sum += next;
15         }
16         double average = (double) sum / numDays;
17         System.out.println();
18         System.out.println("Average = " + average);
19     }
20 }
```

Did You Know?

Buffer Overruns

One of the earliest and still most common sources of computer security problems is a *buffer overrun* (also known as a *buffer overflow*). A buffer overrun is similar to an array index out of bounds exception. It occurs when a program writes data beyond the bounds of the buffer set aside for that data.

For example, you might have space allocated for the 12-character `string` "James T Kirk":

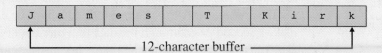

Suppose that you tell the computer to overwrite this buffer with the `string` "Jean Luc Picard". There are 15 letters in Picard's name, so if you write all of those characters into the buffer, you "overrun" it by writing three extra characters:

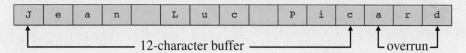

The last three letters of Picard's name ("ard") are being written to a part of memory that is beyond the end of the buffer. This is a very dangerous situation, because it will overwrite any data that is already there. This would be like a fellow student grabbing three sheets of paper from you and erasing anything you had written on them. You are likely to have useful information written on those sheets of paper, so the overrun is likely to cause a problem.

When a buffer overrun happens accidentally, the program usually halts with some kind of error condition. However, buffer overruns are particularly dangerous when they are done on purpose by a malicious program. If the attacker can figure out just the right memory location to overwrite, the attacking software can take over your computer and instruct it to do things you haven't asked it to do.

Three of the most famous internet worms were built on buffer overruns: the 1988 Morris worm, the 2001 Code Red worm, and the 2003 SQLSlammer worm.

Buffer overruns are often written as array code. You might wonder how such a malicious program could be written if the computer checks the bounds when you access an array. The answer is that older programming languages like C and C++ do not check bounds when you access an array. By the time Java was designed in the early 1990s, the danger of buffer overruns was clear and the designers of the language decided to include array-bounds checking so that Java would be more secure. Microsoft included similar bounds checking when it designed the language C# in the late 1990s.

This program does a pretty good job. Here is a sample execution:

```
How many days' temperatures? 5
Day 1's high temp: 78
Day 2's high temp: 81
Day 3's high temp: 75
Day 4's high temp: 79
Day 5's high temp: 71

Average = 76.8
```

But how do you count how many days were above average? You could try to incorporate it into the loop, but that won't work. The problem is that you can't figure out the average until you've gone through all of the data. That means you'll need to make a second pass through the data to figure out how many days were above average. You can't do that with a scanner, because a scanner has no "reset" option that allows you to see the data a second time. You'd have to prompt the user to enter the temperature data a second time, which would be silly.

Fortunately, you can solve the problem with an array. As you read numbers in and compute the cumulative sum, you can fill up an array that stores the temperatures. Then you can use the array to make the second pass through the data.

In the previous temperature example you used an array of double values, but here you want an array of int values. So, instead of declaring a variable of type double[ ], declare a variable of type int[ ]. You're asking the user how many days of temperature data to include, so you can construct the array right after you've read that information:

```
int numDays = console.nextInt();
int[] temps = new int[numDays];
```

The old loop looks like this:

```
for (int i = 1; i <= numDays; i++) {
    System.out.print("Day " + i + "'s high temp: ");
    int next = console.nextInt();
    sum += next;
}
```

Because you're using an array, you'll want to change this to a loop that starts at 0 to match the array indexing. But just because you're using zero-based indexing inside the program doesn't mean that you have to confuse the user by asking for "Day 0's high temp." You can modify the println to prompt for day (i + 1). Furthermore, you no longer need the variable next because you'll be storing the values in the array instead. So, the loop code becomes:

```
for (int i = 0; i < numDays; i++) {
    System.out.print("Day " + (i + 1) + "'s high temp: ");
    temps[i] = console.nextInt();
    sum += temps[i];
}
```

Notice that you're now testing whether the index is strictly less than numDays. After this loop executes, you compute the average as we did before. Then you can write a new loop that counts how many days were above average using our standard traversing loop:

```
int above = 0;
for (int i = 0; i < temps.length; i++) {
    if (temps[i] > average) {
        above++;
    }
}
```

In this loop the test involves temps.length. You could instead have tested whether the variable is less than numDays; either choice works in this program because they should be equal to each other.

If you put these various code fragments together and include code to report the number of days above average, you get the following complete program:

```
 1 // Reads a series of high temperatures and reports the
 2 // average and the number of days above average.
 3
 4 import java.util.*;
 5
 6 public class Temperature2 {
 7     public static void main(String[] args) {
 8         Scanner console = new Scanner(System.in);
 9         System.out.print("How many days' temperatures? ");
10         int numDays = console.nextInt();
11         int[] temps = new int[numDays];
12
13         // record temperatures and find average
14         int sum = 0;
15         for (int i = 0; i < numDays; i++) {
16             System.out.print("Day " + (i + 1)
17                                 + "'s high temp: ");
18             temps[i] = console.nextInt();
19             sum += temps[i];
20         }
21         double average = (double) sum / numDays;
22
23         // count days above average
24         int above = 0;
25         for (int i = 0; i < temps.length; i++) {
26             if (temps[i] > average) {
27                 above++;
28             }
29         }
30
31         // report results
32         System.out.println();
33         System.out.println("Average = " + average);
34         System.out.println(above + " days above average");
35     }
36 }
```

Here is a sample execution:

```
How many days' temperatures? 9
Day 1's high temp: 75
Day 2's high temp: 78
Day 3's high temp: 85
Day 4's high temp: 71
Day 5's high temp: 69
Day 6's high temp: 82
Day 7's high temp: 74
Day 8's high temp: 80
Day 9's high temp: 87

Average = 77.88888888888889
5 days above average
```

Random Access

Most of the algorithms we have seen so for have involved *sequential access.*

> **Sequential Access**
>
> Manipulating values in a sequential manner from first to last.

A `Scanner` object is often all you need for a sequential algorithm, because it allows you to access data in a forward manner from first to last. But as we have seen, there is no way to reset a `Scanner` back to the beginning. The sample program we just looked at uses an array to allow a second pass through the data, but even this is fundamentally a sequential approach because it involves two forward passes through the data.

An array is a powerful data structure that allows a more sophisticated kind of access known as *random access:*

> **Random Access**
>
> Manipulating values in any order whatsoever with quick access to each value.

An array can provide random access because it is allocated as a contiguous block of memory. The computer can quickly compute exactly where a particular value will be stored, because it knows how much space each element takes up in memory and it knows that they are all allocated right next to each other in the array.

Let's explore a problem where random access is important. Suppose that a teacher gives quizzes that are scored on a scale of 0 to 4 and the teacher wants to know the distribution of quiz scores. In other words, the teacher wants to know how many scores of 0 there are, how many scores of 1, how many scores of 2, how many scores of 3, and how many scores of 4. Suppose that the teacher has included all of the scores in a data file like the following:

```
1 4 1 0 3 2 1 4 2 0
3 0 2 3 0 4 3 3 4 1
2 4 1 3 1 4 3 3 2 4
2 3 0 4 1 4 4 1 4 1
```

Common Programming Error:	

Off-by-One Bug

In converting the `Temperature1` program to one that uses an array, you modified the `for` loop to start with an index of 0 instead of 1. The original `for` loop was written this way:

```
for (int i = 1; i <= numDays; i++) {
    System.out.print("Day " + i + "'s high temp: ");
    int next = console.nextInt();
    sum += next;
}
```

Because you were storing the values into an array rather than reading them into a variable called `next`, you replaced `next` with `temps[i]`:

```
// wrong loop bounds
for (int i = 1; i <= numDays; i++) {
    System.out.print("Day " + i + "'s high temp: ");
    temps[i] = console.nextInt();
    sum += temps[i];
}
```

Because the array is indexed starting at 0, you changed the bounds of the `for` loop to start at 0 and adjusted the `print` statement. Suppose those were the only changes you made:

```
// still wrong loop bounds
for (int i = 0; i <= numDays; i++) {
    System.out.print("Day " + (i + 1) + "'s high temp: ");
    temps[i] = console.nextInt();
    sum += temps[i];
}
```

This loop generates an error when you run it. It asks for an extra day's worth of data and then throws an exception, as in the following sample execution:

```
How many days' temperatures? 5
Day 1's high temp: 82
Day 2's high temp: 80
Day 3's high temp: 79
Day 4's high temp: 71
Day 5's high temp: 75
Day 6's high temp: 83
Exception in thread "main"
    java.lang.ArrayIndexOutOfBoundsException: 5
        at Temperature2.main(Temperature2.java:18)
```

The problem is that if you're going to start the `for` loop variable at 0, you need to test for it being strictly less than the number of iterations you want. You changed the 1 to a 0 but left the <= test. As a result, the loop is performing an extra iteration and trying to make a reference to an array element `temps[5]` that doesn't exist.

This is a classic off-by-one error. The fix is to change the loop bounds to use a strictly less-than test:

```
// correct bounds
for (int i = 0; i < numDays; i++) {
    System.out.print("Day " + (i + 1) + "'s high temp: ");
    temps[i] = console.nextInt();
    sum += temps[i];
}
```

The teacher could hand-count the scores, but it would be much easier to use a computer to do the counting. How can you solve the problem? First you have to recognize that you are doing five separate counting tasks: You are counting the occurrences of the number 0, the number 1, the number 2, the number 3, and the number 4. You will need five counters to solve this problem, which means that an array is a great way to store the data. In general, whenever you find yourself thinking that you need *n* of some kind of data, you should think about using an array of length *n*.

Each counter will be an `int`, so you want an array of five `int` values:

```
int[] count = new int[5];
```

This will allocate the array of five integers and will auto-initialize each to 0:

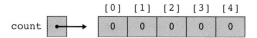

You're reading from a file, so you'll need a `Scanner` and a loop that reads scores until there are no more scores to read:

```
Scanner input = new Scanner(new File("tally.dat"));
while (input.hasNextInt()) {
    int next = input.nextInt();
    // process next
}
```

To complete this code, you need to figure out how to process each value. You know that `next` will be one of five different values: 0, 1, 2, 3, or 4. If it is 0 you want to increment the counter for 0, which is `count[0]`, if it is 1, you want to increment the counter for 1, which is `count[1]`, and so on. We have been solving problems like this one with nested `if`/`else` statements:

```
if (next == 0) {
    count[0]++;
} else if (next == 1) {
    count[1]++;
} else if (next == 2) {
    count[2]++;
} else if (next == 3) {
    count[3]++;
} else { // next == 4
    count[4]++;
}
```

But with an array, you can solve this problem much more directly:

```
count[next]++;
```

This line of code is so short compared to the nested if/else construct that you might not realize at first that it does the same thing. Let's simulate exactly what happens as various values are read from the file.

When the array is constructed, all of the counters are initialized to 0:

The first value in the input file is a 1, so the program reads that into next. Then it executes this line of code:

```
count[next]++;
```

Because next is 1, this becomes:

```
count[1]++;
```

So the counter at index [1] is incremented:

Then a 4 is read from the input file, which means count[4] is incremented:

Next, another 1 is read from the input file, which increments count[1]:

Then a 0 is read from the input file, which increments count[0]:

Notice that in just this short set of data you've jumped from index 1 to index 4, then back down to index 1, then to index 0. The program continues executing in this manner, jumping from counter to counter as it reads values from the file. This ability to jump around in the data structure is what's meant by random access.

After processing all of the data, the array ends up looking like this:

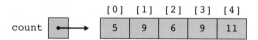

After this loop finishes executing, you can report the total for each score by using the standard traversing loop with a `println`:

```
for (int i = 0; i < count.length; i++) {
    System.out.println(i + "\t" + count[i]);
}
```

If you put this all together and add a header for the output, you get the following complete program:

```
 1 // Reads a series of values and reports the frequency of
 2 // occurrence of each value.
 3
 4 import java.io.*;
 5 import java.util.*;
 6
 7 public class Tally {
 8     public static void main(String[] args)
 9             throws FileNotFoundException {
10         Scanner input = new Scanner(new File("tally.dat"));
11         int[] count = new int[5];
12         while (input.hasNextInt()) {
13             int next = input.nextInt();
14             count[next]++;
15         }
16         System.out.println("Value\tOccurrences");
17         for (int i = 0; i < count.length; i++) {
18             System.out.println(i + "\t" + count[i]);
19         }
20     }
21 }
```

Given the sample input file shown earlier, it produces the following output:

```
Value   Occurrences
0       5
1       9
2       6
3       9
4       11
```

It is important to realize that a program written with an array is much more flexible than programs written with simple variables and `if/else` statements. For example, suppose you wanted to adapt this program to process an input file with exam scores that range from 0 to 100. The only change you would would have to make would be to allocate a larger array:

```
int[] count = new int[101];
```

If you had written the program with an `if/else` approach, you would have to add 96 new branches to account for the new range of values. With the array solution, you just have to modify the overall size of the array. Notice that the array size is one more than the highest score (101 rather than 100) because the array is zero-based and because you can actually get 101 different scores on the test when 0 is a possibility.

Arrays and Methods

You've spent so much time learning how to manipulate variables of type `int` and `double` that it will probably take you awhile to get used to some of the differences that arise when you manipulate arrays. Remember that primitive types like `int` and `double` have value semantics. For example, in Chapter 3 we examined the following method that was intended to double a number:

```
public static void doubleNumber(int number) {
    System.out.println("Initial value of number = " + number);
    number *= 2;
    System.out.println("Final value of number = " + number);
}
```

The `println`s made it clear that the method successfully doubles the local variable called `number`, but we found that it did not double a variable that we included as a parameter in the call. That is because with the value semantics of primitive types like `int`, parameters are copies that have no effect on the original.

Because arrays are objects, they have *reference* semantics, which means that array variables store references to array objects and parameter passing involves copying references. Let's explore a specific example to better understand this. Earlier in the chapter we saw the following code for constructing an array of odd numbers and incrementing each array element:

```
int[] list = new int[5];
for (int i = 0; i < list.length; i++) {
    list[i] = 2 * i + 1;
}

for (int i = 0; i < list.length; i++) {
    list[i]++;
}
```

Let's see what happens when we move the incrementing loop into a method. It will need to take the array as a parameter. We'll rename it `data` instead of `list` to make it easier to distinguish it from the original array variable. Remember that the array is of type `int[]`, so we would write the method as follows:

```
public static void incrementAll(int[] data) {
    for (int i = 0; i < data.length; i++) {
        data[i]++;
    }
}
```

You might think this method, like the `doubleNumber` method, will have no effect whatsoever, or that we have to return the array to cause the change to be remembered. But with an array as a parameter, this approach actually works. We can replace the incrementing loop in the original code with a call on our method:

```
int[] list = new int[5];
for (int i = 0; i < list.length; i++) {
    list[i] = 2 * i + 1;
}
incrementAll(list);
```

This code produces the same result as the original. Let's see why it works. After executing the `for` loop, the array will contain the first five odd numbers:

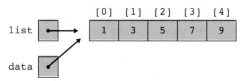

Then we call the `incrementAll` method, passing it the array as a parameter. At this point we see the critical difference between the behavior of a simple `int` and the behavior of an array. In effect, we make a copy of the variable `list`. But the variable `list` is not itself the array; rather, it stores a reference to the array. So, when we make a copy of that reference, we end up with two references to the same object:

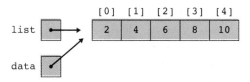

Because `data` and `list` both refer to the same object, when we change `data` by saying `data[i]++`, we end up changing the object that `list` refers to. So, after the loop increments each element of data, we end up with the following:

Then we call the `incrementAll` method, passing it the array as a parameter. At this point the method finishes executing and the parameter `data` goes away. We return to the original code with an array that has been changed by the method.

The key lesson to draw from this is that when we pass an array as a parameter to a method, that method has the ability to change the contents of the array. We don't need to return the array to allow this to happen.

Now let's rewrite the `Tally` program to demonstrate a complete array program with methods and parameter passing. The program begins by constructing a `Scanner` and an array, and then it has two loops: one to read the input file and one to report the results. We can put each loop in its own method. The first loop reads from the `Scanner` and stores its result in the array, so it will need both objects as parameters. The second reports the values in the array, so it needs just the array as a parameter. Thus, the `main` method can be rewritten as follows:

```
public static void main(String[] args)
        throws FileNotFoundException {
    Scanner input = new Scanner(new File("tally.dat"));
    int[] count = new int[5];
    readData(input, count);
    reportResults(count);
}
```

To write the `readData` method, we just need to move the file-processing loop into the method and provide an appropriate header:

```
public static void readData(Scanner input, int[] count) {
    while (input.hasNextInt()) {
        int next = input.nextInt();
        count[next]++;
    }
}
```

As with the `incrementAll` method, this method would change the array even though it does not return it. But this isn't the best approach to use in this situation. It seems odd that the `readData` method requires you to construct an array and pass it as a parameter. Why doesn't `readData` construct the array itself? That would simplify the call to the method, particularly if we ended up calling it multiple times.

If `readData` is going to construct the array, it will have to return a reference to it. Otherwise, only the method will have a reference to the newly constructed array. In its current form, the `readData` method assumes that the array has already been constructed, which is why we wrote these two lines of code in `main`:

```
int[] count = new int[5];
readData(input, count);
```

If the method is going to construct the array, it doesn't have to be passed as a parameter, but it will have to be returned by the method. Thus, we can rewrite these two lines of code from `main` as a single line:

```
int[] count = readData(input);
```

and we can rewrite the `readData` method so that it constructs and returns the array:

```
public static int[] readData(Scanner input) {
    int[] count = new int[5];
    while (input.hasNextInt()) {
```

```
                int next = input.nextInt();
                count[next]++;
            }
            return count;
        }
    }
```

Pay close attention to the header of this method. It no longer has the array as a parameter, and its return type is `int[]` rather than `void`. It also ends with a `return` statement that returns a reference to the array that it constructs.

If we combine this new version of the method with an implementation of the `reportResults` method, we end up with the following complete program:

```
 1 // Variation of Tally program with methods.
 2
 3 import java.io.*;
 4 import java.util.*;
 5
 6 public class Tally2 {
 7     public static void main(String[] args)
 8             throws FileNotFoundException {
 9         Scanner input = new Scanner(new File("tally.dat"));
10         int[] count = readData(input);
11         reportResults(count);
12     }
13
14     public static int[] readData(Scanner input) {
15         int[] count = new int[5];
16         while (input.hasNextInt()) {
17             int next = input.nextInt();
18             count[next]++;
19         }
20         return count;
21     }
22
23     public static void reportResults(int[] count) {
24         System.out.println("Value\tOccurrences");
25         for (int i = 0; i < count.length; i++) {
26             System.out.println(i + "\t" + count[i]);
27         }
28     }
29 }
```

This version produces the same output as the original.

The For-Each Loop

Java 5 introduced a new loop construct that simplifies certain array loops. It is known as the enhanced `for` loop, or the for-each loop. It can be used whenever you find yourself wanting to examine each value in an array. For example, in the program `Temperature2` had an array variable called `temps` and the following loop:

```
for (int i = 0; i < temps.length; i++) {
    if (temps[i] > average) {
```

```
        above++;
    }
}
```

We can rewrite this as a for-each loop:

```
for (int n : temps) {
    if (n > average) {
        above++;
    }
}
```

This loop is normally read as, "For each int n in temps. . . ." The basic syntax of the for-each loop is:

```
for (<type> <name> : <array>) {
    <statement>;
    <statement>;
    . . .
    <statement>;
}
```

There is nothing special about the variable name, as long as you are consistent in the body of the loop. For example, the previous loop could be written with the variable x instead of the variable n:

```
for (int x : temps) {
    if (x > average) {
        above++;
    }
}
```

The for-each loop is most useful when you simply want to examine each value in sequence. There are many situations where a for-each loop is not appropriate. For example, the following loop would double every value in an array called list:

```
for (int i = 0; i < list.length; i++) {
    list[i] *= 2;
}
```

Because the loop is changing the array, you can't replace it with a for-each loop:

```
for (int n : list) {
    n *= 2; // changes only n, not the array
}
```

As the comment indicates, the preceding loop doubles the variable n without changing the array elements.

Also, in some cases the for-each loop isn't the most convenient even when the code involves examining each array element in sequence. Consider, for example, this loop from the Tally program:

```
for (int i = 0; i < count.length; i++) {
    System.out.println(i + "\t" + count[i]);
}
```

A for-each loop could be used to replace the array access:

```
for (int n : count) {
    System.out.println(i + "\t" + n); // not quite legal
}
```

However, this would cause a problem. We want to print the value of i, but we eliminated i when we converted this to a for-each loop. We would have to add extra code to keep track of the value of i, as in:

```
// legal but clumsy
int i = 0;
for (int n : count) {
    System.out.println(i + "\t" + n);
    i++;
}
```

In this case, the for-each loop doesn't really simplify things, and the original version is probably clearer.

Initializing Arrays

Java has a special syntax for initializing an array when you know exactly what you want to put into it. For example, you could write the following code to initialize an array of integers to keep track of how many days are in each month ("Thirty days hath September ... ") and an array of `strings` to keep track of the abbreviations for the names of the days of the week:

```
int[] daysIn = new int[12];
daysIn[0] = 31;
daysIn[1] = 28;
daysIn[2] = 31;
daysIn[3] = 30;
daysIn[4] = 31;
daysIn[5] = 30;
daysIn[6] = 31;
daysIn[7] = 31;
daysIn[8] = 30;
daysIn[9] = 31;
daysIn[10] = 30;
daysIn[11] = 31;

String[] dayNames = new String[7];
dayNames[0] = "Mon";
dayNames[1] = "Tue";
dayNames[2] = "Wed";
dayNames[3] = "Thu";
dayNames[4] = "Fri";
dayNames[5] = "Sat";
dayNames[6] = "Sun";
```

This works, but it's a rather tedious way to declare these arrays. Java provides a shorthand:

```
int[] daysIn = {31, 28, 31, 30, 31, 30, 31, 31, 30, 31, 30, 31};
String[] dayNames = {"Mon", "Tue", "Wed", "Thu", "Fri",
                     "Sat", "Sun"};
```

The general syntax for array initialization is as follows:

```
<element type>[] <name> = {<value>, <value>, . . . , <value>};
```

You use the curly braces to enclose a series of values that will be stored in the array. Order is important. The first value will go into index 0, the second value will go into index 1, and so on. Java counts how many values you include and constructs an array of just the right size. It then stores the various values into the appropriate spots in the array.

This is one of only two examples we have seen in which Java will construct an object without the new keyword. The other place we saw this was with String literals, where Java constructs String objects for you without you having to call new. Both of these are conveniences for programmers. These tasks are so common that the designers of the language wanted to make it easy to do them.

Limitations of Arrays

You should be aware of some general limitations of arrays:

- You can't change the size of an array in the middle of program execution.
- You can't compare arrays for equality using a simple == test. Remember that arrays are objects, so if you ask whether one array is == to another array, you are asking whether they are the same object, not whether they store the same values.
- You can't print an array using a simple print or println statement. You will get odd output when you do so.

These limitations have existed in Java since the language was first introduced. Over the years, Sun has introduced several additions to the Java class libraries to address them. The Arrays class provides a solution to the second and third limitations. You can compare two arrays for equality by calling the method Arrays.equals, and you can convert an array into a useful text equivalent by calling the method Arrays.toString. Both of these methods will be discussed in detail in the next section, when we explore how they are written.

The first limitation is more difficult to overcome. Because an array is allocated as a contiguous block of memory, it is not easy to make it larger. To make an array bigger, you'd have to construct a new array that is larger than the old one and copy values from the old to the new array. Java provides a class called ArrayList that does this growing operation automatically. It also provides methods for inserting values in and deleting values from the middle of a list. We will explore how to use the ArrayList class in Chapter 10.

The `Arrays` class is part of the `java.util` package that also includes `Scanner`, so to use it you must include an `import` declaration in your program.

7.2 Array-Traversal Algorithms

The last section presented two standard patterns for manipulating an array. The first is the traversing loop, which uses a variable of type `int` to index each array value:

```
for (int i = 0; i < <array>.length; i++) {
    <do something with array[i]>;
}
```

The second is the for-each loop:

```
for (<type> <name> : <array>) {
    <statement>;
    <statement>;
    . . .
    <statement>;
}
```

In this section we will explore some common array algorithms that can be implemented with these patterns. Of course, not all array operations can be implemented this way—the section ends with an example that requires a modified version of the standard code.

We will implement each operation as a method. Java does not allow you to write generic array code, so we have to pick a specific type. We'll assume that you are operating on an array of `int` values. If you are writing a program to manipulate a different kind of array, you'll have to modify the code for the type you are using (e.g., changing `int[]` to `double[]` if you are manipulating an array of `double` values).

Printing an Array

Suppose you have an array of `int` values like the following:

```
       [0]  [1]  [2]  [3]  [4]  [5]  [6]
list ──▶ 17  -3   42   8   12    2   103
```

How would you go about printing the values in the array? For other types of data you can use a `println` statement, as in:

```
System.out.println(list);
```

Unfortunately, with an array this produces strange output like the following:

```
[I@6caf43
```

This is not helpful output, and it tells us nothing about the contents of the array. Java provides a solution to this problem in the form of a method called

```java
public static void rotateRight(int[] list) {
    int last = list[list.length - 1];
    for (int i = list.length - 1; i > 0; i--) {
        list[i] = list[i - 1];
    }
    list[0] = last;
}
```

Arrays of Objects

All of the arrays we have looked at so far have stored primitive values like simple
int values, but you can have arrays of any Java type. Arrays of objects behave
slightly differently, though, because objects are stored as references rather than as
data values. Constructing an array of objects is usually a two-step process, because
you normally have to construct both the array and the individual objects.

Consider, for example, the following statement:

```java
Point[] points = new Point[3];
```

This declares a variable called `points` that refers to an array of length 3 that stores
references to `Point` objects. The `new` keyword doesn't construct any actual `Point`
objects. Instead it constructs an array of length 3, each element of which can store a
reference to a `Point`. When Java constructs the array, it auto-initializes these array
elements to the zero-equivalent for the type. The zero-equivalent for all reference
types is the special value `null`, which indicates "no object":

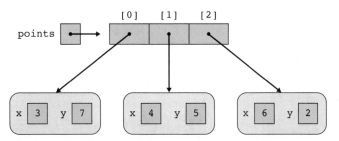

The actual `Point` objects must be constructed separately with the `new` keyword, as in:

```java
Point[] points = new Point[3];
points[0] = new Point(3, 7);
points[1] = new Point(4, 5);
points[2] = new Point(6, 2);
```

After these lines of code execute, you would have individual `Point` objects
referred to by the various array elements:

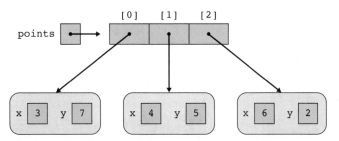

Notice that the `new` keyword is required in four different places, because there are
four objects to be constructed: the array itself and the three individual `Point` objects.

You could also use the curly brace notation for initializing the array, in which case you don't need the new keyword to construct the array itself:

```
Point[] points = {new Point(3, 7), new Point(4, 5),
                  new Point(6, 2)};
```

Command-Line Arguments

As you've seen since Chapter 1, whenever you define a main method, you're required to include as its parameter String[] args, which is an array of String objects. Java itself initializes this array if the user provides what are known as *command-line arguments* when invoking Java. For example, a Java class called DoSomething would normally be started from the command interface by a command like this:

```
java DoSomething
```

The user has the option to type extra arguments, as in:

```
java DoSomething temperature.dat temperature.out
```

In this case the user has specified two extra arguments that are file names that the program should use (e.g., the names of an input and output file). If the user types these extra arguments when starting up Java, the String[] args parameter to main will be initialized to an array of length 2 storing these two strings:

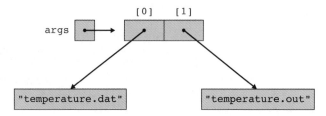

7.4 Multidimensional Arrays (Optional)

The array examples in the previous sections all involved what are known as one-dimensional arrays (a single row or a single column of data). Often, you'll want to store data in a multidimensional way. For example, you might want to store a two-dimensional grid of data that has both rows and columns. Fortunately, you can form arrays of arbitrarily many dimensions:

- double: one double
- double[]: a one-dimensional array of doubles
- double[][]: a two-dimensional grid of doubles
- double[][][]: a three-dimensional collection of doubles
- ...

Arrays of more than one dimension are called *multidimensional arrays.*

> **Multidimensional Array**
>
> An array of arrays, the elements of which are accessed with multiple integer indexes.

Rectangular Two-Dimensional Arrays

The most common use of a multidimensional array is a two-dimensional array of a certain width and height. For example, suppose that on three separate days you took a series of five temperature readings. You can define a two-dimensional array that has three rows and five columns as follows:

```
double[][] temps = new double[3][5];
```

Notice that on both the left and right sides of this assignment statement, you have to use a double set of square brackets. When describing the type on the left, you have to make it clear that this is not just a one-dimensional sequence of values, which would be of type `double[]`, but instead a two-dimensional grid of values, which is of type `double[][]`. On the right, in constructing the array, you must specify the dimensions of the grid. The normal convention is to list the row first followed by the column. The resulting array would look like this:

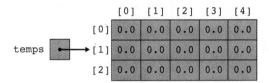

As with one-dimensional arrays, the values are initialized to `0.0` and the indexes start with 0 for both rows and columns. Once you've created such an array, you can refer to individual elements by providing specific row and column numbers (in that order). For example, to set the fourth value of the first row to `98.3` and to set the first value of the third row to `99.4`, you would say:

```
temps[0][3] = 98.3;   // fourth value of first row
temps[2][0] = 99.4;   // first value of third row
```

After executing these lines of code, the array would look like this:

	[0]	[1]	[2]	[3]	[4]
[0]	0.0	0.0	0.0	98.3	0.0
[1]	0.0	0.0	0.0	0.0	0.0
[2]	99.4	0.0	0.0	0.0	0.0

It is helpful to think of this in a stepwise fashion, starting with the name of the array. For example, if you want to refer to the first value of the third row, you obtain that through the following steps:

```
temps              the entire grid
temps[2]           the entire third row
temps[2][0]        the first element of the third row
```

You can pass multidimensional arrays as parameters just as you pass one-dimensional arrays. You need to be careful about the type, though. To pass the temperature grid, you would have to use a parameter of type `double[][]` (with both sets of brackets). For example, here is a method that prints the grid:

```java
public static void print(double[][] grid) {
    for (int i = 0; i < grid.length; i++) {
        for (int j = 0; j < grid[i].length; j++) {
            System.out.print(grid[i][j] + " ");
        }
        System.out.println();
    }
}
```

Notice that to ask for the number of rows you ask for `grid.length` and to ask for the number of columns you ask for `grid[i].length`.

The `Arrays.toString` method mentioned earlier in this chapter does work on multidimensional arrays, but it produces a poor result. When used with the preceding array `temps`, it can be used to produce output such as the following:

```
[[D@14b081b, [D@1015a9e, [D@1e45a5c]
```

This is because `Arrays.toString` works by concatenating the `String` representations of the array's elements. In this case the elements are arrays themselves, so they do not convert into `String`s properly. To correct the problem you can use a different method, called `Arrays.deepToString` that will return better results for multidimensional arrays:

```java
System.out.println(Arrays.deepToString(temps));
```

The call produces the following output:

```
[[0.0, 0.0, 0.0, 98.3, 0.0], [0.0, 0.0, 0.0, 0.0, 0.0],
[99.4, 0.0, 0.0, 0.0, 0.0]]
```

Arrays can have as many dimensions as you want. For example, if you want a three-dimensional 4 by 4 by 4 cube of integers, you would say:

```java
int[][][] numbers = new int[4][4][4];
```

The normal convention would be to assume that this is the plane number followed by the row number followed by the column number, although you can use any convention you want as long as your code is written consistently.

Jagged Arrays

The previous examples have involved rectangular grids that have a fixed number of rows and columns. It is also possible to create a jagged array, where the number of columns varies from row to row.

To construct a jagged array, divide the construction into two steps: Construct the array for holding rows first, and then construct each individual row. For example, to construct an array that has two elements in the first row, four elements in the second row, and three elements in the third row, you can say:

```
int[][] jagged = new int[3][];
jagged[0] = new int[2];
jagged[1] = new int[4];
jagged[2] = new int[3];
```

This would construct an array that looks like this:

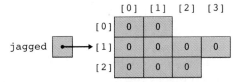

We can explore this technique by writing a program that produces the rows of what is known as *Pascal's Triangle*. The numbers in the triangle have many useful mathematical properties. For example, row *n* of Pascal's triangle contains the coefficients obtained when you expand:

$(x + y)^n$

Here are the results for *n* between 0 and 4:

$(x + y)^0 = 1$
$(x + y)^1 = x + y$
$(x + y)^2 = x^2 + 2xy + y^2$
$(x + y)^3 = x^3 + 3x^2y + 3xy^2 + y^3$
$(x + y)^4 = x^4 + 4x^3y + 6x^2y^2 + 4xy^3 + y^4$

If you pull out just the coefficients, you get the following:

1
1 1
1 2 1
1 3 3 1
1 4 6 4 1

This is Pascal's triangle. One of the properties of the triangle is that given any row, you can use it to compute the next row. For example, let's start with the last row from the preceding triangle:

1 4 6 4 1

We can compute the next row by adding adjacent pairs of values together. So, we add together the first pair of numbers (1 + 4), then the second pair of numbers (4 + 6), and so on:

$$\underbrace{(1 + 4)}_{5} \quad \underbrace{(4 + 6)}_{10} \quad \underbrace{(6 + 4)}_{10} \quad \underbrace{(4 + 1)}_{5}$$

Then we put a 1 at the front and back of this list of numbers, and we end up with the next row of the triangle:

```
1
1 1
1 2 1
1 3 3 1
1 4 6 4 1
1 5 10 10 5 1
```

This property of the triangle provides a technique for computing it. We can construct it row by row, computing each new row from the values in the previous row. In other words, we are going to write a loop like this (assuming we have a two-dimensional array called `triangle` in which to store the answer):

```
for (int i = 0; i < triangle.length; i++) {
    construct triangle[i] using triangle[i - 1].
}
```

We just need to flesh out the details of how a new row is constructed. This is going to be a jagged array because each row has a different number of elements. Looking at the triangle, you'll see that the first row (row 0) has one value in it, the second row (row 1) has two values in it, and so on. In general, row `i` has (`i` + 1) values, so we can refine our pseudocode as follows:

```
for (int i = 0; i < triangle.length; i++) {
    triangle[i] = new int[i + 1];
    fill in triangle[i] using triangle[i - 1].
}
```

We know that the first and last values in the row should be 1:

```
for (int i = 0; i < triangle.length; i++) {
    triangle[i] = new int[i + 1];
    triangle[i][0] = 1;
    triangle[i][i] = 1;
    fill in the middle of triangle[i] using triangle[i - 1]
}
```

And we know that the middle values comes from the previous row. To figure out how to do this, let's draw a picture of the array we are attempting to build:

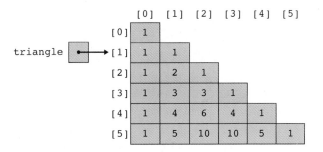

We have already written code to fill in the 1 that appears at the beginning and end of each row. We now need to write code to fill in the middle values. Look at row 5 for an example. The value 5 in column 1 comes from the sum of the values 1 and 4 in columns 0 and 1 in the previous row. The value 10 in column 2 comes from the sum of the values in columns 1 and 2 in the previous row.

More generally, each of these middle values is the sum of the two values from the previous row that appear just above and just above and to the left of it. In other words, for column j:

```
triangle[i][j] = (value above and left) + (value above);
```

We can turn this into actual code by using the appropriate array indexes:

```
triangle[i][j] = triangle[i - 1][j - 1] + triangle[i - 1][j];
```

We need to include this statement in a for loop so that it assigns all of the middle values, which allows us to finish converting our pseudocode into actual code:

```
for (int i = 0; i < triangle.length; i++) {
    triangle[i] = new int[i + 1];
    triangle[i][0] = 1;
    triangle[i][i] = 1;
    for (int j = 1; j < i; j++) {
        triangle[i][j] = triangle[i - 1][j - 1]
                       + triangle[i - 1][j];
    }
}
```

If we include this code in a method along with a printing method similar to the grid-printing method described earlier, we end up with the following complete program:

```
 1 // This program constructs a jagged two-dimensional array
 2 // that stores Pascal's Triangle. It takes advantage of the
 3 // fact that each value other than the 1s that appear at the
 4 // beginning and end of each row is the sum of two values
 5 // from the previous row.
 6
 7 public class PascalsTriangle {
 8     public static void main(String[] args) {
 9         int[][] triangle = new int[11][];
10         fillIn(triangle);
11         print(triangle);
```

```
12        }
13
14      public static void fillIn(int[][] triangle) {
15          for (int i = 0; i < triangle.length; i++) {
16              triangle[i] = new int[i + 1];
17              triangle[i][0] = 1;
18              triangle[i][i] = 1;
19              for (int j = 1; j < i; j++) {
20                  triangle[i][j] = triangle[i - 1][j - 1]
21                      + triangle[i - 1][j];
22              }
23          }
24      }
25
26      public static void print(int[][] triangle) {
27          for (int i = 0; i < triangle.length; i++) {
28              for (int j = 0; j < triangle[i].length; j++) {
29                  System.out.print(triangle[i][j] + " ");
30              }
31              System.out.println();
32          }
33      }
34 }
```

It produces the following output:

```
1
1 1
1 2 1
1 3 3 1
1 4 6 4 1
1 5 10 10 5 1
1 6 15 20 15 6 1
1 7 21 35 35 21 7 1
1 8 28 56 70 56 28 8 1
1 9 36 84 126 126 84 36 9 1
1 10 45 120 210 252 210 120 45 10 1
```

7.5 Case Study: Hours Worked

Let's look at a more complex program example that involves using arrays. Suppose we have an input file containing data indicating how many hours an employee has worked, with each line of the input file indicating the hours worked for a different week. Each week has seven days, so there could be up to seven numbers listed on each line. We generally consider Monday to be the start of the work week, so let's assume that each line lists hours worked on Monday followed by hours worked on Tuesday, and so on, ending with hours worked on Sunday. But we'll allow the lines to have fewer than seven numbers, because the person may not always work seven days. Here is a sample input file that we'll call hours.txt:

```
8 8 8 8 8
8 4 8 4 8 4 4
8 4 8 4 8
3 0 0 8 6 4 4
8 8
0 0 8 8
8 8 4 8 4
```

Let's write a program that reads this input file, reporting totals for each row and each column. The totals for each row will tell us how many hours the person has worked each week. The totals for each column will tell us how many hours the person worked on Mondays versus Tuesdays versus Wednesdays, and so on.

One way to approach this problem would be to store all of the data in a two-dimensional array and then add up the individual rows and columns. However, we don't need quite such a complicated solution for this particular task.

We have to process the input file one line at a time, so it makes sense to read each line of data into an array and to report the total for that line as soon as we have read it in. This takes care of reporting the sum for each row. To report the sum for each column, we can have a second array that keeps track of the running sum for the columns (the sum up to this line of the input file). This array will have to be constructed before the file-processing loop and can be printed after the loop finishes reading the input file. This approach is an array equivalent of the cumulative sum algorithm.

The basic approach is outlined in the following pseudocode:

```
construct array for total.
for (each line of the input file) {
    transfer the next line of data into an array.
    report the sum of the array (sum for this row).
    add this data to total array.
}
print total array.
```

We will once again develop the program in stages:

1. A program that reads each line of the input file into an array, printing each array to verify that the file is being read correctly

2. A program that reads each line of the input file into an array, adding it into a total array that sums the columns

3. A complete program that reports the sum of each row and that prints the total in an easy-to-read format

Version 1: Reading the Input File

In the first version of the program, we'll write the basic file-processing code that will read each line of data into an array. Eventually we will have to process that data, but for now we will simply print the array to verify that the code is working properly.

The `main` method can be fairly short, opening the input file we want to read and calling a method to process the file:

```
public static void main(String[] args)
        throws FileNotFoundException {
    Scanner input = new Scanner(new File("hours.txt"));
    processFile(input);
}
```

That leaves us the task of writing the code for `processFile`. We saw in Chapter 6 that for line-oriented data, we can generally use the following pattern as a starting point for file-processing code:

```
while (input.hasNextLine()) {
    String text = input.nextLine();
    process text.
}
```

For this version of the program, processing the text involves transferring data from the `String` into an array and printing the contents of the array. We can put the transfer code in its own method to keep `processFile` short and we can use `Arrays.toString` to print the array, which means that the body of `processFile` becomes:

```
while (input.hasNextLine()) {
    String text = input.nextLine();
    int[] next = transferFrom(text);
    System.out.println(Arrays.toString(next));
}
```

The `transferFrom` method is given a `String` as a parameter and is supposed to construct a new array containing the numbers from the `String`. As usual, we will construct a `Scanner` from the `String` that allows us to read the individual numbers. Each input line has at most seven numbers, but it might have fewer. As a result, it makes sense to use a `while` loop that tests whether there are more numbers left to read from the `Scanner`:

```
construct a Scanner and array.
while (the Scanner has a next int) {
    process next int from scanner.
}
```

In this case, processing the next integer from the input means storing it in the array. The first number should go into index 0, the second number in index 1, the third number in index 2, and so on. That means we need some kind of integer counter that increments by one each time through the loop:

```
construct a Scanner and array.
initialize i to 0.
while (the Scanner has a next int) {
    store data.nextInt() in position i of the array.
    increment i.
}
```

This is now fairly easy to translate into actual code:

```
Scanner data = new Scanner(text);
int[] result = new int[7];
int i = 0;
while (data.hasNextInt()) {
    result[i] = data.nextInt();
    i++;
}
```

If we put these pieces together, we end up with the following program:

```
 1  // First version of program that simply reads and echos.
 2
 3  import java.io.*;
 4  import java.util.*;
 5
 6  public class Hours1 {
 7      public static void main(String[] args)
 8              throws FileNotFoundException {
 9          Scanner input = new Scanner(new File("hours.txt"));
10          processFile(input);
11      }
12
13      public static void processFile(Scanner input) {
14          while (input.hasNextLine()) {
15              String text = input.nextLine();
16              int[] next = transferFrom(text);
17              System.out.println(Arrays.toString(next));
18          }
19      }
20
21      public static int[] transferFrom(String text) {
22          Scanner data = new Scanner(text);
23          int[] result = new int[7];
24          int i = 0;
25          while (data.hasNextInt()) {
26              result[i] = data.nextInt();
27              i++;
28          }
29          return result;
30      }
31  }
```

The program produces the following output:

```
[8, 8, 8, 8, 8, 0, 0]
[8, 4, 8, 4, 8, 4, 4]
[8, 4, 8, 4, 8, 0, 0]
[3, 0, 0, 8, 6, 4, 4]
[8, 8, 0, 0, 0, 0, 0]
[0, 0, 8, 8, 0, 0, 0]
[8, 8, 4, 8, 4, 0, 0]
```

If you compare this output to the original input file, you'll see that it is properly reading each line of data into an array of length 7. When the input line has fewer than seven numbers the array is padded with 0s, which is exactly the behavior that we want.

Notice that none of this output will be included in the final version of the program. Programmers often include output like this that helps to debug a program while it is being developed.

Version 2: Cumulative Sum

The primary change we want to make in this version of the program is to introduce the second array that keeps track of the column sums. That means we're going to extend the code for processFile, which currently looks like this:

```
while (input.hasNextLine()) {
    String text = input.nextLine();
    int[] next = transferFrom(text);
    System.out.println(Arrays.toString(next));
}
```

We need to construct the total array before the loop, and we want to print it after the loop. Inside the loop, we want to add the next line of data into the overall total. To keep this method short, we can introduce another method that will perform the addition:

```
int[] total = new int[7];
while (input.hasNextLine()) {
    String text = input.nextLine();
    int[] next = transferFrom(text);
    addTo(total, next);
}
System.out.println(Arrays.toString(total));
```

This version drops the println inside the loop because we have already verified that the individual rows of data are being read properly into an array.

At this point it is worth noting that we have already used the number 7 twice in the program to construct the two arrays. It is essential that the two arrays be of the same length, so it makes sense to define a class constant that we can use instead:

```
public static final int DAYS = 7; // # of days in a week
```

We can also use this constant for our various for loops instead of the usual array length.

To complete the second version, we have to write the addTo method. We will be given two arrays, one with the total hours and one with the next week's hours. Let's consider where we'll be in the middle of processing the sample input file. The first three lines of input are as follows:

```
8 8 8 8 8
8 4 8 4 8 4 4
8 4 8 4 8
```

Suppose we have properly processed the first two lines and have just read in the third line for processing. Our two arrays will look like this:

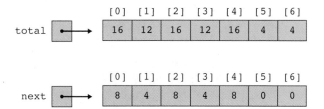

It would be nice if we could just say:

```
total += next; // does not compile
```

Unfortunately, we can't use operations like + and += on arrays. However, those operations can be performed on simple integers, and these arrays are composed of simple integers. So, we basically just have to tell the computer to do seven different += operations on the individual array elements. This can be easily written with a for loop:

```java
public static void addTo(int[] total, int[] next) {
    for (int i = 0; i < DAYS; i++) {
        total[i] += next[i];
    }
}
```

So, our second version ends up looking like this:

```java
1  // Second version of program that computes column sums.
2
3  import java.io.*;
4  import java.util.*;
5
6  public class Hours2 {
7      public static final int DAYS = 7; // # of days in a week
8
9      public static void main(String[] args)
10             throws FileNotFoundException {
11         Scanner input = new Scanner(new File("hours.txt"));
12         processFile(input);
13     }
14
15     public static void processFile(Scanner input) {
16         int[] total = new int[DAYS];
17         while (input.hasNextLine()) {
18             String text = input.nextLine();
19             int[] next = transferFrom(text);
20             addTo(total, next);
21         }
22         System.out.println(Arrays.toString(total));
23     }
24
25     public static int[] transferFrom(String text) {
26         Scanner data = new Scanner(text);
27         int[] result = new int[DAYS];
28         int i = 0;
29         while (data.hasNextInt()) {
30             result[i] = data.nextInt();
```

```
31                      i++;
32              }
33          return result;
34      }
35
36      public static void addTo(int[] total, int[] next) {
37          for (int i = 0; i < DAYS; i++) {
38              total[i] += next[i];
39          }
40      }
41 }
```

This version produces the following single line of output:

```
[43, 32, 36, 40, 34, 8, 8]
```

You can use a calculator to verify that these are the correct column totals, which means that we are ready to move on to version 3.

Version 3: Row Sum and Column Print

The core of the program has already been written. It properly reads each line of the input file into an array, and it uses a second array to keep track of the sums of the different columns. In this final version we are simply finishing some of the minor details of the output.

We want to make two changes to our existing code: We want to report the sum for each row and we want to print the column sums in a format that is easier to read. Each of these changes will require changing the central processFile method. To keep processFile short, we can write a method for each of these changes.

The body of the processFile method currently looks like this:

```
int[] total = new int[DAYS];
while (input.hasNextLine()) {
    String text = input.nextLine();
    int[] next = transferFrom(text);
    addTo(total, next);
}
System.out.println(Arrays.toString(total));
```

We need to add a call on a new method to report the sum of the row inside the loop, and we need to replace the simple println after the loop with a call on a method that will print the total in a more meaningful way:

```
int[] total = new int[DAYS];
while (input.hasNextLine()) {
    String text = input.nextLine();
    int[] next = transferFrom(text);
    System.out.println("Total hours = " + sum(next));
    addTo(total, next);
}
System.out.println();
print(total);
```

Now we just have to write the `sum` and `print` methods. For the `sum` method, we want to add up the numbers stored in the array. This is a classic cumulative sum problem, and we can use a for-each loop to accomplish the task:

```
public static int sum(int[] numbers) {
    int sum = 0;
    for (int n : numbers) {
        sum += n;
    }
    return sum;
}
```

The `print` method should print the column totals (the totals for each day of the week). We could accomplish this with a for-each loop, as in:

```
for (int n : total) {
    System.out.println(n);
}
```

But we don't want to simply write out seven lines of output each with a number on it. It would be nice to give some information about what the numbers mean. We know that `total[0]` represents the total hours worked on various Mondays, `total[1]` represents the total hours worked on Tuesdays, and so on, but somebody reading the output might not know that. So, it would be helpful to label the output with some information about which day goes with each total. We can do this by defining our own array of `String` literals:

```
String[] dayNames = {"Mon", "Tue", "Wed", "Thu",
                     "Fri", "Sat", "Sun"};
```

Given that we want to manipulate two arrays at once, we need to switch from a for-each loop to a `for` loop with an index:

```
for (int i = 0; i < DAYS; i++) {
    System.out.println(dayNames[i] + " hours = " + total[i]);
}
```

We can also call the `sum` method to write out the overall total hours worked after the `for` loop, which results in the following complete method:

```
public static void print(int[] total) {
    String[] dayNames = {"Mon", "Tue", "Wed", "Thu",
                         "Fri", "Sat", "Sun"};
    for (int i = 0; i < DAYS; i++) {
        System.out.println(dayNames[i] + " hours = "
                           + total[i]);
    }
    System.out.println("Total hours = " + sum(total));
}
```

Putting all the pieces together, we end up with the following complete program:

```
 1  // This program reads an input file with information about
 2  // hours worked and produces a list of total hours worked each
 3  // week and total hours worked for each day of the week.
 4
 5  import java.io.*;
 6  import java.util.*;
 7
 8  public class Hours3 {
 9      public static final int DAYS = 7; // # of days in a week
10
11      public static void main(String[] args)
12              throws FileNotFoundException {
13          Scanner input = new Scanner(new File("hours.txt"));
14          processFile(input);
15      }
16
17      // contains the overall file-processing loop
18      public static void processFile(Scanner input) {
19          int[] total = new int[DAYS];
20          while (input.hasNextLine()) {
21              String text = input.nextLine();
22              int[] next = transferFrom(text);
23              System.out.println("Total hours = " + sum(next));
24              addTo(total, next);
25          }
26          System.out.println();
27          print(total);
28      }
29
30      // constructs an array of integers and transfers
31      // data from the given String into the array in order
32      // pre: text has at most DAYS integers
33      public static int[] transferFrom(String text) {
34          Scanner data = new Scanner(text);
35          int[] result = new int[DAYS];
36          int i = 0;
37          while (data.hasNextInt()) {
38              result[i] = data.nextInt();
39              i++;
40          }
41          return result;
42      }
43
44      // returns the sum of the integers in the given array
45      public static int sum(int[] numbers) {
46          int sum = 0;
47          for (int n : numbers) {
48              sum += n;
49          }
50          return sum;
51      }
52
53      // adds the values in next to their corresponding
54      // entries in total
55      public static void addTo(int[] total, int[] next) {
56          for (int i = 0; i < DAYS; i++) {
57              total[i] += next[i];
58          }
```

Chapter **8**

Classes

Introduction

Now that you've mastered the basics of procedural-style programming in Java, you're finally ready to explore what Java was designed for: object-oriented programming. This chapter introduces the basic terminology used when talking about objects and shows you how to declare your own classes to create your own objects.

You'll see that objects are entities that contain state and behavior and can be used as parts of larger programs. We'll discuss the concepts of abstraction and encapsulation, which allow you to use objects at a high level without understanding their inner details. We'll also discuss ideas for designing new classes of objects and implementing the programs that utilize them.

8.1 Object-Oriented Programming Concepts

Most of our focus so far has been on procedural decomposition, or breaking complex tasks into smaller subtasks. This is the oldest style of programming, and even in a language like Java we still use procedural techniques. But Java also provides a different approach to programming that we call *object-oriented programming.*

> **Object-Oriented Programming (OOP)**
> Reasoning about a program as a set of objects rather than as a set of actions.

Object-oriented programming involves a particular view of programming that has its own terminology. Let's explore that terminology with non-programming examples first. Recall the definition of *object* from Chapter 3.

> **Object**
> A programming entity that contains state and behavior.

To truly understand this definition, you have to understand the terms "state" and "behavior." These are some of the most fundamental concepts in object-oriented programming.

Let's consider the class of objects we call radios. What are the different states a radio can be in? It can be turned on or turned off. It can be tuned to one of many different stations, and it can be set to different volumes. Any given radio has to "know" what state it is in, which means that it has to keep track of this information internally. We call the collection of such internal values the *state* of an object.

> **State**
> A set of values (internal data) stored in an object.

What are the behaviors of a radio? The most obvious one is that it produces sound when it is turned on and the volume is turned up. But it has other behaviors that involve the manipulation of its internal state. We can turn a radio on or off, and we can change the station or volume. We can also check what station the radio is set to right now. We call the collection of these operations the *behavior* of an object.

> **Behavior**
> A set of actions an object can perform, often reporting or modifying its internal state.

Objects themselves are not complete programs; they are components that are given distinct roles and responsibilities. Objects can be used as part of larger programs to solve problems. The pieces of code that create and use objects are known as *clients.*

> **Client (or Client Code)**
>
> Code that interacts with a class or objects of that class.

Client programs interact with objects by sending messages to them, asking them to perform behaviors. A major benefit of objects is that they provide reusable pieces of code that can be used in many client programs. You've already used several interesting objects, such as those of type `String`, `Point`, `Scanner`, `Random`, and `File`. In other words, you and your programs have been clients of these objects. Java's class libraries contain over 3000 existing classes of objects.

As you write larger programs, however, you'll find cases where Java doesn't have a pre-existing object for the problem you're solving. For example, if you were creating a calendar application, you might want objects to represent dates, contacts, and appointments. If you were creating a three-dimensional graphical simulation, you might want objects to represent 3D points, vectors, and matrices. If you were writing a financial program, you might want classes to represent your various assets, transactions, and expenses. In this chapter you'll learn how to create your own classes of objects that can be used by client programs like these.

Our definition of object-oriented programming is somewhat simplified. A full exploration of this programming paradigm includes other advanced concepts, called polymorphism and inheritance, that will be discussed in the next chapter.

Classes and Objects

In the previous chapters, we've considered the words "class" and "program" to be roughly synonymous. We wrote programs by creating new classes and placing static `main` methods into them.

But classes have another use in Java: to serve as blueprints for new types of objects. To create a new type of object in Java, we must create a class and add code to it that specifies the following things:

- The state stored in each object
- The behavior each object can perform
- How to construct objects of that type

Once we have written the appropriate code, we can use the class to create objects of its type. We can then use those objects in our client programs. We say that the created objects are *instances* of the class because one class can be used to construct many objects. This is similar to the way that a blueprint works: One blueprint can be used to create many similar houses, each of which is an instance of the original blueprint.

In the next several sections we'll explore the structure of a class by writing a new class incrementally. We'll write our own version of the `Point` class from the `java.awt` package. A `Point` object represents a two-dimensional (x, y) location. `Point` objects are useful for applications that store many 2D locations, such as maps of cities, graphical animations, and games.

Did You Know?

Operating Systems History and Objects

If you went back to 1983, you'd find that the IBM PC and its "clones" dominated the PC market and that most people were running an operating system called DOS. DOS uses what we call a "command-line interface," in which the user types commands at a prompt. The console window we have been using is a similar interface. To delete a file in DOS, for example, you would give the command "del" (short for "delete") followed by the file name, as in:

```
del data.txt
```

This interface can be described in simple terms as "verb noun." In fact, if you look at a DOS manual, you will find that it is full of verbs. This closely parallels the procedural approach to programming. When we want to accomplish some task, we issue a command (the verb) and then mention the object of the action (the noun, the thing we want to affect).

In 1984, Apple Computer released a new computer called a Macintosh that had a different operating system that used what we call a graphical user interface, or GUI. The GUI interface uses a graphical "desktop" metaphor that has become so well known that people now tend to forget it is a metaphor. The Macintosh was not the first computer to use the desktop metaphor and a GUI, but it was the first such computer that became a major commercial success. Later, Microsoft brought this functionality to IBM PCs with its Windows operating system.

So, how do you delete a file on a Macintosh or on a Windows machine? You locate the icon for the file and click on it. Then you have several options. You can drag it to the trash/recycling bin, or you can give a "delete" command from the main or context (right-click) menu. Either way, you start with the object you want to delete and then give the command you want to perform. This is a reversal of the fundamental paradigm: In DOS it was "verb noun," but with a GUI it's "noun verb." This different method of interaction is the core of object-oriented programming.

Most modern programs use GUIs because we have learned that people find it more natural to work this way. We are used to pointing at things, picking up things, grabbing things. Starting with the object is very natural for us. This approach has also proved to be a helpful way to structure our programs, enabling us to divide our programs up into different objects that each can do certain tasks rather than dividing up the central task into subtasks.

The main components of a class that we'll see in these sections are:

- Fields (the data stored in each object)
- Methods (the behavior each object can execute)
- Constructors (special methods used to construct objects with the new keyword)
- Encapsulation (protecting an object's data from outside access)

We'll focus on these concepts by creating four major versions of the Point class. The first version will give us Point objects that contain only data. The second version will add behavior to the objects. The third version will allow us to construct Points at any initial position. The fourth version will encapsulate each Point object's internal data from unwanted outside access. Only the fourth version of the Point class will be written in proper object-oriented style; the others will be incomplete and used to illustrate each feature of a class in isolation.

8.2 Object State: Fields

The first version of our Point class will contain state only. To specify each object's state, we declare special variables inside the class called *fields*. There are many synonyms for "field" that come from other programming languages and environments, such as "instance variable," "data member," and "attribute."

> **Field**
>
> A variable inside an object that makes up part of its internal state.

The syntax for declaring a field is the same as for declaring normal variables: a type followed by a name and a semicolon. The difference with fields is where they're declared: directly inside the { and } braces of your class. When we declare a field, we're saying that we want every object of this class to have that variable inside it.

In previous chapters we've seen that every class should be placed into its own file. The following code, written in the file Point.java, defines the first version of our Point class. Each Point object will contain two fields (an integer called x and an integer called y):

```
1 // A Point object represents a pair of (x, y) coordinates.
2 // First version: state only.
3
4 public class Point {
5     int x;
6     int y;
7 }
```

Though the syntax for fields makes them look like local variables, they have different properties. The preceding code does not declare a single pair of int variables, x and y. Instead, it indicates that each Point object will contain its own int fields called x and y. For example, if we create 100 Point objects, we'll have 100 pairs of x and y fields, one in each instance of the class.

The Point class isn't itself an executable Java program; it simply defines a new class of objects for client programs to use. The client code that uses Point will be a separate class that we will store in a separate file. Client programs can create Point objects using the new keyword and empty parentheses, as in:

```
Point origin = new Point();
```

When a Point object is constructed, its fields are given default initial values of 0, so a new Point object always begins at the origin of (0, 0) unless you change its x or y value. This is another example of auto-initialization, similar to the way that array elements are automatically given default values.

The following is the first version of a client program that uses our Point class. The code is saved in a file called PointMain.java, which should be in the same folder or project as Point.java for the program to compile successfully.

```
 1 // A program that deals with 2D points.
 2 // First version, to accompany Point class with state only.
 3
 4 public class PointMain {
 5     public static void main(String[] args) {
 6         // create two Point objects
 7         Point p1 = new Point();
 8         p1.x = 7;
 9         p1.y = 2;
10
11         Point p2 = new Point();
12         p2.x = 4;
13         p2.y = 3;
14
15         // print each point and its distance from the origin
16         System.out.println("p1 is (" + p1.x + ", " + p1.y + ")");
17         double dist1 = Math.sqrt(p1.x * p1.x + p1.y * p1.y);
18         System.out.println("distance from origin = " + dist1);
19
20         System.out.println("p2 is (" + p2.x + ", " + p2.y + ")");
21         double dist2 = Math.sqrt(p2.x * p2.x + p2.y * p2.y);
22         System.out.println("distance from origin = " + dist2);
23         System.out.println();
24
25         // translate each point to a new location
26         p1.x += 11;
27         p1.y += 6;
28         p2.x += 1;
29         p2.y += 7;
30
31         // print the points again
32         System.out.println("p1 is (" + p1.x + ", " + p1.y + ")");
33         System.out.println("p2 is (" + p2.x + ", " + p2.y + ")");
34     }
35 }
```

The code produces the following output:

```
p1 is (7, 2)
distance from origin = 7.280109889280518
p2 is (4, 3)
distance from origin = 5.0

p1 is (18, 8)
p2 is (5, 10)
```

The client program has some redundancy that we'll eliminate as we improve our `Point` class in the next sections.

Our initial `Point` class essentially serves as a way to group two `int` values into one object. This is somewhat useful for the client program, but the client could have been written using primitive `int`s instead. Using `Point` objects is not yet substantially better than using primitive `int` values, because our `Point` objects do not yet have any behavior. Such an object that contains state but no behavior is sometimes called a *record* or *struct*. In the following sections, we'll grow our `Point` class from a minimal implementation into a proper Java class.

8.3 Object Behavior: Methods

The second version of our `Point` class will contain both state and behavior. Behavior of objects is specified by writing *instance methods*. The instance methods of an object describe the messages to which that object can respond.

> **Instance Method**
> A method inside an object that operates on that object.

The objects introduced in previous chapters all contained instance methods representing their behavior. For example, a `String` object has a `length` method and a `Scanner` object has a `nextInt` method.

Our client program from the previous section translates the position of two `Point` objects. It does this by manually adjusting their x and y values:

```
p1.x += 11; // client code translating a Point
p1.y += 6;
```

Since translating points is a common operation, we should represent it as a method. One option would be to write a static `translate` method in the client code that accepts a `Point`, a delta-x, and a delta-y as parameters. Its code would look like this:

```
// a static method to translate a Point;
// not a good choice in this case
public static void translate(Point p, int dx, int dy) {
    p.x += dx;
    p.y += dy;
}
```

A call to the static method would look like this:

```
translate(p1, 11, 6);  // calling a translate static method
```

However, a static method isn't the best way to implement the translate behavior. One of the biggest benefits of programming with objects is that we can put related data and behavior together. The ability for a `Point` to translate is closely related to that `Point` object's (x, y) data, so it is better to specify that each `Point` object will know how to translate itself. We'll do this by writing an instance method in the `Point` class.

We know from experience with objects that you can call an instance method called `translate` using "dot notation":

```
p1.translate(11, 6); // calling a translate instance method
```

Notice that the instance method needs just two parameters: `dx` and `dy`. The client doesn't pass the `Point` as a parameter, because the call begins by indicating which `Point` object it wants to translate (p1). In this way, the client is sending a `translate` message to the object referred to by `p1`.

Instance method headers do not have the static keyword found in static method headers, but they still include the public keyword, the method's return type, its name, and any parameters the method accepts. Here's the start of a `Point` class with a `translate` method, with the header declared but the body blank:

```
public class Point {
    int x;
    int y;

    public void translate(int dx, int dy) {
        . . .
    }
}
```

Remember that when we declare a `translate` method in the `Point` class, we are saying that each `Point` object has its own copy of that method. Each `Point` object also has its own x and y values. A `Point` object would look like the following:

```
x 7   y 2
public void translate(int dx, int dy) {
    . . .
}
```

Whenever an instance method is called, it is called on a particular object. So, when we're writing the body of the `translate` method, we'll think of that code from the perspective of the particular `Point` object that receives the message: "The client has given me a `dx` and `dy` and wants me to change my x and y values by those amounts." Essentially, we need to write code to match the following pseudocode:

```
public void translate(int dx, int dy) {
    add dx to this Point object's x value.
    add dy to this Point object's y value.
}
```

A helpful thing to know at this point is that an object's instance methods can refer to its fields. In previous chapters we've talked about *scope,* the range in which a variable can be seen and used. The scope of a variable is the set of braces in which it is declared. The same rule applies to fields: Since they are declared directly inside a class, their scope is the entire class.

This means that the `translate` method can directly refer to the fields x and y. For example, the statement `x += 3;` would increase the `Point` object's x value by 3.

Here is a working `translate` method that adjusts the `Point` object's location:

```java
public void translate(int dx, int dy) {
    x += dx;
    y += dy;
}
```

It might seem strange that the `translate` method can refer to x and y directly without being more specific about which object it is affecting. As a non-programming analogy, if you were riding inside a car and wanted the driver to turn left, you'd simply say, "Turn left." Though there are millions of cars in the world, you wouldn't feel a need to specify which car you meant. It is implied that you mean the car you're currently occupying. Similarly, in instance methods we don't need to specify which object's x or y we're using, because it is implied that we want to use the fields of the object that receives the message.

Here's the complete `Point` class that contains the `translate` method. Sun's Java style guidelines suggest declaring fields at the top of the class, with methods below, but in general it is legal for a class's contents to appear in any order.

```java
public class Point {
    int x;
    int y;

    // shifts this point's location by the given amount
    public void translate(int dx, int dy) {
        x += dx;
        y += dy;
    }
}
```

The general syntax for instance methods is the following:

```java
public <type> <name>(<type> <name>, . . . , <type> <name>) {
    <statement>;
    <statement>;
    . . .
    <statement>;
}
```

Methods like `translate` are useful because they give our objects useful behavior that lets us write more expressive and concise client programs. Having the client code manually adjust the x and y values of `Point` objects to move them is tedious, especially in larger client programs that translate many times. By adding the `translate` method, we have provided a clean way to adjust the location of a `Point` object in a single statement.

The Implicit Parameter

We said a moment ago that an object's methods can refer to its fields. From a code perspective, this means that the code for an instance method has an implied knowledge of what object it is operating upon. This knowledge is sometimes called the *implicit parameter.*

Implicit Parameter

The object being referenced during an instance method call.

Let's walk through an example to demonstrate exactly how instance methods use the implicit parameter. First we'll write some client code that constructs two `Point` objects and sets initial locations for them:

```
// construct two Point objects
Point p1 = new Point();
p1.x = 7;
p1.y = 2;
Point p2 = new Point();
p2.x = 4;
p2.y = 3;
```

After the preceding code, a diagram of the variables and objects in memory would look like the following. Remember that each object has its own copy of the `translate` method:

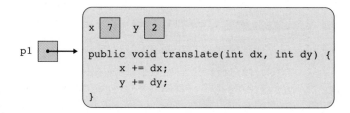

Now we'll call the `translate` method on each object. First, `p1` is translated. During this call, `p1`'s `translate` method is passed the parameters `11` and `6`. The implicit parameter here is `p1`'s object, so the statements `x += dx;` and `y += dy;` affect `p1.x` and `p1.y`:

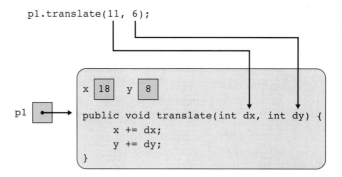

During the second method call p2's `translate` method is executed, so the lines in the body of the `translate` method change `p2.x` and `p2.y`:

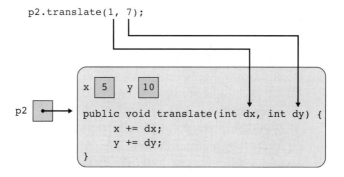

Mutators and Accessors

The `translate` method is an example of a *mutator*.

> **Mutator**
>
> An instance method that modifies the object's internal state.

Generally, a mutator assigns a new value to one of the object's fields. Going back to the radio example, the mutators would be the switches and knobs that turn the radio on and off or change the station or volume.

It is a common convention for a mutator method's name to begin with "set," as in `setID` or `setTitle`. Usually a mutator method will have a `void` return type. Mutators often accept parameters that specify the new state of the object or the amount by which to modify its current state.

A second important category of instance methods is known as *accessors*.

> **Accessor**
>
> An instance method that provides information about the state of an object without modifying it.

Generally an accessor returns the value of one of the object's fields. For a radio, an accessor might return the current station or volume. Examples of accessor methods you have seen in previous chapters include the `length` and `substring` methods of `String` objects and the `exists` method of `File` objects.

Our client program computes how far two `Point`s are from the origin, (0, 0). Since this is a common operation related to the data in a `Point`, let's give each `Point` object an accessor called `distanceFromOrigin` that computes and returns that `Point` object's distance from the origin. The method accepts no parameters and returns the distance as a `double`.

The distance from the origin is computed using the Pythagorean Theorem, taking the square root of the sum of the squares of the x and y values. As in the `translate` method, we'll refer to the `Point` object's x and y fields directly in our computation:

```
// returns the distance between this point and (0, 0)
public double distanceFromOrigin() {
    return Math.sqrt(x * x + y * y);
}
```

Note that the `distanceFromOrigin` method doesn't change the `Point` object's x or y values. Accessors are not used to change the state of the object—they only report information about the object. You can think of accessors as read-only operations while mutators are read-write operations.

A typical accessor will have no parameters and a non-void return type, because it must return a piece of information. An accessor returns a value that is part of the state of the object or is derived from it. The names of many accessors begin with "get" or "is," as in `getBalance` or `isEmpty`.

Here's the complete second version of our `Point` class that now contains both state and behavior:

```
 1 // A Point object represents a pair of (x, y) coordinates.
 2 // Second version: state and behavior.
 3
 4 public class Point {
 5     int x;
 6     int y;
 7
 8     // returns the distance between this point and (0, 0)
 9     public double distanceFromOrigin() {
10         return Math.sqrt(x * x + y * y);
11     }
12
13     // shifts this point's location by the given amount
14     public void translate(int dx, int dy) {
15         x += dx;
16         y += dy;
17     }
18 }
```

The client program can now use the new behavior of the `Point` class. The resulting program produces the same output as before but is shorter and more readable than the original:

```
 1 // A program that deals with 2D points.
 2 // Second version, to accompany Point class with behavior.
 3
 4 public class PointMain {
 5     public static void main(String[] args) {
 6         // create two Point objects
 7         Point p1 = new Point();
 8         p1.x = 7;
 9         p1.y = 2;
10
11         Point p2 = new Point();
12         p2.x = 4;
13         p2.y = 3;
14
15         // print each point and its distance from the origin
16         System.out.println("p1 is (" + p1.x + ", " + p1.y + ")");
17         System.out.println("distance from origin = " +
18                             p1.distanceFromOrigin());
19
20         System.out.println("p2 is (" + p2.x + ", " + p2.y + ")");
21         System.out.println("distance from origin = " +
22                             p2.distanceFromOrigin());
23
24         // translate each point to a new location
25         p1.translate(11, 6);
26         p2.translate(1, 7);
27
28         // print the points again
29         System.out.println("p1 is (" + p1.x + ", " + p1.y + ")");
30         System.out.println("p2 is (" + p2.x + ", " + p2.y + ")");
31     }
32 }
```

8.4 Object Initialization: Constructors

Our third version of the Point class will contain the ability to create Point objects at any initial location. The initial state of objects is specified by writing special methods called *constructors*.

Constructor

A special method that initializes the state of new objects as they are created.

A clumsy aspect of our existing client code is that it takes three lines to create and initialize the state of one Point object:

```
// client needs 3 statements to initialize one Point object
Point p1 = new Point();
p1.x = 7;
p1.y = 2;
```

Recall that in Chapter 3 we were able to create Java Point objects with initial locations in a single statement. We did this by writing their initial (x, y) values in parentheses as we constructed the objects:

```
Point p = new Point(10, 27); // legal with Java's Point class
```

Such a statement wouldn't be legal for our `Point` class, though, because we haven't written any code specifying how to create a `Point` with an initial (x, y) location. We can specify how to do this by writing a constructor in our `Point` class. A constructor is the piece of code that executes when the client uses the `new` keyword to create a new object.

A constructor's header begins with the keyword `public` followed by the class's name and any parameters. It looks like a method header, but its name must match the name of the class and may not have a return type. A constructor often has parameters that specify the object's initial state. Our constructor for the `Point` class will accept initial x and y values as parameters and store them into the new `Point` object's x and y fields:

```
// constructs a new point with the given (x, y) location
public Point(int initialX, int initialY) {
    x = initialX;
    y = initialY;
}
```

Like instance methods, constructors execute on a particular object (the one that's being created with the `new` keyword) and can refer to that object's fields and methods directly. In this case, we store `initialX` and `initialY` parameter values into the new `Point` object's x and y fields.

Now that we are exploring constructors, it makes sense to think about the process of creating objects in more detail. The following statement actually performs several operations:

```
Point p = new Point(1, 2);
```

It creates a `Point` reference named p, it creates a new `Point` object, and it calls the `Point` constructor on the newly created object, passing 1 and 2 as the `initialX` and `initialY` parameter values. Finally, it assigns the newly created object to be stored in the reference variable p.

Here is the complete code for the third version of our `Point` class:

```
 1 // A Point object represents a pair of (x, y) coordinates.
 2 // Third version: state and behavior with constructor.
 3
 4 public class Point {
 5     int x;
 6     int y;
 7
 8     // constructs a new point with the given (x, y) location
 9     public Point(int initialX, int initialY) {
10         x = initialX;
11         y = initialY;
12     }
13
14     // returns the distance between this point and (0, 0)
15     public double distanceFromOrigin() {
16         return Math.sqrt(x * x + y * y);
```

```
17        }
18
19        // shifts this point's location by the given amount
20        public void translate(int dx, int dy) {
21            x += dx;
22            y += dy;
23        }
24 }
```

Calling a constructor with parameters is similar to ordering a car from a factory: "I'd like the yellow one with power windows and a CD player." You might not specify every detail about the car, such as the fact that it should have four wheels and headlights, but you do specify some initial attributes that are important you.

The general syntax for constructors is the following:

```
public <class name>(<type> <name>, . . . , <type> <name>) {
    <statement>;
    <statement>;
    . . .
    <statement>;
}
```

After we add the constructor our client code becomes shorter and simpler, because it can create a Point and initialize its (x, y) coordinates in a single line:

```
 1 // A program that deals with 2D points.
 2 // Third version, to accompany Point class with constructor.
 3
 4 public class PointMain {
 5     public static void main(String[] args) {
 6         // create two Point objects
 7         Point p1 = new Point(7, 2);   // calling the constructor
 8         Point p2 = new Point(4, 3);   // calling the constructor
 9
10         // print each point and its distance from the origin
11         System.out.println("p1 is (" + p1.x + ", " + p1.y + ")");
12         System.out.println("distance from origin = " +
13                            p1.distanceFromOrigin());
14
15         System.out.println("p2 is (" + p2.x + ", " + p2.y + ")");
16         System.out.println("distance from origin = " +
17                            p2.distanceFromOrigin());
18
19         // translate each point to a new location
20         p1.translate(11, 6);
21         p2.translate(1, 7);
22
23         // print the points again
24         System.out.println("p1 is (" + p1.x + ", " + p1.y + ")");
25         System.out.println("p2 is (" + p2.x + ", " + p2.y + ")");
26     }
27 }
```

When a class doesn't have a constructor, as with our previous versions of the Point class, Java automatically supplies a *default constructor* with no parameters.

Common Programming Error

Using `void` with a Constructor

Many new programmers accidentally include the keyword `void` in the header of a constructor, since they've gotten so used to writing a return type for every method:

```
// this code has a bug
public void Point(int initialX, int initialY) {
    x = initialX;
    y = initialY;
}
```

This is actually a very tricky and annoying bug. Constructors aren't supposed to have return types. When you write a return type such as `void`, what you've created is not a constructor, but rather a normal instance method called `Point` that accepts `x` and `y` parameters and has a `void` return type. This error is tough to catch, because the `Point.java` file still compiles successfully.

You will see an error when you try to call the constructor you thought you just wrote, though, because it isn't actually a constructor. The client code that tries to construct the `Point` object will complain that it can't find an `(int, int)` constructor for a `Point`:

```
PointMain.java:7: cannot find symbol
symbol : constructor Point(int,int)
location: class Point
        Point p1 = new Point(7, 2);
```

If you see "cannot find symbol" constructor errors and you were positive that you wrote a constructor, double-check its header to make sure there's no return type.

That is why it was previously legal to construct a `new Point()`. (The default constructor auto-initializes all fields to zero-equivalent values.) However, Java doesn't supply the default empty constructor when we supply one of our own, so it is now illegal to construct `Point` objects without passing in the initial `x` and `y` parameters:

```
Point p1 = new Point(); // will not compile for this version
```

In a later section of this chapter, we'll write additional code to restore this ability.

Redeclaring Fields in a Constructor

Another common bug with constructors is to mistakenly redeclare fields by writing their types. Here's an example that shows this mistake:

```
// this constructor code has a bug
public Point(int initialX, int initialY) {
    int x = initialX;
    int y = initialY;
}
```

The preceding code behaves oddly. It compiles successfully, but when the client code constructs a `Point` object its initial coordinates are always (0, 0), regardless of what parameter values are passed to the constructor:

```
// this client code will print that p1 is (0, 0)
Point p1 = new Point(7, 2);
System.out.println("p1 is (" + p1.x + ", " + p1.y + ")");
```

The problem is that rather than storing `initialX` and `initialY` in the `Point` object's x and y fields, we've actually declared local variables called x and y inside the `Point` constructor. We store `initialX` and `initialY` in those local variables, which are thrown away when the constructor finishes running. No values are ever assigned to the x and y fields in the constructor, so they are automatically initialized to 0. We say that these local x and y variables *shadow* our x and y fields because they obscure the fields we intended to set.

If you observe that your constructor doesn't seem to be setting your object's fields, check closely to make sure that you didn't accidentally declare local variables that shadow your fields. The key thing is not to include a type at the front of the statement when assigning a field a value.

8.5 Encapsulation

Our fourth version of the `Point` class will protect its data from unwanted access using a concept known as *encapsulation*.

> **Encapsulation**
>
> Hiding the implementation details of an object from the clients of the object.

To understand the notion of encapsulation, recall the non-programming analogy of radios as objects. Almost everyone knows how to use a radio, but few know how to build a radio or how the circuitry inside a radio works. It is a benefit of the radio's design that we don't need to know those details.

The internal and external views of a radio.

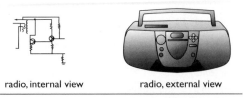

radio, internal view   radio, external view

Figure 8.1   The internal and external views of a radio.

We all understand the essential properties of a radio (what it does), but only a few of us understand the internal details of the radio (how it works). This leads to an important dichotomy of external versus internal views of an object. From the outside, we just see behavior. From the inside, we see internal state that is used to accomplish that behavior (Figure 8.1).

Focusing on the radio's external behavior enables us to use it easily while ignoring the details of its inner workings that are unimportant to us. This is an example of an important computer science concept known as *abstraction.*

> **Abstraction**
>
> Focusing on essential properties rather than inner details.

In fact, a radio (like most other electronic devices) has a case or chassis that houses all of the electronics so that we don't see them from the outside. A set of dials and buttons and displays on the case allow us to manipulate the radio without having to deal with all of the circuitry that makes it work. In fact, you wouldn't want someone to give you a fully functional radio that had wires and capacitors hanging out of it, because they would make the interface to the radio less pleasant to use.

When applied to programming, the concept of hiding internal state from outside view is called encapsulation. When an object is properly encapsulated, its clients cannot directly access or modify its internal workings, nor do they need to do so. Only the implementer of the class needs to know about those details. Encapsulation leads to abstraction; an encapsulated object presents a more pure abstraction than one whose data can be accessed directly.

In previous chapters you have already taken advantage of the abstraction provided by well-encapsulated objects. For example, you have used `Scanner` objects to read data from the console without knowing exactly how the `Scanner` stores and tokenizes the input data, and you have used `Random` objects to create random numbers without knowing exactly what algorithm the random number generator uses.

But so far, our `Point` class is not encapsulated. We've built a working radio, but its wires (its x and y fields) are still hanging out. Using encapsulation, we'll put a casing around our `Point` objects so that clients will only need to use the objects' methods and not access the fields directly.

Private Fields

To encapsulate fields of an object, we declare them to be private by writing the key-word `private` at the start of the declaration of each field. The fields of our `Point` class would thus be declared as follows:

```
// encapsulated fields of Point objects
private int x;
private int y;
```

We haven't yet shown a syntax template for fields because we wanted to show the preferred style with the fields private. The syntax for declaring encapsulated fields is the following:

```
private <type> <name>;
```

Fields can also be declared with an initial value:

```
private <type> <name> = <value>;
```

Declaring fields as private encapsulates the state of the object, in the same way that a radio's casing protects the user from seeing the wires and circuitry inside it. Private fields are visible to all of the code inside the `Point` class (i.e., inside the `Point.java` file), but not anywhere else. This means that we can no longer directly refer to a `Point` object's x or y fields in our client code. The following client code will not compile successfully:

```
// this client code doesn't work with encapsulated points
System.out.println("p1 is (" + p1.x + ", " + p1.y + ")");
```

The compiler produces error messages such as the following:

```
PointMain.java:11: x has private access in Point
PointMain.java:11: y has private access in Point
```

To preserve the functionality of our client program, we need to provide a way for client code to access a `Point` object's field values. We will do this by adding some new accessor methods to the `Point` class. If the value of an object's field might be useful externally, it is common to write an accessor to return that value. Here are the methods that provide access to a `Point` object's x and y fields:

```
// returns the x-coordinate of this point
public int getX() {
    return x;
}

// returns the y-coordinate of this point
public int getY() {
    return y;
}
```

The client code to print a `Point` object's x and y values must be changed to the following:

```
// this code works with our encapsulated Points
System.out.println("p1 is (" + p1.getX() + ", " +
                         p1.getY() + ")");
```

It probably seems odd to grant access to a `Point` object's x and y fields when we said our goal was to encapsulate those fields, but having accessors like `getX` and `getY` doesn't actually violate the encapsulation of the object. The accessor methods just return a copy of the fields' values to the client, so the client can see the x or y values but doesn't have any way to change them. In other words, these accessor methods give the client read-only access to the state of the object.

Another benefit of encapsulating our `Point` objects is that we can later change the internal structure of our `Point` class without having to modify our client code. For example, sometimes it is useful to express 2D points in polar coordinates using a radius *r* and an angle *theta.* In this representation, a point's (x, y) coordinates are not stored directly but can be computed as (*r* cos *theta, r* sin *theta*). With the `Point` class encapsulated, we could modify it to use *r* and *theta* fields internally, then modify the `getX` and `getY` methods to compute and return the appropriate values.

One drawback of encapsulating the `Point` class is that it is no longer easy for the client code to set a `Point` to a new location. For convenience, we'll add a new mutator to our encapsulated `Point` class that sets both the x and y fields of the object to new values passed as parameters:

```
// sets this point's (x, y) location to the given values
public void setLocation(int newX, int newY) {
    x = newX;
    y = newY;
}
```

Another possibility would have been to write separate methods called `setX` and `setY`. We have chosen `setLocation` partly for brevity and partly because it matches Java's `Point` class. Writing `setX` and `setY` is left as an exercise.

Notice that the `Point` class now has some redundancy between its constructor and its `setLocation` method. The two bodies are essentially the same, setting the `Point` to have new x- and y-coordinates. We can eliminate this redundancy by having the constructor call `setLocation` rather than setting the field values manually. It is legal for an object to call its own instance methods from a constructor or another instance method:

```
// constructs a new point with the given (x, y) location
public Point(int initialX, int initialY) {
    setLocation(initialX, initialY);
}
```

We can eliminate a bit more redundancy using this technique. Translating a `Point` can be thought of as setting its location to the old location plus the dx and dy, so we can modify the `translate` method to call the `setLocation` method:

```
// shifts this point's location by the given amount
public void translate(int dx, int dy) {
    setLocation(x + dx, y + dy);
}
```

Now that we've introduced all the major elements of a well-encapsulated class, it's time to look at a proper syntax template for an entire class. Sun's Java style guidelines suggest putting fields at the top of the class, followed by constructors, followed by methods:

```
public class <class name> {
    // fields
    private <type> <name>;
    private <type> <name>;
    ...

    // constructors
    public <class name>(<type> <name>, ..., <type> <name>) {
        <statement>;
        <statement>;
        ...
        <statement>;
    }
    ...

    // methods
    public <type> <name>(<type> <name>, ..., <type> <name>) {
        <statement>;
        <statement>;
        ...
        <statement>;
    }
    ...
}
```

Class Invariants

Another benefit of encapsulated objects is that you can place constraints on their state. For example, suppose we want to ensure that every Point object's x and y values are non-negative. This might be useful if Point objects were being used to represent coordinates on the screen, which are never negative. A property that is true of every object of a class is called a *class invariant*.

> **Class Invariant**
>
> An assertion about an object's state that is true for the lifetime of that object.

Class invariants are related to preconditions, postconditions, and assertions, as presented in Chapters 4 and 5. A class invariant should be treated as an implicit postcondition of every instance method of the class. The invariant may also add preconditions to constructors and mutator methods of the class.

To enforce our class invariant, we must ensure that a client cannot create a Point object with a negative x or y value. We must also ensure that client code cannot move a Point to a negative x or y value. This means that the (x, y) coordinates must be checked every time the constructor, translate method, or setLocation method is called.

Since we removed redundancy by having the constructor and translate method call setLocation, we can actually enforce the invariant with a single check in the

setLocation method. If the new x or y value is negative, we'll throw an
IllegalArgumentException to notify the client of the error:

```
// sets this point's (x, y) location to the given values
// pre: newX >= 0 && newY >= 0
public void setLocation(int newX, int newY) {
    if (newX < 0 || newY < 0) {
        throw new IllegalArgumentException();
    }

    x = newX;
    y = newY;
}
```

If the Point class weren't encapsulated, we wouldn't be able to properly enforce
our invariant. Client code would be able to make a Point object's location negative
by setting its x or y fields' values directly. For example, this piece of malicious client
code would succeed in setting the Point object's x value to −1:

```
// if our Point objects were not encapsulated,
// this client code would violate the class invariant
Point p1 = new Point(7, 2);
p1.x = -1;
System.out.println("Haha, I set its x value to " + p1.x);
```

With encapsulation, the Point class has much better control over how clients can
use Point objects, making it impossible for a misguided client program to violate our
class invariant. We can now be sure that a Point object will never have a corrupt state.

Here is the fourth (complete) version of our Point class, including encapsulation and our class invariant. Because all code to set the Point object's location
calls the setLocation method, we only have to check once for the x and y values
being less than 0:

```
 1 // A Point object represents a pair of (x, y) coordinates.
 2 // Fourth version: encapsulated.
 3 // Class invariant: x >= 0 && y >= 0.
 4
 5 public class Point {
 6     private int x;
 7     private int y;
 8
 9     // constructs a new point with the given (x, y) location
10     // pre: initialX >= 0 && initialY >= 0
11     public Point(int initialX, int initialY) {
12         setLocation(initialX, initialY);
13     }
14
15     // returns the distance between this point and (0, 0)
16     public double distanceFromOrigin() {
17         return Math.sqrt(x * x + y * y);
18     }
19
20     // returns the x-coordinate of this point
21     public int getX() {
22         return x;
23     }
```

```
24
25         // returns the y-coordinate of this point
26         public int getY() {
27             return y;
28         }
29
30         // sets this point's (x, y) location to the given values
31         // pre: newX >= 0 && newY >= 0
32         public void setLocation(int newX, int newY) {
33             if (newX < 0 || newY < 0) {
34                 throw new IllegalArgumentException();
35             }
36
37             x = newX;
38             y = newY;
39         }
40
41         // shifts this point's location by the given amount
42         // pre: x + dx >= 0 && y + dy >= 0
43         public void translate(int dx, int dy) {
44             setLocation(x + dx, y + dy);
45         }
46 }
```

Here's the corresponding fourth version of our client program:

```
 1 // A program that deals with 2D points.
 2 // Fourth version, to accompany encapsulated Point class.
 3
 4 public class PointMain {
 5     public static void main(String[] args) {
 6         // create two Point objects
 7         Point p1 = new Point(7, 2);
 8         Point p2 = new Point(4, 3);
 9
10         // print each point and its distance from the origin
11         System.out.println("p1 is (" + p1.getX() + ", " +
12                             p1.getY() + ")");
13         System.out.println("distance from origin = " +
14                             p1.distanceFromOrigin());
15
16         System.out.println("p2 is (" + p2.getX() + ", " +
17                             p2.getY() + ")");
18         System.out.println("distance from origin = " +
19                             p2.distanceFromOrigin());
20
21         // translate each point to a new location
22         p1.translate(11, 6);
23         p2.translate(1, 7);
24
25         // print the points again
26         System.out.println("p1 is (" + p1.getX() + ", " +
27                             p1.getY() + ")");
28         System.out.println("p2 is (" + p2.getX() + ", " +
29                             p2.getY() + ")");
30     }
31 }
```

The client is actually a bit more verbose now, because it must call the getX and getY methods on a Point to print its coordinates. However, this moderate inconvenience to the client code is necessary to preserve the encapsulation and class invariant on our Point objects.

8.6 More Instance Methods

In this section we'll add some special instance methods to our Point class to make it easier and more convenient to use in client code. We'll write a method to make it easy to print Point objects and another to compare them to each other for equality.

The toString Method

The designers of Java felt it was important for all types of values to work well with Strings. You've seen that you can concatenate Strings with any other type of value, such as primitive ints or other objects. Consider the following code:

```java
int i = 42;
String s = "hello";
Point p = new Point(7, 2);

System.out.println("i is " + i);
System.out.println("s is " + s);
System.out.println("p is " + p);
```

Using the Point class we've written so far, the preceding code produces output like the following:

```
i is 42
s is hello
p is Point@119c082
```

Notice the strange result when printing the Point p. We'd rather have it print the object's state of (7, 2), but Java doesn't know how to do so unless we write a special method in our Point class.

When a Java object is being printed or concatenated with a String, a special method called toString is called on the object to convert it into a String. The toString method is an instance method that returns a String representation of the object. A toString method accepts no parameters and has a String return type:

```java
public String toString() {
    code to produce and return the desired string.
}
```

If you don't write a toString method in your class, your class will receive a default version that returns the class name followed by an @ sign and some letters and numbers. If you define your own toString method, it replaces this default version.

Did You Know?

Perils of Poor Encapsulation

Many novices (as well as many professional programmers) do not fully appreciate the concepts of abstraction and encapsulation. It is tempting to write classes that directly expose their data for clients to use, since private fields introduce some complexity and restrictions in a program. However, there have been some famous examples where a lack of proper encapsulation and abstraction caused a large problem.

One such example is the "Y2K" or "millennium bug" scare of late 1999. The issue arose because a large number of programs represented years using only two digits, such as 72 for 1972. This was done largely to save memory, since many of these were older programs written in COBOL during a time when memory was more scarce. Once the year became 2000, the programs would incorrectly think the year was 1900 and therefore could fail.

Making matters worse was the fact that many of these programs contained their own hand-written logic for representing dates, which sometimes appeared in many places in the code. In order to represent a year with more than two digits, many places in the code needed to be changed. In total, over $300 billion was spent on repairing old programs and systems to correct the Y2K problem.

An encapsulated `Date` class would have greatly reduced the work needed to fix the Y2K bug. If the old programs had used a `Date` class with a field to represent the year, the class could have been updated once and all the client code would have received the benefits.

Surprisingly, Java's class libraries also contain examples of poorly encapsulated classes. In the `java.awt` package, for example, the `Point` and `Dimension` classes have public fields. (A `Dimension` object stores `width` and `height` fields to represent the size of an onscreen region.) Many client programs access the fields directly when using these objects. Java's developers regret this decision:

> Several classes in the Java platform libraries violate the advice that public classes should not expose fields directly. Prominent examples include the Point and Dimension classes in the `java.awt` package. Rather than examples to be emulated, these classes should be regarded as cautionary tales. [. . .] The decision to expose the internals of the Dimension class resulted in a serious performance problem that could not be solved without affecting clients.

—Joshua Bloch, *Effective Java*

The following code implements a `toString` method for our `Point` objects. It returns a `String` such as `"(7, 2)"`:

```
// returns a String representation of this point
public String toString() {
    return "(" + x + ", " + y + ")";
}
```

Now that our class has this method, the preceding client code now produces the following output.

```
i is 42
s is hello
p is (7, 2)
```

Note that the client code didn't explicitly call the `toString` method; the compiler did it automatically because the `Point` object was being concatenated with a `String`. The `toString` method is also implicitly called when printing an object by itself, as in:

```
System.out.println(p);
```

For this implicit calling behavior to work properly, your `toString` method's signature must exactly match the one shown in this section. Changing the name or signature even slightly (for example, naming the method `ToString` with a capital T, or `convertToString`) will cause the class to produce the old output (e.g., `"Point@119c082"`). This has to do with concepts called inheritance and overriding that we will explore in the next chapter.

It is also legal to call `toString` explicitly if you prefer. The following client code uses an explicit `toString` call and produces the same output as the original client code:

```
System.out.println("p is " + p.toString());
```

Sun's Java guidelines recommend writing a `toString` method in every class you write.

The `equals` Method

For several chapters now, you have used the `==` operator to compare for equality. You also saw that this operator does not behave as expected when used on objects. This is because of the possibility of having two distinct objects with equivalent state, such as two `Point` objects with the coordinates (5, 2). This gets at the idea that an object has an *identity* and is distinct from other objects, even if another object happens to have the same state.

A non-programming analogy would be if you and your friend both owned identical iPods that held the same set of songs. They are in some ways equivalent, but you still consider them distinct and separate items. You certainly wouldn't want to have to share.

The `==` operator does not behave as expected with objects because it tests whether two objects have the same identity. The `==` comparison actually tests whether two

---

Common Programming Error

println Statement in toString Method

Since the toString method is closely related to printing, some students mistakenly think that they should place println statements in their toString methods, as in:

```java
// this toString method is flawed;
// it should return the String rather than printing it
public String toString() {
    System.out.println("(" + x + ", " + y + ")");
    return "";
}
```

A key idea to understand about toString is that it doesn't directly print anything: It simply returns a String that the client can use in a println statement.

In fact, many well-formed classes of objects do not contain any println statements at all. Having println statements in a class binds it to a particular style of output. For example, the preceding code prints a Point object on its own line, making the class unsuitable for a client that doesn't want the output to appear exactly this way (say, a client that wants to print many Point objects on the same line).

You may wonder why the designers of Java chose to use a toString method rather than, say, a print method that would output the object to the console. The reason is that toString is more versatile. You can use toString to output the object to a file, display it on a graphical user interface, or even send the text over a network.

---

variables refer to the same object, not whether two distinct objects have the same state. Consider the following three variable declarations:

```java
Point p1 = new Point(7, 2);
Point p2 = new Point(7, 2);
Point p3 = p2;
```

The following diagram represents the state of these objects and the variables that refer to them. Notice that p3 is not a reference to a third object but a second reference to the object referred to by p2. This means that a change to p2, such as a call of its translate method, would also be reflected in p3:

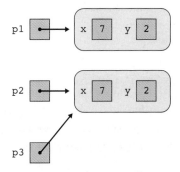

With the preceding `Point` objects, the expression `p1 == p2` would evaluate to `false` because `p1` and `p2` do not refer to the same object. The object referred to by `p1` has the same state as `p2`'s object, but they have different identities. The expression `p2 == p3` would evaluate to `true`, though, because `p2` does refer to the same object as `p3`.

Often when comparing two objects we instead want to know whether the objects have the same state. To perform such a comparison, we use a special method called `equals`. Every Java object contains an instance method called `equals` that it uses to compare itself to other objects.

The previous section mentioned that a class without a `toString` method receives a default version of the method. Similarly, a class without an `equals` method receives a default version that uses the most conservative definition of equality, considering two objects to be equal only if they have the same identity. This means that the default `equals` method behaves identically to the `==` operator. If you want different behavior than this, you must write your own `equals` method to replace the default behavior.

A proper `equals` method performs a comparison of two objects' states and returns `true` if the states are the same. With the preceding `Point` objects, we'd like the expressions `p1.equals(p2)`, `p1.equals(p3)`, and `p2.equals(p3)` to evaluate to `true` because the `Point`s all have the same (x, y) coordinates.

You can imagine a piece of client code that examines two `Point` objects and returns whether they have the same state. Two `Point` objects have the same state if they have the same x and y field values. Therefore, such code might look like this:

```
if (p1.getX() == p2.getX() && p1.getY() == p2.getY()) {
    return true;
} else {
    return false;
}
```

The `equals` functionality should actually be implemented in the `Point` class itself, though, not in the client code. Rather than having two `Point`s p1 and p2, the `equals` method considers the first object to be the "implicit parameter" and accepts the second object as a parameter. It returns a `boolean` value of `true` if the two objects are equal.

The following is an initial implementation of the `equals` method that has several flaws:

```
// a flawed implementation of an equals method
public boolean equals(Point p2) {
    if (x == p2.getX() && y == p2.getY()) {
        return true;
    } else {
        return false;
    }
}
```

An initial flaw we can correct is that the preceding code doesn't make good use of "Boolean zen," described in Chapter 5. Recall that when your code uses an `if/else` statement to return a `boolean` value of `true` or `false`, often you can directly return the value of the `if` statement's condition:

```
return x == p2.getX() && y == p2.getY();
```

It's legal for the `equals` method to access `p2`'s fields directly, so we can optionally modify this further. Private fields are visible to their entire class, including to other objects of that same class, so it is legal for one `Point` object to examine the fields of another:

```
return x == p2.x && y == p2.y;
```

Some programmers respect `p2`'s encapsulation even against other `Point` objects and therefore would not make the preceding change.

To be consistent with other Java classes, we must also make a change to the header of our `equals` method. The `equals` method's parameter should not be of type `Point`. The method must instead accept a parameter of type `Object`:

```
public boolean equals(Object o) {
```

A variable or parameter of type `Object` can refer to any Java object, which means that any object may be passed as the parameter to the `equals` method. Thus, we can compare `Point` objects against any type of object, not just other `Point`s. For example, an expression such as `p1.equals("hello")` would now be legal. The `equals` method should return `false` in such a case because the parameter isn't a `Point`.

You might think that the following code would correctly compare the two `Point` objects and return the proper result. Unfortunately, it does not even compile successfully:

```
return x == o.x && y == o.y; // does not compile
```

The Java compiler doesn't allow us to write an expression such as `o.x` because it doesn't know ahead of time whether `o`'s object will have a field called `x`. The preceding code produces errors such as the following for each of `o`'s fields we try to access:

```
Point.java:36: cannot find symbol
symbol : variable x
location: class java.lang.Object
```

If we want to treat `o` as a `Point` object, we must cast it from type `Object` to type `Point`. We've already discussed typecasting to convert between primitive types, such as casting `double` to `int`. Casting between object types has a different meaning. A cast of an object is a promise to the compiler. The cast is your assurance that the reference actually refers to a different type and that the compiler can treat it as that type. In our method, we'll write a statement that casts `o` into a `Point` object, so the compiler will trust that we can access its `x` and `y` fields:

```
// returns whether the two Points have the same (x, y) values
public boolean equals(Object o) {
    Point other = (Point) o;
    return x == other.x && y == other.y;
}
```

The `instanceof` Keyword

By changing our `equals` method's parameter to type `Object`, we have allowed non-`Point` objects to be passed. However, our method still doesn't behave properly when clients pass non-`Point` objects. An expression in client code such as `p.equals("hello")` will produce an exception like the following at runtime:

```
Exception in thread "main"
java.lang.ClassCastException: java.lang.String
        at Point.equals(Point.java:25)
        at PointMain.main(PointMain.java:25)
```

The exception occurs because it is illegal to cast a `String` into a `Point`, since these are not compatible types of objects. To prevent the exception, our `equals` method will need to examine the type of the parameter and return `false` if it isn't a `Point`. The following pseudocode shows the pattern to follow:

```
public boolean equals(Object o) {
    if (o is a Point object) {
        compare the x and y values.
    } else {
        return false. // not a Point object
    }
}
```

There is an operator called `instanceof` that tests whether a variable refers to an object of a given type. An `instanceof` test is a binary expression that takes the following form and produces a `boolean` result:

```
<expression> instanceof <type>
```

Table 8.1 lists some example expressions using `instanceof` and their results, given the following variables:

```
String s = "carrot";
Point p = new Point(8, 1);
```

The `instanceof` operator is unusual because it looks like the name of a method but is used more like a relational operator, such as > or ==. It is separated from its

Table 8.1   Sample `instanceof` expressions

Expression	Result
s instanceof String	true
s instanceof Point	false
p instanceof String	false
p instanceof Point	true
"hello" instanceof String	true
null instanceof Point	false

operands by spaces but doesn't require parentheses, dots, or any other notation. The operand on the left side is generally a variable, and the operand on the right is the name of the class you wish to test against.

In our `equals` method, we must examine the parameter o to see whether it is a `Point` object. The following code uses the `instanceof` keyword to implement the equals method correctly:

```
// returns whether o refers to a Point with the same (x, y)
// coordinates as this Point
public boolean equals(Object o) {
    if (o instanceof Point) {
        Point other = (Point) o;
        return x == other.x && y == other.y;
    } else { // not a Point object
        return false;
    }
}
```

You might think that our `instanceof` test would allow us to remove the type cast below it. After all, the `instanceof` test ensures that the comparison occurs only when o does refer to a `Point` object. However, the type cast cannot be removed because the compiler doesn't allow the code to compile without it.

A nice side benefit of the `instanceof` operator is that it produces a `false` result when o is `null`. Thus, if the client code contains an expression such as `p1.equals(null)`, it will correctly return `false` rather than throwing a `NullPointerException`.

Many classes implement an `equals` method like ours, so much of the preceding equals code can be reused as boilerplate code. The following is a template for a well-formed `equals` method. The `instanceof` test and type cast are likely the first two things you'll want to do in any `equals` method you write:

```
public boolean equals(Object o) {
    if (o instanceof <type>) {
        <type> other = (<type>) o;
        compare the data and return the result.
    } else {
        return false;
    }
}
```

Here is the fifth version of our `Point` class that includes the `toString` and `equals` methods:

```
1 // A Point object represents a pair of (x, y) coordinates.
2 // Fifth version: toString and equals.
3 // Class invariant: x >= 0 && y >= 0.
4
5 public class Point {
6     private int x;
7     private int y;
8
9     // constructs a new point with the given (x, y) location
```

```
10        // pre: initialX >= 0 && initialY >= 0
11        public Point(int initialX, int initialY) {
12            setLocation(initialX, initialY);
13        }
14
15        // returns the distance between this point and (0, 0)
16        public double distanceFromOrigin() {
17            return Math.sqrt(x * x + y * y);
18        }
19
20        // returns whether o refers to a Point with the same (x, y)
21        // coordinates as this Point
22        public boolean equals(Object o) {
23            if (o instanceof Point) {
24                Point other = (Point) o;
25                return x == other.x && y == other.y;
26            } else { // not a Point object
27                return false;
28            }
29        }
30
31        // returns the x-coordinate of this point
32        public int getX() {
33            return x;
34        }
35
36        // returns the y-coordinate of this point
37        public int getY() {
38            return y;
39        }
40
41        // sets this point's (x, y) location to the given values
42        // pre: newX >= 0 && newY >= 0
43        public void setLocation(int newX, int newY) {
44            if (newX < 0 || newY < 0) {
45                throw new IllegalArgumentException();
46            }
47
48            x = newX;
49            y = newY;
50        }
51
52        // returns a String representation of this point
53        public String toString() {
54            return "(" + x + ", " + y + ")";
55        }
56
57        // shifts this point's location by the given amount
58        // pre: x + dx >= 0 && y + dy >= 0
59        public void translate(int dx, int dy) {
60            setLocation(x + dx, y + dy);
61        }
62 }
```

Here is the final version of the client program, which now takes advantage of the toString method when printing Point objects:

```
1  // A program that deals with 2D points.
2  // Fifth version, to accompany Point class with toString method.
3
4  public class PointMain {
5      public static void main(String[] args) {
6          // create two Point objects
7          Point p1 = new Point(7, 2);
8          Point p2 = new Point(4, 3);
9
10         // print each point and its distance from origin
11         System.out.println("p1 is " + p1);
12         System.out.println("distance from origin = " +
13                            p1.distanceFromOrigin());
14
15         System.out.println("p2 is " + p2);
16         System.out.println("distance from origin = " +
17                            p2.distanceFromOrigin());
18
19         // translate each point to a new location
20         p1.translate(11, 6);
21         p2.translate(1, 7);
22
23         // print the points again
24         System.out.println("p1 is " + p1);
25         System.out.println("p2 is " + p2);
26     }
27 }
```

8.7 The Keyword this

When we discussed instance methods we mentioned that an object's instance methods can refer to its other methods and fields, because the instance method code knows which object it's operating on. We called this idea the "implicit parameter." In this section, we'll explore the mechanics behind the implicit parameter and introduce a keyword that allows us to refer to it directly.

The implicit parameter is actually a special reference that is set each time an instance method is called. You can access this reference in your code using the keyword this.

> **this**
> A Java keyword that allows you to refer to the implicit parameter inside a class.

When you refer to a field such as x in your code, you are actually using shorthand. The compiler converts an expression such as x to this.x. You can use the longer form in your code if you want be more explicit. For example, our translate method could be rewritten as follows:

```
public void translate(int dx, int dy) {
    this.x += dx;
```

```
      this.y += dy;
}
```

The code behaves the same as the original version of the method. The explicit style is less common, but some programmers prefer it because it's clearer. It also more closely matches the style used in client code, where all messages to objects begin with a variable name and a dot.

The general syntax for using the keyword `this` to refer to fields is the following:

```
this.<field name>
```

Similarly, when you call an instance method such as `setLocation`, you're actually using shorthand for a call of `this.setLocation`. You can use the longer form if you prefer. It has the following general syntax:

```
this.<method name>(<expression>,<expression>, . . . , <expression>);
```

In the earlier section about the implicit parameter, we diagrammed the behavior of some method calls on two `Point` objects. Let's revisit the same example using the keyword `this`. Consider the following two `Point` objects:

```
Point p1 = new Point(7, 2);
Point p2 = new Point(4, 3);
```

After constructing the `Point` objects, we make the following method calls:

```
p1.translate(11, 6);
p2.translate(1, 7);
```

Essentially, the behavior of these two method calls is the following:

- Set `this` to refer to the same object as `p1`, and execute the `translate` method with parameters (`11, 6`).
- Set `this` to refer to the same object as `p2`, and execute the `translate` method with parameters (`1, 7`).

During the first call, `this` refers to the same object as `p1`. Therefore, the method call adjusts the (`x,y`) coordinates of `p1`'s object:

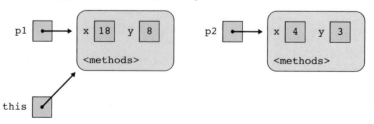

During the second method call `this` refers to the same object as `p2`, so the lines in the body of the `translate` method change the x and y fields of `p2`'s object:

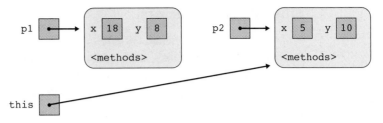

One common usage of the keyword this is to deal with shadowed variables. As described earlier, shadowing occurs when a field is obscured by another variable with the same name. This can happen when a field has the same name as a parameter or local variable in a class. For example, the following is a legal header for our setLocation method, even though our fields are also called x and y:

```java
public void setLocation(int x, int y) {
```

As explained at the beginning of this section, Java would normally interpret the expression x to mean this.x. However, if a parameter or local variable called x exists, that will be used instead if you just write x because the field x is shadowed by the parameter/variable. If you write this.x, though, the field x will always be used:

```java
// sets this point's (x, y) location to the given values
// pre: x >= 0 && y >= 0
public void setLocation(int x, int y) {
    if (x < 0 || y < 0) {
        throw new IllegalArgumentException();
    }

    this.x = x;
    this.y = y;
}
```

Of course, you can avoid this situation by naming parameters and local variables differently from fields. However, some programmers prefer the style where a variable takes the same name as a closely related field, because it saves them from having to concoct separate parameter names like initialX or newY.

With that in mind we can also modify our Point constructor's parameter names to be x and y, since the constructor's body passes their values to setLocation:

```java
// constructs a new point with the given (x, y) location
// pre: x >= 0 && y >= 0
public Point(int x, int y) {
    setLocation(x, y);
}
```

In most cases, the compiler will not allow two variables to have the same name at the same point in a program. Fields are a special case that present the risk of shadowing. Java's designers decided to allow this so that parameter names could match their related fields.

Multiple Constructors

A class can have multiple constructors, to provide multiple ways for clients to construct objects of that class. Each constructor must have a different signature (i.e., number and type of parameters).

Our existing `Point` constructor requires two parameters (the `Point` object's initial x- and y-coordinates):

```
// constructs a new point with the given (x, y) location
// pre: x >= 0 && y >= 0
public Point(int x, int y) {
    setLocation(x, y);
}
```

The initial version of the `Point` class had no constructor. In such cases, Java provides a parameterless default constructor that initializes the fields to 0. When we added our two-parameter constructor, we lost the default constructor. This is unfortunate, because it provided a useful shorter notation for constructing a `Point` at the origin. We can restore this ability by adding a second, parameterless constructor to our `Point` class. Our new constructor might look like this:

```
// constructs a Point object with location (0, 0)
public Point() {
    x = 0;
    y = 0;
}
```

(To eliminate redundancy, we could have called `setLocation(0, 0)` in the body of the constructor instead of setting x and y manually.)

Now it's possible to construct `Point`s in two ways:

```
Point p1 = new Point(5, -2);   // (5, -2)
Point p2 = new Point();        // (0, 0)
```

Returning to the non-programming example of purchasing cars, you can imagine that some customers wish to specify many details about their new cars (e.g., "I'd like a yellow Civic with gold trim, upgraded stereo system, and a sun roof."), while other customers wish to specify fewer details and receive default options instead. Having multiple constructors gives clients similar flexibility when asking for new objects of your class.

Notice that both constructors perform similar actions; the only difference is what initial values the x and y fields receive. Another way of saying this is that the new constructor can be expressed in terms of the old constructor. The following two lines have the same effect:

```
Point p1 = new Point();        // construct Point at (0, 0)
Point p2 = new Point(0, 0);    // construct Point at (0, 0)
```

A common programming paradigm in classes with multiple constructors is for one constructor to contain the true initialization code and for all others to call it. This means that every object created passes through a common code path, which can be useful for testing and debugging later. The syntax for one constructor to call another is to write the keyword this, followed by the parameters to pass to the other constructor in parentheses:

```
this(<expression>, <expression>, ..., <expression>);
```

This is really just the normal syntax for a method call, except that we use the special keyword this where we would normally put the name of a method. In our case, we want to pass parameter values of 0 and 0 to initialize each field:

```
// constructs a new point at the origin, (0, 0)
public Point() {
    this(0, 0); // calls Point(int, int) constructor
}
```

The following diagram depicts the behavior of one constructor calling another. Notice that the keyword this is used in multiple ways in our code, both to call a constructor and to refer to fields in the setLocation method:

```
public Point() {
    this(0, 0);
}
```

```
public Point(int x, int y) {
    setLocation(x, y);
}
```

```
public void setLocation(int x, int y) {
    this.x = x;
    this.y = y;
}
```

Here is the final version of our Point class incorporating all of the changes in this section. This version of the class uses the keyword this in its constructor and setLocation method:

```
1  // A Point object represents a pair of (x, y) coordinates.
2  // Sixth version: multiple constructors and this keyword.
3  // Class invariant: x >= 0 && y >= 0.
4
5  public class Point {
6      private int x;
7      private int y;
8
9      // constructs a new point at the origin, (0, 0)
10     public Point() {
11         this(0, 0); // calls Point(int, int) constructor
```

```
12        }
13
14        // constructs a new point with the given (x, y) location
15        // pre: x >= 0 && y >= 0
16        public Point(int x, int y) {
17            setLocation(x, y);
18        }
19
20        // returns the distance between this Point and (0, 0)
21        public double distanceFromOrigin() {
22            return Math.sqrt(x * x + y * y);
23        }
24
25        // returns whether o refers to a point with the same (x, y)
26        // coordinates as this point
27        public boolean equals(Object o) {
28            if (o instanceof Point) {
29                Point other = (Point) o;
30                return x == other.x && y == other.y;
31            } else { // not a Point object
32                return false;
33            }
34        }
35
36        // returns the x-coordinate of this point
37        public int getX() {
38            return x;
39        }
40
41        // returns the y-coordinate of this point
42        public int getY() {
43            return y;
44        }
45
46        // sets this point's (x, y) location to the given values
47        // pre: x >= 0 && y >= 0
48        public void setLocation(int x, int y) {
49            if (x < 0 || y < 0) {
50                throw new IllegalArgumentException();
51            }
52
53            this.x = x;
54            this.y = y;
55        }
56
57        // returns a String representation of this point
58        public String toString() {
59            return "(" + x + ", " + y + ")";
60        }
61
62        // shifts this point's location by the given amount
63        // pre: x + dx >= 0 && y + dy >= 0
64        public void translate(int dx, int dy) {
65            setLocation(x + dx, y + dy);
66        }
67 }
```

The client program is unmodified because it does not construct any `Points` at $(0, 0)$.

8.8 More Classes

Many key concepts about classes were illustrated during the development of our Point class. But since there are so many new ideas and so much new syntax, one example class is insufficient. In this section we will explore the creation of some additional small classes.

Participant

In Chapters 2 and 4 we wrote code to compute a person's body mass index (BMI). What if you wanted to write a program that conducted a study of the BMIs of many participating people? You'd read a set of names, heights, and weights and compute each participant's BMI value.

This programming problem has related state and behavior for each participant, so it would benefit from having a Participant class. The state of each Participant object would be its name, height, and weight:

```java
public class Participant {
    private String name;
    private double height;
    private double weight;

    . . .
}
```

You can compute the BMI based on this state. Write a method named getBMI that computes and returns the body mass index:

```java
// returns the participant's body mass index (BMI)
public double getBMI() {
    return weight / (height * height) * 703;
}
```

The class should also have a constructor. None of the three pieces of state has a sensible default value; the client must supply all three. Therefore, the Participant constructor should have these three values as parameters.

Here is a complete version of the Participant class, including accessors for the Participant's fields:

```java
 1 // A Participant object represents data about one person in a
 2 // body mass index (BMI) study program.
 3
 4 public class Participant {
 5     private String name;
 6     private double height;
 7     private double weight;
 8
 9     // constructs a participant with the given state
10     public Participant(String name, double height, double weight) {
11         this.name = name;
12         this.height = height;
13         this.weight = weight;
14     }
```

```
15
16      // returns the participant's BMI
17      public double getBMI() {
18          return weight / (height * height) * 703;
19      }
20
21      // returns the participant's height
22      public double getHeight() {
23          return height;
24      }
25
26      // returns the participant's name
27      public String getName() {
28          return name;
29      }
30
31      // returns the participant's weight
32      public double getWeight() {
33          return weight;
34      }
35 }
```

Because no mutators (e.g., `setName` or `setWeight`) are provided in the `Participant` class, a `Participant` object's state cannot be modified after it is constructed. Such an object is called an *immutable object*. As you'll recall from Chapter 3, `String` objects are also immutable.

Immutable Object

An object whose state cannot be modified.

Not supplying mutators might seem restrictive, but immutable objects have some advantages. Immutability helps the author of a class ensure adherence to any conditions or invariants placed on the class. Also, a client that has created an immutable object can pass it as a parameter to any other piece of code without fear that the code will modify the object.

A good rule of thumb when writing classes is not to provide any functionality that does not have a clear use. This is especially true of mutator methods. If client programs are unlikely to need a given mutator, it is often best omitted. If a client needs to modify a `Participant` object, a workaround is simply to discard it and create a new one with the new information. Since `Participant` objects do not retain much state, this is not a very costly operation.

We sometimes call small objects with simple state *lightweight objects*. Many lightweight objects are made immutable for simplicity.

It is possible to make a class's objects immutable while still retaining operations that seem to modify the objects. The most famous example of such an immutable class is the `String` class. As discussed in Chapter 3, it is impossible to modify a `String` once it has been created. Any operations that change the `String`, such as `toUpperCase`, actually return a new `String`. Recall that when modifying a `String`, you must reassign the `String` into its variable, as in:

```
str = str.toUpperCase();
```

It would be possible to make our `Point` class immutable, using this idea of return-ing a new object on operations that modify state. For example, its `translate` method would create a new `Point` object at the translated location instead of adjusting the `x` and `y` values of the existing point:

```
// a possible translate method for an immutable Point class
public Point translate(int dx, int dy) {
    return new Point(x + dx, y + dy);
}
```

Client code using `Point` objects would require slight modifications to use the new immutable `Point` class. Any call to a mutator method would have to store the call's result by reassigning it into the same variable. For example, the call in our `PointMain` client to translate `Point` `p1` would have to be changed to the following:

```
p1 = p1.translate(11, 6);
```

Making the `Point` class immutable is left as an exercise.

TimeSpan

Consider a program that measures or deals with elapsed intervals of time, such as a stopwatch, a scheduler, a TV recorder, or an airline flight system. A useful abstrac-tion in such a program would be an object representing an elapsed span of time.

Let's write a class called `TimeSpan`, where each `TimeSpan` object represents an interval of elapsed hours and minutes. For example, we could construct a `TimeSpan` representing an interval of 6 hours and 15 minutes. We'll represent only hours and minutes, ignoring larger or smaller units such as days or seconds.

Since we're representing intervals of hours and minutes, it seems natural to have these two quantities as fields in our class:

```
// represents a time span of elapsed hours and minutes
public class TimeSpan {
    private int hours;
    private int minutes;

    . . .
}
```

The constructor for a `TimeSpan` object will accept `hours` and `minutes` as parame-ters and store the values into the object's fields. However, there is a potential problem: What should we do about values of `minutes` that are 60 or greater? Should the client program be allowed to construct a `TimeSpan` object representing 0 hours and 157 min-utes? A more natural representation of this amount would be 2 hours and 37 minutes.

Let's make a design decision that we will only store `TimeSpans` with `minutes` less than 60. If the user tries to construct a `TimeSpan` object with more than 60 minutes, we will convert the excess minutes into hours. You might be tempted to use an if/else statement or a loop to handle minutes above 60, but there is a simpler solution. Recall that in a large number of minutes such as 157, dividing by 60 will produce the hours (2) and using the % operator by 60 will produce the remaining minutes (37). The hours field should really store the hours parameter plus the minutes parameter divided by 60, and the minutes field should store the remaining minutes.

The following code implements the constructor. We'll assume as a precondition that negative values (such as −12 minutes) are not entered:

```java
// initial version of TimeSpan constructor
// pre: hours >= 0 && minutes >= 0
public TimeSpan(int hours, int minutes) {
    this.hours = hours + minutes / 60;
    this.minutes = minutes % 60;
}
```

We can express our design decision as a class invariant, that the value of every TimeSpan object's minutes field will always be less than 60.

A useful behavior of a TimeSpan object would be the ability to add more hours and minutes to the span. An airline scheduling program might use this to add the elapsed times for two flights to determine the total travel time for a passenger's trip. Let's implement this behavior as a method called add that accepts hours and minutes as parameters. Here's an initial (incorrect) version of that method:

```java
// an incorrect version of add method
// pre: hours >= 0 && minutes >= 0
public void add(int hours, int minutes) {
    this.hours += hours;
    this.minutes += minutes;
}
```

The problem with the preceding code is that it allows the client to violate our class invariant. If the client passes a value of minutes large enough to make the total minutes greater than 60, the minutes field can have an invalid value. For example, if 45 minutes are added to a time span of 1 hour and 30 minutes, the result will be 1 hour and 75 minutes. We must write code at the end of the add method to deal with minutes above 60. The following code implements the behavior:

```java
// adds the given interval to this time span
// pre: hours >= 0 && minutes >= 0
public void add(int hours, int minutes) {
    this.hours += hours;
    this.minutes += minutes;

    // converts each 60 minutes into one hour
    this.hours += this.minutes / 60;
    this.minutes = this.minutes % 60;
}
```

The code now has to resolve the issue of minutes values above 60 in two places, but it would be preferable to solve this problem in one place rather than redundantly checking for it throughout the class. A more elegant solution is to have the constructor initialize the fields to 0 and then call the add method:

```
// constructs a time span with the given interval
// pre: hours >= 0 && minutes >= 0
public TimeSpan(int hours, int minutes) {
    this.hours = 0;
    this.minutes = 0;
    add(hours, minutes);
}
```

(The fields would have been auto-initialized to 0 anyway, but many programmers prefer to explicitly initialize field values for clarity.)

Since our add method is a mutator, TimeSpan objects are not immutable. If we had wanted to create immutable TimeSpan objects, we could have written the add method to create and return a new TimeSpan object rather than modifying the current TimeSpan object.

Another useful operation for TimeSpan objects would be the ability to print them on the console. As we have seen in this chapter, to make objects printable we can write a toString method. First we must decide on the format we'd like the String to have, such as "2h35m" for 2 hours and 35 minutes. Next, we'll write the toString method to build and return this String based on the state of the TimeSpan object:

```
// returns a String for this time span, such as "6h15m"
public String toString() {
    return hours + "h" + minutes + "m";
}
```

It might also be useful to be able to compare TimeSpan objects to see whether they represent the same amount of elapsed time. We'll add an equals method to the TimeSpan class to allow such comparisons. Recall the boilerplate code for equals presented earlier in this chapter. First we must perform an instanceof test, and if it succeeds, we must cast the parameter from an Object to a TimeSpan. After casting we can compare the hours and minutes of the current TimeSpan object with those of the parameter. The following code implements the method:

```
// returns whether o is a TimeSpan representing the same
// number of hours and minutes as this TimeSpan object
public boolean equals(Object o) {
    if (o instanceof TimeSpan) {
        TimeSpan other = (TimeSpan) o;
        return hours == other.hours &&
                minutes == other.minutes;
    } else { // not a TimeSpan object
        return false;
    }
}
```

The following is the code for the complete TimeSpan class:

```
1 // Represents a time span of hours and minutes elapsed.
2 // Class invariant: minutes < 60
3
```

```
 4 public class TimeSpan {
 5     private int hours;
 6     private int minutes;
 7
 8     // constructs a time span with the given interval
 9     // pre: hours >= 0 && minutes >= 0
10     public TimeSpan(int hours, int minutes) {
11         this.hours = 0;
12         this.minutes = 0;
13         add(hours, minutes);
14     }
15
16     // adds the given interval to this time span
17     // pre: hours >= 0 && minutes >= 0
18     public void add(int hours, int minutes) {
19         this.hours += hours;
20         this.minutes += minutes;
21
22         // converts each 60 minutes into one hour
23         this.hours += this.minutes / 60;
24         this.minutes = this.minutes % 60;
25     }
26
27     // returns whether o is a TimeSpan representing the same
28     // number of hours and minutes as this TimeSpan object
29     public boolean equals(Object o) {
30         if (o instanceof TimeSpan) {
31             TimeSpan other = (TimeSpan) o;
32             return hours == other.hours &&
33                     minutes == other.minutes;
34         } else { // not a TimeSpan object
35             return false;
36         }
37     }
38
39     // returns a String for this time span, such as "6h15m"
40     public String toString() {
41         return hours + "h" + minutes + "m";
42     }
43 }
```

There are some additional features that should be included in the class, such as accessors for the field values, but these are left as exercises.

Changing Internal Implementations

Something that may not be obvious is that the internal representation of our TimeSpan does not necessarily have to match the external view the client sees. The client wishes to think of time as hours and minutes, but the TimeSpan object does not have to store time with those two data fields. In fact, the code for TimeSpan becomes much simpler if we simply store a total number of minutes. We can absorb each hour into this total by adding 60 minutes to it:

```
// alternate implementation using only total minutes
public class TimeSpan {
    private int totalMinutes;
    ...
}
```

Recall that encapsulation allows us to change the internal implementation of a class without changing any client code. We can implement the same add, toString, and equals behavior using total minutes. We'll make modifications to the code to account for the new representation.

For example, the add method needs to combine the hours and minutes together and add both of them into the totalMinutes. We'll scale the hours by 60:

```
// adds the given interval to this time span
// pre: hours >= 0 && minutes >= 0
public void add(int hours, int minutes) {
    totalMinutes += 60 * hours + minutes;
}
```

The constructor, toString, and equals methods also require minor modifications to account for our new representation. Here is the complete class, implemented with total minutes instead of hours and minutes:

```
 1  // Represents a time span of elapsed hours and minutes.
 2  // Alternate implementation using only total minutes.
 3
 4  public class TimeSpan {
 5      private int totalMinutes;
 6
 7      // constructs a time span with the given interval
 8      // pre: hours >= 0 && minutes >= 0
 9      public TimeSpan(int hours, int minutes) {
10          totalMinutes = 0;
11          add(hours, minutes);
12      }
13
14      // adds the given interval to this time span
15      // pre: hours >= 0 && minutes >= 0
16      public void add(int hours, int minutes) {
17          totalMinutes += 60 * hours + minutes;
18      }
19
20      // returns whether o is a TimeSpan representing the same
21      // number of hours and minutes as this TimeSpan object
22      public boolean equals(Object o) {
23          if (o instanceof TimeSpan) {
24              TimeSpan other = (TimeSpan) o;
25              return totalMinutes == other.totalMinutes;
26          } else { // not a TimeSpan object
27              return false;
28          }
29      }
30
31      // returns a String for this time span, such as "6h15m"
```

```
32      public String toString() {
33          return (totalMinutes / 60) + "h" +
34                  (totalMinutes % 60) + "m";
35      }
36 }
```

The main benefit of this new internal representation is that the code is shorter and simpler. We do not need to separate the time interval into two pieces or worry about the `minutes` value becoming too large. Encapsulation is what enables us to make a design change like this without fear that a client program will break. The clients will see the same behavior for this version of the class.

8.9 Case Study: Designing a Stock Class

So far we have written several classes, but we have not talked about how to design a class or how to break apart a programming problem into classes. In this section we'll examine a larger programming problem and design a class and client to solve it. We will create a class called `Stock` and a client program that compares the performance of stocks the user has purchased.

Consider the task of writing a financial program to record purchases of shares of two stocks and report which has the greatest profit. The investor may have made several purchases of the same `Stock` at different times and prices. The interaction with the program would look like this:

```
First stock's symbol: AMZN
How many purchases did you make? 2
1: How many shares, at what price per share? 50 35.06
2: How many shares, at what price per share? 25 38.52
What is today's price per share? 37.29
Net profit/loss: $80.75

Second stock's symbol: INTC
How many purchases did you make? 3
1: How many shares, at what price per share? 15 16.50
2: How many shares, at what price per share? 10 18.09
3: How many shares, at what price per share? 20 17.15
What is today's price per share? 17.82
Net profit/loss: $29.75

AMZN was more profitable than INTC.
```

The program must perform several actions: prompting the user for input, reporting profits, and so on. The client program could perform all of these actions and could keep track of the financial data using existing types such as `doubles` and `Strings`. However, recall that we began this chapter by talking about object-oriented reasoning. With complex programs it is often useful to think about the problem in terms of the relevant objects that could solve it, rather than placing all behavior in the client program. In this particular program, we must perform several computations that involve keeping track of purchases of shares of a particular stock, so it would be useful to store the purchase information in an object.

One possible design would be to create a `Purchase` class that records information about a single purchase of shares of a particular stock. For example, if the user specified that three purchases were made, three `Purchase` objects would be constructed. However, a more useful abstraction here would be to hold the overall information about all purchases of one stock. The investor may make many purchases of the same stock, so it would be nice to have an easy way to accumulate these shares and their total cost into a single object.

Therefore, instead of a `Purchase` class, we'll write a `Stock` class. Each `Stock` object will keep track of the investor's accumulated shares of one stock and can provide profit/loss information. Our `Stock` class will reside in a file called `Stock.java`, and the client program itself will reside in a separate file called `StockMain.java`.

Object-Oriented Design Heuristics

We now face the important task of deciding what the contents of our `Stock` class should be. To do this, let's look at the overall set of responsibilities (things a class knows or does) that are necessary to solve the programming problem:

- The user must be prompted for each stock's symbol. The information must be stored somewhere.
- The user must be prompted for the number of purchases of each stock.
- Each purchase (number of shares and price per share) must be read from the console. The information must be stored somewhere.
- The total profit/loss of each stock must be computed.
- The total profit/loss of each stock must be printed to the console.
- The two total profits/losses must be compared, and a message must be printed about which stock performed better.

It might be tempting to make most or all of these responsibilities of our `Stock` class. We could make a `Stock` object store all the purchases of both stocks, prompt for information from the console, print the results, and so on. But a key idea when writing classes is that they should have *cohesion*.

> **Cohesion**
>
> The extent to which the code for a class represents a single abstraction.

Striving for high cohesion is an example of an object-oriented *design heuristic,* a rule of thumb or guideline to follow when designing object-oriented programs. Placing all the responsibilities in the `Stock` class would not represent a clear abstraction. The abstraction we want to represent is the accumulated purchases of a single stock.

One set of responsibilities that `Stock` objects should not handle is producing the console input and output. We need to prompt the user for information and print messages, but this is specific to the current client program. Objects are meant to be reusable pieces of software, and other programs might wish to track stock purchases without using these exact messages or prompts. If the `Stock` class handles the prompts and printing, it will be heavily intertwined with this client program and not easily reusable by other clients.

In general, we want to reduce unnecessary dependencies between classes. Dependencies between classes in an object-oriented program contribute to *coupling*.

> **Coupling**
>
> The degree to which one part of a program depends on another.

Striving to avoid unnecessary coupling is a second design heuristic commonly used in object-oriented programming. A design that avoids this problem is sometimes said to have *loose coupling*.

Let's divide some of the responsibilities now, based on our heuristics. Since the `StockMain` client program will perform the console I/O, it should handle the responsibilities listed here:

StockMain

- Prompt for each stock's symbol.
- Prompt for the number of purchases of each stock.
- Read each purchase (number of shares and price per share) from the console.
- Print the total profit/loss of each stock.
- Compare the two total profits/losses and print a message about which stock performed better.

If the `StockMain` client program is to perform the console I/O, it might also seem natural for it to store the information about each stock purchase (that is, the number of shares and price paid). But our `Stock` object should contain the functionality to compute a stock's total profit or loss, and it will need to have the data about all purchases to do so. This leads us to a third design heuristic: Related data and behavior should be in the same place. With that in mind, we can write out the responsibilities for the `Stock` class as follows:

Stock

- Store a stock's symbol.
- Store accumulated information about the investor's purchases of the stock.
- Record a purchase of the stock.
- Compute the total profit/loss for the stock.

When designing large object-oriented programs, many software engineers write information on index cards similar to the tables shown in this section. Each card is called a *CRC card* because it lists the Class, its Responsibilities, and any Collaborators (other classes to which it is coupled).

The following list summarizes the design heuristics discussed in this section:

- A class should be cohesive, representing only one abstraction.
- A class should avoid unnecessary coupling.
- Related data and behavior should be in the same class.

Note that we began our design by looking at responsibilities rather than by specifying fields, as we did when developing our `Point` class. We began the `Point` evolution with fields because the data associated with a point is more obvious than the data associated with multiple stock purchases. Fields are also conceptually simpler than instance methods.

Stock Fields and Method Headers

In this section we'll decide on a design for the method names and signatures the `Stock` should use to implement its behavior. We'll use this design to determine what fields are required to implement the behavior.

We've decided that a `Stock` object should allow clients to record purchases and request the total profit or loss. Each of these tasks can be represented as a method. The recording of a purchase can be represented as a method called `purchase`. The retrieval of the total profit or loss can be represented as a method called `getProfit`.

The `purchase` method should record information about a single purchase. A purchase consists of a number of shares bought (which we can assume is a whole number) and a price per share (which can include real numbers with both dollars and cents). Therefore, our `purchase` method should accept two parameters: an `int` for the number of shares bought and a `double` for the price per share. The method can use a `void` return type, since nothing needs to be returned after each purchase is recorded:

```
public void purchase(int shares, double pricePerShare) {
```

The `getProfit` method needs to return the amount of money that has been made or lost on all accumulated purchases of this stock. Consider an investor who has made the following three purchases of a stock:

Purchase #1: 20 shares * $10 per share = $ 200 cost
Purchase #2: 20 shares * $30 per share = $ 600 cost
Purchase #3: 10 shares * $20 per share = $ 200 cost
              50 total shares, $1000 total cost

If today's price per share is $22.00, the current market value of the investor's 50 shares is (50 * 22) or $1100. Since the investor paid $1000 total for the shares and they are now worth $1100, the investor has made (1100 − 1000), or $100 of profit. The general formula for the profit is the following:

profit = ((total shares) * (current share price)) − (total cost)

The total shares and total cost needed for this calculation are the accumulated information from all purchases that have been made of this stock. This means that information will need to be stored during each call of the `purchase` method to be used later in the `getProfit` method. A key observation here is that we do not need to store the number of shares, price per share, and cost for every purchase: We only need to store cumulative sums of the total shares purchased so far and the total dollars spent so far to acquire those values.

The third value we need in order to calculate the profit is the current share price. We could choose to make this a field in the `Stock` class as well, but the share price is a dynamic value that changes regularly. We use it during a single call to the `getProfit` method, but the next call may come at a later date when the price per share has changed.

This leads us to another design heuristic: Fields should represent values of core importance to the object and values that are used in multiple methods. Adding too many fields clutters a class and can make its code harder to read. If a value is used in only one method of the class, it's best to make it a parameter to that method rather than a field. Therefore, we'll make the share price a parameter to the `getProfit` method.

```
public double getProfit(double currentPrice) {
```

One piece of state that we haven't discussed yet is that each stock has a symbol, such as `"AMZN"`. We'll store the symbol as a `String` field in each `Stock` object.

Here's a skeleton of our `Stock` class so far:

```
// incomplete Stock class
public class Stock {
    private String symbol;
    private int totalShares;
    private double totalCost;
    . . .

    public double getProfit(double currentPrice) {
        . . .
    }

    public void purchase(int shares, double pricePerShare) }
        . . .
    }
}
```

Stock Method and Constructor Implementation

Now that we've decided on some of the `Stock`'s state and behavior, let's think about how to construct `Stock` objects. The client program will need the ability to create two `Stocks` and record purchases of them.

It may be tempting to write a constructor that accepts three parameters: the symbol, total shares purchased, and total cost. But our `Stock` objects are accumulators of purchases, and we may want to be able to create new `Stock` objects before initial purchases are recorded. Let's design our class to require only the symbol as a parameter and initialize the other fields to 0:

```
// initializes a new Stock with no shares purchased
public Stock(String theSymbol) {
    symbol = theSymbol;
    totalShares = 0;
    totalCost = 0.0;
}
```

When a constructor takes an object as a parameter (such as the String theSymbol), it might make sense to check that parameter's value to make sure it isn't null. One possible way to handle this case would be to throw an exception if a null symbol is passed when creating a Stock object. We could do this by inserting the following lines at the start of the Stock's constructor:

```
if (theSymbol == null) {
    throw new NullPointerException();
}
```

Sun recommends that you throw a NullPointerException when a parameter's value is null but should not be. For other invalid parameter values, throw an IllegalArgumentException.

Now let's write the body of the purchase method. Recording the purchase consists of adding the number of shares to the total shares and adding the price paid for these shares to the total cost. The price paid is equal to the number of shares times the price per share. Here's the code for the purchase method to implement this behavior:

```
// records a purchase of the given number of shares of this stock
// at the given price per share
public void purchase(int shares, double pricePerShare) {
    totalShares += shares;
    totalCost += shares * pricePerShare;
}
```

As with the constructor, it might make sense here to check the parameters passed in to make sure they are valid. In this case, valid numbers of shares and prices per share must be non-negative. To perform this test, we can insert the following lines at the start of our purchase method:

```
if (shares < 0 || pricePerShare < 0) {
    throw new IllegalArgumentException();
}
```

Next, we'll write the body of the getProfit method. As discussed previously, the profit of a Stock is equal to its current market value minus what was paid for it:

profit = ((total shares) * (current share price)) − (total cost)

We can implement this formula in a straightforward manner using the totalShares and totalCost fields and the currentPrice parameter:

```
// Returns the total profit or loss earned on this stock,
// based on the given price per share.
public double getProfit(double currentPrice) {
    return totalShares * currentPrice - totalCost;
}
```

Note that parentheses are not needed in the code because multiplication has a higher precedence than subtraction.

As with the other methods, we should check for illegal parameter values. In this case, we shouldn't allow a negative current price per share. To ensure this, we can place the following code at the start of the method:

```
if (currentPrice < 0.0) {
    throw new IllegalArgumentException();
}
```

After we've written all the fields, the constructor, and the methods of our Stock, it will look like this:

```
1 // A Stock object represents purchases of shares of a stock.
2
3 public class Stock {
4      private String symbol;       // stock symbol, e.g. "YHOO"
5      private int totalShares;     // total shares purchased
6      private double totalCost;    // total cost for all shares
7
8      // initializes a new Stock with no shares purchased
9      // Precondition: symbol != null
10     public Stock(String theSymbol) {
11         if (theSymbol == null) {
12             throw new NullPointerException();
13         }
14
15         symbol = theSymbol;
16         totalShares = 0;
17         totalCost = 0.0;
18     }
19
20     // returns the total profit or loss earned on this stock,
21     // based on the given price per share
22     // pre: currentPrice >= 0.0
23     public double getProfit(double currentPrice) {
24         if (currentPrice < 0.0) {
25             throw new IllegalArgumentException();
26         }
27
28         double marketValue = totalShares * currentPrice;
29         return marketValue - totalCost;
30     }
31
32     // records purchase of the given shares at the given price
33     // pre: shares >= 0 && pricePerShare >= 0.0
34     public void purchase(int shares, double pricePerShare) {
35         if (shares < 0 || pricePerShare < 0.0) {
36             throw new IllegalArgumentException();
37         }
38
39         totalShares += shares;
40         totalCost += shares * pricePerShare;
41     }
42 }
```

The client code to use the Stock class would be written as follows:

```
1  // This program tracks the user's purchases of two stocks,
2  // computing and reporting which stock is more profitable.
3
4  import java.util.*;
5
6  public class StockMain {
7      public static void main(String[] args) {
8          Scanner console = new Scanner(System.in);
9
10         // first stock
11         System.out.print("First stock's symbol: ");
12         String symbol1 = console.next();
13         Stock stock1 = new Stock(symbol1);
14         double profit1 = makePurchases(stock1, console);
15
16         // second stock
17         System.out.print("Second stock's symbol: ");
18         String symbol2 = console.next();
19         Stock stock2 = new Stock(symbol2);
20         double profit2 = makePurchases(stock2, console);
21
22         // report which stock made more money
23         if (profit1 > profit2) {
24             System.out.println(symbol1 + " was more " +
25                     "profitable than" + symbol2 + ".");
26         } else if (profit2 > profit1) {
27             System.out.println(symbol2 + " was more " +
28                     "profitable than " + symbol1 + ".");
29         } else { // profit1 == profit2
30             System.out.println(symbol1 + " and " + symbol2 +
31                     " are equally profitable.");
32         }
33     }
34
35     // make purchases of stock and return the profit
36     public static double makePurchases(Stock currentStock,
37                                        Scanner console) {
38         System.out.print("How many purchases did you make? ");
39         int numPurchases = console.nextInt();
40
41         // ask about each purchase
42         for (int i = 1; i <= numPurchases; i++) {
43             System.out.print(i +
44                 ": How many shares, at what price per share? ");
45             int numShares = console.nextInt();
46             double pricePerShare = console.nextDouble();
47
48             // ask the Stock object to record this purchase
49             currentStock.purchase(numShares, pricePerShare);
50         }
51
52         // use the Stock object to compute profit
53         System.out.print("What is today's price per share? ");
54         double currentPrice = console.nextDouble();
55
```

```
56            double profit = currentStock.getProfit(currentPrice);
57            System.out.println("Net profit/loss: $" + profit);
58            System.out.println();
59            return profit;
60       }
61 }
```

There are other methods that would be useful to have in our `Stock` objects. For example, it would be good to implement accessors for the `Stock`'s data (the symbol, number of shares, and so on), and a `toString` method to enable `Stock` objects to be printed easily would be handy. We could even add a second constructor that would accept an initial number of shares and cost. These features are left for you to implement as exercises.

Chapter Summary

Object-oriented programming is a different philosophy of writing programs that focuses on nouns or entities in a program, rather than verbs or actions of a program. In object-oriented programming, state and behavior are grouped into objects that communicate with each other.

A class serves as the blueprint for a new type of object, specifying the object's data and behavior. The class can be asked to construct many objects (also called "instances") of its type.

The data for each object is specified using special variables called fields.

The behavior of each object is specified by writing instance methods in the class. Instance methods exist inside an object and can access and act on that object's internal state.

A class can define a special method called a constructor that creates and returns a new object and initializes its state. The constructor is the method that will be called when external client code creates a new object of your type using the `new` keyword. You can specify more than one constructor in a class; if none is specified, Java provides a default constructor.

Usually, an object can communicate with other objects despite not knowing all the details about how they work. This principle is known as abstraction. Most objects protect their internal data from unwanted external modification, which is known as encapsulation. You can provide encapsulation by declaring fields with the `private` modifier, which prevents other classes from directly modifying their values.

Two common categories of object methods are accessors and mutators. Accessors, such as the `length` method of a `String` object or the `getX` method of a `Point` object, provide information about the object. Mutators, such as the `translate` method of a `Point` object, allow us to modify the state of the object.

To make objects easily printable, write a `toString` method. To make objects testable for equality, write an `equals` method.

The keyword this can be used when an object wishes to refer to itself. It is also used when a class has multiple constructors and one constructor wishes to call another.

A class should represent only one key abstraction with related data and behavior, and it should be independent from its clients.

_____

_____

An immutable object is one whose state cannot be changed after it has been constructed.

_____

Self-Check Problems

Section 8.1: Object-Oriented Programming Concepts

1. Describe the difference between object-oriented programming and procedural programming.

2. What is an object? How is an object different from a class?

3. What is the state of a String object? What is its behavior?

4. Imagine that you are creating a class called Calculator. A Calculator object could be used to program a simple mathematical calculator device like the ones you have used in math classes in school. What state might a Calculator object have? What might its behavior be?

Section 8.2: Object State: Fields

5. Explain the differences between a field and a parameter. What is the difference in their syntax? What is the difference in their scope and how they may be used?

6. Create a class named Name that represents a person's name. The class should have fields representing the person's first name, last name, and middle initial. (Your class should contain only fields for now.)

Section 8.3: Object Behavior: Methods

7. What is the difference between an accessor and a mutator? What are the naming conventions used with accessors and mutators?

8. Add the following method to the Point class we developed in this chapter:

```
public double distance(Point other)
```

Returns the distance between the current Point object and the given other Point object. The distance between two points is equal to the square root of the sum of the squares of the differences of their x- and y-coordinates. In other words, the distance between two points $(x1, y1)$ and $(x2, y2)$ can be expressed as the square root of $(x2 - x1)^2 + (y2 - y1)^2$. Two points with the same (x, y) coordinates should return a distance of 0.0.

9. (You must complete self-check problem 6 before answering this question.)

Add the following methods to the Name class:

```
public String getNormalOrder()
```

Returns the person's name in normal order, with the first name followed by the middle initial and last name. For example, if the first name is "John", the middle initial is "Q" and the last name is "Public", returns "John Q. Public".

```
public String getReverseOrder()
```

Returns the person's name in reverse order, with the last name before the first name and middle initial. For example, if the first name is `"John"`, the middle initial is `"Q"`, and the last name is `"Public"`, returns `"Public, John Q."`.

Section 8.4: Object Initialization: Constructors

10. What is a constructor? How is a constructor different from other methods?

11. What are two major problems with the following constructor?

```
public void Point(int initialX, int initialY) {
    int x = initialX;
    int y = initialY;
}
```

12. (You must complete self-check problems 6 and 9 before answering this question.)

    Add a constructor to the `Name` class that accepts a first name, middle initial, and last name as parameters and initializes the `Name` object's state with those values.

Section 8.5: Encapsulation

13. What is abstraction? How do objects provide abstraction?

14. What is the difference between the `public` and `private` keywords? What items should be declared `private`?

15. When fields are made private, client programs cannot see them directly. How do you allow classes access to read these fields' values, without letting the client break the object's encapsulation?

16. Add methods named `setX` and `setY` to the `Point` class that allow clients to change a `Point` object's x- and y-coordinates, respectively.

17. (You must complete self-check problem 12 before answering this question.)

    Encapsulate the `Name` class. Make its fields private and add appropriate accessor methods to the class.

Section 8.6: More Instance Methods

18. How do you write a class whose objects can easily be printed on the console?

19. What is the potential problem with using the `==` operator with objects? How can you specify a way to compare objects of your class for equality?

20. The `Point` class in the `java.awt` package has a `toString` method that returns a `String` in the following format:

```
java.awt.Point[x=7,y=2]
```

    Write a modified version of the `toString` method on our `Point` class that returns a result in this format.

21. (You must complete self-check problem 6 before answering this question.)

    Write `toString` and `equals` methods for the `Name` class. The `toString` method should return a `String` such as `"John Q. Public"`. The `equals` method should return `true` if the two `Name`s have the same first name, last name, and middle initial.

Section 8.7: The Keyword `this`

22. What is the meaning of the keyword `this`? Describe three ways that the keyword can be used.

23. Add a constructor to the `Point` class that accepts another `Point` as a parameter and initializes this new `Point` to have the same (x, y) values. Use the keyword `this` in your solution.

24. (You must complete self-check problem 6 before answering this question.)

Add methods called `setFirstName`, `setMiddleInitial`, and `setLastName` to your `Name` class. Name the parameters the same as your fields, and use the `this` keyword in your solution.

Section 8.8: More Classes

25. What is an immutable object? What is a benefit of using immutable objects?

26. (You must complete self-check problem 24 before answering this question.)

Is your `Name` class immutable? Why or why not? You developed `Name` in several preceding problems. Was the `Name` class immutable in any of its previous versions?

27. How does encapsulation allow you to change the internal implementation of a class?

28. Add `toString` and `equals` methods to the `Participant` class. The `toString` method should return a `String` such as `"John Doe (height=70.0 weight=195.0)"`. The `equals` method should return `true` if two participants have the same name, height, and weight.

Section 8.9: Case Study: Designing a `Stock` Class

29. What is cohesion? How can you tell whether a class is cohesive?

30. Why didn't we choose to put the console I/O code into the `Stock` class?

31. Add accessor methods to the `Stock` class to return the stock's symbol, total shares, and total cost.

Exercises

1. Add the following method to the `Point` class:

```
public int manhattanDistance(Point other)
```

Returns the "Manhattan distance" between the current `Point` object and the given other `Point` object. The Manhattan distance refers to how far apart two places are if one can only travel between them by moving horizontally or vertically, as though driving on the streets of Manhattan. In our case, the Manhattan distance is the sum of the absolute values of the differences in their coordinates; in other words, the difference in x plus the difference in y between the points.

2. Add the following method to the `Point` class:

```
public boolean isVertical(Point other)
```

Returns `true` if the given `Point` lines up vertically with this `Point`; that is, if their x-coordinates are the same.

3. (myCodeMate) Add the following method to the `Point` class:

```
public double slope(Point other)
```

Returns the slope of the line drawn between this `Point` and the given other `Point`. Use the formula $(y2 - y1) / (x2 - x1)$ to determine the slope between two points $(x1, y1)$ and $(x2, y2)$. Note that this formula fails for points with identical x-coordinates, so throw an `IllegalArgumentException` in this case.

4. Add the following method to the `Point` class:

```
public boolean isCollinear(Point p1, Point p2)
```

Returns whether this `Point` is collinear with the given two other `Points`. Points are collinear if a straight line can be drawn that connects them. Two basic examples are three points that have the same x- or y-coordinate. The more general case can be determined by calculating the slope of the line between each pair of points and checking whether this slope is the same for all pairs of points. Use the formula $(y2 - y1) / (x2 - x1)$ to determine the slope between two points $(x1, y1)$ and $(x2, y2)$. (Note that this formula fails for points with identical x-coordinates so this will have to be special-cased in your code.)

Since Java's `double` type is imprecise, round all slope values to a reasonable accuracy such as four digits past the decimal point before you compare them.

5. Write an immutable version of the `Point` class. Any mutating operations should instead return new `Point` objects.

6. Add the following methods to the `TimeSpan` class:

```
public void add(TimeSpan span)
```

Adds the given amount of time to this time span.

```
public void subtract(TimeSpan span)
```

Subtracts the given amount of time from this time span.

```
public void scale(int factor)
```

Scales this time span by the given factor. For example, 1 hour and 45 minutes scaled by 2 equals 3 hours and 30 minutes.

7. Add the following method to the `Stock` class:

```
public void clear()
```

Resets this `Stock`'s number of shares purchased and total cost to 0.

8. Add the following method to the `Stock` class:

```
public boolean equals(Object o)
```

Returns `true` if the given object o is a `Stock` object with the same symbol, number of shares purchased, and total cost as this one.

9. Write a class called `Line` that represents a line segment between two `Points`. Your `Line` objects should have the following methods:

```
public Line(Point p1, Point p2)
```

Constructs a new `Line` that contains the given two `Points`.

```
public Point getP1()
```

Returns this `Line`'s first endpoint.

```
public Point getP2()
```

Returns this `Line`'s second endpoint.

Chapter 9

Inheritance and Interfaces

Introduction

In this chapter we will explore two of the most important techniques the Java language provides to help you write better structured solutions. Inheritance allows you to share code between classes to reduce redundancy, as well as letting you treat different classes of objects in the same way. Interfaces allow you to treat several different classes of objects the same way without sharing code.

It is difficult to show the usefulness of inheritance and interfaces in small examples, but in larger and more complex projects they are invaluable. In fact, the classes we will see and use in the rest of this textbook (as well as several we have already used) make extensive use of these two features. Inheritance and interfaces make it possible to create well-structured code on a scale as large as the entire Java class libraries.

9.1 Inheritance Basics

We'll begin our discussion of inheritance by looking at why the concept came about and considering a non-programming example. This will lead us toward programming with inheritance in Java.

Large programs demand the ability to write versatile and clear code on a large scale. In this textbook, we've examined several ways to express programs more concisely and elegantly on a small scale. Features like static methods, parameterization, loops, and classes help us organize our programs and extract common features that can be used in many places. This general practice is called *code reuse.*

> **Code Reuse**
>
> The practice of writing program code once and using it in many contexts.

Did You Know

The Software Crisis

Software has been getting more and more complicated since the advent of programming. By the early 1970s, teams writing larger and more complex programs began to encounter some common problems. Despite much effort, software projects were running over budget and were not finishing on time; the software also often had bugs, didn't do what it was supposed to do, or was otherwise of low quality. In his 1975 book *The Mythical Man-Month: Essays on Software Engineering*, software engineer Fred Brooks argued that adding manpower to a late software project often made it finish even later. Collectively, these problems came to be called the "software crisis."

A particularly sticky issue involved program maintenance. Companies found that they spent much of their time not writing new code but modifying and maintaining existing code (also called *legacy code*). This proved to be a difficult task, because it was easy to write disorganized and redundant code. Code maintenance was likely to take a long time and to introduce new bugs into the system.

The negative effects of the software crisis and maintenance programming were particularly noticeable when graphical user interfaces came into prominence in the 1980s. User interfaces in graphical systems like Microsoft Windows and Apple's Mac OS were much more sophisticated than the text interfaces that preceded them. The original graphical programs were prone to redundancy because they had to describe in detail how buttons, text boxes, and other onscreen components were implemented. Also, the graphical components themselves contained a lot of common state and behavior, such as a particular size, shape, color, position, or scrollbar.

Object-oriented programming provides us with a feature called inheritance that increases our ability to reuse code by allowing one class to be an extension of another. Inheritance also gives us the benefit of writing programs with hierarchies of related object types.

Non-Programming Hierarchies

When you start to think about inheritance, you'll want to be able to identify similarities between different objects and classes in your programs. Let's start by looking at a non-programming example: a hierarchy of employees at a company.

Imagine a large law firm that hires several classes of employees: lawyers, general secretaries, legal secretaries, and marketers. The company has a bunch of employee rules about vacation and sick days, medical benefits, harassment regulations, and so on. Each subdivision of the company also has a few of its own rules; for example, lawyers may ask for vacation leave with a different form than secretaries.

Imagine that all the employees attend a common orientation where they learn the general rules. Each employee is given a 20-page manual of these rules to read. A mixed group of employees could attend the orientation together: Lawyers, secretaries, and marketers all might sit in the same orientation group.

Afterward, the employees go to their subdivisions and receive second, smaller orientations covering any rules specific to those divisions. Each employee receives a smaller manual, two or three pages in length, covering that subdivision's specific rules. Some rules are added to those in the general 20-page manual, and a few are replaced. For example, perhaps one class of employees gets three weeks of vacation instead of two, and perhaps one class uses a pink form to apply for time off, not the yellow form listed in the 20-page manual. Each class has its own submanual with a unique length and contents as shown in Figure 9.1.

An alternative solution would be to give every employee a large manual containing both the applicable general rules and the rules of their subdivisions. For example, there would be a 22-page manual for the lawyers, a 21-page manual for secretaries,

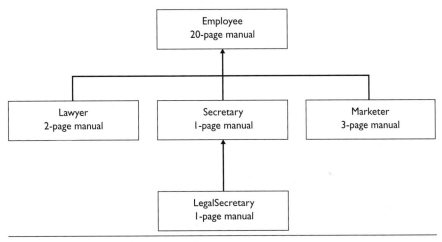

Figure 9.1 A hierarchy of employee manuals

and a 23-page manual for marketers. In fact, the consolidation might even save a few pages. So why does the company bother with two manuals for every employee?

The main issues are with redundancy and maintenance. The 22-page lawyer manual contains a lot of the same text as the 21-page secretary manual. If a common rule is changed, all the manuals need to be updated individually, which is a tedious process. Making the same change to many manuals is also error-prone, because it is easy to make the change in one copy but forget to do it in another.

There's also a certain practical appeal to the shorter, more specific manuals. Someone who wants to know all the rules that are specific to lawyers can simply read the 2-page lawyer manual, rather than combing through a 22-page lawyer manual trying to spot differences.

There are two key ideas here:

1. It's useful to be able to specify a broad set of rules that will apply to many related groups (the 20-page manual).

2. It's also useful to be able to specify a smaller set of rules specific to a particular group, and to be able to replace some rules from the broad set (e.g., "use the pink form instead of the yellow form").

An important thing to notice about the categories is that they are hierarchical. For example, every legal secretary is also a secretary, and every marketer is also an employee. In a pinch, you could ask a legal secretary to work as a standard secretary for a short period, because a legal secretary is a secretary. We call such a connection an *is-a relationship*.

> **Is-a Relationship**
>
> A hierarchical connection between two categories where one type can be treated as a specialized version of the other.

An is-a relationship is similar to the idea of a role. A legal secretary can fill the role of a secretary and the role of an employee. A lawyer can also fill the role of an employee. A member of a subcategory can add to or change behavior from the larger category. For example, a legal secretary adds the ability to file legal briefs to the secretary role and may change the way in which dictation is taken.

When applying these concepts to programming, each group of employees can be represented as a class. The different employee groups represent a set of related classes connected by is-a relationships. We call such a set of classes an *inheritance hierarchy*.

> **Inheritance Hierarchy**
>
> A set of hierarchical relationships between classes of objects.

As you'll see, inheritance hierarchies are commonly used in Java to group related classes of objects and reuse code between them.

Extending a Class

The previous section presented a non-programming example of hierarchies. But as an exercise, we could write small Java classes to represent those categories of employees. The code will be a bit silly but will illustrate some important concepts.

Let's imagine that we have the following rules for our employees:

- Employees work 40 hours per week.

- Employees make $40,000 salary per year, with the exception of marketers, who make $50,000 per year.

- Employees have two weeks of paid vacation leave per year, with the exception of lawyers, who have three weeks of vacation leave.

- Employees use a yellow form to apply for vacation leave, with the exception of lawyers, who use a special pink form.

- Each type of employee has unique behavior: Lawyers know how to sue, marketers know how to advertise, and secretaries know how to take dictation.

Let's write a class to represent the common behavior of all employees. (Think of this as the 20-page employee manual.) We'll write methods called `showHours`, `showSalary`, `showVacation`, and `applyForVacation` to represent these behaviors. To keep things simple, each method will just print a short relevant `String` representing the default employee behavior, such as the $40,000 salary and the yellow form for vacation leave. We won't declare any fields for now. Here is the code for the basic `Employee` class:

```
1   // A class to represent employees in general.
2   public class Employee {
3       public void applyForVacation() {
4           System.out.println("Use the yellow vacation form.");
5       }
6
7       public void showHours() {
8           System.out.println("I work 40 hours per week.");
9       }
10
11      public void showSalary() {
12          System.out.println("My salary is $40,000.");
13      }
14
15      public void showVacation() {
16          System.out.println("I receive 2 weeks vacation.");
17      }
18  }
```

Now let's think about implementing the `Secretary` subcategory. As mentioned in the previous section, every `Secretary` is also an `Employee`, and they should retain the abilities that `Employee`s have. Secretaries also have one additional ability: The ability to take dictation. If we wrote `Secretary` as a standalone class, its code would not reflect this relationship very elegantly. We would be forced to repeat all of the same methods from `Employee` with identical behavior. Here is the redundant class:

```
 1  // A redundant class to represent secretaries.
 2  public class Secretary {
 3      public void applyForVacation() {
 4          System.out.println("Use the yellow vacation form.");
 5      }
 6
 7      public void showHours() {
 8          System.out.println("I work 40 hours per week.");
 9      }
10
11      public void showSalary() {
12          System.out.println("My salary is $40,000.");
13      }
14
15      public void showVacation() {
16          System.out.println("I receive 2 weeks vacation.");
17      }
18
19      // this is the only added behavior
20      public void takeDictation() {
21          System.out.println("I know how to take dictation.");
22      }
23  }
```

The only code unique to the `Secretary` class is its `takeDictation` method. What we'd really like to be able to write is the following:

```
public class Secretary {
    copy all the methods from the Employee class.

    // this is the only added behavior
    public void takeDictation() {
        System.out.println("I know how to take dictation.");
    }
}
```

Fortunately, Java provides a mechanism called *inheritance* that can help us remove this sort of redundancy between similar classes of objects. Inheritance allows the programmer to specify a relationship between two classes where one class includes ("inherits") the state and behavior of another.

> **Inheritance (Inherit)**
>
> A programming technique in which a derived class extends the functionality of a base class, inheriting all of its state and behavior.

The child class, more commonly called the *subclass*, inherits all of the state and behavior of its parent class, commonly called the *superclass*.

> **Superclass**
>
> The parent class in an inheritance relationship.

> **Subclass**
>
> The child class in an inheritance relationship.

We say that the subclass *extends* the superclass because it not only receives the superclass's state and behavior but can also add new state and behavior of its own. The subclass can also replace inherited behavior with new behavior as needed, which we'll discuss in the next section.

A Java class can have only one superclass; it is not possible to extend more than one class. This is called *single inheritance*. On the other hand, one class may have many subclasses extending it.

To declare one class as the subclass of another, place the extends keyword followed by the superclass name at the end of the subclass header. The general syntax is the following:

```
public class <subclass name> extends <superclass name> {
    . . .
}
```

We can rewrite the Secretary class to extend the Employee class. This will create an is-a relationship where every Secretary also is an Employee. Secretary objects will inherit copies of the applyForVacation, showHours, showSalary, and showVacation methods, so we won't need to write these methods in the Secretary class. This will remove the redundancy.

It's legal and expected for a subclass to add new behavior that wasn't present in the superclass. We said previously that secretaries add an ability not seen in other employees: the ability to take dictation. We can add this to our otherwise empty Secretary class. The following is the complete Secretary class:

```
1  // A class to represent secretaries.
2  public class Secretary extends Employee {
3      public void takeDictation() {
4          System.out.println("I know how to take dictation.");
5      }
6  }
```

This concise new version of the Secretary class has the same behavior as the longer class shown before. Like the two-page specialized manual, this class shows only the things that are unique to the specific job class. In this case, it is very easy to see that the unique behavior of secretaries in our system is to take dictation.

The following client code would work with our new Secretary class:

```
1  public class EmployeeMain {
2      public static void main(String[] args) {
3          System.out.println("Employee:");
4          Employee employee1 = new Employee();
5          employee1.applyForVacation();
6          employee1.showHours();
7          employee1.showSalary();
8          employee1.showVacation();
9          System.out.println();
```

```
10
11              System.out.println("Secretary:");
12              Secretary employee2 = new Secretary();
13              employee2.applyForVacation();
14              employee2.showHours();
15              employee2.showSalary();
16              employee2.showVacation();
17              employee2.takeDictation();
18        }
19  }
```

The code would produce the following output:

```
Employee:
Use the yellow vacation form.
I work 40 hours per week.
My salary is $40,000.
I receive 2 weeks vacation.

Secretary:
Use the yellow vacation form.
I work 40 hours per week.
My salary is $40,000.
I receive 2 weeks vacation.
I know how to take dictation.
```

Notice that the first four methods produce the same output for both objects, because `Secretary` inherits that behavior from `Employee`. The fifth line of `Secretary` output reflects the new extended behavior of the `takeDictation` method.

Overriding Methods

We can use inheritance in our other types of `Employees`, making `Lawyer` and `Marketer` classes that are subclasses of `Employee`. But while the `Secretary` class merely adds behavior to the standard `Employee` behavior, the `Lawyer` and `Marketer` classes also need to replace some of the standard `Employee` behavior with their own. `Lawyers` receive three weeks of vacation and use a pink form to apply for vacation. `Marketers` receive $50,000 salaries, not $40,000.

It's legal to replace superclass behavior by writing new versions of the relevant method(s) in the subclasses. The new version in the subclass will replace the one inherited from `Employee`. This idea of replacing behavior from the superclass is called *overriding*.

> **Override**
>
> To implement a new version of a method to replace code that would otherwise have been inherited from a superclass.

Overriding requires no special syntax. To override a method, just write the method you want to replace in the subclass. No special syntax is required, but the method's name and signature must exactly match those of the method from the superclass.

Here are the `Lawyer` and `Marketer` classes that extend `Employee` and override the relevant methods:

```
1   // A class to represent lawyers.
2   public class Lawyer extends Employee {
3       public void applyForVacation() {
4           System.out.println("Use the pink vacation form.");
5       }
6
7       public void showVacation() {
8           System.out.println("I receive 3 weeks vacation.");
9       }
10
11      public void sue() {
12          System.out.println("I'll see you in court!");
13      }
14  }
```

```
1   // A class to represent marketers.
2   public class Marketer extends Employee {
3       public void advertise() {
4           System.out.println("Act now, while supplies last!");
5       }
6
7       public void showSalary() {
8           System.out.println("My salary is $50,000.");
9       }
10  }
```

The following client program uses our `Lawyer` and `Marketer` classes:

```
1   public class EmployeeMain2 {
2       public static void main(String[] args) {
3           System.out.println("Lawyer:");
4           Lawyer employee1 = new Lawyer();
5           employee1.applyForVacation();
6           employee1.showHours();
7           employee1.showSalary();
8           employee1.showVacation();
9           employee1.sue();
10          System.out.println();
11
12          System.out.println("Marketer:");
13          Marketer employee2 = new Marketer();
14          employee2.applyForVacation();
15          employee2.showHours();
16          employee2.showSalary();
17          employee2.showVacation();
18          employee2.advertise();
19      }
20  }
```

The program produces the following output:

```
Lawyer:
Use the pink vacation form.
I work 40 hours per week.
My salary is $40,000.
```

```
I receive 3 weeks vacation.
I'll see you in court!

Marketer:
Use the yellow vacation form.
I work 40 hours per week.
My salary is $50,000.
I receive 2 weeks vacation.
Act now, while supplies last!
```

Be careful not to confuse overriding with overloading. Overloading, introduced in Chapter 3, is where one class contains multiple methods with the same name but different parameter signatures. Overriding is when a subclass substitutes its own version of an otherwise inherited method, with exactly the same name and the same parameters.

Polymorphism

One very interesting and odd thing about inherited classes is that it's legal for a variable of a superclass type to refer to an object of one of its subclasses. For example, the following is a legal assignment statement:

```
Employee employee1 = new Lawyer();
```

When studying the primitive types, we saw cases where a variable of one type could store a value of another type (for example, an `int` value can be stored in a `double` variable). In such cases, a conversion between types occurred: the `int` value was automatically converted to a `double` when it was assigned.

When a subclass object is stored in a superclass variable, no such conversion occurs. The object referred to by `employee1` really is a `Lawyer` object, not an `Employee` object. If we call methods on it, it will behave like a `Lawyer` object. For example, the call:

```
employee1.applyForVacation();
```

produces the following output, which is the `Lawyer`'s behavior, not the `Employee`'s:

```
Use the pink vacation form.
```

This ability for variables to refer to subclass objects is one of the most crucially important ideas in object-oriented programming. It allows us to write flexible code that can interact with many types of objects in the same way. For example, we can write a method that accepts an `Employee` as a parameter, or returns an `Employee`, or creates an array of `Employee` objects. In any of these cases, we can substitute a `Secretary`, `Lawyer`, or other subclass object of `Employee`, and the code will still work.

Even more importantly, code will actually behave differently depending on which type of object is used, because each subclass overrides and changes some of the behavior from the superclass. This important ability for the same code to be used with several different types of objects is called *polymorphism*.

> **Polymorphism**
>
> The ability for the same code to be used with several different types of objects and behave differently depending on the actual type of object used.

Here is an example test file that uses `Employee` objects polymorphically as parameters to a static method:

```
1  public class EmployeeMain3 {
2      public static void main(String[] args) {
3          Employee empl = new Employee();
4          Lawyer law = new Lawyer();
5          Marketer mark = new Marketer();
6          Secretary sec = new Secretary();
7
8          printInfo(empl);
9          printInfo(law);
10         printInfo(mark);
11         printInfo(sec);
12     }
13
14     public static void printInfo(Employee employee) {
15         employee.applyForVacation();
16         employee.showHours();
17         employee.showSalary();
18         employee.showVacation();
19         System.out.println();
20     }
21 }
```

Notice that the static method lets us pass many different types of `Employees` as parameters, and it produces different behavior depending on which type is passed. Polymorphism gives us this flexibility. The program produces the following output:

```
Use the yellow vacation form.
I work 40 hours per week.
My salary is $40,000.
I receive 2 weeks vacation.

Use the pink vacation form.
I work 40 hours per week.
My salary is $40,000.
I receive 3 weeks vacation.

Use the yellow vacation form.
I work 40 hours per week.
My salary is $50,000.
I receive 2 weeks vacation.

Use the yellow vacation form.
I work 40 hours per week.
My salary is $40,000.
I receive 2 weeks vacation.
```

The word "polymorphism" comes from the Greek words "poly" and "morph," which mean "many" and "forms," respectively. The lines of code in the `printInfo` method are polymorphic because their behavior will take many forms depending on what type of employee is passed as the parameter.

The program doesn't know which `applyForVacation` or `showSalary` method to call until it's actually running. When the program reaches a particular call to an object's method, it examines the actual object to see which method to call. This idea has taken many names over the years, such as *late binding*, *virtual binding*, and *dynamic dispatch*.

When sending messages to an object through a reference of a superclass type, it is only legal to call methods known to the superclass. For example, the following code will not compile because the `Employee` class has no `advertise` method:

```
// does not compile
public static void badStuff(Employee e) {
    e.advertise();
}
```

The compiler does not allow this code because the variable e could theoretically refer to an `Employee` object or an object of any `Employee` subclass. The actual object is not guaranteed to have an `advertise` method.

9.2 The Mechanics of Polymorphism

Inheritance and polymorphism introduce some complex new mechanics and behavior into programs. One useful way to get the hang of these mechanics is to perform some exercises to interpret the behavior of programs with inheritance. The main goal of these exercises is to help you understand in detail what happens when a Java program with inheritance executes.

The `EmployeeMain3` program developed in the last section serves as a template for inheritance hierarchies. Looking at this template, one can formulate a generic question about instance hierarchies: Given the following hierarchy of classes, what behavior would result if we created several objects of the different types and called various methods on them?

To achieve some polymorphism in this type of question, we'll store the objects being examined into an array. In the case of the `Employee` hierarchy, it's legal for an object of class `Lawyer`, `Secretary`, or any other subclass of `Employee` to reside as an element of an `Employee[]`.

The following program produces the same output as the `EmployeeMain3` program from last section:

```
1  public class EmployeeMain4 {
2      public static void main(String[] args) {
3          Employee[] employees = {new Employee(), new Lawyer(),
4                  new Marketer(), new Secretary()};
5
6          // print information about each employee
7          for (int i = 0; i < employees.length; i++) {
8              employees[i].applyForVacation();
9              employees[i].showHours();
10             employees[i].showSalary();
11             employees[i].showVacation();
```

```
12                        System.out.println();
13              }
14         }
15   }
```

Even if you didn't understand inheritance, you might be able to deduce some things about the hierarchy from the classes' names and the relationships between employees in the real world. So let's take this exercise one step further. Instead of using descriptive names for the classes, we'll use letters so that one has to read the code to determine the class relationships and behavior.

Assume that the following classes have been defined:

```
1    public class A {
2         public void method1() {
3              System.out.println("A 1");
4         }
5
6         public void method2() {
7              System.out.println("A 2");
8         }
9
10        public String toString() {
11             return "A";
12        }
13   }
```

```
1    public class B extends A {
2         public void method2() {
3              System.out.println("B 2");
4         }
5    }
```

```
1    public class C extends A {
2         public void method1() {
3              System.out.println("C 1");
4         }
5
6         public String toString() {
7              return "C";
8         }
9    }
```

```
1    public class D extends C {
2         public void method2() {
3              System.out.println("D 2");
4         }
5    }
```

Consider the following client code, which uses these classes. It takes advantage of the fact that every other class extends class A (either directly or indirectly), so the array can be of type A[]. When you call methods on the elements of the array, you should observe polymorphic behavior:

```
1    // Client program to use the A, B, C, and D classes.
2    public class ABCDMain {
```

```
 3        public static void main(String[] args) {
 4            A[] elements = {new A(), new B(), new C(), new D()};
 5
 6            for (int i = 0; i < elements.length; i++) {
 7                System.out.println(elements[i]);
 8                elements[i].method1();
 9                elements[i].method2();
10                System.out.println();
11            }
12        }
13  }
```

How does one go about interpreting such code and determining its correct output?

Diagramming Polymorphic Code

To determine the output of a polymorphic program like the one in the previous section, you must determine what happens when each element is printed (i.e., when its toString method is called) and when its method1 and method2 methods are called. One way to get started is to draw a diagram. Draw each type as a box listing its methods, and connect subclasses to their superclasses with arrows (this type of diagram is a simplified version of the commonly used UML class diagram).

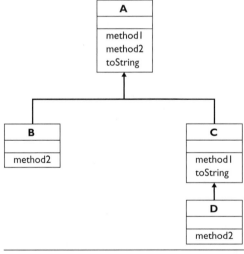

Figure 9.2 Hierarchy of classes A, B, C, and D

Now, enhance the diagram by writing the methods' output next to their names. Write the output not just for the methods defined in each class, but also for the ones that the class inherits.

Start by filling in the methods from the A class with their output. When someone calls method1 on an A object, the resulting output is "A 1". When someone calls method2 on an A object, the resulting output is "A 2". When someone prints an A object with toString, the resulting output is "A". Fill in this output as a note on your diagram in Figure 9.3.

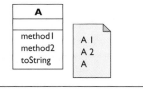

Figure 9.3 A class with method output

Next, look at the B class. B inherits all the behavior from A, except that it overrides the `method2` output to say `"B 2"`. That means you can fill in the B output on your diagram in Figure 9.4 identically to the A output, replacing `"A 2"` with `"B 2"`.

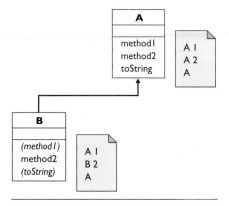

Figure 9.4 A and B classes with method output

Third, look at the C class. C also inherits all the behavior from A, but it overrides the `method1` output to say `"C 1"` and it overrides the `toString` method to say `"C"`. Thus, the C output on your diagram will have the same second line as the A output, but you'll replace `"A 1"` on the first line with `"C 1"` and `"A"` on the third line with `"C"` as shown in Figure 9.5.

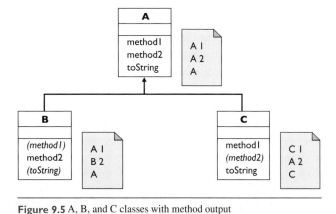

Figure 9.5 A, B, and C classes with method output

Treat the D class similarly. D inherits all the behavior from C, except that it overrides the `method2` output to say `"D 2"`. Following the pattern, you'll get this final diagram shown in Figure 9.6.

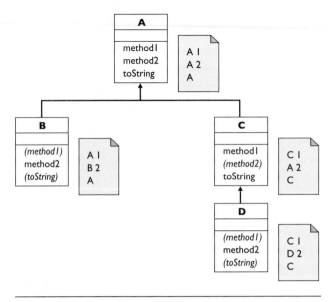

Figure 9.6 A, B, C, and D classes with method output

Another way to do this is to make a table of behavior for the methods of each type, listing each type horizontally and each method name vertically as shown in Table 9.1.

TABLE 9.1   Method Output for Each Class

	A	B	C	D
toString	A	A	C	C
method1	A 1	A 1	C 1	C 1
method2	A 2	B 2	A 2	D 2

Once you've created a diagram or table, you can figure out the output of the code. The array contains an A object, a B object, a C object, and a D object. For each of these it prints the `toString` output, then calls `method1`, then calls `method2`, then prints a blank line. When a method gets called on an object, you can just look up the output of that method for that type on the diagram or table. For example, you'll see that the output for these methods on an A object (element 0 of the array) is the following:

```
A
A 1
A 2
```

Using the table/diagram in this way for all four types, you'll get the following complete output for the exercise:

```
A
A 1
A 2
```

```
A
A 1
B 2

C
C 1
A 2

C
C 1
D 2
```

9.3 Interacting with the Superclass

The classes in the previous sections demonstrated inheritance with methods, but now you'll want to write more meaningful classes that use inheritance with fields, methods, and constructors. These subclasses require more complex interaction with the state and behavior they inherit from their superclass. To show you how to perform this interaction properly, we'll need to introduce a new keyword called super.

Inherited Fields

In the previous chapter's case study, we built a Stock class representing purchased shares of a given stock. Here's the code for that class, which has been shortened a bit for this section by removing tests for illegal arguments:

```
1    // A Stock object represents purchases of shares of a stock.
2    public class Stock {
3        private String symbol;
4        private int totalShares;
5        private double totalCost;
6
7        // initializes a new Stock with no shares purchased
8        public Stock(String theSymbol) {
9            symbol = theSymbol;
10           totalShares = 0;
11           totalCost = 0.0;
12       }
13
14       // returns the total profit or loss earned on this stock
15       public double getProfit(double currentPrice) {
16           double marketValue = totalShares * currentPrice;
17           return marketValue − totalCost;
18       }
19
20       // records purchase of the given shares at the given price
21       public void purchase(int shares, double pricePerShare) {
22           totalShares += shares;
23           totalCost += shares * pricePerShare;
24       }
25   }
```

Now let's imagine you want to create a type of object for stocks that pay dividends. Dividends are profit-sharing payments made by a corporation to its shareholders. The amount the shareholder receives is proportional to the number of shares owned. Not every stock pays dividends, so you wouldn't want to add this functionality directly to the Stock class. Instead, create a new class called DividendStock that extends Stock and adds this new behavior.

Each DividendStock object will inherit the symbol, total shares, and total cost from the Stock superclass. You'll simply need to add a field to record the amount of dividends paid:

```
public class DividendStock extends Stock {
    private double dividends;     // amount of dividends paid

    . . .
}
```

Using the dividends field, you can write a method in the DividendStock class that lets the shareholder receive a per-share dividend. Your first thought might be to write code like the following, but this won't compile:

```
// this code does not compile
public void payDividend(double amountPerShare) {
    dividends += amountPerShare * totalShares;
}
```

A DividendStock cannot access the totalShares field it has inherited, because totalShares is declared private in Stock. A subclass may not refer directly to any private fields that were declared in its superclass, so you'll get a compiler error like the following:

```
DividendStock.java:17: totalShares has private access in Stock
```

The solution is to use the accessor or mutator methods associated with those fields to access or change their values. The Stock class doesn't have a public accessor method for the totalShares field, but you can now add a getTotalShares method to the Stock class:

```
// returns the total shares purchased of this stock
public int getTotalShares() {
    return totalShares;
}
```

Here is a corrected version of the payDividend method that uses the getTotalShares method from Stock:

```
// records a dividend of the given amount per share
public void payDividend(double amountPerShare) {
    dividends += amountPerShare * getTotalShares();
}
```

The DividendStock subclass is allowed to call the public getTotalShares method, so the code now behaves properly.

Calling a Superclass's Constructor

Unlike other behavior, constructors are not inherited. You'll have to write your own constructor for the `DividendStock` class, and when you do this the problem of the inability to access private fields will arise again.

The `DividendStock` constructor should accept the same parameter as the `Stock` constructor: the stock symbol. It should have the same behavior as the `Stock` constructor, but also initialize the `dividends` field to `0.0`. The following constructor implementation might seem like a good start, but it is redundant with `Stock`'s constructor and won't compile successfully:

```
// this constructor does not compile
public DividendStock(String theSymbol) {
    symbol = theSymbol;
    totalShares = 0;
    totalCost = 0.0;
    dividends = 0.0;   // this line is the new code
}
```

The compiler produces four errors: one error for each line that tries to access an inherited private field, and a message about a missing `Stock()` constructor:

```
DividendStock.java:5: cannot find symbol
symbol   : constructor Stock()
location: class Stock
    public DividendStock(String theSymbol) {
                        ^
DividendStock.java:6: symbol has private access in Stock
DividendStock.java:7: totalShares has private access in Stock
DividendStock.java:8: totalCost has private access in Stock
```

The first problem is that even though a `DividendStock` does contain the `symbol`, `totalShares`, and `totalCost` fields by inheritance, it cannot refer to them directly because they were declared private in the `Stock` class. This was done intentionally so that inheritance would not provide a loophole for a malicious subclass to break a `Stock` object's encapsulation.

The second problem—the missing `Stock()` constructor—is a subtle and confusing detail of inheritance. The problem is that a subclass's constructor must call a constructor from the superclass. Essentially, the `DividendStock` partially consists of a `Stock` object, and you must initialize the state of that `Stock` object by calling a constructor for it. If you don't specify how to do so, the compiler assumes that `Stock` has a parameterless `Stock()` constructor and tries to initialize the `Stock` data by calling this constructor. Since the `Stock` class doesn't actually have a parameterless constructor, the bizarre error message about a missing `Stock()` constructor occurs. (It's a shame the error message isn't more informative.)

The solution to this problem is to explicitly call the `Stock` constructor that accepts a `String` symbol as its parameter. Java uses the keyword `super` for a subclass to refer to behavior from its superclass. To call a constructor of a superclass, write the keyword `super`, followed by the constructor's parameter values in parentheses:

```
super(<expression>, <expression>, ... , <expression>);
```

In the case of the `DividendStock` constructor, the following code does the trick. Use the `super` keyword to call the superclass constructor, passing it the same `theSymbol` value passed to the `DividendStock` constructor. This will initialize the `symbol`, `totalShares`, and `totalCost` fields. Then set the initial dividends to `0.0`:

```
// constructs a new dividend stock with the given symbol
// and no shares purchased
public DividendStock(String theSymbol) {
    super(theSymbol);  // call Stock constructor
    dividends = 0.0;
}
```

The call to the superclass's constructor using `super` must be the first statement in a subclass's constructor. If you reverse the order of the statements in `DividendStock`'s constructor and set the dividends before calling `super`, you'll get a compiler error like the following:

```
Call to super must be first statement in constructor
        super(theSymbol);   // call Stock constructor
            ^
```

Here's the `DividendStock` class so far. The class isn't complete yet because you haven't yet implemented the behavior to make dividend payments:

```
// A DividendStock object represents a stock purchase that also pays
// dividends.
public class DividendStock extends Stock {
    private double dividends;  // amount of dividends paid

    // constructs a new dividend stock with the given symbol
    // and no shares purchased
    public DividendStock(String theSymbol) {
        super(theSymbol);   // call Stock constructor
        this.dividends = 0.0;
    }

    ...
}
```

Calling Overridden Methods

To implement dividend payments, begin by writing a method called `payDividend` that accepts a dividend amount per share and adds the proper amount to `DividendStock`'s dividends field. The amount per share should be multiplied by the number of shares held:

```
// records a dividend of the given amount per share
public void payDividend(double amountPerShare) {
    dividends += amountPerShare * getTotalShares();
}
```

The dividend payments being recorded should be considered profit for the stockholder. The overall profit of a `DividendStock` object is equal to the profit from the stock's price plus any dividends. This is computed as the market value (number of shares times current price) minus the total cost paid for the shares, plus the amount of dividends paid.

Notice that you don't need to use `super.getTotalShares` in the preceding code. You only have to use the `super` keyword when accessing overridden methods or constructors from the superclass. `DividendStock` doesn't override the `getTotalShares` method, so you can call it without the `super` keyword.

Because the profit of a `DividendStock` object is computed differently from that of a regular `Stock` object, you should override the `getProfit` method in the `DividendStock` class to implement this new behavior. An incorrect initial attempt might look like this:

```
// this code does not compile
public double getProfit(double currentPrice) {
    double marketValue = totalShares * currentPrice;
    return marketValue - totalCost + dividends;
}
```

The preceding code has two problems. For one, you can't refer directly to the various fields that were declared in `Stock`. To get around this, you can add accessor methods for each field. The second problem is that the code is redundant: It duplicates much of the functionality from `Stock`'s `getProfit` method, shown earlier. The only new behavior is the adding of dividends into the total.

To remove this redundancy, you can have `DividendStock`'s `getProfit` method call `Stock`'s `getProfit` method as part of its computation. However, since the two methods share the same name, you must disambiguate them by explicitly telling the compiler you want to call `Stock`'s version. Again, you do this using the super keyword.

The general syntax for calling an overridden method using the `super` keyword is:

```
super.<method name>(<expression>, <expression>, . . . , <expression>)
```

Here is the corrected code, which does compile and eliminates the previous redundancy:

```
// returns the total profit or loss earned on this stock,
// including profits made from dividends
public double getProfit(double currentPrice) {
    return super.getProfit(currentPrice) + dividends;
}
```

And here is the code for the completed `DividendStock` class:

```
1   // A DividendStock object represents a stock purchase that also pays
2   // dividends.
3   public class DividendStock extends Stock {
4       private double dividends;   // amount of dividends paid
5
6       // constructs a new dividend stock with the given symbol
7       // and no shares purchased
8       public DividendStock(String theSymbol) {
9           super(theSymbol);   // call Stock constructor
```

```
10                dividends = 0.0;
11        }
12
13        // returns the total profit or loss earned on this stock,
14        // including profits made from dividends
15        public double getProfit(double currentPrice) {
16                return super.getProfit(currentPrice) + dividends;
17        }
18
19        // records a dividend of the given amount per share
20        public void payDividend(double amountPerShare) {
21                dividends += amountPerShare * getTotalShares();
22        }
23    }
```

It's possible to have a deeper inheritance hierarchy with multiple layers of inheritance and overriding. However, the super keyword reaches just one level upward to the most recently overridden version of the method. It's not legal to use super more than once in a row; you cannot make calls like super.super.getProfit. If you need such a solution, you'll have to find a workaround such as using different method names.

Another Example: MeteredPoint

Let's consider another example of extending a class where super is useful. Say you want to write a program that deals with a person's movements in 2D space, such as a pedometer program that measures the number of steps a person has taken, an application for a traveling salesman to track sales visits to cities, or a game. In writing such programs, it would be useful to have a class representing a person's position as well as a meter of total distance traveled.

In Chapter 8 we wrote a Point class to represent a point in 2D space. You can extend the Point class into a new class called MeteredPoint that adds a totalDistance measure:

```
1   // A MeteredPoint object represents a Point that counts
2   // the total distance it has been moved.
3
4   public class MeteredPoint extends Point {
5        private double totalDistance;
6
7        ...
8   }
```

MeteredPoint's constructor needs to set the x and y fields, just as the Point constructor does. But MeteredPoint adds a totalDistance field, which must also be set. Calling super(x, y) sets the first two fields. The third, totalDistance, is initialized to 0.0 separately:

```
// constructs a new point with the given coordinates
public MeteredPoint(int x, int y) {
    super(x, y);
    totalDistance = 0.0;
}
```

The main behavior you'll have to add to `MeteredPoint` is to accumulate the distance traveled every time the `Point` moves. Luckily, every piece of code in the `Point` class that adjusts a `Point` object's position (including the constructors and the `translate` method) ends up calling the `setLocation` method. Therefore, `MeteredPoint` can override `setLocation` and add code to calculate how far the `Point` is moving. You can use the Pythagorean Theorem to compute the distance and add it into your `totalDistance` field:

```
public void setLocation(int x, int y) {
    // accumulates distance moved from old to new location
    int dx = x - getX();
    int dy = y - getY();
    totalDistance += Math.sqrt(dx * dx + dy * dy);

    ...
}
```

You have to call the `getX` and `getY` methods to examine the point's coordinates, because those fields are private in the `Point` superclass.

After accumulating the distance traveled, you have to set the object to the new location. But you cannot set the x and y fields directly, since they are private in the `Point` superclass. The correct way to set the fields is to call the superclass's version of `setLocation` to adjust the x- and y-coordinates:

```
super.setLocation(x, y);
```

It's important to do this at the end of the `setLocation` method so that x and y still contain the old location values for computing the distance traveled. Here is the complete code for the method:

```
// sets the location of this MeteredPoint object to the
// given coordinates and accumulates the distance moved
public void setLocation(int x, int y) {
    // accumulates distance moved from old to new location
    int dx = x - getX();
    int dy = y - getY();
    totalDistance += Math.sqrt(dx * dx + dy * dy);

    super.setLocation(x, y);
}
```

The last addition to `MeteredPoint` is a `getTotalDistance` method that returns the `totalDistance` value. Client code that has translated a `MeteredPoint` many times can call `getTotalDistance` to find out how far it has traveled.

Here is the complete code for the `MeteredPoint` class:

```
1   // A MeteredPoint object represents a Point that counts
2   // the total distance it has been moved.
3
4   public class MeteredPoint extends Point {
5       private double totalDistance;
6
7       // constructs a new point with the given coordinates
```

```
 8        public MeteredPoint(int x, int y) {
 9            super(x, y);
10            totalDistance = 0.0;
11        }
12
13        // returns the total distance traveled by this point
14        public double getTotalDistance() {
15            return totalDistance;
16        }
17
18        // sets the location of this MeteredPoint object to the
19        // given coordinates and accumulates the distance moved
20        public void setLocation(int x, int y) {
21            // accumulate distance moved from old to new location
22            int dx = x - getX();
23            int dy = y - getY();
24            totalDistance += Math.sqrt(dx * dx + dy * dy);
25
26            super.setLocation(x, y);
27        }
28    }
```

The Object Class

There is a class called Object that serves as the ultimate superclass for all other Java classes, even those that do not declare explicit superclasses in their headers. In fact, classes whose headers do not have extends clauses are treated as though their headers say extends Object when they are compiled. (You can optionally explicitly write the extends Object in a class header, but this is unnecessary and not a common style.)

The Object class contains methods that are common to all objects. Table 9.2 summarizes the methods of the Object class. Note that some of the methods are not public and therefore cannot be called externally.

TABLE 9.2 Methods of the Object Class

Method	Description
clone()	Creates and returns a copy of the object (not a public method)
equals(obj)	Indicates whether the other object is equal to this one
finalize()	Called automatically by Java when objects are destroyed (not a public method)
getClass()	Returns information about the type of the object
hashCode()	Returns a number associated with the object; used with certain data structures
toString()	Returns the state of the object as a String
notify(), notifyAll(), wait()	Advanced methods for multithreaded programming

In Chapter 8 we mentioned that without a `toString` method in a class, the objects will not print properly. For example, our `Point` class printed `Point@119c082` by default before we wrote its `toString` method. This default message was the behavior of the `Object` class's `toString` method, which we inherited in our `Point` class. The `Object` class provides a generic `toString` output that will work for every class: the class name followed by some internal numeric information about the object. When we wrote our own `toString` method, we overrode this default behavior.

The `equals` method also has a default implementation in the `Object` class. The default `equals` behavior considers two objects equal only if they are literally the same object. When we wrote our own `equals` methods, we overrode this behavior to also consider two objects equal if they have the same state.

It is sometimes useful to refer to the `Object` class in your programs. For example, if you wish to write a method that can accept any object as a parameter, you can declare a parameter of type `Object`:

```
// this method can accept any object as its parameter
public static void myMethod(Object o) {
    ...
```

Of course, since your parameter can be anything, you are only allowed to call the methods from the `Object` class on it, such as `toString` or `getClass`. It is also legal to have a method whose return type is `Object`.

The `Object` class is used extensively in the Java class libraries. For example, the `println` method of the `PrintStream` class (the class of which `System.out` is an instance) accepts a parameter of type `Object`, which allows you to print any object to the console.

9.4 Inheritance and Design

Inheritance affects the thought processes you should use when designing object-oriented solutions to programming problems. You should be aware of similarities between classes and potentially capture those similarities with inheritance relationships and hierarchies. The designers of the Java class libraries have followed these principles, as we'll see when we examine a graphical subclass in this section.

However, there are also situations where using inheritance seems like a good choice but turns out to produce poor results. Misuse of inheritance can introduce some pitfalls and problems that we'll now examine.

A Misuse of Inheritance: `Point3D`

Imagine that you want to write a program that deals with points in three-dimensional space, such as a 3D game, rendering program, or simulation. A `Point3D` class would be useful for storing the positions of objects in such a program.

This seems to be a case where inheritance will be useful to extend the functionality of existing code. Many programmers would be tempted to have `Point3D` extend

Point and simply add the new code for the z-coordinate. Here's a quick implementation of a minimal Point3D class that extends Point:

```
1   // A Point3D object represents an (x, y, z) location.
2   // This is not a good design to follow.
3
4   public class Point3D extends Point {
5       private int z;
6
7       // constructs a new 3D point with the given coordinates
8       public Point3D(int x, int y, int z) {
9           super(x, y);
10          this.z = z;
11      }
12
13      // returns the z-coordinate of this Point3D
14      public int getZ() {
15          return z;
16      }
17  }
```

On the surface, this seems to be a reasonable implementation. However, consider the equals method defined in the Point class. It compares the x- and y-coordinates of two Point objects and returns true if they are the same:

```
// returns whether o refers to a Point with the same
// (x, y) coordinates as this Point
public boolean equals(Object o) {
    if (o instanceof Point) {
        Point other = (Point) o;
        return x == other.x && y == other.y;
    } else { // not a Point object
        return false;
    }
}
```

You might also want an equals method for the Point3D class. Two Point3D objects are equal if they have the same x-, y-, and z-coordinates. The following is a working implementation of equals that is correct, but stylistically unsatisfactory:

```
// initial flawed version
public boolean equals(Object o) {
    if (o instanceof Point3D) {
        Point3D p = (Point3D) o;
        return getX() == p.getX() && getY() == p.getY() && z == p.z;
    } else {
        return false;
    }
}
```

The preceding code compiles and runs correctly in many cases, but it has a subtle problem that occurs when you compare Point objects to Point3D objects. The Point class's equals method tests whether the parameter is an instance of Point and returns false if not. However, it turns out that the instanceof operator will return true not only if the variable refers to that type, but also if it refers to any of its subclasses. Consider the following test in the `equals` method of the `Point` class:

```
if (o instanceof Point) {
    ...
}
```

The test will evaluate to `true` if `o` refers to a `Point` object or a `Point3D` object. The `instanceof` operator can be thought of as an is-a test, asking whether the variable refers to any type that can fill the role of a `Point`. By contrast, `Point3D`'s `equals` method tests whether the parameter is an instance of `Point3D` and rejects it if not. A `Point` cannot fill the role of a `Point3D` (not every `Point` is a `Point3D`), so the method will return `false` if the parameter is of type `Point`.

Consequently, the `equals` behavior is not symmetric when used with a mixture of `Point` and `Point3D` objects. The following client code demonstrates the problem:

```
Point p = new Point(12, 7);
Point3D p3d = new Point3D(12, 7, 11);
System.out.println("p.equals(p3d) is " + p.equals(p3d));
System.out.println("p3d.equals(p) is " + p3d.equals(p));
```

The code produces the following output. The first test is `true` because a `Point` can accept a `Point3D` as the parameter to `equals`, but the second test is `false` because a `Point3D` cannot accept a `Point` as its parameter to `equals`:

```
p.equals(p3d) is true
p3d.equals(p) is false
```

This is a problem, because the contract of the `equals` method requires it to be a symmetric operation. You'd encounter other problems if you added more behavior to `Point3D`, such as a `setLocation` or `distance` method.

Proper object-oriented design would say that `Point3D` should not extend `Point`, because any code that asks for a `Point` object should be able to work correctly with a `Point3D` object as well. We call this principle *substitutability* (it is also sometimes called the Liskov substitution principle, in honor of the author of a 1993 paper describing the idea).

> **Substitutability**
> The ability for an object of a subclass to be used successfully anywhere an object of the superclass is expected.

Fundamentally, a `Point3D` isn't the same thing as a `Point`, so an is-a relationship with inheritance is the wrong choice. In this case, you're better off writing `Point3D` from scratch and avoiding these thorny issues.

Is-a Versus Has-a Relationships

There are ways to connect related objects without using inheritance. Consider the task of writing a `Circle` class, where each `Circle` object is specified by a center point and a radius. It might be tempting to have `Circle` extend `Point` and add the radius field. However, this is a poor choice because a class is only supposed to capture one abstraction, and a circle simply isn't a point.

A point does make up a fundamental part of the state of each `Circle` object, though. To capture this relationship in the code, you can have each `Circle` object hold a `Point` object in a field to represent its center. One object containing another as state is called a *has-a relationship*.

> **Has-a Relationship**
>
> A connection between two objects where one has a field that refers to the other. The contained object acts as part of the containing object's state.

Has-a relationships are preferred over is-a relationships in cases where your class cannot or should not substitute for the other class. As a non-programming analogy, many people have a need for legal services in their lives, but most of them will choose to *have* a lawyer rather than *be* a lawyer themselves.

The following code presents a potential initial implementation of the `Circle` class:

```
1   // Represents circular shapes.
2   public class Circle {
3       private Point center;
4       private double radius;
5
6       // constructs a new circle with the given radius
7       public Circle(Point center, double radius) {
8           this.center = center;
9           this.radius = radius;
10      }
11
12      // returns the area of this circle
13      public double getArea() {
14          return Math.PI * radius * radius;
15      }
16  }
```

This design presents a `Circle` object as a single clear abstraction and prevents awkward commingling of `Circle` and `Point` objects.

Graphics2D (Optional)

Use of inheritance is prevalent in the Java class libraries. One notable example is in the drawing of 2D graphics. In this section we'll discuss a class that uses inheritance to draw complex 2D shapes and colors.

In Chapter 3's supplement on graphics, we introduced an object called `Graphics` that acts like a pen you can use to draw shapes and lines onto a window. When Java's designers wanted additional graphical functionality, they extended the `Graphics` class into a more powerful class called `Graphics2D`. This is a good example of one of the more common uses of inheritance: to extend and reuse functionality from a powerful existing object.

TABLE 9.3   Useful Methods of `Graphics2D` Objects

Method	Description
`rotate(angle)`	Rotates subsequently drawn items by the given angle in radians with respect to the origin
`scale(sx, sy)`	Adjusts the size of any subsequently drawn items by the given factors (1.0 means equal size)
`shear(shx, shy)`	Gives a slant to any subsequently drawn items
`translate(dx, dy)`	Shifts the origin by (dx, dy) in the current coordinate system

Why didn't Sun simply add the new methods into the existing `Graphics` class? The `Graphics` class already worked properly, so Sun decided it was best not to perform unnecessary surgery on it. John Vlissides, part of a famous foursome of software engineers affectionately called the "Gang of Four," once described the idea this way: "I've said it before and I'll say it again: A hallmark—if not the hallmark—of good object-oriented design is that you can modify and extend a system by adding code rather than by hacking it. In short, change is additive, not invasive."

Making `Graphics2D` extend `Graphics` retains *backward compatibility*. Backward compatibility is the ability for new code to work correctly with old code without modification. Leaving `Graphics` untouched ensured that old programs would keep working properly, while giving new programs the option to use the new `Graphics2D` functionality.

Sun's documentation for `Graphics2D` describes the purpose of the class as follows. "This `Graphics2D` class extends the `Graphics` class to provide more sophisticated control over geometry, coordinate transformations, color management, and text layout. This is the fundamental class for rendering 2-dimensional shapes, text, and images on the Java(tm) platform." To be specific, `Graphics2D` adds the ability to perform transformations such as scaling and rotation when you're drawing. These capabilities can lead to some fun and interesting images on the screen.

If you used the `DrawingPanel` class from Chapter 3's graphical supplement, you previously wrote statements like the following to get access to the panel's `Graphics` object:

```
Graphics g = panel.getGraphics();
```

Actually, the `getGraphics` method doesn't return a `Graphics` object at all, but rather a `Graphics2D` object. Because of polymorphism, though, it is legal for your program to treat it as a `Graphics` object, because every `Graphics2D` object "is" a `Graphics` object. To use it as a `Graphics2D` object instead, simply say:

```
Graphics2D g2 = panel.getGraphics();
```

Table 9.3 lists some of `Graphics2D`'s extra methods.

The following program demonstrates `Graphics2D`. The `rotate` method's parameter is an angle of rotation measured in radians instead of degrees. Rather than memorizing the conversion between degrees and radians, we can use a static method from the `Math` class called `toRadians` that converts a degree value into the equivalent radian value:

```java
 1  // Draws a picture of rotating squares using Graphics2D.
 2
 3  import java.awt.*;
 4
 5  public class FancyPicture {
 6      public static void main(String[] args) {
 7          DrawingPanel panel = new DrawingPanel(250, 220);
 8          Graphics2D g2 = panel.getGraphics();
 9          g2.translate(100, 120);
10          g2.fillRect(-5, -5, 10, 10);
11
12          for (int i = 0; i <= 12; i++) {
13              g2.setColor(Color.BLUE);
14              g2.fillRect(20, 20, 20, 20);
15
16              g2.setColor(Color.BLACK);
17              g2.drawString("" + i, 20, 20);
18
19              g2.rotate(Math.toRadians(30));
20              g2.scale(1.1, 1.1);
21          }
22      }
23  }
```

Figure 9.7 shows the program's output:

Figure 9.7 Output of FancyPicture

9.5 Interfaces

Inheritance is a very useful tool because it enables polymorphism and code sharing, but it does have several limitations. Because Java uses single inheritance, a class can extend only one superclass. This makes it impossible to use inheritance to set up multiple is-a relationships for classes that share multiple characteristics, such as an employee who is both part-time and a secretary. There are also situations where you want is-a relationships and polymorphism without sharing code, in which case inheritance isn't the right tool for the job.

To this end, Java provides a construct called an *interface* that can represent a common supertype between several classes without code sharing.

Interface

A set of methods that classes can promise to implement, allowing you to treat those classes similarly in your code.

An interface is like a class, but it contains only method headers without bodies. A class can promise to *implement* an interface, meaning that the class promises to provide implementations of all methods declared in the interface. Classes that implement an interface form an is-a relationship with it. In a system with an interface that is implemented by several classes, polymorphic code can be written that will handle objects from any classes implementing that interface.

A non-programming analogy for an interface is that of a certification. It's possible for a person to become certified as a teacher, nurse, accountant, or doctor. To do this, the person must demonstrate certain abilities required of members of those professions. Employers can hire anyone who has received the proper certification and know that person will be able to perform certain job duties. An interface acts as a certification that classes can meet by implementing all behavior described in the interface. Code that receives an object implementing an interface can rely on the object having certain behavior.

Interfaces are also used to define roles that objects can play; for example, a `Rectangle` class might implement the `Comparable` interface to indicate that `Rectangle` objects can be compared to each other, or a `Point` class might implement the `Cloneable` interface to indicate that a `Point` object can be replicated.

An Interface for Shape Classes

In this section we'll use an interface to define a polymorphic hierarchy of shape classes without sharing code between them. Imagine that we are creating classes to represent many different types of shapes, such as rectangles, circles, and triangles. We might be tempted to use inheritance with these shape classes because they seem to share some common behavior (all shapes have an area and a perimeter, for example).

It may seem as though there is an is-a relationship here, because a rectangle, a circle, and a triangle are all shapes. But code sharing isn't useful in this case because each class implements its behavior differently. As depicted in Figure 9.8 and Table 9.4, each shape computes its area and perimeter in a totally different way. The w and h represent the rectangle's width and height; the r represents the circle's radius; and the a, b, and c represent the lengths of the triangle's three sides.

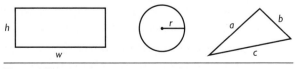

Figure 9.8 Three types of shapes

TABLE 9.4   Area amd Perimeter of Each Shape Type

	Rectangle	Circle	Triangle
Area	$w * h$	πr^2	$\sqrt{s(s - a)(s - b)(s - c)}$ where $s = \dfrac{a + b + c}{2}$
Perimeter	$2 (w + h)$	$2 \pi r$	$a + b + c$

Since no code is shared between these classes, we should not create a common superclass to represent their is-a relationship. Java uses single inheritance, and we don't want to use up our only potential inheritance relationship here. A better solution would be to write an interface called `Shape` to represent the common functionality of all shapes: the ability to ask for an area and a perimeter. Our various shape classes will implement this interface.

To write an interface, we create a new file with the same name as the interface's name; our `Shape` interface, for example, would be stored in `Shape.java`. We give the interface a header with the keyword `interface` in place of the word `class`:

```
public interface Shape {
    ...
}
```

Inside the interface we write headers for each method we want shapes to contain. But instead of writing method bodies with braces, we simply place a semicolon at the end of each header. We don't specify how the methods are implemented. Instead, we're requiring that any class that wants to be considered a shape must implement these methods. In fact, it isn't legal for an interface to contain method bodies; an interface can only contain method headers and class constants.

The following is the complete code for our `Shape` interface. It declares that shapes have methods to compute their areas and perimeters as type `double`:

```
1   // A general interface for shape classes.
2   public interface Shape {
3       public double getArea();
4       public double getPerimeter();
5   }
```

The methods of an interface are sometimes called *abstract methods* because we only declare their names and signatures; we don't specify how they will be implemented.

> **Abstract Method**
>
> A method that is declared (as in an interface) but not implemented. Abstract methods represent the behavior a class promises to implement when it implements an interface.

Writing the `public` keyword on an interface's method headers is optional. We chose to include the `public` keyword so that the declarations in the interface would match the headers of the method implementations in the classes. The general syntax we'll use for declaring an interface is the following:

```
public interface <name> {
    public <type> <name>(<type> <name>, ..., <type> <name>);
    public <type> <name>(<type> <name>, ..., <type> <name>);
    ...
    public <type> <name>(<type> <name>, ..., <type> <name>);
}
```

While superficially classes and interfaces look alike, an interface cannot be instantiated. In our case, any code trying to create a `new Shape()` would not compile. It is, however, legal to create variables of type `Shape` that can refer to any object that implements the `Shape` interface, as we'll explore in a moment.

Implementing the Shape Interface

Now that we've written a `Shape` interface, we want to connect the various classes of shapes to it. To connect a class to our interface with an is-a relationship, we must do two things:

1. Declare that the class "implements" the interface.

2. Implement each of the interface's methods in the class.

The general syntax for declaring that a class implements an interface is the following:

```
public class <name> implements <interface> {
    ...
}
```

We must modify the headers of our various shape classes to indicate that they implement all of the methods in the `Shape` interface. The file `Rectangle.java`, for example, should begin like this:

```
public class Rectangle implements Shape {
    ...
}
```

When we claim that our `Rectangle` class implements `Shape`, we are promising that the `Rectangle` class will contain implementations of the `getArea` and `getPerimeter` methods. If a class claims to implement `Shape` but does not have a suitable `getArea` or `getPerimeter` method, it will not compile. For example, if we leave the body of our `Rectangle` class empty and try to compile it, the compiler will give errors like the following:

```
Rectangle.java:2: Rectangle is not abstract and does not override abstract
    method getPerimeter()
```

```
public class Rectangle implements Shape {
              ^
1 error
```

The solution is to implement the `getArea` and `getPerimeter` methods in our `Rectangle` class. we'll define a `Rectangle` object by a width and height. Since the area of a rectangle is equal to its width times its height, we'll implement the `getArea` method by multiplying its fields. We'll then use the perimeter formula 2 * (w + h) to implement `getPerimeter`. Here is the complete `Rectangle` class that implements the `Shape` interface:

```
1   // Represents rectangular shapes.
2   public class Rectangle implements Shape {
3       private double width;
4       private double height;
5
6       // constructs a new rectangle with the given dimensions
7       public Rectangle(double width, double height) {
8           this.width = width;
9           this.height = height;
10      }
11
12      // returns the area of this rectangle
13      public double getArea() {
14          return width * height;
15      }
16
17      // returns the perimeter of this rectangle
18      public double getPerimeter() {
19          return 2.0 * (width + height);
20      }
21  }
```

The other classes of shapes are implemented in a similar fashion. We'll define a `Circle` object to have a field called `radius`. (We'll abandon the center `Point` object used in the `Circle` class earlier in the chapter, since we don't need it here.) We can determine the area by multiplying π by the radius squared. To find the perimeter, we'll use the equation 2 * π * r. Notice that there is no common code between `Circle` and `Rectangle`, so inheritance is unnecessary. Here is the complete `Circle` class:

```
1   // Represents circular shapes.
2   public class Circle implements Shape {
3       private double radius;
4
5       // constructs a new circle with the given radius
6       public Circle(double radius) {
7           this.radius = radius;
8       }
9
10      // returns the area of this circle
11      public double getArea() {
12          return Math.PI * radius * radius;
```

```
13            }
14
15            // returns the perimeter of this circle
16            public double getPerimeter() {
17                return 2.0 * Math.PI * radius;
18            }
19    }
```

Finally, we'll specify a `triangle`'s shape by its three side lengths, *a*, *b*, and *c*. The perimeter of the triangle is simply the sum of the three side lengths. The `getArea` method is a bit trickier, but there is a useful geometric formula called Heron's formula that says that the area of a triangle with sides of lengths *a*, *b*, and *c* is related to a value *s* equal to half the triangle's perimeter:

$$\text{area} = \sqrt{s(s-a)(s-b)(s-c)} \quad \text{where} \quad s = \frac{a+b+c}{2}$$

Here is a complete version of the `Triangle` class:

```
1    // Represents triangular shapes.
2    public class Triangle implements Shape {
3            private double a;
4            private double b;
5            private double c;
6
7            // constructs a new triangle with the given side lengths
8            public Triangle(double a, double b, double c) {
9                this.a = a;
10               this.b = b;
11               this.c = c;
12           }
13
14           // returns this triangle's area using Heron's formula
15           public double getArea() {
16               double s = (a + b + c) / 2.0;
17               return Math.sqrt(s * (s - a) * (s - b) * (s - c));
18           }
19
20           // returns the perimeter of this triangle
21           public double getPerimeter() {
22               return a + b + c;
23           }
24   }
```

Benefits of Interfaces

Classes that implement a common interface form a type hierarchy similar to those created by inheritance. The interface serves as a parent type for the classes that implement it. The following simplified UML diagram represents our type hierarchy after our modifications. We'll represent an interface similarly to a class, but with the word "interface" for clarity. Its methods are italicized to emphasize that they are abstract. Figure 9.9 shows our use of dashed lines to connect the classes and the interface they implement:

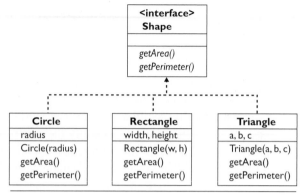

Figure 9.9 Hierarchy of shape classes

The major benefit of interfaces is that we can use them to achieve polymorphism. We can create an array of `Shapes`, pass a `Shape` as a parameter to a method, return a `Shape` from a method, and so on. The following program uses the shape classes in an example similar to the polymorphism exercises in Section 9.2:

```
1   // Demonstrates shape classes.
2   public class ShapesMain {
3       public static void main(String[] args) {
4           Shape[] shapes = new Shape[3];
5           shapes[0] = new Rectangle(18, 18);
6           shapes[1] = new Triangle(30, 30, 30);
7           shapes[2] = new Circle(12);
8
9           for (int i = 0; i < shapes.length; i++) {
10              System.out.println("area=" + shapes[i].getArea() +
11                                  ", perimeter=" +
12                                  shapes[i].getPerimeter());
13          }
14      }
15  }
```

This program produces the following output:

```
area=324.0, perimeter=72.0
area=389.7114317029974, perimeter=90.0
area=452.3893421169302, perimeter=75.39822368615503
```

It would be fairly easy to modify our client program if another shape class, such as `Hexagon` or `Ellipse`, were added to the hierarchy. This is another example of the desired property of "additive, not invasive" change mentioned earlier in this chapter.

It may seem odd that we can have interface variables, arrays, and parameters when it isn't possible to construct an object of an interface type, but all this means is that any object of a type that implements that interface may be used. In our case, any type that implements `Shape` (such as `Circle`, `Rectangle`, or `Triangle`) may be used.

Also recall that interfaces help us cope with the limitations of single inheritance. A class may extend only one superclass but may implement arbitrarily many interfaces. The following is the general syntax for headers of classes that extend a superclass and implement one or more interfaces:

```
public class <name> extends <superclass name>
    implements <interface name>, <interface name>, . . . , <interface name> {
    ...
}
```

There are many classes in the Java class libraries that both extend a superclass and implement one or more interfaces. For example, the `PrintStream` class (of which `System.out` is an instance) has the following header:

```
public class PrintStream extends FilterOutputStream
        implements Appendable, Closeable, Flushable
```

Interfaces in the Java Class Libraries

Interfaces are used in many other places in Java's class libraries. Here are just a few of Java's important interfaces:

- The `ActionListener` interface in the `java.awt` package is used to assign behavior to events when a user clicks on a button or other graphical control.

- The `Serializable` interface in the `java.io` package denotes classes whose objects are able to be saved to files and transferred over a network.

- The `Comparable` interface allows you to describe how to compare objects of your type to see which are less than, greater, or equal to each other. This can be used to search or sort a collection of objects.

- The `Formattable` interface lets objects describe different ways they can be printed by the `System.out.printf` command.

- The `Runnable` interface is used for multithreading, which allows a program to execute two pieces of code at the same time.

- Interfaces such as `List`, `Set`, `Map`, and `Iterator` in the `java.util` package describe data structures you can use to store collections of objects.

We will cover some of these interfaces in later chapters.

9.6 Case Study: Designing a Hierarchy of Financial Classes

As you write larger and more complex programs, you will end up with more classes and more opportunities to use inheritance and interfaces. It is important to get practice devising sensible hierarchies of types, so that you will be able to solve large problems by breaking them down into good classes in the future.

When designing an object-oriented system, you should ask yourself the following questions:

- What classes of objects should I write?

- What behavior does the client want each of these objects to have?

- What data do the objects need to store in order to implement this behavior?
- Are the classes related? If so, what is the nature of the relationships?

Having good answers to these questions, along with a good knowledge of the necessary Java syntax, is a good start toward designing an object-oriented system. Such a process is called *object-oriented design.*

> **Object-Oriented Design (OOD)**
>
> Modeling a program or system as a collection of cooperating objects, implemented as a set of classes using class hierarchies.

Let's consider the problem of gathering information about a person's financial investments. We've already explored a `Stock` example in this chapter and the previous chapter as well as a `DividendStock` class to handle stocks that pay dividends. But stocks are not the only type of asset that investors might have in their financial portfolios. Other investments might include mutual funds, real estate, or cash.

How would you design a complete portfolio system? What new types of objects would you write? Take a moment to consider the problem. We'll discuss an example design next.

Designing the Classes

Each type of asset deserves its own class. We already have the `Stock` class from the last chapter and its `DividendStock` subclass from earlier in this chapter, and we can add classes like `MutualFund` and `Cash`. Each object of each of these types will represent a single investment of that type: for example, a `MutualFund` object will represent a purchase of a mutual fund, and a `Cash` object will represent a sum of money in the user's portfolio. The available types are shown in Figure 9.10. What data and behavior is necessary in each of these types of objects? Take a moment to consider it.

Though each type of asset is unique, the types do have some common behavior: Each asset should be able to compute its current market value and profit or loss, if any. These values are computed in different ways for different asset types, though. For instance, a stock's market value is the total number of shares purchased times the current price per share, while cash is always worth exactly its own amount.

In terms of data, we decided previously that a `Stock` object should store the stock's symbol, the number of shares purchased, the total cost paid for all shares, and the current price of the stock. Dividend stocks also need to store the amount of dividends paid. A `MutualFund` object should store the same data as a `Stock` object, but mutual funds can hold partial shares. Cash only needs to store its amount. Figure 9.11 updates our diagram of types to reflect this data and behavior.

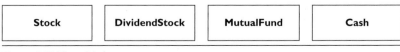

Figure 9.10 Financial classes

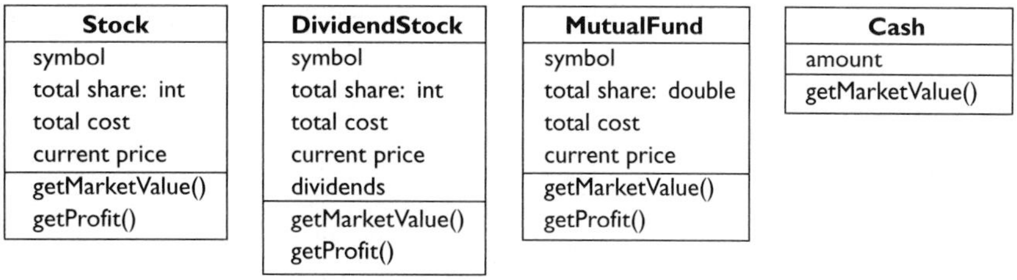

Stock	DividendStock	MutualFund	Cash
symbol	symbol	symbol	amount
total share: int	total share: int	total share: double	getMarketValue()
total cost	total cost	total cost	
current price	current price	current price	
getMarketValue()	dividends	getMarketValue()	
getProfit()	getMarketValue()	getProfit()	
	getProfit()		

Figure 9.11 Financial classes with state and behavior

Are the asset types related? It seems so. Perhaps we'd want to gather and store a person's portfolio of assets in an array. It would be convenient to be able to treat any asset the same way, insofar as they share similar functionality. For example, every asset has a market value, so it would be nice to be able to compute the total market value of all assets in an investor's portfolio, without worrying about the exact type of each asset.

One hurdle is that different assets compute their market values in different ways. Stocks' values are based on the current share price, while the market value of cash is always exactly equal to its amount. This implies that we should use an interface to represent the notion of an asset and have every class previously listed implement the asset interface. Our interface will demand that all assets have methods to get the market value and profit. The interface is a way of saying, "Classes that want to consider themselves assets must have `getMarketValue` and `getProfit` methods." Our interface for financial assets would be saved in a file called `Asset.java` and would look like this:

```
1   // Represents financial assets that investors hold.
2   public interface Asset {
3       // how much the asset is worth
4       public double getMarketValue();
5
6       // how much money has been made on this asset
7       public double getProfit();
8   }
```

We'll have our various classes certify that they are assets by making them implement the `Asset` interface. For example, let's look at the `Cash` class. We didn't write a `getProfit` method in our previous diagram of `Cash`, because the value of cash doesn't really change and therefore it doesn't have a profit. To indicate this, we can write a `getProfit` method for `Cash` that returns `0.0`. The `Cash` class should look like this:

```
1   // A Cash object represents an amount of money held by an investor.
2   public class Cash implements Asset {
3       private double amount; // amount of money held
4
5       // constructs a cash investment of the given amount
6       public Cash(double amount) {
7           this.amount = amount;
8       }
9
10      // returns this cash investment's market value, which
```

```
11        // is equal to the amount of cash
12        public double getMarketValue() {
13            return amount;
14        }
15
16        // since cash is a fixed asset, it never has any profit
17        public double getProfit() {
18            return 0.0;
19        }
20
21        // sets the amount of cash invested to the given value
22        public void setAmount(double amount) {
23            this.amount = amount;
24        }
25  }
```

As discussed earlier in this chapter, a DividendStock is very similar to a normal Stock, but with a small amount of behavior added. Let's display DividendStock as a subclass of Stock through inheritance, matching the design from earlier in the chapter. Figure 9.12 shows how our hierarchy should now look.

What about the similarity between mutual funds and stocks? They both store assets based on shares, with a symbol, total cost, and current price. It wouldn't work very well to make one of them a subclass of the other, though, because the type of shares (integer or real number) isn't the same, and also because it's not a sensible is-a relationship: stocks aren't really mutual funds, and vice versa.

Let's modify our design by making a new superclass called ShareAsset that represents any asset that has shares and contains the common behavior of Stock and MutualFund. Then we can have both Stock and MutualFund extend ShareAsset, to reduce redundancy.

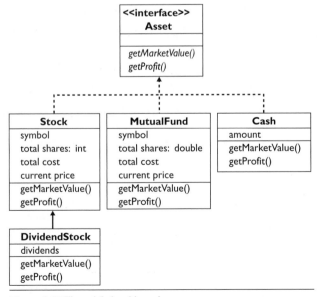

Figure 9.12 Financial class hierarchy

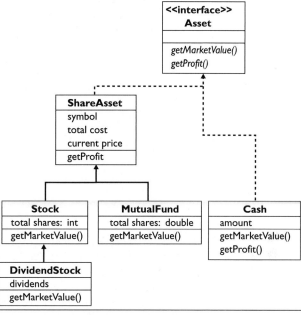

Figure 9.13 Updated financial class hierarchy

Our previous versions of the Stock and DividendStock classes each had a getProfit method that required a parameter for the current price per share. In order to implement the Asset interface with its parameterless getMarketValue and getProfit methods, we'll change our design and make the current price a field. We'll also add methods to get and set its value.

The updated type hierarchy should look like that shown in Figure 9.13.

This practice of redesigning code to meet new requirements is sometimes called *refactoring*.

Initial Redundant Implementation

Here's some potential code for the ShareAsset class:

```
1   // A ShareAsset object represents a general asset that has a symbol
2   // and holds shares. Initial version.
3   public class ShareAsset {
4       private String symbol;
5       private double totalCost;
6       private double currentPrice;
7
8       // constructs a new share asset with the given symbol
9       // and current price
10      public ShareAsset(String symbol, double currentPrice) {
11          this.symbol = symbol;
12          this.currentPrice = currentPrice;
13          totalCost = 0.0;
```

```
14          }
15
16          // adds a cost of the given amount to this asset
17          public void addCost(double cost) {
18              totalCost += cost;
19          }
20
21          // returns the price per share of this asset
22          public double getCurrentPrice() {
23              return currentPrice;
24          }
25
26          // returns this asset's total cost for all shares
27          public double getTotalCost() {
28              return totalCost;
29          }
30
31          // sets the current share price of this asset
32          public void setCurrentPrice(double currentPrice) {
33              this.currentPrice = currentPrice;
34          }
35      }
```

We stole some code from the `Stock` class, but to fit this interface, the code underwent a few changes. Our `Stock` code accepted the current share price as a parameter to its `getProfit` method. Since the `getProfit` method cannot accept any parameters if we wish to implement the interface, we'll instead store the current share price as a field in the `ShareAsset` class and supply a `setCurrentPrice` mutator method that can be called to set its proper value. We also include a constructor that can initialize a `Stock` object with any number of shares and a total cost.

One last modification we made in creating `ShareAsset` was to include an `addCost` method, which we'll use to add a given amount to the asset's total cost. We will need this because purchases of `Stocks` and `MutualFunds` need to update the `totalCost` field, but they cannot do so directly since it is private.

The `Stock` class can now extend `ShareAsset` to implement its remaining functionality. Notice that we both extend `ShareAsset` and implement the `Asset` interface in the class's header:

```
1   // A Stock object represents purchases of shares of a stock.
2   // Initial version.
3   public class Stock extends ShareAsset implements Asset {
4       private int totalShares;
5
6       // constructs a new Stock with the given symbol and
7       // current price per share
8       public Stock(String symbol, double currentPrice) {
9           super(symbol, currentPrice);
10          totalShares = 0;
11      }
12
13      // returns the market value of this stock, which is
14      // the number of total shares times the share price
```

```
15      public double getMarketValue() {
16          return totalShares * getCurrentPrice();
17      }
18
19      // returns the total number of shares purchased
20      public int getTotalShares() {
21          return totalShares;
22      }
23
24      // returns the profit made on this stock
25      public double getProfit() {
26          return getMarketValue() - getTotalCost();
27      }
28
29      // records a purchase of the given number of shares of
30      // the stock at the given price per share
31      public void purchase(int shares, double pricePerShare) {
32          totalShares += shares;
33          addCost(shares * pricePerShare);
34      }
35  }
```

The `MutualFund` class receives similar treatment, but with a `double` for its total shares (the two classes are highly redundant; we'll improve them in the next section):

```
1   // A MutualFund object represents a mutual fund asset.
2   // Initial version.
3   public class MutualFund extends ShareAsset implements Asset {
4       private double totalShares;
5
6       // constructs a new MutualFund investment with the given
7       // symbol and price per share
8       public MutualFund(String symbol, double currentPrice) {
9           super(symbol, currentPrice);
10          totalShares = 0.0;
11      }
12
13      // returns the market value of this mutual fund, which
14      // is the number of shares times the price per share
15      public double getMarketValue() {
16          return totalShares * getCurrentPrice();
17      }
18
19      // returns the number of shares of this mutual fund
20      public double getTotalShares() {
21          return totalShares;
22      }
23
24      // returns the profit made on this mutual fund
25      public double getProfit() {
26          return getMarketValue() - getTotalCost();
27      }
28
29      // records purchase of the given shares at the given price
30      public void purchase(double shares, double pricePerShare) {
31          totalShares += shares;
```

```
32                addCost(shares * pricePerShare);
33       }
34  }
```

The `DividendStock` simply adds an amount of dividend payments to a normal `Stock`, which affects its market value. We don't need to override the `getProfit` method in `DividendStock`, because `DividendStock` already inherits a `getProfit` method with the following body:

```
return getMarketValue() - getTotalCost();
```

Notice that `getProfit`'s body calls `getMarketValue`. `DividendStock` overrides the `getMarketValue` method, and a convenient side effect is that any other method that calls `getMarketValue` (such as `getProfit`) will also behave differently. This occurs because of polymorphism; since `getMarketValue` is overridden, `getProfit` calls the new version of the method. The profit will be correctly computed with dividends because these are added to the market value.

The following code implements the `DividendStock` class:

```
1   // A DividendStock object represents a stock purchase that also pays
2   // dividends.
3   public class DividendStock extends Stock {
4       private double dividends;   // amount of dividends paid
5
6       // constructs a new dividend stock with the given symbol
7       // and no shares purchased
8       public DividendStock(String symbol, double currentPrice) {
9           super(symbol, currentPrice);   // call Stock constructor
10          dividends = 0.0;
11      }
12
13      // returns this DividendStock's market value, which is
14      // a normal stock's market value plus any dividends
15      public double getMarketValue() {
16          return super.getMarketValue() + dividends;
17      }
18
19      // records a dividend of the given amount per share
20      public void payDividend(double amountPerShare) {
21          dividends += amountPerShare * getTotalShares();
22      }
23  }
```

Abstract Classes

So far we have written classes, which are concrete implementations of state and behavior, and interfaces, which are completely abstract declarations of behavior. There is an entity that exists between these two extremes, allowing us to define some concrete state and behavior while leaving some abstract without defined method bodies. Such an entity is called an *abstract class*.

> **Abstract Class**
>
> A Java class that cannot be instantiated, but instead serves as a superclass to hold common code and declare abstract behavior.

You probably noticed a lot of redundancy between the `Stock` and `MutualFund` code in the last section. For example, the `getMarketValue` and `getProfit` methods, while they have identical code, can't be moved up into the `ShareAsset` superclass because they depend on the number of shares, which is different in each child class. Ideally, we should get rid of this redundancy somehow.

There is also a problem with our current `ShareAsset` class. A `ShareAsset` isn't really a type of asset that a person can buy; it's just a concept that happens to be represented in our code. It would be undesirable for a person to actually try to construct a `ShareAsset` object—we wrote the class to eliminate redundancy, not for clients to instantiate it.

We can resolve these issues by designating the `ShareAsset` class as abstract. Writing `abstract` in a class's header will modify the class in two ways. First, the class becomes non-instantiable, so client code will not be allowed to construct an object of that type with the `new` keyword. Second, the class is enabled to declare abstract methods without bodies. Unlike an interface, though, an abstract class can also declare fields and implement methods with bodies, so the `ShareAsset` class can retain its existing code.

The general syntax for declaring an abstract class is:

```java
public abstract class <name> {
    ...
}
```

Thus, our new `ShareAsset` class header will be:

```java
public abstract class ShareAsset {
    ...
}
```

An attempt to create a `ShareAsset` object will now produce a compiler error such as the following:

```
ShareAsset is abstract; cannot be instantiated
        ShareAsset asset = new ShareAsset("MSFT", 27.46);
        ^
1 error
```

Really, the `Employee` class introduced earlier in this chapter should also have been an abstract class. We did not especially want client code to construct `Employee` objects. No one is *just* an employee; the `Employee` class just represented a general category to be extended.

Abstract classes are allowed to implement interfaces if so desired. Rather than requiring all subclasses of `ShareAsset` to implement the `Asset` interface, we can specify that `ShareAsset` implements `Asset`:

```
public abstract class ShareAsset implements Asset {
    ...
}
```

This will save `ShareAsset` subclasses from having to write `implements Asset` in their class headers.

`ShareAsset` does not implement the `getMarketValue` method required by `Asset`; that functionality is left for its subclasses. We can instead declare `getMarketValue` as an abstract method in the `ShareAsset` class. Abstract methods declared in abstract classes need the keyword `abstract` to appear in their headers to compile properly. Otherwise, the syntax is the same as when declaring an abstract method in an interface, with a semicolon replacing the method's body:

```
// returns the current market value of this asset
public abstract double getMarketValue();
```

The general syntax for an abstract method declaration in an abstract class is the following:

```
public abstract <type> <name> (<type> <name>, ... ,
                               <type> <name>);
```

Another benefit of this design is that code in the abstract class can actually call any of its abstract methods, even if they don't have implementations in that file. This is allowed because the abstract class can count on its subclasses to implement the abstract methods. Now that `ShareAsset` implements `Asset`, we can move the common redundant `getProfit` code up to `ShareAsset` and out of `Stock` and `MutualFund`:

```
// returns the profit earned on shares of this asset
public double getProfit() {
    // calls an abstract getMarketValue method
    // (the subclass will provide its implementation)
    return getMarketValue() - totalCost;
}
```

`ShareAsset` objects can call `getMarketValue` from their `getProfit` methods even though that method isn't present in `ShareAsset`. The code compiles because the compiler knows that whatever class extends `ShareAsset` will have to implement `getMarketValue`.

The following is the final version of the `ShareAsset` abstract class:

```
1   // A ShareAsset represents a general asset that has a symbol and
2   // holds shares.
3   public abstract class ShareAsset implements Asset {
4       private String symbol;
5       private double totalCost;
6       private double currentPrice;
7
```

```
 8          // constructs a new share asset with the given symbol
 9          // and current price
10          public ShareAsset(String symbol, double currentPrice) {
11              this.symbol = symbol;
12              this.currentPrice = currentPrice;
13              totalCost = 0.0;
14          }
15
16          // adds a cost of the given amount to this asset
17          public void addCost(double cost) {
18              totalCost += cost;
19          }
20
21          // returns the price per share of this asset
22          public double getCurrentPrice() {
23              return currentPrice;
24          }
25
26          // returns the current market value of this asset
27          public abstract double getMarketValue();
28
29          // returns the profit earned on shares of this asset
30          public double getProfit() {
31              // calls an abstract getMarketValue method
32              // (the subclass will provide its implementation)
33              return getMarketValue() - totalCost;
34          }
35
36          // returns this asset's total cost for all shares
37          public double getTotalCost() {
38              return totalCost;
39          }
40
41          // sets the current share price of this asset
42          public void setCurrentPrice(double currentPrice) {
43              this.currentPrice = currentPrice;
44          }
45  }
```

An abstract class is a useful hybrid that can contain both abstract and non-abstract methods. All methods declared in an interface are implicitly abstract; they can be declared with the abstract keyword if so desired. Declaring them without the abstract keyword as we have done in this chapter is a commonly used shorthand for the longer explicit form. Unfortunately, abstract classes disallow this shorthand to avoid ambiguity.

Non-abstract classes like Stock and MutualFund are sometimes called *concrete classes* to differentiate them from abstract classes. We can modify the Stock and MutualFund classes to take advantage of ShareAsset and reduce the redundancy. The following are the final versions of the Stock and MutualFund classes. (DividendStock is unmodified.) Notice that the subclasses of ShareAsset must implement getMarketValue, or we'll receive a compiler error:

```
1    // A Stock object represents purchases of shares of a stock.
2    public class Stock extends ShareAsset {
3        private int totalShares;
4
5        // constructs a new Stock with the given symbol and
6        // current price per share
7        public Stock(String symbol, double currentPrice) {
8            super(symbol, currentPrice);
9            totalShares = 0;
10       }
11
12       // returns the market value of this stock, which is
13       // the number of total shares times the share price
14       public double getMarketValue() {
15           return totalShares * getCurrentPrice();
16       }
17
18       // returns the total number of shares purchased
19       public int getTotalShares() {
20           return totalShares;
21       }
22
23       // records a purchase of the given number of shares of
24       // the stock at the given price per share
25       public void purchase(int shares, double pricePerShare) {
26           totalShares += shares;
27           addCost(shares * pricePerShare);
28       }
29   }
```

```
1    // A MutualFund object represents a mutual fund asset.
2    public class MutualFund extends ShareAsset {
3        private double totalShares;
4
5        // constructs a new MutualFund investment with the given
6        // symbol and price per share
7        public MutualFund(String symbol, double currentPrice) {
8            super(symbol, currentPrice);
9            totalShares = 0.0;
10       }
11
12       // returns the market value of this mutual fund, which
13       // is the number of shares times the price per share
14       public double getMarketValue() {
15           return totalShares * getCurrentPrice();
16       }
17
18       // returns the number of shares of this mutual fund
19       public double getTotalShares() {
20           return totalShares;
21       }
22
23       // records purchase of the given shares at the given price
24       public void purchase(double shares, double pricePerShare) {
25           totalShares += shares;
26           addCost(shares * pricePerShare);
27       }
28   }
```

9. Using the same classes from the previous problem, what is the output produced by the following code fragment?

```java
public static void main(String[] args) {
    SeaCreature[] elements = {new SeaCreature(),
            new Squid(), new Mammal(), new Whale()};
    for (int i = 0; i < elements.length; i++) {
        elements[i].method2();
        System.out.println(elements[i]);
        elements[i].method1();
        System.out.println();
    }
}
```

Section 9.3: Interacting with the Superclass

10. Explain the difference between the this keyword and the super keyword. When should each be used?

11. For the next three problems, consider the following class:

```java
1   // Represents a university student.
2   public class Student {
3       private String name;
4       private int age;
5
6       public Student(String name, int age) {
7           this.name = name;
8           this.age = age;
9       }
10
11      public void setAge(int age) {
12          this.age = age;
13      }
14  }
```

and the following partial implementation of a subclass of Student to represent undergraduate students at a university:

```java
public class UndergraduateStudent extends Student {
    private int year;

    ...
}
```

Can the code in the UndergraduateStudent class access the name and age fields it inherits from Student? Can it call the setAge method?

12. Write a constructor for the UndergraduateStudent class that accepts a name as a parameter and initializes the UnderGraduateStudent's state with that name, an age value of 18, and a year value of 0.

13. Write a version of the setAge method in the UndergraduateStudent class that not only sets the age but also increments the year field's value by one.

14. Add the following constructor to the MeteredPoint class developed in this section:

```java
public MeteredPoint()
```

Constructs a new metered point at the origin of (0, 0). Use the super keyword or the this keyword as part of your solution.

Section 9.4: Inheritance and Design

15. What is the difference between an is-a and a has-a relationship? How do you create a has-a relationship in your code?

16. Imagine a `Rectangle` class whose objects represent 2D rectangles. The `Rectangle` has `width` and `height` fields with appropriate accessors and mutators, as well as `getArea` and `getPerimeter` methods.

You would like to add a `Square` class into your system. Is it a good design to make `Square` a subclass of `Rectangle`? Why or why not?

17. Imagine that you are going to write a program to play card games. Consider a design with a `Card` class and 52 subclasses, one for each of the unique playing cards (for example, `NineOfSpades` and `JackOfClubs`). Is this a good design? If so, why? If not, why not, and what might be a better design?

18. In this section we discussed adding functionality for dividend payments to the `Stock` class developed in Chapter 8. Why was it preferable to create a `DividendStock` class rather than editing the `Stock` class and adding this feature directly to it?

Section 9.5: Interfaces

19. What is the difference between implementing an interface and extending a class?

20. Consider the following interface and class:

```
public interface I {
    public void m1();
    public void m2();
}

public class C implements I {
    // code for class C
}
```

What must be true about the code for class `C` in order for it to compile successfully?

21. What's wrong with the code for the following interface? What should be changed to make a valid interface for objects that have a color?

```
public interface Colored {
    private Color color;

    public Color getColor() {
        return color;
    }
}
```

22. Modify the `Point` class from Chapter 8 so that it implements the `Colored` interface and `Point`s have colors. (You may wish to create a `ColoredPoint` class that extends `Point`.)

23. Declare a method called `getSideCount` in the `Shape` interface that returns how many sides the shape has. Implement the method in all shape classes.

Section 9.6: Case Study: Designing a Hierarchy of Financial Classes

24. What is an abstract class? How is an abstract class like a normal class, and how does it differ? How is it like an interface?

25. Consider writing a program to be used to manage a collection of movies. There are three kinds of movies in the collection: dramas, comedies, and documentaries. The collector would like to keep track of each movie's name, the name of its director, and the date when it was made. Some operations are to be implemented for all movies, and there will also be special operations for each of the three different kinds of movies. How would you design the class(es) to represent this system of movies?

Exercises

1. **myCodeMate** For the next four problems, consider the task of representing types of tickets to school campus events. Each ticket has a unique number and a price. There are three types of tickets: walk-up tickets, advance tickets, and student advance tickets. Figure 9.14 illustrates the types:

   - Walk-up tickets are purchased the day of the event and cost $50.
   - Advance tickets purchased 10 or more days before the event cost $30, and advance tickets purchased fewer than 10 days before the event cost $40.
   - Student advance tickets are sold at half the price of normal advance tickets: ones 10 days early cost $15, and fewer than 10 days early cost $20.

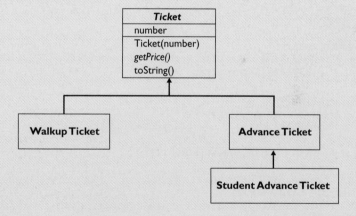

   Implement a class called `Ticket` that will serve as the superclass for all three types of tickets. Define all common operations in this class, and specify all differing operations in such a way that every subclass must implement them. No actual objects of type `Ticket` will be created: Each actual ticket will be an object of a subclass type. Define the following operations:

   - The ability to construct a ticket by number.
   - The ability to ask for a ticket's price.
   - The ability to `println` a ticket object as a `String`. An example string would be `"Number: 17, Price: 50.0"`.

2. Implement a class called `WalkupTicket` to represent a walk-up event ticket. Walk-up tickets are also constructed by number, and they have a price of $50.00.

3. Implement a class called `AdvanceTicket` to represent tickets purchased in advance. An advance ticket is constructed with a ticket number and with how many days in advance the ticket was purchased. Advance tickets purchased 10 or more days before the event cost $30, and advance tickets purchased fewer than 10 days before the event cost $40.

4. Implement a class called `StudentAdvanceTicket` to represent tickets purchased in advance by students. A student advance ticket is constructed with a ticket number and with how many days in advance the ticket was purchased. Student advance tickets purchased 10 or more days before the event cost $15, and student advance tickets purchased fewer than 10 days before the event cost $20 (half of a normal advance ticket). When a student advance ticket is printed, the string should mention that the student must show his or her student ID (for example, `"Number: 17, Price: 15.0 (ID required)"`).

5. For the next six problems, consider the task of representing types of birds in an aviary simulation. Each bird has an (x, y) position and a color, and each bird can fly. Different types of birds have different flight behavior.

Write an interface called `Bird` to represent different types of birds. The interface should have methods to do the following:

- Get the bird's color.
- Get the bird's (x, y) position as a `Point`.
- Tell a bird to fly. (Each time a bird is told to fly, it will move its position once.)

Your `Bird` interface should work with the following client program:

```
1   import java.awt.*;
2
3   public class Aviary {
4       public static final int SIZE = 20;
5       public static final int PIXELS = 10;
6
7       public static void main(String[] args) {
8           // create a drawing panel
9           DrawingPanel panel = new DrawingPanel(SIZE * PIXELS,
10                                                 SIZE * PIXELS);
11          Graphics g = panel.getGraphics();
12
13          // create several birds
14          Bird[] birds = {
15              new Cardinal(7, 4),      new Cardinal(3, 8),
16              new Hummingbird(2, 9),   new Hummingbird(16, 11),
17              new Bluebird(4, 15),     new Bluebird(8, 1),
18              new Vulture(3, 2),       new Vulture(18, 14)
19          };
20
21          while (true) {
22              // clear screen
23              g.setColor(Color.WHITE);
24              g.fillRect(0, 0, SIZE * PIXELS, SIZE * PIXELS);
25
26              // tell each bird to fly, and redraw the bird
27              for (Bird bird : birds) {
28                  bird.fly();
29                  g.setColor(bird.getColor());
30                  Point pos = bird.getPosition();
31                  g.fillOval(pos.getX() * PIXELS,
```

```
32                                    pos.getY() * PIXELS,
33                                    PIXELS, PIXELS);
34                  }
35
36              panel.sleep(500);
37          }
38      }
39  }
```

6. Write a class called `Cardinal` that represents cardinals. A cardinal is red in color. The cardinal's movement is vertical. Initially a cardinal is moving up. Each time the cardinal is told to fly, it will move its position one unit upward on the y-axis (remember that upward is negative). If the cardinal hits the edge of the aviary (a y-coordinate of 0 or 19), it turns around and flies in the opposite direction.

   Assume that the aviary's size of 20 is stored in a static constant called `Aviary.SIZE`. You may wish to introduce an abstract class to hold behavior that will be common to all bird classes.

7. Write a class called `Hummingbird` that represents hummingbirds. A hummingbird is magenta in color. The hummingbird's movement is random; each time the hummingbird is told to fly, it will pick a new random (x, y) position in the range of (0, 0) to (19, 19).

8. Write a class called `Bluebird` that represents bluebirds. A bluebird is blue in color. The bluebird's movement is in a zig-zag pattern. Initially the bluebird faces right. The bluebird moves in an alternating pattern of up-right, down-right, up-right, down-right, and so on until it hits the right edge of the aviary (x-coordinate of 19), at which point it turns around. Subsequent calls to `fly` will cause the bird to move up-left, down-left, up-left, down-left, and so on until it hits the left edge of the aviary.

9. Write a class called `Vulture` that represents vultures. A vulture is black in color. The vulture's movement is in a counter-clockwise circle pattern. Initially the vulture faces up. The first time the vulture flies, it moves up by one, then it turns to face left. Its second move, it moves left by one and turns to face down. Its third move, it moves down and turns to face right. Its fourth move, it moves right by one and turns to face up. The pattern repeats in this fashion.

10. What changes will you have to make if you want to count the number of times each bird has flown?

11. **myCodeMate** Declare an interface called `Incrementable` that represents items that store an integer that can be incremented in some way. The interface has a method called `increment` that increments the value and a method called `getValue` that returns the value. Once you have written the interface, write two classes called `SequentialIncrementer` and `RandomIncrementer` that implement the interface. The `SequentialIncrementer` begins its value at 0 and increases it by one each time it is incremented. The `RandomIncrementer` begins its value at a random integer and changes it to a new random integer each time it is incremented.

Programming Projects

1. Write an inheritance hierarchy of three-dimensional shapes. Make a top-level shape interface that has methods for getting information such as the volume and surface area of a 3D shape. Then make classes and subclasses that implement various shapes such as cubes, rectangular prisms, spheres, triangular prisms, cones, and cylinders. Place common behavior in superclasses whenever possible, and use abstract classes as appropriate. Add methods to the subclasses to represent the unique behavior of each 3D shape, such as a method to get a sphere's radius.

2. **myCodeMate** Write a set of classes that define the behavior of certain animals. They can be used in a simulation of a world with many animals moving around in it. Different kinds of animals will move in different ways (you are defining those differences). As the simulation runs, animals can "die" by ending up in the same location, in which case the simulator randomly selects one animal to survive the collision.

The behavior of each animal class is the following:

Class	getChar	getMove
Bird	B	Randomly selects one of the four directions each time
Frog	F	Picks a random direction, moves 3 in that direction, repeat (same as bird, but staying in a single direction longer)
Mouse	M	West 1, north 1, repeat (zig-zag to the NW)
Turtle	T	South 5, west 5, north 5, east 5, repeat (clockwise box)
Wolf	W	Has custom behavior that you define

Your classes should be stored in files called `Bird.java`, `Frog.java`, `Mouse.java`, `Turtle.java`, and `Wolf.java`.

3. Write an inheritance hierarchy that models sports players. Create a common superclass and/or interface to store information common to any player regardless of sport, such as name, number, and salary. Then create subclasses for players of your favorite sports, such as basketball, soccer, or tennis. Place sport-specific information and behavior (such as kicking or vertical jump height) into subclasses whenever possible.

4. Write an inheritance hierarchy to model items at a library. Include books, magazines, journal articles, videos, and electronic media such as CDs. Include in a superclass and/or interface common information that the library must have for every item, such as a unique identification number and title. Place item-type-specific behavior and information, such as a video's runtime length or a CD's musical genre, into the subclasses.

Chapter 10

ArrayLists

Introduction

One of the most fundamental data structures you will encounter in programming is a list. You'll want to be able to store lists of words, lists of numbers, lists of names, and so on. Chapter 7 demonstrated using arrays to store sequences of values, but arrays are fixed-size structures that require you to declare in advance exactly how many elements you want to store in them. In this chapter we'll explore a new structure, known as an `ArrayList`, that provides more functionality than an array. An `ArrayList` is a dynamic structure with a variable length, so it can grow and shrink as the program executes.

The `ArrayList` structure is the first example we have discussed of a generic structure that can be used to store values of different types. As a result, we will need to explore some issues related to generic structures in this chapter. We will also look at how to use primitive data with such structures, using what are known as the wrapper classes. Finally, we will demonstrate how the `Comparable` interface is used to describe how to put values of a particular type into sorted order and how to write classes that implement the `Comparable` interface.

10.1 ArrayLists

In our daily lives, we often find ourselves manipulating lists of one kind or another. For example, on social networking sites like Facebook.com, students are asked to list the bands they like. Suppose someone listed the following bands:

Tool, U2, Phish, Pink Floyd, Redefining the Moment

You saw in Chapter 7 that you can declare an array to store a sequence of values. For example, to store the preceding list, you could declare an array of `String`s of length 5. But what happens if you want to change the list later (say, to remove Tool and U2 from the list)? You would have to shift values over, and you'd be left with empty array slots at the end. And what if you wanted to add to the list, so that it ended up with more than five names? You wouldn't have room to store more than five values in the original array, so you would have to construct a new array with a larger size to store the list.

Most of us think of lists as being more flexible. We don't want to have to worry about the kind of low-level details that come up when manipulating an array. We want to be able to just say, "Add something here to the list" or "Remove this value from the list," and we want the lists to be able to grow and shrink over time as we add or remove values. Computer scientists would say that we have in mind a *list abstraction* that enables us to specify certain operations to be performed (add, remove) without having to worry about the details of how those operations are performed (shifting, constructing new arrays).

Java provides this functionality in a class called `ArrayList`. Internally, each `ArrayList` object uses an array to store its values. As a result, an `ArrayList` provides the same fast random access as an array. But unlike with an array, with an `ArrayList` you can make simple requests to add or remove values, and the `ArrayList` takes care of all of the details for you: if you add values to the list it makes the array bigger, and it handles any shifting that needs to be done if you remove values.

Remember that you can declare arrays of different types. If you want an array of `int` values, you declare a variable of type `int[]`. For an array of `String` values, you use the type `String[]`. This is a special syntax that works just for arrays, but Sun introduced a new mechanism as part of Java 5 that allows the `ArrayList` class to have almost the same flexibility. If you read the API documentation for `ArrayList`, you'll see that it is actually listed as `ArrayList<E>`. This is an example of a *generic class* in Java.

> **Generic Class (Generic)**
> A class such as `ArrayList<E>` that takes a type parameter to indicate what kind of values will be used.

The "E" in `ArrayList<E>` is short for "Element," and it indicates the type of elements that will be included in the `ArrayList`. Generic classes are similar to parameterized methods. Remember from Chapter 3 that using a parameter, you can define a family of related tasks that differ just by a particular characteristic like height or width. In this case, the parameter is a type and it is used to declare another type. The type `ArrayList<E>` represents a family of types that differ just by the type of element they store: you would use `ArrayList<String>` to store a list of `Strings`, `ArrayList<Point>` to store a list of `Points`, `ArrayList<Color>` to store a list of `Colors`, and so on. Notice that you would never actually declare something to be of type `ArrayList<E>`. As with any parameter, you have to replace the `E` with a specific value to make it clear which of the many possible `ArrayList` types you are using.

Basic **ArrayList** Operations

The `ArrayList` class is part of the `java.util` package, so to include it in a program you must include an import declaration. The syntax for constructing an `ArrayList` is more complicated than what we've seen before because of the type parameter. For example, you would construct an `ArrayList` of `Strings` as follows:

```
ArrayList<String> list = new ArrayList<String>();
```

This code constructs an empty `ArrayList<String>`. This syntax is complicated, but it will be easier to remember if you keep in mind that the `<String>` notation is actually part of the type: This isn't simply an `ArrayList`, it is an `ArrayList<String>` (often read as "an `ArrayList` of `String`"). Notice how the type appears in declaring the variable and in calling the constructor:

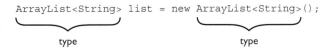

```
ArrayList<String> list = new ArrayList<String>();
```

           type   type

If you think in terms of the type being `ArrayList<String>` you'll see that this line of code isn't all that different from the code used to construct an object like a `Point`:

```
Point p = new Point();
```

    type   type

Once you've constructed an `ArrayList`, you can add values to it by calling the add method:

```
ArrayList<String> list = new ArrayList<String>();
list.add("Tool");
list.add("Phish");
list.add("Pink Floyd");
```

Java will make sure that you add values of an appropriate type. In this case, because you requested an `ArrayList<String>`, you can add `Strings` to the list. When you ask an `ArrayList` to add a new value to the list, it appends the new value to the end of the list.

Unlike with simple arrays, printing an `ArrayList` is straightforward because the `ArrayList` class overrides Java's `toString` method. The `ArrayList` version of `toString` constructs a `String` that includes the contents of the list inside square brackets, with the values separated by commas. Remember that the `toString` method is called when you print an object or concatenate an object to a `String`. As a result, you can print `ArrayLists` with a simple `println`, as in:

```
System.out.println("list = " + list);
```

For example, you can add `println` statements as you add values to the list:

```
ArrayList<String> list = new ArrayList<String>();
System.out.println("list = " + list);
list.add("Tool");
System.out.println("list = " + list);
list.add("Phish");
System.out.println("list = " + list);
list.add("Pink Floyd");
System.out.println("list = " + list);
```

Executing this code produces the following output:

```
list = []
list = [Tool]
list = [Tool, Phish]
list = [Tool, Phish, Pink Floyd]
```

Notice that you can print the `ArrayList` even when it is empty and that new values are added to the end of the list. The `ArrayList` class also provides an overloaded version of the `add` method for adding a value at a particular index in the list. It preserves the order of the other list elements, shifting values right to make room for the new value. This version of `add` takes two parameters, an index and a value to insert. `ArrayLists` use zero-based indexing, just as arrays and `Strings` do. For example, given the preceding list, consider the effect of inserting a value at index 1:

```
list.add(1, "U2");
System.out.println("now list = " + list);
```

The call on `add` instructs the computer to insert the new `String` at index 1. That means that the old value at index 1 and everything that comes after it gets shifted to the right. So, the following output is produced:

```
now list = [Tool, U2, Phish, Pink Floyd]
```

The `ArrayList` also has a method for removing a value at a particular index. The `remove` method also preserves the order of the list by shifting values left to fill in any gap. For example, consider what happens to the previous list if we remove the value at position 0 and then remove the value at position 1:

```
System.out.println("before remove list = " + list);
list.remove(0);
list.remove(1);
System.out.println("after remove list = " + list);
```

This code produces the following output:

```
before remove list = [Tool, U2, Phish, Pink Floyd]
after remove list = [U2, Pink Floyd]
```

This result is a little surprising. We asked the list to remove the value at position 0 and then to remove the value at position 1. You might imagine that this would get rid of the `Strings` `"Tool"` and `"U2"`, since they were at positions 0 and 1, respectively, before this code was executed. However, an `ArrayList` is a dynamic structure whose values can move around and shift into new positions in response to your commands. This is demonstrated more clearly if we include a second `println` statement:

```
System.out.println("before remove list = " + list);
list.remove(0);
System.out.println("after 1st remove list = " + list);
list.remove(1);
System.out.println("after 2nd remove list = " + list);
```

This code produces the following output:

```
before remove list = [Tool, U2, Phish, Pink Floyd]
after 1st remove list = [U2, Phish, Pink Floyd]
after 2nd remove list = [U2, Pink Floyd]
```

The first call on `remove` removes the `String` `"Tool"` because it's the value currently in position 0. But once that value has been removed, everything else shifts over: The `String` `"U2"` moves to the front (to position 0), the `String` `"Phish"` shifts into position 1, and the `String` `"Pink Floyd"` moves into position 2. So, when the second call on `remove` is performed, Java removes `"Phish"` from the list because it is the value that is in position 1 at that point in time.

If you want to find out how many elements are in an `ArrayList`, you can call its `size` method. If you want to obtain an individual item from the list, you can call its `get` method, passing it a specific index. For example, the following loop would add up the lengths of the `Strings` in an `ArrayList<String>`:

```
int sum = 0;
for (int i = 0; i < list.size(); i++) {
    String s = list.get(i);
    sum += s.length();
}
System.out.println("Total of lengths = " + sum);
```

This loop looks similar to the kind of loop you would use to access the various elements of an array, but instead of asking for `list.length` as you would for an array, you ask for `list.size()`, and instead of asking for `list[i]` as you would with an array, you ask for `list.get(i)`.

Calling `add` and `remove` can be expensive because of the shifting of values. To replace a value you can use a method called `set`, which takes an index and a value and replaces the value at the given index with the given value without doing any shifting. For example, you could replace the value at the front of the sample list by saying:

```
list.set(0, "The Flaming Lips");
```

As noted earlier, when you construct an `ArrayList` it will initially be empty. After you have added values to a list, you can remove them one at a time. But what if you

TABLE 10.1   Basic **ArrayList** Methods

Method	Description	**ArrayList<String> example**
add(value)	adds the given value at the end of the list	list.add("end");
add(index, value)	adds the given value at the given index, shifting subsequent values right	list.add(1, "middle");
clear()	removes all elements from the list	list.clear();
get(index)	gets the value at the given index	list.get(1)
remove(index)	removes the value at the given index, shifting subsequent values left	list.remove(1);
set(index, value)	replaces the value at the given index with the given value	list.set(2, "hello");
size()	returns the current number of elements in the list	list.size()

want to remove all of the values from the list? In that case, you can call the clear method of the ArrayList.

Table 10.1 summarizes the ArrayList operations introduced in this section. A more complete list can be found in the online Java documentation.

ArrayList Searching Methods

Once you have built up an ArrayList, you might be interested in searching for a specific value in the list. The ArrayList class provides several mechanisms for doing so. If you just want to know whether or not something is in the list, you can call the contains method, which returns a Boolean value. For example, suppose you have an input file of names that has some duplicates, and you want to get rid of the duplicates. The file might look like this:

```
Maria Derek Erica
Livia Jack Anita
Kendall Maria Livia Derek
Jamie Jack
Erica
```

You can construct an ArrayList<String> to hold these names and use the contains method to avoid adding any duplicates:

```
// removes duplicates from a list
Scanner input = new Scanner(new File("names.txt"));
ArrayList<String> list = new ArrayList<String>();
while (input.hasNext()) {
    String name = input.next();
```

```
    if (!list.contains(name)) {
        list.add(name);
    }
}
System.out.println("list = " + list);
```

Given the sample input file, this code produces the following output:

```
list = [Maria, Derek, Erica, Livia, Jack, Anita, Kendall, Jamie]
```

Notice that only 8 of the original 13 names appear in this list, because the various duplicates have been eliminated.

Sometimes it is not enough to know that a value appears in the list. You may want to know exactly where it occurs. For example, suppose you want to write a method to replace the first occurrence of one word in an `ArrayList<String>` with another word. You can call the `set` method to replace the value, but you have to know where it appears in the list. You can find out the location of a value in the list by calling the `indexOf` method.

The `indexOf` method takes a value to search for and returns the index of the first occurrence of the value in the list. If it doesn't find the value, it returns –1. So, you could write the `replace` method as follows:

```
public static void replace(ArrayList<String> list,
                           String target, String replacement) {
    int index = list.indexOf(target);
    if (index >= 0) {
        list.set(index, replacement);
    }
}
```

Notice that the return type of this method is `void`, even though it changes the contents of an `ArrayList` object. Some novices think that you have to return the changed `ArrayList`, but the method doesn't actually create a new `ArrayList`; it merely changes the contents of the list. As you've seen with arrays and other objects, a parameter is all you need to be able to change the current state of an object.

You can test the method with the following code:

```
ArrayList<String> list = new ArrayList<String>();
list.add("to");
list.add("be");
list.add("or");
list.add("not");
list.add("to");
list.add("be");
System.out.println("initial list = " + list);
replace(list, "be", "beep");
System.out.println("final list = " + list);
```

This code produces the following output:

```
initial list = [to, be, or, not, to, be]
final list = [to, beep, or, not, to, be]
```

TABLE 10.2   ArrayList Searching Methods

Method	Description	ArrayList<String> example
contains(value)	returns true if the given value appears in the list	list.contains("hello")
indexOf(value)	returns the index of the first occurrence of the given value in the list (–1 if not found)	list.indexOf("world")
lastIndexOf(value)	returns the index of the last occurrence of the given value in the list (–1 if not found)	list.lastIndexOf("hello")

There is also a variation of indexOf known as lastIndexOf. As its name implies, this method returns the index of the last occurrence of a value. There are many situations where you might be more interested in the last occurrence rather than the first occurrence. For example, if a bank finds a broken automated teller machine, it might want to find out the name and account number of the last customer to use that machine. Table 10.2 summarizes the ArrayList searching methods.

All of the ArrayList searching methods call the equals method for comparing values. The method names are fairly standard and appear elsewhere in the Java class libraries. For example, the String class also has methods called indexOf and lastIndexOf that allow you to search for the position of a character or substring inside a string.

A Complete ArrayList Program

Before we go further, let's look at a complete ArrayList program. Search engines like Google use a list of what are called *stop words* that are ignored when users make queries. The idea is that certain words like "a" and "the" appear so often that they aren't worth indexing. Google won't disclose the exact list of words used, although a few examples are listed on the web site and other people have speculated about what they think is on the list.

Google's full list of stop words is believed to have at least 35 entries, but we'll settle for 15 of the most obvious choices. To explore how removing stop words can affect a text, our program will read a file called speech.txt that contains the first part of Hamlet's famous speech:

```
To be or not to be - that is the question:
Whether 'tis nobler in the mind to suffer
The slings and arrows of outrageous fortune
Or to take arms against a sea of troubles,
And by opposing end them.
```

The program constructs a list of stop words and then reads the file word by word, printing every word that is not a stop word. To avoid issues of case, the stop words are all in lowercase and the call on contains is passed a lowercase version of each word from the input file. Here is the complete program:

```
1    // This program constructs a list of stop words and echos
2    // Hamlet's famous speech with the stop words removed.
3
4    import java.util.*;
5    import java.io.*;
6
7    public class StopWords {
8        public static void main(String[] args)
9                throws FileNotFoundException {
10           // build the list of stop words
11           ArrayList<String> stopWords = new ArrayList<String>();
12           stopWords.add("a");
13           stopWords.add("be");
14           stopWords.add("by");
15           stopWords.add("how");
16           stopWords.add("in");
17           stopWords.add("is");
18           stopWords.add("it");
19           stopWords.add("of");
20           stopWords.add("on");
21           stopWords.add("or");
22           stopWords.add("that");
23           stopWords.add("the");
24           stopWords.add("this");
25           stopWords.add("to");
26           stopWords.add("why");
27
28           // process the file, printing all but stop words
29           Scanner input = new Scanner(new File("speech.txt"));
30           while (input.hasNext()) {
31               String next = input.next();
32               if (!stopWords.contains(next.toLowerCase())) {
33                   System.out.print(next + " ");
34               }
35           }
36       }
37   }
```

It produces the following output:

```
not - question: Whether 'tis nobler mind suffer slings and
arrows outrageous fortune take arms against sea troubles,
And opposing end them.
```

This output represents the search view of the original text (the core set of words that will be used by a search engine).

Adding To and Removing From an `ArrayList`

In this section we will explore some of the issues that come up when you dynamically add values to or remove values from the middle of an `ArrayList`. The results are often surprising, so it is worth exploring the common pitfalls.

Consider the following code, which creates an `ArrayList` and stores several words in it:

```
ArrayList<String> words = new ArrayList<String>();
words.add("four");
words.add("score");
words.add("and");
words.add("seven");
words.add("years");
words.add("ago");
System.out.println("words = " + words);
```

This code produces the following output:

```
words = [four, score, and, seven, years, ago]
```

We'll explore the problem of inserting a tilde ("~") in front of each word, doubling the size of the list. Inserting tildes isn't the most exciting operation you can imagine doing with a list, but we want to keep things simple so we can focus on the programming issues, and you'll find that you often want to perform operations like this. For example, in Google, if you put a tilde in front of a search term it does a different search, including synonyms of the word. Searching for "~four ~score" yields more than 10 times the results of searching for just "four score."

In our case we want to keep the tildes separate from the words themselves, so we want to insert a new `String` containing just a tilde in front of each word in the list. Here is a first attempt that makes sense intuitively but doesn't work:

```
// doesn't work properly
for (int i = 0; i < words.size(); i++) {
    words.add(i, "~");
}
System.out.println("after loop words = " + words);
```

This `for` loop is a slight variation of the standard array-traversal loop. It has an index variable `i` whose value starts at `0` and goes up by one each time. In this case it is inserting a tilde at position `i` each time through the loop. The problem is that the loop never terminates (if you're patient enough, you will find that the program does eventually terminate with an "out of memory" error).

The loop fails to terminate because of the dynamic nature of the `ArrayList` structure. Let's think about this carefully to see what's happening. Initially we have this list, with the `String` "four" in position 0:

```
[four, score, and, seven, years, ago]
```

The first time through the loop, we insert a tilde at position 0. To make room for the tilde at position 0, the `ArrayList` has to shift all of the other values one to the right. As a result, the `String` "four" ends up in position 1:

```
[~, four, score, and, seven, years, ago]
```

Then we come around the `for` loop, increment `i` to be 1, and insert a tilde at position 1. But because the word "four" is currently at position 1, this second tilde also goes in front of the word "four", shifting it into position 2:

```
[~, ~, four, score, and, seven, years, ago]
```

We then go around the loop again, incrementing i to be 2 and inserting a tilde at that position, which is once again in front of the word "four":

```
[~, ~, ~, four, score, and, seven, years, ago]
```

This continues indefinitely, because we keep inserting tildes in front of the first word in the list. The for loop test compares i to the size of the list, but because the list is growing, the size keeps going up. So, this process continues until all available memory is exhausted.

To fix this loop, we have to take into account that inserting a tilde at position i is going to shift everything one to the right. So, on the next iteration of the loop, we will want to deal with the position two to the right, not the position one to the right. We can fix the code simply by changing the update part of the for loop to add 2 to i instead of adding 1 to i:

```
for (int i = 0; i < words.size(); i += 2) {
    words.add(i, "~");
}
System.out.println("after loop words = " + words);
```

When we execute this version of the code, we get the following output:

```
after loop words = [~, four, ~, score, ~, and, ~, seven, ~,
years, ~, ago]
```

As another example, let's consider what code we would need to write to undo this operation. We want to write code that will remove every other value from the list, starting with the first value—in other words, the values that are currently at indexes 0, 2, 4, 6, 8, and 10. That might lead us to write code like the following:

```
// doesn't work properly
for (int i = 0; i < words.size(); i += 2) {
    words.remove(i);
}
System.out.println("after second loop words = " + words);
```

Looking at the loop, you can see that i starts at 0 and goes up by 2 each time, which means it produces a sequence of even values (0, 2, 4, and so on). That would seem to be right, given that the values to be removed are at those indexes. But this code doesn't work. It produces the following output:

```
after second loop words = [four, ~, ~, and, seven, ~, ~, ago]
```

Again, the problem comes from the fact that in the ArrayList values are shifted dynamically from one location to another. The first tilde we want to remove is at index 0:

```
[~, four, ~, score, ~, and, ~, seven, ~, years, ~, ago]
```

But once we remove the tilde at position 0, everything is shifted one to the left. The second tilde moves into index 1:

```
[four, ~, score, ~, and, ~, seven, ~, years, ~, ago]
```

so the second remove should be at index 1, not index 2. And once we perform that second remove, the third tilde will be in index 2:

```
[four, score, ~, and, ~, seven, ~, years, ~, ago]
```

So, in this case, we don't want to increment i by 2 each time through the loop. Here, the simple loop that increments by 1 is the right choice:

```
for (int i = 0; i < words.size(); i++) {
    words.remove(i);
}
System.out.println("after second loop words = " + words);
```

After executing this code, we obtain the following output:

```
after second loop words = [four, score, and, seven, years, ago]
```

Putting all of these pieces together gives us the following complete program:

```
 1  // Builds up a list of words, adds tildes, and removes them.
 2
 3  import java.util.*;
 4
 5  public class TildeFun {
 6      public static void main(String[] args) {
 7          // construct and fill up ArrayList
 8          ArrayList<String> words = new ArrayList<String>();
 9          words.add("four");
10          words.add("score");
11          words.add("and");
12          words.add("seven");
13          words.add("years");
14          words.add("ago");
15          System.out.println("words = " + words);
16
17          // insert one tilde in front of each word
18          for (int i = 0; i < words.size(); i += 2) {
19              words.add(i, "~");
20          }
21          System.out.println("after loop words = " + words);
22
23          // remove tildes
24          for (int i = 0; i < words.size(); i++) {
25              words.remove(i);
26          }
27          System.out.println("after second loop words = "
28                             + words);
29      }
30  }
```

If we want to write the loops in a more intuitive manner, we can run them backwards. The loops we have written go from left to right, from the beginning of the list to the end of the list. We could instead go from right to left, from the end of the list to the beginning of the list. By going backwards, we ensure that any changes we are making occur in parts of the list that we have already visited.

For example, we found that this loop did not work properly even though it seemed like the intuitive approach:

```
// doesn't work properly
for (int i = 0; i < words.size(); i++) {
    words.add(i, "~");
}
```

But if we turn this loop around and have it go backwards rather than going forwards, it does work properly:

```
// works properly because loop goes backwards
for (int i = words.size() - 1; i >= 0; i--) {
    words.add(i, "~");
}
```

The problem we had with the original code was that we were inserting a value into the list and then moving our index variable onto that spot in the list. If instead we work backwards, the changes that we make affect only those parts of the list that we have already processed.

Similarly, we wanted to write the second loop this way:

```
// doesn't work properly
for (int i = 0; i < words.size(); i += 2) {
    words.remove(i);
}
```

Again, the problem was that we were changing a part of the list that we were about to process. We can keep the overall structure intact by running the loop backwards:

```
// works properly because loop goes backwards
for (int i = words.size() - 2; i >= 0; i -= 2) {
    words.remove(i);
}
```

Using the For-Each Loop with ArrayLists

You saw in Chapter 7 that you can use a for-each loop to iterate over the elements of an array. You can do the same with an `ArrayList`. For example, earlier we mentioned that the following code could be used to add up the lengths of the `Strings` stored in an `ArrayList<String>` called `list`:

```
int sum = 0;
for (int i = 0; i < list.size(); i++) {
    String s = list.get(i);
    sum += s.length();
}
System.out.println("Total of lengths = " + sum);
```

We can simplify this code with a for-each loop. Remember that its syntax is as follows:

```
for (<type> <name> : <structure>) {
    <statement>;
    <statement>;
    . . .
    <statement>;
}
```

Thus, the preceding loop can be rewritten as follows:

```
int sum = 0;
for (String s : list) {
    sum += s.length();
}
System.out.println("Total of lengths = " + sum);
```

You can think of this loop as saying, "For each `String` s contained in list . . . ."

Because the for-each loop has such a simple syntax, you should use it whenever you find yourself wanting to process each value stored in a list sequentially. You will find, however, that the for-each loop is not appropriate for more complex list problems. For example, there is no simple way to skip around in a list using a for-each loop. You must process the values in sequence from first to last. Also, you cannot modify the list while you are iterating over it.

Consider, for example, the following sample code:

```
// this doesn't work
for (String s : words) {
    System.out.println(s);
    words.remove(0);
}
```

This code prints each `String` from the list and then attempts to remove the value at the front of the list. When you execute this code, the program halts with a `ConcurrentModificationException`. Java is letting you know that you are not allowed to iterate over the list and to modify the list at the same time (concurrently). Because of this limitation, neither of the problems discussed in the previous section could be solved using a for-each loop.

Wrapper Classes

So far, all of the `ArrayList` examples we have looked at have involved `ArrayLists` of `String` objects. What if you wanted to form a list of integers? Given that `ArrayList<E>` is a generic class, you'd think that Java would allow you to define an `ArrayList<int>`, but that is not the case. The `E` in `ArrayList<E>` can be filled in with any object or reference type (i.e., the name of a class). The primitive types (e.g., `int`, `double`, `char`, and `boolean`), cannot be used as type parameters for an `ArrayList`.

Instead, Java defines a series of *wrapper classes* that allow you to store primitive data as objects.

Wrapper Class

A class that "wraps" primitive data as an object.

To understand the role of a wrapper class, think about why we so often put candy in a wrapper. Pieces of candy can be sticky and inconvenient to handle directly, so we put them inside wrappers that make handling them more convenient. When we want the actual candy, we open up the wrapper to get the candy out. The Java wrapper classes fill a similar role.

Consider, for example, simple integers. They are of type `int`, which is a primitive type. Primitive types are not objects, which means that we can't use values of type `int` in an object context. To allow this, we must wrap up each `int` into an object of type `Integer`. `Integer` objects are very simple. They have just one field: an `int` value. When we construct an `Integer`, we pass an `int` value to be wrapped; when we want to get the `int` back, we call a method called `intValue` that returns the `int`.

To understand the distinction, consider the following variable declarations:

```
int x = 38;
Integer y = new Integer(38);
```

This code leads to the following situation in memory:

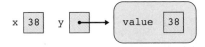

Primitive data is stored directly (the variable x stores the actual value 38), while objects are stored as references (the variable y stores a reference to an object that contains 38).

If we later want to get the 38 out of the object (to unwrap it and remove the candy inside), we call the method `intValue`:

```
int number = y.intValue();
```

The wrapper classes are of particular interest for this chapter because if you want to have an `ArrayList<E>`, the E needs to be a reference type. You can't form an `ArrayList<int>`, but you can form an `ArrayList<Integer>`. For example, you can write code like the following that puts several integer values into a list and adds them up:

```
ArrayList<Integer> list = new ArrayList<Integer>();
list.add(13);
list.add(47);
list.add(15);
list.add(9);
int sum = 0;
for (int n : list) {
    sum += n;
}
System.out.println("list = " + list);
System.out.println("sum = " + sum);
```

This code produces the following output:

```
list = [13, 47, 15, 9]
sum = 84
```

The code takes advantage of a mechanism that Java provides for simplifying code that involves the use of wrapper classes: For example, Java will convert between `Integer` values and `int` values for you when your intent seems clear. Given the declaration of the variable `list` as an `ArrayList<Integer>`, Java would normally expect you to add values of type `Integer` to the list. But in the preceding code you were adding simple `int` values, as in:

```
list.add(13);
```

In this line of code, Java sees that you are adding an `int` to a structure that is expecting an `Integer`. Because Java knows the relationship between `int` and `Integer` (that each `Integer` is simply an `int` wrapped up as an object), it will automatically convert the `int` value into a corresponding `Integer` object. This process is known as *boxing*.

> **Boxing**
>
> An automatic conversion from primitive data to a wrapped object of the appropriate type (e.g., an `int` boxed to form an `Integer`).

Similarly, you don't have to do anything special to unwrap an `Integer` to get the `int` inside. You could write code like the following:

```
int product = list.get(0) * list.get(1);
```

This code multiplies two values from the `ArrayList<Integer>` and stores the result in a variable of type `int`. The calls on `get` will return an `Integer` object, so normally these values would be incompatible. However, because Java knows about the relationship between `int` and `Integer` it will unwrap the `Integer` objects for you and give you the `int` values stored inside. This process is known as *unboxing*.

> **Unboxing**
>
> An automatic conversion from a wrapped object to its corresponding primitive data (e.g., an `Integer` unboxed to yield an `int`).

Notice that you can write a for-each loop to use a variable of type `int` even though the `ArrayList` stores values of type `Integer`. Java will unbox the objects and perform the appropriate conversions for you.

Because of boxing and unboxing, you will find that the only place you generally need to use the wrapper class is in defining a type like `ArrayList<Integer>`. You can't actually define it to be of type `ArrayList<int>`, but even though it is of type `ArrayList<Integer>` you can manipulate it as if it is of type `ArrayList<int>`.

Table 10.3 lists the major primitive types and their corresponding wrapper classes.

TABLE 10.3 Common Wrapper Classes

Primitive type	Wrapper class
int	Integer
double	Double
char	Character
boolean	Boolean

10.2 The Comparable Interface

There is a method that can be used to sort an `ArrayList` called `Collections.sort`. It is part of the `java.util` package. The following short program demonstrates how to use `Collections.sort`:

```
1   // Constructs an ArrayList of Strings and sorts it.
2
3   import java.util.*;
4
5   public class SortExample {
6       public static void main(String[] args) {
7           ArrayList<String> words = new ArrayList<String>();
8           words.add("four");
9           words.add("score");
10          words.add("and");
11          words.add("seven");
12          words.add("years");
13          words.add("ago");
14
15          // show list before and after sorting
16          System.out.println("before sort, words = " + words);
17          Collections.sort(words);
18          System.out.println("after sort, words = " + words);
19      }
20  }
```

This program produces the following output:

```
before sort, words = [four, score, and, seven, years, ago]
after sort, words = [ago, and, four, score, seven, years]
```

If you try to do something similar with an `ArrayList<Point>`, you will find that the program does not compile. Why can you sort a list of `String` objects but not a list of `Point` objects? The answer is that the `String` class implements the `Comparable` interface, while the `Point` class does not. In this section we will explore the details of the `Comparable` interface and explain how to write classes that implement it.

Did You Know?

Controversy over Boxing and Unboxing

Not all software developers are happy with Sun's decision to add boxing and unboxing to the Java language. The ability to manipulate an `ArrayList<Integer>` almost as if it were an `ArrayList<int>` can simplify code, and everyone agrees that simplification is good. The disagreement comes from the fact that it is *almost* like an `ArrayList<int>`. Some argue that "almost" isn't good enough. Because it comes close, programmers are likely to use it and eventually come to count on it. That can prove disastrous when "almost" isn't "always."

For example, suppose someone told you that you could use a device that is almost like a potholder to pick up hot objects. In most cases, it will protect your hand from heat. So you start using it, and while you might be nervous at first, you soon find that it seems to work just fine. And then one day you pick up a different object, and you get burned. You can think of similar scenarios with aircraft landing gear that almost works or vests that are almost bulletproof.

For a programming example, consider the following code:

```java
int n = 420;
ArrayList<Integer> list = new ArrayList<Integer>();
list.add(n);
list.add(n);
if (list.get(0) == list.get(1)) {
    System.out.println("equal");
} else {
    System.out.println("unequal");
}
```

It's difficult to know exactly what this code will do. If you think of the `ArrayList<Integer>` as being "almost" like an `ArrayList<int>`, you'd probably be inclined to think that the code would print the message that the two values are equal. In fact, there is no guarantee as to what it will do. In the current release of Java, it prints the message "unequal."

Remember that testing for object equality is not as simple as testing for equality of primitive data. Two `Strings` might store the same text but not be the same object, which is why we call the `equals` method to compare `Strings`. The same applies here: The two `list` elements might store the same `int` but not be the same object. The code prints "unequal" in the current release of Java because the program creates two different `Integer` objects that each store the value `420`. However, to add to the confusion, if we change the value from `420` to `42` the program will print that the two values are equal.

The Java Language Specification guarantees that this code will work for any value of n between −128 and 127, but it provides no guarantee as to how the code will behave for other values of n. For those other values, it could print either message, and this might change from one implementation of Java to another. It might be that in the next release of Java, the code will print "equal" for 420 but not for a value like 420000.

Some have argued that because boxing and unboxing cover up what is happening underneath, that it is better not to use them at all. Boxing and unboxing don't necessarily simplify anything if they work only "sometimes," because you have to be able to understand the cases where they don't work.

Natural Ordering and compareTo

We are all familiar with many kinds of data that can be sorted. For example, we are used to putting numbers into order from lowest to highest or alphabetizing lists of names. We describe types that can be sorted as having a *natural ordering* of values. To have such an ordering of values, a type needs a well-defined *comparison function* that indicates the relationship between any pair of values.

> **Comparison Function**
> A well-defined procedure for deciding, given a pair of values, the relative order of the two values (less than, equal, or greater than).

> **Natural Ordering**
> The order imposed on a type by its comparison function.

Not all types have natural orderings because not all types have comparison functions. For example, in this chapter we have been exploring how to construct a variety of ArrayList objects. How would you compare two ArrayList objects to determine whether one is less than another? What would it mean for one ArrayList to be less than another? You might decide to use the lengths of the lists to determine which one is less, but what would you do with two ArrayList objects of equal length that store different values? You wouldn't want to describe them as "equal." There is no obvious way that we could all agree on to order ArrayLists, and therefore there is no comparison function for this type. As a result, we say that the ArrayList type does not have a natural ordering.

Java has a convention for indicating the natural ordering of a type. Any type that has such an ordering should implement the Comparable interface:

```
public interface Comparable<T> {
    public int compareTo(T other);
}
```

This interface provides a second example of a generic type in Java. In the case of `ArrayList`, Sun decided to use the letter "E," which is short for "Element." In the case of `Comparable`, Sun used the letter "T," which is short for "Type."

The `compareTo` method is the comparison function for the type. A boolean return type can't be used because there are three possible answers: less than, equal, or greater than. The convention for `compareTo` is that an object should return:

- A negative number to indicate a less-than relationship
- 0 to indicate equality
- A positive number to indicate a greater-than relationship

Let's look at a few examples to help you understand this better. We have seen that Java has `Integer` objects that serve as wrappers for individual `int` values. We know how to compare `int` values to determine their relative order, so it is not surprising that the `Integer` class implements the `Comparable` interface. Consider the following code:

```
Integer x = 7;
Integer y = 42;
Integer z = 7;
System.out.println(x.compareTo(y));
System.out.println(x.compareTo(z));
System.out.println(y.compareTo(x));
```

This code begins by constructing three `Integer` objects:

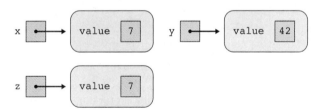

Then it includes a series of `println` statements that report the results of various pairwise comparisons. In the first `println` we ask x to compare itself to y, which involves comparing the `int` value 7 to the `int` value 42. This pair has a less-than relationship (x is less than y), so the method call returns a negative integer. In the second `println` we ask x to compare itself to z, which involves comparing one occurrence of the `int` value 7 with another occurrence of the `int` value 7. This second pair has an equality relationship (x equals z), so the method call returns 0. In the final `println` we ask y to compare itself to x, which involves comparing the `int` value 42 to the `int` value 7. This final pair has a greater-than relationship (y is greater than x), so the method call returns a positive integer.

Here is the actual output of the code:

```
-1
0
1
```

The values −1, 0, and 1 are the standard values to return, but the `compareTo` method is not required to return these specific values. For example, consider a similar piece of code that compares `String` values:

```
String x = "hello";
String y = "world";
String z = "hello";
System.out.println(x.compareTo(y));
System.out.println(x.compareTo(z));
System.out.println(y.compareTo(x));
```

There are similar relationships in this code: x is less than y ("hello" is less than "world"), x is equal to z (the two occurrences of "hello" are equal), and y is greater than x ("world" is greater than "hello"). But the output produced is slightly different from that produced by the `Integer` example:

```
−15
0
15
```

Instead of −1 and 1, we get −15 and 15. You don't really need to know where these numbers come from—the only important fact is whether they are negative or positive—but for those of you who are curious, the −15 and 15 represent the distance between the positions of the characters 'h' and 'w' in type char ('w' appears 15 positions later than 'h').

So while the values −1 and 1 are often returned by a comparison function, that won't always be the case. The important thing to remember is that "less-than" relationships are indicated by a negative number and "greater-than" relationships are indicated by a positive number.

Also keep in mind that the relationship operators that we've been using since Chapter 4 have a different syntax. For example, you've seen that if you have two variables x and y that are of type int or double, you can compare them using operators like < and >, as in:

```
int x = 7;
int y = 42;
if (x < y) {
    System.out.println("x less than y");
}
```

Even though the `String` class implements the `Comparable` interface, you can't use the relational operators to compare `Strings`. The following code will not compile:

```
// illegal--can't compare objects this way
String s1 = "hello";
String s2 = "world";
if (s1 < s2) {
    System.out.println("s1 less than s2");
}
```

Instead, call the `compareTo` method, as in:

```
String s1 = "hello";
String s2 = "world";
if (s1.compareTo(s2) < 0) {
    System.out.println("s1 less than s2");
}
```

You can use a relational operator in this context because the `compareTo` method returns an `int`. Notice that the specific value of −1 isn't used for `compareTo` because you are only guaranteed to get a negative value for a less-than relationship. Table 10.4 summarizes the standard way to compare objects that implement the `Comparable` interface.

Implementing Comparable

Many of the standard Java classes, such as `String`, implement the `Comparable` interface. You can have your own classes implement the interface as well. Implementing the `Comparable` interface will open up a wealth of off-the-shelf programming solutions that are included in the Java class libraries. For example, there are built-in methods for sorting lists and for speeding up searches. Many of these features will be discussed in the next chapter.

As a fairly simple example, let's explore a class that can be used to keep track of a

TABLE 10.4   Comparing Values Summary

Relationship	Primitive data (int, double, etc.)	Objects (Integer, String, etc.)

less than	`if (x < y) {`
	`    . . .`
	`}`
		`if (x.compareTo(y) < 0) {`
		`    . . .`
		`}`

less than or equal	`if (x <= y) {`
	`    . . .`
	`}`
		`if (x.compareTo(y) <= 0) {`
		`    . . .`
		`}`

equal	`if (x == y) {`
	`    . . .`
	`}`
		`if (x.compareTo(y) == 0) {`
		`    . . .`
		`}`

not equal	`if (x != y) {`
	`    . . .`
	`}`
		`if (x.compareTo(y) != 0) {`
		`    . . .`
		`}`

greater than	`if (x > y) {`
	`    . . .`
	`}`
		`if (x.compareTo(y) > 0) {`
		`    . . .`
		`}`

greater than or equal	`if (x >= y) {`
	`    . . .`
	`}`
		`if (x.compareTo(y) >= 0) {`
		`    . . .`
		`}`

calendar date. The idea is to keep track of a particular month and day, but not the year. For example, the United States celebrates its independence on July 4th each year. Similarly, an organization might want a list of its employees' birthdays that doesn't include information about how old they are.

We can implement this as a class with two fields to store the month and day:

```java
public class CalendarDate {
    private int month;
    private int day;

    public CalendarDate(int month, int day) {
        this.month = month;
        this.day = day;
    }

    //other methods
}
```

Remember that to implement an interface, you include an extra notation in the class header. Implementing the `Comparable` interface is a little more challenging because it is a generic interface (`Comparable<T>`). We can't simply say:

```java
// not correct
public class CalendarDate implements Comparable {
    . . .
}
```

We have to replace the `<T>` in `Comparable<T>`. Whenever you implement `Comparable`, you will be comparing pairs of values from the same class. So a class called `CalendarDate` should implement `Comparable<CalendarDate>`. If you look at the header for the `Integer` class, you will find that it implements `Comparable<Integer>`. Likewise, the `String` class implements `Comparable<String>`. So, we need to change the header to the following:

```java
public class CalendarDate implements Comparable<CalendarDate> {
    . . .
}
```

Of course, claiming to implement the interface is not enough. We also have to include appropriate methods. In this case, the `Comparable` interface has just a single method for us to include:

```java
public interface Comparable<T> {
    public int compareTo(T other);
}
```

Because we are using `CalendarDate` in place of `T`, we need to write a `compareTo` method that takes a parameter of type `CalendarDate`:

```java
public int compareTo(CalendarDate other) {
    . . .
}
```

Now we have to figure out how to compare two dates. Each `CalendarDate` object will have fields storing the month and day. With calendars, the month takes precedence over the day. If we want to compare January 31 (1/31) with April 5 (4/5), we don't care that 5 comes before 31, we care more about the fact that January comes before April. So, as a first attempt, we could write the method as follows:

```
// doesn't work
public int compareTo(CalendarDate other) {
    if (month < other.month) {
        return -1;
    } else if (month == other.month) {
        return 0;
    } else { // month > other.month
        return 1;
    }
}
```

There are two problems with this approach. First, while this code uses a nested `if/else` construct to return the standard values of -1, 0, and 1, a simpler option is available. We can simply return the difference between `month` and `other.month`, because it will be negative when `month` is less than `other.month`, it will be 0 when they are equal, and it will be positive when `month` is greater than `other.month`. So, we can simplify the code as follows:

```
// still doesn't quite work
public int compareTo(CalendarDate other) {
    return month - other.month;
}
```

It is a good idea to keep things simple when you can, so this version is preferable. It returns slightly different values than the earlier version, but it satisfies the contract of the `Comparable` interface just as well. However, the code still has a problem.

While it's true that months are more important than days in a calendar, the days can be important. Consider, for example, April 1 (4/1) versus April 5 (4/5). The current version of `compareTo` would subtract the months and return a value of 0, indicating that these two dates are equal. However, the dates aren't equal: April 1 comes before April 5.

The day of the month becomes important only when the months are equal. If the months differ, we can use the months to determine order. Otherwise (when the months are equal), we must use the day of the month to determine order. This is a common ordering principle that you will find in many tasks. We can implement this strategy as follows:

```
public int compareTo(CalendarDate other) {
    if (month != other.month) {
        return month - other.month;
    } else {
        return day - other.day;
    }
}
```

It might seem that this code would never return 0, but it does. Suppose that we have two `CalendarDate` objects that both store the date April 5 (4/5). The months are equal, so we return the difference between the dates. That difference is 0, so we return 0, which correctly indicates that the two dates are equal.

Here is a complete `CalendarDate` class with the `compareTo` method, two accessor methods, and a `toString` method:

```
1   // The CalendarDate class stores information about a single
2   // calendar date (month and day but no year).
3
4   public class CalendarDate implements Comparable<CalendarDate> {
5       private int month;
6       private int day;
7
8       public CalendarDate(int month, int day) {
9           this.month = month;
10          this.day = day;
11      }
12
13      // Compares this calendar date to another date.
14      // Dates are compared by month and then by day.
15      public int compareTo(CalendarDate other) {
16          if (month != other.month) {
17              return month - other.month;
18          } else {
19              return day - other.day;
20          }
21      }
22
23      public int getMonth() {
24          return month;
25      }
26
27      public int getDay() {
28          return day;
29      }
30
31      public String toString() {
32          return month + "/" + day;
33      }
34  }
```

One of the major benefits of implementing the `Comparable` interface is that it gives you access to built-in utilities like `Collections.sort`. As mentioned previously, you can use `Collections.sort` to sort an `ArrayList<String>` but not to sort an `ArrayList<Point>`, because the `Point` class does not implement `Comparable`. The `CalendarDate` class implements the `Comparable` interface, so, as the following short program demonstrates, we can use `Collections.sort` for an `ArrayList<CalendarDate>`:

```
1   // Short program that creates a list of the birthdays of the
2   // first 5 US Presidents and that puts them into sorted order.
3
4   import java.util.*;
5
6   public class CalendarDateTest {
7       public static void main(String[] args) {
```

```
 8            ArrayList<CalendarDate> dates =
 9                    new ArrayList<CalendarDate>();
10            dates.add(new CalendarDate(2, 22));    // Washington
11            dates.add(new CalendarDate(10, 30));   // Adams
12            dates.add(new CalendarDate(4, 13));    // Jefferson
13            dates.add(new CalendarDate(3, 16));    // Madison
14            dates.add(new CalendarDate(4, 28));    // Monroe
15
16            System.out.println("birthdays = " + dates);
17            Collections.sort(dates);
18            System.out.println("birthdays = " + dates);
19        }
20  }
```

This program produces the following output:

```
birthdays = [2/22, 10/30, 4/13, 3/16, 4/28]
birthdays = [2/22, 3/16, 4/13, 4/28, 10/30]
```

Notice that the dates appear in increasing calendar order after the call on `Collections.sort`.

10.3 Case Study: Vocabulary Comparison

In this section we will use `ArrayLists` to solve a complex problem. We will develop a program that will read two different text files and compare their vocabulary. In particular, we will determine the set of words used in each file and compute how much overlap they have. Researchers in the humanities often perform such comparisons to answer questions like, "Did Christopher Marlowe actually write Shakespeare's plays?"

As we have done with most of our case studies, we will develop the program in stages:

1. The first version will read the two files and report the unique words in each. We will use short testing files for this stage.

2. The second version will also compute the overlap between the two files (i.e., the set of words that appear in both). We will continue to use short testing files for this stage.

3. The third version will read from large text files and will include some analysis of the results.

Version 1: Compute Vocabulary

The program we are writing will only be interesting when we compare large input files, but while we are developing the program it will be easier to use short input files so we can easily check whether we are getting the right answer. Using short input files also means that we don't have to worry about execution time. When you use a large input file and the program takes a long time to execute, it is difficult to know whether the program will ever finish executing. If we develop the program with short input files, we'll know that it should never take a long time to execute. So, if we accidentally introduce an infinite loop into our program, we'll know right away that the problem is with our code, not with the fact that we have a lot of data to process.

Did You Know?

Why Not −1, 0, and 1 for `compareTo`?

As discussed earlier, some types like `Integer` return the values −1, 0, and 1 when you call `compareTo`. These are the *canonical* values for `compareTo` to return, because they correspond to a function in mathematics known as the *signum* function (sometimes abbreviated "sgn"). However, other types like `String` do not return the standard values. You might wonder why Sun didn't require that all classes return −1, 0 and 1 when you call `compareTo`.

One answer to this question is that Java doesn't have a convenient ternary type. For any binary decision, we can use `boolean` as the return type. But what type do we turn to if we want to return exactly one of three different values? There is no predefined type with just three values, so it's more honest in a sense to use Sun's rule that any negative number will do and any positive number will do. Suppose that Sun said that `compareTo` should return just −1, 0, and 1. What should happen when someone writes a `compareTo` that returns something else? Ideally any code calling that `compareTo` would throw an exception when it gets an illegal return value, but that would require programmers to write a lot of error-checking code. By saying that all negatives will be interpreted one way, all positives will be interpreted a second way, and 0 will be interpreted a third way, Sun provided a complete definition for all values of type `int` which makes the `compareTo` method easier for programmers to work with.

A second reason for having `compareTo` behave this way is that many comparison tasks can be easily expressed directly in this way. We saw that it simplified our `CalendarDate` code to return either the difference in the months (when the months were unequal) or the difference in the days (when the months were equal). This pattern occurs in many places. For example, the `String` class uses *lexicographic* order (also called "dictionary" or "alphabetic" order). To determine the relationship between two `String`s, you scan through them trying to find the first pair of letters that differ. For example, if you were comparing `"nattering"` and `"nabobs,"` you'd find that the first pair of characters that differ is the third pair (`"nat . . . "` versus `"nab . . . "`). You would then return the difference between the character values (`'t'` − `'b'`). If you don't find such a pair, then you return the difference between the lengths. For example, `"nattering"` will be considered greater than `"nat"` based on length.

The `compareTo` behavior for the `String` class can be described with the following pseudocode:

```
search for a pair of characters in corresponding positions that differ.
if (such a pair exists) {
    return difference between the two characters.
```

(continues)

```
} else {
    return difference between the two lengths.
}
```

Notice that this approach returns 0 in just the right case, when there are no character pairs that differ and when the strings have the same length. Having the flexibility to return any negative integer for "less than" and any positive integer for "greater than" makes it easier to implement this approach.

The final reason not to specify the return values for compareTo is efficiency. By having a less strict rule, Sun allows programmers to write faster compareTo methods. The compareTo method in the String class is one of the most frequently called methods. All sorts of data comparisons are built on String comparisons, and performing a task like sorting thousands of records will lead to thousands of calls on the String class's compareTo method. As a result, it's important that the method runs quickly. We wouldn't want to unnecessarily complicate the code by requiring that it always return −1, 0, or 1.

We'll use the first two stanzas of a popular children's song as our input files. We'll create a file called test1.txt that contains the following text:

```
The wheels on the bus go Round and round
Round and round
Round and round.
The wheels on the bus go Round and round
All through the town.
```

and a file called test2.txt that contains the following text:

```
The wipers on the bus go Swish, swish, swish,
Swish, swish, swish,
Swish, swish, swish.
The wipers on the bus go Swish, swish, swish,
All through the town.
```

We need to open each of these files with a Scanner, so our main method will begin with:

```
Scanner in1 = new Scanner(new File("test1.txt"));
Scanner in2 = new Scanner(new File("test2.txt"));
```

Then we want to compute the unique vocabulary contained in each file. We can store this in an ArrayList<String>. The operation will be the same for each file, so it makes sense to write a single method that we call twice. The method should take the Scanner as a parameter and it should convert that into an ArrayList<String> that contains the vocabulary. So, after opening the files, we can execute the following code:

```
ArrayList<String> list1 = getWords(in1);
ArrayList<String> list2 = getWords(in2);
```

This initial version is meant to be fairly simple, so after we have computed the vocabulary for each file, we can simply report it:

```
System.out.println("list1 = " + list1);
System.out.println("list2 = " + list2);
```

The difficult work for this version of the program reduces to writing the getWords method. It should read all of the words from the Scanner, building up an ArrayList<String> that contains those words and eliminating any duplicates. We can achieve this fairly easily with the ArrayList contains method. For our purposes, we don't care about capitalization, so we can convert each word to lowercase before we add it to the list. We can build up the list using the following code:

```
ArrayList<String> words = new ArrayList<String>();
while (input.hasNext()) {
    String next = input.next().toLowerCase();
    if (!words.contains(next)) {
        words.add(next);
    }
}
```

This code behaves fairly well. When we execute it, we get the following output:

```
list1 = [the, wheels, on, bus, go, round, and, round., all, through, town.]
list2 = [the, wipers, on, bus, go, swish,, swish., all, through, town.]
```

The original input files each have 28 words in them. We have reduced the first file to 11 unique words and the second to 10 unique words. The program is correctly ignoring differences in case, but it isn't ignoring differences in punctuation. For example, it considers "round" and "round." to be different words (one with a period, one without). We will explore how to fix that when we get to version 3.

This approach works, but it is not likely to work fast enough for large text files. The problem is that calling contains becomes increasingly expensive as the word list grows. For example, suppose that you have added a thousand words to the list. If you read a new word that isn't in the list, the contains method will have to examine all 1000 words to figure out that the new word is not there. And even if you read a word that is already in the list, a call on contains will have to examine half of the words on average before it can verify that the word is in the list.

There is another approach that uses more memory but will run faster. Instead of trying to eliminate the duplicates as we are reading words, we can instead just read all of the words directly into an ArrayList. That way we won't make any expensive calls on the contains method. After we have read everything in, we can put the list into sorted order. When we do that, all of the duplicates will appear right next to each other, so we can fairly easily get rid of them.

When we get to Chapter 13 we'll see how to analyze a problem like this more formally to figure out which approach is likely to be faster. Using the techniques discussed in that chapter, you'd discover that the calls on `contains` will turn out to be more expensive than sorting the complete list and then eliminating duplicates from the sorted list.

The bigger issue is the fact that the second approach takes more memory. This is a classic tradeoff often found in computing: We can make programs run faster if we are willing to have them use more memory. Eventually, that could become a problem. In Chapter 11, we'll see yet another way to approach this problem that would work in those situations.

We can rewrite the beginning of the method to store all the words into the `ArrayList`, and then, because we are using an `ArrayList<String>`, we can call `Collections.sort` to put the list into sorted order:

```
while (input.hasNext()) {
    String next = input.next().toLowerCase();
    words.add(next);
}
Collections.sort(words);
```

Once the list has been sorted, duplicates of any words will be grouped together. To eliminate them, we can simply compare adjacent elements and remove any duplicates that we encounter. Here is a pseudocode description of this approach:

```
for (each i) {
    if (value at i equals value at i+1) {
        remove value at i+1.
    }
}
```

While this approach can work, it's also slow. Remember that a call on `remove` requires shifting values. If the list has thousands of words in it, each call on `remove` is likely to be time-consuming.

Instead of removing duplicates from this list, we can build up a new list that contains only the unique words. If we add the words in alphabetical order, each new word will be added to the end of the new list, which is a very fast operation.

In the first approach we were looking for duplicates to remove. In this second approach, we need to look for unique words. The simplest way to do this is to look for transitions between words. For example, if we have 5 occurrences of one word followed by 10 occurrences of another word, most of the pairs of adjacent words will be equal to each other. However, in the middle of those equal pairs, when we make the transition from the first word to the second word, there will be a pair that are not equal. Whenever we see such a transition, we know that we are seeing a new word that should be added to our new list.

Looking for transitions leads to a classic fencepost problem. For example, if there are 10 unique words, there will be 9 transitions. We can solve the fencepost problem by adding the first word before the loop begins. Then we can look for words that are not equal to the words that come before them and add them to the list. Expressed as pseudocode, we get the following:

```
construct a new empty list.
add first word to new list.
for (each i) {
    if (value at i does not equal value at i-1) {
        add value at i.
    }
}
```

This can be converted into actual code fairly directly, but we have to be careful to start i at 1 rather than 0 because in the loop we compare each word to the one that comes before it and the first word has nothing before it. We also have to be careful to call the `ArrayList get` method to obtain individual values and to use the `equals` method to compare `Strings` for equality:

```
ArrayList<String> result = new ArrayList<String>();
result.add(words.get(0));
for (int i = 1; i < words.size(); i++) {
    if (!words.get(i).equals(words.get(i - 1))) {
        result.add(words.get(i));
    }
}
```

There is still one minor problem with this code: If the input file is empty, there won't be a first word to add to the new list. So, we need an extra `if` to make sure that we don't try to add values to the new list if the first list is empty.

Putting all of these changes together, we get the following program:

```
 1  // First version of vocabulary program that reads two files and
 2  // determines the unique words in each.
 3
 4  import java.util.*;
 5  import java.io.*;
 6
 7  public class Vocabulary1 {
 8      public static void main(String[] args)
 9              throws FileNotFoundException {
10          Scanner in1 = new Scanner(new File("test1.txt"));
11          Scanner in2 = new Scanner(new File("test2.txt"));
12
13          ArrayList<String> list1 = getWords(in1);
14          ArrayList<String> list2 = getWords(in2);
15
16          System.out.println("list1 = " + list1);
17          System.out.println("list2 = " + list2);
18      }
19
20      public static ArrayList<String> getWords(Scanner input) {
21          // read all words and sort
22          ArrayList<String> words = new ArrayList<String>();
23          while (input.hasNext()) {
24              String next = input.next().toLowerCase();
25              words.add(next);
26          }
27          Collections.sort(words);
28
```

```
29                // add unique words to new list and return
30                ArrayList<String> result = new ArrayList<String>();
31                if (words.size() > 0) {
32                    result.add(words.get(0));
33                    for (int i = 1; i < words.size(); i++) {
34                        if (!words.get(i).equals(words.get(i - 1))) {
35                            result.add(words.get(i));
36                        }
37                    }
38                }
39                return result;
40        }
41   }
```

The program produces the following output:

```
list1 = [all, and, bus, go, on, round, round., the, through, town., wheels]
list2 = [all, bus, go, on, swish,, swish., the, through, town., wipers]
```

Version 2: Compute Overlap

The first version of the program produces two sorted `ArrayLists` containing sets of unique words. For the second version, we want to compute the overlap between the two lists of words and report it. This operation will be complex enough that it deserves to be in its own method. So, we can add the following line of code to the `main` method right after the two word lists are constructed:

```
ArrayList<String> common = getOverlap(list1, list2);
```

The primary task for the second version of our program is to implement the `getOverlap` method. Look closely at the two lists of words produced by the first version:

```
list1 = [all, and, bus, go, on, round, round., the, through, town., wheels]
list2 = [all, bus, go, on, swish,, swish., the, through, town., wipers]
```

People are pretty good at finding matches, so you can probably see exactly what words overlap. Both lists begin with `"all"`, so that is part of the overlap. Skipping past the word `"and"` in the first list, we find the next match is for the word `"bus"`. Then we have another two matches with the words `"go"` and `"on"`. Next there are a few words in a row in both lists that don't match, followed eventually by the match with the word `"the"`, two more matches, and a final unique word in each list. So, the complete set of matches is as follows:

```
list1 = [all, and, bus, go, on, round, round., the, through, town., wheels]
```

```
list2 = [all, bus, go, on, swish,, swish., the, through, town., wipers]
```

We want to design an algorithm that parallels what we do when we look for such matches. Imagine putting a finger from your left hand on the first word in the first list and putting a finger from your right hand on the first word in the second list to keep track of where you are in each list. We will compare the words you are pointing at, and depending upon how they compare, we will move one or both fingers forward.

We start with the left finger on the word "all" in the first list and the right finger on the word "all" in the second list.

```
list1 = [all, and, bus, go, on, round, round., the, through, town., wheels]
          ▲
list2 = [all, bus, go, on, swish,, swish., the, through, town., wipers]
          ▲
```

The words match, so we'll add that word to the overlap and move both fingers forward:

```
list1 = [all, and, bus, go, on, round, round., the, through, town., wheels]
               ▲
list2 = [all, bus, go, on, swish,, swish., the, through, town., wipers]
               ▲
```

These words don't match. So what do you do? It turns out that the word "bus" in list2 is going to match a word in list1. So how do you know to move the left finger forward? We are pointing at the word "and" from the first list and the word "bus" from the second list. Because the lists are sorted and because the word "and" comes before the word "bus", we know there can't be a match for the word "and" in the second list. Every word that comes after "bus" in the second list will be alphabetically greater than "bus", so the word "and" can't be there. Thus, we can move the left finger forward to skip the word "and":

```
list1 = [all, and, bus, go, on, round, round., the, through, town., wheels]
                    ▲
list2 = [all, bus, go, on, swish,, swish., the, through, town., wipers]
               ▲
```

This gets us to the second match, and the algorithm proceeds. In general, we will find ourselves in one of three situations when we compare the current word in list1 with the current word in list2:

- The words might be equal, in which case we've found a match that should be included in the overlap and we should advance to the next word in each list.
- The word from the first list might be alphabetically less than the word from the second list, in which case we can skip it because it can't match anything in the second list.
- The word from the second list might be alphabetically less than the word from the first list, in which case we can skip it because it can't match anything in the first list.

Thus, the basic approach we want to use can be described with the following pseudocode:

```
if (word from list1 equals word from list2) {
    record match.
```

```
        skip past word in each list.
} else if (word from list1 < word from list2) {
        skip past word in list1.
} else {
        skip past word in list2.
}
```

We can refine this pseudocode by introducing two index variables and putting this code inside of a loop:

```
i1 = 0.
i2 = 0.
while (more values to compare) {
    if (list1.get(i1) equals list2.get(i2)) {
        record match.
        increment i1.
        increment i2.
    } else if (list.get(i1) less than list.get(i2)) {
        increment i1.
    } else {
        increment i2.
    }
}
```

This is now fairly close to actual code. First, we have to figure out an appropriate loop test. We start the two index variables at 0 and increment one or both each time through the loop. Eventually we'll run out of values in one or both lists, and when that happens there won't be any more matches to find. So, we want to continue in the while loop as long as the two index variables haven't reached the end of the list. We also have to figure out how to compare the two words. Because the String class implements the Comparable interface, we can use its compareTo method. Finally, we have to construct an ArrayList to store the overlap, and we have to return it after the loop.

Thus, we can turn our pseudocode into the following actual code:

```
ArrayList<String> result = new ArrayList<String>();
int i1 = 0;
int i2 = 0;
while (i1 < list1.size() && i2 < list2.size()) {
    int num = list1.get(i1).compareTo(list2.get(i2));
    if (num == 0) {
        result.add(list1.get(i1));
        i1++;
        i2++;
    } else if (num < 0) {
        i1++;
    } else { // num > 0
        i2++;
    }
}
return result;
```

Turning this into a method and modifying `main` to call this method and to report the overlap, we end up with the following new version of the program:

```
1    // Second version of vocabulary program which reads two files
2    // and reports the overlap between them.
3
4    import java.util.*;
5    import java.io.*;
6
7    public class Vocabulary2 {
8        public static void main(String[] args)
9                throws FileNotFoundException {
10           Scanner in1 = new Scanner(new File("test1.txt"));
11           Scanner in2 = new Scanner(new File("test2.txt"));
12
13           ArrayList<String> list1 = getWords(in1);
14           ArrayList<String> list2 = getWords(in2);
15           ArrayList<String> common = getOverlap(list1, list2);
16
17           System.out.println("list1 = " + list1);
18           System.out.println("list2 = " + list2);
19           System.out.println("overlap = " + common);
20       }
21
22       public static ArrayList<String> getWords(Scanner input) {
23           // read all words and sort
24           ArrayList<String> words = new ArrayList<String>();
25           while (input.hasNext()) {
26               String next = input.next().toLowerCase();
27               words.add(next);
28           }
29           Collections.sort(words);
30
31           // add unique words to new list and return
32           ArrayList<String> result = new ArrayList<String>();
33           if (words.size() > 0) {
34               result.add(words.get(0));
35               for (int i = 1; i < words.size(); i++) {
36                   if (!words.get(i).equals(words.get(i - 1))) {
37                       result.add(words.get(i));
38                   }
39               }
40           }
41           return result;
42       }
43
44       public static ArrayList<String> getOverlap(
45               ArrayList<String> list1, ArrayList<String> list2) {
46           ArrayList<String> result = new ArrayList<String>();
47           int i1 = 0;
48           int i2 = 0;
49           while (i1 < list1.size() && i2 < list2.size()) {
50               int num = list1.get(i1).compareTo(list2.get(i2));
51               if (num == 0) {
52                   result.add(list1.get(i1));
```

```
53                        i1++;
54                        i2++;
55                 } else if (num < 0) {
56                        i1++;
57                 } else { // num > 0
58                        i2++;
59                 }
60          }
61          return result;
62      }
63  }
```

It produces the following output:

```
list1 = [all, and, bus, go, on, round, round., the, through, town., wheels]
list2 = [all, bus, go, on, swish,, swish., the, through, town., wipers]
overlap = [all, bus, go, on, the, through, town.]
```

Version 3: Complete Program

Our program now correctly builds a vocabulary list for each of two files and computes the overlap between them. The second version of the program printed the three lists of words, but that won't be very convenient for large text files containing thousands of different words. We can instead report overall statistics including the number of words in each list, the number of words of overlap, and the percentage of overlap.

The program also should have at least a brief introduction to explain what it does, and we can write it so that it prompts for file names rather than using hard-coded file names.

This also seems like a good time to think about punctuation. The first two versions allowed words to contain punctuation characters such as commas, periods, and dashes that we wouldn't normally consider part of a word.

We can improve our solution by telling the Scanner what parts of the input file to ignore. Scanner objects have a method called useDelimiter that you can call to tell them what characters to use for breaking the input file into tokens. When you call the method, you pass it what is known as a *regular expression.* Regular expressions are a highly flexible way to describe patterns of characters. There is some documentation about them in the API pages for the class called Pattern.

For our purposes, we want to form a regular expression that will instruct the Scanner to look just at characters that are part of what we consider words. That is, we want the Scanner to look at letters and apostrophes. The following regular expression is a good starting point:

```
[a-zA-Z']
```

This regular expression would be read as, "Any character in the range of a to z or in the range of A to Z or an apostrophe." This is a good description of the kind of characters we want the Scanner to include. But we actually need to tell the Scanner what characters to *ignore,* so we need to indicate that it should use the opposite set of characters. The easy way to do this is by including a caret (∧) in front of the list of legal characters:

```
[∧a-zA-Z']
```

This regular expression would be read as, "Any character other than the characters that are in the range of a to z or in the range of A to Z or an apostrophe." Even this expression isn't quite right, though, because there might be many such characters in a row. For example, there might be several spaces or dashes or other punctuation characters separating two words. We can indicate this by putting a plus after the square brackets to indicate "Any sequence of one or more of these characters":

```
[∧a-zA-Z']+
```

We pass this regular expression as a `String` to a call on `useDelimiter`. We can add this at the beginning of the `getWords` method:

```
public static ArrayList<String> getWords(Scanner input) {
    input.useDelimiter("[∧a-zA-Z']+");
    . . .
}
```

The following is a complete program that incorporates all of these changes and includes more extensive commenting:

```
1   // This program reads two text files and compares the
2   // vocabulary used in each.
3
4   import java.util.*;
5   import java.io.*;
6
7   public class Vocabulary3 {
8       public static void main(String[] args)
9               throws FileNotFoundException {
10          Scanner console = new Scanner(System.in);
11          giveIntro();
12
13          System.out.print("file #1 name? ");
14          Scanner in1 = new Scanner(new File(console.nextLine()));
15          System.out.print("file #2 name? ");
16          Scanner in2 = new Scanner(new File(console.nextLine()));
17          System.out.println();
18
19          ArrayList<String> list1 = getWords(in1);
20          ArrayList<String> list2 = getWords(in2);
21          ArrayList<String> common = getOverlap(list1, list2);
22
23          reportResults(list1, list2, common);
24      }
25
26      // post: reads words from the Scanner, converts them to
27      //       lowercase, returns a sorted list of unique words
28      public static ArrayList<String> getWords(Scanner input) {
```

```
29          // ignore all but alphabetic characters and apostrophes
30          input.useDelimiter("[^a-zA-Z']+");
31          // read all words and sort
32          ArrayList<String> words = new ArrayList<String>();
33          while (input.hasNext()) {
34              String next = input.next().toLowerCase();
35              words.add(next);
36          }
37          Collections.sort(words);
38
39          // add unique words to new list and return
40          ArrayList<String> result = new ArrayList<String>();
41          if (words.size() > 0) {
42              result.add(words.get(0));
43              for (int i = 1; i < words.size(); i++) {
44                  if (!words.get(i).equals(words.get(i - 1))) {
45                      result.add(words.get(i));
46                  }
47              }
48          }
49          return result;
50      }
51
52      // pre : list1 and list2 are sorted and have no duplicates
53      // post: constructs and returns an ArrayList containing
54      //       the words in common betweeen list1 and list2
55      public static ArrayList<String> getOverlap(
56              ArrayList<String> list1, ArrayList<String> list2) {
57          ArrayList<String> result = new ArrayList<String>();
58          int i1 = 0;
59          int i2 = 0;
60          while (i1 < list1.size() && i2 < list2.size()) {
61              int num = list1.get(i1).compareTo(list2.get(i2));
62              if (num == 0) {
63                  result.add(list1.get(i1));
64                  i1++;
65                  i2++;
66              } else if (num < 0) {
67                  i1++;
68              } else { // num > 0
69                  i2++;
70              }
71          }
72          return result;
73      }
74
75      // post: explains program to user
76      public static void giveIntro() {
77          System.out.println("This program compares two files,");
78          System.out.println("reporting the number of words in");
79          System.out.println("common and the percent overlap.");
80          System.out.println();
81      }
82
83      // pre : common contains overlap between list1 and list2
84      // post: reports statistics about lists and their overlap
```

```
85       public static void reportResults(ArrayList<String> list1,
86              ArrayList<String> list2, ArrayList<String> common) {
87           System.out.println("file #1 words = " + list1.size());
88           System.out.println("file #2 words = " + list2.size());
89           System.out.println("common words  = " + common.size());
90
91           double pct1 = 100.0 * common.size() / list1.size();
92           double pct2 = 100.0 * common.size() / list2.size();
93           System.out.println("% of file 1 in overlap =" + pct1);
94           System.out.println("% of file 2 in overlap =" + pct2);
95       }
96   }
```

The following is an execution of the program that compares the texts of Shakespeare's *Hamlet* and *King Lear:*

```
This program compares two files,
reporting the number of words in
common and the percent overlap.

file #1 name? hamlet.txt
file #2 name? lear.txt

file #1 words = 4874
file #2 words = 4281
common words  = 2108
% of file 1 in overlap = 43.24989741485433
% of file 2 in overlap = 49.24083158140621
```

Notice that the two files have about the same number of unique words and that about half of them appear in both files. Here is a second execution that compares the text of Herman Melville's *Moby Dick* to the text of *Hamlet:*

```
This program compares two files,
reporting the number of words in
common and the percent overlap.

file #1 name? moby.txt
file #2 name? hamlet.txt

file #1 words = 17305
file #2 words = 4874
common words  = 3079
% of file 1 in overlap = 17.792545507078877
% of file 2 in overlap = 63.17193270414444
```

In this case, it is obvious that *Moby Dick* has a much larger vocabulary. As a result, only a small fraction of the words from *Moby Dick* appear in *Hamlet.* But a large proportion of the words from *Hamlet* appear in *Moby Dick.* It is well known that Melville admired Shakespeare, so it is not surprising that his novel has such a high overlap with one of Shakespeare's plays.

As we mentioned in Chapter 6, you can obtain classic texts like these from the Project Gutenberg web site at http://www.gutenberg.com.

Chapter Summary

The `ArrayList` class in Java's `java.util` package represents a growable list of objects implemented using an array. You can use an `ArrayList` to store objects in a sequential order. Each element has a zero-based index.

———————

`ArrayList` is a generic class. A generic class is one that accepts a data type as a parameter when created, as in `ArrayList<String>`.

———————

An `ArrayList` maintains its own size for you; elements can be added and removed at any index up to the size of the list. Other `ArrayList` operations include `get`, `set`, `clear`, and `toString`.

———————

`ArrayList`s can be searched using methods named `contains`, `indexOf`, and `lastIndexOf`.

———————

Java's for-each loop can be used to examine each element of an `ArrayList`. The list cannot be modified during the execution of the for-each loop.

———————

When storing primitive values such as `int`s or `double`s into an `ArrayList`, you must declare the list with special wrapper types such as `Integer` and `Double`.

———————

The `Comparable` interface defines a natural ordering for the objects of a class using its method `compareTo`. Objects that implement `Comparable` can be placed into an `ArrayList` and sorted. Many common types (such as `String` and `Integer`) implement `Comparable`, and you can implement `Comparable` in your own classes.

———————

Self-Check Problems

Section 10.1: ArrayLists

1. What is an `ArrayList`? In what cases should you use an `ArrayList` rather than an array?

2. The next five questions refer to the following `String` elements:

   ```
   ["It", "was", "a", "stormy", "night"]
   ```

   Write the code to declare an `ArrayList` containing these elements. What is the size of the list? What is its type?

3. Write code to insert two additional elements, `"dark"` and `"and"`, at the proper places in the list to produce the following `ArrayList` as the result:

   ```
   ["It", "was", "a", "dark", "and", "stormy", "night"]
   ```

4. Write code to change the second element's value to `"IS"`, producing the following `ArrayList` as the result:

   ```
   ["It", "IS", "a", "dark", "and", "stormy", "night"]
   ```

5. Write code to remove from the list any `String`s that contain the letter "a". The following should be the list's contents after your code has run:

   ```
   ["It", "IS", "stormy", "night"]
   ```

Chapter 11

Java Collections Framework

Introduction

The previous chapter explored the `ArrayList` class. An `ArrayList` is one of many ways to store data in Java. In this chapter we'll explore Java's framework of collections, including lists, sets, and maps. We'll see how to use these structures together to manipulate and examine data in many ways to solve programming problems. This chapter will examine a trio of smaller interesting programs as case studies rather than presenting a unified case study at the end of the chapter.

We'll introduce a new type of list called a linked list that stores its data differently from an `ArrayList` but supports the same operations. We'll also discuss collections called sets that don't allow duplicate elements and are good for searching. Another collection type we'll explore is the map, which creates associations between pairs of data values. We'll also delve into the notion of abstract data types as a way to separate the capabilities of a collection from the details of its implementation.

11.1 Lists

The `ArrayList` class from Chapter 10 has several advantages over an array: it keeps track of its size for you, it allows insertion and removal at arbitrary places in the array, and it resizes itself for you if it gets full.

In this section we'll learn about an object called a `LinkedList`, which is similar to an `ArrayList`. We'll also explore some concepts about generalizing collections and discuss a useful object called an iterator that lets you examine the elements of any collection.

Collections

In Chapters 7 and 8 we discussed ways to use arrays and classes to store data. The notion of organizing and structuring data is an important one that helps us solve complex problems. Entities that store and manage data are also called *data structures*. Data structures can be used to implement sophisticated data storage objects called *collections*.

> **Collection**
>
> An object that stores a group of other objects, called its *elements*.

An `ArrayList` is an example of a collection. A collection uses a data structure internally to store its elements, such as an array or a set of objects that refer to each other. For example, an `ArrayList` is implemented using an array as its data structure, and a `TreeSet` (a collection introduced later in this chapter) is implemented using a data structure called a binary search tree.

Collections are categorized by the types of elements they store, the operations they allow you to perform on those elements, and the speed or efficiency of those operations. Some examples of collections are:

- *List:* An ordered collection of elements accessed by integer indexes.
- *Stack:* A collection where the last element added is the first one to be removed.
- *Queue:* A collection where elements are removed in the order in which they were added.
- *Set:* A collection of elements that is guaranteed to contain no duplicates and generally can be searched efficiently.
- *Map:* A collection of (key, value) pairs in which each key is associated with a corresponding value.

Java provides a large group of useful collections that allow you to store, access, search, sort, and manipulate data in a variety of ways. Together, these collections and

TABLE 11.1 Useful Methods of the `Collection` Interface

Method	Description
add(element)	adds the specified element to this collection
addAll(collection)	adds all elements from the given collection to this collection
clear()	removes all elements from this collection
contains(element)	returns true if this collection contains the given element
containsAll(collection)	returns true if this collection contains all elements of the given collection
isEmpty()	returns true if this collection contains no elements
iterator()	returns an object that can be used to traverse the elements of this collection
remove(element)	removes one occurrence of the specified element, if it is contained in this collection
removeAll(collection)	removes all elements of the given collection from this collection
retainAll(collection)	removes all elements not found in the given collection from this collection
size()	returns the number of elements in this collection
toArray()	returns an array containing the elements of this collection

classes are known as the *Java Collections Framework*. This framework is largely contained in the package `java.util`.

The `java.util` package contains an interface called `Collection` that every collection implements. This interface specifies the operations that most collections support. Table 11.1 lists those operations.

The `Collection` interface is extended and implemented by the other interfaces and classes in the Java Collections Framework. Figure 11.1 summarizes the various interfaces and what classes implement them. These classes will be discussed in this chapter.

Now we'll look at a collection called `LinkedList` and compare and contrast it with `ArrayList`.

LinkedList Versus ArrayList

`ArrayList` is a powerful and useful collection, but there are some cases where using an `ArrayList` isn't ideal. For example, suppose we want to write a program to remove each `String` of even length from an `ArrayList` of `Strings`. We can do this using a loop that looks at each element of the list and either removes it if its length is even or advances to the next string if not:

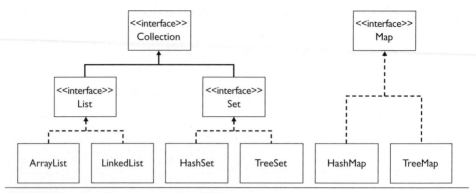

FIGURE 11.1   An abridged view of the Java Collections Framework

```
// Removes all strings of even length from
// the given array list.
public static void removeEvenLength(ArrayList<String> list) {
    int i = 0;
    while (i < list.size()) {
        String element = list.get(i);
        if (element.length() % 2 == 0) {
            list.remove(i);
        } else {
            i++;    // skip to next element
        }
    }
}
```

The preceding code is correct, but it doesn't perform well when the list has a lot of elements. On a relatively modern machine, it can take several minutes to process a list of a million elements. The reason it is so slow is that every time we remove an element from the list, we have to shift all subsequent elements to the left by one. This repeated shifting results in a slow program.

Another case when an ArrayList behaves slowly is when it's used to model a waiting line or queue, where elements (customers) are always added to the end of the list (line) and always removed from the front. As customers arrive, they are added to the end of the list. Customers are removed from the front of the list and processed in turn. Removing an element from the front of a large ArrayList is a slow operation because each other element has to be shifted to the left.

There is another type of collection, called a *linked list,* that can give better performance in problems like these that involve a lot of additions to or removals from the front or middle of a list. A linked list provides the same operations as an array list, such as add, remove, isEmpty, size, and contains. But a linked list stores its elements in a fundamentally different way. Elements of a linked list are stored in small individual containers called *nodes.* The nodes are "linked" together, with each node storing a reference to the next node in the list. The overall linked list object keeps references to the front and back nodes.

> **Linked List**
>
> A collection that stores a list of elements in small object containers called *nodes,* which are linked together.

One way to think of a linked list is as an array list that's been "broken apart," with each element stored in a small box (a node) connected to its neighboring box by an arrow:

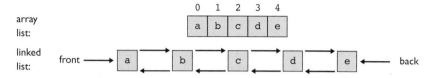

One major advantage of using a linked list is that elements can generally be added at the front of the list quickly, because rather than shifting all the elements in an array, the list just creates a new node object and links it with the others in the list. We don't have to do this ourselves; we simply call methods on the list, which takes care of it for us internally. Figure 11.2 shows what happens inside a linked list when an element is added at the front.

To use a linked list in Java, create an object of type `LinkedList` instead of type `ArrayList`. `LinkedList` objects have the same methods you've used when working with `ArrayLists`:

```
LinkedList <String> words = new LinkedList<String>();
words.add("hello");
words.add("goodbye");
words.add("this");
words.add("that");
```

We could write a version of our `removeEvenLength` method that accepts a `LinkedList<String>` as its parameter rather than an `ArrayList<String>`. However, this change alone won't have much impact on performance. Since the

1. Make a new node to hold the new element.

2. Connect the new node to the other nodes in the list.

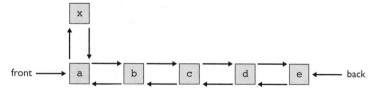

3. Change the front of the list to point to the new node.

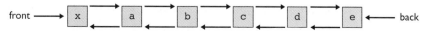

FIGURE 11.2 Adding an element to the front of a linked list

removeEvenLength method examines each element of the list in sequential order, we can make the code more efficient by employing another type of object, called an iterator.

Iterators

As discussed in Chapter 7, arrays provide a nice property called *random access,* meaning that we can efficiently access or modify arbitrary array elements in any order. This is possible because arrays are stored as large contiguous blocks of memory, so the computer can quickly compute the memory location of any of the array's elements. Linked lists, unfortunately, do not provide fast random access. Since a linked list is made up of many small node objects and generally keeps a direct reference only to the front element, it is not possible to quickly access arbitrary elements of the list. A linked list is somewhat like a VHS tape or audio cassette tape in this way; if we wish to access an element, we must "fast-forward" or "rewind" through the list to the proper position.

When you call methods like get, set, add, or remove on a linked list, the code internally creates a temporary reference that begins at the front of the list and traverses the links between nodes until reaching the desired index. The time this takes is dependent on the index used: if you ask for the element at index 5 it will be returned quickly, but if you ask for the element at index 9,000 the loop inside the get method must advance through 9,000 nodes, which will take much longer.

These methods tend to perform slowly on a linked list, especially if you call them many times or call them on a list with many elements. Imagine that after the preceding example call of get(9000) you decided to call get(9001). The linked list doesn't remember its previous position, and it will have to start from the front again and advance 9,001 times. The only case where the methods run quickly is when you pass an index near the front or back of the list.

Earlier, we wrote a method to remove strings of even length from an ArrayList. If we adapted this code to use a LinkedList and made no other modifications we would find that it still runs very slowly on large lists, because it calls the get and remove methods many times:

```java
// performs poorly on a linked list
public static void removeEvenLength(LinkedList<String> list) {
    int i = 0;
    while (i < list.size()) {
        String element = list.get(i);      // slow
        if (element.length() % 2 == 0) {
            list.remove(i);                 // slow
        } else {
            i++;
        }
    }
}
```

However, there's an efficient way to examine every element of a linked list if we want sequential access (i.e., if we want to examine each element in order from the front to the back). To do this, we can use a special object called an *iterator* that keeps track of our current position in the list.

> **Iterator**
>
> An object that allows you to efficiently retrieve the elements of a list in sequential order.

Using an iterator, when we move from one element to the next, we don't have to go back to the beginning at each call and follow the links all the way from the front of the list to the desired index. As we'll see in this chapter, iterators are central to the Java Collections Framework. Every collection provides iterators to access its elements. This means that there's a familiar interface for examining the elements of any collection. An iterator object has the methods listed in Table 11.2.

To get an iterator from most collections, such as an `ArrayList` or a `LinkedList`, you can call the method called `iterator` on the list, which returns an `Iterator` object for that list's elements. (You don't use the new keyword.) Generally, a variable named `list` storing elements of type `E` would use an iterator in the following way:

```
Iterator<E> itr = list.iterator();
while (itr.hasNext()) {
    do something with itr.next().
}
```

The example of removing strings of even length from a collection can be implemented much more efficiently using an iterator:

```
// removes all strings of even length from the given linked list
public static void removeEvenLength(LinkedList<String> list) {
    Iterator<String> i = list.iterator();
    while (i.hasNext()) {
        String element = i.next();
        if (element.length() % 2 == 0) {
            i.remove();
        }
    }
}
```

TABLE 11.2   Methods of Iterator Objects

Method	Description
hasNext()	returns `true` if there are more elements to be examined
next()	returns the next element from the list and advances the position of the iterator by one
remove()	removes the element most recently returned by `next()`

While the original `ArrayList` version took up to several minutes to process a list of one million elements on a modern computer, this new code finishes a million-element list in under one-tenth of a second. It performs so quickly because the iterator retains the current position in the list between getting or removing each element.

Iterators are also used internally by Java's for-each loop. When you use a for-each loop like the following, Java is actually accessing the elements using an iterator under the hood:

```
for (String word : list) {
    System.out.println(word + " " + word.length());
}
```

Common Programming Error

Calling `next` on an Iterator Too Many Times

Iterators can be a bit confusing to new programmers, so you have to be careful to use them correctly. The following code attempts to use an iterator to find and return the longest string in a linked list, but it has a bug:

```
// returns the longest string in the list (does not work!)
public static String longest(LinkedList<String> list) {
    Iterator<String> itr = list.iterator();
    String longest = itr.next(); // initialize to first element

    while (itr.hasNext()) {
        if (itr.next().length() > longest.length()) {
            longest = itr.next();
        }
    }
    return longest;
}
```

The problem with the previous code is that the `next` method is called on the iterator in two places: once when testing its length, and again when trying to store the string as the longest. Each time you call `next`, the iterator advances by one position, so if it's called twice in the loop, you'll skip an element when you find a match. For example, if the list contains the elements ("oh", "hello", "how", "are", "you"), you might see the "hello" and intend to store it, but the second call to `next` would cause you to actually store the following element, "how".

The solution is to save the result of the `itr.next()` call into a variable. The following code would replace the previous `while` loop:

```
// this version of the code is now correct
while (itr.hasNext()) {
    String current = itr.next();
    if (current.length() > longest.length()) {
        longest = current;
    }
}
```

As the compiler processes the for-each loop, it essentially converts it into the following code:

```
Iterator<String> i = list.iterator();
while (i.hasNext()) {
    String word = i.next();
    System.out.println(word + " " + word.length());
}
```

There's a more advanced version of `Iterator` called `ListIterator` that works only on lists. A `ListIterator` provides operations like adding elements, setting element values, and reverse iteration from back to front. Because it is more complex, we won't discuss `ListIterator` in detail in this book.

In summary, the following are some of the major benefits of `ArrayList` and `LinkedList`:

Collection	Strengths
ArrayList	• random access: any element can be accessed quickly
	• adding and removing at the end of the list is fast
LinkedList	• adding and removing at either end of the list is fast
	• fast add/remove during a sequential access with an iterator
	• no need to expand an array when full
	• can be more easily used as a queue

Abstract Data Types (ADTs)

It's no accident that the `LinkedList` collection provides the same methods as the `ArrayList`. They're both considered to be implementations of the same kind of collection: a *list*. At a high level, the most important thing isn't the way the list is implemented internally, but the operations we can perform on it. This set of operations is an example of an *abstract data type,* or ADT.

> **Abstract Data Type (ADT)**
>
> A specification of a type of data and the operations that can be performed on it.

An ADT specifies operations that can be performed on data without specifying exactly how those operations are implemented. Linked lists and array lists are both examples of the list ADT because they both provide the same operations, such as storing data by index, adding and removing data at particular indexes, and so on.

In Java, ADTs are specified by interfaces. Each ADT's operations are specified by the methods of its interface. For example, both `LinkedList` and `ArrayList` implement an interface in the `java.util` package called `List`. The `List` interface declares all the common methods that both types of lists implement.

It's considered a good practice to declare any variables and parameters of a collection type using the appropriate interface type for that ADT rather than the actual class type. For example, the following code declares a `LinkedList` object but stores it in a variable of type `List`:

```
List<Integer> list = new LinkedList<Integer>();
```

Joshua Bloch, one of the authors of the Java Collections Framework, calls this "a strongly recommended programming practice because it gives you the flexibility to change implementations." Note that you cannot create an object of type `List`, but you can use `List` as the type of a variable.

You can also use the interface types for ADTs like `List` when declaring parameters, return types, or fields. Doing so is useful when you're writing a method that accepts a collection as a parameter, because it means that method will be able to operate successfully on any collection that implements that ADT's interface. For example, the following method can accept a `LinkedList<String>` or an `ArrayList<String>` as its actual parameter:

```
// returns the longest string in the given list
// pre: list.size() > 0
public static String longest(List<String> list) {
    Iterator<String> i = list.iterator();
    String result = i.next();
    while (i.hasNext()) {
        String next = i.next();
        if (next.length() > result.length()) {
            result = next;
        }
    }
    return result;
}
```

It works with either type of list and is efficient for both. This flexibility is another benefit of polymorphism (as discussed in Chapter 9).

The `java.util` package has a class called `Collections` that contains several useful methods related to all collections. (Note that this is not the same as the `Collection` interface that all collection classes implement.) The `Collections` class contains static methods that operate on lists. These methods' headers specify parameters of type `List` rather than `LinkedList` or `ArrayList`. The methods perform common tasks on lists, such as sorting, shuffling, and searching. Table 11.3 presents a short list of useful methods from the `Collections` class that operate on lists.

Notice that these methods are static, so they must be called by writing the word `Collections` followed by a dot and the method's name. For example, if you had a `LinkedList` variable called `list` and you wanted to reverse the list's contents, you'd write:

```
Collections.reverse(list);
```

There are several other interfaces representing ADTs in the Collections Framework besides `List`, such as `Queue`, `Set`, and `Map`. We'll explore several of them in this chapter.

TABLE 11.3 Useful Static Methods of the `Collections` Class

Method	Description
`binarySearch(list, value)`	searches a sorted list for a given element value and returns its index
`copy(destinationList, sourceList)`	copies all elements from the source list to the destination list
`fill(list, value)`	replaces every element in the given list with the given value
`max(list)`	returns the element with the highest value
`min(list)`	returns the element with the lowest value
`replaceAll(list, oldValue, newValue)`	replaces all occurrences of the old value with the new value
`reverse(list)`	reverses the order of the elements in the given list
`rotate(list, distance)`	shifts each element to the right by the given number of indexes, moving the final elements to the front
`shuffle(list)`	rearranges the elements into random order
`sort(list)`	rearranges the elements into sorted (nondecreasing) order
`swap(list, index1, index2)`	switches the element values at the given two indexes

LinkedList Case Study: Sieve

Consider the task of finding all prime numbers up to a given maximum. Prime numbers are integers with no factors other than 1 and themselves. The number 2 is defined as the smallest prime number.

To build a list of prime numbers, you could just write a brute-force solution using `for` loops:

```
for (each number from 2 to maximum) {
    if (number is prime) {
        add number to list of prime numbers.
    }
}
```

But you would need a way to figure out whether each number is prime. One option would be to write another `for` loop that tested all lower integers to see whether they were factors of that number. However, there's an easier way.

The *Sieve of Eratosthenes,* named for the Ancient Greek mathematician who devised it, is a classic algorithm for finding prime numbers. The sieve algorithm starts by creating two lists of numbers: one list of numbers to process (some of which may be prime), and another list of numbers known to be prime. Initially, the list of numbers to process can contain every number from 2 to the maximum, while the list of primes will be empty. Here is the initial state of the two lists for a maximum of 25:

```
numbers:  (2, 3, 4, 5, 6, 7, 8, 9, 10, 11, 12, 13, 14, 15, 16, 17, 18, 19,
          20, 21, 22, 23, 24, 25)
primes:   ()
```

The sieve algorithm begins by removing the first element from the numbers list and adding it to the primes list. This number will be prime because of the nature of the algorithm. Next, the algorithm filters out all other elements from the numbers list that are multiples of this prime number. On the first pass of the algorithm, for example, 2 is the number chosen from the numbers list, so 2 is placed into the primes list and all multiples of 2 are removed from the numbers list. The number now at the front of the numbers list is 3. This number will be placed into the primes list during the next pass of the algorithm, and all its multiples that appear in the numbers list will be removed.

The numbers taken from the front of the numbers list are guaranteed to be prime. A non-prime number cannot reach the front of the numbers list because every non-prime number must be a multiple of some prime number, and any such multiples will have been removed by a previous pass of the algorithm.

Here are the states of the two lists after the first three passes of the algorithm:

```
numbers:  (3, 5, 7, 9, 11, 13, 15, 17, 19, 21, 23, 25)
primes:   (2)

numbers:  (5, 7, 11, 13, 17, 19, 23, 25)
primes:   (2, 3)

numbers:  (7, 11, 13, 17, 19, 23)
primes:   (2, 3, 5)
```

Now let's implement the sieve algorithm. We'll use LinkedLists to represent the lists of numbers and primes. This is preferable to using ArrayLists because, as discussed previously, removing elements from the front of an ArrayList is inefficient.

First we'll create an empty list of primes and a list of all numbers up to the given maximum. Since we've discussed ADTs and the List interface, we'll declare our variables as the ADT interface type List<Integer>:

```java
List<Integer> primes = new LinkedList<Integer>();
List<Integer> numbers = new LinkedList<Integer>();
for (int i = 2; i <= max; i++) {
    numbers.add(i);
}
```

Next, we'll process the list of numbers as described previously. We'll use an iterator to make passes over the numbers list and remove elements that are multiples of the front element:

```
while (!numbers.isEmpty()) {
    // remove a prime number from the front of the list
    int front = numbers.remove(0);
    primes.add(front);

    // remove all multiples of this prime number
    Iterator<Integer> itr = numbers.iterator();
    while (itr.hasNext()) {
        int current = itr.next();
        if (current % front == 0) {
            itr.remove();
        }
    }
}
```

The following is the complete program. The most significant addition is a `main` method that prompts the user for the maximum number to examine:

```
 1  // Uses a linked list to implement the Sieve of
 2  // Eratosthenes algorithm for finding prime numbers.
 3
 4  import java.util.*;
 5
 6  public class Sieve {
 7      public static void main(String[] args) {
 8          System.out.println("This program will tell you all prime");
 9          System.out.println("numbers up to a given maximum.");
10          System.out.println();
11
12          Scanner console = new Scanner(System.in);
13          System.out.print("Maximum number? ");
14          int max = console.nextInt();
15
16          List<Integer> primes = sieve(max);
17          System.out.println("Prime numbers up to " + max + ":");
18          System.out.println(primes);
19      }
20
21      // Returns a list of all prime numbers up to given max
22      // using the Sieve of Eratosthenes algorithm.
23      public static List<Integer> sieve(int max) {
24          List<Integer> primes = new LinkedList<Integer>();
25
26          // add all numbers from 2 to max to a list
27          List<Integer> numbers = new LinkedList<Integer>();
28          for (int i = 2; i <= max; i++) {
29              numbers.add(i);
30          }
31
32          while (!numbers.isEmpty()) {
33              // remove a prime number from the front of the list
34              int front = numbers.remove(0);
35              primes.add(front);
36
37              // remove all multiples of this prime number
38              Iterator<Integer> itr = numbers.iterator();
39              while (itr.hasNext()) {
```

```
40                       int current = itr.next();
41                       if (current % front == 0) {
42                           itr.remove();
43                       }
44                   }
45               }
46
47           return primes;
48       }
49   }
```

The following is a sample log of execution of the program:

```
This program will tell you all prime
numbers up to a given maximum.

Maximum number? 50
Prime numbers up to 50:
[2, 3, 5, 7, 11, 13, 17, 19, 23, 29, 31, 37, 41, 43, 47]
```

Our version of the sieve algorithm has been simplified. The real algorithm stops once the front element of the `numbers` list is greater than the square root of the maximum, because any number this large that remains in the list cannot have any multiples remaining in the list. For example, when the maximum is 25, once the item at the front of the `numbers` list exceeds 5, all remaining numbers in the list are known to be prime and can be placed into the `primes` list.

The algorithm can be improved in other ways. For example, the initial list of numbers doesn't actually need to store every integer from 2 through the maximum. It can instead store 2 and each odd integer up to the maximum. This makes the algorithm more efficient because it requires fewer numbers to be processed. These two improvements to the algorithm are left as an exercise.

11.2 Sets

A major limitation of both linked and array lists is that they're slow to search. Generally, if you want to search a list you have to look at each element sequentially to see if you've found the target. This can take a long time for a large list.

Another limitation of lists is that it's not easy to prevent a list from storing duplicate values. In many cases this isn't a problem, but if, for example, you are storing a collection to count the number of unique words in a book, you don't want any duplicates to exist. To prevent duplicates in a list, you have to sequentially search the list on every add operation to make sure you aren't adding a word that's already present.

When you want to maintain a collection of elements that prevents duplicates and can be searched quickly, you're better off using another abstract data type called a *set*.

Set

A collection that stores a group of elements and prevents duplicates.

The Set collection is very much like the mathematical notion of a set. Sets do not support all of the operations you can perform on lists (namely, any operation that requires an index), but they do offer the benefits of fast searching and effortless elimination of duplicates.

Set Concepts

The two primary implementations of the Java Collections Framework's Set interface are called HashSet and TreeSet. HashSet is the general-purpose set class, while TreeSet offers a few advantages that will be discussed later. If you wanted to store a set of String values, you could write code like the following:

```
Set<String> stooges = new HashSet<String>();
stooges.add("Larry");
stooges.add("Moe");
stooges.add("Curly");
stooges.add("Moe"); // duplicate, won't be added
stooges.add("Shemp");
stooges.add("Moe"); // duplicate, won't be added
```

The set would contain only four elements, because "Moe" would be placed into the set only once. Notice that, as with lists, you can declare your collection variable to be of type Set rather than type HashSet.

A Set provides all of the operations from the Collection interface introduced earlier in this chapter, such as add, contains, and remove. It's generally assumed that the Set performs these operations efficiently, so you can add many elements to a Set and search it many times without incurring poor performance. A Set also provides a toString method that lets you see its elements. Printing the preceding stooges set would produce the following output:

```
[Moe, Shemp, Larry, Curly]
```

One of the most important benefits of using a Set such as HashSet is that it can be searched incredibly quickly. Recall that the contains method of an ArrayList or LinkedList must examine every element of the list in order until it finds the target value. By contrast, the contains method of a HashSet is implemented in such a way that it often needs to examine just one element, making it a much more efficient operation.

A HashSet is implemented using a special internal array called a *hash table* that places elements into specific positions based upon integers called *hash codes*. (Every Java object has a hash code that can be accessed through its hashCode method.) You don't need to understand the details of HashSet's implementation to use it—the bottom line is that it's implemented in such a way that you can add, remove, and search for elements very quickly.

One drawback of the HashSet is that it stores its elements in an unpredictable order. The elements of the stooges set were not alphabetized, nor did they match the order in which they were inserted. This unusual behavior is a tradeoff for the HashSet's fast performance.

Sets are very useful for examining lots of data while ignoring duplicates. For example, if you wanted to see how many unique words appear in the book *Moby Dick,* you could write code such as the following:

```java
Set<String> words = new HashSet<String>();
Scanner in = new Scanner(new File("mobydick.txt"));
while (in.hasNext()) {
    String word = in.next();
    word = word.toLowerCase();
    words.add(word);
}
System.out.println("Number of unique words = " + words.size());
```

This code produces the following output when run on a copy of the text of *Moby Dick* (available from http://www.gutenberg.org):

```
Number of unique words = 30368
```

The `HashSet` class has a convenient constructor that accepts another collection as a parameter and puts all unique elements from that collection into the `Set`. One clever usage of this constructor is to find out whether a `List` contains any duplicates. To do so, simply construct a `HashSet` from it and see if the sizes differ. The following code demonstrates this:

```java
// returns true if the given list contains any duplicate elements
public static boolean hasDuplicates(List<Integer> list) {
    Set<Integer> set = new HashSet<Integer>(list);
    return set.size() < list.size();
}
```

One drawback of a `Set` is that it doesn't store elements by indexes. The following loop doesn't compile on a `Set`, because it doesn't have a `get` method:

```java
// this code does not compile
for (int i = 0; i < words.size(); i++) {
    String word = words.get(i); // error -- no get method
    System.out.println(word);
}
```

Instead, if you want to loop over the elements of a `Set`, you must do so using an iterator. Like other collections, `Sets` have an `iterator` method that creates an `Iterator` object to examine their elements. You can then use the familiar `hasNext`/`next` loop to examine each element:

```java
// this code works correctly
Iterator<String> itr = words.iterator();
while (itr.hasNext()) {
    String word = itr.next();
    System.out.println(word);
}
```

A shorter alternative to the preceding code is to use a for-each loop over the elements of the set. As mentioned previously, the code behaves the same way but is easier to write and read:

```
for (String word : words) {
    System.out.println(word);
}
```

TreeSet Versus HashSet

The examples in the preceding section used `HashSet`, but there's another class called `TreeSet` that also implements the `Set` interface. A `TreeSet` stores its elements in sorted order using an internal linked data structure called a *binary search tree.* A `TreeSet` is efficient for adding, removing, and searching, though it is a bit slower than a `HashSet`.

A `TreeSet` can be useful if you want to print the set and have the output ordered. For example, the following code displays the sorted set of all three-letter words in *Moby Dick* that start with "a":

```
Set<String> words = new TreeSet<String>();
Scanner in = new Scanner(new File("mobydick.txt"));
while (in.hasNext()) {
    String word = in.next();
    word = word.toLowerCase();
    if (word.startsWith("a") && word.length() == 3) {
        words.add(word);
    }
}
System.out.println("Three-letter 'a' words = " + words);
```

The code produces the following output:

```
Three-letter 'a' words = [act, add, ado, aft, age, ago, ah!,
ah,, aid, aim, air, alb, ale, ali, all, am,, am-, am:, and,
ant, any, apt, arc, are, ark, arm, art, as,, as-, as., ash,
ask, ass, at,, at., at;, at?, ate, awe, axe, aye]
```

A `TreeSet` can be used with data that has a natural ordering. This means it will work if its elements are of any type that implements the `Comparable` interface, such as `Integer` or `String`. You can also provide your own object that specifies how to compare elements, called a comparator. Comparators will be discussed in Chapter 13 when we cover searching and sorting.

You should not try to construct a `TreeSet` of objects without a natural ordering, such as `Point` objects:

```
// this code compiles but will lead to a runtime error
Set<Point> points = new TreeSet<Point>();
```

The preceding code compiles (unfortunately), but it generates an exception when you run it because it doesn't know how to order the `Point` objects in the `TreeSet`:

```
Exception in thread "main"
    java.lang.ClassCastException: java.awt.Point
        at java.util.TreeMap.compare(Unknown Source)
        at java.util.TreeMap.put(Unknown Source)
        at java.util.TreeSet.add(Unknown Source)
```

You'd be better off using a `HashSet` in this case.

In summary, the following are some of the major differences between `HashSet` and `TreeSet`:

Collection	Strengths
HashSet	• extremely fast performance for add, contains, remove
	• can be used with any type of objects as its elements
TreeSet	• elements are stored in sorted order
	• must be used with elements that can be compared (such as `Integer`, `String`)

Set Operations

Consider the case where you have two sets and you need to figure out how many unique elements appear in them. You cannot just add the sets' sizes, since they might have some elements in common that should not be counted twice in your total. You could count all elements from the first set and then count only the unique elements of the second, by checking to see whether each element from the second is also in the first:

```java
// Returns the number of unique elements contained
// in either set1 or set2. Not a good model to follow.
public static int totalElements(Set<String> set1,
                                Set<String> set2) {
    int count = set1.size();
    for (String element : set2) {
        if (!set2.contains(element)) {
            count++;
        }
    }
    return count;
}
```

However, a more elegant way to perform this calculation is to compute a *union* between the sets. The union of two sets A and B is the set of all elements that are contained in either A, B, or both. Union is an example of a *set operation;* many set operations combine two sets to produce a new set as their result. Other examples of set operations are *intersection* (the set of all elements that are in both A and B) and *difference* (the set of all elements that are in A but not in B).

Set operations are often depicted by drawings called Venn diagrams, where sets are shown as circles and shaded overlapping between the circles represents set operations. Figure 11.3 shows some examples.

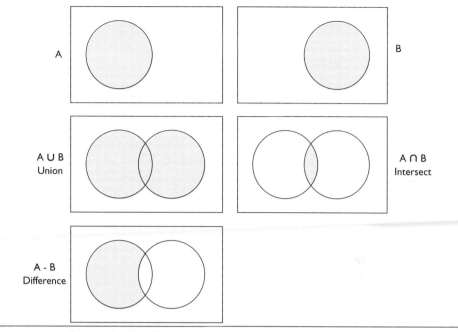

FIGURE 11.3   Set operation Venn diagrams

TABLE 11.4   Common Set Operations, Given Two Sets A and B

Set operation	Method	Description
union	addAll	set of all elements that are in A, B, or both
intersection	retainAll	set of all elements that are in both A and B
difference	removeAll	set of all elements that are in A but not in B
superset, subset	containsAll	returns true if A is a superset of (contains all elements of) B

You can write code to perform set operations by calling methods whose names end with "All" using the relevant pair of sets. Table 11.4 summarizes which methods correspond to which set operations.

For example, we could rewrite the totalElements code to use a union with the addAll method:

```
// returns the number of elements contained in both set1 and set2
public static int totalElements(Set<String> set1, Set<String> set2) {
    Set<String> union = new HashSet<String>(set1);
    union.addAll(set2);
    return union.size();
}
```

An important thing to note about the set operations in Java is that they modify the existing sets on which you call them, rather than creating new sets for you. Notice that in the preceding code, we initialize a new `HashSet` that contains all the elements from `set1` and then add `set2`'s contents to the new set, rather than combining `set1` and `set2` directly. We do this because the caller might not want us to disturb the sets' original contents.

Set Case Study: Lottery

Consider the task of writing a lottery program. The program should randomly generate a winning lottery ticket, then prompt the player to enter lotto numbers. Depending on how many numbers match, the player wins various cash prizes.

Sets make excellent collections for storing the winning lotto numbers and the player's numbers. They prevent the possibility of duplicates, and they allow us to efficiently test whether a number in one set is in the other. This will help us to count the number of winning numbers the player has entered.

The following code uses a `Random` object to initialize a set of six winning lottery numbers between 1 and 40. The code uses a `while` loop because the same number might be randomly generated more than once:

```
Set<Integer> winningNumbers = new TreeSet<Integer>();
Random r = new Random();
while (winningNumbers.size() < 6) {
    int number = r.nextInt(40) + 1;
    winningNumbers.add(number);
}
```

Once the winning number set is generated, we'll read the player's lottery numbers into a second set. To figure out how many numbers the player has chosen correctly, we could search the winning number set to see whether it contains each number from the ticket. However, a more elegant way to perform this test is to determine the intersection between the winning numbers set and the player's ticket set. The following code creates the intersection of the player's ticket and the winning numbers by copying the ticket and then removing any elements from it that aren't winning numbers:

```
// find the winning numbers from the user's ticket
Set<Integer> intersection = new TreeSet<Integer>(ticket);
intersection.retainAll(winningNumbers);
```

Once we have the intersection, we can ask for its size to see how many of the player's numbers were winning numbers; we can then calculate the appropriate cash prize amount for the player based on that number. (Our version starts with a $100 prize and doubles that figure for each winning number.)

Here is a complete implementation of the lottery program. We've created a few static methods for structure and added a few constants for the number of numbers, maximum number, and lotto prize amounts:

```
1  // Plays a lottery game with the user, reading
2  // the user's lottery numbers and printing how many
3  // matched a winning lottery ticket.
4
```

```
5   import java.util.*;
6
7   public class Lottery {
8       public static final int NUMBERS = 6;
9       public static final int MAX_NUMBER = 40;
10
11      public static void main(String[] args) {
12          // get winning number and ticket sets
13          Set<Integer> winningNumbers = createWinningNumbers();
14          Set<Integer> ticket = getTicket();
15          System.out.println();
16
17          // keep only winning numbers from user's ticket
18          Set<Integer> intersection =
19                  new TreeSet<Integer>(ticket);
20          intersection.retainAll(winningNumbers);
21
22          // print results
23          System.out.println("Your ticket numbers are " +
24                              ticket);
25          System.out.println("The winning numbers are " +
26                              winningNumbers);
27          System.out.println();
28          System.out.println("You had " + intersection.size() +
29                              " matching numbers." );
30          if (intersection.size() > 0) {
31              double prize = 100 * Math.pow(2,
32                      intersection.size());
33              System.out.println("The matched numbers are " +
34                              intersection);
35              System.out.println("Your prize is $" + prize);
36          }
37      }
38
39      // generates a set of the winning lotto numbers
40      public static Set<Integer> createWinningNumbers() {
41          Set<Integer> winningNumbers = new TreeSet<Integer>();
42          Random r = new Random();
43          while (winningNumbers.size() < NUMBERS) {
44              int number = r.nextInt(MAX_NUMBER) + 1;
45              winningNumbers.add(number);
46          }
47          return winningNumbers;
48      }
49
50      // reads the player's lottery ticket from the console
51      public static Set<Integer> getTicket() {
52          Set<Integer> ticket = new TreeSet<Integer>();
53          Scanner console = new Scanner(System.in);
54          System.out.print("Type your " + NUMBERS +
55                          " unique lotto numbers: ");
56          while (ticket.size() < NUMBERS) {
57              int number = console.nextInt();
58              ticket.add(number);
59          }
60          return ticket;
61      }
62  }
```

Here's one example output from running the program:

```
Type your 6 unique lotto numbers: 2 8 15 18 21 32

Your ticket numbers are [2, 8, 15, 18, 21, 32]
The winning numbers are [1, 3, 15, 16, 18, 39]

You had 2 matching numbers.
The matched numbers are [15, 18]
Your prize is $400.0
```

11.3 Maps

Consider the task of writing a telephone book program that allows users to type a person's name and search for that person's phone number. You could store the data in an array, a list, or a set. Perhaps you'd make a small class called `PhoneBookRecord` that stores a person's name and phone number and a list to contain the `PhoneBookRecord` objects. When searching for a phone number, you'd traverse the list looking for the `PhoneBookRecord` matching the name entered by the user and return the associated phone number.

A solution such as the one just described isn't very practical. With a large list of records, it would take the program a long time to look at each one to find the right record to retrieve the phone number.

There are many data-processing tasks in which it's useful to link pairs of objects (such as a name and a telephone number). We often find ourselves saying, "I'd like to associate every A with a B." Perhaps we'd like to associate names with addresses so that when the user types a name, we can quickly look up that person's address. Or perhaps we want to count the number of occurrences of every word in a book by associating each word with its count of occurrences.

The abstract data type *map* describes a collection that allows you to create one-way associations between pairs of objects to solve problems such as these.

> **Map**
>
> A collection that associates objects called keys with objects called values.

Maps can be used to solve a surprisingly large number of problems. A map can group all the words in a book by length and report how many words there are of each length. Maps can associate chat users with their set of friends/buddies. Maps can even represent a family tree where each person knows the identity of his/her mother and father.

We say that a map associates *keys* with *values*. A key can map to only one value, but it's possible for multiple keys to map to the same value. Java's Collections Framework includes an interface called `Map` representing this ADT.

A map can be thought of as a pair of connected collections: a set of keys and a collection of values associated with those keys. Figure 11.4 is an example of this idea, mapping first names to last names.

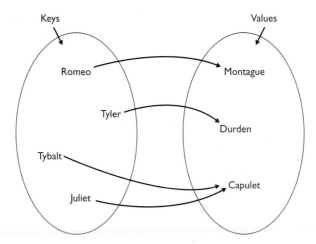

FIGURE 11.4   Mapping keys (first names) to values (last names)

Basic Map Operations

The two primary classes that implement the `Map` interface are called `HashMap` and
`TreeMap`. `HashMap` is the more general-purpose map; a `TreeMap` stores comparable
keys in sorted order.

A `Map` is constructed with not one but two generic type parameters, separated by a
comma. The first type parameter represents the type of the keys, and the second represents the type of the values. This makes for a lengthy declaration line in your code.
The following is an example of constructing a salary map (which associates people's
names with their salaries). Notice that we have to use the wrapper type `Double` rather
than the primitive type `double`:

```
Map<String, Double> salaryMap = new HashMap<String, Double>();
```

Key/value pairings are added to a map using its `put` method, which is roughly similar to the `add` method of most other collections. The `put` method accepts a key and a
value as parameters and stores a mapping between the key and value in the map. If the
key was previously associated with some other value, the new association replaces the
old one. We can add key/value pairs to our salary map using code like the following:

```
salaryMap.put("Stuart Reges", 20000.00);
salaryMap.put("Marty Stepp", 15500.00);
salaryMap.put("Jenny", 86753.09);
```

Once you've added key/value pairs to a map, you can look up a value later by calling the map's `get` method, which accepts a key as a parameter and returns the value
associated with that key:

```
double jenSalary = salaryMap.get("Jenny");
System.out.println("Jenny's salary is $" + jenSalary);
```

To see whether a map contains a mapping for a given key, you can use the containsKey method, or you can call the get method and test for a null result:

```
Scanner console = new Scanner(System.in);
System.out.print("Type a person's name: ");
String name = console.nextLine();

// search the map for the given name
if (salaryMap.containsKey(name)) {
    double salary = salaryMap.get(name);
    System.out.println(name + "'s salary is $" + salary);
} else {
    System.out.println("I don't have a record for " + name);
}
```

Table 11.5 lists several useful Map methods.

A Map's toString method displays a comma-separated list of its key/value pairs. The order in which the keys appear depends on the type of map used, which we'll get to in a moment. Here's what the salary map declared previously would look like when printed:

```
{Jenny=86753.09, Stuart Reges=20000.0, Marty Stepp=15500.0}
```

Map Views (keySet and values)

Unlike most collections, a map doesn't have an iterator method, because exactly what you wanted to iterate over wouldn't be clear. The keys? The values? Both? Instead, maps have a pair of methods called keySet and values that respectively return a Set of all keys in the map and a Collection of all values in the map. These are sometimes called *collection views* of a map because they are each collections that conceptually exist inside of the map.

TABLE 11.5 Useful Methods of Maps

Method	Description
clear()	removes all keys and values from a map
containsKey(key)	returns true if the given key maps to some value in this map
containsValue(value)	returns true if some key maps to the given value in this map
get(key)	returns the value associated with this key, or null if not found
isEmpty()	returns true if this collection contains no keys or values
keySet()	returns a Set of all keys in this map
put(key, value)	associates the given key with the given value
putAll(map)	adds all key/value mappings from the given map to this map
remove(key)	removes the given key and its associated value from this map
size()	returns the number of key/value mappings in this map
values()	returns a Collection of all values in this map

For example, consider a map that associates people's names with their Social Security Numbers. In other words, the map's keys are names and its values are Social Security Numbers. We could create the map as follows:

```
Map<String, Integer> ssnMap = new HashMap<String, Integer>();
ssnMap.put("Stuart Reges", 439876305);
ssnMap.put("Marty Stepp", 504386382);
ssnMap.put("Jenny", 867530912);
```

If we wanted to write a loop that printed the names of every person in the map, we could then call the keySet method on the map. This method returns a Set containing every key from the hash table—in this case, every String for a person's name. If you store the keySet in a variable, you should declare that variable as type Set, with the map's keys' type between the < and >:

```
Set<String> nameSet = ssnMap.keySet();
for (String name : nameSet) {
    System.out.println("Name: " + name);
}
```

The preceding code would produce the following output (the keys are in an unpredictable order since a HashMap is used):

```
Name: Jenny
Name: Stuart Reges
Name: Marty Stepp
```

If we instead wanted to loop over every Social Security Number (every value) stored in the map, we'd instead call the values method on the map. The values method returns a reference of type Collection, not of type Set, because the values may contain duplicates (it's legal for two keys to map to the same value). If you store the keySet in a variable, you should declare that variable as type Collection, with the map's values' type between the < and >:

```
Collection<Integer> ssnValues = ssnMap.values();
for (int ssn : ssnValues) {
    System.out.println("SSN: " + ssn);
}
```

The preceding code would produce the following output:

```
SSN: 867530912
SSN: 439876305
SSN: 504386382
```

The keys and values are often combined by looping over the keys and then getting the value for each key:

```
for (String name : ssnMap.keySet()) {
    int ssn = ssnMap.get(name);
    System.out.println(name + "'s SSN is " + ssn);
}
```

Notice that this code doesn't declare a variable to store the key set, but instead calls keySet directly in the for-each loop. The resulting output is the following:

```
Jenny's SSN is 867530912
Stuart Reges's SSN is 439876305
Marty Stepp's SSN is 504386382
```

There's a related method called entrySet that returns objects of a type called Entry that represents key/value pairs, but we won't explore this here.

TreeMap Versus HashMap

Just as there are two set implementations, HashSet and TreeSet, there are two flavors of Map collections in Java: HashMap and TreeMap. A HashMap performs a bit faster than a TreeMap and can store any type of data, but it keeps its keys in a somewhat haphazard order. A TreeMap can store only comparable data and performs a bit slower, but it keeps its keys in sorted order.

If we declared the Social Security Number map from the previous section to use a TreeMap as follows:

```
Map<String, Integer> ssnMap = new TreeMap<String, Integer>();
ssnMap.put("Stuart Reges", 439876305);
ssnMap.put("Marty Stepp", 504386382);
ssnMap.put("Jenny", 867530912);
System.out.println(ssnMap);
```

we'd see a different ordering to the keys when we print it.

```
{Jenny=867530912, Marty Stepp=504386382, Stuart Reges=439876305}
```

Notice that the names (the map's keys) are in sorted alphabetical order. This can be useful for certain applications, but HashMap is still the flavor Sun recommends for general use. Many applications don't care about the order of the keys and benefit from the better performance of HashMap. HashMap also works even on data without a natural ordering.

Map Case Study: WordCount

In an earlier example, we counted the number of unique words in the book *Moby Dick*. What if we were asked to find the words that occur the most frequently in the book? It seems like for each word in the book, we should count how many times that word occurs. If we then examine all of those counts and print the ones with large values, we'd have our answer.

Maps are very useful for solving problems like this. We can create a word-count map where each key is a word and its associated value is the number of occurrences of that word in the book:

```
wordCountMap = empty.
for (each word from file) {
    if (I have never seen this word before) {
        set this word's count to 1.
```

```
    } else {
        increase this word's count by one.
    }
}
```

We'll need a `Scanner` to read the appropriate file and a `Map` to store the word counts:

```
Map<String, Integer> wordCountMap = new TreeMap<String, Integer>();
Scanner in = new Scanner(new File("mobydick.txt"));
```

We can now read the file's contents and store each word that's encountered in the map. If we come across a word that's been seen before, we retrieve its old `count` value, increment it by 1, then put the new value back into the map. Recall that when you put a key/value mapping into a map that already contains that key, the old mapping is replaced. For example, if the word `"ocean"` was mapped to the number 25 and we put in a new mapping from `"ocean"` to 26, the old mapping from `"ocean"` to 25 would be replaced; we don't have to remove it manually. Here's the code to build up the map:

```
while (in.hasNext()) {
    String word = in.next().toLowerCase();
    if (!wordCountMap.containsKey(word)) {      // never seen before
        wordCountMap.put(word, 1);
    } else {                                    // seen before
        int count = wordCountMap.get(word);
        wordCountMap.put(word, count + 1);
    }
}
```

Once we've built the word-count map, if we want to print all words that appear more than, say, 2,000 times in the book, we can write code like the following:

```
for (String word : wordCountMap.keySet()) {
    int count = wordCountMap.get(word);
    if (count > 2000) {
        System.out.println(word + " occurs " +
                           count + " times.");
    }
}
```

Here's the complete program, with a method added for structure and a constant for the number of occurrences needed for a word to be printed:

```
 1  // Uses maps to implement a word count, so that the user
 2  // can see which words occur the most in the book Moby Dick.
 3
 4  import java.io.*;
 5  import java.util.*;
 6
 7  public class WordCount {
 8      // minimum number of occurrences needed to be printed
 9      public static final int OCCURRENCES = 2000;
10
11      public static void main(String[] args)
12              throws FileNotFoundException {
13          System.out.println("This program displays the most");
```

```
14              System.out.println("frequently occurring words from");
15              System.out.println("the book Moby Dick.");
16              System.out.println();
17
18              // read the book into a map
19              Scanner in = new Scanner(new File("mobydick.txt"));
20              Map<String, Integer> wordCountMap = getCountMap(in);
21
22              for (String word: wordCountMap.keySet()) {
23                  int count = wordCountMap.get(word);
24                  if (count > OCCURRENCES) {
25                      System.out.println(word + " occurs  " +
26                                               count + " times.");
27                  }
28              }
29          }
30
31          // Reads book text and returns a map from words to counts.
32          public static Map<String, Integer> getCountMap(Scanner in) {
33              Map<String, Integer> wordCountMap =
34                      new TreeMap<String, Integer>();
35
36              while (in.hasNext()) {
37                  String word = in.next().toLowerCase();
38                  if (!wordCountMap.containsKey(word)) {
39                      // never seen this word before
40                      wordCountMap.put(word, 1);
41                  } else {
42                      // seen this word before; increment count
43                      int count = wordCountMap.get(word);
44                      wordCountMap.put(word, count + 1);
45                  }
46              }
47
48              return wordCountMap;
49          }
50  }
```

The program produces the following output for our copy of *Moby Dick:*

```
This program displays the most
frequently occurring words from
the book Moby Dick.

a occurs 4509 times.
and occurs 6138 times.
his occurs 2451 times.
in occurs 3975 times.
of occurs 6405 times.
that occurs 2705 times.
the occurs 13991 times.
to occurs 4433 times.
```

Collection Overview

We've discussed three major abstract data types in this chapter: lists, sets, and maps. It's important to understand the differences between them and when each should be

These diagrams included just four individuals for the sake of brevity, but you can imagine this process working if there were 30 or even 300 people in the line.

One of the key aspects to notice here is that recursion involves many cooperating entities that each solve a little bit of the problem. Instead of one person doing all of the counting, each individual asks one question as we go towards the front of the line and answers one question as we come back out.

In programming, the iterative solution of having one person do all the counting is like having a loop that repeats some action. The recursive solution of having many people each do a little bit of work translates into many different method calls, each of which performs a little bit of work. Let's look at an example of how a simple iterative solution can be turned into a recursive solution.

An Iterative Solution Converted to Recursion

Suppose you want to create a method called `writeStars` that will take an integer parameter n and will produce a line of output with exactly n stars on it. You can solve this problem with a simple `for` loop:

```
public static void writeStars(int n) {
    for (int i = 1; i <= n; i++) {
        System.out.print("*");
    }
    System.out.println();
}
```

The action being repeated here is the call on `System.out.print` that prints a star. To write this recursively, you need to think about different cases. You might ask the method to produce a line with 10 stars, 20 stars, or 50 stars. Of all of the possible star-writing tasks you might ask it to perform, which is the simplest?

Students often answer that printing a line of one star is very easy and they're right that it's easy. But there is a task that is even easier. Printing a line of zero stars requires almost no work at all. You can create such a line by calling `System.out.println`, so you can begin your recursive definition with a test for this case:

```
public static void writeStars(int n) {
    if (n == 0) {
        System.out.println();
    } else {
        . . .
    }
}
```

In the `else` part, you want to deal with lines that have more than zero stars on them. Your instinct will probably be to fill in the `else` part with the `for` loop shown earlier, but you'll have to fight the instinct to solve the entire problem that way. To solve this second part of the problem, it is important to think about how you can do just a small amount of work that will get you closer to the solution. If the number of stars is greater than zero, you know you have to print at least one star, so you can add that to the code:

```
public static void writeStars(int n) {
    if (n == 0) {
        System.out.println();
    } else {
        System.out.print("*");
        // what is left to do?
        ...
    }
}
```

At this point in the process you have to make a leap of faith: You have to believe that recursion actually works. Once you've printed a single star, what's left to do? The answer is that you want to write (n − 1) more stars along with a println. In other words, after writing one star, what's left to do is to write a line of (n − 1) stars. You should find yourself thinking, "If only I had a method that would produce a line of (n − 1) stars, I could call that method." But you *do* have such a method—the method you're writing. So, after writing a single star, you can call the writeStars method itself to complete the line of output:

```
public static void writeStars(int n) {
    if (n == 0) {
        System.out.println();
    } else {
        System.out.print("*");
        writeStars(n − 1);
    }
}
```

Many novices complain that this seems like cheating. You're supposed to be writing the method called writeStars, so how can you call writeStars from inside of writeStars? Welcome to the world of recursion.

In the earlier non-programming example, we talked about many people standing in a line solving a problem together. To understand a recursive method like writeStars, it is useful to imagine each method invocation as being like a person in the line. The key insight is that there isn't just one person who can do the writeStars task; there's an entire army of people who can each do the task.

Let's think about what happens when you call the method and request a line of three stars:

```
writeStars(3);
```

Imagine that you're calling up the first person from the writeStars army and saying, "I want a line of three stars." That person looks at the code in the method and sees that the way you write a line of three stars is:

```
System.out.print("*");
writeStars(2);
```

In other words, the first member of the army writes a star and calls up the next member of the army to write a line of two stars, and so on down the line. Just as you had a series of people figuring out what places they were at in line, you have a series of people who each print one star and then call on someone else to write the rest of the line. With the people standing in line, you eventually reached the person at the front of the line. In this case, you reach a point where the request is to write a line of zero stars, which leads you into the `if` branch rather than the `else` branch. At this point, you complete the task with a simple `println`.

Here is a trace of the calls that would be made to print the line:

```
writeStars(3); // n > 0, execute else
    System.out.print("*");
    writeStars(2); // n > 0, execute else
        System.out.print("*");
        writeStars(1); // n > 0, execute else
            System.out.print("*");
            writeStars(0); // n == 0, execute if
                System.out.println();
```

A total of four different calls are made on the method. Continuing the analogy, you could say that a total of four members of the army are called up to solve the task together. Each one solves a star-writing task, but the tasks are slightly different (three stars, two stars, one star, zero stars). This is similar to the non-programming example, in which the various people standing in line were all answering the same kind of question but were solving slightly different problems because of where they were standing in the line (closer to or further from the front).

Structure of Recursive Solutions

Writing recursive solutions requires a certain leap of faith, but there is nothing magical about recursion. Let's look a bit more closely at the structure of a recursive solution. The following method is not a solution to the task of writing a line of n stars:

```
//does not work
public static void writeStars(int n) {
    writeStars(n);
}
```

This version never finishes executing, which we refer to as *infinite recursion*. For example, if you ask the method to write a line of 10 stars, it tries to accomplish that by asking the method to write a line of 10 stars, which asks the method to write a line of 10 stars, which asks the method to write a line of 10 stars, and so on. In other words, this solution is the recursive equivalent of an infinite loop.

Every recursive solution that you write will have two key ingredients: a *base case* and a *recursive case*.

Base Case

A case that is so simple that it can be solved directly without a recursive call.

> **Recursive Case**
>
> A case that involves reducing the overall problem to a simpler problem of
> the same kind that can be solved by a recursive call.

Here is the `writeStars` method again, with its base case and recursive case indicated with comments:

```java
public static void writeStars(int n) {
    if (n == 0) {
        // base case
        System.out.println();
    } else {
        // recursive case
        System.out.print("*");
        writeStars(n - 1);
    }
}
```

The base case is the task of writing a line of zero stars. This task is so simple that
it can be done immediately. The recursive case is the task of writing lines with one or
more stars. To solve the recursive case, you begin by writing a single star, which
reduces the remaining task to that of writing a line of (n - 1) stars. This is the task
that the `writeStars` method is designed to solve and it is simpler than the original
task, so you can solve it by making a recursive call.

As an analogy, suppose you're at the top of a ladder with n rungs on it. If you have
a way to get from one rung to the one below and if you can recognize when you've
reached the ground, you can handle a ladder of any height. Stepping from one rung to
the one below is like the recursive case where you perform some small amount of
work that reduces the problem to a simpler one of the same form (get down from rung
(n - 1) versus get down from rung n). Recognizing when you reach the ground is
like the base case that can be solved directly (stepping off the ladder).

Some problems involve multiple base cases and some problems involve multiple
recursive cases, but there will always be at least one of each. If you are missing either,
you run into trouble. Without the ability to step down from one rung to the one below,
you'd be stuck at the top of the ladder. Without the ability to recognize when you
reach the ground, you'd keep trying to step down even when there are no rungs left in
the ladder.

Because recursive solutions include some combination of base cases and recursive
cases, you will find that they are often written with `if`/`else` statements, nested `if`
statements, or some minor variation thereof. You will also find that recursive programming generally involves a case analysis, where you categorize the possible forms
the problem might take into different cases and write a solution for each case.

12.2 A Better Example of Recursion

While solving the `writeStars` task with recursion may have been an interesting exercise, it isn't a very compelling example. Let's look in detail at a problem where recursion simplifies the work to be done.

Suppose you have a `Scanner` that is tied to an external input file and you want to print the lines of the file in reverse order. For example, the file might contain the following four lines of text:

```
this
is
fun
no?
```

Printing these lines in reverse order would produce this output:

```
no?
fun
is
this
```

To solve the problem iteratively, you'd need some kind of data structure for storing the lines of text. You might, for example, use an `ArrayList<String>`. However, with recursion you can solve the problem without using a data structure.

Remember that recursive programming involves thinking about cases. What would be the simplest file to reverse? A one-line file would be fairly easy to reverse, but it would be even easier to reverse an empty file. So, you can begin writing your method as follows:

```
public static void reverse(Scanner input) {
    if (!input.hasNextLine()) {
        // base case (empty file)
        . . .
    } else {
        // recursive case (nonempty file)
        . . .
    }
}
```

For this problem, the base case is so simple that there isn't anything to do. An empty file has no lines to reverse. Thus, in this case it makes more sense to turn around the `if`/`else` statement so that you test for the recursive case. That way you can make it a simple `if` that has an implied "`else` there is nothing to do":

```
public static void reverse(Scanner input) {
    if (input.hasNextLine()) {
        // recursive case (nonempty file)
        . . .
    }
}
```

Again, the challenge is to solve a little bit of the problem. How do you get a bit closer to being done? You can read one line of text from the file:

```java
public static void reverse(Scanner input) {
    if (input.hasNextLine()) {
        // recursive case (nonempty file)
        String line = input.nextLine();
        ...
    }
}
```

For the sample file, this would read the line `"this"` into the variable `line` and leave you with these three lines of text in the `Scanner`:

```
is
fun
no?
```

Recall that your aim is to produce this overall output:

```
no?
fun
is
this
```

You might be asking yourself questions like, "Is there another line of input to process?" But that's not how to think recursively. If you're thinking recursively, you'll be thinking about what a call on the method will get you. Since the `Scanner` is positioned in front of the three lines `"is"`, `"fun"`, and `"no?"`, a call on `reverse` should read in those lines and produce the first three lines of output that you're looking for. If that works, you'll just have to write out the line `"this"` afterwards to complete the output.

This is where the leap of faith comes in—you have to believe that the `reverse` method actually works. If it does, this code can be completed as follows:

```java
public static void reverse(Scanner input) {
    if (input.hasNextLine()) {
        // recursive case (nonempty file)
        String line = input.nextLine();
        reverse(input);
        System.out.println(line);
    }
}
```

It turns out that this works. To reverse a sequence of lines, you read in the first one, reverse the others, and then write out the first one. It doesn't seem that it should be that simple, but it is.

Mechanics of Recursion

Novices seem to understand recursion better when they know more about the underlying mechanics that make it work. Before we examine a recursive method in detail,

So Java sets aside this version of the method as well and brings up a third version:

```
public static void reverse(Scanner input) {
  public static void reverse(Scanner input) {
    public static void reverse(Scanner input) {
        if (input.hasNextLine()) {
            String line = input.nextLine();
            reverse(input);
            System.out.println(line);
        }
    }
    line [          ]
```

Again, notice that it has its own variable called line that is independent of the other variables called line. This version of the method also finds that there is a line to reverse (the third line, "fun"), so it reads it in and reaches a recursive call on reverse:

```
public static void reverse(Scanner input) {
  public static void reverse(Scanner input) {
    public static void reverse(Scanner input) {
        if (input.hasNextLine()) {
            String line = input.nextLine();
    →       reverse(input);
            System.out.println(line);
        }
    }
    line "fun"
```

This brings up a fourth version of the method:

```
public static void reverse(Scanner input) {
  public static void reverse(Scanner input) {
    public static void reverse(Scanner input) {
      public static void reverse(Scanner input) {
          if (input.hasNextLine()) {
              String line = input.nextLine();
              reverse(input);
              System.out.println(line);
          }
      }
      line [          ]
```

This one finds a fourth line of input ("no?"), so it reads that in and reaches the recursive call:

```
public static void reverse(Scanner input) {
  public static void reverse(Scanner input) {
    public static void reverse(Scanner input) {
      public static void reverse(Scanner input) {
          if (input.hasNextLine()) {
              String line = input.nextLine();
      →       reverse(input);
              System.out.println(line);
          }
      }
      line │ "no?"
```

This brings up a fifth version of the method:

```
public static void reverse(Scanner input) {
  public static void reverse(Scanner input) {
    public static void reverse(Scanner input) {
      public static void reverse(Scanner input) {
        public static void reverse(Scanner input) {
            if (input.hasNextLine()) {
                String line = input.nextLine();
                reverse(input);
                System.out.println(line);
            }
        }
        line │        │
```

This one turns out to have the easy task, like the final person who was asked to print a line of zero stars. This time around the `Scanner` is empty (`input.hasNextLine()` returns `false`). This is our very important base case that stops this process from going on indefinitely. This version of the method recognizes that there are no lines to reverse, so it simply terminates.

Then what? We're done with this call, so we throw it away and go back to where we were just before:

```
public static void reverse(Scanner input) {
  public static void reverse(Scanner input) {
    public static void reverse(Scanner input) {
      public static void reverse(Scanner input) {
          if (input.hasNextLine()) {
              String line = input.nextLine();
              reverse(input);
      →       System.out.println(line);
          }
      }
      line │ "no?"
```

We've finished the call on reverse and are positioned at the println right after it, so we print the text in the line variable ("no?") and terminate. Where does that leave us? This method goes away and we return to where we were just before:

```
public static void reverse(Scanner input) {
    public static void reverse(Scanner input) {
        public static void reverse(Scanner input) {
            if (input.hasNextLine()) {
                String line = input.nextLine();
                reverse(input);
        ⟶       System.out.println(line);
            }
        }
        line "fun"
```

We then print the current line of text, which is "fun", and this version goes away:

```
public static void reverse(Scanner input) {
    public static void reverse(Scanner input) {
        if (input.hasNextLine()) {
            String line = input.nextLine();
            reverse(input);
    ⟶       System.out.println(line);
        }
    }
    line "is"
```

Now we execute this println, for the text "is", and eliminate one more call:

```
public static void reverse(Scanner input) {
    if (input.hasNextLine()) {
        String line = input.nextLine();
        reverse(input);
⟶       System.out.println(line);
    }
}
line "this"
```

Notice that we've written out three lines of text so far:

```
no?
fun
is
```

Our leap of faith was justified. The recursive call on reverse read in the three lines of text that came after the first line of input and printed them in reverse order. We complete the task by printing the first line of text, which leads to this overall output:

```
no?
fun
```

```
is
this
```

Then this version of the method terminates, and we're done.

12.3 Recursive Functions

Both of the examples of recursion we have looked at so far have been action-oriented methods with a return type of void. In this section we will examine some of the issues that come up when you want to write methods that compute values and return a result.

Integer Exponentiation

Java provides a method, Math.pow, that allows you to compute an exponent. If you want to know what x^y is equal to, you can call Math.pow(x, y). Let's consider how we could implement the pow method. To keep things simple, we'll limit ourselves to the domain of integers. But because we are limiting ourselves to integers, we have to recognize an important precondition of our method: We won't be able to compute negative exponents because the results would not be integers.

The method we want to write will look like this:

```
// pre : y >= 0
// post: returns x^y
public static int pow(int x, int y) {
    . . .
}
```

We could obviously solve this problem by writing a loop, but we want to explore how to write the method recursively. Again, the right place to start is to think about different cases. What would be the easiest exponent to compute? It's pretty easy to compute x^1, so that's a good candidate, but there is an even more basic case. The simplest possible exponent is 0. By definition, any integer to the 0 power is considered to be 1. So we can begin our solution as follows:

```
public static int pow(int x, int y) {
    if (y == 0) {
        // base case with y == 0
        return 1;
    } else {
        // recursive case with y > 0
        . . .
    }
}
```

In the recursive case we know that y is greater than 0. In other words, there will be at least one factor of x to be included in the result. We know from mathematics that:

$$x^y = x \cdot x^{y-1}$$

This equation expresses x to the y power in terms of x to a smaller power, (y - 1). Therefore, it can serve as our recursive case. All we have to do is to translate it into its Java equivalent:

```java
public static int pow(int x, int y) {
    if (y == 0) {
        // base case with y == 0
        return 1;
    } else {
        // recursive case with y > 0
        return x * pow(x, y - 1);
    }
}
```

This is a complete recursive solution. Tracing the execution of a recursive function is a little more difficult than with a void method because we have to keep track of the values being returned by each recursive call. The following is a trace of execution showing how we would compute 3^5:

```
pow(3, 5) = 3 * pow(3, 4)
      pow(3, 4) = 3 * pow(3, 3)
            pow(3, 3) = 3 * pow(3, 2)
                  pow(3, 2) = 3 * pow(3, 1)
                        pow(3, 1) = 3 * pow(3, 0)
                              pow(3, 0) = 1
                        pow(3, 1) = 3 * 1 = 3
                  pow(3, 2) = 3 * 3 = 9
            pow(3, 3) = 3 * 9 = 27
      pow(3, 4) = 3 * 27 = 81
pow(3, 5) = 3 * 81 = 243
```

Notice that we make a series of six recursive calls in a row until we get to the base case of computing 3 to the 0 power. That call returns the value 1, and then the recursion unwinds, computing the various answers as it returns from each method call.

It is useful to think about what will happen if someone violates the precondition by asking for a negative exponent. For example, what if someone asked for pow(3, -1)? The method would recursively ask for pow(3, -2), which would ask for pow(3, -3), which would ask for pow(3, -4), and so on. In other words, it would lead to an infinite recursion. In a sense this is okay, because the person calling the method should pay attention to the precondition. But it's not much work for us to handle this case in a more elegant manner. Our solution is structured as a series of cases, so we can simply add a new case for illegal exponents:

```java
public static int pow(int x, int y) {
    if (y < 0) {
        throw new IllegalArgumentException("negative exponent");
    } else if (y == 0) {
        // base case with y == 0
        return 1;
    } else {
```

```
        // recursive case with y > 0
        return x * pow(x, y - 1);
    }
}
```

One of the advantages of writing functions recursively is that if we can identify other cases, we can potentially make the function more efficient. For example, suppose that you want to compute 2^{16}. In its current form, the method will multiply 2 by 2 by 2 a total of 16 times. But we can do better than that. If y is an even exponent, then:

$$x^y = (x^2)^{\frac{y}{2}}$$

So instead of computing 2^{16}, we can compute 4^8. Adding this case to our method is relatively simple:

```
public static int pow(int x, int y) {
    if (y < 0) {
        throw new IllegalArgumentException("negative exponent");
    } else if (y == 0) {
        // base case with y == 0
        return 1;
    } else if (y % 2 == 0) {
        // recursive case with y > 0, y even
        return pow(x * x, y / 2);
    } else {
        // recursive case with y > 0, y odd
        return x * pow(x, y - 1);
    }
}
```

This version of the method is more efficient than the original. The following is a trace of execution for computing 2^{16}:

```
pow(2, 16) = pow(4, 8)
     pow(4, 8) = pow(16, 4)
          pow(16, 4) = pow(256, 2)
               pow(256, 2) = pow(65536, 1)
                    pow(65536, 1) = 65536 * pow(65536, 0)
                         pow(65536, 0) = 1
                    pow(65536, 1) = 65536 * 1 = 65536
               pow(256, 2) = 65536
          pow(16, 4) = 65536
     pow(4, 8) = 65536
pow(2, 16) = 65536
```

Greatest Common Divisor

In mathematics, we often want to know the largest integer that goes evenly into two different integers, which is known as the *greatest common divisor* (or GCD) of the two integers. Let's explore how to write a GCD method recursively.

For now, let's not worry about negative values of x and y. We want to write this method:

```
// pre : x >= 0, y >= 0
// post: returns the greatest common divisor of x and y
```

```java
public static int gcd(int x, int y) {
    . . .
}
```

To introduce some variety, let's try to figure out the recursive case first and then figure out the base case. Suppose, for example, that we are asked to compute the GCD of 20 and 132. The GCD is 4, because 4 is the largest integer that goes evenly into both numbers.

There are many ways to compute the GCD of two numbers. One of the most efficient algorithms dates back at least to the time of Euclid, and perhaps even farther. The idea is to eliminate any multiples of the smaller integer from the larger integer. For our example of 20 and 132, we know that:

$$132 = 20 \cdot 6 + 12$$

There are six multiples of 20 in 132, with a remainder of 12. Euclid's algorithm says that we can ignore the six multiples of 20 and just focus on the value 12. In other words, we can replace 132 with 12:

$$gcd(132, 20) = gcd(12, 20)$$

The proof of this principle is beyond the scope of this book, but that is the basic idea. This is easy to express in Java terms because the mod operator gives us the remainder when one number is divided by another. Expressing this principle in general terms, we know that:

$$gcd(x, y) = gcd(x \ \% \ y, y) \quad \text{when} \quad y > 0$$

Again, the proof is beyond the scope of this book, but given this basic principle we can produce a recursive solution to the problem. We might now try to write the method as follows:

```java
public static int gcd(int x, int y) {
    if ( . . . ) {
        // base case
        . . .
    } else {
        // recursive case
        return gcd(x % y, y);
    }
}
```

This isn't a bad first attempt, but it has a problem. It's not enough to be mathematically correct. We have to know that our recursive solution keeps reducing the overall problem to a simpler problem. If we start with 132 and 20, the method makes progress on the first call, but then it starts repeating itself:

```
gcd(132, 20) = gcd(12, 20)
       gcd(12, 20) = gcd(12, 20)
              gcd(12, 20) = gcd(12, 20)
```

```
gcd(12, 20) = gcd(12, 20)
               . . .
```

This will lead to infinite recursion. The Euclidean trick helped the first time around, because for the first call x was greater than y (132 is greater than 20). But the algorithm makes progress only if the first number is larger than the second number.

The line of code that is causing us problems is this one:

```
return gcd(x % y, y);
```

When we compute (x % y), we are guaranteed to get a result that is smaller than y. That means that on the recursive call, the first value will always be smaller than the second value. To make the algorithm work, we need the opposite to be true. We can achieve this goal simply by reversing the order of the arguments:

```
return gcd(y, x % y);
```

On this call we are guaranteed to have a first value that is larger than the second value. If we trace this version of the method for computing the GCD of 132 and 20, we get the following:

```
gcd(132, 20) = gcd(20, 12)
       gcd(20, 12) = gcd(12, 8)
               gcd(12, 8) = gcd(8, 4)
                       gcd(8, 4) = gcd(4, 0)
                           . . .
```

At this point we have to decide what the GCD of 4 and 0 is. It may seem strange, but the answer is 4. In general, gcd(n, 0) is always n. Obviously, the GCD can't be any larger than n, and n goes evenly into n. But n also goes evenly into 0, because 0 can be written as an even multiple of n: (0 * n).

This observation leads us to the base case. If y is 0, the GCD is x:

```
public static int gcd(int x, int y) {
    if (y == 0) {
        // base case with y == 0
        return x;
    } else {
        // recursive case with y > 0
        return gcd(y, x % y);
    }
}
```

With this base case, we also solve the potential problem that the Euclidean formula depends on y not being 0. However, we still have to think about the case where one or both of x and y is negative. We could keep the precondition and throw an exception when this occurs, but it is more common in mathematics to return the GCD of the absolute value of the two values. We can accomplish this with one extra case for negatives:

```
public static int gcd(int x, int y) {
    if (x < 0 || y < 0) {
```

```
      // recursive case with negative value(s)
      return gcd(Math.abs(x), Math.abs(y));
  } else if (y == 0) {
      // base case with y == 0
      return x;
  } else {
      // recursive case with y > 0
      return gcd(y, x % y);
  }
}
```

Common Programming Error

Infinite Recursion

Everyone who uses recursion to write programs eventually accidentally writes a solution that leads to infinite recursion. For example, the following is a slight variation of the gcd method that doesn't work:

```
// flawed definition
public static int gcd(int x, int y) {
    if (x <= 0 || y <= 0) {
        // recursive case with negative value(s)
        return gcd(Math.abs(x), Math.abs(y));
    } else if (y == 0) {
        // base case with y == 0
        return x;
    } else {
        // recursive case with y > 0
        return gcd(y, x % y);
    }
}
```

This solution is just slightly different than the one we wrote previously. In the test for negative values, this code tests whether x and y are less than or equal to 0. The original code tests whether they are strictly less than 0. It doesn't seem like this should make much difference, but it does. If we execute this version of the code on our original problem of finding the GCD of 132 and 20, the program produces many lines of output that look like this:

```
at Bug.gcd(Bug.java:9)
at Bug.gcd(Bug.java:9)
at Bug.gcd(Bug.java:9)
at Bug.gcd(Bug.java:9)
at Bug.gcd(Bug.java:9)
at Bug.gcd(Bug.java:9)
at Bug.gcd(Bug.java:9)
```

The first time you see this, you are likely to think that something has broken on your computer because you will get so many lines of output. The number of lines of output will vary from one system to another, but it's likely to be hundreds, if not

(continues)

thousands. If you scroll all the way back up, you'll see that the output begins with this message:

```
Exception in thread "main" java.lang.StackOverflowError
        at Bug.gcd(Bug.java:9)
        at Bug.gcd(Bug.java:9)
        at Bug.gcd(Bug.java:9)
        . . .
```

Java is letting you know that the call stack has gotten too big. Why is this happening? Remember the trace of execution for this case:

```
gcd(132, 20) = gcd(20, 12)
        gcd(20, 12) = gcd(12, 8)
                gcd(12, 8) = gcd(8, 4)
                        gcd(8, 4) = gcd(4, 0)
                            . . .
```

Think of what happens at this point, when we call gcd(4, 0). The value of y is 0, which is our base case, so normally we would expect the method to return the value 4 and terminate. But the method begins by checking whether either x or y is less than or equal to 0. Since y is 0, this test evaluates to true, so we make a recursive call with the absolute values of x and y. But the absolute values of 4 and 0 are 4 and 0. In other words, we decide that gcd(4, 0) must be equal to gcd(4, 0), which must be equal to gcd(4, 0):

```
gcd(132, 20) = gcd(20, 12)
        gcd(20, 12) = gcd(12, 8)
                gcd(12, 8) = gcd(8, 4)
                        gcd(8, 4) = gcd(4, 0)
                                gcd(4, 0) = gcd(4, 0)
                                        gcd(4, 0) = gcd(4, 0)
                                                gcd(4, 0) = gcd(4, 0)
                                                        gcd(4, 0) = gcd(4, 0)
                                                            . . .
```

In other words, this version generates infinitely many recursive calls. Java allows you to make a lot of recursive calls, but eventually it runs out of space. When it does, it gives you a backtrace to let you know how you got to the error. In this case, the backtrace is not nearly as helpful as usual because almost all of the calls will involve the infinite recursion.

Again, think in terms of stacking pieces of paper on top of each other as methods are called. You'd wind up with a stack containing hundreds or even thousands of sheets, and you would have to look back through all of these to find the problem.

To handle these situations, you have to look closely at the line number to see which line of your program generated the infinite recursion. In this simple case, we know that it is the recursive call for negative x and y values. That alone might be enough to allow us to pinpoint the error. If the problem isn't obvious, though, you might need to include `println` statements to figure out what is going on. For example, in this code, we could add a `println` just before the recursive call:

```java
public static int gcd(int x, int y) {
    if (x <= 0 || y <= 0) {
        // recursive case with negative value(s)
        System.out.println("x = " + x + " and y = " + y);
        return gcd(Math.abs(x), Math.abs(y));
    } else if (y == 0) {
        . . .
}
```

With that `println` in place, the code produces hundreds of lines of output of the form:

```
x = 4 and y = 0
```

If we examine that case closely, we'll see that we don't have negative values and will realize that we have to fix the test we are using.

Directory Crawler

Recursion is particularly useful when you're working with data that is itself recursive. For example, think of how files are stored on a computer. Each file is kept in a folder or directory. But directories can contain more than just files: Directories can contain other directories, those inner directories can contain directories, and even those directories can contain directories. Directories can be nested to an arbitrary depth. This is an example of recursive data.

In Chapter 6, you learned to use `File` objects to keep track of files stored on your computer. For example, if you have a file called `data.txt`, you can construct a `File` object that can be used to get information about that file:

```java
File f = new File("data.txt");
```

Several useful methods for the `File` class were introduced in Chapter 6. For example, there is a method called `exists` that indicates whether or not a certain file exists, and there is a method called `isDirectory` that indicates whether or not the name supplied corresponds to a file or a directory.

Let's write a program that will prompt the user for the name of a file or directory and recursively explore all files that can be reached from that starting point. If the user provides the name of a file, we will simply print the name. But if the user gives us the name of a directory, we will print the directory name along with a listing of all the directories and files inside that directory.

We can write a fairly simple `main` method that prompts for a file/directory name and checks to make sure it exists. If not, it tells the user that there is no such file or directory. If so, it calls a method to print the information for that `File` object:

```
public static void main(String[] args) {
    Scanner console = new Scanner(System.in);
    System.out.print("directory or file name? ");
    String name = console.nextLine();
    File f = new File(name);
    if (!f.exists()) {
        System.out.println("No such file/directory");
    } else {
        print(f);
    }
}
```

Our job will be to write the `print` method. The method should begin by printing the name of the file or directory:

```
public static void print(File f) {
    System.out.println(f.getName());
    . . .
}
```

If the `File` object `f` represents a simple file, that's all we want to do. But if `f` represents a directory, we also want to print the names of all the files contained in the directory:

```
public static void print(File f) {
    System.out.println(f.getName());
    if (f.isDirectory()) {
        // print contents of directory
    }
}
```

We can accomplish this using the `listFiles` method, which returns an array of `File` objects that represent the contents of the directory. We can use a for-each loop to process each one:

```
public static void print(File f) {
    System.out.println(f.getName());
    if (f.isDirectory()) {
        for (File subF : f.listFiles()) {
            // print information for subF
        }
    }
}
```

To complete the method, we have to figure out how to print information about each of the individual `subF` objects in the directory. An obvious thing to do is to simply print the names:

```
// not quite right
public static void print(File f) {
    System.out.println(f.getName());
    if (f.isDirectory()) {
        for (File subF : f.listFiles()) {
```

```
                      System.out.println(subF.getName());
            }
        }
    }
```

This works in that it prints the name of the subfiles inside the directory. But remember that there can be directories inside this directory, so some of those subfiles might actually be directories whose contents also need to be printed. We could try to fix our code with an additional test:

```
// getting worse, not better
public static void print(File f) {
    System.out.println(f.getName());
    if (f.isDirectory()) {
        for (File subF : f.listFiles()) {
            System.out.println(subF.getName());
            if (subF.isDirectory()) {
                // print contents of subdirectory
            }
        }
    }
}
```

But even this won't work, because there might be directories within those inner directories, and those directories might have subdirectories. There is no simple way to solve this problem with standard iterative techniques.

The solution is to think recursively. You might be tempted to think of the possibilities as many different cases: a file, a directory with files, a directory with subdirectories, a directory with subdirectories that have subdirectories, and so on. However, there are really only two cases to consider: We either have a file or a directory. If it's a file, we simply print its name. If it's a directory, we print its name and then print information about every file and directory inside of it. How do we get the code to recursively explore all of the possibilities? We recognize that we can call our own `print` method to process whatever appears inside a directory:

```
public static void print(File f) {
    System.out.println(f.getName());
    if (f.isDirectory()) {
        for (File subF : f.listFiles()) {
            print(subF);
        }
    }
}
```

This version of the code recursively explores the structure. Each time we find something inside a directory, we make a recursive call that can handle either a file or a directory; that recursive call might make yet another recursive call to handle either a file or directory, and so on.

One problem this program might encounter that is worth addressing is that there are some directories that your Java program might not be able to read. For example, on most computer systems there are protected directories that contain files considered sensitive, so you aren't even allowed to ask for their names. To allow for this situation, we can add an extra test for our loop that processes the contents of a directory. There is a method called `canRead` that will let us know whether the directory's contents are readable:

```java
public static void print(File f) {
    System.out.println(f.getName());
    if (f.isDirectory() && f.canRead()) {
        for (File subF : f.listFiles()) {
            print(subF);
        }
    }
}
```

The following is a complete program that incorporates this code. It includes an extra parameter for the `print` method to indicate a level of indentation to use. That way, the contents of a directory will be indented relative to the name of the directory. Here's our directory-crawling program:

```java
 1  // This program prompts the user for a file or directory name
 2  // and shows a listing of all files and directories that can be
 3  // reached from it (including subdirectories).
 4
 5  import java.io.*;
 6  import java.util.*;
 7
 8  public class DirectoryCrawler {
 9      public static void main(String[] args) {
10          Scanner console = new Scanner(System.in);
11          System.out.print("directory or file name? ");
12          String name = console.nextLine();
13          File f = new File(name);
14          if (!f.exists()) {
15              System.out.println("No such file/directory");
16          } else {
17              print(f, 0);
18          }
19      }
20
21      // Prints information for the given file/directory using the
22      // given level of indentation
23      public static void print(File f, int level) {
24          for (int i = 0; i < level; i++) {
25              System.out.print("    ");
26          }
27          System.out.println(f.getName());
28          if (f.isDirectory() && f.canRead()) {
29              for (File subF : f.listFiles()) {
30                  print(subF, level + 1);
31              }
32          }
33      }
34  }
```

12.4 Recursive Graphics (Optional)

There has been a great deal of interest in the past 30 years about an emerging field of mathematics called *fractal geometry*. A fractal is a geometric object that is recursively constructed or self-similar. A fractal shape contains smaller versions of itself, so that it looks similar at all magnifications.

Benoit Mandelbrot created the field of fractals in 1975 with his first publication about fractals in general and about a specific fractal that has come to be known as the Mandelbrot set. The most impressive aspect of fractal geometry is that extremely intricate and complex phenomena can be described with a simple set of rules. When Mandelbrot and others began drawing pictures of their fractals, they were an instant hit.

Many fractals can be described easily with recursion. As an example, we will explore a recursive method for drawing what is known as the Sierpinski triangle. We can't draw the actual fractal, because it is composed of infinitely many subtriangles. Instead, we will write a method that produces various levels that approximate the actual fractal.

At level 1, we draw an equilateral triangle as shown in Figure 12.1:

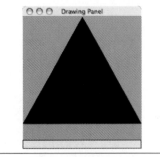

Figure 12.1 Sierpinski triangle, level 1

In going to level 2, we draw three smaller triangles that are contained within the original triangle as in Figure 12.2:

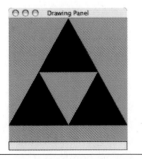

Figure 12.2 Sierpinski triangle, level 2

We apply this principle in a recursive manner. Just as we replaced the original triangle with three inner triangles, we replace each of these three triangles with three inner triangles to obtain Figure 12.3 with nine triangles in level 3:

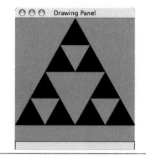

Figure 12.3 Sierpinski triangle, level 3

This process continues indefinitely, making a more intricate pattern at each new level. Figure 12.4 shows what we get at level 7:

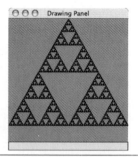

Figure 12.4 Sierpinski triangle, level 7

We can solve this problem using the `DrawingPanel` class from Supplement 3G. We'll pass the `Graphics` object for the panel to the method that is to draw the triangles. The method will also need to know the level to use and the three vertices of the triangle, which we can pass as `Point` objects. So, our method will look like this:

```
public static void drawFigure(int level, Graphics g,
                              Point p1, Point p2, Point p3) {
    . . .
}
```

Our base case will be to draw the basic triangle for level 1. The `Graphics` class has methods for filling rectangles and ovals, but not for filling triangles. Fortunately, there is a `Polygon` class in the `java.awt` package. You construct a `Polygon` and then add a series of points to it. Once we've specified the three vertices, we can use the `fillPolygon` method of the `Graphics` class to fill the polygon. So, our base case will look like this:

```
public static void drawFigure(int level, Graphics g,
                              Point p1, Point p2, Point p3) {
    if (level == 1) {
        // base case: simple triangle
        Polygon p = new Polygon();
        p.addPoint(p1.x, p1.y);
        p.addPoint(p2.x, p2.y);
        p.addPoint(p3.x, p3.y);
        g.fillPolygon(p);
    } else {
        // recursive case, split into 3 triangles
        ...
    }
}
```

Most of the work happens in the recursive case. We have to split the triangle into three smaller triangles. We'll label the vertices of the overall triangle as in Figure 12.5. We then need to compute three new points that are the midpoints of the three sides of this triangle as shown in Figure 12.6.

There are three different midpoint computations involved here, so clearly it will be helpful to first write a method that will compute the midpoint of a segment given two endpoints:

```
public static Point midpoint(Point p1, Point p2) {
    return new Point((p1.x + p2.x) / 2, (p1.y + p2.y) / 2);
}
```

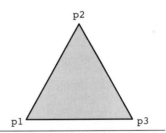

Figure 12.5 Triangle before splitting

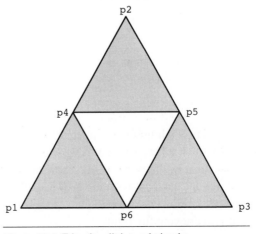

Figure 12.6 Triangle split into subtriangles

Given this method, we can easily compute the three midpoints. Looking at Figure 12.6, we see that:

- p4 is the midpoint of p1 and p2.
- p5 is the midpoint of p2 and p3.
- p6 is the midpoint of p1 and p3.

Once we have computed those points, we can describe the smaller triangles as follows:

- In the lower-left corner is the triangle formed by p1, p4, and p6.
- On top is the triangle formed by p4, p2, and p5.
- In the lower-right corner is the triangle formed by p6, p5, and p3.

The final detail we have to think about is the level. If you look again at the level 2 version of the figure, you will notice that it is composed of three simple triangles. In other words, the level 2 figure is composed of three level 1 figures. Similarly, the level 3 figure is composed of three level 2 figures, which in turn are each composed of three level 1 figures. In general, if we are asked to draw a level n figure, we do so by drawing three level (n - 1) figures.

By turning these observations into code, we can complete the recursive method:

```java
public static void drawFigure(int level, Graphics g,
                              Point p1, Point p2, Point p3) {
    if (level == 1) {
        // base case: simple triangle
        Polygon p = new Polygon();
        p.addPoint(p1.x, p1.y);
        p.addPoint(p2.x, p2.y);
        p.addPoint(p3.x, p3.y);
        g.fillPolygon(p);
    } else {
        // recursive case, split into 3 triangles
        Point p4 = midpoint(p1, p2);
        Point p5 = midpoint(p2, p3);
        Point p6 = midpoint(p1, p3);

        // recurse on 3 triangular areas
        drawFigure(level - 1, g, p1, p4, p6);
        drawFigure(level - 1, g, p4, p2, p5);
        drawFigure(level - 1, g, p6, p5, p3);
    }
}
```

There is a limit to how many levels deep we can go. The DrawingPanel has a finite resolution, so at some point we won't be able to subdivide our triangles any further. Also bear in mind that at each new level the number of triangles that we draw triples, which means that the number of triangles increases exponentially with the level.

The following is a complete program that allows the user to decide what level to use in drawing the figure:

```
 1 // This program draws the Sierpinski fractal.
 2
 3 import java.awt.*;
 4 import java.util.*;
 5
 6 public class Sierpinski {
 7     public static final int SIZE = 256;
 8
 9     public static void main(String[] args) {
10         // prompt for level
11         Scanner console = new Scanner(System.in);
12         System.out.print("What level do you want? ");
13         int level = console.nextInt();
14
15         // initialize drawing panel
16         DrawingPanel p = new DrawingPanel(SIZE, SIZE);
17         p.setBackground(Color.CYAN);
18         Graphics g = p.getGraphics();
19
20         // compute triangle endpoints and begin recursion
21         int height = (int) Math.round(SIZE * Math.sqrt(3) / 2);
22         Point p1 = new Point(0, height);
23         Point p2 = new Point(SIZE / 2, 0);
24         Point p3 = new Point(SIZE, height);
25         drawFigure(level, g, p1, p2, p3);
26     }
27
28     // draws a Sierpinski fractal to the given level inside the
29     // triangle whose vertices are (p1, p2, p3)
30     public static void drawFigure(int level, Graphics g,
31             Point p1, Point p2, Point p3) {
32         if (level == 1) {
33             // base case: simple triangle
34             Polygon p = new Polygon();
35             p.addPoint(p1.x, p1.y);
36             p.addPoint(p2.x, p2.y);
37             p.addPoint(p3.x, p3.y);
38             g.fillPolygon(p);
39         } else {
40             // recursive case, split into 3 triangles
41             Point p4 = midpoint(p1, p2);
42             Point p5 = midpoint(p2, p3);
43             Point p6 = midpoint(p1, p3);
44
45             // recurse on 3 triangular areas
46             drawFigure(level - 1, g, p1, p4, p6);
47             drawFigure(level - 1, g, p4, p2, p5);
48             drawFigure(level - 1, g, p6, p5, p3);
49         }
50     }
51
52     // returns the midpoint of p1 and p2
53     public static Point midpoint(Point p1, Point p2) {
54         return new Point((p1.x + p2.x) / 2, (p1.y + p2.y) / 2);
55     }
56 }
```

12.5 Case Study: Prefix Evaluator

In this section we will explore the use of recursion to evaluate complex numeric expressions. We will begin by exploring the different conventions for specifying numeric expressions and then we will see how recursion makes it relatively easy to implement one of the standard conventions.

Infix, Prefix, and Postfix Notation

When we write numeric expressions in a Java program we typically put numeric operators like + and * between the two operands, as in:

```
3.5 + 8.2
9.1 * 12.7
7.8 * (2.3 + 2.5)
```

Putting the operator between the operands is a convention known as *infix notation*. A second convention is to put the operator in front of the two operands, as in:

```
+ 3.5 8.2
* 9.1 12.7
* 7.8 + 2.3 2.5
```

Putting the operator in front of the operands is a convention known as *prefix notation*. Prefix notation looks odd for symbols like + and *, but it resembles mathematical function notation, where the name of the function goes first. For example, if we were calling methods instead of using operators, we would write:

```
plus(3.5, 8.2)
times(9.1, 12.7)
times(7.8, plus(2.3, 2.5))
```

There is also a third convention where the operator appears after the two operands, as in:

```
3.5 8.2 +
9.1 12.7 *
7.8 2.3 2.5 + *
```

This convention is known as *postfix notation*. It is also sometimes referred to as Reverse Polish Notation, or RPN. For many years Hewlett-Packard has sold scientific calculators that use RPN rather than normal infix notation.

We are so used to infix notation that it takes a while to get used to the other two conventions. One of the interesting facts you will discover if you take the time to learn the prefix and postfix conventions is that infix is the only notation that requires parentheses. The other two notations are unambiguous. Table 12.1 summarizes the three notations.

TABLE 12.1 **Arithmetic Notations**

Notation	Description	Examples
infix	operator between operands	2.3 + 4.7
		2.6 * 3.7
		(3.4 + 7.9) * 18.6 + 2.3 / 4.7
prefix	operator before operands	+ 2.3 4.7
	(functional notation)	* 2.6 3.7
		+ * + 3.4 7.9 18.6 / 2.3 4.7
postfix	operator after operands	2.3 4.7 +
	(Reverse Polish Notation)	2.6 3.7 *
		3.4 7.9 + 18.6 * 2.3 4.7 / +

Evaluating Prefix Expressions

Of the three standard notations, prefix notation is the one most easily implemented with recursion. In this section we will write a method that reads a prefix expression from a `Scanner` and computes its value. Our method should look like this:

```
// pre : input contains a legal prefix expression
// post: expression is consumed and the result is returned
public static double evaluate(Scanner input) {
    . . .
}
```

Before we can begin writing the method, we have to consider what kind of input we are going to get. As the precondition indicates, we will assume that the `Scanner` contains a legal prefix expression. The simplest possible expression would be a number, as in:

```
38.9
```

There isn't much to evaluate in this case—we can simply read and return the number. More complex prefix expressions will involve one or more operators. Remember that the operator goes in front of the operands in a prefix expression. A slightly more complex expression would have two numbers as operands with an operator in front, as in:

```
+ 2.6 3.7
```

This expression could itself be an operand in a larger expression. For example, we might ask for:

```
* + 2.6 3.7 + 5.2 18.7
```

At the outermost level, we have a multiplication operator with two operands:

```
  *        + 2.6 3.7    + 5.2 18.7
  ↑        ‿‿‿‿‿‿‿      ‿‿‿‿‿‿‿‿
operator   operand #1    operand #2
```

In other words, this expression is computing the product of two sums. Here is the same expression in the more familiar infix notation:

```
(2.6 + 3.7) * (5.2 + 18.7)
```

These expressions can become arbitrarily complex. The key observation to make about them is that they all begin with an operator. In other words, every prefix expression is of one of two forms:

- A simple number

- An operator followed by two operands

This observation will become a roadmap for our recursive solution. The simplest prefix expression will be a number, and we can distinguish it from the other case because any other expression will begin with an operator. So, we can begin our recursive solution by looking to see if the next token in the Scanner is a number. If so, we have a simple case and we can simply read and return the number:

```
public static double evaluate(Scanner input) {
    if (input.hasNextDouble()) {
        // base case with a simple number
        return input.nextDouble();
    } else {
        // recursive case with an operator and two operands
        . . .
    }
}
```

Turning our attention to the recursive case, we know that the input must be composed of an operator followed by two operands. We can begin by reading the operator:

```
public static double evaluate(Scanner input) {
    if (input.hasNextDouble()) {
        // base case with a simple number
        return input.nextDouble();
    } else {
        // recursive case with an operator and two operands
        String operator = input.next();
        . . .
    }
}
```

At this point we reach a critical decision. We have read in the operator, and now we need to somehow read in the first operand and then the second operand. If we knew that the operands were simple numbers, we could say:

```
// not the right approach
public static double evaluate(Scanner input) {
    if (input.hasNextDouble()) {
        // base case with a simple number
        return input.nextDouble();
    } else {
        // recursive case with an operator and two operands
```

```
        String operator = input.next();
        double operand1 = input.nextDouble();
        double operand2 = input.nextDouble();
        . . .
    }
}
```

But we have no guarantee that the operands are simple numbers. They might be complex expressions that begin with operators. Your instinct might be to test whether or not the original operator is followed by another operator (in other words, whether the first operand begins with an operator), but that reasoning won't lead you to a satisfactory outcome. Remember that the expressions can be arbitrarily complex, so there might be dozens of operators to be processed in either of the operands.

The solution to this puzzle involves recursion. We need to read two operands from the Scanner, and they might be very complex. But we know that they are in prefix form and we know that they aren't as complex as the original expression we were asked to evaluate. The key is to recursively evaluate each of the two operands:

```
public static double evaluate(Scanner input) {
    if (input.hasNextDouble()) {
        // base case with a simple number
        return input.nextDouble();
    } else {
        // recursive case with an operator and two operands
        String operator = input.next();
        double operand1 = evaluate(input);
        double operand2 = evaluate(input);
        . . .
    }
}
```

Simple as it is, this solution works. Of course, we still have the task of evaluating the operator. After the two recursive calls we will have an operator and two numbers (say, + and 3.4 and 2.6). It would be nice if we could just say:

```
return operand1 operator operand2; // does not work
```

Unfortunately, Java doesn't work that way. We have to use a nested if/else statement to test what kind of operator we have and to return an appropriate value, as in:

```
if (operator.equals("+")) {
    return operand1 + operand2;
} else if (operator.equals("-")) {
    return operand1 - operand2;
} else if (operator.equals("*")) {
    . . .
```

We can include this code in its own method so that our recursive method stays fairly short:

```
public static double evaluate(Scanner input) {
    if (input.hasNextDouble()) {
        // base case with a simple number
```

```
            return input.nextDouble();
    } else {
        // recursive case with an operator and two operands
        String operator = input.next();
        double operand1 = evaluate(input);
        double operand2 = evaluate(input);
        return apply(operator, operand1, operand2);
    }
}
```

Complete Program

When you program with recursion, you'll notice two things. First, the recursive code that you write will tend to be fairly short even though it might be solving a very complex task. Second, you will generally find that most of your program ends up being supporting code for the recursion that does low-level tasks. For this problem we have a short and powerful prefix evaluator, but we need to include some supporting code that explains the program to the user, prompts for a prefix expression, and reports the result. We also found that we needed a method that would apply an operator to two operands. The nonrecursive parts of the program are fairly straightforward, so they are included in the following code without detailed discussion:

```
 1  // This program prompts for and evaluates a prefix expression.
 2
 3  import java.util.*;
 4
 5  public class PrefixEvaluator {
 6      public static void main(String[] args) {
 7          Scanner console = new Scanner(System.in);
 8          System.out.println("This program evaluates prefix");
 9          System.out.println("expressions that include the");
10          System.out.println("operators +, -, *, / and %");
11          System.out.print("expression? ");
12          double value = evaluate(console);
13          System.out.println("value = " + value);
14      }
15
16      // pre : input contains a legal prefix expression
17      // post: expression is consumed and the result is returned
18      public static double evaluate(Scanner input) {
19          if (input.hasNextDouble()) {
20              return input.nextDouble();
21          } else {
22              String operator = input.next();
23              double operand1 = evaluate(input);
24              double operand2 = evaluate(input);
25              return apply(operator, operand1, operand2);
26          }
27      }
28
29      // pre : operator is one of +, -, *, / or %
30      // post: returns the result of applying the given operator
31      //       to the given operands
32      public static double apply(String operator, double operand1,
```

in a list of books sorted by the author's last name. If the dictionary is large or the list of books is long, you probably won't want to sequentially examine all the items it contains.

There's a better algorithm called *binary search* that searches sorted data much faster than a sequential search. A normal sequential search of a million-element array may have to examine all the elements, but a binary search will need to look at only around 20 of them. Java's class libraries contain methods that implement the binary search algorithm for arrays and lists.

The binary search algorithm begins by examining the center element of the array or list. If the center element is smaller than the target you're searching for, there's no reason to examine any elements to the left of the center (at lower indexes). If the center element is larger than the target you're searching for, there's no reason to examine any elements to the right of the center (at greater indexes). On each pass of the algorithm, half the search space is eliminated from consideration, so in most cases the target value is found much faster than it would be with a sequential search.

The logic of the binary search algorithm is similar to the strategy people use in a high/low guessing game where the computer generates a random number between 1 and 100 and the user tries to guess it. After each incorrect guess, the program gives a hint about whether the user's guess was too high or too low. A poor algorithm for this game is to guess 1, 2, 3, and so on. A smarter algorithm is to guess the middle number and cut the range in half each time based on whether the guess was too high or too low. Figure 13.1 shows how this works.

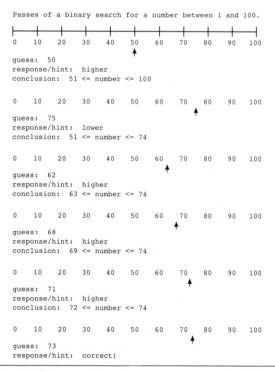

FIGURE 13.1   Passes of a binary search for a number between 1 and 100

A binary search uses this same approach when searching a sorted array for a target value. The algorithm scales extremely well to large input data; when searching a list with a million elements, a binary search will have to examine only around 20 elements to find the target value.

The `Arrays` class in the `java.util` package contains a static method called `binarySearch` that implements the binary search algorithm. It accepts an array of any suitable type and a target value as its parameters and returns the index where you can find the target element. If the element isn't found, a negative index is returned.

The following code uses the `Arrays.binarySearch` method to find a number in an array of integers. It needs to examine only indexes 4, 6, and then 5 to find the target value at index 5:

```
// binary search on an array
int[] numbers = {-3, 2, 8, 12, 17, 29, 44, 58, 79};
int index = Arrays.binarySearch(numbers, 29);
System.out.println("29 is found at index " + index);
```

If you're using a list such as an `ArrayList` instead, you can call the static method `Collections.binarySearch` to search the list of elements. If you had an `ArrayList` called `list` containing the same elements as the array in the previous example, the following code would similarly search the elements at indexes 4, 6, and then 5 before assigning the value 5 to the variable `index`:

```
// binary search on an ArrayList
int index = Collections.binarySearch(list, 29);
System.out.println("29 is found at index " + index);
```

With either an array or a list the data must be in sorted order to use the `binarySearch` method, because it relies on the ordering to more quickly find the target value. If you call `binarySearch` on unsorted data, the results are undefined and the algorithm doesn't guarantee that it will return the right answer.

The following program demonstrates a binary search for a word in a dictionary file. The input file's words occur in sorted order, so the list can be properly searched using `Collections.binarySearch`.

```
 1   // Searches for a word in a dictionary text file
 2   // and reports that word's position in the file.
 3
 4   import java.io.*;
 5   import java.util.*;
 6
 7   public class FindWords {
 8       public static void main(String[] args)
 9               throws FileNotFoundException {
10           // read sorted dictionary file into an ArrayList
11           Scanner in = new Scanner(new File("words.txt"));
12           ArrayList<String> words = new ArrayList<String>();
13           while (in.hasNext()) {
14               String word = in.next();
15               words.add(word);
16           }
```

Now that we've written a length comparator, we can pass one when sorting an array or list of String objects:

```
// sort array of strings by length using Comparator
Arrays.sort(strings, new LengthComparator());
System.out.println(Arrays.toString(strings));
```

Here's the output when used on the String array from earlier in this section. Notice that the strings appear in order of increasing length:

```
[echo, golf, alpha, bravo, hotel, DELTA, Foxtrot, Charlie]
```

Sometimes you'll want to search or sort a collection of objects that don't implement the Comparable interface. For example, the Point class doesn't implement Comparable, but you might want to sort an array of Point objects by x-coordinate, breaking ties by y-coordinate. The following is an example Comparator that compares Point objects in this way:

```
1   import java.awt.*;
2   import java.util.*;
3
4   // compares Point objects by x-coordinate and then by y-coordinate
5   public class PointComparator implements Comparator<Point> {
6       public int compare(Point p1, Point p2) {
7           int dx = p1.x - p2.x;
8           int dy = p1.y - p2.y;
9
10          if (dx == 0) {
11              return dy;
12          } else {
13              return dx;
14          }
15      }
16  }
```

The following code uses the PointComparator to sort an array of four Point objects:

```
Point[] points = {
    new Point(4, -2),
    new Point(3, 9),
    new Point(-1, 15),
    new Point(3, 7)
};
Arrays.sort(points, new PointComparator());
```

After this code, the points appear in the following order: $(-1, 15), (3, 7), (3, 9), (4, -2)$.

If you have a group of objects with a natural ordering and you want to sort them in reverse order, you can call the method Collections.reverseOrder to receive a Comparator that inverts the objects' natural ordering. For example, the following code would sort the preceding array of strings used earlier in reverse alphabetical order:

```
Arrays.sort(strings, Collections.reverseOrder());
```

For types without a natural ordering, you can ask for the reverse of a `Comparator`'s order by calling `Collections.reverseOrder` and passing the `Comparator` to be reversed. For example, the following code would sort the preceding array of `Point` objects by decreasing x-coordinate:

```
Arrays.sort(points, Collections.reverseOrder(new PointComparator()));
```

This would sort the points in the following order: $(4, -2), (3, 9), (3, 7), (-1, 15)$.

Table 13.2 summarizes several useful places comparators appear in the Java class libraries. Comparators can also be used with various collections that use element ordering, such as `TreeSets` or `TreeMaps`.

TABLE 13.2   Useful Comparators and Methods

Comparator/Method	Description
`Arrays.binarySearch(array, value, comparator)`	returns the index of the given value in the given array, assuming that the array is currently sorted in the ordering of the given comparator, returns a negative number if not found
`Arrays.sort(array, comparator)`	sorts the given array in the ordering of the given comparator
`Collections.binarySearch(list, value, comparator)`	returns the index of the given value in the given list, assuming that the list is currently sorted in the ordering of the given comparator; returns a negative number if not found
`Collections.max(collection, comparator)`	returns the largest value in the collection according to the ordering of the given comparator
`Collections.min(collection, comparator)`	returns the smallest value in the collection according to the ordering of the given comparator
`Collections.reverseOrder()`	returns a comparator that compares objects in the opposite of their natural order
`Collections.reverseOrder (comparator)`	returns a comparator that compares objects in the opposite of the ordering of the given comparator
`Collections.sort(list, comparator)`	sorts the given list in the ordering of the given comparator
`String.CASE_INSENSITIVE_ORDER`	sorts strings alphabetically, ignoring capitalization

13.2 Program Efficiency

In Chapter 8 we talked about client code, the code that interacts with a class or object. In this chapter we've looked at how to be a client of Java's powerful methods for searching and sorting data. Since searching and sorting are important programming ideas, it's worthwhile to understand how they are implemented as well. But before we dive into this, let's discuss some background ideas about how to analyze the efficiency of code.

As you progress in this textbook, you're writing increasingly complex programs. You're also seeing that there are often many ways to solve the same problem. How do you compare different solutions to the same problem to see which is better?

We say that an algorithm that solves a problem quickly is efficient or has high *efficiency*.

> **Efficiency**
>
> A measure of the computing resources used by a piece of code such as time, memory or disk space.

Often when we talk about a program's efficiency we are talking about how long the program takes to run, or its *time efficiency*. The time efficiency needed for a program to be considered "fast enough" depends on the task. A program running on a modern computer that requires five minutes to look up a dictionary word is probably too slow. An algorithm that renders a complex three-dimensional movie scene in five minutes is probably very fast.

One way to determine an algorithm's time efficiency is to program it, run the program, and measure how long it takes to run. This is sometimes called an *empirical analysis* of the algorithm. For example, consider two algorithms to search an array: one that sequentially searches for the desired target element, and one that first sorts the array and then performs a binary search on the sorted array. You could empirically analyze the algorithms by writing both as programs, running them on the same input, and timing them.

But empirically analyzing an algorithm isn't a very reliable measure, because on a different computer with a different processor speed and more or less memory the program may not run in the same amount of time. Also, to empirically test an algorithm you must write it and time it, which can be a chore.

A more neutral way to measure a program's performance is to examine its code or pseudocode and count roughly how many statements are executed. This is a form of *algorithm analysis,* which consists of applying techniques to mathematically approximate the performance of various computing algorithms. Algorithm analysis is an important tool in computer science. One of the fundamental principles of science in general is that we can make predictions and hypotheses using formal models, which we can then test by experimentation.

It's hard to know exactly how to count how many statements a piece of code executes, because not all statements require the same amount of time to execute. For example, a CPU can handle addition faster than multiplication, and a method call is generally slower than evaluating the Boolean test of an `if`/`else` statement. But for the purposes of simplification, let's consider the following actions as requiring an equal and fixed amount of time to execute:

- Variable declarations and assignments
- Evaluating mathematical and logical expressions
- Accessing or modifying an individual element of an array
- Simple method calls (where the method does not perform a loop)

From the preceding simple rules, we can extrapolate the runtimes of larger and more complex pieces of code. For example, the runtime of a group of statements in sequential order is the sum of the individual runtimes of the statements:

```
statement1.
statement2.   } 3
statement3.
```

The runtime of a loop is roughly equal to the runtime of its body times the number of iterations of the loop. For example, a loop whose body contains K simple statements that repeats N times will have a runtime of roughly $(K * N)$:

```
for (N times) {
    statement1.
    statement2.   } 3N
    statement3.
}
```

The runtime of multiple loops placed sequentially (not nested) with other statements is the sum of the loops' runtimes and the other statements' runtimes:

```
statement1.
for (N times) {
    statement2.   } N
}
                            } M + N + 3
for (M times) {
    statemnt3.    } M
}
statement4.
statement5.
```

The runtime of a loop containing a nested loop is roughly equal to the runtime of the inner loop multiplied by the number of repetitions of the outer loop:

```
for (M times) {
    for (N times) {
        statement1.
        statement2.      3      3N      3MN
        statement3.
    }
}
```

Normally, the loops in long-running algorithms are processing some kind of data. Many algorithms run very quickly if the input dataset is small, so we generally worry about the performance only for large datasets. For example, consider the following set of loops that process an array of N elements:

```
for (N times) {
    for (N times) {
        statement1.         N²
    }
}
                                          N² + 2N
for (N times) {
    statement2.
    statement3.         2N
}
```

When analyzing code like this, we often think about which line is the most frequently executed in the code. In programs with several sequential blocks of code that all relate to some common value N (such as the size of an input dataset), the block raised to the highest power of N usually dominates the overall runtime. In the preceding code, the first N^2 loop executes its statement far more times than the second N loop executes its two statements. For example, if N is 1,000, `statement1` executes (1,000 * 1,000) or 1,000,000 times, while `statement2` and `statement3` each execute only 1,000 times.

When performing algorithm analysis, we often ignore all but the most frequently executed part of the code, because its runtime will outweigh the runtime of the other parts of the code. For example, we might refer to the preceding code as being "on the order of" N^2, ignoring the extra $2N$ statements altogether. We'll revisit this idea later in the chapter.

One key concept to take away from this brief discussion of algorithm analysis is how expensive it is to perform nested loops over large sets of input data. Algorithms that make many nested passes over a very large dataset tend to perform poorly, so it's important to come up with efficient algorithms that don't loop over data needlessly.

Now let's take a look at algorithm efficiency in action, observing the runtimes of some actual algorithms that can be used to solve a programming problem on a large dataset.

Empirical Analysis

Consider the task of computing the statistical range of numbers in an array. The range is the difference between the lowest and highest numbers in the array. An initial solution might use nested loops to examine every pair of elements in the array, computing their difference and remembering the largest difference found:

```
max = 0.
for (each index i) {
    for (each index j) {
        update max, if elements i and j differ by more than max.
    }
}
```

The following code implements the `range` method as described:

```
// returns the range of numbers in the given array
public static int range(int[] numbers) {
    int maxDiff = 0;
    for (int i = 0; i < numbers.length; i++) {
        for (int j = 0; j < numbers.length; j++) {
            int diff = Math.abs(numbers[j] - numbers[i]);
            maxDiff = Math.max(maxDiff, diff);
        }
    }
    return maxDiff;
}
```

Since the code has two `for` loops that each process the entire array, we can hypothesize that the algorithm executes roughly N^2 statements, or some multiple thereof.

We can measure the speed of this range algorithm in milliseconds by calling `range` on various arrays and measuring the time elapsed. The timing is done by acquiring the current time before and after calling `range` on a large array and subtracting the start time from the end time.

As you can see in Figure 13.2, as the input size N doubles, the runtime of the `range` method approximately quadruples. This is consistent with our hypothesis. If the algorithm takes N^2 statements to run and we increase the input size to $2N$, the new runtime is roughly $(2N)^2$ or $4N^2$, which is four times as long as the original runtime.

Our code isn't very efficient for a large array. It requires over 12 seconds to examine 32,000 integers on a modern computer. In real-world data-processing situations we would expect to see far larger input datasets than this, so this runtime isn't acceptable for general use.

Looking at a piece of code and trying to figure out how to speed it up can be deceptively difficult. It's tempting to approach the problem by looking at each line of code and trying to reduce the amount of computation it performs. For example, you may have noticed that our `range` method actually examines every pair of elements in the array twice: For unique integers `i` and `j`, we examine the pair of elements at indexes (`i`, `j`) as well as the pair at (`j`, `i`).

N	Runtime (ms)
1000	15
2000	47
4000	203
8000	781
16000	3110
32000	12563
64000	49937

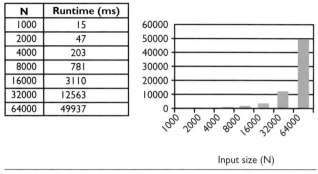

Input size (N)

FIGURE 13.2 Runtimes for first version of range algorithm

We can perform a minor modification to our `range` methods code by starting each inner `j` loop ahead of `i`, so that we won't examine any pair (`i`, `j`) where `i` ≥ `j`. Performing minor modifications like this is sometimes called *tweaking* an algorithm. The following code implements our tweaked version of the range algorithm:

```java
// returns the largest integer in the given array
public static int range2(int[] numbers) {
    int maxDiff = 0;
    for (int i = 0; i < numbers.length; i++) {
        for (int j = i + 1; j < numbers.length; j++) {
            int diff = Math.abs(numbers[j] - numbers[i]);
            maxDiff = Math.max(maxDiff, diff);
        }
    }
    return maxDiff;
}
```

Since about half of the possible pairs of `i`/`j` values are eliminated by this tweak, we'd hope that the code would run about twice as fast. Figure 13.3 shows its actual measured runtime. As we estimated, the second version is about twice as fast as the first. We could implement other minor tweaks, such as replacing the `Math.max` call with a simple `if` test (which would speed up the algorithm by around 10% more), but

N	Runtime (ms)
1000	16
2000	16
4000	110
8000	406
16000	1578
32000	6265
64000	25031

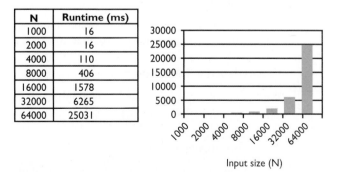

Input size (N)

FIGURE 13.3 Runtimes for second version of range algorithm

there's a more important point to be made. When the input size doubles, the runtime of either version of the algorithm roughly quadruples. Consequently, regardless of which version we use, if the input array is very large the method will be too slow.

Rather than trying to further tweak our nested loop solution, let's try to think of a more efficient algorithm. As stated earlier, the range of values in an array is the difference between the array's largest and smallest elements. We don't really need to examine all pairs of values to find this range; we just need to discover the pair representing the largest and smallest values. We can discover both of these values in a single loop over the array by using a `min`/`max` loop, as discussed in Chapter 4. The following new algorithm demonstrates this idea:

```
// returns the largest of all integers in the given array
public static int range3(int[] numbers) {
    int max = numbers[0];
    int min = max;
    for (int i = 1; i < numbers.length; i++) {
        if (numbers[i] > max) {
            max = numbers[i];
        } else if (numbers[i] < min) {
            min = numbers[i];
        }
    }

    return max - min;
}
```

Since this algorithm passes over the array only once, we'd hope that its runtime is proportional to the array's length. If the array length doubles, the runtime should double, not quadruple. Figure 13.4 shows its runtime.

Our runtime predictions were roughly correct. As the size of the array doubles, the runtime of this new range algorithm approximately doubles as well. The overall runtime of this algorithm is much better; we can examine over a hundred million integers in under one second.

There are some important observations to take away from this exercise:

- Tweaking an algorithm's code often isn't as powerful an optimization as finding a better algorithm.

- An algorithm's rate of growth, or the amount its runtime increases as the input dataset grows, is one of the most important measures of the efficiency of the algorithm.

Complexity Classes

We categorize rates of growth based on their proportion to the input data size *N*. We call these categories *complexity classes* or *growth rates*.

> **Complexity Class**
>
> A category of algorithm efficiency based upon the algorithm's relationship to the input data size.

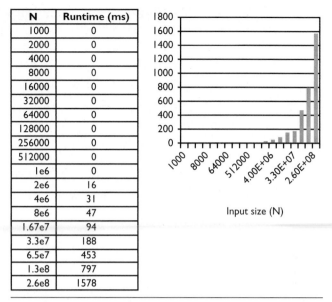

N	Runtime (ms)
1000	0
2000	0
4000	0
8000	0
16000	0
32000	0
64000	0
128000	0
256000	0
512000	0
1e6	0
2e6	16
4e6	31
8e6	47
1.67e7	94
3.3e7	188
6.5e7	453
1.3e8	797
2.6e8	1578

FIGURE 13.4 Runtimes for third version of range algorithm

The complexity class of a piece of code is determined by looking at the most frequently executed line of code, determining the number of times it is executed, and extracting the highest power of N. For example, if the most frequent line executes ($2N^3 + 4N$) times, we say that the algorithm is in the "order N^3" complexity class, or $O(N^3)$ for short. The shorthand notation with the capital O is called *big-Oh notation* and is used commonly in algorithm analysis.

Here are some of the most common complexity classes, listed in order from slowest to fastest growth (i.e., from most to least efficient):

- *Constant-time* or $O(1)$ algorithms are those whose runtimes don't depend on input size. Some examples of constant-time algorithms would be code to convert Fahrenheit temperatures to Celsius or numerical functions such as `Math.abs`.

- *Logarithmic* or $O(\log N)$ algorithms typically divide a problem space in half repeatedly until the problem is solved. Binary search is an example of a logarithmic-time algorithm.

- *Linear* or $O(N)$ algorithms are those whose runtimes are directly proportional to N (i.e., roughly double when N doubles). The last version of the `range` method in the previous section is a linear algorithm.

- *Log-linear* or $O(N \log N)$ algorithms typically perform a combination of logarithmic and linear operations, such as executing a logarithmic algorithm over every element of a dataset of size N. Many efficient sorting algorithms, such as merge sort (discussed later in this chapter), are log-linear.

Did You Know?

Timing Code and the Epoch

The current time is found in Java using a method called `System.currentTimeMillis`. It returns the number of milliseconds that have passed since 12:00 AM on January 1, 1970. Over one trillion milliseconds have passed since this time, so the value is too large to store in a simple `int` value. The milliseconds are instead returned as a value of type `long`, which is a primitive type that's similar to `int` but capable of holding much larger values. A `long` can store any number up to 9,223,372,036,854,775,807, or roughly 2^{63}.

The following code shows an example of how a piece of code can be timed:

```
long startTime = System.currentTimeMillis();
<code to be timed>
long endTime = System.currentTimeMillis();
System.out.println("Elapsed time: " + (endTime - startTime));
```

The choice of January 1, 1970 as the point of reference for system times is an example of an *epoch,* or an instant chosen as the origin of a particular time scale. This particular epoch was chosen because it matches the epochs of many popular operating systems, including Unix.

For historical reasons, many older Unix operating systems store the time passed since the epoch as a 32-bit integer value. However, unspecified problems may occur when this number exceeds its capacity, which is not necessarily a rare event. The clocks of some Unix systems will overflow on January 19, 2038, creating a Year 2038 problem similar to the famous Year 2000 or Y2K problem.

- *Quadratic* or $O(N^2)$ algorithms are those whose runtimes are proportional to the square of the input size. This means that quadratic algorithms' runtimes roughly quadruple when N doubles. The initial versions of the range algorithm developed in the previous section were quadratic algorithms.
- *Cubic* or $O(N^3)$ algorithms are those whose runtimes are proportional to the cube of the input size. Such algorithms often make triply nested passes over the input data. Code to count the number of colinear trios of points in a large `Point` array would be an example of a cubic algorithm.
- *Exponential* or $O(2^N)$ algorithms are those whose runtimes are proportional to 2 raised to the power of the input size. This means that if the input size increases by just one, the algorithm will take roughly twice as long to execute. One example would be code to print the "power set" of a dataset, which is the set of all possible subsets of the data. Exponential algorithms are so slow that they should be executed only on very small input datasets.

TABLE 13.3   Algorithm Runtime Comparison Chart

Input size (N)	O(1)	O(log N)	O(N)	O(N log N)	O(N²)	O(N³)	O(2ⁿ)
100	100 ms	100 ms	100 ms	100 ms	100 ms	100 ms	100 ms
200	100 ms	115 ms	200 ms	240 ms	400 ms	800 ms	32.7 sec
400	100 ms	130 ms	400 ms	550 ms	1.6 sec	6.4 sec	12.4 days
800	100 ms	145 ms	800 ms	1.2 sec	6.4 sec	51.2 sec	36.5 million years
1600	100 ms	160 ms	1.6 sec	2.7 sec	25.6 sec	6 min 49.6 sec	$4.21 * 10^{24}$ years
3200	100 ms	175 ms	3.2 sec	6 sec	1 min 42.4 sec	54 min 36 sec	$5.6 * 10^{61}$ years

The column header row reads: Input size (N) $O(1)$ $O(\log N)$ $O(N)$ $O(N \log N)$ $O(N^2)$ $O(N^3)$ $O(2^N)$

Table 13.3 presents several hypothetical algorithm runtimes as the input size N grows, assuming that each algorithm requires 100 ms to process 100 elements. Notice that even though they all start at the same runtime for a small input size, as N grows the algorithms in higher complexity classes become so slow as to be impractical.

Looking at the numbers in Table 13.3, one might wonder why anyone bothers to use $O(N^3)$ or $O(2^N)$, algorithms when $O(1)$ and $O(N)$ algorithms are so much faster. The answer is that not all problems can be solved in $O(1)$ or even $O(N)$ time. Computer scientists have been studying classic problems such as searching and sorting for many years, trying to find the most efficient algorithms possible. However, there will likely never be a constant-time algorithm that can sort 1,000,000 elements as quickly as it can sort 10 elements.

For large datasets it's very important to choose the most efficient algorithms possible (i.e., those with the lowest complexity classes). Algorithms with complexity classes of $O(N^2)$ or worse will take a long time to run on extremely large datasets. Keeping this in mind, we'll now examine algorithms to search and sort data.

13.3 Implementing Searching and Sorting Algorithms

In this section we'll implement methods that search and sort data. We'll start by writing code to search for an integer in an array of integers and return the index where it is found. If the integer doesn't appear in the array, we'll return a negative number. We'll examine two major searching algorithms, sequential and binary search, and discuss the tradeoffs between them.

While there are literally hundreds of algorithms to sort data, we'll cover two in detail in this chapter. The first, seen later in this section, is one of the more intuitive algorithms, although it performs poorly on large datasets. The second, examined as a case study in the next section, is one of the fastest sorting algorithms used in practice today.

Sequential Search

Perhaps the simplest way to search an array is to loop over the elements of the array and check each one to see if it is the target number. As mentioned earlier, this is called a sequential search because it examines every element in sequence.

We implemented a sequential search of an array of integers in Chapter 7. The code uses a `for` loop and is relatively straightforward. The algorithm returns −1 if the loop completes without finding the target number:

```
// Sequential search algorithm.
// Returns the index at which the given target number first
// appears in the given input array, or -1 if it not found.
public static int indexOf(int[] list, int target) {
    for (int i = 0; i < list.length; i++) {
        if (list[i] == target) {
            return i;
        }
    }
    return -1;    // not found
}
```

Based on the rules stated in the previous section, we predict that the sequential search algorithm is a linear, $O(N)$ algorithm because it contains one loop that traverses at most N elements in an array. (We say "at most" because if the algorithm finds the target element, it stops and immediately returns.) Next we'll time it to verify our prediction.

Figure 13.5 shows actual results of running the sequential search algorithm on randomly generated arrays of integers. Searches were conducted for a value known to be in the array and for a value not in the array.

When searching for an integer that isn't in the array the algorithm runs somewhat slower, because it can't exit its loop early by finding the target. This raises the question of whether we should judge the algorithm by its fastest or slowest runtime. Often what's most important is the expected behavior for a typical input, or the average of its runtime over all possible inputs. This is called an *average case analysis*. But in certain conditions, we also care about the fastest possible outcome, the *best case analysis,* and/or the slowest possible outcome, the *worst case analysis.*

Binary Search

Consider a modified version of the searching problem, where we can assume that the elements of the input array are in sorted order. Does this affect our algorithm? Our existing algorithm will still work correctly, but now we know that we can stop searching if we ever get to a number larger than our target without finding the target. For example, if we're searching an array containing the elements (1, 4, 5, 7, 7, 9, 10, 12, 56) for the target value 8, we can stop searching once we see the 9.

N	Runtime when element is found (ms)	Runtime when element is not found (ms)
100000	0	0
200000	0	0
400000	0	0
800000	0	0
1.6e6	0	16
3.2e6	15	16
6.4e6	16	31
1.3e7	32	47
2.6e7	37	93
5.1e7	45	203
1.0e8	72	402
2.0e8	125	875

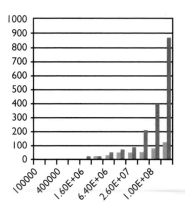

Input size (N)

FIGURE 13.5　Runtimes for sequential search algorithm

It might seem that such a modification to our sequential search algorithm would lead to a significant speedup, but in actuality it doesn't make much difference. The only case in which it speeds up the algorithm noticeably is when searching for a relatively small value that isn't found in the array. In fact, when searching for a large value that requires the code to examine most or all of the array elements, the modified algorithm actually performs slower than the original because it has to perform a few more Boolean tests. Most importantly, the algorithm is still $O(N)$, which isn't the optimal solution.

Once again, tweaking the algorithm won't make as much difference as finding another, more efficient algorithm. If the input array is in sorted order, a sequential search isn't the best choice. If you had to instruct a robot on how to look up a person's phone number in a phone book, would you tell the robot to read through all the entries on the first page, then the second, and so on until it found the person's name? Not unless you wanted to torture the poor robot. You know that the entries are sorted by name, so you'd tell the robot to flip open the book to somewhere near the middle, then narrow its search down toward the first letter of the person's name.

The binary search algorithm discussed previously in this chapter takes advantage of the ordering of the array. A binary search keeps track of the range of the array that is currently of interest. (Initially, this range is the whole array.) The algorithm repeatedly examines the center element of the array and uses its value to eliminate half of the range of interest. If the center element is smaller than the target, the lower half of the range is eliminated; if the center element is larger than the target, the upper half is eliminated.

As the algorithm runs, we must keep track of three indexes:

- The minimum index of interest (`min`)
- The maximum index of interest (`max`)
- The middle index, halfway between the minimum and maximum, which will be examined during each pass of the algorithm (`mid`)

The algorithm repeatedly examines the element at the middle index and uses it to trim the range of indexes of interest in half. If we examine the middle element and find it's too small, we will eliminate all elements between `min` and `mid` from consideration. If the middle element is too large, we will eliminate all elements between `mid` and `max` from consideration.

Consider the following array:

```
int[] numbers = {11, 18, 29, 37, 42, 49, 51, 63,
                 69, 72, 77, 82, 88, 91, 98};
```

0	1	2	3	4	5	6	7	8	9	10	11	12	13	14
11	18	29	37	42	49	51	63	69	72	77	82	88	91	98

Let's binary search the array for a target value of 77. We'll start at the middle element, which is at index (15 / 2), or 7 by integer division. The following diagrams show the `min`, `mid`, and `max` at each step of the algorithm:

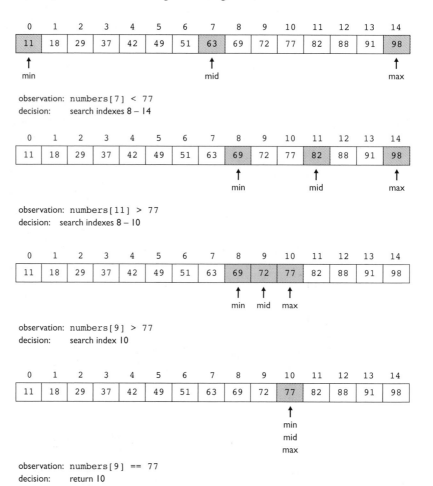

observation: `numbers[7] < 77`
decision: search indexes 8 – 14

observation: `numbers[11] > 77`
decision: search indexes 8 – 10

observation: `numbers[9] > 77`
decision: search index 10

observation: `numbers[9] == 77`
decision: return 10

What about when we're searching for an element that isn't found in the array? Let's say we're searching for the value 78 instead of 77. The steps of the algorithm will be the same, except on the fourth pass 77 will be seen instead of the desired value, 78. The algorithm will have eliminated the entire range without finding the target and will know that it should stop. Another way to describe the process is that the algorithm loops until the min and max have crossed each other.

The following code implements the binary search algorithm. Its loop repeats until the target is found or until the min and max have crossed:

```
// Binary search algorithm.
// Returns an index at which the target
// appears in the given input array, or -1 if not found.
// pre: array is sorted.
public static int binarySearch(int[] numbers, int target) {
    int min = 0;
    int max = numbers.length - 1;

    while (min <= max) {
        int mid = (max + min) / 2;
        if (numbers[mid] == target) {
            return mid;        // found it!
        } else if (numbers[mid] < target) {
            min = mid + 1;   // too small
        } else {    // numbers[mid] > target
            max = mid - 1;   // too large
        }
    }

    return -1;               // not found
}
```

We won't bother to show a runtime chart for the binary search algorithm, because there would be nothing to draw on the chart. This algorithm is so fast that the computer's clock has trouble measuring its runtime. On a modern computer, even an array of over 100,000,000 elements registers as taking 0 ms to search!

While this is an impressive result, it makes it harder for us to empirically examine the runtime. What is the complexity class of the binary search algorithm? The fact that it finishes so quickly tempts us to conclude that it's a constant-time, or $O(1)$, algorithm. But it doesn't seem right that a method with a loop in it would take a constant amount of time to execute. There is a relation between the runtime and the input size, because the larger the input is, the more times we must divide our min–max range in half to arrive at a single element. We could make the following statement about the number of repetitions as related to the input size N:

$$2^{\text{repetitions}} \cong N$$

Using some algebra and taking a logarithm base-2 of both sides of the equation:

$$\text{repetitions} \cong \log_2 N$$

we conclude that the binary search algorithm is in the logarithmic complexity class, or $O(\log N)$.

The runtime of the binary search algorithm doesn't differ much between the best and worst cases. In the best case, the algorithm finds its target value in the middle on the first check. In the worst case, the code must perform the full ($\log N$) comparisons. But since logarithms are small numbers ($\log_2$ 1,000,000 is roughly 20), the performance is still excellent in the worst case.

Recursive Binary Search

In the previous section, binary search was implemented using an iterative algorithm with a `for` loop. But the algorithm can also be implemented elegantly using the concept of recursion introduced in Chapter 12. The idea is to write a recursive binary search method that accepts the minimum and maximum indexes of interest as parameters. The method can recursively call itself with different values of `min` and `max` until it finds the target. The following code implements the recursive algorithm:

```
// Recursive binary search algorithm.
// Returns an index at which the target
// appears in the given input array, or -1 if not found.
// pre: array is sorted.
public static int binarySearchR(int[] numbers, int target,
                                int min, int max) {
    // base case
    if (min > max) {
        return -1;    // not found
    } else {
        // recursive case
        int mid = (max + min) / 2;
        if (numbers[mid] == target) {
            return mid;
        } else if (numbers[mid] < target) {
            return binarySearchR(numbers, target, mid + 1, max);
        } else {
            return binarySearchR(numbers, target, min, mid - 1);
        }
    }
}
```

One problem with the preceding method is that its parameters don't match those of the original `binarySearch` method. When client code calls it, the initial minimum and maximum indexes must be passed as parameters. Their values will always be `0` and the last index of the array. For example:

```
int index = binarySearchR(numbers, target, 0, numbers.length - 1);
```

To solve this problem, we can overload the `binarySearchR` method by writing another version that accepts only the array and target value as parameters. This short method will call the other `binarySearchR` method and pass the last two parameters for us:

```
// Recursive binary search algorithm.
// This "helper" method requires fewer parameters.
public static int binarySearchR(int[] numbers, int target) {
    return binarySearchR(numbers, target, 0, numbers.length - 1);
}
```

A method like this is sometimes called a *helper method* because it is used only for convenience.

Some instructors don't like recursive versions of methods like binary search because there is a nonrecursive solution that's fairly easy to write, and because recursion tends to have poor runtime performance. While recursion can be a bit slow because of the extra method calls it generates, that doesn't pose a problem here. The runtime of the recursive version of our binary search method is still $O(\log N)$, because it's essentially performing the same computation; it's still cutting the input in half at each step. In fact, the recursive version is fast enough that the computer still can't time it accurately; it produces a runtime of 0 ms even on arrays of tens of millions of integers.

In general, analyzing the runtimes of recursive algorithms is tricky. Recursive runtime analysis often requires a technique called *recurrence relations*. That's a topic for a later course that won't be covered in this textbook.

Did You Know?

Binary Search Details

There are a few interesting things about Sun's implementation of binary search in `Arrays.binarySearch` and `Collections.binarySearch` that we haven't mentioned yet. Take a look at this text from the Javadoc documentation of Sun's `binarySearch` method:

> The array **must** be sorted (as by the `sort` method, above) prior to making this call. If it is not sorted, the results are undefined. If the array contains multiple elements with the specified value, there is no guarantee which one will be found.

Binary search depends on the array being sorted. If it isn't sorted, Sun says the results are undefined. What does that mean? Why doesn't the algorithm just sort the array for you if it's unsorted?

There are two problems with that idea, both essentially related to runtime performance. For one, sorting takes much longer ($O(N \log N)$ time) than a binary search ($O(\log N)$ time). Second, to even discover that one needs to sort requires looking at each element to determine whether they're in order, which takes $O(N)$ time. Essentially, the cost of examining the array and sorting it if necessary would be too great.

(continues)

Even if the cost of sorting the array weren't so large, the client of the `binarySearch` method probably won't want its array modified by the `binarySearch` method. Searching is supposed to be a read-only operation, not one that rearranges the array.

Let's look at the other part of the previous quote: "If the array contains multiple elements with the specified value, there is no guarantee which one will be found." We didn't mention this earlier when discussing the algorithm, but in the case of duplicates, binary search isn't guaranteed to find the first occurrence of the element, because the moment it finds an occurrence it stops.

Here's another interesting blurb from the `binarySearch` documentation:

Returns: index of the search key, if it is contained in the list; otherwise, `(-(insertion point) - 1)`. The insertion point is defined as the point at which the key would be inserted into the list: the index of the first element greater than the key, or `list.size()`, if all elements in the list are less than the specified key. Note that this guarantees that the return value will be `>= 0` if and only if the key is found.

Rather than returning –1 for an unsuccessful search, the `Arrays.binarySearch` and `Collections.binarySearch` methods return (`-index - 1`), where `index` is the last index the algorithm examined before giving up, which is also the index of the first element whose value is greater than the target. The documentation for these methods calls this value the *insertion point* because if you wanted to add the target to the array in sorted position, you'd place it at that index. For example, because a binary search of the following array for the value 45 would finish at index 5, the algorithm would return –6:

0	1	2	3	4	5	6	7	8	9	10	11	12	13	14
11	18	29	37	42	49	51	63	69	72	77	82	88	91	98

If you were maintaining this sorted array and wanted to add 45 to it at the proper index to retain the sorted order, you could call `Arrays.binarySearch`, get the result of –6, and negate and subtract 1 from it to get the index at which you should insert the value. This is much faster than linearly searching for the place to add the value, or adding the value at the end and re-sorting the array.

We could modify our own binary search code to match Sun's behavior by changing the last line of the method's body to the following:

```
return -min - 1;    // not found
```

Searching Objects

Searching for a particular object in an array of objects requires a few modifications to our searching code from the previous sections. Let's look at a sequential object search first, because it will work with any type of object. The most important modification to make to the code is that it should use the equals method to compare objects for equality:

```
// Sequential search algorithm.
// Returns the index at which the target first
// appears in the given input array, or -1 if not found.
public static int indexOf(Object[] objects, Object target) {
    for (int i = 0; i < objects.length; i++) {
        if (objects[i].equals(target)) {
            return i;   // found it!
        }
    }
    return -1;   // not found
}
```

If we want to do a binary search on objects, the objects must have a natural ordering (in other words, must be of a type that implements the Comparable interface), and the elements in the array or collection must be in sorted order. One common example would be an array of Strings. Since we can't use relational operators like < and >= on objects, we must call the compareTo method on pairs of String objects and examine its return value. The following code implements a binary search on an array of Strings:

```
// Binary search algorithm that works with Strings.
// Returns the index at which the given target String
// appears in the given input array, or -1 if not found.
// pre: array is sorted
public static int binarySearch(String[] strings, String target) {
    int min = 0;
    int max = strings.length - 1;

    while (min <= max) {
        int mid = (max + min) / 2;
        int compare = strings[mid].compareTo(target);
        if (compare == 0) {
            return mid;      // found it!
        } else if (compare < 0) {
            min = mid + 1;   // too small
        } else { // compare > 0
            max = mid - 1;   // too large
        }
    }

    return -1;   // not found
}
```

Selection Sort

Selection sort is a well-known sorting algorithm that makes many passes over an input array to put its elements into sorted order. Each time through a loop, the smallest value is selected and put in the proper place near the front of the array. Consider the following array:

```
int[] nums = {12, 123, 1, 28, 183, 16};
```

	0	1	2	3	4	5
	12	123	1	28	183	16

How would you put its elements into order from smallest to largest? The selection sort algorithm conceptually divides the array into two pieces: sorted elements at the front and unsorted elements at the end. The first step of the selection sort makes a pass over the array and finds the smallest number. In the sample array the smallest is nums[2], which equals 1. The algorithm then swaps the smallest value into its proper place at the front of the array. In this case, nums[0] and nums[2] are swapped:

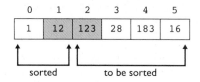

The element at index 0 now has the value it should, and only the elements at indexes 1 through 5 remain to be ordered. The algorithm now repeats this process of scanning the unsorted portion of the array and looking for the smallest element. On the second pass the remaining five elements are scanned and nums[2], which equals 12, is found to be the smallest element. It is swapped with nums[1]. After this swap, the sorted area of the array consists of its first two indexes:

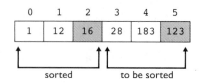

Now nums[0] and nums[1] have the correct values. The third pass of the algorithm scans the remaining four unsorted elements and finds the smallest to be nums[5], which equals 16. It swaps this element with nums[2]:

	0	1	2	3	4	5
	1	12	16	28	183	123

sorted   to be sorted

The algorithm continues this process until all elements have the proper values. Each pass involves a scan followed by a swap. The scan/swap occurs five times to process six elements. You don't need to perform a sixth scan/swap because if the first five elements have the correct values the sixth will as well.

Here is a pseudocode description of the execution of the selection sort algorithm over an array nums that has six elements:

Subarrays								Next include		Merged array							

```
 0   1   2   3    0   1   2   3                       0   1   2   3   4   5   6   7
14  32  67  76   23  41  58  85     85 from right    14  23  32  41  58  67  76  85
                           ↑                                                  ↑
                           i2                                                 i
```

The following code is an initial attempt to implement the merge algorithm just described:

```java
// initial incorrect attempt
public static void merge(int[] result,
                         int[] left, int[] right) {
    int i1 = 0;    // index into left array
    int i2 = 0;    // index into right array

    for (int i = 0; i < result.length; i++) {
        if (left[i1] <= right[i2]) {
            result[i] = left[i1];     // take from left
            i1++;
        } else {
            result[i] = right[i2];    // take from right
            i2++;
        }
    }
}
```

The preceding code is incorrect and will cause an `ArrayIndexOutOfBoundsException`. After the seventh step of the preceding diagram, all of the elements in the left subarray have been consumed, and the left index `i1` runs off the end of the subarray. This means that the code will crash when it tries to access element `left[i1]`. A similar problem would occur if the right index `i2` exceeded the bounds of the right array.

We need to modify our code to remain within the bounds of the arrays. The `if/else` logic needs to ensure that the index `i1` or `i2` is within the array bounds before accessing the appropriate element. The simple test in the pseudocode needs to be expanded:

```
if (i2 has passed the end of the right array, or
    left element at i1 < right element at i2) {
    take from left.
} else {
    take from right.
}
```

The following second version of the code correctly implements the merging behavior. The preconditions and postconditions of the method are documented in comments:

```java
// Merges the given left and right arrays into the given
// result array. Second, working version.
```

```
// pre : result is empty; left/right are sorted
// post: result contains result of merging sorted lists.
public static void merge(int[] result,
                         int[] left, int[] right) {
    int i1 = 0;    // index into left array
    int i2 = 0;    // index into right array

    for (int i = 0; i < result.length; i++) {
        if (i2 >= right.length || (i1 < left.length &&
                left[i1] <= right[i2])) {
            result[i] = left[i1];    // take from left
            i1++;
        } else {
            result[i] = right[i2];    // take from right
            i2++;
        }
    }
}
```

Recursive Merge Sort

We've written the code to split an array into halves and to merge the sorted halves into a sorted whole. The overall merge sort method now looks like this:

```
public static void mergeSort(int[] array) {
    // split array into two halves
    int[] left = leftHalf(array);
    int[] right = rightHalf(array);

    // sort the two halves
    ...

    // merge the sorted halves into a sorted whole
    merge(array, left, right);
}
```

The missing piece is the code to sort each half of the array. How can we sort the halves? We could call the selectionSort method created earlier in this chapter on the two halves, a better approach would be to merge sort them. We can recursively call our own mergeSort method on the array halves, and if it's written correctly, it'll put each of them into sorted order. Our original pseudocode can now be rewritten as the following:

```
split the array into two halves.
merge sort the left half.
merge sort the right half.
merge the two halves.
```

If we're making our merge sort algorithm recursive, it needs a base case and a recursive case. The preceding pseudocode specifies the recursive case, but for the base case, what are the simplest arrays to sort? An array with either no elements or just one element doesn't need to be sorted at all. At least two elements must be present in order for them to appear in the wrong order, so the simple cases are arrays of length less than 2. This means that our final pseudocode for the merge sort method is the following:

```
if (array length is at least 1) {
    split the array into two halves.
    merge sort the left half.
    merge sort the right half.
    merge the two halves.
}
```

No `else` case is needed because if the array size is 0 or 1, we don't need to do anything to the array. This recursive algorithm has an empty base case.

The following method implements the complete merge sort algorithm:

```java
// Places the elements of the given array into sorted order
// using the merge sort algorithm.
// post: array is in sorted (nondecreasing) order
public static void mergeSort(int[] array) {
    if (array.length > 1) {
        // split array into two halves
        int[] left = leftHalf(array);
        int[] right = rightHalf(array);

        // recursively sort the two halves
        mergeSort(left);
        mergeSort(right);

        // merge the sorted halves into a sorted whole
        merge(array, left, right);
    }
}
```

To get a better idea of the algorithm in action, we'll temporarily insert a few `println` statements into its code and run the method on the eight-element sample array shown previously in this section. We'll insert the following `println` statement at the start of the `mergeSort` method:

```java
// at start of mergeSort method
System.out.println("sorting " + Arrays.toString(array));
```

and the following `println` statement at the start of the `merge` method:

```java
// at start of merge method
System.out.println("merging " + Arrays.toString(left) +
                   " and " + Arrays.toString(right));
```

Here is the output from running `mergeSort` on the example array:

```
sorting [14, 32, 67, 76, 23, 41, 58, 85]
sorting [14, 32, 67, 76]
sorting [14, 32]
sorting [14]
sorting [32]
merging [14] and [32]
sorting [67, 76]
sorting [67]
```

```
sorting [76]
merging [67] and [76]
merging [14, 32] and [67, 76]
sorting [23, 41, 58, 85]
sorting [23, 41]
sorting [23]
sorting [41]
merging [23] and [41]
sorting [58, 85]
sorting [58]
sorting [85]
merging [58] and [85]
merging [23, 41] and [58, 85]
merging [14, 32, 67, 76] and [23, 41, 58, 85]
```

It's also important to test the code on an array that doesn't divide into subarrays of exactly equal size (i.e., one whose overall length is not a power of 2). Because it employs integer division, our code makes the left subarray one element smaller than the right when the size is odd. Given an initial five-element list of (14, 32, 67, 76, 23) the algorithm prints the following:

```
sorting [14, 32, 67, 76, 23]
sorting [14, 32]
sorting [14]
sorting [32]
merging [14] and [32]
sorting [67, 76, 23]
sorting [67]
sorting [76, 23]
sorting [76]
sorting [23]
merging [76] and [23]
merging [67] and [23, 76]
merging [14, 32] and [23, 67, 76]
```

Complete Program

The following is the complete program containing the merge sort code. Its main method constructs a sample array and sorts it using the algorithm:

```
1   // This program implements the merge sort algorithm for
2   // arrays of integers.
3
4   import java.util.*;
5
6   public class MergeSort {
7       public static void main(String[] args) {
8           int[] list = {14, 32, 67, 76, 23, 41, 58, 85};
9           System.out.println("before: " + Arrays.toString(list));
10          mergeSort(list);
11          System.out.println("after:  " + Arrays.toString(list));
12      }
13
14      // Places the elements of the given array into sorted order
15      // using the merge sort algorithm.
```

```
16        // post: array is in sorted (nondecreasing) order
17        public static void mergeSort(int[] array) {
18            if (array.length > 1) {
19                // split array into two halves
20                int[] left = leftHalf(array);
21                int[] right = rightHalf(array);
22
23                // recursively sort the two halves
24                mergeSort(left);
25                mergeSort(right);
26
27                // merge the sorted halves into a sorted whole
28                merge(array, left, right);
29            }
30        }
31
32        // Returns the first half of the given array.
33        public static int[] leftHalf(int[] array) {
34            int size1 = array.length / 2;
35            int[] left = new int[size1];
36            for (int i = 0; i < size1; i++) {
37                left[i] = array[i];
38            }
39            return left;
40        }
41
42        // Returns the second half of the given array.
43        public static int[] rightHalf(int[] array) {
44            int size1 = array.length / 2;
45            int size2 = array.length - size1;
46            int[] right = new int[size2];
47            for (int i = 0; i < size2; i++) {
48                right[i] = array[i + size1];
49            }
50            return right;
51        }
52
53        // Merges the given left and right arrays into the given
54        // result array.
55        // pre : result is empty; left/right are sorted
56        // post: result contains result of merging sorted lists;
57        public static void merge(int[] result,
58                                 int[] left, int[] right) {
59            int i1 = 0;    // index into left array
60            int i2 = 0;    // index into right array
61
62            for (int i = 0; i < result.length; i++) {
63                if (i2 >= right.length || (i1 < left.length &&
64                        left[i1] <= right[i2])) {
65                    result[i] = left[i1];  // take from left
66                    i1++;
67                } else {
68                    result[i] = right[i2]; // take from right
69                    i2++;
70                }
71            }
72        }
73    }
```

The program produces the following output:

```
before: [14, 32, 67, 76, 23, 41, 58, 85]
after:  [14, 23, 32, 41, 58, 67, 76, 85]
```

Figure 13.7 demonstrates the performance of our merge sort algorithm on a modern computer. The merge sort algorithm's performance is much better than that of the selection sort algorithm. What is its complexity class? It looks almost like an $O(N)$ algorithm, because the runtime only slightly more than doubles when we double the array size.

However, merge sort is actually an $O(N \log N)$ algorithm. A formal proof of this is beyond the scope of this book, but the intuition is the following: We have to split the array in half repeatedly until we hit the algorithm's base case, when the subarrays each contain 1 element. For an array of size N, we must split the array $\log_2 N$ times. At each of those $\log N$ steps, we have to do a linear operation of order N (merging the halves after they're sorted). Multiplying these operations' runtimes together produces a $O(N \log N)$ overall runtime.

The preceding algorithm runtime analysis is informal and not rigorous. As with other recursive algorithms, a precise analysis of merge sort's performance is complicated and requires mathematical techniques such as recurrence relations, which are not discussed in this book.

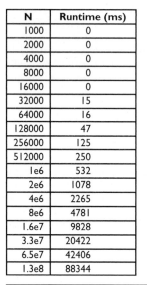

N	Runtime (ms)
1000	0
2000	0
4000	0
8000	0
16000	0
32000	15
64000	16
128000	47
256000	125
512000	250
1e6	532
2e6	1078
4e6	2265
8e6	4781
1.6e7	9828
3.3e7	20422
6.5e7	42406
1.3e8	88344

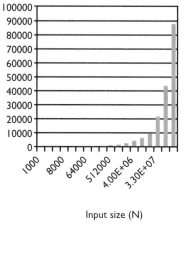

FIGURE 13.7   Runtimes for merge sort algorithm

Chapter 14

Graphical User Interfaces

Introduction

In this chapter we will explore the creation of graphical user interfaces (GUIs). While console programs like those we have written in the preceding chapters are still very important, the majority of modern desktop applications have graphical user interfaces. Supplement 3G introduced a `DrawingPanel` class that allowed you to draw 2D graphics on the screen. While this is useful for certain applications, writing a GUI is not the same as drawing shapes and lines onto a canvas. A real graphical user interface involves the creation of your own window frames that contain buttons, text input fields, and other onscreen components.

14.1 GUI Basics

GUIs are potentially very complex entities because they involve a large number of interacting objects and classes. Each onscreen component and window is represented by an object, so a programmer starting out with GUIs must learn many new class, method, and package names. In addition, if the GUI is to perform sophisticated tasks the objects must interact with each other and call each other's methods, which raises tricky communication and scoping issues.

Another factor that makes writing GUIs challenging is that the path of code execution becomes nondeterministic. In a GUI program, the user can click any of the buttons and interact with any of the other onscreen components in any order. Because the program's execution is driven by the series of events that occur, we say that programs with GUIs are *event-driven*. In this chapter you'll learn how to handle user events so that your event-driven graphical programs will respond appropriately to user interaction.

Graphical Input and Output with Option Panes

The simplest way to create a graphical window in Java is to pop up an *option pane,* which is a simple message box that appears on the screen and presents a message or a request for input to the user.

The Java class used to show option panes is called `JOptionPane`. `JOptionPane` belongs to the `javax.swing` package, so you'll need to import this package to use it. ("Swing" is the name of one of Java's GUI libraries.) Note that the package name starts with `javax` this time, not `java` (the x is because in Java's early days, Swing was an extension to Java's feature set).

```
import javax.swing.*; // for GUI components
```

`JOptionPane` can be thought of as a rough graphical equivalent of `System.out.println` output and `Scanner` console input. The following program creates a "Hello, world!" message on the screen:

```
1  // A graphical equivalent of the classic "Hello world" program.
2
3  import javax.swing.*; // for GUI components
4
5  public class HelloWorld {
6      public static void main(String[] args) {
7          JOptionPane.showMessageDialog(null, "Hello, world!");
8      }
9  }
```

It produces the following graphical "output" (we'll show screenshots for the output of the programs in this chapter).

The window may look slightly different depending on your operating system, but the message will be the same.

The preceding program uses a static method in the JOptionPane class called showMessageDialog. This method accepts two parameters: a parent window and a message string to display. We don't have a parent window in this case, so we passed null.

JOptionPane can be used in three major ways: to display a message (as shown previously), to present a list of choices to the user, and to ask the user to type input. The three methods that implement these three behaviors are called showMessageDialog, showConfirmDialog, and showInputDialog, respectively. These methods are detailed in Table 14.1.

TABLE 14.1 Useful Methods of the JOptionPane Class

Method	Description
showConfirmDialog(parent, message)	shows a Yes/No/Cancel message box containing the given message on the screen and returns the choice as an int with one of the following constant values: • JOptionPane.YES_OPTION (user clicked "Yes") • JOptionPane.NO_OPTION (user clicked "No") • JOptionPane.CANCEL_OPTION (user clicked "Cancel")
showInputDialog(parent, message)	shows an input box containing the given message on the screen and returns the user's input value as a String
showMessageDialog(parent, message)	shows the given message string in a message box on the screen

The following program briefly demonstrates all three types of option panes:

```
1   // Shows several JOptionPane windows on the screen.
2
3   import javax.swing.*; // for GUI components
4
5   public class UseOptionPanes {
6       public static void main(String[] args) {
7           // read the user's name graphically
8           String name = JOptionPane.showInputDialog(null,
9                   "What is your name?");
10
11          // ask the user a yes/no question
12          int choice = JOptionPane.showConfirmDialog(null,
13                  "Do you like cake, " + name + "?");
```

```
14
15              // show different response depending on answer
16              if (choice == JOptionPane.YES_OPTION) {
17                  JOptionPane.showMessageDialog(null,
18                          "Of course! Who doesn't?");
19              } else { // choice == NO_OPTION or CANCEL_OPTION
20                  JOptionPane.showMessageDialog(null,
21                          "We'll have to agree to disagree.");
22              }
23          }
24      }
```

The graphical input and output of this program is a series of windows, which pop up one at a time:

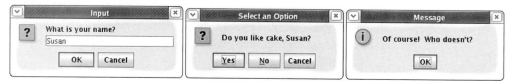

One limitation of `JOptionPane` is that its `showConfirmDialog` method always returns the user's input as a `String`. If you'd like to graphically request user input that is a number instead, your program must convert the `String` using the `Integer.parseInt` or `Double.parseDouble` method. These static methods accept a `String` as a parameter and return an `int` or `double` value, respectively.

The following program demonstrates using `JOptionPane` to read numbers from the user:

```
1   // Uses JOptionPane windows for numeric input.
2
3   import javax.swing.*; // for GUI components
4
5   public class UseOptionPanes2 {
6       public static void main(String[] args) {
7           String ageText = JOptionPane.showInputDialog(null,
8                   "How old are you?");
9           int age = Integer.parseInt(ageText);
10
11          String moneyText = JOptionPane.showInputDialog(null,
12                  "How much money do you have?");
13          double money = Double.parseDouble(moneyText);
14
15          JOptionPane.showMessageDialog(null,
16                  "If you can double your money each year,\n" +
17                  "You'll have " + (money * 32) +
18                  " dollars at age " + (age + 5) + "!");
19      }
20  }
```

The `Integer.parseInt` and `Double.parseDouble` methods throw exceptions of type `NumberFormatException` if you pass them `String`s that cannot be converted into

TABLE 14.2 Useful Methods of Wrapper Classes

Method	Description
`Integer.parseInt(str)`	returns the integer represented by the given `String` as an `int`
`Double.parseDouble(str)`	returns the real number represented by the given `String` as a `double`
`Boolean.parseBoolean(str)`	returns the `boolean` value represented by the given `String` (if the text is `"true"`, returns `true`; otherwise, returns `false`)

valid numbers, such as `"abc"`, `"five"`, or `"2×2"`. To make your code robust against such invalid input, you can enclose the code in a `try`/`catch` statement such as the following:

```
try {
    int age = Integer.parseInt(ageText);
} catch (NumberFormatException nfe) {
    JOptionPane.showMessageDialog(null,
            "Invalid integer.");
}
```

Table 14.2 summarizes the static methods in the wrapper classes that can be used to convert `String`s.

Working with Frames

`JOptionPane` is useful, but on its own it is not flexible or powerful enough to create rich graphical user interfaces. To do that, you'll need to learn about the various types of widgets that can be placed on the screen in Java.

An onscreen window is called a *frame*.

> **Frame**
>
> A graphical window on the screen.

The graphical widgets inside a frame, such as buttons or text input fields, are collectively called *components*.

> **Component**
>
> A widget, such as a button or text field, that resides inside a graphical window.

Technically a frame is also a component, but we will treat frames differently from other components because frames form the physical windows seen onscreen. Frames also have a large number of methods not found in other components.

Figure 14.1 illustrates some of Java's more commonly used graphical components, listed by class name. A more complete pictorial reference of the available graphical components can be found in Sun's Java Tutorial at http://java.sun.com/docs/books/tutorial/uiswing/components/components.html.

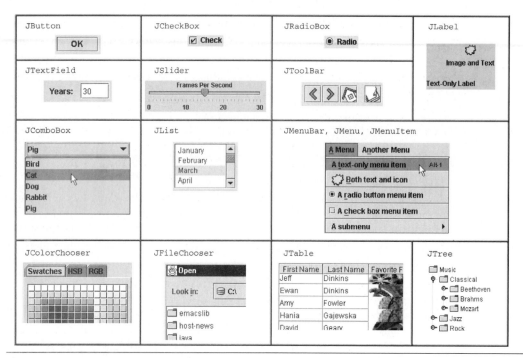

Figure 14.1   Some of Java's graphical components

Frames are represented by objects of the `JFrame` class. Any complex graphical program must construct a `JFrame` object to represent its main graphical window. Once you've constructed a `JFrame` object you can tell it to display itself on the screen by calling its `setVisible` method and passing it the `boolean` value `true`. Here's a simple program that constructs a frame and places it onscreen:

```
 1   // Shows an empty window frame on the screen.
 2
 3   import javax.swing.*;
 4
 5   public class SimpleFrame {
 6       public static void main(String[] args) {
 7           JFrame frame = new JFrame();
 8           frame.setVisible(true);
 9       }
10   }
```

The program's output is a bit silly, producing only a tiny window:

In fact, there is another problem with the program: When you close the window, it doesn't actually terminate the Java program. When you display a `JFrame` on the screen, by default Java does not exit the program when the frame is closed. You can tell that the program hasn't exited because a console window will remain on your screen (if you're using certain Java editors) or because your editor does not show its usual message that the program has terminated. If you want the program to exit when the window closes, you have to say so explicitly.

To make a more interesting frame, you'll have to learn about the properties of `JFrame`s. A *property* of a GUI component is a field or attribute it possesses internally that you may wish to examine or change. A frame's properties control things like the size of the window or the text that appears in the title bar. You can set or examine these properties' values by calling methods on the frame.

Table 14.3 lists several useful `JFrame` properties. For example, to set the title text of the frame in the `SimpleFrame` program to "A window frame", you'd write:

```
frame.setTitle("A window frame");
```

TABLE 14.3 **Useful Properties Specific to `JFrame`s**

Property	Type	Description	Methods
default close operation	int	what should happen when the frame is closed; choices include: • JFrame.DO_NOTHING_ON_ CLOSE (don't do anything) • JFrame.HIDE_ON_CLOSE (hide the frame) • JFrame.DISPOSE_ON_CLOSE (hide and destroy the frame so that it cannot be shown again) • JFrame.EXIT_ON_CLOSE (exit the program)	getDefaultCloseOperation, setDefaultCloseOperation(int)
icon image	Image	the icon that appears in the title bar and Start menu or Dock	getIconImage, setIconImage(Image)
layout	LayoutManager	an object that controls the positions and sizes of the components inside this frame	getLayout, setLayout(LayoutManager)
resizable	boolean	whether or not the frame allows itself to be resized	isResizable, setResizable(boolean)
title	String	the text that appears in the frame's title bar	getTitle, setTitle(String)

TABLE 14.4   Useful Properties of All Components (Including `JFrame`s)

Property	Type	Description	Methods
background	`Color`	background color	`getBackground`, `setBackground(Color)`
enabled	`boolean`	whether the component can be interacted with	`isEnabled`, `setEnabled(boolean)`
focusable	`boolean`	whether the keyboard can send input to the component	`isFocusable`, `setFocusable(boolean)`
font	`Font`	font used to write text	`getFont, setFont(Font)`
foreground	`Color`	foreground color	`getForeground`, `setForeground(Color)`
location	`Point`	(x, y) coordinate of component's top-left corner	`getLocation`, `setLocation(Point)`
size	`Dimension`	current width and height of the component	`getSize`, `setSize(Dimension)`
preferred size	`Dimension`	"preferred" width and height of the component; that is, the size it should be to make it appear naturally on the screen (used with layout managers, seen later)	`getPreferredSize`, `setPreferredSize(Dimension)`
visible	`boolean`	whether the component can be seen on the screen	`isVisible`, `setVisible(boolean)`

It turns out that all graphical components and frames share a common set of properties, because they exist in a common inheritance hierarchy. The Swing GUI framework is a powerful example of the code sharing of inheritance, since many components share features represented in common superclasses. Table 14.4 lists several useful common properties of frames/components and their respective methods.

There are various types of objects in Table 14.4. The background and foreground properties are `Color` objects, which you may have seen previously in Supplement 3G. The location property is a `Point` object; the `Point` class was discussed in Chapter 3. The font property is a `Font` object; we'll discuss fonts later in this chapter. All of these types are found in the `java.awt` package, so be sure to import it, just as you did when drawing graphical programs with `DrawingPanel` in previous chapters:

```
import java.awt.*; // for various graphical objects
```

The size property is an object of type `Dimension`, which simply stores a width and height and is constructed with two integers representing those values. We'll use this property several times in this chapter. We only need to know a bit about the `Dimension`

TABLE 14.5   Useful Methods of Dimension Objects

public Dimension(int width, int height)
Constructs a Dimension representing the given size

public int getWidth()
Returns the width represented by this Dimension

public int getHeight()
Returns the height represented by this Dimension

class, such as how to construct it. Table 14.5 lists the methods with which you should be familiar.

The following new version of the SimpleFrame program creates a frame and sets several of the properties listed in Table 14.4. In this version, we give the frame a color, set its location and size on the screen, and place text into its title bar. We also set the "default close operation" of the frame, telling it to shut down our Java program when it is closed:

```
1   // Sets several properties of a window frame.
2
3   import java.awt.*;    // for Dimension
4   import javax.swing.*; // for GUI components
5
6   public class SimpleFrame2 {
7       public static void main(String[] args) {
8           JFrame frame = new JFrame();
9           frame.setForeground(Color.WHITE);
10          frame.setDefaultCloseOperation(JFrame.EXIT_ON_CLOSE);
11          frame.setLocation(new Point(10, 50));
12          frame.setSize(new Dimension(300, 120));
13          frame.setTitle("A frame");
14          frame.setVisible(true);
15      }
16  }
```

When the program is run, the following window appears:

When the window is closed, the program exits.

Buttons, Labels, and Text Fields

Our empty frames are not very interesting without anything inside them. Let's look at some graphical components that can be placed in a frame.

The first component we'll examine is the *button*. You most likely know that a button is an onscreen component that can be clicked to cause an action. Buttons are represented by the JButton class. Each JButton object you create represents one button on the screen; if you want three buttons, you must create three JButton objects and place them in your frame.

You can construct a button either with no parameters (a button with no text), or with a String representing the text on the button. Of course, you can always change the button's text by calling the setText method on it. You can also set other properties of the button, such as its background color:

```
JButton button1 = new JButton();
button1.setText("I'm the first button");

JButton button2 = new JButton("The second button");
button2.setBackground(Color.YELLOW);
```

A *label* is a string of text that is displayed on the GUI. Labels exist to provide information and are not generally clicked to perform actions. A label is represented by a JLabel object, which can be constructed with a parameter specifying the label's text:

```
JLabel label = new JLabel("This is a label");
```

This is a label

A *text field* is a box into which the user can type text strings. A text field is represented by a JTextField object, which can be constructed with a parameter specifying the number of characters that should be able to fit in the text field:

```
// creates a field 8 characters wide
JTextField field = new JTextField(8);
```

The character width you specify (8, in the preceding code) is not enforced by the program; the user can type more than the specified number of characters if so desired. The parameter value just affects the size of the text field on the screen.

Merely constructing various component objects does not place them onto the screen; you must add them to the frame so it will display them. A frame acts as a *container,* or a region to which you can add graphical components. To add a component to a JFrame, call the frame's add method and pass the appropriate component as a parameter.

The following program creates a frame and places two buttons inside it:

```
1  // Creates a frame containing two buttons.
2
3  import java.awt.*;
```

```
4   import javax.swing.*;
5
6   public class ComponentsExample {
7       public static void main(String[] args) {
8           JFrame frame = new JFrame();
9           frame.setDefaultCloseOperation(JFrame.EXIT_ON_CLOSE);
10          frame.setSize(new Dimension(300, 100));
11          frame.setTitle("A frame");
12
13          JButton button1 = new JButton();
14          button1.setText("I'm a button.");
15          button1.setBackground(Color.BLUE);
16          frame.add(button1);
17
18          JButton button2 = new JButton();
19          button2.setText("Click me!");
20          button2.setBackground(Color.RED);
21          frame.add(button2);
22
23          frame.setVisible(true);
24      }
25  }
```

You'll notice a pattern in this code. When creating a component, you must do the following things:

- Construct it.
- Set its properties, if necessary.
- Place it on the screen (in this case, by adding it to the frame).

The program produces the following graphical output:

This program's output is probably not what you expected. The first button isn't visible; it's hidden beneath the second button, which has been stretched to fill the entire frame. Let's explore the cause of this problem and how to solve it.

Changing a Frame's Layout

The problem in the previous program has to do with the *layout* of the components, or how they are positioned, sized, and so on. We didn't tell the frame how to lay out the buttons, so it used a default behavior in which each component is positioned in the center of the frame and fills the entire frame's space. When multiple components are added to the frame, the last component added is placed on top and gets all the onscreen space.

Each button has size and location properties, but setting these in our code won't fix the problem. To fix the window's appearance, we must use an object called a *layout manager.*

> **Layout Manager**
>
> A Java object that decides the positions, sizes, and resizing behavior of the components within a frame or other container on the screen.

The frame has a layout manager object that it uses to position all of the components inside it. Even if we set the positions and sizes of the buttons, the frame's layout manager will set them back to the values it prefers. To position the components in a different way, we must set a new layout manager for the frame and let it position the components.

Java contains many layout manager classes in its `java.awt` package, so make sure to import that package (along with `javax.swing` for the `JFrame` and other component classes):

```
import java.awt.*;    // for layout managers
import javax.swing.*; // for GUI components
```

The default type of layout manager for a `JFrame` is called a `BorderLayout`, which we'll explore later in this chapter. If we want the buttons to flow in a left-to-right order instead, we can set the frame to use a different layout manager called `FlowLayout`. We do this by inserting the following line in the program before adding the buttons:

```
frame.setLayout(new FlowLayout());
```

Setting the layout in this manner ensures that both components will be visible in the frame. The program now produces the following graphical output:

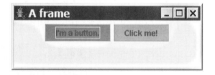

We'll discuss layout managers in detail in Section 14.2.

You may have noticed that the frame currently isn't sized quite right to fit its buttons — there's extra space at the bottom and on the sides. `JFrame` objects have a useful method called `pack` that tells them to resize themselves exactly to fit their contents. If you call `pack`, you don't need to call `setSize` on the frame because `pack` will set its size for you. Calling this method just before showing the frame on the screen will ensure that the components fit snugly within it, without excess whitespace:

```
frame.pack();
frame.setVisible(true);
```

The new, packed frame has the following onscreen appearance:

Handling an Action Event

The user interfaces we've created so far are not interactive—nothing happens when the user clicks the buttons or types on the components. In order to create useful interactive GUIs, you must learn how to handle Java events. When the user clicks on a component, moves the mouse over it, or otherwise interacts with it, Java's GUI system creates a special kind of object called an *event* to represent this action.

> **Event**
>
> An object representing a user's interaction with a GUI component, which can be handled by your programs to create interactive components.

By default, if you don't specify how to react to an event, it goes unnoticed by your program. Therefore, nothing happens when the user clicks your buttons or types in your text fields. You can cause a response to a particular event (such as the user clicking a particular button) using a kind of object called a *listener.*

> **Listener**
>
> An object that is notified when an event occurs and executes code to respond to that event.

To handle an event, create a listener object and attach it to the component of interest. The listener object contains the code you want to run when the appropriate event occurs.

The first kind of event we'll handle in this chapter is called an action event. An *action event* is a fairly general type of event that occurs when the user interacts with many standard components (for example clicking on a button or pressing Enter when a `JTextField` has the focus).

In Java, event listeners are written by implementing particular interfaces. The interface for handling action events in Java is called `ActionListener`. The `ActionListener` interface is located in the `java.awt.event` package, which you'll need to import.

```
import java.awt.event.*; // for action events
```

Even if you've already imported the `java.awt` package, you'll still need to separately import the `java.awt.event` package; one does not contain the other.

The `ActionListener` interface contains only the following method:

```
public void actionPerformed(ActionEvent event)
```

To listen to an event, you write a class that implements the `ActionListener` interface and place into its `actionPerformed` method the code you want to run when the event occurs. Then you attach an object of your listener class to the appropriate component.

Here is a simple example of an `ActionListener` class that responds to an event by displaying a message box on the screen:

```
1   // Responds to a button click by displaying a message box.
2
3   import java.awt.event.*;
```

```
 4   import javax.swing.*;
 5
 6   public class MessageListener implements ActionListener {
 7       public void actionPerformed(ActionEvent event) {
 8           JOptionPane.showMessageDialog(null,
 9                   "You clicked the button!");
10       }
11   }
```

Now that we've written this class, we can attach a `MessageListener` object to any button or other component of interest, and it will respond to action events on that component. For example, if we attach a `MessageListener` to a button, an option pane will pop up whenever that button is clicked. To attach the listener, we'll use a method called `addActionListener` found in several Swing components that accepts a parameter of type `ActionListener`.

For example, we can add the following line to the `ComponentsExample` program we developed earlier to attach the listener to the first button:

```
// attach a listener to handle events on this button
button1.addActionListener(new MessageListener());
```

Here is the result when the program is executed and the user clicks on the button:

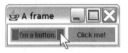 

Note that a listener only responds to events on components to which it is added. If the user clicks the "Click me!" button, nothing will happen. If we wanted the same event to occur when the user clicks this button, we'd have to add a `MessageListener` to it. If we wanted a different response to occur on a click of this button, we could write a second class that implements `ActionListener` and attach one of its objects to the button.

To summarize, here are the necessary steps to handle an event in Java:

- Write a class that implements `ActionListener`.
- Place the code to handle the event into its `actionPerformed` method.
- Attach an object of your listener class to the component of interest using its `addActionListener` method.

14.2 Laying Out Components

Earlier, we used a `FlowLayout` to position the components in our frame. In this section, we will explore several different layout manager objects that can be used to position components in a variety of ways.

There are a few problems with this output. First of all, because a grid layout forces every component inside it to take the same size, the labels, text fields, and buttons are not the proper sizes. You want each label to be the same size as the other labels and each text field and button to be the same size as the others, but you don't want the different kinds of components to all be the same size.

The simplest way to resolve this size problem is to create three separate panels with grid layout in the north region of the frame, each with three rows and only one column. You can then put the labels into the first grid, the text fields into the second, and the buttons into the third. (Even though there are only two buttons, make the layout 3×1 so a blank space is left to match the expected output.)

To position the three grids next to each other, add another layer of compositing by creating a master north panel with a border layout to store all three grids. The labels will occupy the panel's west region, the text fields the center, and the buttons the east region. Place this master north panel in the north region of the frame.

The other problem with the previous output is that the Send button is stretched. Because it was placed directly in the south region of a BorderLayout, the button is stretched horizontally to fill the frame. To avoid this problem, put the Send button into a panel with a FlowLayout. FlowLayout doesn't stretch the components inside it, so the button won't grow to such an odd size. Then add the panel to the south region of the frame, rather than adding the Send button directly.

Here's a complete version of the program that contains these corrections and produces the proper graphical output:

```
1   // Creates a GUI that resembles an email Compose Message window.
2
3   import java.awt.*;
4   import javax.swing.*;
5
6   public class EmailMessage {
7       public static void main(String[] args) {
8           JFrame frame = new JFrame();
9           frame.setDefaultCloseOperation(JFrame.EXIT_ON_CLOSE);
10          frame.setSize(new Dimension(400, 300));
11          frame.setTitle("Send Message");
12          frame.setLayout(new BorderLayout());
13
14          JPanel northWest = new JPanel(new GridLayout(3, 1));
15          northWest.add(new JLabel("From: "));
16          northWest.add(new JLabel("To: "));
17          northWest.add(new JLabel("Subject: "));
18
19          JPanel northCenter = new JPanel(new GridLayout(3, 1));
20          northCenter.add(new JTextField());
21          northCenter.add(new JTextField());
22          northCenter.add(new JTextField());
23
24          JPanel northEast = new JPanel(new GridLayout(3, 1));
25          northEast.add(new JButton("Browse..."));
26          northEast.add(new JButton("Browse..."));
27
```

```
28              JPanel north = new JPanel(new BorderLayout());
29              north.add(northWest, BorderLayout.WEST);
30              north.add(northCenter, BorderLayout.CENTER);
31              north.add(northEast, BorderLayout.EAST);
32
33              JPanel south = new JPanel(new FlowLayout());
34              south.add(new JButton("Send"));
35
36              frame.add(north, BorderLayout.NORTH);
37              frame.add(new JTextArea(), BorderLayout.CENTER);
38              frame.add(south, BorderLayout.SOUTH);
39
40              frame.setVisible(true);
41          }
42      }
```

14.3 Interaction Between Components

In this section we'll write some larger and more complex graphical programs. These programs will raise new issues about communication between components and event listeners.

Example 1: BMI GUI

Consider the task of writing a graphical program to compute a person's body mass index (BMI). The program should have a way for the user to type in a height and a weight and should use these values to compute the person's BMI. A reasonable appearance for the GUI would be the following, using text fields for input and a button to trigger computation of the body mass index:

Let's figure out how to create a GUI with the proper components and layout first, and worry about event handling after. Since we want text fields with labels next to them, aligned in a row/column format, a 2×2 GridLayout is a good choice. But we'll want to use a composite layout, because we don't want the central label and the Compute button to have the same size and position as the grid squares. We'll use a BorderLayout on our frame and add the central "Type your height and weight" label and Compute button directly to it. We'll also create a panel with a 2×2 GridLayout and place it in the north region of the frame.

The following code implements the initial BMI user interface. The program sets the frame's title by passing it as a parameter to its constructor.

```
1   // A GUI to compute a person's body mass index (BMI).
2   // Initial version without event handling.
3
```

```
4    import java.awt.*;
5    import javax.swing.*;
6
7    public class BmiGui1 {
8        public static void main(String[] args) {
9            // set up components
10           JTextField heightField = new JTextField(5);
11           JTextField weightField = new JTextField(5);
12           JLabel bmiLabel = new JLabel(
13                   "Type your height and weight");
14           JButton computeButton = new JButton("Compute");
15
16           // layout
17           JPanel north = new JPanel(new GridLayout(2, 2));
18           north.add(new JLabel("Height: "));
19           north.add(heightField);
20           north.add(new JLabel("Weight: "));
21           north.add(weightField);
22
23           // overall frame
24           JFrame frame = new JFrame("BMI");
25           frame.setDefaultCloseOperation(JFrame.EXIT_ON_CLOSE);
26           frame.setLayout(new BorderLayout());
27           frame.add(north, BorderLayout.NORTH);
28           frame.add(bmiLabel, BorderLayout.CENTER);
29           frame.add(computeButton, BorderLayout.SOUTH);
30           frame.pack();
31           frame.setVisible(true);
32       }
33   }
```

The program currently does nothing when the user presses the Compute button.

Object-Oriented GUIs

Let's think about the task of making our BMI GUI respond to clicks on the Compute button. Clicking a button causes an action event, so we might try putting an `ActionListener` on the button. But in the code for the listener's `actionPerformed` method, we'd need to read the text from the height and weight text fields and use that information to compute the BMI and display it as the text of the central label. This is a problem because the GUIs we've written so far were not built to allow so much interaction between components.

To enable listeners to access each of its components, we need to make our GUI itself into an object. We'll declare the onscreen components as fields inside that object and initialize them in the GUI's constructor. In our `BmiGui1` example, we can convert much of the code currently in the `main` method into the constructor for the GUI.

The following class implements the new object-oriented version of the GUI. For the moment, it still has no event handling:

```
1    // A GUI to compute a person's body mass index (BMI).
2    // Object-oriented version without event handling.
3
4    import java.awt.*;
5    import javax.swing.*;
```

```
6
7   public class BmiGui2 {
8       // onscreen components stored as fields
9       private JFrame frame;
10      private JTextField heightField;
11      private JTextField weightField;
12      private JLabel bmiLabel;
13      private JButton computeButton;
14
15      public BmiGui2() {
16          // set up components
17          heightField = new JTextField(5);
18          weightField = new JTextField(5);
19          bmiLabel = new JLabel(
20                  "Type your height and weight");
21          computeButton = new JButton("Compute");
22
23          // layout
24          JPanel north = new JPanel(new GridLayout(2, 2));
25          north.add(new JLabel("Height: "));
26          north.add(heightField);
27          north.add(new JLabel("Weight: "));
28          north.add(weightField);
29
30          // overall frame
31          frame = new JFrame("BMI");
32          frame.setDefaultCloseOperation(JFrame.EXIT_ON_CLOSE);
33          frame.setLayout(new BorderLayout());
34          frame.add(north, BorderLayout.NORTH);
35          frame.add(bmiLabel, BorderLayout.CENTER);
36          frame.add(computeButton, BorderLayout.SOUTH);
37          frame.pack();
38          frame.setVisible(true);
39      }
40  }
```

Now that the GUI is an object, we can write a separate client class to hold the `main` method to construct it. The following short class does the job:

```
1   // Shows a BMI GUI on the screen.
2
3   public class RunBmiGui2 {
4       public static void main(String[] args) {
5           BmiGui2 gui = new BmiGui2(); // construct/show GUI
6       }
7   }
```

The advantage of having an object-oriented GUI is that we can make it into an event listener. We want to add a listener to the Compute button to compute the user's BMI, and this listener will need to access the height and weight text fields and the central BMI label. These components are fields within the BmiGui2 object, so if the BmiGui2 class itself implements ActionListener, it will have access to all the information it needs.

Let's write a third version of our BMI GUI that handles action events. We'll change our class name to BmiGui3 and change our class header to implement the ActionListener interface:

```
public class BmiGui3 implements ActionListener {
```

To implement `ActionListener`, we must write an `actionPerformed` method. Our `actionPerformed` code will read the two text fields' values, convert them into type `double`, compute the BMI using the standard BMI formula of weight / height^2 * 703, and set the text of the central BMI label to show the BMI result. The following code implements the listener:

```
// Handles clicks on Compute button by computing the BMI.
public void actionPerformed(ActionEvent event) {
    // read height/weight info from text fields
    String heightText = heightField.getText();
    double height = Double.parseDouble(heightText);
    String weightText = weightField.getText();
    double weight = Double.parseDouble(weightText);

    // compute BMI and display it onscreen
    double bmi = weight / (height * height) * 703;
    bmiLabel.setText("BMI: " + bmi);
}
```

Now we have to attach the action listener to the Compute button. Since the GUI is the listener, the parameter we pass to the button's `addActionListener` method is the GUI itself. Because this code is inside the GUI object's constructor, we pass the GUI as a parameter using the keyword `this`:

```
// attach GUI as event listener to Compute button
computeButton.addActionListener(this);
```

The second version of our BMI GUI used a separate class called `RunBmiGui2` as a client to run the GUI. However, using a second class for such a minimal client program is a bit of a waste. It is actually legal to have the same `main` method in the BMI GUI class itself and not use the `RunBmiGui2` class. If we do this, the class becomes its own client, and we can just compile and run the GUI class to execute the program. (Static methods like `main` are generally placed above any fields, constructors, and instance methods in the same file.)

After implementing the listener code and incorporating the `main` method, our final version of the BMI GUI is the following:

```
 1   // A GUI to compute a person's body mass index (BMI).
 2   // Final version with event handling.
 3
 4   import java.awt.*;
 5   import java.awt.event.*;
 6   import javax.swing.*;
 7
 8   public class BmiGui3 implements ActionListener {
 9       // BmiGui3 is its own runnable client program
10       public static void main(String[] args) {
11           BmiGui3 gui = new BmiGui3();
12       }
13
14       // onscreen components stored as fields
```

```
15        private JFrame frame;
16        private JTextField heightField;
17        private JTextField weightField;
18        private JLabel bmiLabel;
19        private JButton computeButton;
20
21        public BmiGui3() {
22            // set up components
23            heightField = new JTextField(5);
24            weightField = new JTextField(5);
25            bmiLabel = new JLabel("Type your height and weight");
26            computeButton = new JButton("Compute");
27
28            // attach GUI as event listener to Compute button
29            computeButton.addActionListener(this);
30
31            // layout
32            JPanel north = new JPanel(new GridLayout(2, 2));
33            north.add(new JLabel("Height: "));
34            north.add(heightField);
35            north.add(new JLabel("Weight: "));
36            north.add(weightField);
37
38            // overall frame
39            frame = new JFrame("BMI");
40            frame.setDefaultCloseOperation(JFrame.EXIT_ON_CLOSE);
41            frame.setLayout(new BorderLayout());
42            frame.add(north, BorderLayout.NORTH);
43            frame.add(bmiLabel, BorderLayout.CENTER);
44            frame.add(computeButton, BorderLayout.SOUTH);
45            frame.pack();
46            frame.setVisible(true);
47        }
48
49        // Handles clicks on Compute button by computing the BMI.
50        public void actionPerformed(ActionEvent event) {
51            // read height/weight info from text fields
52            String heightText = heightField.getText();
53            double height = Double.parseDouble(heightText);
54            String weightText = weightField.getText();
55            double weight = Double.parseDouble(weightText);
56
57            // compute BMI and display it onscreen
58            double bmi = weight / (height * height) * 703;
59            bmiLabel.setText("BMI: " + bmi);
60        }
61    }
```

Example 2: Credit Card GUI

You may not know that credit card numbers contain several pieces of information for performing validity tests. For example, Visa card numbers always begin with 4, and a valid Visa card number always passes a digit-sum test known as the Luhn checksum algorithm. Luhn's algorithm states that if you sum the digits of any valid credit card number in a certain way, the total sum will be a multiple of 10. Systems that accept credit cards perform a Luhn test before contacting the credit card company for final verification. This allows them to filter out fake or mistyped credit card numbers.

The algorithm for summing the digits can be described as follows. Consider each digit of the credit card number to have a zero-based index: The first is at index 0, and the last is at index 15. Start from the rightmost digit and process each digit one at a time. For each digit at an odd-numbered index (the 15th digit, 13th digit, etc.), simply add that digit to the cumulative sum. For each digit at an even-numbered index (the 14th, 12th, etc.), double the digit's value. If that doubled value is less than 10, add it to the sum; if the doubled value is 10 or greater, add each of its digits separately into the sum.

The following pseudocode describes the Luhn algorithm to sum the digits:

```
sum = 0.
for (each digit of credit card number, starting from right) {
    if (digit's index is odd) {
        add digit to sum.
    } else {
        double the digit's value.
        if (doubled value < 10) {
            add doubled value to sum.
        } else {
            split doubled value into its two digits.
            add first digit to sum.
            add second digit to sum.
        }
    }
}
```

4111111111111111 and 4408041274369853 are example credit card numbers that pass the Luhn algorithm. Figure 14.3 shows the algorithm summing the latter number in detail. Notice how digits at even indexes are doubled and split into two digits if their new values are 10 or higher. For example, the number 7 at index 8 is doubled to 14, which is then split to make 1 + 4.

```
CC #     4408 0412 7436 9853

         4    4    0    8    0    4    1    2    7    4    3    6    9    8    5    3
Scale   ×2        ×2        ×2        ×2        ×2        ×2        ×2        ×2
        ─────────────────────────────────────────────────────────────────────────
         8    4    0    8    0    4    2    2   14    4    6    6   18    8   10    3

Sum    = 8 + 4 + 0 + 8 + 0 + 4 + 2 + 2 + 1+4 + 4 + 6 + 6 + 1+8 + 8 + 1+0 + 3
       = 70

70 is divisible by 10, therefore, this card number is valid.
```

Figure 14.3 Example checksum using the Luhn algorithm

Let's write a GUI where the user can type in a credit card number, press a button to verify it, then receive a message stating whether the number was valid. The GUI will have the following appearance:

To validate the credit card number, we'll place a listener on the Verify CC Number button. In the code for the listener's `actionPerformed` method, we'll need to read the text from the text field, decide whether the number is valid, and use that information to set the text of the label. Since the listener involves interaction between components, we'll make it object-oriented and make it its own listener.

As usual, let's deal with components and layout first before worrying about event handling. The frame can use a `FlowLayout` that wraps the text label to a second line.

The following is an initial version of the program that does not respond to events. As with the previous `BmiGui3` example, we'll make the GUI be its own client program by incorporating a `main` method:

```
1   // Presents a GUI to verify credit card numbers.
2   // Initial version without event handling.
3
4   import java.awt.*;
5   import javax.swing.*;
6
7   public class CreditCardGUI1 {
8       public static void main(String[] args) {
9           CreditCardGUI1 gui = new CreditCardGUI1();
10      }
11
12      // fields
13      private JFrame frame;
14      private JTextField numberField;
15      private JLabel validLabel;
16      private JButton verifyButton;
17
18      // creates components, does layout, shows window onscreen
19      public CreditCardGUI1() {
20          numberField = new JTextField(16);
21          validLabel = new JLabel("not yet verified");
22          verifyButton = new JButton("Verify CC Number");
23
24          frame = new JFrame("Credit card number verifier");
25          frame.setDefaultCloseOperation(JFrame.EXIT_ON_CLOSE);
26          frame.setSize(new Dimension(350, 100));
27          frame.setLayout(new FlowLayout());
28          frame.add(numberField);
29          frame.add(verifyButton);
30          frame.add(validLabel);
31          frame.setVisible(true);
32      }
33  }
```

Now let's write a second version of the GUI that listens for action events on the Verify CC Number button. The code to validate credit card numbers is complex enough to merit making it into its own method. The code will loop over each digit starting from the extreme right, doubling the ones at even indexes and splitting doubled numbers of 10 or larger into separate digits before adding them to the total. We can achieve this by adding the `digit / 10` and the `digit % 10` to the sum. We can actually add these same two values to the sum even if the number does not exceed 10, because for single-digit numbers, `digit / 10` is 0 and `digit % 10` is the digit itself. Here is the code that implements the validation:

```java
// returns whether the given string is a valid Visa
// card number according to the Luhn checksum algorithm
public boolean isValidCC(String text) {
    int sum = 0;
    for (int i = text.length() - 1; i >= 0; i--) {
        int digit = Integer.parseInt(
                text.substring(i, i + 1));
        if (i % 2 == 0) { // double even digits
            digit *= 2;
        }
        sum += (digit / 10) + (digit % 10);
    }

    // valid numbers add up to a multiple of 10
    return sum % 10 == 0 && text.startsWith("4");
}
```

Now that we have a method to tell us whether a given string represents a valid Visa card number, we can write the code to listen for events. First, we'll modify our class header:

```java
public class CreditCardGUI2 implements ActionListener {
```

Next, we need to write the `actionPerformed` method. The method is short and simple, because the `isValidCC` method does the bulk of the work:

```java
// Sets label's text to show whether CC number is valid.
public void actionPerformed(ActionEvent event) {
    String text = numberField.getText();
    if (isValidCC(text)) {
        validLabel.setText("Valid number!");
    } else {
        validLabel.setText("Invalid number.");
    }
}
```

Putting it all together, here is the complete version of the program:

```java
1   // Presents a GUI to verify credit card numbers.
2   // Final version with event handling.
3
4   import java.awt.*;
5   import java.awt.event.*;
6   import javax.swing.*;
7
8   public class CreditCardGUI2 implements ActionListener {
9       public static void main(String[] args) {
10          CreditCardGUI2 gui = new CreditCardGUI2();
11      }
12
13      // fields
14      private JFrame frame;
15      private JTextField numberField;
```

```
16          private JLabel validLabel;
17          private JButton verifyButton;
18
19          // creates components, does layout, shows window onscreen
20          public CreditCardGUI2() {
21              numberField = new JTextField(16);
22              validLabel = new JLabel("not yet verified");
23              verifyButton = new JButton("Verify CC Number");
24
25              // event listeners
26              verifyButton.addActionListener(this);
27
28              frame = new JFrame("Credit card number verifier");
29              frame.setDefaultCloseOperation(JFrame.EXIT_ON_CLOSE);
30              frame.setSize(new Dimension(350, 100));
31              frame.setLayout(new FlowLayout());
32              frame.add(numberField);
33              frame.add(verifyButton);
34              frame.add(validLabel);
35              frame.setVisible(true);
36          }
37
38          // Returns whether the given string is a valid Visa
39          // card number according to the Luhn checksum algorithm.
40          public boolean isValidCC(String text) {
41              int sum = 0;
42              for (int i = text.length() - 1; i >= 0; i--) {
43                  int digit = Integer.parseInt(
44                          text.substring(i, i + 1));
45                  if (i % 2 == 0) { // double even digits
46                      digit *= 2;
47                  }
48                  sum += (digit / 10) + (digit % 10);
49              }
50
51              // valid numbers add up to a multiple of 10
52              return sum % 10 == 0 && text.startsWith("4");
53          }
54
55          // Sets label's text to show whether CC number is valid.
56          public void actionPerformed(ActionEvent event) {
57              String text = numberField.getText();
58              if (isValidCC(text)) {
59                  validLabel.setText("Valid number!");
60              } else {
61                  validLabel.setText("Invalid number.");
62              }
63          }
64  }
```

14.4 Additional Components and Events

The GUIs we have developed so far use only a few components (buttons, labels, text fields) and can respond to only one kind of event (action events). In this section we'll look at some other useful components and events that GUI programs can use and respond to.

Text Areas, Scrollbars, and Fonts

Text fields are useful for single-line text input, but they don't work well when the user wants to type a larger or more complex message. Fortunately, there is another kind of component called a *text area* that represents a multi-line text input box. Text areas are represented by `JTextArea` objects. You can construct a `JTextArea` by passing the number of rows and columns (i.e., the number of lines and the number of letters in each line):

```
JTextArea area = new JTextArea(5, 20);
```

This creates a text area 5 lines tall and 20 letters wide:

A `JTextArea` object

The following program constructs a frame and adds a text area to it:

```
1   // Demonstrates the JTextArea component.
2
3   import java.awt.*;
4   import javax.swing.*;
5
6   public class TextFrame {
7       public static void main(String[] args) {
8           JFrame frame = new JFrame();
9           frame.setDefaultCloseOperation(JFrame.EXIT_ON_CLOSE);
10          frame.setLayout(new FlowLayout());
11          frame.setSize(new Dimension(300, 150));
12          frame.setTitle("Text frame");
13
14          JTextArea area = new JTextArea(5, 20);
15          frame.add(area);
16
17          frame.setVisible(true);
18      }
19  }
```

The program produces the following graphical output (shown both before and after typing some text in the text area):

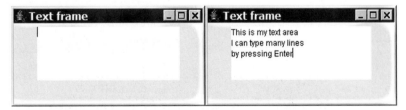

In a larger GUI example, an event listener might examine the text written in a text area using its `getText` method or set new text in the text area by calling its `setText` method.

Currently, when the user types too much text to fit in the text area, the text simply vanishes off the bottom:

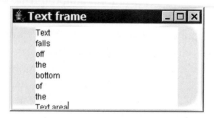

To fix this, we can make the text area scrollable by adding familiar navigation components called *scrollbars* to it. Scrollbars are represented by instances of a special container component called a `JScrollPane`. To make a component scrollable, create a `JScrollPane`, add the component to the scroll pane, and then add the scroll pane to the overall frame. A `JScrollPane` object is constructed by passing the relevant component as a parameter:

```
// use scrollbars on this text area
frame.add(new JScrollPane(area));
```

We add the `JScrollPane` to the frame instead of the `JTextArea` itself, and the scroll pane causes scrollbars to appear along the right and bottom edges of the text area when its text becomes too large to display:

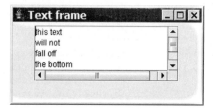

The appearance of onscreen text is determined by *fonts,* which are sets of descriptions for how to display text characters. If you don't like the default font of the text area, remember that every component has a font property that you can set. As discussed previously in Supplement 3G, fonts are represented by `Font` objects. A `Font` object can be constructed by passing its name, style (such as bold or italic), and size in pixels. For example, the following line of code tells the text area to use a size 14 serifed font:

```
area.setFont(new Font("Serif", Font.BOLD, 14));
```

The text area now has the following appearance:

See Supplement 3G for a more lengthy discussion of `Font` objects.

Icons

Many Java components, including buttons and labels, have an icon property that can be set to place an image on the component. This property is of type `Icon`.

The `getIcon` and `setIcon` methods use values that implement the `Icon` interface. The easiest way to get an object that implements `Icon` is to create an object of type `ImageIcon`. The `ImageIcon` constructor accepts a `String` parameter representing the image file to load. The image is a file on your hard disk, such as a GIF, JPG, or PNG image. Place your image files in the same folder as your program files.

The following code places an icon onto a button. The file `smiley.jpg` has already been saved to the same folder as the code:

```
// create a smiley face icon for this button
JButton button = new JButton("Have a nice day");
button.setIcon(new ImageIcon("smiley.jpg"));
```

When placed in a frame, the button has the following appearance. It is enlarged to accommodate both its text and its new icon:

Another way to create an icon is to draw one for yourself. You can create a blank image buffer using a `BufferedImage` object and draw onto it using a `Graphics` pen, as was done with the `DrawingPanel` in Supplement 3G. (In fact, the `DrawingPanel` is implemented with an internal `BufferedImage`.) `BufferedImage` is a class in the `java.awt.image` package, so if you want to use it, you must import this package:

```
import java.awt.image.*; // for BufferedImage
```

Here is the header for the `BufferedImage` constructor:

TABLE 14.6   Useful Methods of `BufferedImage` Objects

`public BufferedImage(int width, int height, int type)`
Constructs an image buffer of the given size and type. Valid types are:

- `BufferedImage.TYPE_INT_ARGB`: An image with a transparent background.

- `BufferedImage.TYPE_INT_RGB`: An image with a solid black background.

`public Graphics getGraphics()`
Returns the pen for drawing on this image buffer.

To use a `BufferedImage`, construct one of a particular size and type (we recommend `BufferedImage.TYPE_INT_ARGB`), then get the `Graphics` object from it using the `getGraphics` method. You can then issue standard drawing commands such as `drawRect` or `fillOval`. Once you're done drawing on the `BufferedImage`, create a new `ImageIcon` object and pass the `BufferedImage` to the `ImageIcon` constructor. You can set this `ImageIcon` as the icon for an onscreen component by calling `setIcon` on that component and passing the `ImageIcon` as the parameter, as demonstrated in the following code:

```
JButton button = new JButton();
button.setText("My drawing");

// create a shape image icon for this button
BufferedImage image = new BufferedImage(100, 100,
        BufferedImage.TYPE_INT_ARGB);
Graphics g = image.getGraphics();
g.setColor(Color.YELLOW);
g.fillRect(10, 20, 80, 70);
g.setColor(Color.RED);
g.fillOval(40, 50, 25, 25);

ImageIcon icon = new ImageIcon(image);
button.setIcon(icon);
```

You can also use a `BufferedImage` as the icon image for a frame, by calling its `setIconImage` method:

```
frame.setIconImage(image);
```

This is a case where Java's designers chose confusing names, because the `setIconImage` method doesn't accept an `ImageIcon` as its parameter.

When placed into a frame, the button's appearance is the following. Notice that a smaller version of the icon also appears in the top-left corner of the window, because of the `setIconImage` call:

Mouse Events

So far, we've worked exclusively with `ActionListener` objects. When we want to listen to mouse clicks or movements, we use another type of listener called a `MouseInputListener`. The `MouseInputListener` interface resides in the `javax.swing.event` package, which you'll need to import:

```
import javax.swing.event.*; // for mouse events
```

The `MouseInputListener` interface methods for handling mouse input are listed in Table 14.6. There are quite a few methods, and you probably won't want to implement them all. Many programs only want to handle button presses or cursor

TABLE 14.7   The Methods of the `MouseInputListener` Interface

`public void mouseClicked(MouseEvent event)`
Invoked when the mouse button has been clicked (pressed and released) on a component.

`public void mouseDragged(MouseEvent event)`
Invoked when a mouse button is pressed on a component and then dragged.

`public void mouseEntered(MouseEvent event)`
Invoked when the mouse enters a component.

`public void mouseExited(MouseEvent event)`
Invoked when the mouse exits a component.

`public void mouseMoved(MouseEvent event)`
Invoked when the mouse has been moved onto a component but no buttons have been pushed.

`public void mousePressed(MouseEvent event)`
Invoked when a mouse button has been pressed on a component.

`public void mouseReleased(MouseEvent event)`
Invoked when a mouse button has been released on a component.

---

movements. In these cases, you have to write empty versions of all the other `MouseInputListener` methods, because otherwise the class doesn't implement the interface properly and won't compile.

To avoid this annoyance, Java provides a class named `MouseInputAdapter` that implements default empty versions of all the methods from the `MouseInputListener` interface. You can extend `MouseInputAdapter` and override only the methods that correspond to the mouse event types you want to handle. We'll make all the mouse listeners we write subclasses of `MouseInputAdapter` so that we don't have to write the methods we aren't interested in.

For example, let's write a mouse listener class that responds only when the mouse cursor moves over a component. To do this, we'll extend the `MouseInputAdapter` class and override only the `mouseEntered` method

```
1   // Responds to a mouse event by showing a message dialog.
2
3   import java.awt.event.*;
4   import javax.swing.*;
5   import javax.swing.event.*;
6
7   public class MovementListener extends MouseInputAdapter {
8       public void mouseEntered(MouseEvent event) {
9           JOptionPane.showMessageDialog(null, "Mouse entered!");
10      }
11  }
```

Unfortunately, attaching this new listener to a component isn't so straightforward. The designers of the GUI component classes decided to separate the various types of mouse actions into two categories, mouse button clicks and mouse movements, and created two separate interfaces (MouseListener and MouseMotionListener) to represent these types of actions. Later, the MouseInputListener and MouseInputAdapter were added to merge the two listeners, but GUI components still need mouse listeners to be attached in two separate ways for them to work.

If we wish to hear about mouse enter, exit, press, release, and click events, we must call the addMouseListener method on the component. If we wish to hear about mouse move and drag events, we must call the addMouseMotionListener method on the component. If we want to hear about all the events, we can add the mouse input adapter in both ways. (This is what we'll do in the examples in this section.)

TABLE 14.8   Useful Methods of Components

```
public void addMouseListener(MouseListener listener)
```
Attaches a listener to hear mouse enter, exit, press, release, and click events.

```
public void addMouseMotionListener(MouseMotionListener listener)
```
Attaches a listener to hear mouse move and drag events.

Here is an entire program that uses our MovementListener to respond to the mouse being moved over a label:

```
 1  // A GUI that listens to mouse movements over a label.
 2
 3  import java.awt.*;
 4  import javax.swing.*;
 5
 6  public class MouseGUI {
 7      public static void main(String[] args) {
 8          JFrame frame = new JFrame();
 9          frame.setDefaultCloseOperation(JFrame.EXIT_ON_CLOSE);
10          frame.setLayout(new FlowLayout());
11          frame.setSize(new Dimension(200, 100));
12          frame.setTitle("A frame");
13
14          JLabel label = new JLabel();
15          label.setText("Move the mouse over me!");
16          frame.add(label);
17
18          MovementListener mListener = new MovementListener();
19          label.addMouseListener(mListener);
20          label.addMouseMotionListener(mListener);
21
22          frame.setVisible(true);
23      }
24  }
```

TABLE 14.9 Useful Methods of `MouseEvent` Objects

```
public int getButton()
```
Returns the number of the mouse button that was pressed or released (1 for the left button, 2 for the right button, and so on).

```
public int getClickCount()
```
Returns the number of times the user clicked the button; useful for detecting double-clicks.

```
public int getPoint()
```
Returns the (x, y) point where the mouse event occurred.

```
public int getX()
```
Returns the x-coordinate where the mouse event occurred.

```
public int getY()
```
Returns the y-coordinate where the mouse event occurred.

The program produces the following graphical output, shown both before and after the user moves the mouse onto the `JLabel`:

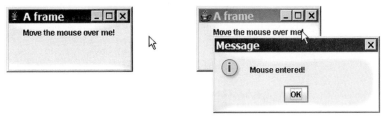

When dealing with action listeners, the `actionPerformed` method accepts a parameter of type `ActionEvent` that represents the action that occurs. We didn't use this object for anything in our programs. However, the corresponding parameter in mouse listeners, which is of type `MouseEvent`, is very useful. Several handy pieces of information are stored in the `MouseEvent` parameter. Table 14.9 lists some of its methods.

For example, the following mouse listener could be attached to any component, even the frame itself. It would make a message appear any time the user pressed the mouse button:

```
 1  // Responds to a mouse click by showing a message
 2  // indicating where the user clicked
 3
 4  import java.awt.event.*;
 5  import javax.swing.*;
 6  import javax.swing.event.*;
 7
 8  public class ClickListener extends MouseInputAdapter {
 9      public void mousePressed(MouseEvent event) {
10          JOptionPane.showMessageDialog(null,
11              "Mouse pressed at position ("
12              + event.getX() + ", " + event.getY() + ")");
13      }
14  }
```

As another example, the following program uses a mouse listener to set a label's text to show the mouse's position as it moves over the label. As with our previous examples, the GUI is object-oriented and serves as its own listener:

```
 1  // A GUI that displays the position of the mouse over a label.
 2
 3  import java.awt.*;
 4  import java.awt.event.*;
 5  import javax.swing.*;
 6  import javax.swing.event.*;
 7
 8  public class MousePointGUI extends MouseInputAdapter {
 9      public static void main(String[] args) {
10          MousePointGUI gui = new MousePointGUI();
11      }
12
13      // fields
14      private JFrame frame;
15      private JLabel label;
16
17      // sets up the GUI, components, and events
18      public MousePointGUI() {
19          label = new JLabel();
20          label.setText("Move the mouse over me!");
21
22          // listen for mouse events
23          label.addMouseListener(this);
24          label.addMouseMotionListener(this);
25
26          frame = new JFrame();
27          frame.setDefaultCloseOperation(JFrame.EXIT_ON_CLOSE);
28          frame.setSize(new Dimension(200, 100));
29          frame.setTitle("A frame");
30          frame.add(label);
31          frame.setVisible(true);
32      }
33
34      // responds to mouse movement events
35      public void mouseMoved(MouseEvent event) {
36          label.setText("(" + event.getX() + ", " +
37                                event.getY() + ")");
38      }
39  }
```

The program produces the following graphical output, shown after the user moves the mouse onto a few different points on the label:

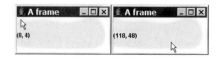

14.5 2D Graphics

In Supplement 3G, we introduced a graphical class called `DrawingPanel`. The `DrawingPanel` was kept simple so that you did not need to learn a lot of details about graphical user interfaces. Now that we're starting to uncover those details, we can examine how to draw our own 2D graphics manually. This will lead us to the point where we can understand the code for `DrawingPanel` and even reimplement it ourselves.

Drawing onto Panels

Earlier in this chapter we discussed the `JPanel` component, which we used as an invisible container for laying out other components. Panels have one other important function: they serve as surfaces onto which we can draw. The `JPanel` object has a method called `paintComponent` that draws the panel on the screen. By default this method draws nothing, so the panel is transparent.

We can use inheritance to change the drawing behavior for a panel. If we want to make a panel onto which we can draw shapes, we can extend `JPanel` and override the `paintComponent` method. Here is the header of the `paintComponent` method we must override:

```
public void paintComponent(Graphics g)
```

Its parameter, `Graphics g`, should look familiar to you if you read Supplement 3G. `Graphics` is a class in Java's `java.awt` package with methods for drawing shapes, lines, and images onto a surface. Think of the `Graphics` object as a pen and the panel as a sheet of paper.

There is one quirk when writing a `paintComponent` method. Remember that when you override a method, you replace the superclass method's previous functionality. We don't want to lose the behavior of `paintComponent` from `JPanel`, though, because it does important things on the interior of the panel; we just want to add additional behavior to it. Therefore, the first thing you should do when overriding `paintComponent` is to call `super.paintComponent` and pass it your `Graphics` object `g` as its parameter. (If you don't, you can get strange ghosty afterimages when you drag or resize your window.)

Here's a small class that represents a panel with two rectangles drawn on it:

```
 1  // A panel that draws two rectangles on its surface.
 2
 3  import java.awt.*;
 4  import javax.swing.*;
 5
 6  public class RectPanel extends JPanel {
 7      public void paintComponent(Graphics g) {
 8          super.paintComponent(g); // call JPanel's version
 9
10          g.setColor(Color.RED);
11          g.fillRect(20, 40, 70, 30);
12          g.setColor(Color.BLUE);
```

```
13              g.fillRect(60, 10, 20, 80);
14      }
15  }
```

We can now write a separate class for a GUI that incorporates this panel. In the GUI class, we create a `RectPanel` object and add it to the frame. It will appear on the screen with the two shapes drawn on it. Here's the example client code that uses our `RectPanel`:

```
 1  // Demonstrates the RectPanel class by placing one into a GUI.
 2
 3  import java.awt.*;
 4  import javax.swing.*;
 5
 6  public class UseRectPanel {
 7      public static void main(String[] args) {
 8          JFrame frame = new JFrame();
 9          frame.setDefaultCloseOperation(JFrame.EXIT_ON_CLOSE);
10          frame.setSize(200, 200);
11          frame.setTitle("A panel with rectangles");
12
13          RectPanel panel = new RectPanel();
14          panel.setBackground(Color.WHITE);
15          frame.add(panel);
16
17          frame.setVisible(true);
18      }
19  }
```

The program produces the following graphical output:

You might ask yourself, why not just use a `DrawingPanel` rather than going to all this trouble? There are several reasons. One is that `DrawingPanel` isn't actually a standard part of Java, so you can't rely on it outside of a classroom setting. Also, while it's a nice tool for simple drawing, you can't make a `DrawingPanel` part of a larger GUI with other components. The following modified code for the previous client program achieves a mixture of components that would be impossible to replicate with a `DrawingPanel`:

```
public static void main(String[] args) {
    JFrame frame = new JFrame();
    frame.setDefaultCloseOperation(JFrame.EXIT_ON_CLOSE);
    frame.setSize(400, 200);
    frame.setTitle("A panel with rectangles");
    frame.setLayout(new BorderLayout());
```

The `DrawingPanel`'s stateful painting is achieved by painting onto a `BufferedImage` object. The `DrawingPanel` declares a `BufferedImage` as a field and initializes it in its constructor. When the client calls `getGraphics` on the `DrawingPanel`, a reference to the buffered image's graphics pen is returned. To place the buffered image onto the screen, it is set as the icon for a `JLabel`.

The start of the `DrawingPanel` class looks a lot like the code for the GUIs developed in this chapter. It begins by declaring various graphical components as fields. The fields are the overall window frame, the `Graphics` object for the onscreen buffered image, and a panel to hold the image:

```
public class DrawingPanel {
    private JFrame frame;        // overall window frame
    private JPanel panel;        // drawing surface
    private Graphics g;          // drawing pen


    . . .

}
```

The constructor of the `DrawingPanel` accepts two parameters representing the panel's width and height. It initializes the fields, as well as constructing the `BufferedImage` to serve as the persistent buffer where shapes and lines can be drawn. The class also adds a few methods for the client, such as `getGraphics`, `setBackground`, and `setVisible`. The following is an initial version of its complete code:

```
 1  // A simple interface for drawing persistent images.
 2  // Initial version without events.
 3
 4  import java.awt.*;
 5  import java.awt.image.*;
 6  import javax.swing.*;
 7
 8  public class DrawingPanel {
 9      private JFrame frame;   // overall window frame
10      private JPanel panel;   // drawing surface
11      private Graphics g;     // drawing pen
12
13      // constructs a drawing panel of given size
14      public DrawingPanel(int width, int height) {
15          // set up the empty image onto which we will draw
16          BufferedImage image = new BufferedImage(width, height,
17                  BufferedImage.TYPE_INT_ARGB);
18          g = image.getGraphics();
19          g.setColor(Color.BLACK);
20
21          // enclose the image in a label inside a panel
22          JLabel label = new JLabel();
23          label.setIcon(new ImageIcon(image));
24          panel = new JPanel(new FlowLayout());
25          panel.setBackground(Color.WHITE);
26          panel.setPreferredSize(new Dimension(width, height));
27          panel.add(label);
28
29          // set up the JFrame
30          frame = new JFrame("Drawing Panel");
```

```
31              frame.setDefaultCloseOperation(JFrame.EXIT_ON_CLOSE);
32              frame.setResizable(false);
33              frame.add(panel);
34              frame.pack();
35              frame.setVisible(true);
36          }
37
38          // obtains the Graphics object to draw on the panel
39          public Graphics getGraphics() {
40              return g;
41          }
42
43          // sets the background color of the drawing panel
44          public void setBackground(Color c) {
45              panel.setBackground(c);
46          }
47
48          // shows or hides the drawing panel on the screen
49          public void setVisible(boolean visible) {
50              frame.setVisible(visible);
51          }
52  }
```

The code places the buffered image onto a label as its icon, then stores the buffered image into a panel that is placed inside the frame. Using this intermediate panel enables background colors to be set properly.

Second Version with Events

A more sophisticated version of `DrawingPanel` will also act as an event listener for mouse events, so that as the user hovers the mouse over the panel, a status bar at the bottom will display the cursor's (x, y) position for debugging. To achieve this, the `DrawingPanel` can be modified to act as a mouse listener and attach itself to listen to its central panel. Whenever the mouse moves, the mouse listener will receive the event and the status bar text will be updated to show the mouse position.

To implement these capabilities, we'll begin by changing our class header to the following:

```
public class DrawingPanel extends MouseInputAdapter {
```

We'll then add a new field called `statusBar` of type `JLabel`, which we'll place in the south region of the frame. Initially the status bar's text will be empty, but if the mouse moves, its listener will change the text to reflect the cursor's position. The following code implements the mouse listener's `mouseMoved` method:

```
// draws status bar text when mouse moves
public void mouseMoved(MouseEvent e) {
    statusBar.setText("(" + e.getX() + ", " +
                            e.getY() + ")");
}
```

We'll also add the following code to the constructor to attach the `DrawingPanel` as a listener to its inner panel:

```
// attach listener to observe mouse movement
panel.addMouseListener(this);
panel.addMouseMotionListener(this);
```

There's another kind of event we should handle in the DrawingPanel. When the client code using DrawingPanel takes a long time (such as when it uses console input to guide what shapes will be drawn), we may need to repaint the DrawingPanel periodically to reflect any new shapes the client has drawn. To keep things simple, we don't want to force the client to call repaint itself.

To force the DrawingPanel to refresh at a given interval, we must use a Timer to periodically call repaint. Since a Timer requires an action listener as a parameter, we'll make the DrawingPanel implement the ActionListener interface. Its increasingly long header will now look like this:

```
public class DrawingPanel extends MouseInputAdapter
        implements ActionListener {
```

The actionPerformed method simply needs to call repaint on the main onscreen panel:

```
// used for timer that repeatedly repaints screen
public void actionPerformed(ActionEvent e) {
    panel.repaint();
}
```

Lastly, we'll add the following lines to the DrawingPanel's constructor to create and start the timer:

```
// start a repaint timer to refresh the screen
Timer timer = new Timer(250, this);
timer.start();
```

Putting it all together, here is the complete code for the second version of the DrawingPanel class:

```
 1  // A simple interface for drawing persistent images.
 2  // Final version with events.
 3
 4  import java.awt.*;
 5  import java.awt.event.*;
 6  import java.awt.image.*;
 7  import javax.swing.*;
 8  import javax.swing.event.*;
 9
10  public class DrawingPanel extends MouseInputAdapter
11          implements ActionListener {
12      private JFrame frame; // overall window frame
13      private JPanel panel; // drawing surface
14      private JLabel statusBar; // status bar
15      private Graphics g; // drawing pen
16
17      // constructs a drawing panel of given size
18      public DrawingPanel(int width, int height) {
19          // set up the empty image onto which we will draw
```

```
20              BufferedImage image = new BufferedImage(width, height,
21                      BufferedImage.TYPE_INT_ARGB);
22              g = image.getGraphics();
23              g.setColor(Color.BLACK);
24
25              // enclose the image in a label inside a panel
26              JLabel label = new JLabel();
27              label.setIcon(new ImageIcon(image));
28              panel = new JPanel(new FlowLayout());
29              panel.setBackground(Color.WHITE);
30              panel.setPreferredSize(new Dimension(width, height));
31              panel.add(label);
32
33              // the status bar that shows the mouse position
34              statusBar = new JLabel(" ");
35
36              // attach listener to observe mouse movement
37              panel.addMouseListener(this);
38              panel.addMouseMotionListener(this);
39
40              // set up the JFrame
41              frame = new JFrame("Drawing Panel");
42              frame.setDefaultCloseOperation(JFrame.EXIT_ON_CLOSE);
43              frame.setResizable(false);
44              frame.setLayout(new BorderLayout());
45              frame.add(panel, BorderLayout.CENTER);
46              frame.add(statusBar, BorderLayout.SOUTH);
47              frame.pack();
48              frame.setVisible(true);
49
50              // start a repaint timer to refresh the screen
51              Timer timer = new Timer(250, this);
52              timer.start();
53          }
54
55          // obtains the Graphics object to draw on the panel
56          public Graphics getGraphics() {
57              return g;
58          }
59
60          // sets the background color of the drawing panel
61          public void setBackground(Color c) {
62              panel.setBackground(c);
63          }
64
65          // shows or hides the drawing panel on the screen
66          public void setVisible(boolean visible) {
67              frame.setVisible(visible);
68          }
69
70          // used for timer that repeatedly repaints screen
71          public void actionPerformed(ActionEvent e) {
72              panel.repaint();
73          }
74
75          // draws status bar text when mouse moves
76          public void mouseMoved(MouseEvent e) {
```

```
77                    statusBar.setText("(" + e.getX() + ", " +
78                                       e.getY() + ")");
79       }
80   }
```

This version of the code can be used to draw any of the example programs from Supplement 3G. For example, the following is the output when the Pyramids case study from Supplement 3G is run using the `DrawingPanel` we have just implemented:

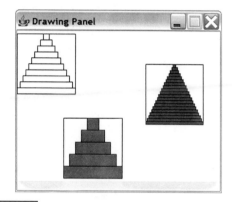

Chapter Summary

A graphical user interface (GUI) has a window frame that contains buttons, text input fields, and other onscreen components.

The `JOptionPane` class is a simple GUI class that can be used to display messages and prompt for input values, enabling graphical output and input.

Some of the most common graphical components are buttons (`JButton` objects), text input fields (`JTextField` objects), and text labels (`JLabel` objects).

All graphical components in Java belong to a common inheritance hierarchy, so they share a common set of methods that can be used to get and set properties such as background color, size, and font.

Components are positioned in a frame or container by objects called layout managers, such as `BorderLayout`, `FlowLayout`, and `GridLayout`. The features of the

layout managers can be combined by nesting them in different containers to form a composite layout.

Java generates special objects called events when the user interacts with onscreen graphical components. To write an interactive GUI, you must respond to these events.

The most common type of event is an `ActionEvent`, which you can handle by writing a class that implements the `ActionListener` interface. You can also respond to `MouseEvents` by writing a class that extends the `MouseInputAdapter` class.

To draw lines and shapes, you must write a class that extends `JPanel` and write a method called `paintComponent`.

GUIs can be animated using objects called timers that cause events to fire on an action listener at regular intervals.

Self-Check Problems

Section 14.1: GUI Basics

1. This section introduced three new packages that you must import when writing graphical programs. What are they? Write the `import` statements necessary to use these classes.

2. Write Java code to pop up an option pane asking the user for his or her age. If the user types a number less than 40, respond with a message box saying that he or she is young. Otherwise, tease the user for being old. For example:

 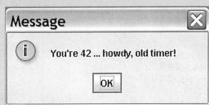

3. What is a component? How is a frame different from other components?

4. Name two properties of frames. Give an example piece of code that creates a new frame and sets these two properties to have new values of your choice.

5. Identify the Java class used to represent each of the following graphical components.

6. Write a piece of Java code that creates two buttons, one with a green background and the text "Click me" and the other with a yellow background and the text "Do not touch!".

Section 14.2: Laying Out Components

7. Identify the layout manager that would produce each of the following onscreen appearances:

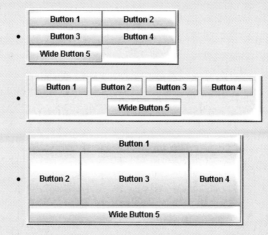

8. Write the code that would produce each of the layouts pictured in problem 7 given the following variable declarations:

```java
JButton b1 = new JButton("Button 1");
JButton b2 = new JButton("Button 2");
JButton b3 = new JButton("Button 3");
JButton b4 = new JButton("Button 4");
JButton b5 = new JButton("Wide Button 5");
```

Section 14.3: Interaction Between Components

9. What is an event? What is a listener? What interface is used when handling standard action events?

10. Describe the code that must be written to handle an event. What class(es) and method(s) must be written? What messages must be sent to the component in question (such as the button to be clicked)?

11. Write an `ActionListener` that could be attached to a button, so that whenever that button is clicked, an option pane will pop up that says, `"Greetings, Earthling!"`.

12. Why should complex GUIs that handle events be written in an object-oriented way?

Section 14.4: Additional Components and Events

13. What classes and interfaces are used when implementing mouse listeners? In what ways is the process of handling mouse events different from that of handling action events?

14. Modify the `MousePointGUI` program's mouse listener so that it sets the frame's background color to blue if the mouse pointer is in the upper half of the frame and red if it is in the lower half of the frame. (*Hint*: Use the label's `getHeight` and `setForeground` methods in your solution.)

Section 14.5: 2D Graphics

15. What class should be extended when drawing 2D graphics? What method should be overwritten to do the drawing?

16. Write a panel class that paints a red circle on itself when drawn on the screen.

17. What is a timer? How are timers used with panels when drawing 2D graphics?

18. Modify your red circle panel from problem 16 so the color changes to blue and back again, alternating every 1 second. Use a timer to "animate" the color changes of the panel.

Exercises

1. 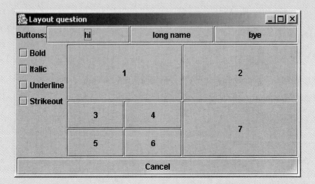 Write a complete Java program that creates the following window layout. The window title is "Good thing I studied!" and the window size is 285 by 200 pixels.

2. Write a complete Java program that creates the following window layout. The window title is "Layout question" and the window size is 420 by 250 pixels.

```
Inside second method
Inside first method
Inside second method
Inside first method
Inside third method
Inside first method
Inside second method
Inside first method
```

17.
```
Inside first method
Inside first method
Inside second method
Inside first method
Inside third method
Inside second method
Inside first method
Inside first method
Inside second method
Inside first method
Inside third method
```

18.
```
Inside second method
Inside first method
Inside first method
Inside second method
Inside first method
Inside third method
Inside first method
Inside second method
Inside first method
```

19.
```
I am method 1.
I am method 1.
I am method 2.
I am method 3.
I am method 1.
I am method 1.
I am method 2.
I am method 1.
I am method 2.
I am method 3.
I am method 1.
```

20.
```
I am method 1.
I am method 1.
```

```
I am method 1.
I am method 2.
I am method 3.
I am method 1.
I am method 2.
I am method 1.
I am method 1.
I am method 2.
I am method 3.
```

21.
```
I am method 1.
I am method 2.
I am method 1.
I am method 1.
I am method 2.
I am method 3.
I am method 1.
I am method 1.
I am method 2.
```

22.
- On line 1, the class name should be `LotsOfErrors` (no space).
- On line 2, the word `void` should appear after `static`.
- On line 2, `String` should be `String[]`.
- On line 3, `System.println` should be `System.out.println`.
- On line 3, `"Hello, world!)` should be `"Hello, world!")`.
- On line 4, there should be a semicolon after `message()`.
- On line 7, there should be a `()` after `message`.
- On line 8, `System.out println` should be `System.out.println`.
- On line 8, `cannot";` should be `cannot")`.
- On line 9, the phrase `"errors"` cannot appear inside a `String`. `'errors'` would work.
- On line 11, there should be a closing `}` brace.

23.
- Syntax error: The program would not compile because its class name (`Demonstration`) would not match its file name (`Example.java`).
- Different program output: The program would not run because Java would be unable to find the `main` method.
- Different program output: There would now be a blank line between the two printed messages.
- Syntax error: The program would not compile because the `main` method would be calling a method (`displayRule`) that no longer existed.
- No effect: The program would still compile successfully and produce the same output.

- Different program output: The output would now have no line break between "The first rule" and "of Java Club is," in its output.

24.
```java
public class GiveAdvice {
    public static void main(String[] args) {
        System.out.println("Programs can be easy or");
        System.out.println("difficult to read, depending");
        System.out.println("upon their format.");
        System.out.println();
        System.out.println("Everyone, including yourself,");
        System.out.println("will be happier if you choose");
        System.out.println("to format your programs.");
    }
}
```

25.
```java
public class Messy {
    public static void main(String[] args) {
        message();
        System.out.println();
        message();
    }

    public static void message() {
        System.out.println("I really wish that");
        System.out.println("I had formatted my source");
        System.out.println("code correctly!");
    }
}
```

Chapter 2

1. 22, -1, and -6875309 are legal int literals.

2.
- 8
- 11
- 6
- 4
- 33
- -16
- 6.4
- 6
- 30
- 1

- 7
- 5
- 2
- 18
- 3
- 4
- 4
- 15
- 8
- 1

3. • 9.0
  • 9.6
  • 2.2
  • 6.0
  • 6.0
  • 2.2
  • 8.0
  • 1.25
  • 3.0
  • 3.0

• 3.0
• 5.0
• 6.4
• 37.0
• 9.0
• 8.5
• 9.6
• 4.0
• 4.8

4. • 11
  • `"2 + 2 34"`
  • `"2 2 + 3 4"`
  • `"7 2 + 2"`
  • `"2 + 2 7"`
  • `"(2 + 2) 7"`
  • `"hello 34 8"`

5.
```
int age;
String gender;
double height;
int weight;
```

6.
```
String year;
int numberOfCourses;
double gpa;
```

7. Last digit: `number % 10`

8. Second-to-last digit: `(number % 100) / 10` or `(number / 10) % 10`
Third-to-last digit: `(number % 1000) / 100` or `(number / 100) % 10`

9.
```
first: 19
second: 8
```

The code swaps the values of the variables `first` and `second`.

10.
```
int first = 8, second = 19;
first += second;
second = first - second;
first -= second;
```

11. a: 6
   b: 9
   c: 16

12. • 15 * count - 11
   • -10 * count + 40
   • 4 * count - 11
   • -3 * count + 100

13.
```
for (int i = 1; i <= 6; i++) {
     // your code here
     System.out.println(18 * i - 22);
}
```

14.
```
System.out.println("Twas brillig and the ");
System.out.println("   slithy toves did gyre and");
System.out.println("gimble");
System.out.println();
System.out.println("in the wabe.");
```

15. • The loop prints every third number, not every odd number. The statement count = count + 2 on line 8 should be moved into the loop header instead of count++.
   • On line 12, the variable count is no longer defined (its scope is limited to the for loop). It should be declared before the loop begins rather than inside the loop's header.
   • On line 12, too large a value is printed for the final odd number; count should be printed, not count + 2.
   • On line 20, it is illegal to try to assign a new value to a constant such as MAX_ODD. One way to fix this would be to write two methods: one to print the odds up to 21 and a second to print the odds up to 11. (Admittedly, this solution is redundant. A better solution to this kind of problem involves parameter passing, which will be demonstrated in later chapters.)

16. 4
   2

17. The result is: 55

18. 24   1
   22   2
   19   3
   15   4
   10   5

19.
```
+----+
 \    /
 /    \
 \    /
 /    \
 \    /
 /    \
+----+
```

20.
```
How many lines
How many lines
How many lines
are printed?
```

21. `T-minus 5, 4, 3, 2, 1, Blastoff!`

22.
```
1  2  3  4  5  6  7  8  9  10
2  4  6  8  10  12  14  16  18  20
3  6  9  12  15  18  21  24  27  30
4  8  12  16  20  24  28  32  36  40
5  10  15  20  25  30  35  40  45  50
```

23.
```
         *
        ***
       *****
      *******
     *********
    ***********
   *************
  ***************
 *****************
*******************
```

24.
```
****!****!****!
****!****!****!
```

25.
```
***********!
***********!
```

26.
```
*!*!*!*!
*!*!*!*!
*!*!*!*!
*!*!*!*!
*!*!*!*!
*!*!*!*!
```

2. The black rectangle is being drawn second, so it's covering up the white inner circle. The following code fixes the problem:

```
DrawingPanel panel = new DrawingPanel(200, 100);
Graphics g = panel.getGraphics();
g.setColor(Color.BLACK);
g.fillRect(10, 10, 50, 50);
g.setColor(Color.WHITE);
g.fillOval(10, 10, 50, 50);
```

3. The problem is that the parameters for the `drawRect` and `drawLine` methods have different meanings. In `drawRect`, the parameters are (`x, y, width, height`); in `drawLine`, they are (`x1, y1, x2, y2`). To fix the problem, the third and fourth parameters passed to `drawRect` should be changed to 40 and 20 so that the rectangle's bottom-left corner will be at (50, 40). The following code fixes the problem:

```
DrawingPanel panel = new DrawingPanel(200, 100);
Graphics g = panel.getGraphics();
g.drawRect(10, 20, 40, 20);
g.drawLine(10, 20, 50, 40);
```

4. The `Draw7` program draws a series of progressively smaller black circles, each with its right and bottom edges touching the right and bottom corners of the window. Its output looks like this:

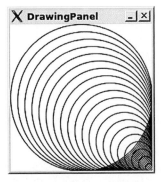

Chapter 4

1. The `sum` variable needs to be declared outside the `for` loop. The following code fixes the problem:

```
public static int sumTo(int n) {
    int sum = 0;
    for (int i = 1; i <= n; i++) {
        sum += i;
```

```
        }
        return sum;
    }
```

2. The code has a fencepost problem; a comma will be printed after the last number.
The following code fixes the problem:

```
System.out.print(1);
for (int i = 2; i <= n; i++) {
    System.out.print(", " + i);
}
System.out.println(); // end the line of output
```

3.
```
Scanner console = new Scanner(System.in);
System.out.print("How many numbers? ");
int count = console.nextInt();
int product = 1;

for (int i = 1; i <= count; i++) {
    System.out.print("Next number --> ");
    int num = console.nextInt();
    product *= num;
}
System.out.println("Product = " + product);
```

4.
- `z % 2 == 1`
- `z <= Math.sqrt(y)`
- `y > 0`
- `x % 2 != y % 2`
- `y % z == 0`
- `z != 0`
- `Math.abs(y) > Math.abs(z)`
- `(x >= 0) == (z < 0)`
- `y % 10 == y`
- `z >= 0`
- `x % 2 == 0`
- `Math.abs(x - y) < Math.abs(z - y)`

5.
- `true`
- `false`
- `true`
- `false`
- `true`
- `false`
- `false`

- true
- true

6. The code incorrectly uses an if/else/if/else/if pattern, but it should really use an if/if/if pattern because the three conditions are not mutually exclusive. The given code answers correctly only when zero or one of the numbers is odd; if more than one is odd, the code enters only one branch and does not properly increment the counter multiple times.

The following version of the code fixes the problem:

```
if (n1 % 2 == 1) {
    count++;
}
if (n2 % 2 == 1) {
    count++;
}
if (n3 % 2 == 1) {
    count++;
}
```

This version achieves the same thing without the need for if/else statements:

```
count = n1 % 2 + n2 % 2 + n3 % 2;
```

7.
```
Scanner console = new Scanner(System.in);

System.out.print("Type a number: ");
int number = console.nextInt();

if (number % 2 == 0) {
    System.out.println("even");
} else {
    System.out.println("odd");
}
```

8. The code incorrectly prints that even numbers not divisible by 3 are odd. This is because the else statement matches the most closely nested if statement (number % 3 == 0), not the outer if statement.

The following change corrects the problem. Note the braces around the outer if statement:

```
if (number % 2 == 0) {
    if (number % 3 == 0) {
        System.out.println("Divisible by 6.");
    }
```

```
    }
    else {
        System.out.println("Odd.");
    }
```

9. The code shouldn't return the factor i when found; it should instead count how many factors it finds. This is a cumulative sum, so the count variable should be declared outside the for loop. The following code fixes the problem:

```
public static int countFactors(int n) {
    int count = 0;
    for (int i = 1; i <= n; i++) {
        if (n % i == 0) { // factor
            count++;
        }
    }
    return count;
}
```

10.
```
    Scanner console = new Scanner(System.in);
    System.out.print(
            "Is your money multiplied 1 or 2 times? ");
    int times = console.nextInt();

    System.out.print(
            "And how much are you contributing? ");
    int donation = console.nextInt();
    sum += times * donation;
    total += donation;

    if (times == 1) {
        count1++;
    }
    else if (times == 2) {
        count2++;
    }
```

If the user could type any number, the code might need additional if statements to increment the proper count variable. If the user could type anything, even a non-integer, the code might need to use the hasNextInt method of the Scanner to ensure valid input before proceeding.

11.
```
// Prompts for two people's money and reports
// how many $20 bills the person would need.

import java.util.*;
```

```
public class Bills {
    public static void main(String[] args) {
        Scanner console = new Scanner(System.in);

        int numBills1 = getBills(console, "John");
        int numBills2 = getBills(console, "Jane");

        System.out.println("John needs " + numBills1 +
                          " bills");
        System.out.println("Jane needs " + numBills2 +
                          " bills");
    }

    public static int getBills(Scanner console,
                               String name) {
        System.out.print("How much will " + name +
                          " be spending? ");
        double amount = console.nextDouble();
        System.out.println();

        int numBills = (int) (amount/20.0);
        if (numBills * 20.0 < amount) {
            numBills++;
        }

        return numBills;
    }
}
```

12. The code won't ever print "Mine, too!" because Strings cannot be compared with the == operator. The fourth line of the code should be changed to the following:

```
if (name.equals("blue")) {
```

13. The code's output is the following, because the == operator was used instead of the equals method:

```
non-equal
```

14. ```
second
third
```

15. ```
Scanner console = new Scanner(System.in);
System.out.print("What color do you want? ");
String choice = console.nextLine();
if (choice.equalsIgnoreCase("r")) {
```

```java
            System.out.println("You have chosen Red.");
        } else if (choice.equalsIgnoreCase("g")) {
            System.out.println("You have chosen Green.");
        } else if (choice.equalsIgnoreCase("b")) {
            System.out.println("You have chosen Blue.");
        } else {
            System.out.println("Unknown color: " + choice);
        }
```

16.
```java
    Scanner console = new Scanner(System.in);
    System.out.print("Enter a card: ");
    String rank = console.next();
    String suit = console.next();

    if (rank.equals("2")) {
        rank = "Two";
    } else if (rank.equals("3")) {
        rank = "Three";
    } else if (rank.equals("4")) {
        rank = "Four";
    } else if (rank.equals("5")) {
        rank = "Five";
    } else if (rank.equals("6")) {
        rank = "Six";
    } else if (rank.equals("7")) {
        rank = "Seven";
    } else if (rank.equals("8")) {
        rank = "Eight";
    } else if (rank.equals("9")) {
        rank = "Nine";
    } else if (rank.equals("10")) {
        rank = "Ten";
    } else if (rank.equals("J")) {
        rank = "Jack";
    } else if (rank.equals("Q")) {
        rank = "Queen";
    } else if (rank.equals("K")) {
        rank = "King";
    } else { // rank.equals("A")
        rank = "Ace";
    }

    if (suit.equals("C")) {
        suit = "Clubs";
    } else if (suit.equals("D")) {
        suit = "Diamonds";
```

```
    } else if (suit.equals("H")) {
        suit = "Hearts";
    } else { // suit.equals("S")
        suit = "Spades";
    }

    System.out.println(rank + " of " + suit);
```

17. The expression equals 6.800000000000001 because the limited precision of the double type led to a roundoff error.

18. The expression gpa * 3 equals 9.600000000000001 because of a roundoff error. A fix would be to test that the value is close to 9.6 rather than exactly equal to it:

```
double gpa = 3.2;
if (Math.abs(gpa * 3 - 9.6) < 0.1) {
    System.out.println("You earned enough credits.");
}
```

19. efg
    nopqrs

    qr

20.
```
if (Character.isUpperCase(theString.charAt(0))) {
    ...
}
```

21. The toLowerCase method cannot be called on a char value, which is what the charAt method returns. A better solution would be to call the Character.toLowerCase method on the characters of the string:

```
int count = 0;
for (int i = 0; i < s.length(); i++) {
    if (Character.toLowerCase(s.charAt(i)) == 'e') {
        count++;
    }
}
```

Another solution would be to lowercase the entire string once before the loop:

```
s = s.toLowerCase();
int count = 0;
for (int i = 0; i < s.length(); i++) {
    if (s.charAt(i) == 'e') {
        count++;
    }
}
```

22. The following expression would produce the desired result:

```
String name = "Marla Singer";
int space = name.indexOf(" ");
String lastName = name.substring(space + 1);
String firstInitial = name.substring(0, 1);
String lastNameFirstInitial = lastName + ", " +
                                   firstInitial + ".";
System.out.println(lastNameFirstInitial);
```

Alternatively, you could use this shorter version:

```
String name = "Marla Singer";
System.out.println(name.substring(name.indexOf(" ") + 1) +
        ", " + name.charAt(0) + ".");
```

23.
```
// assuming that the String is stored in the variable str
int count = 0;
for (int i = 0; i < str.length(); i++) {
    if (Character.toLowerCase(str.charAt(i)) >= 'n') {
        count++;
    }
}
System.out.println(count + " letters come after n.");
```

24.
```
public static void printTriangleType(int s1, int s2,
                                      int s3) {
    if (s1 == s2 && s2 == s3) {
        System.out.println("equilateral");
    } else if (s1 == s2 || s1 == s3 || s2 == s3) {
        System.out.println("isosceles");
    } else {
        System.out.println("scalene");
    }
}
```

Invalid values are when a side's length is negative, or when any one side length is greater than the sum of the other two side lengths, because this cannot be a valid triangle. The precondition of the printTriangleType method is that the side lengths constitute a valid triangle.

25. The preconditions of this method are that the grade parameter's value is between 0 and 100.

26. The code fails when n3 is the smallest of the three numbers; for example, when the parameters' values are (4, 7, 2), the code should return 4 but instead returns 2. The method could be correctly written as:

```java
public static int medianOf3(int n1, int n2, int n3) {
    if (n1 < n2 && n1 < n3) {
        if (n2 < n3) {
            return n2;
        } else {
            return n3;
        }
    } else if (n2 < n1 && n2 < n3) {
        if (n1 < n3) {
            return n1;
        } else {
            return n3;
        }
    } else { // (n3 < n1 && n3 < n2)
        if (n1 < n2) {
            return n1;
        } else {
            return n2;
        }
    }
}
```

or the following shorter version:

```java
public static int medianOf3(int n1, int n2, int n3) {
    return Math.max(Math.max(Math.min(n1, n2),
                             Math.min(n2, n3)),
                    Math.min(n1, n3));
}
```

27.
```java
// Throws an exception if a, b, c are invalid
public static void quadratic(int a, int b, int c) {
    double determinant = b * b - 4 * a * c;

    if (a == 0) {
        throw new IllegalArgumentException(
                "Invalid a value of 0");
    }
    if (determinant < 0) {
        throw new IllegalArgumentException(
                "Invalid determinant");
    }

    . . .
}
```

Invalid values are when $a = 0$ (because it makes the denominator of the equation equal 0), or when $b^2 - 4ac < 0$, because then it has no real square root.

Chapter 5

1. • Executes body 10 times.
Output is:
```
1 11 21 31 41 51 61 71 81 91
```
• Executes body 0 times.
No output.
• Loops infinitely.
Output is:
```
250
250
250

. . .
```
• Executes body 3 times.
Output is:
```
2 4 16
```
• Executes body 5 times.
Output is:
```
bbbbbabbbbb
```
• Executes body 7 times.
Output is:
```
10
5
2
1
0
0
0
```

2. •
```java
int n = 1;
while (n <= max) {
    System.out.println(n);
    n++;
}
```

•
```java
int total = 25;
int number = 1;
while (number <= (total / 2)) {
    total = total - number;
    System.out.println(total + " " + number);
    number++;
}
```

-
```java
int i = 1;
while (i <= 2) {
    int j = 1;
    while (j <= 3) {
        int k = 1;
        while (k <= 4) {
            System.out.print("*");
            k++;
        }
        System.out.print("!");
        j++;
    }
    System.out.println();
    i++;
}
```

-
```java
int number = 4;
int count = 1;
while (count <= number) {
    System.out.println(number);
    number = number / 2;
    count++;
}
```

3.

Method call	Output
`mystery(1);`	1 0
`mystery(6);`	4 2
`mystery(19);`	16 4
`mystery(39);`	32 5
`mystery(74);`	64 6

4.

Method call	Output
`mystery(19);`	19 0
`mystery(42);`	21 1
`mystery(48);`	3 4
`mystery(40);`	5 3
`mystery(64);`	1 6

5.
```java
int SENTINEL = -1;
System.out.print("Type a number (or " + SENTINEL +
                 " to stop): ");
Scanner console = new Scanner(System.in);
int input = console.nextInt();
int min = input;
int max = input;
```

```java
    while (input != SENTINEL) {
        if (input < min) {
            min = input;
        } else if (input > max) {
            max = input;
        }

        System.out.print("Type a number (or " + SENTINEL +
                         " to stop): ");
        input = console.nextInt();
    }

    if (min != SENTINEL) {
        System.out.println("Maximum was " + max);
        System.out.println("Minimum was " + min);
    }
```

6.
```java
public static int zeroDigits(int number) {
    int count = 0;
    do {
        if (number % 10 == 0) {
            count++;
        }
        number = number / 10;
    } while (number > 0);
    return count;
}
```

7.
```java
Scanner console = new Scanner(System.in);
System.out.print("Type a number: ");
int number = console.nextInt();
String textNumber = String.valueOf(number);

// print odd digits
for (int i = 0; i < textNumber.length(); i++) {
    int digit = Character.getNumericValue(
            textNumber.charAt(i));
    if (digit % 2 == 1) {
        System.out.print(digit);
    }
}

// print even digits
for (int i = 0; i < textNumber.length(); i++) {
    int digit = Character.getNumericValue(
            textNumber.charAt(i));
```

```
        if (digit % 2 == 0) {
            System.out.print(digit);
        }
    }
```

8. a: 0 through 99 inclusive
   b: 50 through 69 inclusive
   c: 0 through 69 inclusive
   d: −20 through 79 inclusive
   e: 0, 4, 8, 16, 20, 24, 28, 32, or 36

9. ```
   Random rand = new Random();
   int num = rand.nextInt(11);
   ```

10. ```
    Random rand = new Random();
    int num = rand.nextInt(25) * 2 + 51;
    ```

11. • true
    • true
    • false
    • true
    • true
    • false
    • false
    • true
    • true
    • true
    • true
    • false

12. ```
    public static boolean isVowel(char c) {
        c = Character.toLowerCase(c); // case-insensitive
        return c == 'a' || c == 'e' || c == 'i' ||
               c == 'o' || c == 'u';
    }
    ```

    or:

    ```
    public static boolean isVowel(char c) {
        String vowels = "aeiouAEIOU";
        return vowels.indexOf(c) >= 0;
    }
    ```

13. In this code the `boolean` flag isn't being used properly, because if the code finds a factor of the number `prime` will be set to `false`, but on the next pass through the loop, if the next number isn't a factor, `prime` will be reset to `true` again. The following code fixes the problem:
    ```

```java
public static boolean isPrime(int n) {
    boolean prime = true;
    for (int i = 2; i < n; i++) {
        if (n % i == 0) {
            prime = false;
        }
    }

    return prime;
}
```

14. In this code the `boolean` flag isn't being used properly, because if the code finds the character `found` will be set to `true`, but on the next pass through the loop, if the next character isn't `ch`, `found` will be reset to `false` again. The following code fixes the problem:

```java
public static boolean contains(String str, char ch) {
    boolean found = false;
    for (int i = 0; i < str.length(); i++) {
        if (str.charAt(i) == ch) {
            found = true;
        }
    }

    return found;
}
```

15.
```java
public static boolean startEndSame(String str) {
    return str.charAt(0) == str.charAt(str.length() - 1);
}
```

16.
```java
public static boolean hasPennies(int cents) {
    return cents % 5 != 0;
}
```

17.
Method call	Value returned
`mystery(3, 3)`	3
`mystery(5, 3)`	1
`mystery(2, 6)`	2
`mystery(12, 18)`	6
`mystery(30, 75)`	15

18. The code should reprompt for a valid integer for the user's age and a valid real number for the user's GPA. If the user types a token of the wrong type, the line of input should be consumed and the user should be reprompted.

The following code implements the corrected behavior:

```
Scanner console = new Scanner(System.in);
System.out.print("Type your age: ");
while (!console.hasNextInt()) {
    console.nextLine(); // throw away offending token
    System.out.print("Type your age: ");
}
int age = console.nextInt();

System.out.print("Type your GPA: ");
while (!console.hasNextDouble()) {
    console.nextLine(); // throw away offending token
    System.out.print("Type your GPA: ");
}
double gpa = console.nextDouble();
```

19. • Type something for me! **Jane**
      Your name is Jane
    • Type something for me! **56**
      Your IQ is 56
    • Type something for me! **56.2**
      Your name is 56.2

20.
```
Scanner console = new Scanner(System.in);
System.out.print("Type a number: ");
if (console.hasNextInt()) {
    int value = console.nextInt();
    System.out.println("You typed the integer " +
                        value);
} else if (console.hasNextDouble()) {
    double value = console.nextDouble();
    System.out.println(
        "You typed the real number " + value);
}
```

21.
```
String prompt = "Please enter a number: ";
Scanner console = new Scanner(System.in);

int num1 = getInt(console, prompt);
int num2 = getInt(console, prompt);
int num3 = getInt(console, prompt);

double average = (num1 + num2 + num3) / 3.0;
System.out.println("Average: " + average);
```

22. • Executes body 10 times.
    Output is:
    ```
    1 11 21 31 41 51 61 71 81 91
    ```

• Loops infinitely.
    Output is:
    ```
    count down: 10
    count down: 9
    . . . .
    ```

• Loops infinitely.
    Output is:
    ```
    250
    250
    250
    . . . .
    ```

• Executes body 2 times.
    Output is:
    ```
    100
    50
    ```

• Executes body 3 times.
    Output is:
    ```
    2  4  16
    ```

• Executes body 5 times.
    Output is:
    ```
    bbbbbabbbbb
    ```

• Executes body 7 times.
    Output is:
    ```
    10
    5
    2
    1
    0
    0
    0
    ```

• Executes body 3 times.
    Output is:
    ```
    /\/\/\/\/\/\/\
    ```

23.
```
Scanner console = new Scanner(System.in);
String response;
do {
    System.out.println(
            "She sells seashells by the seashore.");
```

```
        System.out.print("Do you want to hear it again? ");
        response = console.nextLine();
    } while (response.equals("y"));
```

24.
```
Scanner console = new Scanner(System.in);
Random rand = new Random();
int num;
do {
    num = rand.nextInt(1000);
    System.out.println("Random number: " + num);
} while (num < 900);
```

25.
```
int SENTINEL = -1;
Scanner console = new Scanner(System.in);
System.out.print("Type a number (or " + SENTINEL +
                " to stop): ");
int input = console.nextInt();
int min = input;
int max = input;

while (true) {
    System.out.print("Type a number (or " + SENTINEL +
                    " to stop): ");
    input = console.nextInt();
    if (input == SENTINEL) {
        break;
    }

    if (input < min)
        min = input;
    else if (input > max)
        max = input;
}

if (min != SENTINEL) {
    System.out.println("Maximum was " + max);
    System.out.println("Minimum was " + min);
}
```

26.

	y < x	y == 0	count > 0
Point A:	SOMETIMES	SOMETIMES	NEVER
Point B:	ALWAYS	SOMETIMES	SOMETIMES
Point C:	ALWAYS	ALWAYS	ALWAYS
Point D:	SOMETIMES	SOMETIMES	SOMETIMES
Point E:	NEVER	SOMETIMES	SOMETIMES

27.

	n > b	a > 1	b > a
Point A:	SOMETIMES	SOMETIMES	SOMETIMES
Point B:	ALWAYS	SOMETIMES	SOMETIMES
Point C:	SOMETIMES	ALWAYS	ALWAYS
Point D:	SOMETIMES	ALWAYS	NEVER
Point E:	NEVER	SOMETIMES	SOMETIMES

28.

	next == 0	prev == 0	next == prev
Point A:	SOMETIMES	ALWAYS	SOMETIMES
Point B:	NEVER	SOMETIMES	SOMETIMES
Point C:	NEVER	NEVER	ALWAYS
Point D:	SOMETIMES	NEVER	SOMETIMES
Point E:	ALWAYS	SOMETIMES	SOMETIMES

Chapter 6

1. A file is a named collection of information stored on a computer. We can read a file with a Scanner using the following syntax:

```
Scanner input = new Scanner(new File("input.txt"));
```

2. The Scanner should read a new File with the name test.dat. The correct line of code is:

```
Scanner input = new Scanner(new File("test.dat"));
```

3. `Scanner input = new Scanner(new File("input.txt"));`

4. The file name String should use / or \\ instead of \. The \ is used to create escape sequences, and \\ represents a literal backslash. The correct String is:

```
Scanner input = new Scanner(new File("C:/temp/new files/
test.dat"));
```

5. • "numbers.dat" or "C:/Documents and Settings/amanda/
    My Documents/numbers.dat".
  • "data/homework6/input.dat" or "C:/Documents and
    Settings/amanda/My Documents/programs/data/homework6/
    input.dat".
  • There is only one legal way to refer to this file: by its absolute path,
    "C:/Documents and Settings/amanda/My Documents/homework/
    data.txt".

6. • "names.txt" or "/home/amanda/Documents/hw6/names.txt".
  • "data/numbers.txt" or "/home/amanda/Documents/hw6/data/
    numbers.txt".
  • There is only one legal way to refer to this file: by its absolute path,
    "/home/amanda/download/saved.html".

7. ```
   input: 6.7        This file has
   input:   several input lines.
   input:
   input:    10 20 30 40
   input:
   input: test
   6 total
   ```

8. ```
   input: 6.7
   input: This
   input: file
   input: has
   input: several
   input: input
   input: lines.
   input: 10
   input: 20
   input: 30
   input: 40
   input: test
   12 total
   ```

9. • Using `hasNextInt` and `nextInt`:
   ```
   0 total
   ```
   • Using `hasNextDouble` and `nextDouble`:
   ```
   input: 6.7
   1 total
   ```

10. ```java
    import java.io.*;
    import java.util.*;

    public class PrintMyself {
        public static void main(String[] args)
                throws FileNotFoundException {
            Scanner input = new Scanner(
                    new File("PrintMyself.java"));
            while (input.hasNextLine()) {
                System.out.println(input.nextLine());
            }
        }
    }
    ```
    ```

11. ```java
public static void printEntireFile()
        throws FileNotFoundException {
    Scanner console = new Scanner(System.in);
    System.out.print("Type a file name: ");
    String filename = console.nextLine();

    Scanner input = new Scanner(new File(filename));
    while (input.hasNextLine()) {
        System.out.println(input.nextLine());
    }
}
```

12. A `PrintStream` object is used to write to an external file. It has methods such as `println` and `print`.

13. ```java
PrintStream out = new PrintStream(new File("message.txt"));
out.println("Testing,");
out.println("1, 2, 3.");
out.println();
out.println("This is my output file.");
```

14. ```java
public static String getFileName() {
    Scanner console = new Scanner(System.in);
    String filename = null;
    do {
        System.out.print("Type a file name: ");
        filename = console.nextLine();
    } while (!(new File(filename).exists()));

    return filename;
}
```

15. ```java
// reprompts until file name is valid
public static void printEntireFile2()
        throws FileNotFoundException {
    String filename = getFileName();
    Scanner input = new Scanner(new File(filename));
    while (input.hasNextLine()) {
        System.out.println(input.nextLine());
    }
}
```

```
public class Name {
    String firstName;
    char middleInitial;
    String lastName;
}
```

7. An accessor provides the client access to some data in the object, while a mutator lets the client change the object's state in some way. Accessors' names often
   begin with "get" or "is", while mutators' names often begin with "set".

8. ```
   // Returns the distance from this point to the
   // given other point.
   public double distance(Point other) {
       int dx = x - other.x;
       int dy = y - other.y;
       return Math.sqrt(dx * dx + dy * dy);
   }
   ```

9. ```
   // A Name object represents a name such as "John Q. Public".

   public class Name {
       String firstName;
       char middleInitial;
       String lastName;

       // The name in normal order such as "John Q. Public".
       public String getNormalOrder() {
           return firstName + " " + middleInitial +
                   ". " + lastName;
       }
       // The name in reverse order such as "Public, John Q.".
       public String getReverseOrder() {
           return lastName + ", " + firstName +
                   " " + middleInitial + ".";
       }
   }
   ```

10. A constructor is a special method that creates an object and initializes its state.
    It's the method that is called when you use the new keyword. A constructor is
    declared without a return type.

11. • The constructor shouldn't have the void keyword in its header, because con-
    structors have no return type. The header should be:

    ```
    public Point(int x, int y) {
    ```

- The fields x and y shouldn't have their types redeclared in front of them. This bug causes shadowing of the fields. Here are the corrected lines:

```
x = initialX;
y = initialY;
```

12. ```
// A Name object represents a name such as "John Q. Public".

public class Name {
    String firstName;
    char middleInitial;
    String lastName;

    // Initializes a new Name with the given values.
    public Name(String initialFirst, char initialMiddle,
            String initialLast) {
        firstName = initialFirst;
        middleInitial = initialMiddle;
        lastName = initialLast;
    }

    // The name in normal order such as "John Q. Public".
    public String getNormalOrder() {
        return firstName + " " + middleInitial +
                ". " + lastName;
    }

    // The name in reverse order such as "Public, John Q.".
    public String getReverseOrder() {
        return lastName + ", " + firstName +
                " " + middleInitial + ".";
    }
}
```

13. Abstraction is the ability to focus on a problem at a high level without worrying about the minor details. Objects provide abstraction by giving us more powerful pieces of data that have sophisticated behavior without having to manage and manipulate the data directly.

14. Items declared `public` may be seen and used from any class. Items declared `private` may be seen and used only from within their own classes. Objects' fields should be declared `private` to provide encapsulation, so that external code can't make unwanted direct modifications to the fields' values.
```

15. To access private fields, create accessor methods that return their values. For example, add a `getName` method to access the `name` field of an object.

16.
```java
// Sets this Point's x coordinate to the given value.
public void setX(int newX) {
    x = newX;
}

// Sets this Point's y coordinate to the given value.
public void setY(int newY) {
    y = newY;
}
```

17.
```java
// A Name object represents a name such as "John Q. Public".

public class Name {
    private String firstName;
    private char middleInitial;
    private String lastName;

    // Initializes a new Name with the given values.
    public Name(String initialFirst, char initialMiddle,
                String initialLast) {
        firstName = initialFirst;
        middleInitial = initialMiddle;
        lastName = initialLast;
    }

    // Returns the person's first name.
    public String getFirstName() {
        return firstName;
    }

    // Returns the person's middle initial.
    public char getMiddleInitial() {
        return middleInitial;
    }

    // Returns the person's last name.
    public String getLastName() {
        return lastName;
    }
```

```java
        // The name in normal order such as "John Q. Public".
        public String getNormalOrder() {
            return firstName + " " + middleInitial +
                    ". " + lastName;
        }

        // The name in reverse order such as "Public, John Q.".
        public String getReverseOrder() {
            return lastName + ", " + firstName +
                    " " + middleInitial + ".";
        }
    }
```

18. To make the objects of your class printable, define a `toString` method in it.

19. The `==` operator doesn't work with objects because it just compares references to see whether they point to exactly the same object. It doesn't compare two objects to see whether they have the same state, which is usually what you want. If you want your objects to be compared correctly, define an `equals` method in your class and use `equals` instead of `==` in the client code.

20.
```java
// Returns a String representation of this point.
public String toString() {
    return "java.awt.Point[x=" + x + ", y=" + y + "]";
}
```

21.
```java
// Returns the name in normal order such as "John Q. Public".
public String toString() {
        return firstName + " " + middleInitial +
                ". " + lastName;
}
```

or:

```java
// Returns a String representation of this Name.
public String toString() {
    return getNormalOrder();
}
// Returns true if o refers to a Name object with
// the same first/last/middle name as this Name object.
public boolean equals(Object o) {
    if (o instanceof Name) {
        Name other = (Name) o;
        return firstName.equals(other.firstName) &&
                middleInitial == other.middleInitial &&
                lastName == other.lastName;
```

```
        } else { // not a Name object
            return false;
        }
    }
}
```

22. The keyword this refers to the object on which a method or constructor has been called (sometimes called the "implicit parameter"). It is used to access or set the object's field values, to call the object's methods, or to call one constructor from another.

23.
```
// Constructs a Point object with the same x and y
// coordinates as the given Point.
public Point(Point p) {
    this.x = p.x;
    this.y = p.y;
}
```

or:

```
// Constructs a Point object with the same x and y
// coordinates as the given Point.
public Point(Point p) {
    this(p.x, p.y); // call the (int, int) constructor
}
```

24.
```
// Sets the first name to the given value.
public void setFirstName(String firstName) {
    this.firstName = firstName;
}
```

```
// Sets the last name to the given value.
public void setLastName(String lastName) {
    this.lastName = lastName;
}
```

```
// Sets the middle initial to the given value.
public void setMiddleInitial(char middleInitial) {
    this.middleInitial = middleInitial;
}
```

25. An immutable object is one whose state cannot be changed after it has been created. A benefit of using immutable objects is that they are "read-only" and can be passed to other code without worrying that the code will somehow change them. Also, immutable objects allow class authors to enforce invariants more easily without worrying about changes to the state of the objects.

26. The completed `Name` class is not immutable because it has mutator methods such as `setFirstName`. In the previous version of the `Name` class, which was encapsulated but did not have the mutator methods, `Name` objects were immutable.

27. Encapsulation allows you to change a class's internal implementation without changing its external view to clients. When a class is encapsulated clients cannot directly access its fields, so changing those fields will not disturb client behavior as long as the external view (method behavior) is consistent.

28.
```java
// Returns a String representation of this Participant.
public String toString() {
    return name + " (height=" + height +
            " weight=" + weight + ")";
}


// Returns true if o refers to a Participant object
// with the same name, height, and weight as this one.
public boolean equals(Object o) {
    if (o instanceof Participant) {
        Participant other = (Participant) o;
        return name.equals(other.name) &&
                height == other.height &&
                weight == other.weight;
    } else { // not a Participant object
        return false;
    }
}
```

29. Cohesion is the concept of how well a class's contents go together. You can tell that a class is cohesive when each of its fields stores important state related to the object and each method interacts with that state in some way to produce useful behavior.

30. We did not place console I/O code into our `Stock` class because doing so would force clients to use those exact I/O messages. By keeping I/O code out of `Stock`, we kept it independent from its clients.

31.
```java
// Returns this Stock's symbol value.
public String getSymbol() {
    return symbol;
}


// Returns this Stock's total number of shares purchased.
public int getTotalShares() {
    return totalShares;
}
```

```
// Returns this Stock's total cost for all shares.
public double getTotalCost() {
    return totalCost;
}
```

Chapter 9

1. Code reuse is the practice of writing a single piece of code and using it many times in different programs and contexts. Inheritance is useful for code reuse because it allows you to write a class that captures common useful code and then extend that class to add more features and behavior to it.

2. Overloading a method involves creating two methods in the same class that have the same name but different parameters. Overriding a method involves creating a new version of an inherited method in a subclass, with identical parameters but new behavior to replace the old.

3. The following statements are legal:
   - `Vehicle v = new Car();`
   - `Vehicle v = new SUV();`
   - `Car c = new SUV();`
   - `SUV s = nev SUV();`

4. ```
// A class to represent legal secretaries.
public class LegalSecretary extends Employee {
    public void fileLegalBriefs() {
        System.out.println("I could file all day!");
    }

    public void showSalary() {
        System.out.println("My salary is $45,000.");
    }
}
```

5. B 2
   A
   A 1

   D 2
   C
   C 1
```

```
A 2
A
A 1

A 2
C
C 1
```

6.
```
flute
shoe 1
flute 2

flute
blue 1
flute 2

moo
moo 1
moo 2

moo
blue 1
moo 2
```

7.
```
moo 2
blue 1
moo

moo 2
moo 1
moo

flute 2
shoe 1
flute

flute 2
blue 1
flute
```

8.
```
squid
creature 1
tentacles

BIG!
spout
creature 2
```

```
    ocean-dwelling
    creature 1
    creature 2

    ocean-dwelling
    warm-blooded
    creature 2
```

9. ```
    creature 2
    ocean-dwelling
    creature 1

    tentacles
    squid
    creature 1

    creature 2
    ocean-dwelling
    warm-blooded

    creature 2
    BIG!
    spout
```

10. The `this` keyword refers to the current object, while the `super` keyword refers to the current class's superclass. Use the `super` keyword when calling a method or constructor from the superclass that you've overridden, and use the `this` keyword when accessing your object's other fields, constructors, and methods.

11. `UndergraduateStudent` can call the `setAge` method but cannot directly access the `name` or `age` fields from `Student`.

12. ```java
    public UndergraduateStudent(String name) {
        super(name, 18);
        year = 0;
    }
```

13. ```java
    public void setAge(int age) {
        super.setAge(age);
        year++;
    }
```

14. ```java
    // Constructs a Metered Point at the origin of (0, 0).
    public MeteredPoint() {
        super(0, 0);
        totalDistance = 0.0;
```

```
    }
```

or:

```
// Constructs a Metered Point at the origin of (0, 0).
public MeteredPoint() {
    this(0, 0);
}
```

15. An is-a relationship is a subclass relationship such as those created by inheritance. A has-a relationship is when one object contains a reference to another as a field.

16. Having `Square` extend `Rectangle` is a poor design because a `Square` cannot substitute for a `Rectangle`. If the client thinks the `Square` is a `Rectangle` and calls `setWidth` or `setHeight` on it, unexpected results will occur.

17. Having each of the 52 playing cards in its own class is not a good design because it will result in a clutter of code files without significant differences between them. A better design would have one `Card` class with fields for rank and suit.

18. We made `DividendStock` a separate subclass from `Stock` for two major reasons. First, not all stocks pay dividends, so it does not make sense for every `Stock` object to have a `dividends` field and a `payDividend` method. Second, the `Stock` code already worked correctly, so we did not want to tamper with it needlessly. Making `DividendStock` a separate class constituted an additive and noninvasive change.

19. Extending a class causes your class to inherit all methods and data from that class. Implementing an interface forces you to write your own code to implement all the methods in that interface.

20. The code for class `C` must contain implementations of the methods `m1` and `m2` to compile correctly, because `C` claims to implement the `I` interface.

21. The interface is incorrect because interfaces can't declare fields or write bodies for methods. The following is a correct interface:

```
import java.awt.*;

// Represents items that have a color that can be retrieved.
public interface Colored {
    public Color getColor();
}
```

22. // Represents a point with a color.

```
import java.awt.*;

public class ColoredPoint extends Point implements Colored {
    private Color color;

    // Constructs a new colored point with the given
    // coordinates and color.
    public ColoredPoint(int x, int y, Color color) {
        super(x, y);
        this.color = color;
    }

    // Returns this point's color.
    public Color getColor() {
        return color;
    }
}
```

23. // A general interface for shape classes.
```
public interface Shape {
    public double getArea();
    public double getPerimeter();
    public int getSideCount();
}
```

The following are the implementations of the method in the `Circle`, `Rectangle`, and `Triangle` classes:

```
// Returns the number of sides a circle has (0).
public int getSideCount() {
    return 0;
}

// Returns the number of sides a rectangle has (4).
public int getSideCount() {
    return 4;
}

// Returns the number of sides a triangle has (3).
public int getSideCount() {
    return 3;
}
```

24. An abstract class is a class intended to be used only as a superclass for inheritance. It's like a normal class in that it can have fields, methods, constructors, and so on. It's different from a normal class in that it can have abstract methods, which are like methods of an interface because only their headers are given, not their bodies. It's also different from a normal class because it can't be instantiated (used to create objects).

25. One good design would be to have an abstract superclass named `Movie` with data such as `name`, `director`, and `date`. There would be subclasses of `Movie` to represent particular movie types, such as `Drama`, `Comedy`, and `Documentary`. Each subclass would store its specific data and behavior.

Chapter 10

1. An `ArrayList` is a structure that stores a collection of objects inside itself as elements. Each element is associated with an integer index starting from 0. You should use an `ArrayList` instead of an array if you don't know how many elements you'll need in advance, or if you plan to add items to or remove items from the middle of your dataset.

2.
```
ArrayList<String> list = new ArrayList<String>();
list.add("It");
list.add("was");
list.add("a");
list.add("stormy");
list.add("night");
```

The list's type is `ArrayList<String>` and its size is 5.

3.
```
list.add(3, "dark");
list.add(4, "and");
```

4.
```
list.set(1, "IS");
```

5.
```
for (int i = 0; i < list.size(); i++) {
    if (list.get(i).indexOf("a") >= 0) {
        list.remove(i);
        i--;     // so the new element i will be checked
    }
}
```

6.
```
ArrayList<Integer> numbers = new ArrayList<Integer>();
for (int i = 0; i < 10; i++) {
    numbers.add(2 * i);
}
```

7.
```java
public static int maxLength(ArrayList<String> list) {
    int max = 0;
    for (int i = 0; i < list.size(); i++) {
        String s = list.get(i);
        if (s.length() > max) {
            max = s.length();
        }
    }
    return max;
}
```

8.
```java
System.out.println(list.contains("IS"));
```

9.
```java
System.out.println(list.indexOf("stormy"));
System.out.println(list.indexOf("dark"));
```

10.
```java
for (String s : list) {
    System.out.println(s.toUpperCase());
}
```

11. The code throws a `ConcurrentModificationException` because it is illegal to modify the elements of an `ArrayList` while for-eaching over it.

12. The code doesn't compile because primitives cannot be specified as type parameters for generic types. The solution is to use the "wrapper" type `Integer` instead of `int`. Change the line declaring the `ArrayList` to the following:

```java
ArrayList<Integer> numbers = new ArrayList<Integer>();
```

13. A wrapper class is one whose main purpose is to act as a bridge between primitive values and objects. An `Integer` is an object that holds an `int` value. Wrappers are useful in that they allow primitive values to be stored into collections.

14. To arrange an `ArrayList` into sorted order, call the `Collections.sort` method on it. For example, if your `ArrayList` is stored in a variable named `list`:

```java
Collections.sort(list);
```

For this to work, the type of the objects stored in the list must be `Comparable`.

15. A natural ordering is an order for objects of a class where "lesser" objects come before "greater" ones, as determined by a procedure called the class's comparison function. To give your own class a natural ordering, declare it to implement the `Comparable` interface and define a comparison function for it by writing an appropriate `compareTo` method.

16.
```java
n1.compareTo(n2) > 0
n3.compareTo(n1) == 0
n2.compareTo(n1) < 0
```

```
    s1.compareTo(s2) < 0
    s3.compareTo(s1) > 0
    s2.compareTo(s2) == 0
```

17.
```java
Scanner console = new Scanner(System.in);
System.out.print("Type a name: ");
String name1 = console.nextLine();
System.out.print("Type a name: ");
String name2 = console.nextLine();

if (name1.compareTo(name2) < 0) {
    System.out.println(name1 + " goes before " + name2);
} else if (name1.compareTo(name2) > 0) {
    System.out.println(name1 + " goes after " + name2);
} else { // equal
    System.out.println(name1 + " is the same as " + name2);
}
```

18.
```java
Scanner console = new Scanner(System.in);
System.out.print("Type a message to sort: ");
String message = console.nextLine();

ArrayList<String> words = new ArrayList<String>();
Scanner lineScan = new Scanner(message);
while (lineScan.hasNext()) {
    words.add(lineScan.next());
}

System.out.print("Your message sorted: ");
Collections.sort(words);
for (String word : words) {
    System.out.print(word + " ");
}
System.out.println(); // to end the line of output
```

Chapter 11

1. You should use a `LinkedList` when you plan to add or remove many values at the front or back of the list, or when you plan to make many filtering passes over the list in which you remove certain elements.

2. The code shown would perform better with an `ArrayList`, because it calls the `get` method many times using indexes in the middle of the list. This is a slow operation for a `LinkedList`.

3. An iterator is an object that represents a position within a list and enables you to view or make changes to the elements at that position. Iterators are often used with linked lists because they retain the position in the list, so you don't have to call expensive list methods like get, add, or remove many times.

4.
```java
public static int countDuplicates(LinkedList<Integer> list) {
    int count = 0;

    Iterator<Integer> i = list.iterator();
    int prev = i.next();

    while (i.hasNext()) {
        int next = i.next();
        if (prev == next) {
            count++;
        }
        prev = next;
    }

    return count;
}
```

5.
```java
public static void insertInOrder(LinkedList<String> list,
        String value) {
    int index = 0;

    Iterator<String> i = list.iterator();
    String next = i.next();

    // advance until the proper index
    while (i.hasNext() && next.compareTo(value) < 0) {
        next = i.next();
        index++;
    }

    list.add(index, value);
}
```

6.
```java
public static void removeAll(LinkedList<Integer> list,
        int value) {
    Iterator<Integer> i = list.iterator();
    while (i.hasNext()) {
        if (i.next() == value) {
            i.remove();
        }
    }
}
```

7.
```
public static void wrapHalf(LinkedList<Integer> list) {
    int halfSize = (list.size() + 1) / 2;
    for (int i = 0; i < halfSize; i++) {
        // wrap around one element
        int element = list.remove(list.size() - 1);
        list.add(0, element);
    }
}
```

8. An abstract data type defines the type of data a collection can hold and the operations it can perform on that data. Linked lists implement the `List` abstract data type.

9. The `countDuplicates` code is identical to that provided for problem 4, but the method's header should be changed to the following:

```
public static int countDuplicates(List<Integer> list) {
```

10. You should use a `Set` rather than a `List` if you wanted to avoid duplicates or wanted to be able to search the collection quickly.

11. You should use a `TreeSet` when you want to keep the data in sorted natural order. You should use `HashSets` with non-`Comparable` types or when order doesn't matter, to get the fastest searching time.

12. You can examine every element of a `Set` using an iterator.

13. `[32, 90, 9, 182, 29, 12]`

14. `[79, 8, 132, 50, 98, 86]`

15. `[94, 4, 11, 84, 42, 12, 247]`

16. To do a union, use the `addAll` method to add one set's contents to the other. To do an intersection, use the `retainAll` method to remove elements not common to both sets.

17.
```
Map<String, Integer> ageMap = new TreeMap<String, Integer>();
ageMap.put("Stuart", 85);
ageMap.put("Marty", 12);
ageMap.put("Amanda", 25);
```

18. You can examine every key of a Map by calling the keySet method and then iterating or for-eaching over the keySet. You can examine every value of a Map by calling the values method and then iterating or for-eaching over that collection of values, or by looking up each associated value using the keys from the keySet.

19. {17=Steve, 34=Louann, 15=Moshe, 2350=Orlando, 7=Ed, 5=Moshe, 27=Donald}

20. {79=Seventy-nine, 8=Ocho, 132=OneThreeTwo, 50=Fifty, 98=Ninety-eight, 86=Eighty-six}

21. The following method implements the new behavior in the wordCount program:

```
public static void reverseMap(
        Map<String, Integer> wordCountMap) {

    Map<Integer, String> reverseMap =
            new TreeMap<Integer, String>();

    // reverse the original map
    for (String word : wordCountMap.keySet()) {
        int count = wordCountMap.get(word);
        if (count > OCCURRENCES) {
            reverseMap.put(count, word);
        }
    }

    // print the words sorted by count
    for (int count : reverseMap.keySet()) {
        String word = reverseMap.get(count);
    }
}
```

Chapter 12

1. Recursion is a technique where an algorithm is expressed in terms of itself. A recursive method differs from a regular method in that it contains one or more calls to itself within its body.

2. A base case is a situation where a recursive method does not need to make a recursive call to solve the problem. A recursive case is a situation where the recursive method does call itself. Recursive methods need both cases because the recursive case is called repeatedly until the base case is reached, stopping the chain of recursive calls.

3. • 1
   • 1, 2
   • 1, 3
   • 1, 2, 4
   • 1, 2, 4, 8, 16
   • 1, 3, 7, 15, 30
   • 1, 3, 6, 12, 25, 50, 100

4.
```
public static void doubleReverse(String s) {
    if (s.length() > 0) {
        char last = s.charAt(s.length() - 1);
        System.out.print(last);
        System.out.print(last);
        doubleReverse(s.substring(0, s.length() - 1));
    }
}
```

5. A call stack is the structure of information about all methods that have currently been called by your program. Recursion produces a tall call stack in which each recursive call is represented.

6. The new code would print the lines in their original order, not reversed.

7. The new code would cause infinite recursion, because each recursive call just makes another recursive call and doesn't progress toward the base case.

8. The second version of the pow method is more efficient than the first because it requires fewer recursive calls. Both versions are recursive.

9.
```
public static int factorial(int n) {
    if (n == 0) {
        return 1;
    } else {
        return n * factorial(n - 1);
    }
}
```

10. • 6
   • 4
   • 7
   • 0
   • 1

11. The base case if statement has a bug: It should test for numbers less than 10, not greater. The following is the correct line:

```
if (n < 10) {
```

12. A fractal is an image that is recursively constructed to contain smaller versions of itself. Recursive methods are useful when drawing fractal images because they can elegantly express the recursive nature of the images.

13.
```
public static void drawHexagon(Graphics g, Point position,
        int size) {
    Polygon poly = new Polygon();
    poly.addPoint(position.x, position.y + size / 2);
    poly.addPoint(position.x + size / 3, position.y);
    poly.addPoint(position.x + 2 * size / 3, position.y);
    poly.addPoint(position.x + size, position.y + size / 2);
    poly.addPoint(position.x + 2 * size / 3, position.y +
            size);
    poly.addPoint(position.x + size / 3, position.y + size);
    g.drawPolygon(poly);
}
```

Chapter 13

1. You can perform a sequential search over the array using a `for` loop, or you can sort the array using `Arrays.sort` and then perform a binary search over it using `Arrays.binarySearch`.

2. A sequential search should be used on an array of `Point` objects because they do not implement `Comparable`.

3. `Arrays.binarySearch` and `Collections.binarySearch` can be used successfully if the array or collection contains elements that are sorted, according to either their natural ordering or the ordering of a `Comparator`.

4. • $O(\log N)$
  • $O(N)$
  • $O(N^2)$

5. • $O(N)$
  • $O(N^2)$
  • $O(N)$
  • $O(N)$
  • $O(\log B)$
  • $O(N^3)$
  • $O(N)$, where N is the number of lines or bytes in the file
  • $O(1)$

6. The runtime complexity of both sequential searches is $O(N)$.

7. Binary search requires a sorted dataset because it uses the ordering to jump to the next index. If the elements are out of order, the search isn't guaranteed to find the target element.

8. A binary search of 60 elements examines at most 6 elements, because log 60 (when rounded up) equals 6.

9. • The algorithm will examine index 4 and will return 4.
  • The algorithm will examine indexes 4 and 6 and will return 6.
  • The algorithm will examine indexes 4, 6, and 7 and will return 7.
  • The algorithm will examine indexes 4, 2, 1, and 0 and will return 0.

10. Because the input isn't sorted, the algorithm will examine indexes 4, 6, and 5 and will return -1.

11. The parameter array type should be changed to `double`. Also, a new `swap` method will be needed that accepts a `double[]` as the first parameter. Here's the new code:

```java
public static void selectionSort(double[] a) {
    for (int i = 0; i < a.length - 1; i++) {
        // find index of smallest element
        int smallest = i;
        for (int j = i + 1; j < a.length; j++) {
            if (a[j] < a[smallest]) {
                smallest = j;
            }
        }

        swap(a, i, smallest); // swap smallest to front
    }
}
```

12. A merge sort of 32 elements will generate 63 total calls to `mergeSort` and will perform the merge operation 31 times.

13. {1, 2, 3, 4, 5, 11, 9, 7, 8, 10}
   {7, 2, 8, 4, 1, 11, 9, 5, 3, 10}
   {7, 2, 8, 4, 1}, {11, 9, 5, 3, 10}
   {7, 2}, {8, 4, 1}, {11, 9}, {5, 3, 10}
   {7, 2}, {8, 4, 1}, {11, 9}, {5, 3, 10}
   {7}, {2}, {8}, {4, 1}, {11}, {9}, {5}, {3, 10}
              {4}, {1},   {3}, {10}
   {2, 7},   {8}, {1, 4}, {9, 11}, {5}, {3, 10}

```
{2, 7},    {1, 4, 8},    {9, 11}, {3, 5, 10}
{1, 2, 4, 7, 8},            {3, 5, 9, 10, 11}
{1, 2, 3, 4, 5, 7, 8, 9, 10, 11}
```

Chapter 14

1. The packages are `java.awt`, `java.awt.event`, and `javax.swing`. The statements to import these packages are:

```java
import java.awt.*;
import java.awt.event.*;
import javax.swing.*;
```

2.
```java
String response = JOptionPane.showInputDialog(null,
        "What's your age, cowboy?");
int age = Integer.parseInt(response);
if (age < 40) {
    JOptionPane.showMessageDialog(null, "Only " + age +
            " . . . still a young'n.");
} else {
    JOptionPane.showMessageDialog(null, "You're " +
            age + " . . . howdy, old timer!");
}
```

3. A component is an onscreen item such as a button or text field. A frame is different from other components because it is a first-class citizen of the user's operating system. Frames hold other components inside them.

4. Some properties of frames are `size`, `location`, and `title`. The following code creates a frame and sets these properties:

```java
JFrame frame = new JFrame();
frame.setSize(new Dimension(400, 300));
frame.setLocation(new Point(20, 10));
frame.setTitle("My favorite frame");
frame.setVisible(true);
```

5.
- `JTextArea`
- `JOptionPane`
- `JLabel`
- `JButton`
- `JTextField`

6.
```
JButton b1 = new JButton("Click me");
b1.setBackground(Color.GREEN);

JButton b2 = new JButton("Do not touch!");
b2.setBackground(Color.YELLOW);
```

7. • GridLayout
   • FlowLayout
   • BorderLayout

8. •
```
frame.setLayout(new GridLayout(3, 2));
frame.add(b1);
frame.add(b2);
frame.add(b3);
frame.add(b4);
frame.add(b5);
```
   •
```
frame.setLayout(new FlowLayout());
frame.add(b1);
frame.add(b2);
frame.add(b3);
frame.add(b4);
frame.add(b5);
```
   •
```
frame.setLayout(new BorderLayout());
frame.add(b1, BorderLayout.NORTH);
frame.add(b2, BorderLayout.WEST);
frame.add(b3, BorderLayout.CENTER);
frame.add(b4, BorderLayout.EAST);
frame.add(b5, BorderLayout.SOUTH);
```

9. An event is an object representing a user's interaction with a graphical component. A listener is an object that handles an event. The `ActionListener` interface is used to handle action events.

10. To handle an event, you must write a class that implements the `ActionListener` interface. It must contain a method named `actionPerformed`. You must call the `addActionListener` method on the component in question to attach your new listener to it.

11.
```
import java.awt.event.*;
import javax.swing.*;

public class GreetingListener implements ActionListener {
    public void actionPerformed(ActionEvent event) {
        JOptionPane.showMessageDialog(null,
```

```
                      "Greetings, Earthling!");
        }
    }
```

12. Object-oriented GUIs store their components as fields. This is useful because such a GUI can also be made into an action listener that has access to these components.

13. The `MouseInputListener` interface and `MouseInputAdapter` class are used when implementing mouse listeners. This differs from using `ActionListener` because you extend a class rather than implementing an interface, due to the large number of methods in the interface. You're also more likely to interact with a mouse listener's `MouseEvent` parameter than with the `ActionEvent` parameter of an action listener.

14.
```
// responds to mouse movement events
public void mouseMoved(MouseEvent event) {
    if (event.getY() < label.getHeight() / 2) {
        label.setForeground(Color.BLUE);
    } else {
        label.setForeground(Color.RED);
    }

    label.setText("(" + event.getX() + ", " +
                      event.getY() + ")");
}
```

15. When drawing 2D graphics, you should extend the `JPanel` class and write a `paintComponent` method.

16.
```
import java.awt.*;
import javax.swing.*;

public class RedCirclePanel extends JPanel {
    public void paintComponent(Graphics g) {
        super.paintComponent(g);
        g.drawOval(10, 30, 50, 50);
    }
}
```

17. A `Timer` is an object that can fire an `ActionListener` event at regular intervals. A `Timer` can be used to animate a panel by having its `ActionListener` change the state of the panel in some way and then repaint it.

18. `// An animated panel that draws a red and blue circle.`

```java
import java.awt.*;
import java.awt.event.*;
import javax.swing.*;

public class RedCirclePanel2 extends JPanel {
    private boolean red;

    public RedCirclePanel2() {
        red = true;
        Timer timer = new Timer(1000, new ColorListener());
        timer.start();
    }

    public void paintComponent(Graphics g) {
        super.paintComponent(g);
        if (red) {
            g.setColor(Color.RED);
        } else {
            g.setColor(Color.BLUE);
        }
        g.drawOval(10, 30, 50, 50);
    }

    private class ColorListener implements ActionListener {
        public void actionPerformed(ActionEvent e) {
            red = !red;
            repaint();
        }
    }
}
```

Java Summary

Java Keywords (Section 1.2)

abstract	continue	for	new	switch
assert	default	goto	package	synchronized
boolean	do	if	private	this
break	double	implements	protected	throw
byte	else	import	public	throws
case	enum	instanceof	return	transient
catch	extends	int	short	try
char	final	interface	static	void
class	finally	long	strictfp	volatile
const	float	native	super	while

Primitive Types (Section 2.1)

Type	Description	Examples
int	integers (whole numbers)	42, -3, 18, 20493, 0
double	real numbers	7.35, 14.9, -19.83423
char	single characters	'a', 'X', '!'
boolean	logical values	true, false

Arithmetic Operators (Section 2.1)

Operator	Meaning	Example	Result
+	addition	2 + 2	4
-	subtraction	53 - 18	35
*	multiplication	3 * 8	24
/	division	4.8 / 2.0	2.4
%	remainder or mod	19 % 5	4

Relational Operators (Section 4.2)

Operator	Meaning	Example	Value
==	equal to	`2 + 2 == 4`	`true`
!=	not equal to	`3.2 != 4.1`	`true`
<	less than	`4 < 3`	`false`
>	greater than	`4 > 3`	`true`
<=	less than or equal to	`2 <= 0`	`false`
>=	greater than or equal to	`2.4 >= 1.6`	`true`

Logical Operators (Section 5.2)

Operator	Meaning	Example	Value
&&	AND (conjunction)	`(2 == 2) && (3 < 4)`	`true`
||	OR (disjunction)	`(1 < 2) || (2 == 3)`	`true`
!	NOT (negation)	`!(2 == 2)`	`false`

Operator Precedence (Sections 2.1, 4.2, and 5.2)

Description	Operators
unary operators	`!, ++, --, +, -`
multiplicative operators	`*, /, %`
additive operators	`+, -`
relational operators	`<, >, <=, >=`
equality operators	`==, !=`
logical AND	`&&`
logical OR	`||`
assignment operators	`=, +=, -=, *=, /=, %=, &&=, ||=`

Common Wrapper Classes (Section 10.1)

Primitive type	Wrapper class
int	Integer
double	Double
char	Character
boolean	Boolean

Syntax Templates

Variable declaration without initialization (Section 2.2):

```
<type> <name>, <name>, <name>, ..., <name>;
```

Variable declaration with initialization (Section 2.2):

```
<type> <name> = <expression>;
```

Assignment (Section 2.2):

```
<variable> = <expression>;
```

Constant declaration (Section 2.4):

```
public static final <type> <name> = <expression>;
```

Static method definition (Sections 1.4 and 3.2):

```
public static <type> <name>(<type> <name>, ..., <type> <name>) {
    <statement>;
    ...
    <statement>;
}
```

Call on static method (Sections 1.4 and 3.1):

```
<method name>(<expression>, <expression>, ..., <expression>)
```

Call on instance method (Section 3.3):

```
<variable>.<method>(<expression>, <expression>, ..., <expression>)
```

Class definition (Section 8.5):

```
public class <class name> {
    // fields
    private <type> <name>;
```

```
    private <type> <name>;
    ...

    // constructors
    public <class name>(<type> <name>, ..., <type> <name>) {
        <statement>;
        ...
        <statement>;
    }
    ...

    // methods
    public <type> <name>(<type> <name>, ..., <type> <name>) {
        <statement>;
        ...
        <statement>;
    }
    ...
}
```

Constructor calling another constructor (Section 8.7):

```
this(<expression>, <expression>, ..., <expression>);
```

Instance method calling superclass method (Section 9.3):

```
super.<method>(<expression>, <expression>, ..., <expression>)
```

Constructor calling superclass constructor (Section 9.3):

```
super(<expression>, <expression>, ..., <expression>);
```

Specifying inheritance relationship (Section 9.1):

```
public class <subclass name> extends <superclass name> {
    ...
}
```

Implementing an interface (Section 9.5):

```
public class <name> implements <interface> {
    ...
}
```

Specifying inheritance relationship and implementing interfaces (Section 9.5):

```
public class <name> extends <superclass name>
    implements <interface name>, <interface name>, ..., <interface name> {
    ...
}
```

Interface definition (Section 9.5):

```
public interface <name> {
    public <type> <name>(<type> <name>, ..., <type> <name>);
```

```
    ...
    public <type> <name>(<type> <name>, ..., <type> <name>);
}
```

Abstract class (Section 9.6):

```
public abstract class <name> {
    ...
}
```

Abstract method (Section 9.6):

```
public abstract <type> <name>(<type> <name>, ..., <type> <name>);
```

return statement (Section 3.2):

```
return <expression>;
```

throw statement (Section 4.5):

```
throw <exception>;
```

assert statement (Section 5.5):

```
assert <boolean test>;
```

Array declaration (Section 7.1):

```
<element type>[] <name> = new <element type>[<size>];
```

Array initialization (Section 7.1):

```
<element type>[] <name> = {<value>, <value>, ..., <value>};
```

Simple if (Section 4.2):

```
if (<test>) {
    <statement>;
    ...
    <statement>;
}
```

if/else (Section 4.2):

```
if (<test>) {
    <statement>;
    ...
    <statement>;
} else {
    <statement>;
    ...
    <statement>;
}
```

Nested `if/else` ending in test (Section 4.2):

```
if (<test1>) {
    <statement1>;
} else if (<test2>) {
    <statement2>;
} else if (<test3>) {
    <statement3>;
}
```

Nested `if/else` ending in `else` (Section 4.2):

```
if (<test1>) {
    <statement1>;
} else if (<test2>) {
    <statement2>;
} else {
    <statement3>;
}
```

`for` loop (Section 2.3):

```
for (<initialization>; <continuation test>; <update>) {
    <statement>;
    ...
    <statement>;
}
```

For-each loop (Section 7.1):

```
for (<type> <name> : <array or collection>) {
    <statement>;
    ...
    <statement>;
}
```

`while` loop (Section 5.1):

```
while (<test>) {
    <statement>;
    ...
    <statement>;
}
```

`do/while` loop (Section 5.4):

```
do {
    <statement>;
    ...
    <statement>;
} while (<test>);
```

try/catch statement (Section 6.4):

```
try {
    <statement>;
    ...
    <statement>;
} catch (<type> <name>) {
    <statement>;
    ...
    <statement>;
}
```

Useful Methods of ArrayList Objects (Section 10.1)

Method	Description	ArrayList<String> example
add(value)	adds the given value at the end of the list	list.add("end");
add(index, value)	adds the given value at the given index, shifting subsequent values right	list.add(1, "middle");
clear()	removes all elements from the list	list.clear();
contains(value)	returns true if the given value appears in the list	list.contains("hello")
get(index)	gets the value at the given index	list.get(1)
indexOf(value)	returns the index of the first occurrence of the given value in the list (−1 if not found)	list.indexOf("world")
lastIndexof(value)	returns the index of the last occurrence of the given value in the list (−1 if not found)	list.lastIndexof("hello")
remove(index)	removes the value at the given index, shifting subsequent values left	list.remove(1);
set(index, value)	replaces the given value at the given index with the given value	list.set(2, "hello");
size()	returns the current number of elements in the list	list.size()

Useful Methods of the Character Class (Section 4.4)

Method	Description	Example
getNumericValue(ch)	converts a character that looks like a number into that number	Character.getNumericValue('6') returns 6
isDigit(ch)	whether or not the character is one of the digits '0' through '9'	Character.isDigit('X') returns false
isLetter(ch)	whether or not the character is in the range 'a' to 'z' or 'A' to 'Z'	Character.isLetter('f') returns true
isLowerCase(ch)	whether or not the character is a lowercase letter	Character.isLowerCase('Q') returns false
isUpperCase(ch)	whether or not the character is an uppercase letter	Character.isUpperCase('Q') returns true
toLowerCase(ch)	the lowercase version of the given letter	Character.toLowerCase('Q') returns 'q'
toUpperCase(ch)	the uppercase version of the given letter	Character.toUpperCase('x') returns 'X'

Useful Methods of the Collection Interface (Section 11.1)

Method	Description
add(element)	adds the specified element to this collection
addAll(collection)	adds all elements from the given collection to this collection
clear()	removes all elements from this collection
contains(element)	returns true if this collection contains the given element
containsAll(collection)	returns true if this collection contains all elements of the given collection
isEmpty()	returns true if this collection contains no elements
iterator()	returns an object that can be used to traverse the elements of this collection
remove(element)	removes one occurrence of the specified element, if it is contained in this collection
removeAll(collection)	removes all elements of the given collection from this collection
retainAll(collection)	removes all elements not found in the given collection from this collection
size()	returns the number of elements in this collection
toArray()	returns an array containing the elements of this collection

Useful Methods of the Collections Class (Section 11.1)

Method	Description
`binarySearch(list, value)`	searches a sorted list for a given element value and returns its index
`copy(destinationList, sourceList)`	copies all elements from the source list to the destination list
`fill(list, value)`	replaces every element in the given list with the given value
`max(list)`	returns the element with the highest value
`min(list)`	returns the element with the lowest value
`replaceAll(list, oldValue, newValue)`	replaces all occurrences of the old value with the new value
`reverse(list)`	reverses the order of the elements in the given list
`rotate(list, distance)`	shifts each element to the right by the given number of indexes, moving the final elements to the front
`shuffle(list)`	rearranges the elements into random order
`sort(list)`	rearranges the elements into sorted (nondecreasing) order
`swap(list, index1, index2)`	switches the element values at the given two indexes

Useful Methods of DrawingPanel Objects (Section 3G.1)

Method	Description
`getGraphics()`	returns a reference to the `Graphics` object that can be used to draw onto the panel
`setBackground(color)`	sets the background color of the panel to the given color (the default is white)

Useful Methods of Graphics Objects (Section 3G.2)

Method	Description
drawLine(x1, y1, x2, y2)	draws a line between the points (x1, y1) and (x2, y2)
drawOval(x, y, width, height)	draws the outline of the largest oval that fits within the specified rectangle
drawRect(x, y, width, height)	draws the outline of the specified rectangle
drawString(message, x, y)	draws the given text with its lower-left corner at (x, y)
fillOval(x, y, width, height)	fills the largest oval that fits within the specified rectangle using the current color
fillRect(x, y, width, height)	fills the specified rectangle using the current color
setColor(color)	sets this graphics context's current color to the specified color (all subsequent graphics operations using this graphics context use this specified color)
setFont(font)	sets this graphics context's current font to the specified font (all subsequent strings drawn using this graphics context use this specified font)

Useful Methods of File Objects (Section 6.1)

Method	Description
delete()	deletes the given file
exists()	indicates whether or not this file exists on the system
getAbsolutePath()	returns the full path where this file is located
getName()	returns the name of this file as a String, without any path attached
isDirectory()	indicates whether this file represents a directory/folder on the system
isFile()	indicates whether this file represents a file (non-folder) on the system
length()	returns the number of characters in this file
mkdirs()	creates the directory represented by this file, if it does not exist
renameTo(file)	changes this file's name to be the given file's name

Methods of Iterator Objects (Section 11.1)

Method	Description
hasNext()	returns true if there are more elements to be examined
next()	returns the next element from the list and advances the position of the iterator by one
remove()	removes the element most recently returned by next()

Useful Methods of Map Objects (Section 11.3)

Method	Description
clear()	removes all keys and values from a map
containsKey(key)	returns true if the given key maps to some value in this map
containsValue(value)	returns true if some key maps to the given value in this map
get(key)	returns the value associated with this key, or null if not found
isEmpty()	returns true if this collection contains no keys or values
keySet()	returns a Set of all keys in this map
put(key, value)	associates the given key with the given value
putAll(map)	adds all key/value mappings from the given map to this map
remove(key)	removes the given key and its associated value from this map
size()	returns the number of key/value mappings in this map
values()	returns a Collection of all values in this map

Constants and Useful Methods of the Math Class (Section 3.2)

Constant	Description
E	base used in natural logarithms (2.71828. . .)
PI	ratio of circumference of a circle to its diameter (3.14159. . .)

Method	Description	Example
abs	absolute value	Math.abs(-308) returns 308
ceil	ceiling (rounds upward)	Math.ceil(2.13) returns 3.0
cos	cosine (radians)	Math.cos(Math.PI) returns -1.0
exp	exponent base e	Math.exp(1) returns 2.7182818284590455
floor	floor (rounds downward)	Math.floor(2.93) returns 2.0
log	logarithm base e	Math.log(Math.E) returns 1.0
log10	logarithm base 10	Math.log10(1000) returns 3.0
max	maximum of two values	Math.max(45, 207) returns 207
min	minimum of two values	Math.min(3.8, 2.75) returns 2.75
pow	power (general exponentiation)	Math.pow(3, 4) returns 81.0
random	random value	Math.random() returns a random double value k such that $0.0 = k < 1.0$
sin	sine (radians)	Math.sin(0) returns 0.0
sqrt	square root	Math.sqrt(2) returns 1.4142135623730951
toDegrees	converts radian angles to degrees	Math.toDegrees(Math.PI) returns 180.0
toRadians	converts degree angles to radians	Math.toRadians(270.0) returns 4.71238898038469

Methods of the Object Class (Section 9.3)

Method	Description
clone()	creates and returns a copy of the object (not a public method)
equals(obj)	indicates whether the other object is equal to this one
finalize()	called automatically by Java when objects are destroyed (not a public method)
getClass()	returns information about the type of the object
hashCode()	returns a number associated with the object; used with certain data structures
toString()	returns the state of the object as a String
notify(), notifyAll(), wait()	advanced methods for multithreaded programming

Useful Methods of Point Objects (Section 3.3)

Method	Description
translate(dx, dy)	translates the coordinates by the given amounts
setLocation(x, y)	sets the coordinates to the given values
distance(p2)	returns the distance from this Point to p2

Useful Methods of Random Objects (Section 5.1)

Method	Description
nextInt()	random integer between -2^{31} and $(2^{31} - 1)$
nextInt(max)	random integer between 0 and (max − 1)
nextDouble()	random real number between 0.0 (inclusive) and 1.0 (exclusive)
nextBoolean()	random logical value of true or false

Useful Methods of Scanner Objects (Sections 3.4 and 5.3)

Method	Description
next()	reads and returns the next token as a String
nextDouble()	reads and returns a double value
nextInt()	reads and returns an int value
nextLine()	reads and returns the next line of input as a String
hasNext()	returns true if there is another token to be read
hasNextDouble()	returns true if there is another token to be read and if it can be interpreted as a double
hasNextInt()	returns true if there is another token to be read and if it can be interpreted as an int
hasNextLine()	returns true if there is another line of input to be read

Useful Methods of String Objects (Section 3.3)

Method	Description	Example (assuming s is "hello")
charAt(index)	character at a specific index	s.charAt(1) returns 'e'
endsWith(text)	whether or not the string ends with some text	s.endsWith("llo") returns true
indexOf(text)	index of a particular character or String (-1 if not present)	s.indexOf("o") returns 4
length()	number of characters in the string	s.length() returns 5
startsWith(text)	whether or not the string starts with some text	s.startsWith("hi") returns false
substring(start, stop)	characters from start index to just before stop index	s.substring(1, 3) returns "el"
toLowerCase()	a new string with all lowercase letters	s.toLowerCase() returns "hello"
toUpperCase()	a new string with all uppercase letters	s.toUpperCase() returns "HELLO"

Javadoc Comments and the Java API Specification

The Java API Specification

Java's Application Programming Interface (API) Specification is a set of web pages that describe the classes, interfaces, and methods of the Java class libraries. You can use these pages to learn class and method names or to find details about a particular method. The API pages can be thought of as a contract between the authors of the class libraries and you, the client of those classes.

The API pages exemplify the idea of the public view of a class versus its private implementation. Each class has a set of constructors, constants, and methods that its clients can access and use. The class also has private fields, methods, and method bodies used to actually implement the behavior specified in the public interface. The main benefit of this separation is that you don't need to know the private implementation of the class libraries to be able to use them.

As of this writing, the current Java API Specification pages can be accessed from the following URL:

http://java.sun.com/j2se/1.5.0/docs/api/

(Each new version of Java has a new specification, so this URL will change as versions 1.6 and onward are released.) When you visit the API pages you'll see a screen that looks like Figure C.1.

The main frame of the page (on the right) shows information about classes you can select using the frames on the left. The lower-left frame lists all of the classes and interfaces, and the upper-left frame lists all of the packages in the class libraries. Recall that packages are groups of related classes that you can use in your program by importing them. If you're looking for a class from a particular package, you can click that package's name in the top-left frame to filter the results in the bottom-left frame.

Once you click a class name in the bottom-left frame, information about that class appears in the main frame. At the start of the page you'll see a tree showing the names of any superclasses and any interfaces it implements, the class's header, and a summary description of the class. The summary description gives general information about the purpose and usage of the class and may link to other relevant documentation or tutorials.

Below the summary is an ordered list of the contents of the class. Listed first will be any public fields and class constants. Next will be the class's constructors, followed by its methods. Each field, method, and constructor has a line showing information such as its name, parameters, and return type, followed by a one-sentence description. You can click the name of the item to see more details about it.

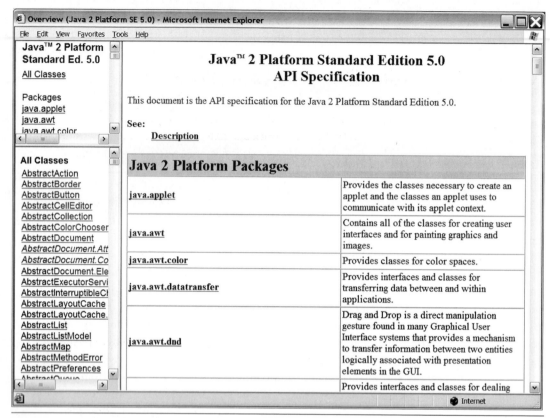

Figure C.1   The Java API Specification

For example, the following is the summary information for the Scanner class's constructor to read input from a file:

Constructor Summary
Scanner (File source)
    Constructs a new Scanner that produces values scanned from the specified file.

Clicking on a method can provide useful details about how to use it, including a longer description, a detailed explanation of each parameter the method requires, a description of what kind of value (if any) the method returns, and a listing of any exceptions the method may throw. These detail views allow you to learn the preconditions and postconditions of the method and to see examples of calls and their results.

For example, the following are the details about the `substring` method of the `String` class:

substring
```
public String substring(int beginIndex,
                        int endIndex)
```

Returns a new string that is a substring of this string. The substring begins at the specified `beginIndex` and extends to the character at index `endIndex` - 1. Thus the length of the substring is `endIndex-beginIndex`.

Examples:
```
"hamburger".substring(4, 8) returns "urge"
"smiles".substring(1, 5) returns "mile"
```

Parameters
  `beginIndex`—the beginning index, inclusive.
  `endIndex`—the ending index, exclusive.

Returns
  the specified substring

Throws
  `IndexOutOfBoundsException`—if the `beginIndex` is negative, or `endIndex` is larger than the length of this `String` object, or `beginIndex` is larger than `endIndex`.

Some of the methods in the API specs are marked as *deprecated*.

Deprecated
Discouraged from use.

Deprecated items are ones that Java's designers want to discourage you from using. Generally these are methods that Sun has either renamed or decided shouldn't be called because they didn't behave correctly or safely. You might think that Sun should just remove these deprecated methods from Java, but doing so would break any older Java programs that call these methods. An example of a deprecated method is the `inside` method in the `Rectangle` class of the `java.awt` package:

```
inside(int X, int Y)
```
  Deprecated. *As of JDK version 1.1, replaced by* `contains(int, int)`.

Writing Javadoc Comments

If you write your comments in a special style called *Javadoc,* they can be used to automatically produce web pages like those in the API Specification. In fact, Sun generates the API Specification by writing Javadoc comments in each class of the class libraries.

The syntax to signify a Javadoc comment is to begin a multi-line comment with `/**` rather than the usual `/*`:

```
/**
 *  This is a Javadoc comment.
 */
```

Javadoc comments can be added to class headers, methods, class constants, public fields, and any other visible members of a class.

Many Javadoc comments also specify additional information using special syntax called tags. A *tag* is an indicator for specific information such as a description of a parameter or return value, the author of a class, the version of a file, and so on. The information in a tag can include boundary conditions, acceptable parameter ranges, and examples.

The syntax for tags is to write an @ sign and a tag name, followed by any additional information. Several common Javadoc tags are described in the following table:

Tag name	Description
`@author <name>`	name(s) of the author(s) who wrote this class
`@param <name> <description>`	details about the given parameter to this method
`@return <description>`	details about what value is returned by this method
`@throws <type> <description>`	a type of exception this method may throw and a description of the circumstances under which it will do so
`@version <number>`	version or revision number of the file; can be a number such as 1.2.5 or a more complex string such as a date

The `@author` and `@version` tags are often used on class headers. For example, the following comment can precede the header for a `Point` class:

```
/**
 *  A Point object represents an ordered pair of
 *  (x, y) coordinates in the 2D Cartesian plane.
 *
 *  @author Marty Stepp (stepp@example.com)
 *  @version 1.2 (January 12, 2007)
 */
public class Point {
    . . .
}
```

The `@param` and `@throws` tags are often used on methods and constructors. Non-void methods may also use the `@return` tag. It is best to use the three preceding tags if they supply valuable additional information that cannot be discerned from the method's header or overall comment header.

For example, the following comment can precede the header for the `distance` method of the `Point` class:

```
/**
 *  Computes and returns the distance between this point
 *  and the given other point.
 *
 *  @param p the point to which the distance is computed
 *  @return the distance, computed as the square root of
 *          the sums of the squares of the differences
 *          between the two points' x-coordinates (dx)
 *          and between their y-coordinates (dy)
 *  @throws NullPointerException if p is null
 */
public double distance(Point p) {
    int dx = x - p.x;
    int dy = y - p.y;
    return Math.sqrt(dx * dx + dy * dy);
}
```

As mentioned previously, Javadoc comments can be converted into web documentation pages. Some Java editing environments include this functionality; check your editor to see whether it is provided. If not, Sun's JDK includes a command-line tool for generating the pages. To use it, open a terminal window to the directory of your source code files and type the following command:

```
javadoc *.java
```

The generated web page for the preceding `Point` class is shown in Figure C.2.

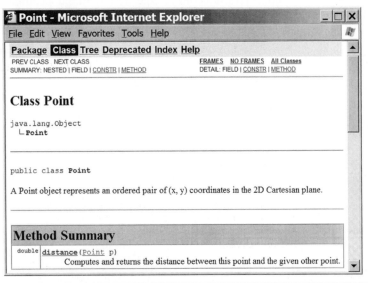

Figure C.2 Generated Javadoc pages for `Point` class

Clicking on the name of a method brings up the method's detail page, as in the API Specification. The generated web page for the preceding `distance` method looks like this:

Method Detail

distance

```
public double distance(Point p)
```

> Computes and returns the distance between this point and the given other point.
>
> **Parameters:**
>> p - the point to which the distance is computed
>
> **Returns:**
>> the distance, computed as the square root of the sums of the squares of the differences between the two points' x-coordinates (dx) and between their y-coordinates (dy)
>
> **Throws:**
>> `java.lang.NullPointerException` - if p is null

Since Javadoc comments are converted into HTML, they can contain HTML tags that will show up in any generated Javadoc pages. You can use these tags to format your comments.

Javadoc comments provide documentation to clients that lets them know how to use your class without needing to read its source code. However, they are lengthy and can take time to write. Writing Javadoc comments is most useful when you know that your class will be used by many clients.

Sun maintains a web site with much more information about writing Javadoc comments at the following URL:

http://java.sun.com/j2se/javadoc/writingdoccomments/

Index